A History of Jazz Music
1900-2000

*

Piero Scaruffi

*

2007

Scaruffi, Piero
A History of Jazz Music
All Rights Reserved © 2007 by Piero Scaruffi

ISBN-10: 0-9765531-3-9
ISBN-13: 978-0-9765531-3-7

Jazz, Swing, Big Band, Bebop, Hard bop, Cool, Free, Creative

For information: www.scaruffi.com

Printed in the USA

Photo credits: Piero Scaruffi

No part of this book may be reproduced or transmitted in any form or by any means, graphic, electronic or mechanical, including photocopying, recording, taping or by any information storage retrieval system, without the written permission of the author (http://www.scaruffi.com)

Contents

1. THE BEGINNINGS: NEW ORLEANS..........................11
2. CHICAGO:WHITE JAZZ...26
3. NEW YORK: STRIDE PIANO....................................28
4. NEW YORK: BIG BANDS..31
5. NEW YORK: THE SWING ERA.................................38
6. NEW YORK: THE SWING SOLOISTS........................42
7. KANSAS CITY: BIG BANDS...................................46
8. BEBOP...49
9. BEBOP PIANIST..55
10. BEBOP BIG BANDS..60
11. COOL JAZZ...64
12. COOL JAZZ IN LOS ANGELES...............................76
13. HARD BOP..80
14. POST-BOP...101
15. FREE JAZZ..118
    FREE JAZZ: THE APOSTLES..............................119
    FREE JAZZ: THE DISCIPLES..............................138
    FREE JAZZ: FREE DRUMMING...........................149
    FREE JAZZ: FREE VOCALS................................152
    WHITE FREE JAZZ..154
    FREE JAZZ: BORDERLINE..................................159
16. CREATIVE MUSIC...163
    CHICAGO'S CREATIVE JAZZ...............................164

CREATIVE MUSIC: THE DISCIPLES..........................177
THE ST LOUIS SCHOOL..187
JAZZ POST-MODERNISM IN NEW YORK..................190
WHITE POST-MODERNISM 202
EUROPEAN CREATIVITY..208
NOISE-JAZZ..232

17. FUSION..235
FUSION JAZZ: THE PIONEERS...................................236
PRE-FUSION PIANISTS..239
WHITE JAZZ BETWEEN FREE JAZZ AND FUSION......248
LATIN JAZZ...255
FUSION GROUPS..258
FUSION STYLISTS..267
GUITAR HEROES..271
POP-FUSION...279
EURO-FUSION..282

18. JAZZ TRADITIONALISM......................................293

19. NON-JAZZ OF THE 1980S....................................304
M-BASE..304
ACID JAZZ...307
NEW-AGE JAZZ..308
POST-FUSION...311

20. POST-JAZZ MUSIC...313
POST-JAZZ CREATIVITY IN NEW YORK....................314
POST-JAZZ SOLOISTS AND HYPER-FUSION...............324

POST-JAZZ BIG BANDS..328

THE GREAT CHICAGO JAZZ REBIRTH...........................334

THE RETURN OF THE JAZZ IMPROVISER....................337

20TH CENTURY POST-CREATIVITY.............................341

FREER JAZZ...343

THE DIGITAL IMPROVISER..347

TURNTABLES..349

RECOMMENDED DISCOGRAPHY................................350

ALPHABETICAL INDEX..355

Almost a Preface

Most books on the history of jazz music, even the ones published very recently (see the bibliography), tend to devote 80-90% of the pages to jazz before the Sixties, and then to quickly summarize (with countless omissions) the last 40 years. Either the authors are very old and stopped listening to new musicians in the 1950s, or jazz historians are affected by some kind of psychological trauma when they enter the 1960s. The paradox, of course, is that a lot more has happened "since" the 1960s than "until" the 1960s, if nothing else because a lot more recordings have been made in the age of the LP and in the age of the CD than in the ages of the 78 RPM and in the age of the 45 RPM. Personally, i also feel that the masterpieces of jazz music have been produced between the 1960s and today, with few exceptions. Thus i felt the need for a history of jazz music from the opposite perspective.

Since i have written a history of rock music of the last 50 years, i can't help wondering what kept jazz historians from doing the same: write a history of jazz from the 1960s to today. i also happen to believe that, by far, the greatest contributions of jazz to the history of humankind came in the second half of the century, for example with composers (repeat: composers) such as Charlie Mingus, Ornette Coleman and John Coltrane. Most of what was done before the 1960s pales in comparison with the giants of the 1960s, who are giants regardless of musical affiliation.

That was the original goal, the gap that my book was supposed to fill. But i quickly realized that i couldn't write a history of jazz for an audience that didn't know how jazz became what it was in the mid 1950s. Therefore i decided to write a short summary of the first 50 years of jazz music. Given that i was already working on a history of blues music, the beginning of that "summary" ended up being a lot more extensive than a mere summary should be. Within two weeks i had written the first 15 chapters of this book, and forgotten that the original focus was meant to be only the last 50 years (the subsequent chapters).

By the way, i made a point of writing a history that could be read by people with little or no mastery of the technical vocabulary (i.e., people whose background is in literature or visual arts or, quite simply, history). i am more interested in discussing how Coltrane introduced Eastern spirituality into popular music and legitimized extended abstract pieces than in discussing how such and such a trumpeter played a fifth or a saxophonist used the keys. It is telling that most jazz books seem to make a point to analyze in detail the tracks that i consider less relevant.

This is now a dangerous book. Jazz historians would forgive me a book that covers the last 50 years, but they are unlikely to forgive a non-jazz historian who writes about the early age of jazz music.

My only excuse is that i didn't write this book for them: i wrote it for an audience that includes listeners of classical, rock and avantgarde music. Sooner or later, i will merge all these "histories" into just one history of 20th century

Preface

music. Having visited more than one hundred countries, i have always hated borders: imagine how i hate it when humans create borders even between arts and even between musical styles.

Now if only a jazz historian wrote a history of rock music...

Thanks to Rocco Stilo for double-checking all the dates (a superhuman task) and to Chris Ford for proof editing part of the book.

piero scaruffi, 2007

Bibliography (in order of relevance):

Gioia Ted: "The History of Jazz" (Oxford Univ Press, 1997)
Shipton, Alyn: "New History of Jazz" (2001)
Southern, Eileen: "The Music of Black Americans" (Norton, 1971)
Gridley, Mark: "Jazz Styles" (Prentice Hall, 1991)
Hardy, Phil & Laing Dave: "Faber Companion to 20th Century Popular Music" (Faber, 1990)
Clarke, Donald: "Penguin Encyclopedia of Popular Music" (Penguin, 1989)
Hodeir, Andre: "Hommes et Problemes du Jazz" (Flammarion, 1954)
Polillo, Arrigo: "Jazz" (Mondadori, 1975)
Roberts, John-Storm: "Black Music of Two Worlds" (1972)

Previous books on the same topic

I will say upfront that i judge Ted Gioia's "The History of Jazz" and Alyn Shipton's "New History of Jazz" as definitive books in their genre (despite Shipton's revisionist attitude towards swindles such as Paul Whiteman and the white swing orchestras, and his focus on tedious reinterpretations instead of original compositions). Jazz historians may argue forever on the early (undocumented) years of jazz, but i doubt that anyone will significantly change the history of the first 50 years of jazz music that Shipton has written. So if you want to buy only one book on jazz, don't buy mine, buy Shipton. If you want two, buy Gioia's too (possibly more perspicacious, just less detailed). If you "also" want a much more comprehensive discussion of the next 50 years, then mine will probably be the only game in town for a while. I've seen Shipton call "modern" the music made in the 1940s (he devotes 640 pages to the first 33 years of jazz music, but only 227 pages to the next 50 years). If you want a book that does not view the history of jazz music as a history of how to play instruments (that is basically the viewpoint of traditional jazz historians), then you might want to read mine before Shipton's (i still think you should read his too). I can't help thinking that Shipton neglects almost all the great achievements of jazz (he hardly mentions Mingus' masterpiece, and perhaps the masterpiece of all jazz, **The Black Saint and the Sinner Lady**) while analyzing in minute detail some rather negligible ditties (one entire page just for Louis Armstrong's *Ain't Misbehavin'*). Relying on (what i consider) an outdated definition of "jazz", too many jazz historians dwell way too much on minor pieces of music while downplaying (and sometimes ignoring tout court) the great compositions of jazz. They do a big disservice to jazz. It is hard to name Armstrong in the same sentence with Mozart or Stravinsky, but not difficult at all to mention Ornette Coleman or Anthony Braxton with those heavy-weights of classical music. If, instead, you want to read about the development of jazz instruments, read Shipton not me. While i acknowledge them, i don't spend much time on musicians who only recorded short pieces, and even less time if they did not compose those pieces, no matter how difficult and innovative their style at the instrument. This is the exact same criterion that i used for the history of rock music.

Notes

- In general, the date of a piece of music is the date in which it was recorded (not the date it was released). The exceptions are "compositions" that were created years before they were first recorded.
- The date of an album is the date its last track was recorded.
- Whenever i couldn't find out when an album was recorded, then i regrettably had to use the date in which it was released (but i welcome input from readers who know the recording date). Whenever my date has the month, then it is the month of recording. If it doesn't have the month, then i am not sure.
- Whenever i do not mention the ethnic group of a musician, s/he's most likely a black USA citizen. I always mention if the musician is not from the USA or is not black. Take it as a way to acknowledge that jazz was invented by black musicians of the USA.
- Whenever i do not mention the birthplace of a musician, s/he's most likely from New York or nearby towns. This is done only to save space: since the vast majority were and are based in New York, it saved quite a bit of space to assume it as a given.
- The albums mentioned in the book are my own favorites. I despise the websites that promote millions of albums as masterpieces. Just about every musician on those websites seems to be a new Beethoven. Just about every musician in the world seems to have produced something comparable to Beethoven's ninth symphony. Most of the "masterpieces" that those websites recommend turned out to be mediocre, and sometimes even terrible. In particular, there is a widespread tendency to promote as masterpiece the most recent recordings. Experience has taught me that it is usually the opposite. Those websites are simply trying to please the record labels that sent them the albums for free. The albums that i mention in this book are the ones that are worth listening to, in my opinion, and they are a tiny minority.

Disclaimer

Only in the USA can one think that the term "African-American" is politically correct. My friend Gerard, a white man from South Africa who relocated to Pennsylvania, is an African-American. My friend Hassan, a Moroccan who relocated to California, is an African-American. The white Zimbabwean businessman whom i met in Argentina and the black Angolan student whom i met in Brazil are African-Americans. But that is not what USA citizens mean when they say "African-American": they mean "black person who lives in the USA". In fact they call "African-American" even people from Haiti, Britain and France, as long as their skin is black. Most USA citizens (particularly the self-appointed African-American ones) think of Africa as being only sub-Saharan Africa, and of America as being only the USA. And they do not consider white people born in Africa as "African". In other words, when they say "African" they really mean "person with a black skin", and when they say "American" they really mean "USA citizen".

I think that "black" (or "negro") is more precise and, ultimately, more politically correct. Thus i use "black musician" to mean what USA citizens refer to as "African-American musician". If no nationality is provided, then it means that the black person is from the USA (this book is mostly about the USA, so it would be redundant to keep repeating "black USA musician"). I write both "black" and "negro" lower case, just like "white". Occasionally i lapse into the "African-American" thing myself, but that should be in a broader context (when i am indeed talking about the two continents).

In my texts on rock music, the reader can safely assume that the musicians are white unless otherwise specified. In this book on jazz music, the reader can safely assume that the musicians are black unless otherwise specified. Thus i will note that Steve Lacy is white and will not note that Miles Davis is black the same way that rock biographers emphasize that Jimi Hendrix was black but do not emphasize that Bob Dylan was white.

THE BEGINNINGS: NEW ORLEANS

Jazz music was, ultimately, the product of New Orleans' melting pot.

At the turn of the century, the streets of New Orleans were awash in blues music, ragtime and the native brass-band fanfares. The latter, used both in the Mardi Gras parades and in funerals, boasted a vast repertory of styles, from military marches to "rags" (not necessarily related to Scott Joplin's ragtime music). The Excelsior Brass Band, formed in 1880, raised the Creole drummer John Robichaux and the Creole clarinetist Alphonse Picou. The Onward Brass Band, formed around 1884, featured Creole cornet player Manuel Perez. Notably missing from this mix was religious music, that played a lesser role in the birth and development of jazz music. Also missing was white popular music, that would define the "commercial" format of jazz music, but not its core technical characteristics.

New Orleans' brass bands eventually spread into the saloons and the dancehalls of "Storyville", the red-light district created by a city ordinance in 1897. These bands (such as Jack "Papa" Laine's Reliance Brass Band, the first major white band, formed in 1892, John Robichaux's band, formed in 1893, the main popularizer of the Creole style, Buddy Bolden's band, formed in 1895, Alphonse Picou's Columbia Brass Band, formed in 1897, Manuel Perez's Imperial Orchestra, formed in 1900) probably played a mixture of blues, ragtime and traditional dance music.

The performers who shared a passion for syncopation and for improvisation were either brass bands (cornet or trumpet for the melody, clarinet for counterpoint, trombone or tuba or percussion for rhythm), that very often were marching bands, or solo pianists, who very often were ragtime pianists.

In 1898 the US defeated Spain (gaining Puerto Rico and "liberating" Cuba). The troops that were coming back from the Caribbean front landed in New Orleans with European brass instruments that were sold cheaply on the black market. Within a few years, every neighborhood in New Orleans boasted a brass band. The influence of blues music could be heard in the way these instruments were played, because they basically imitated the vocal styles of blues music (often on a syncopated rhythm borrowed from ragtime).

A fundamental attribute of New Orleans was the perennial party atmosphere. This was not New York's melting pot, very competitive in nature: this was a melting pot that allowed for a lot of fun. New York was a cosmopolitan financial center. New Orleans was a cosmopolitan amusement park. Thus music was always in demand, not just as paid entertainment but as the soundtrack of a never-ending party. In other cities ethnicity was a problem. In New Orleans ethnicity was an opportunity to improve the party, because each ethnic group brought its different style of partying (e.g., dances) to the party.

During the first decade of the 20th century, these bands would compete in public contests that highlighted the virtuosi. For example, Charles "Buddy" Bolden's trumpet playing became legendary, as did his arrangements (brass instruments playing blues music), as did his division of instrumental roles (the cornet leading the melody, the trombone providing a bass counterpoint and the clarinet dancing around the melody in a higher tone) as did his repertory (*Make me a Pallet on the Floor*, *The House Got Ready*, *Bucket's Got a Hole In It*, *Buddy Bolden's Blues*), but he was locked into a mental hospital in 1907 before he could record any of his music. Bolden's band was probably the first New Orleans band to truly emphasize improvisation. His style was the epitome of "hot jazz", as opposed to the "downtown style" of the Creoles.

The most popular orchestras emphasized the cornet/trumpet (the main melodic instrument) and the clarinet (the counter-melody), while the trombone provided the bass counterpoint and the other instruments (drums, banjo, guitar, contrabass, piano) provided the rhythm section.

In 1911 Bill Johnson, a New Orleans bass player, moved to California and eventually managed to get his orchestra to follow him. From 1913 till 1917 the Original Creole Band was the first black orchestra to tour outside New Orleans.

Unlike blues music, that was exclusively performed by blacks, jazz music was as inter-racial as the melting pot of New Orleans. Blacks were not the only ones who played jazz. Jazz groups were formed by Italians, Creoles and all sorts of European immigrants. The "African" roots of the music may or may not have been obvious to the practitioners, but clearly it did not stop them from adopting it.

In the meantime, the dance craze that swept the northern cities in the 1910s, originating in New York from black musicians such as Ernest Hogan and James Europe, fostered the creation of "syncopated orchestras" both in New York and Chicago.

New York was the epicenter of a fusion of the three great fads of the time: syncopated orchestras, ragtime and blues.

Chicago soon became a middleground of sorts. The soul of the city's black music was Joe Jordan, and the main mentors were the clubs of the "Black Belt", such as the "Pekin Theatre". Tony Jackson's *Pretty Baby* (1915) was the first big hit. The New Orleans Jazz Band was performing at the "Royal Gardens". During World War I, Chicago witnessed the rivalry between the orchestras of Dave Peyton and Erskine Tate. They featured several young talents who had immigrated from the South, such as Joe "King" Oliver, Louis Armstrong, Sidney Bechet. A tour by Will-Marion Cook's orchestra in 1919 introduced Chicago to the syncopated world of New York, and involuntarily led to an exodus of black musicians towards New York. At the end of the war Cook formed the American Syncopated Orchestra.

Well into the 1920s the term "syncopated orchestra" was much more popular than "jazz orchestra", but the term "jazz music" was beginning to spread, among both black and white musicians. The first black musicians who consciously boasted of playing "jazz" were vaudeville artists. For example, Benton Overtstreet's *Jazz Dance* (1917) was for many years one of Estelle Harris' most popular skits.

The Beginnings: New Orleans

In 1917, after relocating to New York from Chicago, some white veterans of New Orleans, led by an Italian-American, Nick LaRocca, who back home had been playing in Jack "Papa" Laine's mixed-race band specializing in private and public events, rechristened themselves <u>Original Dixieland Jass Band</u> and recorded the first jazz record (with their *Dixie Jass Band One Step*). The success of that novelty prompted many other New Orleans musicians to move to New York. The Original Dixieland Jass Band went on to cut many more songs, mostly composed by the members of the band, in a variety of styles: *Barnyard Blues* (august 1917), *Tiger Rag* (august 1917), based on the traditional square dance *Praline*, *Ostrich Walk* (february 1917), *At The Jass Band Ball* (september 1917), *Clarinet Marmalade Blues* (july 1918), *Fidgety Feet* (february 1918), *Lazy Daddy* (july 1918), *Skeleton Jangle* (february 1918), *Satanic Blues* (august 1919), *Bluin' The Blues* (december 1920). But their specialty remained the frantic group improvisation, with a staccato style influenced by syncopated ragtime, the kind of jazz performed by white musicians that came to be called "dixieland jazz". In april 1919 LaRocca took his orchestra to London, where it was equally successful, particularly with *Soudan* (april 1920). The British recordings actually slowed down the tempo a bit, proving that some of the frenzy was simply due to the need to fit a song into the three minutes of a 78 RPM record (in Britain they recorded four-minute 12" records). These songs were "jazz" only insofar as they mimicked negro styles of music.

The term "dixieland jazz" had already been employed by another white band, Tom Brown's Dixieland Jass Band, also based in Chicago, and the first white jazz band to tour the north (although not New York).

The most sophisticated of Chicago's "dixieland" bands was perhaps the <u>New Orleans Rhythm Kings</u>, assembled in 1922 to exploit the popularity of the Original Dixieland Jazz Band and Tom Brown's band. They, too, featured an "Italian" from New Orleans, clarinetist Leon Roppolo, as well as cornetist Paul Mares (the original founder), trombonist George Brunies, pianist Elmer Schoebel (the main composer) and bassist Steve Brown. Initially they recorded as the Friars Society Orchestra: *Oriental* (august 1922), *Bugle Call Blues* (august 1922), *Farewell Blues* (august 1922). But achieved their artistic peak with *Tin Roof Blues* (march 1923), and for the first time Chicago heard white musicians play jazz music worthy of the black masters. Unlike the stormy collective playing of the Original Dixieland Jass Band, these pieces also contained solos.

Chicago had become a major center of ragtime music after the World's Fair of 1893. New Orleans trombonist Tom Brown was the leader of a white ragtime orchestra and moved to Chicago in 1915. He adopted the term "jass" that had been first been used on the West Coast and his success spawned a "jass" trend. "Jass" was identified not so much with a musical style but with a geographical place (New Orleans), with frenzied fun (bordering on slapstick) and with sexual innuendoes in a period when the authorities were trying to crack down on immoral dances. "Jass" was a term with sexual connotations, but the instrumental music of jass bands was tolerated by the moral bigots. Thus it found the right balance between being allowed to reproduce and appealing to an audience that craved morbid entertainment.

The backdrop for the boom of "dixieland jazz" was World War I: while millions of young men were being slaughtered in the trenches of Europe, Chicago was dancing at the sound of this exuberant and clownish music.

The new medium that helped spread the boom of "dixieland jazz" to the rest of the country was the record. It was the first new genre of music that spread thanks to the new medium. Previously a new form of music or dance had required the physical movement of its protagonists who had to personally evangelize the rest of the country. Dixieland jazz spread thanks to the virtual movement of the protagonists via the record. The history of jazz was, from the beginning, also the history of how the music industry learned to make music travel without making its musicians travel, first with the piano rolls of ragtime and then with the records of dixieland jazz. The appeal to see the protagonists live was still very high, but the live performance was becoming less and less indispensable. The market for records had boomed thanks to the dance craze. During the war the price of records had been significantly reduced, making records affordable for a much larger segment of society. In 1919 a law was introduced to break the monopoly of the two majors, Victor and Columbia, and allow their competitors to sell the same kind of "lateral-cut records" that could be played on the most popular phonographs. Despite the fact that the sudden popularity of the radio (followed by the Great Depression) caused a sharp decline in sales of records (that did not recover until the end of the Great Depression), the turmoil in the industry allowed more musicians to record and more fans to listen to them.

Dixieland jazz was a gross misrepresentation of jazz music for the white audience. It was a novelty architected for an unsophisticated audience that was interested only in novelties. New Orleans musicians who emigrated in the 1910s had never heard the term "jass" before they arrived in Chicago.

Black musicians were not recorded partly because of racial discrimination but partly also because they were much more jealous of their style: their aim was to hide their sound from the competition, not to spread it all over the nation.

The Original Creole Band, led by Creole trumpeter <u>Freddie Keppard</u>, was one of the New Orleans bands that never recorded for fear of being copied, but was nonetheless influential in exporting the sound of New Orleans to Los Angeles (1911), where they were lured by bassist Bill Johnson (who already had a Creole Band there), New York (1915) and Chicago (where in 1918 Johnson engineered the mutation of the band sans Keppard into King Oliver's orchestra). Keppard had been raised in Creole bands (that prevailed downtown), but, after Bolden's death, became the archetype of "hot jazz", the style of black musicians (who ruled uptown). Johnson himself popularized the swinging four beats per bar of jazz bass that made the two beats per bar of ragtime bass obsolete.

Bill Johnson transplanted jazz into the West Coast, and may be responsible for exporting the very name of the new music because "jass" was the term used around San Francisco for any kind of black music. The first group to use the term "jazz" in their name was the So Different Jazz Band led by pianist Sid LeProtti in

San Francisco around 1914, seven years after Johnson had first performed there with his pre-Keppard band. A white bandleader of San Francisco, Art Hickman, was billed as playing "jazz" already in 1913.

The first instrumental record by a black orchestra (i.e., the first black jazz record) was in fact cut in Los Angeles: *Ory's Creole Trombone* (july 1922) by Edward "Kid" Ory's Creole Orchestra, formed in 1919 by that veteran New Orleans band-leader with former New Orleans musicians who had relocated to the West Coast. Ory stayed in Los Angeles until 1925, before moving on to Chicago, where he contributed to Louis Armstrong's success (e.g., his *Muskrat Ramble* of 1925).

Black songwriter William Handy (the same man who had inaugurated the age of notated blues) recorded one of the first songs with "jazz" in the title: Benton Overstreet's *Jazz Dance* (november 1917), and performed a "jass concert" in april 1918 at New York's Selwyn Theatre. The word "jazz" began to circulate throughout the dancehalls for white people of the USA. Although initially considered only a new kind of ragtime, jazz became rapidly a sensation both in the USA and abroad.

Harlem musicians were evolving ragtime into a faster and louder syncopated style, that relied a lot more on individual improvisation. Its roots were still in blues music: the soloists were often trying to emulate the singing of the blues, and the counterpoint was trying to emulate the call-and-response of the blues. After all, many jazz musicians cut their teeth accompanying blues singers, and learned to respond to the nuances of those passionate singers. Jazz bands took the piano from ragtime, the saxophone and the trumpet from dancehall bands. But the popularity of blues singers in the 1920s was such that New York's recording industry did not show much interest for jazz orchestras.

If the origins of jazz music were confusing, the difference between New Orleans and the other epicenters was more clear: improvisation. The ragtime pianists, the syncopated orchestras (both black and white), the blues singers and even the various outfits (black and white) that used the proto-term "jass", were playing composed music with minimal (if any) degree of improvisation. The real improvisation was done only in the south, first by blues musicians (who mainly used vocals and guitar) and then by the musicians of New Orleans (who used also the horns). Improvisation introduced a different concept of musician. The musician of written music is, mainly, the composer, whereas the musician of improvised music is, mainly, the player. Because of improvisation, blues and jazz music were emphasizing the persona of the player to a degree unheard of among opera singers or classical violinists. The emphasis shifted from playing (or singing) the exact notes in a sublime manner to playing (or singing) as far as possible from the exact notes while still playing the same tune. Needless to say, the latter allowed the player a greater degree of personal emotion.

Among the early protagonists of New Orleans were: trumpeter Louis "Satchmo" Armstrong, equally famous for his "scat" singing (wordless vocal improvisation); soprano saxophonist Sidney Bechet, another black Creole, the first master of an instrument that had not previously been identified with African-

Americans; trumpeters Bunk Johnson and Freddie Keppard, another black Creole (whose "fat" sound was influential in Chicago); clarinetists Johnny Dodds (one of the wildest soloists of his time), Jimmie Noone (the epitome of elegance) and George Lewis; drummer Warren "Baby" Dodds.

Jazz music was very much a continuation of blues music, except that it took advantage of the instruments of the marching band. The jazz musician was basically "singing" just like the blues singers even though he was playing an instrument instead of using his vocals. The kind of dynamics and of improvisation was identical. The call-and-response structure was replicated in the dialogue between solo instrument and ensemble. Compared with European music, that for centuries had "trained" the voice to sound as perfect as the instruments, jazz music moved in the opposite direction when it trained the instruments to sound as emotional as the human voice of the blues. After all, many jazz instrumentalists made their living accompanying blues singers in the vaudeville circuit. The main difference between jazz and blues, i.e. the heavy syncopation, was the original contribution of ragtime.

Thus the marching bands contributed the instruments, blues singers contributed the improvisation, and ragtime contributed the syncopation (that ragtime had, in turn, taken from the "minstrel shows"). Jazz as a separate genre of music was born at the intersection of collective improvisation and heavy syncopation. Another defining feature was that it was mainly instrumental (blues music was mainly vocal). For some observers of the time jazz music may have sounded simply like the instrumental side of blues music, or the group version of ragtime, or a non-marching club-oriented evolution of the marching bands.

Soon new instruments were incorporated (such as the saxophone) and some habits developed (the "riff", a rhythmic phrase repeated several times, or the "break", a brief solo during a pause by the ensemble). The material that was played came from the most diverse sources: William Handy's songs, Scott Joplin's rags, pop songs, blues songs, and traditional slave songs. Initially, jazz musicians showed little interest in being also composers.

When Storyville was shut down in 1917, jazz simply moved with the black entertainers who had to relocate to Memphis and Chicago (e.g., King Oliver in 1918, Louis Armstrong in 1922). But the exodus of black musicians was also part of the "Great Migration" that saw thousands of blacks leave the South for the northern cities, mostly because of better job opportunities created by World War I in the North (the defense industry was mostly based in the North) and because of a boll weevil infestation that caused great damage to cotton plantations in the South. But also because of more tolerant attitudes: the industrialists of the North were literally luring blacks to their factories while plantation owners were still treating them like slaves. The result of the migration was the establishment of large black communities in Chicago, Detroit and New York, where they displaced white middle-class communities (as in New York's Harlem, that used to be a rich white neighborhood).

Jazz eventually spread to every corner of the USA. In fact, jazz was one of the first musical genres to owe its diffusion to a whole new world of communication of information. The birth of jazz music parallels a revolution in music "media". The first revolution was caused by the networks of vaudeville theaters that were formed by entrepreneurs such as Pericles "Alexander" Pantages in 1902, Martin Beck in 1905 and especially Fred Barrasso in 1907 (whose brainchild, the Theater Owners's Booking Association, or T.O.B.A., became the most important for black performers). These circuits created a low-inertia way to distribute musical novelties to the entire country: the musicians would simply follow the circuit. The dance craze of the 1910s was spread around the USA mainly by "territory bands" (both white and black) that traveled the circuit of vaudeville theaters and other improvised dancehalls. Many of them converted to jazz music after 1917. Another revolution came (in the following decade) with the popularity of the phonographic record, that turned a local phenomenon into a city-wide, state-wide and eventually country-wide phenomenon. And later (in the 1920s) the boom of jazz would come thanks to the radio, that dramatically accelerated that communication from region to region. Jazz was as much the product of New Orleans' melting pot as the product of an organizational and technological revolution.

The founding fathers

Ferdinand "Jelly Roll Morton" LaMothe, a flamboyant black (but very light-skinned) Creole pianist who stands out as the first major jazz composer, blended blues and ragtime styles, a fusion that perhaps represented the origins of jazz music better than anything else. His *Jerry Roll Blues* (september 1915) was the first published piece of jazz music. Morton left New Orleans in 1908, played in California from 1917 until 1922, then in Chicago and moved to New York City in 1928.
Discovered by publisher Walter Melrose, Morton was launched in a sextet fronted by cornet, clarinet, trombone and alto saxophone, that recorded *Big Foot Ham* (june 1923) and *Muddy Water Blues* (june 1923), and coupled with the New Orleans Rhythm Kings in performances of three of his pieces (the first inter-racial records of jazz music): *Mr Jelly Lord*, *London Blues* and *Milenberg Joys* (july 1923). Both recordings displayed Morton's skills in devising a variety of tonal and dynamic solutions.
He laid the foundations of his ensemble music with a handful of early gems, mostly for solo piano, such as *Wolverine Blues* (published in february 1923, solo version recorded in july) and several ragtime-like pieces: *The Pearls* (july 1923), *Kansas City Stomp* (july 1923), *King Porter Stomp* (july 1923), *Shreveport Stomp* (june 1924), *Froggie More* (may 1924), later renamed *Shoe Shiner's Drag* (1928) in the band version. Emblematic is also *King Porter Stomp* (december 1924) with King Oliver, one of the earliest piano-trumpet duets.
Morton perfected his style on the anarchic Chicago recordings with his Red Hot Peppers, a band created solely for studio recordings out of musicians (of different races) who were familiar with the "hot" New Orleans style (some borrowed from Louis Armstrong's Dreamland Syncopators), such as trombonist Edward "Kid" Ory and clarinetist Johnny Dodds: *Black Bottom Stomp* (september 1926), his

masterpiece, that packed a lot of action around three themes, two tempos and seven instruments, the touching *Dead Man Blues* (september 1926), that was another showcase of jazz polyphony (with a clarinet trio), *Sidewalk Blues* (september 1926), that was a rewrite of his *Fish Tail Blues* (1924), *Steamboat Stomp* (september 1926), *Grandpa's Spells* (december 1926), *Jungle Blues* (july 1927), *Mournful Serenade* (july 1928) for a quartet of piano, clarinet, trombone and drums, etc. The band's style was basically orchestrated ragtime, although rich in "decoration" (tonal variety, creative dynamics). No less creative was *Shreveport Stomp* (june 1928), one of the earliest piano-clarinet duets.

While in New York, he still delivered some influential numbers, such as *Freakish* (july 1929), that was one of his most daring solo piano pieces, as well as, with the Red Hot Peppers, *Mint Julep* (november 1929), *Ponchartrain* (march 1930) and *Fickle Fay Creep* (october 1930).

Basically, Morton liberated ragtime music from its own limitation: the clockwork geometry of melody and rhythm. The syncopation of ragtime could be applied only to some themes, while Morton's kind of syncopation could be applied to virtually anything. The secret was in a rhythmic invention that knew no boundaries, at times reminiscent of the blues, of the march, of the square dance, even of Latin-American dances. Nonetheless, Morton's art was still a clockwork art, in the sense that the performance was carefully planned and very little room was left to improvisation. His orchestra was basically an extension of the piano. No other orchestra of the time reached the same level of sonic and rhythmic sophistication. Morton's band arrangements created the stereotype of the three-pronged jazz attack (cornet, clarinet and trombone), although, ironically, the achievement of that line-up was largely due to a calculated studio strategy.

Morton was also the musician who changed the very purpose of jazz music. His recordings were just that: jazz music meant to be recorded. It was conceived and advertised as a recording of jazz music. Thus the careful architecture of group and solo parts. Thus the limit on improvisation: Morton wanted to record the sound that he wanted to record, not the unpredictable sound that improvisers could produce. Thus the studio-driven nature of his band, that basically did not exist outside the studio. There were at least two reasons for Morton's preference for the recording rather than the live performance. The first one was Walter Melrose, one of the first white businessmen to understand that there was a market for such recordings. The second one was Morton's troubles with the mobsters who ran the nightlife of Chicago: Morton's band was only a studio band because he was not welcome in the city's clubs.

The first black band to be well documented on record was actually [Joe "King" Oliver](#)'s Creole Jazz Band (1923), although Oliver too had already left New Orleans for Chicago (in 1918, to replace Freddie Keppard in Bill Johnson's Original Creole Band). King Oliver, who had developed his style at the cornet in Kid Ory's Brownskin Babies since 1914, cemented a group of talents that included cornet player Louis Armstrong, clarinetist Johnny Dodds, drummer Warren "Baby" Dodds, trombonist Honore Dutery, pianist Lil Hardin, Bill Johnson on banjo and bass. This classic line-up recorded *Dippermouth Blues*

The Beginnings: New Orleans

(april 1923), which contains Armstrong's first recorded solo, Armstrong's *Weather Bird Rag* (april 1923), Oliver's *Sugar Foot Stomp* (april 1923), and *Canal Street Blues* (april 1923), which are models of harmonious, disciplined group playing despite the group improvisation: the piano, the drums and the bass provided the rhythmic foundation over which the cornets lead the melody against the petulant counterpoint of the clarinet and the bass ("tailgate") counterpoint of the trombone. Oliver basically perfected the collective improvisation of New Orleans' marching bands. Oliver also strove to produce sounds with his cornet that reflected his vision, thus becoming the first "sound artist" of jazz. His experiments continued with the Dixie Syncopators (1925-27), a larger band with three saxophones and a tuba (Barney Bigard on reeds, Luis Russell on piano, Albert Nicholas on clarinet): *WaWaWa* (may 1926), for example, popularized the "wah-wah" technique (that he had already tested in *Dippermouth Blues*).

If Morton was basically still playing ragtime, Oliver's band was basically still a brass band (with the traditional interplay of cornet, clarinet and trombone). The real innovation was to be found in Oliver's solos: that "was" indeed a new form of music.

Cornet/trumpet player <u>Louis "Satchmo" Armstrong</u> revolutionized both the instrumental and the vocal style of jazz. King Oliver's substitute in Kid Ory's band, Armstrong left New Orleans in 1922 to join King Oliver in Chicago, where he recorded his *Weather Bird Rag* (april 1923), and then (1924) Fletcher Henderson in New York. While in New York, he also accompanied blues singers (notably Bessie Smith's legendary january 1925 recording of *St Louis Blues*) and cut some songs (Clarence Williams' *Texas Moaner Blues* in october 1924) with smaller groups that included clarinetist Sidney Bechet. In fact the classic recording of the age, and perhaps the most faithful to the original sound of New Orleans' jazz, was an interpretation of Benton Overstreet's *Early Every Morn* (december 1924) by a quintet named Red Onion Jazz Babies, organized by Clarence Williams, that featured Armstrong, Bechet, pianist Lil Hardin and blues vocalist Alberta Hunter.

In 1925 he returned to Chicago, formed the drum-less Hot Five a spin-off of King Oliver's Creole Jazz Band (Johnny Dodds on clarinet, Kid Ory on trombone, Johnny St Cyr on banjo, Lil Hardin on piano, but the line-up changed quickly), and cut songs that were celebrated for the smooth and elegant phrasing of his trumpet solos: *Gut Bucket Blues* (november 1925), *Cornet Chop Suey* (february 1926), typical of how the rest of the band was becoming mere background, *Heebie Jeebies* (february 1926), the first black recording of scat singing (already used by white vaudeville singers such as Cliff "Ukulele Ike" Edwards), *Potato Head Blues* (may 1927), with a celebrated chorus, *Wild Man Blues* (may 1927), perhaps their masterpiece recording, the peak of his "vocal" imitation, Kid Ory's *Savoy Blues* (december 1927), featuring blues guitarist Lonnie Johnson, *Muggles* (december 1928) and *A Weather Bird* (december 1928), both featuring Earl Hines on piano (especially the latter, a cornet-piano duet), Spencer Williams' *Basin Street Blues* (december 1928), featuring Earl Hines on celeste, King Oliver's *West End Blues* (july 1928), featuring both Hines on piano and Zutty Singleton on drums, opened by a lengthy and complex solo, and further enhanced by an elegant duet between his scat singing and Jimmy Strong's clarinet. Armstrong's trumpet solos were majestic, phantasmagoric and full of drama. His experience with blues singers had prompted him to develop a trumpet style that was a mirror image of human singing. His trumpet was literally the instrumental counterpart of blues singing. Lil Hardin contributed a lot of material to their repertory: *My Heart* (november 1925), *Skid-Dat-De-Dat* (november 1926), *Struttin' with Some Barbecue* (december 1927), *Hotter Than That* (december 1927), highlighted by a virtuoso vocal duet with guitarist Lonnie Johnson, reminiscent of Adelaide Hall's role in Duke Ellington's *Creole Love Call* (1927), *Two Deuces* (june 1928), etc. These performances contrasted with King Oliver's style because Armstrong's instrument dominated the proceedings: Armstrong had introduced a dose on individualism in jazz that was the antithesis of its original socialist principles. Jelly Roll Morton had used the solos to increase the sophistication of his orchestral music, but his focus was still on the sound of the ensemble. It was Armstrong who shifted the emphasis towards the vocabulary of the extended virtuoso solo. Solos became longer and longer, while displaying an even stronger sense of control.

Armstrong applied a similar technique to his vocals, which did more than just popularize "scat" singing: they invented a way to sing without singing. His singing often sounded like a conversation. Sometimes his vocals were so estranged from the music that it sounded like he didn't know what song he was singing. The voice had always been an instrument, but Armstrong started the trend that would turn it into the most malleable of instruments, away from the passion of blues, the conventions of the opera and the frigidity of pop. Armstrong turned the human voice into not only an instrument but an instrument that was as legitimate for improvising as any other instrument of the orchestra.

Under the direction of his manager Tommy Rockwell, Armstrong left Chicago in 1929 to become a globe-trotter, a veritable evangelist of jazz music around the world, while his repertory became even more commercial: Fats Waller's *Ain't Misbehavin'* (july 1929), the song that made him star, Hoagy Carmichael's *Stardust* (november 1931), the spiritual *When the Saints Go Marching In* (may 1938), *Hello Dolly* (december 1963), his best-selling record, cut with the All Stars, Bob Thiele's *What a Wonderful World* (august 1967), Wilbur Schwandt's *Dream a Little Dream of Me* (july 1968), and even a theme song for a James Bond movie, *We Have All The Time In The World* (october 1969). His fame increased exponentially among the white audience.

Armstrong became famous for his improvisations on covers of blues and pop standards. In many ways, he taught the whole jazz world how to improvise on a theme. At the same time, the charming and flamboyant player knew how to entertain an audience with the humblest of musical tools. But his contributions as a composer are rather dismal. He was more of a popular icon and entertainer than an auteur. This too influenced generations of jazz musicians who cared more for the marginal contribution of their delivery (for the "look and feel" of their music) than for the core contribution of their compositions. With Armstrong jazz became more style than substance. His influence was enormous, but it is debatable what kind of influence it was. He was certainly instrumental in making jazz music acceptable by the white middle class, and in making it a worldwide phenomenon.

After Louis Armstrong, the trumpet revolution was completed by Henry "Red" Allen, a New Orleans trumpeter who moved to New York in 1929 and became the second master of creative phrasing, both with Luis Russell's orchestra and with his own orchestra, that cut *Biff'ly Blues* (july 1929), *Feeling Drowsy* (july 1929) and *It Should Be You* (july 1929). Allen's and Russell's orchestras represented the natural bridge between the New Orleans era and the swing era.

Clarinetist Sidney Bechet was the musician who tamed the soprano saxophone for jazz music. His style at both instruments indulged in a heavy vibrato sound. His saxophone style was exuberant, eloquent and even torrential. After performing in Will-Marion Cook's orchestra during its legendary European tour of 1919, cutting a handful of tracks in 1923-24, including his first tour de force in Clarence Williams' *Kansas City Man Blues* (1923), recording with Louis Armstrong and Alberta Hunter in the Red Onion Jazz Babies (1924), and accompanying Josephine Baker in Paris (1925-29), Bechet recorded sparely, although his style was reaching maturity, as proven by his *Lay Your Racket* (september 1932) and *I Want You Tonight* (same session), and especially by Joe Jordan's *Shag* (same session), that features his most momentous playing (all of them with the seven-piece New Orleans Feetwarmers). In november 1938 his career was reborn thanks to his *Chant In The Night* and *What A Dream* (recorded by an "orchestra" of soprano sax, baritone sax, piano, guitar, drums, bass). He pioneered overdubbing when he played six instruments (clarinet, soprano saxophone, tenor saxophone, piano, bass, drums) on *Sheik of Araby* (april 1941).

A black songwriter, but born in New Orleans, Clarence Williams, claimed to have been the first to use the word "jazz" in a sheet of music. He wrote *Royal Garden Blues* (1919) for the Original Dixieland Jazz Band, before moving to Chicago (1920) and to New York (1923) where he helped bootstrap Bessie Smith's career with *Gulf Coast Blues* (february 1923) and several more hits. Williams, also a pianist himself, was instrumental in organizing the Blue Five series of recording sessions with rising stars of jazz and blues music such as Louis Armstrong and Sidney Bechet. He recorded several of his own compositions in intriguing arrangements: *Bozo* (november 1928), for a big band featuring both cornetists King Oliver and Ed Allen, *Red River Blues* (march 1928), for a quintet with piano, clarinet, cornet, tuba and washboard, *Organ Grinder Blues* (july 1928), etc.

Armstrong's counterpart at the piano was Earl Hines, one of the few early heroes of jazz who was not born in Louisiana (he was born in Pennsylvania and in 1924 moved to Chicago). His technique augmented right-hand delicate virtuoso Armstrong-style phrases with a left-hand rhythmic exuberance that set him apart from the tradition of Jelly Roll Morton. His right hand was basically trying to play the piano like a trumpet or even a trombone, while his left hand was still playing ragtime.

After recording with Louis Armstrong in 1928, and penning with clarinetist Jimmy Noone's Apex Club Orchestra his *A Monday Date* (december 1928) and Noone's *Apex Blues* (july 1929), he delivered a handful of 1928 solo piano interpretations of his own compositions, including *A Monday Date, Caution Blues* (december), *Blues In Thirds* (december), *Stowaway* (december), *Chimes In Blues* (december) and especially the fully improvised *fifty-seven Varieties* (february), that already displayed his mastery at intricate rhythmic patterns and lyrical phrasing. His own band, formed at the end of the year, became one of the best known "big bands" of swing music thanks to live radio broadcasts from their headquarter, Chicago's "Grand Terrace", and thanks to hits such as his own *Deep Forest* (june 1932), *Madhouse* (march 1933), *Rosetta* (february 1933) and *Cavernism* (february 1933), plus *Boogie Woogie on the St Louis Blues* (december 1940), a boogie-woogie adaptation of William Handy's classic, Billy Eckstine's *Jelly Jelly* (1940), also a blues, and T-Bone Walker's *Stormy Monday Blues* (november 1942). Hines later hired vocalist Billy Eckstine (1939), vocalist Sarah Vaughan (1941), trumpeter Dizzy Gillespie (1942) and alto saxophonist Charlie Parker (1943), thus involuntarily laying the foundations for the birth of bebop.

However, these masters of jazz were largely unknown to the masses. Jazz "dance" was popularized by the same white syncopated orchestras (such as Paul Whiteman's) that had popularized previous styles of dancing. Only black communities were familiar with the authentic jazz bands.

The USA, not Africa

Jazz music had been, ultimately, the product of New Orleans' melting pot, and, in general, of the negro culture of the southern states. The big difference between jazz and blues (or the spiritual or the work song) was that jazz was indeed an "American" phenomenon, not an "African" one. The roots of jazz music were in the South of the USA, not in West Africa. There was little relationship between the instruments of jazz and the original instruments of the West African slaves. The instruments of jazz came from the European brass bands. Quite simply, jazz was the product of blacks who had not been slaves, and, in most cases, couldn't even remember the ancestors who originally came from Africa: they were, quite simply, USA citizens (albeit second-class ones). Most blacks were in fact even more "American" than many of the European immigrants who were crossing the Atlantic by the millions in the years before and after World War I. Of course, the condition of blacks in the USA was one of great inferiority. However, jazz was the product of urban blacks from New Orleans, and then Chicago and then New York: the blacks who lived the least segregated life in the USA.

In fact, most jazz musicians were striving to get accepted and integrated in the USA society. They wanted to be like white people. They de facto repudiated the culture of their ancestors and were eager to adopt the culture of the whites.

Jazz music was a USA phenomenon and not an African phenomenon the same way that country music was a USA phenomenon and not a British phenomenon. The fact that country music was a descendant of British folk music does not make it any more British than, say, baseball (derived from cricket). On the other hand the fact that both jazz and country music were born in the South was very relevant: the South was more prone to create the musical identity of the new country than the industrialized North, with its close ties to Europe. In other words, the brass bands of New Orleans' funerals were more important for the development of jazz music than the rituals of West Africa.

The lyrics told the same story. The lyrics of blues songs were emotional and documentary representations of harsh conditions of life. Jazz music had no lyrics or lyrics that were as artificial as the lyrics of pop songs. Jazz lyrics were, ultimately, disposable. In fact, jazz would become a mostly instrumental genre. Blues music, on the other hand, was very much about the lyrics: instrumental-only blues music was almost an oxymoron. Thus, in spirit, jazz was closer to pop than to blues music.

Jazz was born as music to dance to. Blues music was born as music to mourn to. Again, jazz was closer to dance music than to blues music.

Last but not least, there were white jazz musicians from the very beginning, whereas there were no white blues musicians until the 1950s.

All in all, the view that jazz was "African" was a racist view. White intellectuals claimed that jazz was "African" simply because the ancestors of black musicians had come from Africa. But no white intellectual claimed that country music was British. The difference was that white society still identified blacks with a separate race. On the contrary, jazz probably represents better than anything else the historical moment when blacks stopped being an isolated, frozen culture, and became just one of the many ingredients of the melting pot, just one of the many groups of (very poor) immigrants; the moment when blacks started contributing to molding the shape and the soul of the society. Even when they rebelled against that society, they were part of it and wanted to be part of it. After all, few blacks desired to move back to Africa. They wanted to improve the society to reflect their values, just like any other member of that society.

Thus it is not surprising that it would be blues music, not jazz music, to send seismic shock waves into white music, once it began to percolate into white society. Jazz would eventually be assimilated by white pop music (from Broadway show tunes to Tin Pan Alley ballads) without causing any major upheaval. But the assimilation of blues would cause a Copernican revolution.

Early jazz was more properly a descendant of ragtime than of blues. Jazz was about embellishing a melody, an old European paradigm. Blues was more about rhythm than melody, thus remaining closer to the original African paradigm. In its early phase, jazz was recognized by both white and black audiences as a close relative of ragtime. Jazz initially had no name. For a long time, many people called it "ragtime" but they never called it "blues". There were white ragtime musicians, just like there were white jazz musicians. De facto, jazz was an evolution of ragtime, which was an evolution of the "coon song" of the minstrel shows, which were written by white people to make fun of black people: hardly an "African" tradition. The main difference between ragtime and jazz was, of course, the means of transmission. Ragtime was written composition, distributed as sheets. Jazz was improvised music, distributed as records. Other than that, the line between the two was blurred. Only in the 1920s did jazz music begin to employ complex harmonies that went well beyond ragtime harmony.

Last but not least, jazz was another stage in the ongoing process of black assimilation of white technology. Most of the instruments were as "un-African" as possible. And this was going to be the theme of black music for the rest of the century (from the electric guitar of rhythm'n'blues to the organ of gospel to the drum-machines of hip-hop). Jazz was, indirectly, also another stage in the process of black assimilation of white musical styles, because jazz was founded on ragtime, and ragtime was fundamentally the grafting of European musical styles (such as marches and waltzes) onto West-African syncopated rhythms. All in all, jazz was a lot more "white" than it appeared to be on the surface.

The West-African element of jazz music was the emphasis on (syncopated) rhythm and the widespread use of polyrhythms, or, from the viewpoint of instrumentation, the drums. (In fact, the drums remained a distinguishing feature of black musical genres until Bill Haley turned rock'n'roll into a white genre). Also largely West African was the passion for timbral exploration: where European music had always favored crisp tonality and harmonic rules (i.e., only some sounds and some combination of sounds are lawful), black music tended to explore the whole range of timbral and harmonic possibilities (something that white academic music was beginning to do independently and for different reasons at the beginning of the 20th century). This also included the prominence of blue notes (notes that are not part of the European pitch system).

The Primacy Of Improvisation

It is somewhat unfairly claimed that the essence of jazz music is its improvisation. Jazz music is supposed to be the way it is played, not the way it is composed. There is little in jazz music to support this viewpoint, though. Given a chance, many jazz musicians chose to compose, not only to improvise. Improvisation on other people's material was, in fact, more common when the musicians were using "inferior" material (pop or folk songs, or military marches, or religious hymns). The more sophisticated the music is, the less improvisation there seems to be. Thus one simple explanation for the large role of improvisation in early jazz is, quite simply, that the black musicians were forced by society and habit to perform lousy music. Their improvisation was a way to transform it into great music. Whenever jazz musicians started composing their own material, the role of improvisation changed: it became part of the compositional method. And that, perhaps, is the key contribution of jazz music to the overall history of music. It also happens to be a process that paralleled the process of emancipation from traditional compositional methods that was carried out in the 20th century by the classical avantgarde. Both jazz music and the classical avantgarde explored new ways to use melody, rhythm and harmony and to create "sound". If one views jazz improvisation as simply a new form of composition, then the jazz musician is less of an improviser and more of a composer... of sound. The dichotomy between jazz music and Euro-centric music is rather blurred. Jazz musicians began to compose their own material because improvising on other people's material was neither fun nor as rewarding as improvising on one's own material. Even in its most extreme "free" genre, one can find a kind of jazz "composition": the set of rules on how to create the sound desired by the "composer".

The focus on the performer in jazz was real, but perhaps it simply masqueraded the rise of a different kind of composer.

The real dichotomy was to be found in the "composer": it is always singular in classical music, whereas it is often plural in jazz (and rock) music. The sound of a band is rarely due only to the ideas of the leader/composer. More than one member is usually responsible for the "composition". That remained the real difference between jazz and classical composition (but it also applied to rock music).

CHICAGO: WHITE JAZZ

The "Great Migration" from the south to the north, the closure of Storyville (1917) and the rise of Al Capone and other mobsters following the Prohibition (1920) turned Chicago into a bustling center of black entertainment. The gangsters who ruled the city were protectors of music, that was a necessity for their gambling, alcohol and prostitution rackets. The black musicians coming from the south found a new paradise to replace Storyville.

As jazz music moved to Chicago, the role of the soloist became more prominent, and the ensemble playing became more complex. In New Orleans the collective sound had prevailed over the individual sound, in Chicago individual players were allowed more freedom to improvise. This may have been simply a consequence of jazz musicians being more self-assured, or of the influence of the freewheeling spirit of the big city. When jazz musicians arrived in Chicago, they were often employed by gangsters. Their first audience was the mob. It may have been that the scarce musical sophistication of the gangsters made it possible for jazz soloists to break the rules of New Orleans' band playing.

Jazz was immediately successful in Chicago. In the age of Prohibition the "speakeasy" helped whites hear the music of the blacks, and, indirectly, the speakeasy marketed it as fun, exciting music. The first commercial radio station opened the same year that the Prohibition started, in 1920. Within a few years there were several radio stations. Radio stations generally boycotted jazz and blues music, but enough percolated through the air waves to increase the cult status of jazz. However, it was the record that contributed to spread jazz among the white audience.

Cornet player Bix Beiderbecke was the first white jazz master. Born in Iowa, far away from any major source of black music, he was also the first major musician to learn about jazz from records, not first hand. No surprise therefore that his technique was unorthodox. However, his tone was almost baroque. He arrived in Chicago in 1921 and recorded for the first time in 1924, with the Wolverine Orchestra (Tom Delaney's *Jazz Me Blues*). His reputation was rapidly established by a diverse output, mostly in New York: his own *Davenport Blues* (january 1925) for a quintet of cornet, clarinet, trombone, piano and drums (called the Rhythm Jugglers), Con Conrad's *Singin' the Blues* (february 1927), arranged by Bill Challis for Frank Trumbauer's orchestra, that contains Beiderbecke's most celebrated solo, the Original Dixieland Jass Band's *Clarinet Marmalade* (february 1927), also with Trumbauer, *Clementine* (september 1927) with the Jean Goldkette Orchestra, Walter Donaldson's *Changes* (november 1927) with Paul Whiteman, Will Marion Cook's *I'm Coming Virginia* (may 1927), arranged by Irving Riskin again for Trumbauer's orchestra, containing some of his most moving passages. Contemporaries were shocked by the lyrical and pensive quality that Beiderbecke could evoke through his unorthodox handling of timbre and timing.

Chicago: White Jazz

He formed his own orchestra (Gang) and continued to refine his introverted style, particularly via the october 1927 recordings of Spencer Williams' *Royal Garden Blues*, Fletcher Henderson's *Goose Pimples* and Howdy Quicksell's *Sorry* and *Since My Best Girl Turned Me Down*. His own compositions were less famous, and delivered as solo piano pieces, but in reality *In a Mist* (september 1927), perhaps his masterpiece (more influenced by Debussy than by jazz), *Candlelight* (1930), *Flashes* (1931), *In The Dark* (1931), proved the depth of his musical vision. Before his untimely death, Beiderbecke gave several more essays of his lyrical playing: Bill Challis' *San* (january 1928), Fred Fisher's *There Ain't No Sweet Man That's Worth the Salt of My Tears* (september 1927), George Gershwin's *Concerto in F* (october 1928), Bing Crosby's *From Monday On* (february 1928) and Irving Berlin's *Waiting at the End of the Road* (september 1929), all with Paul Whiteman, as well as Harry Barris' *Mississippi Mud* (january 1928) with Trumbauer, and the proto-swing of Maceo Pinkard's *I'll Be a Friend with Pleasure* (september 1930) with his own band. The association with Trumbauer was probably the most fruitful, while the commercial Goldkette orchestra allowed the talents of Beiderbecke, Trumbauer, guitarist Salvatore "Eddie Lang" Massaro and violinist Joe Venuti to come together, despite the limitations of Goldkette's repertory. They all eventually, and sadly, migrated into Paul Whiteman's orchestra, which was even more commercial and which even further diluted and restrained their inspiration. An alcoholic, he died in 1931 at the age of 28. His minimal, tenuous style of improvisation had basically reflected his imploding lifestyle. Needless to say, one wonders what Beiderbecke could have done had he played in black orchestras instead of white ones.

Beiderbecke was the vanguard of a wave of white jazz soloists who gravitated towards Chicago: banjoist Eddie Condon, who moved to New York in 1929; drummer Gene Krupa, the first drummer to experiment with extended solos, who moved to New York with Condon in 1929 and became a star in Benny Goodman's big band formed in 1934; clarinetist Charles "Pee Wee" Russell, who moved to New York in 1927 where he first recorded in 1929; tenor saxophonist Lawrence "Bud" Freeman, who moved to New York in 1928; and especially xylophonist Kenneth "Red Norvo" Norville, who composed and recorded one of the most avantgarde pieces of the time, *Dance Of The Octopus* (november 1933) for a quartet of xylophone, guitar, bass and clarinet (Benny Goodman), and was also the first jazz musician to try the vibraphone.

These white players were actually important to introduce more and more soloing instruments into the canon of jazz (add Jack Teagarden for the trombone, Eddie Lang for the guitar and Joe Venuti for the violin).

Early Chicago big bands of the mid 1920s included: Erskine Tate's Vendome Orchestra, Charles Cooke's, Dave Peyton's.

As far as jazz goes, the rise of Chicago corresponded with the demise of New Orleans, the former cradle of jazz whose jazz scene had all but vanished by the 1930s.

NEW YORK: STRIDE PIANO

One of the most significant innovations in the early history of jazz music was the dramatic transformation of piano playing that took place as jazz migrated from New Orleans to Chicago to New York, the capital of ragtime. In 1920, as the 25-year old fad of ragtime was beginning to wane and the blues was becoming the new fad, New York's jazz pianist began to blend blues and ragtime. The sound that resulted from that fusion was dense and loud, and came to be called "stride" piano.

The place where the synthesis took place might actually have been Atlantic City. Before World War I that was the city where pianists from all over the country converged during the summer to entertain the guests of the various establishments of the red-light district. Pianists who performed in Atlantic City included Eubie Black from Baltimore (from 1906), Luckey Roberts from Philadelphia, Willie "The Lion" Smith and James Johnson (1914) from New York. When the summer season was over, most of these pianists would move to Harlem, the black ghetto of New York, where an entire subculture of night-clubs for black people was booming. In the 1920s, following the vogue of blues music, Harlem was invaded by the white tourists, who came to check out the exotic music of the blacks. So those clubs (and their performers) began to cater to a white audience. They authentic black-piano experience (and innovation) moved to the "rent parties", i.e. parties meant to raise money to pay rent, that became extremely popular after the end of World War II among poor black tenants of Harlem. Those were the years when "stride" piano came into its own.

Philadelphia-born Charles "Luckey" Roberts was in many ways the "founder" of the New York school of pianists. He was the first Harlem pianist to be published (*Junk Man Rag*, 1913) and recorded (october 1916). His most famous and difficult tune was *Ripples of the Nile* (1912), reworked as *Moon Light Cocktail* (may 1942) for Glenn Miller. He also composed classical music: a three-movement *Spanish Suite* (1939), and the "miniature syncopated rhapsody" for piano and orchestra *Whistlin' Pete* (1941).

Jazz music appropriated the instruments that were popular in the community, such as the brass bands of New Orleans. New York (and particularly Harlem, that was rapidly becoming a black ghetto) did not have a musical culture based on brass bands but rather one based on the piano, an instrument that had become extremely popular everywhere during the first decade, and even so in the big cities of the Northeast. Of course, ragtime was the main driver for piano sales in New York. Ragtime pianist and composer Eubie Blake best represents the link between ragtime and "stride". The latter was a style that developed in response to the need of providing both rhythm and melody: the left hand was in charge of the beat, but it was allowed to "stride" all over the keyboard to enliven the piece, while the right hand improvised difficult melodic figures. Stride piano produced an "orchestral" sound, the sound of pianists who could not afford a backing band.

Despite the brisk pace and the syncopation, stride piano was also important in providing the foundations to bring jazz and classical music. These pianists were aware of and intrigued by the European musical tradition.

The three masters of stride piano were James Johnson, probably the "inventor" of the style, Thomas "Fats" Waller, who was by far the most commercially successful and probably the best composer, and Willie "The Lion" Smith.

Stride pianist James Johnson was also one of the greatest composers of the era. Piano rolls and piano solos that he composed in a variety of idioms include: *Steeplechase Rag* (may 1917), the archetype of his dramatic playing, originally published in 1912, *Daintiness Rag* (july 1917), first published in 1914, *Mama's Blues* (july 1917), *Carolina Shout* (february 1918), one of his signature (i.e., technically difficult) rags, composed in 1914, *Keep Off The Grass* (october 1921), *Harlem Strut* (june 1922), *Weeping Blues* (june 1923), *Worried And Lonesome Blues* (june 1923), *You Can't Do What My Last Man Did* (july 1923), *Charleston* (1923), a pop tune written for a Broadway show and soon to become the anthem of the decade, *Snowy Morning Blues* (february 1927), *If I Could Be With You* (march 1927), a duet with Waller, *Feeling Blue* (january 1929), the acrobatic *Riffs* (january 1929). The hits came later: *Liza* (april 1937), *The Mule Walk* (december 1938), *Blueberry Rhyme* (june 1939), His most popular song was *Old Fashioned Love* (recorded by Cliff "Ukulele Ike" Edwards in 1923). But he also tried his hand at classical composition: the four-movement "negro rhapsody" *Yamecraw* (1928), a *Tone Poem* (1930), the *Harlem Symphony* (1932), the piano concerto *Jassamine* (1934), and the opera *De Organizer* (1940).

Harlem native Thomas "Fats" Waller completed the fusion of blues, ragtime and stride piano while also inaugurating a jazz style at the organ. His compositions of the 1920s, that constitute a synthesis of all the (secular and religious, white and black) musical styles he heard while growing up in Harlem, made him the most famous of the jazz pianists: the piano roll of Spencer Williams' *Got to Cool My Doggies Now* (march 1923), Clarence Williams' *Squeeze Me* (february 1926), *Messin' Around With The Blues Blue* (january 1927), *Rusty Pail* and *Soothin' Syrup Stomp* (january 1927), with a typical pipe-organ solo, *The Whiteman Stomp* (1927), the Broadway musical **Connie's Hot Chocolates** (1929), that included *Ain't Misbehavin'* and the protest song *Black And Blue* (both hits for their performer, Louis Armstrong), his canonical piano solo *Handful Of Keys* (march 1929), *Valentine Stomp* (august 1929), *I've Got a Feeling I'm Falling* (august 1929), *Smashing Thirds* (september 1929), still reminiscent of ragtime, *Blue Turning Grey Over You* (published in 1930). During the Great Depression he composed conventional ballads such as *Honeysuckle Rose* (november 1934) with the studio band The Rhythm and *Keepin' Out Of Mischief* (june 1937), besides *The Joint Is Jumping* (1937) and the celebrated *Jitterbug Waltz* (march 1942) with an orchestra, although some of his biggest hits were no longer his own compositions, such as Harry Warren's *Lulu's Back in Town* (1935) and Fred Ahlert's *I'm Gonna Sit Right Down and Write Myself a Letter* (1935). But he also continued to craft austere solo compositions/performances, such as the boogie-woogie *Alligator Crawl* (november 1934), the ragtime *African Ripples* (march 1935), the mini-suite *Clothes Line Ballet* (march 1935), and the *London Suite* (june 1939), whose six movements borrowed from a broad range of exotic, classical and jazz styles. He was one of the most prolific and "poppiest" composers of early jazz.

Willie "The Lion" Smith was the least recorded of the three giants of stride piano. In fact, he was not recorded until well into the Great Depression, and his signature songs *Finger Buster* (january 1939) and *Rippling Waters* (january 1939) date from the end of the decade. But he was probably the authentic stride "animal", living only to display his virtuosity.

Art Tatum, who arrived in New York in 1932 from provincial Ohio, was the man who summarized all of their styles, and went beyond. He very much disengaged jazz piano from the formulas of New York's stride piano and of New Orleans, and opened up unlimited horizons for it, although he personally never ventured into the avantgarde, preferring to stick to his job of ornating the melody with a virtually unlimited arsenal of tricks. His dexterity, introducing a degree of improvisation that had not been known before, resulted not only in a display of piano acrobatics (he could play the most complex passage at a speed of 400 beats per minute) but in a much broader vocabulary and a much more expressive language. He coined the language, but he failed to write the poem: his style was a baroque infrastructure of embellishments. That colossal apparatus of technique was tested mainly on brief pop tunes, it was never adequately employed for a major composition. Fame and respect came in 1933 with a breakneck version of Nick LaRocca's *Tiger Rag* (march 1933), and his first hit came with a solo-piano cover of Vincent Youmans' pop tune *Tea for Two* (march 1933). His repertory would remain of this (very trivial) quality. He mostly performed solo because his quasi-polyphonal playing almost simulated a band, and few musicians could play at his speed anyway.

NEW YORK: BIG BANDS

Another phenomenon, radically opposite in spirit from the soloists of Chicago and to the stride pianists of New York, came to epitomized the "Harlem Renaissance" of the 1920s more than any other.

The flow of musicians from Chicago to New York merged with the local phenomenon of the syncopated orchestra. New Yorkers such as James Europe (who dominated the scene until his untimely death in 1919) had never truly understood the spirit of jazz music, but the Chicago musicians brought it with them. Thus the 1917 novelty of the Original Dixieland Jass Band survived and evolved into a "style", not necessarily representative of the New Orleans sound but certainly a different style from the syncopated orchestra.

As the jazz dance bands became more popular than the traditional syncopated dance bands, jazz bands also became "bigger". They were still smaller than the symphonic orchestra but much larger than the old New Orleans orchestras. It was mainly economic pressure that caused this apparent regression to the pop orchestra: the masses loved to dance, and expected an orchestra to provide the music. They liked the sound of jazz music, but not quite the format of the small group or (worse) soloist. Basically, the big bands of jazz offered a compromise: jazz music (with improvising soloists) played according to the conventions of pop music. The repertory too was often taken or derived from the repertory of Broadway, Tin Pan Alley and the vaudeville. Thus these bands played music that was arranged in sophisticated manners, although it still left room for individual improvisation.

In 1926 the "Savoy Ballroom" had opened in Harlem. It was destined to become the epicenter of the big band phenomenon, and the stage for its first star: Ella Fitzgerald.

The first negro big band of jazz was organized in New York in 1922 by a former blues and stride pianist, Fletcher Henderson (who had arrived in 1920 from Georgia to study chemistry). He and his arranger Don Redman (the alto saxophonist) introduced written scores into jazz music: written music that sounded like improvised music. Tenor saxophonist Coleman Hawkins (who had moved to New York in 1922 and had joined Henderson in 1923) raised the standard of musicianship, incidentally making the saxophone (until then a marginal instrument) one of the distinctive features of jazz music. The partnership among these three giants (all three coincidentally born far away from New York, and college educated) was largely responsible for evolving the early standard of the big band out of the original model of King Oliver's sound. Hawkins learned the art of embellishing a melody from Louis Armstrong (who played with them in 1924 and 1925) and from Art Tatum. Redman's genius developed quickly from *Dicty Blues* (august 1923), the first experiment with separate reed and brass sections, to King Oliver's *Dippermouth Blues* with Armstrong, renamed *Sugar Foot Strut* (may 1925), from Walter Melrose's

Copenhagen (october 1924) to *The Stampede* (may 1926), credited to the Dixie Stompers, a powerful example of how Redman's arrangements smoothly incorporated even the most individual solos and Hawkins' solo that signaled his break with the tradition, from *Tozo* (january 1927), Redman's first experiment with ternary rhythms, to *Rocky Mountain Blues* (january 1927), culminating with the dadaist *The Whiteman Stomp* (may 1927). Clarinetist Buster Bailey, trumpeter Tommy Ladnier, and trombonist Jimmy Harrison (the main stylist between Teagarden and Tommy Dorsey, who adapted Armstrong's innovations to the trombone) also contributed to the sound of the era. Redman and his cohorts invented jazz for orchestra based on the coexistence of written scores and on improvised solos, an epochal change of format for jazz music. He managed to harmonize the language of the sections of the orchestra and the language of the soloing instruments. Redman's passion for saxophones (ignored in New Orleans but already popular in white orchestras) and for clarinets (his specialty) added fire to the texture.

After Redman left in 1927, Henderson took up composing and arranging chores with the collaboration of alto saxophonist Benny Carter (who had joined in 1928), notably on *Keep A Song In Your Soul* (december 1930), *Down South Camp Meeting* (september 1934) and *Wrappin' It Up* (september 1934). Henderson subscribed to the same general philosophy of sound, but greatly simplified Redman's intricate arrangements. The most significant innovation of this period was the replacement of the tuba with John Kirby's double bass, for example in Jean Schwartz's *Chinatown My Chinatown* (october 1930), an act (inspired by Jean Goldkette's bassist Steve Brown) that would change the rhythm section of jazz forever.

In 1932 Carter left, in 1934 Hawkins left and in 1936 Kirby left too, although new talents came in (notably trumpeter Henry "Red" Allen). Henderson's last influential recordings were tenor saxophonist Leon "Chu" Berry's *Christopher Columbus* (march 1936), with Roy Eldridge on trumpet, and Louis Prima's *Sing Sing Sing* (august 1936).

Under the influence of Fletcher Henderson's orchestra, jazz big bands soon came to be dominated by the three-section dogma: a reed section (saxophones, clarinets), a brass section (trumpets, trombones), and a rhythm section (piano, tuba, banjo, drums) that were clearly separated although they operated jointly.

Big-band jazz also adopted a more vibrant rhythm, the "swing" (four beats to the bar).

Artistically the era of "swing" and of the big bands was dominated by Edward "Duke" Ellington's orchestra, Ellington being the first great composer (and self-arranger) of jazz music (and one of the most prolific in the entire history of music). A Washington pianist, raised in a middle-class family, who had moved to New York in 1923, he first proved his skills as a composer with the Washingtonians, that included drummer William "Sonny" Greer: *Choo Choo* (november 1924), a novelty that imitated the sound of a train, *East St Louis Toodle-Oo* (november 1926), originally credited to the Kentucky Club Orchestra, his first major artistic statement and the manifesto of trombonist Joe Nanton's brash ebullience, *New Orleans Low-Down* (february 1927), also by the Kentucky Club Orchestra, with a typical light-hard contrast between the two trumpets, *Black and Tan Fantasy* (april 1927), a metaphysical fantasia that ended with a funeral march and was highlighted (the october version) by a dramatic trumpet solo, *Washington Wobble* (october 1927), the first recording credited to the Duke Ellington's Orchestra, *Creole Love Call* (october 1927), in which Adelaide Hall's wordless singing basically instructs the instruments how to play (thus reenacting the primordial relationship between blues vocals and jazz instruments), *Harlem River Quiver* (december 1927), and, again both credited to the Washingtonians, *Jubilee Stomp* (march 1928), with another epochal trumpet solo, and *The Mooche* (october 1928), another stomp a` la *Black and Tan Fantasy* but featuring blues guitarist Lonnie Johnson.

Bubber Miley's wah-wah trumpet (originally an imitation of the blues shouting of Mamie Smith, whom he accompanied in 1921) was as essential as Ellington's piano. The growling sound of both his trumpet and Joe Nanton's trombone lent the band's sound its "savage" appeal. Couple with Sonny Greer's primordial drumming, they evoked the African-jungle, and therefore was advertised as "jungle music". But Ellington soon dispelled the notion of being a novelty act by debuting his archetypal "mood" (impressionistic) pieces, *Misty Mornin'* (november 1928), *Awful Sad* (october 1928) and *Hot And Bothered* (october 1928). In fact, even the most facile and danceable of Ellington's pieces exhibited the ability to maximize drama and color within a three-minute song that only Jelly Roll Morton had mastered before him.

Between 1927 and 1931 Ellington performed at Harlem's "Cotton Club", in front of an audience that was mostly white. These shows were occasionally broadcasted live, a fact that made Ellington a nation-wide celebrity. He owed it to white manager and publisher Irving Mills, the man who promoted his music as "jungle" music, who found him the contract at the "Cotton Club", and who made sure the shows were broadcasted on the radio.

He seemed capable of delivering tunes like an assembly line: *Doin' The Voom Voom* (january 1929), *Flamin' Youth* (january 1929), *Harlem Flat Blues* (march 1929), credited to the Jungle Band and highlighted by Nanton's "talking" solo, *The Dicty Glide* (march 1929), *Sweet Dreams Of Love* (june 1930), *Sweet Jazz Of Mine* (june 1930), the raunchy stomp *Old Man Blues* (august 1930), *What Good Am I Without You* (november 1930), *I'm So In Love With You* (november 1930). The collective interplay first achieved on *Old Man Blues* (august 1930) crystallized with *Rockin' In Rhythm* (january 1931), *Echoes of the Jungle* (june 1931) and *Mystery Song* (june 1931).

When that engagement came to an end (1931), Ellington began to show the real breadth of his ambitions: *Creole Rhapsody*, that was released in two versions (six minutes in january 1931 and eight minutes in june 1931), both requiring more than a side (the first one took up both sides of a 10" record, the second one took up both sides of a 12" record), the nine-minute suite *Symphony in Black* (october 1934), and the splendid 13-minute *Reminiscing in Tempo* (september 1935), possibly the first thoroughly composed jazz piece (originally recorded over four sides), were the longest jazz pieces ever committed to a record, challenging the limitations of the medium (the 78 RPM record could hardly fit three minutes of music), and felt like jazz music's equivalent of a classical concerto; while his melodic themes, that included *Mood Indigo* (december 1930), in which he turned upside down the conventions of jazz by assigning the highest part to the trumpet, the middle to the trombone and the lowest to the clarinet, *It Don't Mean a Thing If It Ain't Got That Swing* (february 1932), the birth certificate of swing music, the first major hit with a vocalist (Ivie Anderson on wordless scatting), *Sophisticated Lady* (february 1933), *Daybreak Express* (december 1933), *Solitude* (january 1934) and *In A Sentimental Mood* (april 1935), were worthy of the most gifted of Tin Pan Alley's songwriters, but with atmospheric and almost philosophical overtones that harked back to classical music. The group's ambience owed quite a bit to the majestic tones of alto saxophonist Johnny Hodges (the first great master of the instrument) and to the very long notes of baritone saxophonist Harry Carney (both had joined in 1928).

Puerto Rican trombonist Juan Tizol (who had joined in 1929) introduced an exotic element with his compositions: *Caravan* (december 1936), that debuted Afro-Cuban rhythms in a swing context, *A Gypsy Without A Song* (june 1938), and *Perdido* (december 1941).

Ellington composed relatively few songs in the first half of the 1930s, and a lot more at the end of the decade. Not surprisingly, the former are mostly masterpieces and the latter are mostly disposable. However, even the classics of Ellington's later years show how broad his stylistic territory was, ranging from dance numbers to catchy tunes, from mood pieces to abstract meditations: the micro-concerto *Clarinet Lament* (february 1936), also known as *Barney's Concerto*, the ambitious *Crescendo in Blue* (september 1937), the pensive *Lost In Meditation* (january 1938), originally titled *Have a Heart*, *Prelude To A Kiss* (august 1938), another of his paradisiacal melodies, *Braggin' In Brass* (march 1938), a frantic piece which instead dispensed with melody altogether, the dejected *Ko-Ko* (march 1940), *Jack the Bear* (march 1940), propelled by bassist Jimmy Blanton (who had joined in 1939 but died in 1942), the greatest virtuoso yet of the instrument who turned the bass into a melodic vehicle, *Cotton Tail* (may 1940), another tortuous melody with a brainy solo by tenor saxophonist Ben Webster (who had just joined), *Never No Lament* (may 1940), an instrumental later adapted to lyrics as *Don't Get Around Much Anymore*, the ebullient *Harlem Air-shaft* (july 1940), *Bojangles* (may 1940), dedicated to tap dancer Bill Robinson, *Sepia Panorama* (july 1940), a micro-concerto drenched in blues music that displayed Ellington, Blanton and Webster at their best, *Pitter Patter Panther* (october 1940), the ultimate duet between Blanton and Ellington, the tone poems *Dusk* (may 1940) and *Moon Mist* (february 1941), *Take The "A" Train* (january 1941), composed by pianist Billy Strayhorn (who had joined in 1939), *I Got It Bad And That Ain't Good* (june 1941), another showcase for Ivie Anderson's scat singing, *Main Stem* (june 1942), a showcase for Hodges, *The 'C' Jam Blues* (september 1941), *I'm Beginning To See The Light* (december 1944), *Happy Go Lucky Local* (november 1946), and two more experiments with the human voice, *Transbluency* (january 1946), and *On a Turquoise Cloud* (december 1947), Kay Davis' wordless masterpieces.

Ellington lost Williams in 1940, Blanton in 1941, Anderson in 1942, Webster in 1943, Tizol in 1944, cornetist Rex Stewart (who had been with him since 1934) in 1945, Hodges and Greer in 1951. The last hit of his band was *Satin Doll* (april 1953). *Fleurette Africaine* (september 1962), perhaps his last great melody, was a collaboration with Charles Mingus and Max Roach.

His mind and his heart were clearly no longer into songs. To start with, the new format of the long-playing allowed him to think differently. **Masterpieces by Ellington** (december 1950) contained a 15-minute version of *Mood Indigo* that sounded like the belated manifesto of his vision of the entire orchestra as one large instrument, the instrument that he played. Second, he was fascinated by the challenge of creating an extended format for jazz music. He already had under his belt *Echoes Of Harlem* (december 1936), better known as *Concerto For Cootie*, ostensibly a showcase for the trumpet of Cootie Williams (who had replaced Miley in 1929), the three-movement orchestral suite *Black Brown and Beige* (premiered in january 1943), a musical recapitulation to the odyssey of black Americans, the three impressionist suites *Perfume Suite* (december 1944), *Deep South Suite* (november 1946) and *Liberian Suite* (december 1947), *Jam-A-Ditty* (january 1946), ostensibly a "concerto for four jazz horns", and the two musicals **Jump for Joy** (july 1941) and **Beggar's Holiday** (december 1946), an adaptation of John Gay's "Beggar's Opera". Now he proceeded to compose ever more ambitious music: the 14-minute tone poem *Harlem* (composed in 1950), the profound **Piano Reflections** (april 1953), the 12-movement suite **Such Sweet Thunder** (august 1956), inspired by Shakespeare and a collaboration with Billy Strayhorn, the musical *A Drum Is A Woman* (september 1956), co-written with Billy Strayhorn and another artistic peak, the pageant *My People* (august 1963), the *Far East Suite* (december 1966), another Strayhorn collaboration (a suite of songs composed between 1963 and 1966), the three-movement suite *The Golden Broom And The Green Apple* (premiered in july 1965 by the New York Philharmonic with Ellington conducting), the suite *La Plus Belle Africaine* (july 1966), the first *Concert of Sacred Music* (september 1965), the *Second Sacred Concert* (january 1968) and the third *Concert of Sacred Music* (october 1973), that were three colossal compositions for gospel choirs, jazz band and dancers, the *Latin American Suite* (premiered in september 1968), the ballet *The River* (may 1970), the six-movement *The Queen's Suite* (february 1959), perhaps his best suite, the *New Orleans Suite* (april 1970) and the opera comique *Queenie Pie* (unfinished in 1974). He was trying to give a more organic structure to his genius. In the process, he invented the future of jazz.

Ellington was one of the first black beneficiaries of the radio, a medium that dramatically changed the dynamics of jazz music at a time when another major revolution was taking place: the end of the Prohibition (1933). As alcohol became legal again, people didn't need to congregate in the speakeasy anymore. An obvious audience for black musicians was fast disappearing, replaced by the more organized music industry of the night clubs and the publishing houses. At that time the radio was a powerful tool to spread one's music throughout the country but, needless to say, the radio could not deliver the atmosphere of the live performance and the charisma of the players. Thus a musician's fame rested uniquely on the music. At the same time, the black musicians who were successful in making the transition to the radio were finally given a chance to become celebrities, something that had been unthinkable before the age of the radio. The radio propelled sales of records, which became an even more substantial source of revenues than publishing. Thus the landscape changed: recording and broadcasting came to dominate the music industry, and they were both big industries, run by big business. Music lost its regional dimension and acquired a new national dimension.

Bandleaders of New York who mainly employed vocalists included: Chick Webb, Lucky Millinder and Cab Calloway.

The swing orchestra formed by drummer William "Chick" Webb was highlighted by the arrangements of Edgar Sampson (*Let's Get Together* of 1933, *Stompin' At The Savoy* of 1934), by the flute of Wayman Carver (from 1934), the first major flute soloist of jazz music, and by the voice of Ella Fitzgerald (from 1934), notably in Sampson's *I'll Chase the Blues Away* (june 1935), Harry White's *Harlem Congo* (november 1937) and Van Alexander's *A-Tisket A-Tasket* (may 1938). When Webb died in 1939, Fitzgerald took over as bandleader.

Cab Calloway's orchestra, that replaced Ellington's band at the "Cotton Club" in 1931, was famous for the leader's scat-jive vocals that debuted with *Minnie the Moocher* (march 1931), as well as for *Jitterbug* (january 1934), composed by one of his trumpeters, Edwin Swayzee, the song that gave a name to the style of swing dancing. But Calloway also architected the frenzied *Some of These Days* (december 1930), the nonsensical *Scat Song* (february 1932), Harry White's oneiric *Evenin'* (september 1933). He was a virtuoso of singing, combining Louis Armstrong's scat singing with a broader and more powerful vocal range. His ironic scat phrase "hi-de-hi-de-hi-de-ho" not only led the band but also inspired the audience to sing along. His lyrics for the saga of Minnie used the lingo of drug addicts and gangsters (Harold Arlen's *Kicking The Gong Around* of october 1931), while songs like *You Dog* (october 1931) were full of sexual innuendoes. Even in these songs, where the words are clearly sung, Calloway managed to introduce a vocabulary of original vocal effects. The Calloway orchestra of the 1940s was a different beast, relying on bassist Milt Hilton (1936-51), one of the great virtuosi of the instrument, trumpeter Dizzy Gillespie (1939-41), who had replaced Adolphus "Doc" Cheatham (1932-39), and tenor saxophonist Chu Berry (1937-41) to pen sophisticated instrumentals such as Hilton's *Pluckin' the Bass* (august 1939), Don Redman's *Cupid's Nightmare* (july 1940), Benny Carter's *Lonesome Nights* (august 1940) and Victor Young's *Ghost of a Chance* (june 1940).

Lucius "Lucky Millinder" Venable's orchestra featured trumpeter Henry "Red" Allen, vocalist Rosetta Tharpe and pianist Bill Doggett.

Jimmie Lunceford's band was emblematic of the tight and stylish sound of the last phase of swing. That relaxed sound was mostly due to the arrangements of

New York: Big Bands

Sy Oliver (1934-39), the brain behind *Shake Your Head* (october 1934), *My Blue Heaven* (1935), *Organ Grinder's Swing* (august 1936), one of his most eccentric creations, *For Dancers Only* (june 1937), *Honey Keep Your Mind on Me* (1937), with a celebrated solo by guitarist Eddie Durham, *Margie* (january 1938), with a celebrated solo by trombonist James "Trummy" Young, *Tain't What You Do* (january 1939). While in his orchestra, Eddie Durham introduced the amplified guitar into jazz music, for example in their cover of Harold Arlen's *Hittin' The Bottle* (1935). After Sy Oliver left, he was replaced by trumpeter Gerald Wilson, whose *Yard Dog Mazurka* (august 1941) and *Hi Spook* (1941) displayed a proto-bebop approach to arrangement.

Chicago's jazz was an evolution of New Orleans' jazz, still tied to the original tenets of New Orleans. New York's jazz was a much more sophisticated form of music, related not only with pop music but also with classical music.

NEW YORK: THE SWING ERA

In New Orleans and Chicago, jazz had been synonymous with music for "speakeasy" and brothels. The first radio stations had boycotted it. Bigots had warned parents against the demonic effects of jazz on teenagers. Everything changed in june 1924, when a concert organized by the Paul Whiteman orchestra at a classical music venue, legitimized jazz to white America by performing both dixieland classics and the premiere of George Gershwin's *Rhapsody in Blue*. Suddenly, jazz was not only respectable but even highbrow; and white. Trouble is that Whiteman had not performed jazz at all: he had performed the first easy-listening adaptation of jazz music. The public at large never heard of Fletcher Henderson, but everybody knew Whiteman's "jazz". Coincidentally or not, the "Cotton Club" became the hub of black entertainment for white folks in the years following that event. It had become "hip" to listen to jazz music. A few years later, another event contributed to make jazz extremely popular among whites: Al Jolson's performance in **The Jazz singer** (1927), the first "talking" movie. Never mind that Jolson was a minstrel (a white man who painted his face black) and sang sentimental ballads: he was almost the antithesis of the jazz singer. In 1930 George Gershwin completed the assimilation of jazz music by writing *I Got Rhythm* for a successful musical. Among the musicians who played in the pit orchestra of that Broadway show was a young clarinetist, Benny Goodman.

Until then, white New York musicians had been relatively peripheral to the gestation of jazz music. Other than importing dixieland bands from Chicago, New York had not developed a distinctive style of white jazz music. The first home-grown style of New York's white jazz was the invention of cornet player Ernest "Red" Nichols, who had emigrated to the city in 1923. He pioneered "chamber jazz" with his Five Pennies, a rotating cast of white virtuosi that initially featured Miff Mole on trombone and Jimmy Dorsey on alto sax and clarinet, but later, at different times, absorbed Glenn Miller and Jack Teagarden on trombones, Bud Freeman on tenor sax, Pee Wee Russell on clarinet, Eddie Condon on guitar, Gene Krupa on drums. Nichols' compositions were rare: *That's No Bargain* (december 1926), *Hurricane* (march 1927), *Five Pennies* (june 1927), *I May Be Wrong* (august 1929), *They Didn't Believe Me* (august 1929). He was much more interested in sculpting a "white" sound for jazz music, a sound that maintained little of jazz's exuberance and vitality, and instead focused on a more intellectual experience. This idea turned him into one of the most famous (and prolific) musicians of the time. His records sold tens of thousands of copies and influenced scores of white musicians, setting the stage for a bigger revolution.

The French-born bandleader Jean Goldkette organized a white band in Detroit devoted to dance-pop songs that in 1926 commanded Bix Beiderbecke on cornet, Frankie Trumbauer on saxophone, Steve Brown on bass, Eddie Lang on guitar, Joe Venuti on violin, Tommy Dorsey on trombone and Jimmy Dorsey on clarinet, as well as influential arranger Bill Challis. They were mostly absorbed by Paul Whiteman in 1927.

Paul Whiteman, a former violinist with the San Francisco Symphony Orchestra, who organized a band in 1919 in San Francisco band and moved to New York in 1920, was the epitome of white musicians aping the new genre and trying to cash in on it, mixing pop vocalists such as Bing Crosby (1926) with white virtuoso instrumentalists such as cornet player Bix Beiderbecke (1927), saxophonist Frankie Trumbauer (1927), violinist Joe Venuti (1929), guitarist Eddie Lang (1929), trombonist Jack Teagarden (1933), cornet player Red Nichols, trombonist Tommy Dorsey. Whiteman copied from fellow San Francisco bandleader Art Hickman the idea of adding a saxophone section to the traditional brass section. He also used (from 1919) Hickman's pianist Ferde Grofe to embellish his pop hits: trumpeter Henry Busse's *Wang Wang Blues* (september 1920), John Schonberger's *Whispering* (august 1920), that sold over a million copies, Irving Berlin's *My Mammy* (march 1921), Busse's *Hot Lips* (june 1922), that included a quote from Rachmaninov, Julian Robledo's *Three O'Clock In The Morning* (august 1922), that sold almost two million copies, Vincent Rose's *Linger Awhile* (november 1923), Leon Jessel's *Parade of the Wooden Soldiers* (january 1923), Willard Robison's *Peaceful Valley* (september 1925). Whiteman was not a complete rip-off, as he commissioned George Gershwin's *Rhapsody in Blue* (1924), which he premiered with much fanfare (thus legitimizing jazz as a form of highbrow music), the concert made jazz acceptable and credible to the white establishment, and prompted Grofe to compose eclectic pieces that were more reminiscent of classical music than of jazz music in terms of tonal variety and dynamic range (notably the *Grand Canyon Suite* (april 1932). Whether because he was running out of inspiration or because he felt confident enough to parody his own work, Grofe' began to interpolate classical music in pop tunes. Thus his arrangement of George Gershwin's *The Man I Love* (may 1928) quoted Wagner and Gus Kahn's *Nobody's Sweetheart* (october 1929) quoted Stravinsky. As usual with stars that sold millions of records, everything that Whiteman "invented" was considered relevant and everything that he did not invent was considered irrelevant. Whatever (dubious) merits his orchestra had, they were due to Grofe and to the jazz soloists. Despite the very poor average quality of his music, Whiteman's influence was enormous, and not only on white America. For a while, Whiteman (who was as jazz as Al Jolson was black) was marketed to white America as the epitome of jazz music, and therefore ranks as one of the great swindles of the record industry. In reality, he slowed down the progress in jazz music and almost single-handedly destroyed it. Not much of what he recorded, and certainly not Gershwin's (rather mediocre) piece, was worthy of the repertory of so many humble jazz contemporaries.

In 1934 Chicago white clarinetist Benny Goodman, who had moved to New York in 1928, formed the big band (three saxophones, three trumpets, two trombones, and four rhythm instruments) that was to define the swing era, the epitome being Benny Carter's *Take My Word* (august 1934) for four saxophones. National success came from 1935 when Goodman refined his rhythm section, built around white drummer Gene Krupa, and employed Fletcher Henderson to arrange the second-rate material (notably Jelly Roll Morton's *King Porter Stomp*). The band was promoted for six months by a radio program, "Let's Dance", and then a concert at the "Palomar Ballroom" in Los Angeles was broadcast live causing mass hysteria. For several years it continued to be a major attraction on the radio (the new program, "The Camel Caravan," was broadcast in prime time), and in 1938 was given the honor of a concert at New York's "Carnegie Hall". Its audience was mainly made of white teenagers, who perceived the Goodman Orchestra as a social revolution and attended its performances in a state of screaming frenzy. Among the hits were Will Hudson's ballad *Moonglow* (june 1934), Irving Berlin's *Blue Skies* (january 1935), Vincent Youmans' *Sometimes I'm Happy* (july 1935), Edgar Sampson's *Stompin At The Savoy* (january 1936), Irving Berlin's *This Year's Kisses* (january 1937), trumpeter Ziggy Elman's *And the Angels Sing* (january 1938), and especially two "hot" dance numbers arranged by trumpeter Jimmy Mundy, Elmer Schoebel's *Bugle Call Rag* (august 1934) and Louis Prima's *Sing Sing Sing* (january 1938), issued on two sides of a 12" record. But Goodman also continued to lead a second life as a soloist. The Benny Goodman Trio with black pianist Teddy Wilson, Krupa and himself on clarinet, that recorded Turner Layton's *After You've Gone* (july 1935) and Johnny Green's *Body And Soul* (july 1935), later expanded into a Quartet with the addition of black vibraphonist Lionel Hampton (the first virtuoso of an instrument that had just been invented), notably in Harry Akst's *Dinah* (august 1936), Harrington Gibbs' *Runnin' Wild* (february 1937), Vincent Rose's *Avalon* (june 1937) and Hampton's own *Vibraphone Blues* (august 1936), was possibly the first band to mix white and black musicians. It evolved into a Sextet with four white and two black musicians (Goodman on clarinet, Hampton on vibes, Henderson on piano, Charlie Christian on guitar plus bass and drums) that became a launching pad for Christian's solos, as in Hampton's *Flying Home* (november 1939), Art Hickman's *Rose Room* (august 1939), *Seven Come Eleven* (december 1939), *Shivers* (december 1939), *Air Mail Special* (june 1940), *Six Appeal* (june 1940), *Breakfast Feud* (december 1940), *Wholly Cats* (january 1941). These smaller entities were more artistically successful (albeit less commercially successful) than the big band. In 1940 Goodman reorganized the big band with Charlie Christian on the electric guitar and (the following year) Mel "Powell" Epstein on piano and Sid Catlett on drums. Powell contributed elegant detours and highbrow compositions such as *Mission To Moscow* (composed in 1941). Quite the opposite in attitude and style, southerner Christian stole the show in *Solo Flight* (1941), his guitar concerto. Together with bass and drums Powell and Christian created a kind of daring and unpredictable rhythm section that had never been heard before. And the hits, such as *Benny Rides Again* (november 1940) and *Darn That Dream* (debuted in november 1939), were now composed and arranged by Eddie Sauter, a far more competent musician than the average jazz arranger, who tried to blend classical and jazz music in pieces such as *Concerto For Jazz Band And Orchestra* and *Focus* (july 1961) for Stan Getz and a string orchestra.

New York: The Swing Era

White trombonist <u>Tommy Dorsey</u> and clarinetist Jimmy Dorsey from Philadelphia formed a band, later owned only by Tommy, that delivered an even blander form of swing ballads for the white audience, for example with Joe Burke's *On Treasure Island* (september 1935), George Bassman's *I'm Getting Sentimental Over You* (october 1935), the instrumental that established his smooth style (with a trombone sound borrowed from Miff Mole's), Irving Berlin's *Marie* (january 1937), with vocalist Jack Leonard pioneering a sort of call-and-response with the band, and Ruth Lowe's *I'll Never Smile Again* (april 1940), showcasing the young Frank Sinatra, although it helped establish a new genre when it covered Pinetop Smith's *Boogie-Woogie* (september 1938) and shifted towards more swinging rhythms after it hired arranger Sy Oliver, for example with *Well Get It* (1942), and drummer Bernard "Buddy" Rich (1939-42), the most famous of white jazz drummers.

In 1936 white clarinetist <u>Artie "Shaw"</u> Arshawsky organized an octet consisting of a string quartet, a rhythm section, and his clarinet. This chamber orchestra performed his *Interlude in B-flat* (may 1936), one of the most innovative pieces of white jazz, and *Streamline* (december 1936). his full-scale orchestra became more famous for pop ballads such as Cole Porter's *Begin the Beguine* (july 1938), but Shaw continued to compose adventurous music such as *Hold Your Hats* (april 1937), *Back Bay Shuffle* (july 1938), *Nightmare* (september 1938), *Concerto for Clarinet* (december 1940).

<u>Glenn Miller</u>'s was the least "jazz" of all these white big bands, but also the most successful, famous for such ballads as Frankie Carle's *Sunrise Serenade* (november 1938), Miller's own *Moonlight Serenade* (may 1939), and a spirited version of Joe Garland's *In the Mood* (august 1939). Miller had pioneered his arrangements for clarinet and four saxophones (as well as his knack for quoting from classical and folk music) while arranging music for Ray Noble's easy-listening orchestra. Tenor saxophonist Timothy "Tex" Beneke was a staple of the band from inception (1937) till the end (1942).

Benny Goodman's drummer <u>Gene Krupa</u>, who had pioneered the extended drum solo, formed his own orchestra in 1938, initially offering adventurous performances such as *Wire Brush Stomp* (june 1938), *Nagasaki* (july 1938), with virtuoso scat singing by Leo Watson, *Drummin' Man* (november 1940) and *Bolero at the Savoy* (october 1941); but after the war led a schizophrenic life, torn between increasingly trivial pop material and pioneering bebop arrangements.

Swing bands shared the stage with Latin bands that played the rhumba, the tango, the mambo, the samba, the cha-cha, etc. Inevitably rhytmic elements of Latin music were introduced into swing bands.

<u>This was also the era when jazz spread to Europe. Several USA jazzmen traveled or stayed in Europe between the world wars: Sidney Bechet (1925-29), Noble Sissle (1927-33), Duke Ellington (1933), Louis Armstrong (1932-34), Coleman Hawkins (1934-39), Benny Carter (1935-38).</u>

NEW YORK: THE SWING SOLOISTS

The big bands of swing competed to hire the best soloists.

Texas-born white trombonist Jack Teagarden, who was with Paul Whiteman from 1933 till 1938, was (with Miff Mole) the first innovator of the trombone since the New Orleans brass bands. White guitarist Salvatore "Eddie Lang" Massaro from Philadelphia was the first guitar virtuoso, and composed and recorded pieces such as *Black And Blue Bottom* (september 1926), *Stringin'˜The Blues* (november 1926), *Doin' Things* (june 1928) and *Wild Cat* (june 1928) with Joe Venuti, and composed and recorded with black blues guitarist Lonnie Johnson the first guitar duets, such as *Two Tone Stomp* (november 1928), *Blue Guitars* (may 1929), *Guitar Blues* (may 1929) and *A Handful Of Riffs* (may 1929). White violinist Joe Venuti, also from Philadelphia, was the first violin virtuoso, and composed *Tempo di Modernage* (june 1931).

For a time it looked like black trumpeter Cladys "Jabbo" Smith, could compete with Louis Armstrong. His virtuoso style was legendary after a march 1928 session with Fats Waller on organ, James Johnson on piano and Garvin Bushnell on alto (the Louisiana Sugar Babes), and especially after the 1929 recordings of his own compositions by his own quintet, the Rhythm Aces.

Benny Carter was (with Johnny Hodges) one of the most reliable alto saxophonists of the swing era, but mainly he was a composer of relaxed, atmospheric and catchy pieces such as *Blues in My Heart* (september 1931), *Symphony in Riffs* (october 1933), *Dream Lullaby* (december 1934), *When Lights Are Low* (june 1936), *Cow Cow Boogie* (composed in 1942). In 1933 his orchestra featured Wayman Carver, the first major flute soloist of jazz music (*Devil's Holiday*, october 1933). From 1941 Benny Carter became a composer of Hollywood movie soundtracks. When he returned to jazz, he began to compose extended orchestral suites a` la Duke Ellington and he continued until well into his eighties: *Kansas City Suite* (1960) for Count Basie, the six-movement suite *Central City Sketches*, performed by the American Jazz Orchestra on **Central City Sketches** (1987), *Harlem Renaissance* (1992) and *Tales of the Rising Sun* (1992), both on **Harlem Renaissance** (february 1992) performed by a jazz big band and a chamber orchestra with string section.

Oklahoma-raised guitarist Charlie Christian was more of a bluesman than a jazzman because he started playing solo: bluesmen used the guitar as a lead instrument, jazzmen didn't. From the viewpoint of jazz, Christian's guitar was more like a saxophone than like the guitar that had been traditionally played in jazz (a part of the rhythm section). Using Eddie Durham's recent novelty (the electric guitar), Charlie Christian improved over the innovations of acoustic guitarists Lonnie Johnson and Eddie Lang, and perhaps applied to his instrument the lesson of Lester Young. He developed his style in relative isolation in Oklahoma before being discovered (1939) and brought to New York to join Benny Goodman's sextet and band, armed with an electric guitar. Christian was legendary for creating endless series of variations on a theme, during sessions that could last virtually forever, in a manner whose only precedent was pianist Art Tatum. His *Solo Flight* (march 1941) with the Goodman orchestra seemed the prelude to a new kind of music altogether. Alas, he died in 1942 at 26 of turbercolosis.

Black trumpeter Roy Eldridge, who arrived in New York in 1930 from Pennsylvania, heralded a new age (the age of bebop), although he played in swing bands. Eldridge initially emulated Louis Armstrong albeit adding a sense of the narrative dimension to the melodic improvisation. But he began to extend the range of the trumpet in some numbers by his 1936 Chicago-based eight-piece band (with his brother Joe as main arranger): Turner Layton's *After You've Gone* (january 1937), *Wabash Stomp* (january 1937), boasting one of his most celebrated solos, *Heckler's Hop* (january 1937). He trained by playing Coleman Hawkins' saxophone solos on trumpet, i.e. by simulating the keys of the saxophone with the movements of his lips. Eldridge (one of the first black soloists to feature in a white jazz band) reached maturity in Gene Krupa's band from 1941 to 1943, his trumpet highlighting their two hits, Hoagy Carmichael's *Rockin' Chair* (july 1941) and Earl Bostic's *Let Me Off Uptown* (may 1941), as well as his own *Drum Boogie* (composed in 1941). Thanks to Eldridge, the phrasing of the trumpet became much more eloquent, assertive and expressive. His improvisations were more intricate and creative. His melodic lines were almost violent by comparison with the previous generation of trumpeters.

Belgian-born gypsy (or, better, "manouche") guitarist Jean-Baptiste "Django" Reinhardt pioneered the creative use of the guitar in jazz even before Christian. The all-strings Quintette Du Hot Club De France, formed in 1934 with French violinist Stephane Grappelli, a bassist and two more guitarists, influenced by folk and classical music and inspired by Eddie Lang and Joe Venuti, had little in common with the trends of American jazz. At first they revisited American standards such as Philip Braham's *Limehouse Blues* (october 1935) and Harry Akst's *Dinah* (december 1934), but then they began to work on original material in a chamber-jazz style that betrayed the influence of Debussy and Ravel (and gypsy music), not of Armstrong and Ellington: *Runnin' Wild* (april 1935), *Djangology* (september 1935), the solo *Parfum* (april 1937), *Daphne* (september 1937), *Minor Swing* (november 1937), *Swing Guitar* (june 1938), *Nocturne* (february 1938), *Mystery Pacific* (april 1937), *Nuages* (october 1940), *Belleville* (march 1942). Nonetheless some of Reinhardt's most breathtaking solos were variations on other people's material, such as Gus Kahn's *I'll See You In My Dreams* (1939). Extroverted, gentle and warm, Reinhardt relied on acrobatic jazz chording and breakneck finger-picking, as far removed from the blues as a jazz musician could be.

Stephane Grappelli's violin was the perfect counterpart to Reindhart's guitar: Grappelli's multi-layered improvisations, that left a feeling of cascading notes blowing in the wind, were graceful and aristocratic and imbued with a childish verve.

Coleman Hawkins, the man who had coined the jazz language of the tenor saxophone with solos such as the one in Fletcher Henderson's *The Stampede* (may 1926), was also instrumental in changing the way jazz soloists improvised: he improvised (or, better, invented) using the notes of chords in the song, instead of paraphrasing/ embellishing the melody (like everyone else had done). He improvised on the chord structure of a tune rather than on its melody. Somehow the tenor saxophone, that had not been a favorite instrument of jazz soloists, lent itself to this Copernican revolution.

His own complex composition *Queer Notions* (august 1933) predated bebop. He also had a major hit on his own with an atmospheric, and almost lethargic, version of Johnny Green's ballad *Body And Soul* (october 1939), that literally redefined the genre. Other classy interpretations followed: Benny Carter's *When The Lights Are Low* (september 1939), a collaboration with vibraphonist Lionel Hampton featuring a reed section of giants (Hawkins, Benny Carter, Chu Berry, Ben Webster) plus Charlie Christian and Dizzy Gillespie; George Gershwin's *The Man I Love* (december 1943) and Cliff Burwell's *Sweet Lorraine* (december 1943), both in a quartet with pianist Eddie Heywood, a quartet with bassist Oscar Pettiford and drummer Shelly Manne; Harry Warren's *I Only Have Eyes for You* (january 1944) and Jimmy McHugh's *I'm in the Mood for Love* (january 1944), both in a quintet with pianist Teddy Wilson and trumpeter Roy Eldridge. He transitioned into bebop when he hired Thelonious Monk for his quartet (1944) and recorded **Rainbow Mist** (may 1944) with trumpeter Dizzy Gillespie and Max Roach on drums (Gillspie's *Woody'n You* and *Salt Peanuts*, and a lyrical interpretation of Jerome Kern's *Yesterdays*). His *Hawk's Variations* (january 1945) and *Picasso* (1946) were the first major recordings of solo-saxophone pieces.

His main legacy was in the ballad form. His "erotic" vibrato-rich style danced around the melody in order to build tension, and then danced out of it so as to release the tension in a languid swoon.

Two female singers became famous in the swing era: Ella Fitzgerald and Billie Holiday. The former, who sang just about everything that might please an audience in a polished multiple-octave voice, was accepted by the white establishment, and had her greatest hit with Al "Van Alexander" Feldman's *A-Tisket A-Tasket* (may 1938), while the latter, who sang mostly unpleasant topics in a rather unattractive voice, was always sort of a renegade.

Eleanora "Billie Holiday" Fagan was just about the opposite of Ella Fitzgerald. Her singing was all about class (her range was just a little over one octave) and emotion (the sound of pain, of both ancestral and personal pain), not power or virtuosity.

She had a fondness for disturbing material, and none of her classics was joyful: Gus Arnheim's and Abe Lyman's *I Cried For You* (june 1936), Lewis "Abel Meeropol" Allen's *Strange Fruit* (april 1939), a protest song about a lynching, her own *Fine and Mellow* (april 1939), Arthur Herzog's *God Bless the Child* (may 1941), about the "Great Migration", Johnny Green's *I Cover The Waterfront* (august 1941), Rezso Seress' *Gloomy Sunday* (august 1941), about suicide, Roger "Ram" Ramirez's *Lover Man* (april 1944).

The Swing Soloists 45

Instead of simply delivering lines, Holiday would make each note sigh, bleed and cry. They proved her the closest thing to a French chansonnier that American jazz ever had. The backing was not orchestral but rarified, mostly by small combos led by Benny Goodman's pianist Teddy Wilson. She recorded with Lester Young a few numbers in a sophisticated chamber-jazz style: George Gershwin's *The Man I Love* (december 1939) and Seymour Simons' *All of Me* (march 1941).

For her excesses of drugs and alcohol, she was banned from night-clubs and arrested repeatedly. She died poor at 44.

Fletcher Henderson's bassist John Kirby in 1930 revolutionized the rhythm section of jazz. The epitome of chamber jazz in the swing era was the sextet (Charlie Shavers on trumpet, two reeds, Billy Kyle on piano, bass and drums) formed by Kirby after leaving Henderson. Their emphasis on intricate arrangements, clockwork craftmanship and introverted moods contrasted with the prevailing habits of the big-band era and predated cool jazz. Notwithstanding the success of Shavers's *Undecided* (october 1938), most of their repertoire was borrowed from classical music.

Jimmy Blanton (Duke Ellington) and Milt Hinton (Cab Calloway) were the other bassists that brought about one of the most influential changes in the history of jazz ensembles.

Benny Goodman's pianist Teddy Wilson was perhaps the most elegant of the swing era, a less intrepid but more emotional version of Art Tatum. *Blues In C Sharp Minor* (may 1936) was his classic stylistic exhibition.

Fats Waller's tenor saxophonist Gene Sedric had recorded the first piece of solo saxophone in the history of jazz, *Saxophone Doodle* (1937), predating Coleman Hawkins by almost a decade.

The first magazine devoted to jazz music, Down Beat, was published in 1934. Commodore (1938) and Blue Note (1939) were the first labels entirely devoted to jazz music.

During the 1940s the swing big band had become the voice of America abroad. Its dominance of the domestic market had become no less impressive. American music was ruled by African music for the first time in its history.

KANSAS CITY: BIG BANDS

When New Orleans shut down Storyville (1917), many of its black musicians moved to Kansas City that, thanks to Tom Pendergast (1925-38), had become the vice capital of the USA.

Kansas City was for a while the only Midwestern city to keep the pace of New York and Chicago in jazz development, de facto relieving St Louis of the role it played during the "gay nineties". In fact, Kansas City jazz musicians prospered at a time (the "Great Depression") when most jazz musicians of other cities were in trouble.

In the clubs of Kansas City jazz music met a new vocal style (the "shouters") and a new piano style (the "boogie-woogie"), besides the very old bluesy style that was still very much alive in the south. But, mainly, Kansas City avoided the excesses of arrangement that were common in New York, and relished simpler, more immediate rhythmic patterns.

The Kansas City style had debuted in 1923, when the band of pianist Bennie Moten had cut its first record, soon to be followed by hits such as Harlan Leonard's *South* (november 1924), *Kansas City Shuffle* (december 1926) and *Moten Stomp* (june 1927). Several of its members (including the young Count Basie) were later recruited from Walter Page's Blue Devils Besides Basie, in the late 1920s Moten raised trumpeter Oran "Hot Lips" Page, guitarist Eddie Durham (the first guitarist to experiment with proto-amplifiers, for example in the solo of *Band Box Shuffle* in october 1929), saxophonist Ben Webster, and vocalist Jimmy Rushing. It wasn't until *Just Rite* (september 1928), though, that Moten's band clearly switched from ragtime to blues.

The Blue Devils, formed by bassist Walter Page in Oklahoma City in 1925 and that only recorded *Blue Devils Blues* (november 1929), vocalist Jimmy Rushing's debut recording, and Basie's instrumental *Squabblin'* (november 1929), were notable for a rhythm section made of piano, guitar, bass and drums (instead of bass horn, piano and banjo), the epitome of the more elastic rhythm section of the big-band era, and for alto saxophonist and clarinetist Buster Smith. Page was one of the first bassists to play four beats to the bar (as opposed to New Orleans' two beats to the bar) and coined a "walking" style on four strings that became a standard on five-string basses.

William "Count" Basie organized the Barons of Rhythm in 1936, which soon hired tenor saxophonists Lester Young and Herschel Evans, trombonists Dicky Wells and Benny Morton, vocalist Jimmy Rushing, and (replacing Oran "Hot Lips" Page) trumpet player Wilbur "Buck Clayton" Dorsey, propelling them with the formidable rhythm section of Basie on piano, Freddie Green on guitar, Walter Page on bass and Jo Jones on drums. The pillars of that line-up were tested in George Gershwin's *Lady Be Good* (october 1936) and Saul Chaplin's *Shoe Shine Boy* (november 1936), credited to the Jones-Smith Incorporated, a quintet with Basie, Page, Jones, Young and a trumpeter that featured Young's first (revolutionary) solos. Basie's big band indulged in a bluesier style based on the riff (often played in unison) and a "call and response" counterpoint between the brass and reed sections, while emphasizing extended improvisation: *One O'clock Jump* (july 1937), a 12-bar blues that became their first hit, several compositions by Moten's guitarist and trombonist Eddie Durham, notably *Topsy* (august 1937), *Sent For You Yesterday* (february 1938), *Swinging The Blues* (february 1938) and *Every Tub* (february 1938); then Basie's own *Blue And Sentimental* (june 1938), with Evans' most famous solo, *Jumpin' at the Woodside* (august 1938), *Stop Beatin' Round the Mulberry Bush* (august 1938), *Goin' to Chicago Blues* (february 1939), a two-sided version of Ray Noble's *Cherokee* (february 1939). Many of these were Rushing's personal showcases. Young contributed *Taxi War Dance* (march 1939), *Lester Leaps In* (september 1939), reminiscent of George Gershwin's *I Got Rhythm*, and *Tickle Toe* (march 1940). Evans died in 1939 and Young left the orchestra the following year, but the orchestra kept finding new talents and new hits, such as *Open the Door Richard* (january 1947) and *Every Day I Have the Blues* (may 1955), with new vocalist Joe Williams.

Lester Young's intimate, slow, lighter, laconic style (that was more about emotion than about vanity, more about melody than about innovation, and probably more inspired by the blues singers than by jazz trumpeters) made Armstrong' syncopated generation sound outdated. In 1934 Young had briefly replaced Coleman Hawkins in Fletcher Henderson's orchestra, but it was only in the Jones-Smith Incorporated, a quintet with Count Basie, Walter Page, Jo Jones and a trumpeter, that Young's style became a sensation. His first solos in George Gershwin's *Lady Be Good* (october 1936) and Saul Chaplin's *Shoe Shine Boy* (november 1936) introduced Young's tenor saxophone as almost the exact opposite of Coleman Hawkins' saxophone: light, breezy, vibrato-free, more similar to an alto than to Hawkins' tenor, and improvising on the melody rather than on the chords. Young then became a key element in Count Basie's orchestra, to which he contributed *Taxi War Dance* (march 1939), his signature theme *Lester Leaps In* (september 1939) and *Tickle Toe* (march 1940). His artistic peak, though, was perhaps achieved in another small setting, the Kansas City Six (1938) with guitarist Eddie Durham. Young did not seem to belong to the swing age at all: his role was essentially to provide a bridge between Bix Beiderbecke (or, better, Frankie Trumbauer) and cool jazz.

Eddie Durham introduced the electric guitar (just invented in 1931) into jazz music. It was a slow incremental process that started in Kansas City, when Durham was playing trombone in Bennie Moten's orchestra, and continued in Jimmi Lunceford's band (Durham introduced the amplified guitar into jazz music in 1935 via Lunceford's cover of Harold Arlen's *Hittin' The Bottle*) to finally return to Kansas City, with a combo that was drawn from the Count Basie orchestra: the Kansas City Five, formed in 1938 with trumpeter Buck Clayton, drummer Jo Jones, bassist Walter Page and rhythm guitarist Freddie Green, featured Eddie Durham's electric guitar as a replacement for Count Basie's piano. The Kansas City Six of 1938 were augmented by Lester Young on clarinet and tenor sax.

Durham composed for Basie's groups and orchestras: *John's Idea* (july 1937), *Time Out* (august 1937), *Topsy* (august 1937), *Out The Window* (october 1937), *Sent For You Yesterday* (february 1938), *Swinging The Blues* (february 1938), *Every Tub* (february 1938).

Kansas City's most influential tenor saxophonist, Ben Webster served Bennie Moten (1932), Fletcher Henderson (1934), Duke Ellington (1940-43). In the 1950s he became a mainstream entertainer with romantic collections such as **King Of The Tenors** (december 1953), featuring alto saxophonist Benny Carter and pianist Oscar Peterson among others, and **Soulville** (october 1957), again with Peterson on piano.

Pittsburgh's pianist Mary Lou Williams was the most innovative composer of the Kansas City school. She mainly wrote for Andy Kirk's big band, Twelve Clouds of Joy (formed in 1928), where she played piano: the bluesy *Froggy Bottom* (november 1929), *Cloudy* (november 1929), *Mess-A Stomp* (november 1929), the boogie-woogie *Little Joe From Chicago* (february 1938), the subversive *Walkin' and Swingin'* (march 1936), and *Scratchin' In The Gravel* (january 1940). After she retired from jazz, she composed a Duke Ellington-inspired *Zodiac Suite* (1945) for an 18-piece orchestra, the cantata *Black Christ of the Andes* (november 1963), and the *Mary Lou's Mass* (completed in 1970).

The golden age of Kansas City ended in 1938 when Tom Pendergast ended in jail and a wave of moral renewal swept the city. Most night clubs had to shut down and their stars had to move elsewhere or retire.

Bebop

The "swing" era seemed to last an eternity. It was the first negro phenomenon to give a name to an era of the USA (or any western country). Jazz music was acknowledged and imitated throughout the world, even by classical composers such as Stravinsky. But, overall, big bands and swing gave jazz a bad name. Jazz became a "dance craze", a form of light entertainment, a career for musicians who failed at serious music, an industry (not an art) whose only goal was to sell a lot of records (selling a lot of records had become the new trendy way to become rich). Ellington himself was aware of this and was trying to distance himself from swing music.

The first major innovation that destabilized the world order introduced by swing was "bebop".

Swing had been the soundtrack of World War II, a way to vent the angst and to exorcize the fear. It was also a way to capture stability in a time of high instability. At the end of the war, the psychology reverted: swing became a bad memory, and it suddenly sounded anachronistic.

The psychological revolution was particularly felt by the blacks. Before the war, they had tasted success and wealth for the first time in their history. They had discovered that there was money to be made by entertaining white folks. By the end of the war, that capitalist excitement had subsided: blacks wanted to be respected, not only employed. They wanted cultural emancipation to proceed in parallel with material emancipation. (The vast majority, of course, got neither).

At the same time a less visible revolution took place after the end of the Prohibition (december 1933). The "speakeasy" (the club for illicit consumption of alcohol) became legal. By definition, the speakeasy was small and underground (and illegal). It could employ only small combos, and certainly not the big bands that ruled the charts. Thus the speakeasies had been creating a culture of small combos that was alternative to the mainstream culture of big bands. They had been creating a trend without being aware of it. The end of the Prohibition allowed New York's decade-old speakeasies such as the "Onyx Club" (opened in 1927) to cater to a broader audience and to present its musical traditions as more than just "necessity is the mother of necessity".

Whether it was a coincidence or not, bebop also took off in the years of a nation-wide recording ban that affected instrumental jazz. A fight between the union of musicians (the AFM) and the record labels caused a two year ban (from august 1942 till november 1944) on all recordings, an event that certainly did not help the swing orchestras.

The rapid decline of the big bands, and the revival of Tin Pan Alley's pop music, favored the cause of the dissidents within jazz music who were preaching against the commercial sell-out of the big bands. These isolated intellectuals were offering a musical message that did not depend on the taste of the masses. They marked a renewal of the thematic material, away from the (white) pop themes favored by swing orchestras, back to the blues themes of the past and towards original compositions that better reflected the zeitgeist. They marked a regression towards the small club and the small ensemble, and from the big band to the small combo. They also marked a progression towards a more personal, intimate and heartfelt form of music. Bebop was a more "private" form of expression. Bebop was a music to listen to, as opposed to dance to.

Jazz musicians had been, first and foremost, entertainers. Now they became experimenters, explorers, even scientists. Instead of playing what came natural, the bebop improviser tried to play what was not natural. The chamber-jazz detours of the swing era contributed to the advent of bebop, but, mostly, bebop was a completely new phenomenon, that did not quite evolve from the previous tradition but represented a complete subversion of that tradition.

The genre itself was named "bebop" from the nickname of the "flatted fifth", the favorite interval of bebop musicians, but emphasis on it had been virtually unlawful in swing orchestras (the flatted third and seventh were the "blue notes" par excellence, but the flatted fifth wasn't even popular with the blues).

The only reason to consider swing and bebop as branches of the same musical genre is that they shared the same instrumentation and the passion for improvisation (and, mostly, the color of the skin).

The relationship between the new heroes and the old ones was one of estrangement, not inheritance. The new heroes were Benny Goodman's guitarist Charlie Christian, Duke Ellington's bassist Jimmy Blanton, Earl Hines' alto saxophonist Charlie Parker, Cab Calloway's trumpeter Dizzy Gillespie, Coleman Hawkins' pianist Thelonious Monk, Count Basie's saxophonist Lester Young, Louis Armstrong's saxophonist Dexter Gordon. They were not the heirs to their masters' orchestras: they were sidemen, who embodied a different aesthetic. In a sense, they were former slaves who, once liberated, turned their back to their masters and migrated to distant virgin lands. (Armstrong publicly ridiculed bebop).

The core of bebop music was more than just the format: it was an existential mood that almost harked back to the blues. The soloist of bebop was a poet and a philosopher, no longer only an entertainer. Thus the syncopation (meant to facilitate dancing) also became obsolete. In a sense, bebop marked the (temporary) demise of syncopation from jazz music, the emancipation of jazz from the dancehall and its transfer to the loft. It was no longer music for the masses, but music for the elite.

Bebop was structurally and emotionally more complex than swing. Bebop marked a collective growth of awareness within the jazz community. Bebop's looser structure was also another step in the progressive emancipation of jazz from structure.

Bebop downplayed the rhythmic aspect and emphasized the emotional power of the solo. It reduced the complexity of the polyphony and increased the importance of style. It fostered a new degree of melodic invention. Bop phrasing toyed with rhythm in a way that gave meaning even to the pause between two notes. The rhythm section was simplified, anchoring it to bass and drums, thus releasing the guitar and the piano (swing's rhythmic pillars) from their time-keeping duties. As the bass grew in importance (as it had started doing with Jimmy Blanton), the drums began to "accent" the music rather than merely beat a tempo. The rhythm section, that had been the most mechanic part of the ensemble, acquired a new degree of freedom ("no continuity of beat", as Charlie Parker said). This loose, restrained concept of rhythm allowed the soloist to "think". Dissonances, polyrhythms, new tonal colors and irregular phrasing were adopted enthusiastically.

Soloists employed a broad and daring variety of forms, ranges and techniques, and felt bound to melodic themes only in spirit.

For decades jazz music had been moving towards larger and larger orchestras, towards more and more organized music. Bebop made a sharp turn towards smaller ensembles and less organized music.

Even their appearance changed dramatically: the bopper's uniform included a hat, sunglasses and a goatee, not the tuxedo of the swing era.

Among their praxes, the jam session became the equivalent of a religious function, the supernatural moment when art was created.

Ironically, this more sincere and austere strand of black music alienated the original audience of jazz music: the blacks of the ghettos. It attracted a new audience of white intellectuals and eccentrics, an audience that had nothing to do with the historical background of jazz music.

In the 1950s jazz lost its dominant position within the recording industry, first surpassed by the pop vocalists, then by rock music, then even by soul music. The major labels looked elsewhere to increase their profits, while small labels such as Blue Note (founded in 1939), Savoy (founded in 1942) and Prestige (founded in 1949) catered to the niche of jazz fanatics. For the rest of the century, jazz never recovered its prominence.

Jazz and the audience split. Jazz became very much a music about itself, while the audience continued to chase ephemeral fads. Jazz even developed its own iconography. The bebop artist was identified with a "look", a way to dress and a way to speak.

Even more ironically, bebop became "blacker" as it moved away from the big business: while the swing era had been dominated (with few exceptions) by white big bands, the protagonists of the bebop (with the notable exception of Lennie Tristano) era were all black.

Bebop was born in 1941, when trumpeter Dizzy Gillespie, double bass player Milt Hinton, alto saxophonist Charlie Parker, pianist Thelonious Monk and drummer Kenny Clarke began playing informally together. Its official birth place was "Minton's Playhouse", a New York club. Due to a strike by recording artists, very little was documented on record until 1944.

South Carolina's trumpeter <u>John "Dizzy" Gillespie</u>, also an accomplished songwriter, was hired in 1939 by Cab Calloway's orchestra, where he developed a style very influenced by Roy Eldridge (but hardly so in his *Pickin' the Cabbage* of 1940). In 1942 he joined Earl Hines, where in 1943 he played alongside alto saxophonist Charlie Parker and vocalist Sarah Vaughan, and began to display a much more personal style, expanding his habit of improvising new chord changes on a melody to an almost manic form of art, turning dynamics into the very essence of jazz at the expense of intimacy (sometimes replaced by overtones of melodrama and euphoria). Gillespie's *A Night In Tunisia* (composed in 1942 as *Interlude*) was first sung by Vaughan. In 1944 the three young talents (Parker, Gillespie and Vaughan) followed Hines' male vocalist Billy Eckstine when he started his own band. At the same time, in 1944, Dizzy Gillespie's quintet, featuring Max Roach on drums and Oscar Pettiford on bass, and later Charlie Parker, began performing at New York's "Onyx Club" (the first time that the word "bebop" was used to promote a band). Gillespie's first major recordings (january 1945), in a piano-based sextet with Trummy Young on trombone, Pettiford on bass and Don Byas on tenor instead of Parker, showed Gillespie's textural dexterity applied to both material specifically composed for bebop performers, such as *Salt Peanuts*, *Be Bop* and Tadd Dameron's *Good Bait*, and reworked swing classics, such as Vernon Duke's *I Can't Get Started* (january 1945). Another sextet with Dexter Gordon and white pianist Frank Paparelli recorded *Blue 'n' Boogie* (february 1945). The new aesthetic was fully implemented in the tunes (mostly composed by Gillespie) recorded by the All Stars, namely a quintet with Parker on tenor and Al Haig on piano: *Groovin' High* (february 1945), *Dizzy Atmosphere* (february 1945), *Shaw 'Nuff* (may 1945) and Tadd Dameron's *Hot House* (may 1945), based on Cole Porter's *What Is This Thing Called Love*. The Jazzmen, a sextet with Eli "Lucky" Thompson on tenor instead of Parker, Haig on piano and Milt Jackson on vibraphone, debuted *Confirmation* (february 1946). In 1945 Gillespie organized his own band, that lasted till 1950. Hits such as *Things to Come* (june 1946) were arranged by Gil Fuller. Gillespie's band pioneered Cuban bop, a genre born of the wedding between Cuban rhythms and bebop. His association with Cuban conga player Chano Pozo yielded George Russell's *Cubana Be Cubana Bop* (december 1947), possibly the first modal improvisation on record, and their *Manteca* (december 1947). Gillespie's rhythm section of 1947 consisted of John Lewis, Milt Jackson, Kenny Clarke and Ray Brown, that would soon form the Modern Jazz Quartet. After a mediocre decade, Gillespie converted to "third stream" music. Argentinian pianist Boris "Lalo" Schifrin composed for him the five-movement *Gillespiana Suite* (november 1960) and the six-movement suite *The New Continent* (1962), while *Perceptions* (may 1961) came from trombonist James "J.J." Johnson, and Arturo "Chico" O'Farrill scored *Afro-Cuban Jazz Moods* (june 1975).

Kansas City's alto saxophonist <u>Charlie "Bird" Parker</u> grew up in Jay McShann's band, at first influenced by the style of Lester Young. In 1942 he joined Earl Hines and played with Dizzy Gillespie and Sarah Vaughan, and in 1943 the trio (Parker, Gillespie and Vaughan) formed the nucleus of Billy Eckstine's new band. In 1945, besides recording the milestone performances with Gillespie, he formed his own group and proceeded to develop a new tonal vocabulary via *Ko Ko*, a reworking of Ray Noble's *Cherokee*, and his classic compositions *Billie's Bounce, Anthropology/ Thriving on a Riff, Meandering* and *Now's the Time*, all five recorded in november with Miles Davis, Gillespie and Roach. Parker extended both the melodic and the rhythmic range of jazz music in a systematic way. His solos seemed to have no rule, occasionally sounding arbitrary in the context of the group's playing. Thus each solo appeared to be unique in nature, not the repetition of a distinctive pattern. The polyrhythmic essence of his playing was emphasized by the detours of his rhythm section, but made possible by his melodies, that toyed with beats and with the space between beats. Parker was an oxymoron of sorts: the player of a melodic instrument who indirectly focused on rhythm. His music was revolutionary because it was based on discontinuity instead of harmonious flow. His phrasing sounded hysterical and contradictory. His playing did obey a meta-rule, though: emotion. Whatever he was doing with the saxophone, he was trying to secrete as much emotion as possible.

The ambitious *Yardbird Suite* and *Ornithology* were first recorded in march 1946 by a septet (alto, tenor, trumpet, piano, guitar, drums, bass) that included Davis.

In 1947 he formed a New York-based Quintet with Miles Davis on trumpet, Duke Jordan (and later Bud Powell) on piano, Tommy Potter on bass, Max Roach on drums, that recorded spectacular performances of Miles Davis' *Donna Lee* (may), and Bird's own compositions *Dexterity* (october), *Bird of Paradise* (october), *The Hymn* (october), *Klactoveedsedstene* (november), plus *Crazeology*, based on George Gershwin's *I Got Rhythm*, and Drifting On A Reed (both december) with trombonist James "J.J." Johnson added to the quintet. The bluesy *Parker's Mood* (september 1948), featuring John Lewis on piano, stood out as his artistic manifesto, and *Constellation* (same session) was his dizziest group improvisation.

In 1947 Parker's jazz band toured with a philharmonic orchestra, and later three albums titled **Bird With Strings** (1950-52) were made with a small string ensemble. An alcoholic and drug addict, Parker died in 1955 at the age of 30, after having tried twice to commit suicide.

Tenor saxophonist Dexter Gordon adapted Charlie Parker's alto style to the tenor saxophone on **Long Tall Dexter** (january 1946), **Rides Again** (1945) and **The Chase** (june 1947), mostly based on his own themes. He was not shy to employ dissonance. His specialty was the piano-based quartet, starting with **Go** (august 1962) to the European recordings of the 1970s, mostly with Niels Pedersen on bass, notably **The Apartment** (september 1974), containing his *Candlelight Lady* and *The Apartment*, **Bouncing' with Dex** (september 1975), featuring pianist Tete Montoliu, bassist Niels Pedersen and drummer Billy Higgins, and containing *Benji's Bounce* and *Catalonian Nights*, and **Biting the Apple** (november 1976), containing *Apple Jump* and *A La Modal*. He usually failed to master the same energy in other formats, with the notable exception of **Something Different** (september 1975), that did not include a pianist (guitarist Philip Catherine, bassist Niels Pedersen, drummer Billy Higgins) and contained his *Winther's Calling*.

Other notable soloists of the era include drummer Kenny Clarke, famous for his polyrhythmic tricks and for using the cymbal as the timekeeping instrument (like Jo Jones) so as to free the rest of the drum kit; trumpeter Theodore "Fats" Navarro, a prodigy who in january 1945 replaced Dizzy Gillespie in Billy Eckstine's band but who died at the age of 26; trombonist Bennie Green; vocalist Sarah Vaughan, whose greatest hit was *Broken Hearted Melody* (1959); tenor and alto saxophonist Edward "Sonny" Stitt; bassist and cellist Oscar Pettiford, who also composed *Swingin' Till the Girls Come Home* (april 1951), *Tamalpais Love Song* (december 1953), *Tricotism* (march 1954), *Bohemia After Dark* (december 1954), *Laverne Walk* (september 1958).

James "J.J." Johnson, the trombonist of Benny Carter's band (1942-45) and Charlie Parker's quintet (1947), adapted the trombone to the style (if not the mood) of the bebop era. His acrobatic style was documented on **Mad Be Bop** (june 1946), credited to the Beboppers, a quintet with Bud Powell on piano and Max Roach on drums, as well as on the summits of **Trombone By Three** (october 1951) with Bennie Green and Kai Winding and **Four Trombones** (september 1953) with Green, Winding and Willie Dennis. In 1954 he formed a two-trombone quintet with Kai Winding, but his apex were **First Place** (april 1957) and especially **Blue Trombone** (may 1957) both recorded by a quartet with pianist Tommy Flanagan, bassist Paul Chambers and drummer Max Roach.

BEBOP PIANISTS

Just like the saxophone revolution had obscured the double-bass revolution during the swing era, the bebop revolution in playing saxophone and trumpet obscured the revolution in playing the piano. However, it was probably the piano that benefited the most from bebop's harmonic freedom. Once the rhythm section had been opened up, the piano regained the prominence that it had in classical music. Thelonious Monk was not only the most cerebral pianist to enter the history of jazz music but also the greatest composer of the bebop era. *Epistrophy* (1942) and the immortal *Round about Midnight* (1944) were composed for the orchestra of Cootie Williams, *I Mean You* (1946) for Coleman Hawkins' band. *52nd Street Theme* (june 1945) became a classic of bebop when it was recorded by Dizzy Gillespie and Charlie Parker. At the same time that his compositions were leaving a mark on the transition from swing to bebop, his piano style (in Coleman Hawkins' band that he had joined in 1944) was confusing the audience. It was a style that sounded outside the jazz tradition, not only eccentric but also laconic, almost counterproductive in the way it emphasized the pauses instead of the rhythm, and clustered chords instead of linear development.

His recordings of his own compositions established a higher musical standard than jazz music was used to: *Humph* (october 1947), based on George Gershwin's *I Got Rhythm*, and *Thelonious* (october 1947), that exhibits an almost classical geometry while employing both silence and dissonance, for a piano sextet (Idrees Sulieman on trumpet, Danny Quebec West on alto sax, Billy Smith on tenor sax, Gene Ramey on bass, Art Blakey on drums); *Well You Needn't* (1947), *Off Minor* (october 1947) and the tender ballad *Ruby My Dear* (october 1947) for a trio (with Art Blakey on drums); the ballad *Monk's Mood* (november 1947) for a trumpet-sax-piano quintet; *Evidence* (july 1948) and the bluesy *Misterioso* (july 1948) for a piano-based quartet with Milt Jackson on vibraphone.

Monk's art was a calibrated balance of deconstruction and estrangement techniques. On one hand, one could still hear elements of stride jazz, boogie-woogie, blues, even nursery rhymes, although they were diluted in an anarchic patchwork of overtones. On the other hand, the listener was disoriented by the fragile, naked ambiguity of the music. That ambiguity would disappear if one could only appreciate the hidden orchestral quality of Monk's piano playing.

A piano-based quintet with Jackson on vibraphone, Sahib Shihab on alto sax, Blakey on drums, yielded the romantic ballad *Ask Me Now* (july 1951), the blues *Straight No Chaser* (july 1951), *Four in One* (july 1951) and *Criss Cross* (july 1951).

A quintet with French horn player Julius Watkins, Sonny Rollins on tenor sax, Percy Heath on bass, was immortalized on the album **Thelonious Monk and Sonny Rollins** (november 1953) with *Friday the 13th* (1953) and *Think of One* (1953), based on an ostinato trick similar to *Thelonious*.

Hackensack (may 1954) and *Locomotive* (may 1954), with a 20-bar chorus, were due to a quintet of trumpet, tenor sax, piano, drums and bass. In the piano-trio format favored by his friend Bud Powell, Monk sculpted *Bemsha Swing* (december 1952), the Caribbean-sounding *Monk's Dream* (october 1952), *Nutty* (september 1954), *Blue Monk* (september 1954) and the dissonant *Work* (september 1954). Max Roach drummed on the first one, Blakey on all the others.

In the meantime, jazz music had entered the age of the album. his first solo album, **Thelonious Monk** (1954) offered solo-piano versions of his early classics, including *Eronel* (1951) and *Reflections* (1953). After two albums of covers, Monk was allowed to make the album that he was capable of, **Brilliant Corners** (october 1956), a set of complex chamber pieces for tenor saxophone (Sonny Rollins), alto saxophone (Ernie Henry), bass (Oscar Pettiford), drums (Max Roach) and piano, notably *Brilliant Corners* and *Pannonica*, in which Monk played both piano and celeste. This was to remain his masterpiece.

Jazz Connection (may 1957) with Art Blakey's Jazz Messengers revisited several of his classics. **Thelonious Himself** (april 1957) was mostly solo interpretations.

Another historical collaboration, with the young John Coltrane, documented on **Live at the Five Spot** (may 1957), only released in 1993, and **Thelonious Monk with John Coltrane** (july 1957), only released in 1991, that paired two completely opposite souls (the reclusive philosopher and the cosmic virtuoso), yielded a spectacular version of Monk's *Trinkle Tinkle* and his moving ballad *Crepuscule With Nellie*.

After **Mulligan Meets Monk** (august 1957) with white saxophonist Gerry Mulligan and other minor collaborations, Monk joined in a quartet with tenor saxophonist Johnny Griffin that recorded **Thelonious in Action** (july 1958) and especially **Misterioso** (august 1958). The repertory was now fossilized: Monk kept repeating his themes of the golden years.

Earl "Bud" Powell was the pianist who adapted the bebop style of Charlie Parker and Dizzy Gillespie to the piano. He boldly disposed of the left hand striding and of Art Tatum's baroque embellishments to coin an anti-virtuoso style that relied more on melodic invention and on subtle irregularities, and nonetheless releasing an almost demonic energy. His style crystallized through a number of piano trio performances at the turn of the decade: *Bud's Bubble* (january 1947), based on Parker's *Crazeology*, *So Sorry Please* (february 1950), *Celia* (february 1949), *Strictly Confidential* (february 1949) and especially *Tempus Fugit* (february 1949) with Max Roach on drums and Ray Brown on bass; *Hallucinations* (february 1951) and *The Fruit* (february 1951), with Ray Brown on bass and Bernard "Buddy" Rich on drums; *Un Poco Loco* (may 1951) with Curly Russell on bass and Max Roach on drums, one of his artistic peak; and *Glass Enclosure* (august 1953). He also composed *Bouncing with Bud* (august 1949) and especially *Dance of the Infidels* (august 1949), recorded with Theodore "Fats" Navarro on trumpet, Sonny Rollins on tenor saxophone, Tommy Potter on bass and Roy Haynes on drums. These compositions rank among the most refined tunes of the time. His playing was apparently schizophrenic, but in reality Powell was "drumming" with his left hand while unleashing phrases at breakneck speed with the right hand. An alcoholic who had spent several periods of his life in mental hospitals, his major season lasted only those few years.

Chicago's blind pianist Lennie Tristano, of Italian-American descent, who arrived in New York in 1946, fused bebop and 20th-century classical music in his abstract meditations that wove extended melodies over subdued rhythms, the musical equivalent of a renaissance painting with a complex building in the foreground and a simple, pastoral landscape in the background. He was not a poet but an architect: his pieces relied on several levels of counterpoint and even dissonance. They were frigid and lifeless by the standards of jazz music.
Tristano coined that language in 1947, via a series of uncompromising recordings both solo (*Atonement*, *Spontaneous Combustion*) and in a drum-less trio with a guitarist (Billy Bauer) and a bassist (*Dissonance*, *Parallel*, *Apellation*, *Abstraction*, *Palimpsest*, *Freedom*).
Two years later a quintet with Tristano, alto saxophonist Lee Konitz, guitarist Billy Bauer and drummer Shelly Manne laid the foundations for a group version of that art with Konitz's *Subconscious-Lee* and Tristano's *Retrospection* , off **Lennie Tristano Quintet featuring Lee Konitz** (january 1949), as well as Konitz's *Tautology* on **Lee Konitz with Tristano, Marsh and Bauer** (january 1949).
Free jazz was invented in 1949 (ten years before the term was coined) when Tristano's sextet (alto saxophonist Lee Konitz, tenor saxophonist Warne Marsh, guitarist Billy Bauer, bass and drums) recorded *Intuition* and *Digression*, two completely improvised free-form jams. They were but two of the tracks of **Crosscurrents** (1949), that also included *Wow* and *Sax of a Kind*. That album's austere and elegant improvised counterpoint was as pioneering for cool jazz as Miles Davis' **Birth Of The Cool**. The dissonant *Descent into the Maelstrom* (june 1953), for overdubbed pianos, was an even more formidable attack against musical conventions. Two pieces recorded in october 1951 by a piano-bass-drums trio, *Ju-Ju* and *Pastime*, were actually assembled in the studio by Tristano, manipulating and overdubbing sections of music.
After a three-year hiatus, the bluesy and fully improvised *Requiem*, *Line Up*, for another piano-drums-bass trio and accelerated in the studio, and *Turkish Mambo*, that overdubbed three tracks in different meters to create a rhythmic effect that a pianist could not achieve, all three off **Lennie Tristano** (1955), the nine improvisations of **Manhattan Studio** (1956) for piano trio (with *Manhattan Studio* and *Momentum*), *Continuity* (october 1958), with Warne Marsh, bassist Henry Grimes and drummer Paul Motian, off **Continuity**, and **The New Tristano** (1960), a set of breathtaking improvised piano solos (notably *Becoming*, the spectacular *C Minor Complex*, the suite *Scene and Variations*, *Deliberation*, *G Minor Complex*) continued to refine his language, which was now widely understood. The dynamic of his compositions was often cyclic, alternating quiet passages and stormy passages, hinting at an endless cycle of rebirths.

Bebop Pianists

A sort of reaction to bebop came from pianists whose music was far less cerebral and much closer to pop music.

Montreal's pianist Oscar Peterson was a virtuoso (worthy of Art Tatum) in the age of bebop, the antithesis of virtuosity. He mastered the techniques of stride piano, boogie-woogie and pop balladry, and rarely challenged his audience. By 1950 he was widely considered the greatest jazz pianist. **1951** (1951) was a collaboration with trumpeter Austin Roberts. **Pastel Moods** (january 1952) was his first trio album, a typical set of atmospheric themes for piano, guitar and bass. The trio he formed in 1953 with guitarist Herb Ellis and bassist Ray Brown refined that idea via **Recital** (april 1954), **At Zardi's** (november 1955) while Peterson also engaged in countless tedious tribute albums, collaborations with Lionel Hampton, Benny Carter, Roy Eldridge, etc. The subsequent trio of 1958 with only bass (Brown) and drums (Ed Thigpen) started out with **Affinity** (september 1962) and **Night Train** (december 1962), with *Hymn To Freedom*, and perhaps peaked on **Trio Plus One** (august 1964) with trumpeter Clark Terry. They also recorded Peterson's first major composition: the eight-song **Canadiana Suite** (september 1964). Then the classic trio lost its drummer, and the line-up began to fluctuate, although albums such as **Blues Etude** (december 1965) were not much different from the previous ones. After many years of vegetating next to other dinosaurs, a rebirth of sort led Peterson to a handful of inspired recordings: **The Trio** (may 1973) with Joe Pass on guitar and Niels-Henning Orsted Pedersen on bass, five elegant pieces that summarize his style (*Blues Etude, Chicago Blues, Easy Listening Blues, Come Sunday, Secret Love*); **Night Child** (1979) with Pass, Pedersen and a drummer; **Nigerian Marketplace** (1981) with Pedersen on bass and Terry Clark on drums; **If You Could See Me Now** (1983), again with Pedersen, Pass and a drummer; as well as to (finally) composing a few orchestral suites: *African Suite* (1979), *A Royal Wedding Suite* (april 1981) for piano and orchestra; *Easter Suite* (1984), *Trail of Dreams* (2000).

British blind pianist George Shearing represented pop-jazz at its most melodious. His quintet (piano, guitar, bass, drums and Margorie Hyams' vibraphone) scored huge hits with Harry Warren's *September In The Rain* february 1949) and his own *Lullaby Of Birdland* (july 1952). His best album was probably **Spell** (april 1955). He was the epitome of the "light" chamber sound.

New York's pianist Erroll Garner was another master of melody, penning *Laura* (september 1945), *Fantasy on Frankie and Johnny* (june 1947), the pop hit *Misty* (july 1954) and a **Concert by the Sea** (september 1955). While still rooted in swing music and gentle to the point of sounding superficial, Garner's flowing style represented a meeting of the jazz tradition and the impressionistic tradition of classical music, evoking Claude Debussy more than the jazz pioneers.

A follower of Garner's "impressionistic" school, Chicago's pianist Frederick "Ahmad Jamal" Jones (1930) was a master of ambience and dynamics. A sense of existential suspense scars the catchy melodies of *Ahmad's Blues* (may 1952), and, after the fashionable conversion to Islam (1952), *New Rhumba* (may 1955), and the two hits from the live album **But Not for Me** (january 1958), Nat Simon's *Poinciana* and George Gershwin's *But Not for Me*.

Bebop Pianists

The only pianist-composer to stand up to Thelonious Monk during the bebop era was Herbie Nichols, but in his case the composition prevailed over the performance. Nichols pioneered cross-over fusion between jazz music (both the traditional kind and the bop kind) and classical music (the traditional, tonal kind). In fact, he also added doses of Caribbean folk music. He only recorded three albums as a leader, between 1955 and 1956: **The Third World** (may 1955), with Art Blakey on drums, containing *Third World, Dance Line, Cro-Magnon Nights, Amoeba's Dance* and *2300 Skidoo*, and two volumes of **Herbie Nichols Trio** (august 1955 and april 1956), with Max Roach on drums, containing *The Gig, House Party Starting* and *Lady Sings the Blues* (Billie Holiday's theme song). Their unorthodox, whimsical pieces could sound like parodies of the ruling canons or like deconstruction of the pop song.

Hardly a trivial pop-jazz evangelist, California's white pianist Dave Brubeck managed the feat of reconnecting the masses with jazz music. His compositions, such as *The Duke* (august 1955) and *In Your Own Sweet Way* (february 1956), were steeped in jazz tradition but often make him sound like a predecessor of the "third stream". His piano playing, best displayed on **Solo** (1956), could be angular and subversive. The classic Quartet (Brubeck, alto saxophonist Paul Desmond, drummer Joe Morello, black bassist Eugene Wright) crafted **Time Out** (1959), the first million-selling jazz record, but both the hits, Desmond's *Take Five* (in 5/4 time) and *Blue Rondo a la Turk* (in 9/8), indulged in odd time signatures. Brubeck proved his musical ambitions by scoring the ballet *Points on Jazz* (composed in 1960), the oratorio *The Light In The Wilderness* (1968), the cantatas *The Gates of Justice* (1969), *Truth is Fallen* (august 1971) and *La Fiesta de la Posada* (1976), and the mass *To Hope* (1995).

Other noteworthy pianists of the bebop era were Al Haig, Elmo Hope and Richard Twardzik. In Europe, the main bebop pianist was probably the French-based pianist Martial Solal.

BEBOP BIG BANDS

Before he became a ballad singer and the first black pop star, in 1944 Earl Hines' vocalist Billy Eckstine organized the first big band of bebop, featuring Charlie Parker, Dizzy Gillespie and Sarah Vaughan, and, later, Miles Davis, Fats Navarro, Dexter Gordon, Oscar Pettiford, Art Blakey, etc. It was a brief experience (the band folded in 1947 as Eckstine's solo career was taking off) and its main impact was to introduce a new generation of musicians.

Among the white big bands that survived the bebop revolution, saxophonist Charlie Barnet's bridged the swing era and the new era via Ray Noble's *Cherokee* (1939), Andy Gibson's *Shady Lady* (1942) and Ralph Burns' *The Moose* (1943). But the real champions of white big band jazz were now Woody Herman and Stan Kenton.

Reeds player <u>Woody Herman</u>, another white bandleader who had formed his orchestra in 1936 and had already hit the charts with bluesy numbers composed by Joe Bishop, such as *Woodchoppers' Ball* (april 1939) and *Blue Flame* (march 1941), as well as with Harold Arlen's *Blues in the Night* (september 1941), arranged in a traditional manner a` la Duke Ellington or Count Basie, first showed his interest in the new trends when he hired Dizzy Gillespie, who composed *Down Under* (july 1942) for him. In the following years Herman assembled an impressive set of talents, such as bassist Chubby Jackson (1942), drummer Dave Tough (1944), guitarist Billy Bauer (1944), trombonist Bill Harris (1944), pianist Ralph Burns (1944), trumpeter Neal Hefti (1944), vibraphonist Kenneth "Red Norvo" Norville (1945), trumpeter Sonny Berman (1945), trumpeter Shorty Rogers (1945) and formed the first Herd. Burns and Hefti (and later Rogers) were also skilled composers and arrangers, who provided excellent material to top the energetic rhythm section. Hits such as Herman's own novelty *Goosey Gander* (march 1945), Burns' *Bijou Rhumba A La Jazz* (august 1945) Harris' *Your Father's Mustache* (september 1945) Herman's ebullient *Apple Honey* (february 1945), Louis Jordan's caricatural *Caldonia* (february 1945), Herman's *Blowin' Up A Storm* (november 1945) Burns' sprightly *Northwest Passage* (march 1945), Hefti's *Good Earth* (august 1945), Hefti's *Wild Root* (november 1945), made them the most popular band among those trying to assimilate the new language of bebop. Herman's "second herd" of 1947 was characterized by the reed section, the so called "four brothers" whose style pioneered "cool jazz" before the term was invented: three tenor saxophones (enfant prodige Stan Getz, John "Zoot" Sims, Al Cohn) and a baritone saxophone (Serge Chaloff). The reed section became dominant over the brass and the rhythm section, a fact that lent the Second Herd its "modern" quality. Burns was the real genius of the orchestra, as the ambitious multi-part suites *Lady McGowan's Dream* (september 1946) and especially the catchy four-movement *Summer Sequence* (september 1946) proved. The third part of the latter, *Early Autumn*, was the ballad that turned Getz into a star. But this herd had fewer hits:

Jimmy Giuffre's *Four Brothers* (december 1947), Al Cohn's *The Goof and I* (december 1947), Burns' *Keen And Peachy* (december 1947).

Lionel Hampton, who had recorded the first vibraphone solo in october 1930 in Louis Armstrong's version of Eubie Blake's *Memories of You* and who had featured in Benny Goodman's inter-racial quartet (1936-38), formed an orchestra that came to specialize in ebullient jazz music at the border with boogie-woogie and predating rhythm'n'blues. Relying throughout his career on young lions such as alto saxophonist Earl Bostic (1939), tenor saxophonist Jean-Baptiste "Illinois" Jacquet (1941), bassist Charlie Mingus (1947), trumpeter Fats Navarro (1948), trumpeter Quincy Jones (1951), and trumpeter Clifford Brown (1953), Hampton became a staple of the dancehall with Jimmy McHugh's *Sunny Side of the Street* (april 1937), his own *Hot Mallets* (september 1939), featuring tenor saxophonists Coleman Hawkins, Ben Webster and Chu Berry as well as young trumpeter Dizzy Gillespie, a version of Euday Bowman's *Twelfth Street Rag* (june 1939) highlighted by his frantic two-finger piano tour de force, *Down Home Jump* (october 1938), *Central Avenue Breakdown* (may 1940), on which he played piano accompanied by the Nat King Cole trio, *Flying Home* (may 1942), originally recorded in 1939 with Benny Goodman, but now featuring Jacquet's celebrated "honking" solo (the mother of all rhythm'n'blues saxophone solos), *Hamp's Boogie-Woogie* (march 1944), written by the band's exuberant pianist, Milt Buckner, and *Hey Baba Rebop* (december 1945).

A further blow to harmonic stability and to musical entertainment came from another white band, Stan Kenton's orchestra. Los Angeles' pianist Stan Kenton, also a gifted composer (*Suite For Saxophones* from september 1941), became one of the all-time specialists of big bands. His first Orchestra (featuring saxophonist Art Pepper, except in 1944-46) recorded his *Artistry in Rhythm* (november 1943), their first hit, *Eager Beaver* (november 1943), *Harlem Folk Dance* (november 1943), *Painted Rhythm* (october 1945), Buddy Baker's *And Her Tears Flowed Like Wine* (may 1944), another hit, *Opus In Pastels* (may 1945), one of the most intriguing compositions, and Gene Roland's *Tampico* (may 1945), another hit. After the war, Kenton recruited Italian composer Pete Rugolo (1945), who became the orchestra's main arranger, and Danish trombonist Kai Winding (1946): the two were instrumental in crafting the orchestra's "modern" sound, especially since Kenton seemed more interested in format than in style. By 1947 Kenton's Progressive Jazz Orchestra had a brass section of five trumpets and five trombones (and Shelly Manne on drums), and the material had expanded to include Kenton's *Concerto To End All Concertos* (july 1946), Kenton's "hollywoodian" *Theme To The West* (september 1947), Kenton's *Reed Rapture* (july 1946), originally a 1942 three-minute film for a visual juke box, and Bob Graettinger's *Thermopolae* (december 1947).

Rugolo, a consummate composer, was the real hero of Kenton's "progressive" approach. In 1947 he provided a counterweight to Kenton's bombastic musical ego with a set of impressionistic vignettes, notable for their minimalist architectures (*Impressionism, Monotony, Abstraction*), poetic abandon (*Interlude, Collaboration, Lament*), and sheer ingenuity (*Chorale For Piano, Brass And*

Bongos, Fugue For Rhythm Section). Despite being rather subdued compared with Kenton's favorite material, these were extremely powerful pieces of music, boasting a psychological as well as sonic intensity that was more typical of classical than jazz music.

After a hiatus of a few years, in 1950 Kenton organized an even bigger band, the 40-piece Innovations In Modern Music Orchestra, replete with a 16-piece string section and a horn section (but notable soloists were trumpeter Maynard Ferguson and saxophonist Clifford "Bud" Shank). **Innovations In Modern Music Orchestra** (january 1950) was a kaleidoscope of orchestral inventions: Kenton's *Theme For Sunday*, Rugolo's tone poem *Conflict*, Rugolo's five-minute mini-concerto *Mirage*, Johnny Richards' *Soliloquy*, Laurindo Almeida's *Amazonia*, Bob Graettinger's *Incident in Jazz*, trombonist Bill Russo's sentimental *Solitaire* and two gems by Franklyn Marks, *Trajectories* and *Evening In Pakistan*. **Presents** (1950) added Russo's *Halls Of Brass*, Kenton's *Shelly Manne*, Graettinger's *House of Strings*. *June Christy* was an experiment of free-form improvised wordless vocals: vocalist June Christy accompanied by an eight-piece rhythm section. Kenton's strings were almost an insult to the "sweet" string orchestras of the time: they sounded like an army of aliens. Kenton's ambitions were matched by Bob Graettinger, who composed for him the six-movement suite *This Modern World* (may 1953), and the four-movement expressionist, dissonant suite *City Of Glass* (1948), that, greatly revised, became the source for Kenton's album **City of Glass** (1951). Shorty Rogers contributed to the arrangements.

Kenton's New Concepts Of Artistry In Rhythm Orchestra of 1952, that recorded **New Concepts Of Artistry In Rhythm Orchestra** (september 1952) and **Kenton Showcase** (1953) was a smaller entity formed with Russo that featured saxophonists Gerry Mulligan, Lee Konitz, Bill Holman and Zoot Sims. Mulligan and Holman soon became the main composers. The artistic peak of this band was probably Holman's *Invention for Guitar and Trumpet* on the first album. Mel Lewis' drumming from 1954 on bestowed a harder edge on the music, as documented on **Contemporary Concepts** (july 1955).

Cuban Fire (may 1956) was an album of Latin standards, including the hit *Peanut Vendor* (1956), a reworking of a Cuban song, and Johnny Richards originals.

Rugolo's and Kenton's next highbrow project was a string-heavy orchestra that released **Lush Interlude** (july 1958) and **The Kenton Touch** (december 1958).

In 1960 Kenton turned to the Mellophonium Orchestra, featuring four mellophoniums, and opted for the romantic ballad. Their best album was **Adventures in Jazz** (july 1961), that contained Dee Barton's *Waltz Of The Prophets*, Ernesto Lecuona's *Malaguena*, and Bill Holman's *Stairway To The Stars*. **Adventures in Time** (september 1962) was actually Johnny Richards' concerto for orchestra, notable for the insistence on odd time signatures. The Los Angeles Neophonic Orchestra of 1965, instead, specialized in "third stream" repertory. **Conducts the Los Angeles Neophonic** (january 1965) was highlighted by Russ Garcia's five-movement suite *Adventure in Emotion* and by

Clare Fischer's *Piece for Soft Brass, Woodwinds and Percussion*. Throughout his career Stan Kenton seemed to be schizophrenically split in three personalities: the pop charmer, the jazz stylist and the avantgarde experimentalist.

One of the most adventurous jazz bands of the bebop era was led by white Chicago-educated saxophonist Boyd Raeburn, and featured mostly white bop players. Initially, driven by Ed Finckel's compositions, such as *March Of The Boyds* (june 1944) and *Boyd Meets Stravinsky* (february 1946), the orchestra played a progressive form of swing. But the main composer in the golden years from 1944 till 1946 was pianist George Handy, who arranged frequently dissonant scores and penned *Tonsillectomy* (october 1945), *Yerxa* (october 1945) and *Dalvatore Sally* (february 1946), the first movement of a four-movement *Jazz Symphony*.

Cool Jazz

The radical wing of bebop led to "cool jazz", a genre inaugurated in 1948 by Miles Davis with his nine-unit ensemble. Cool jazzists were even more uncompromising than bebop jazzists. They belonged to a younger generation and had been raised playing with the gurus of bebop (Miles Davis with Charlie Parker, the Modern Jazz Quartet with Dizzy Gillespie, Stan Getz with Woody Herman, Gerry Mulligan and Art Pepper with Stan Kenton, Paul Desmond with Dave Brubeck, etc).

Cool jazz was a cerebral kind of music. It was largely independent of the traditional preoccupation with rhythm and melody. It focused on creative sounds in a "cool" (calm, pensive, meditative) fashion. Cool jazz represented the stage at which jazz music joined the general trend towards "soundsculpting" that was the quintessence of 20th century Western music.

Cool jazz represented a dramatic shift in the black psyche. The black musician metamorphosed from being an entertainer to being an explorer. This transition paralleled the social turmoil of the post-war era, when blacks began to enjoy enough (economic and political) freedom to emancipate themselves from the psychological slavery of depending on a white man to make decisions for them. These black musicians were playing for themselves, like they had not done since the birth of the blues. At the same time they were playing "about" themselves in the self-referential sense that the white avantgarde was playing "about" classical music while playing against it. They were, again, explorers of a musical genre, of its structure, of its rules, of its limits. Thus these black jazz musicians became more "white" than their predecessors had ever been.

Cool jazz was particularly popular among white musicians, probably because it downplayed the "African" roots of jazz. One of the founding fathers of cool jazz was a white musician: Lennie Tristano.

The most eccentric sound during the war was produced by the orchestra formed in 1937 by white pianist <u>Claude Thornhill</u>, that in 1942 boasted four vocalists, seven clarinets, two French horns and a tuba. Its arranger, Gil Evans, concocted dreamy and hypnotic textures, such as *Portrait of a Guinea Farm* (april 1941) and *Snowfall* (may 1941), that toyed with timbral and rhythmic mannerism. Their sophisticated chamber jazz even scored a couple of hits, *A Sunday Kind Of Love* (may 1947) and *Love For Love* (september 1947), but the band became even more cryptic after the addition of white alto saxophonist Lee Konitz (1947) and of arranger Gerry Mulligan, who penned *Elevation* (october 1948). Evans, Mulligan and Konitz were defining a white man's version of bebop, much more abstract than swinging.

St Louis' trumpeter <u>Miles Davis</u> left Charlie Parker's band in 1948 and teamed up with white arrangers Gil Evans and Gerry Mulligan, who simply continued what they had been doing with Claude Thornhill's orchestra: emphasize the timbral qualities of instruments. Their inter-racial Nonet (two whites on saxophones, Lee Konitz on alto and Gerry Mulligan on baritone, John Lewis on piano, Max Roach on drums, trombone, French Horn, tuba, bass) disposed of the tenor saxophone, rediscovered the tuba, indulged in the French horn, and removed all barrier between different instrumental sections, thus further upsetting the traditional balance of power within the jazz orchestra. Chalmers MacGregor's *Moon Dreams* (september 1948) and Cleo Henry's *Boplicity* (april 1949), with James "J.J." Johnson on trombone, were Gil Evans' most daring experiments to date. The nonet's album, **Birth of the Cool** (september 1948), originally released as 78 RPM singles and 45 RPM EPs between 1948 and 1950, and eventually released as a 12" LP in 1957, was a self-defining manifesto, and became one of the most influential jazz albums of all times. Featuring Gunther Schuller on French horn, the album included Mulligan's *Venus De Milo* (april 1949) and *Jeru* (january 1949), Lewis' *Rouge* (april 1949), and Davis' *Deception* (march 1950). Davis challenged the fundamental premises of bebop by creating music of haunting tonal qualities without relying on speed, an idea that he had already pioneered while playing with Charlie Parker. This approach dramatically altered the balance between the improviser and the arranger.

After **Dig** (october 1951), his pioneering album in the hard-bop style with a sextet featuring alto saxophonist Jackie McLean, tenor saxophonist Sonny Rollins, pianist Walter Bishop, bassist Tommy Potter and drummer Art Blakey, that contained his compositions *Dig* and *Denial*, Davis retired from the scenes to kick his heroin addiction.

When he returned with **Walkin'** (april 1954), that contains a 13-minute tour de force interpretation of Richard Carpenter's *Walkin'* (1954) with James "J.J." Johnson on trombone, Lucky Thompson on tenor, Horace Silver on piano, Percy Heath on bass and Kenny Clarke on drums, **Bag's Groove**, titled after the eleven-minute version of Milton Jackson's *Bag's Groove* (december 1954) performed with a stellar line-up (Jackson on vibraphone, Thelonious Monk on piano, Clarke and Heath), and containing also three Sonny Rollins compositions performed with Sonny Rollins (tenor sax), Horace Silver (piano), Clarke and Heath, and **Miles Davis and the Modern Jazz Giants**, that contained another Davis-Jackson-Monk collaboration (eleven-minute long) on Davis' own *Swing Spring* (december 1954), Davis had not only a sound that was unique but also a vision for the future of jazz. These works for Quintet redefined jazz as a sensual and haunting music.

Davis became a star in 1955 and formed a new Quintet to much fanfare, featuring tenor saxophonist John Coltrane, pianist Red Garland, bassist Paul Chambers and drummer Philly Joe Jones. The first album, **Miles** (november 1955), with Davis' *The Theme*, was still acerbic, but **Cookin'** (october 1956), that contained only four tracks among which notably Davis' *Blues by Five* and *Tune-Up/ When Lights Are Low*, **Relaxin'** (1956), with their eight-minute reworking of Frank Loesser's *If I Were A Bell* (october 1956), **Workin'** (may 1956), with Davis' *Four* and Coltrane's *Trane's Blues*, and **Steamin'** (may 1956), with their nine-minute reworking of Richard Rodgers' *Surrey With the Fringe on Top*, presented a perfectly integrated unit of imaginative solos and subtle interplay. (Ironically, these innovative recordings of 1956 were due to Davis' need to fulfil a contractual obligation, the easiest way being to cut lengthy spontaneous jams). **Round About Midnight**, titled after the Thelonious Monk original that had become Davis' signature tune, refined the method, particularly in Ray Henderson's *Bye Bye Blackbird* (june 1956): a psychological balance of moods, styles and techniques.

Adding altoist Cannonball Adderley turned the quintet into a Sextet, documented on **Milestones** (february 1958), with Davis' 13-minute *Sid's Ahead* and an eleven-minute version of Monk's *Straight No Chaser*. But the real "milestone" was Davis' modal-based improvisation on his brief *Milestones*. In the meantime, **Miles Ahead** (may 1957) had marked the return of Gil Evans, who arranged a 19-piece Orchestra and provided *Miles Ahead* and *Blues For Pablo*. It was an altogether different format for Davis, one of short, catchy, baroque themes. Davis played flugelhorn on some tracks. During this period Davis also improvised the music for the soundtrack of Louis Malle's film **L'Ascenseur Pour L'Echafaud** (december 1957), one of his most experimental works and the archetype for all future film-noir scores. The collaboration with Evans continued on an album devoted to George Gershwin's **Porgy and Bess** (1958), and peaked with **Sketches of Spain** (march 1960): Davis and Gil Evans merged jazz musicians (Chambers, Cobb, Elvin Jones) and a classical orchestra, and focused on a 16-minute interpretation of Joaquin Rodrigo's *Concierto de Aranjuez*, translucent and sentimental. A 12-minute improvisation around Evans' *Solea* capped the album. The collaboration with Gil Evans ended with the inferior **Quiet Nights** (1962), released only in 1964.

In parallel Davis had been evolving independently his vision of jazz music for small ensembles, and had fully adopted the paradigm of "modal jazz" with **Kind Of Blue** (april 1959). By anchoring the compositions to just one key, chord and mode for several bars, Davis encouraged more freedom and creativity in the solos. Miles, Coltrane, Adderley, Chambers, Bill Evans on piano, Jimmy Cobb on drums improvised in the studio, without any rehearsal. Four lengthy jams, *So What*, *Freddie Freeloader*, *All Blues* and *Flamenco Sketches* (the most adventurous use of modal improvisation), explored their joint soul rather than constructing architectures of sound. The idea of modal jazz was immediately perceived as a revolutionary idea by the younger generation. Modal jazz was fundamentally a reaction to bebop's stereotypical pattern: a rapid succession of chords. Modal jazz created music using modes instead of chords as building blocks, thus greatly simplifying the harmony and emphasizing the melody.

Someday My Prince Will Come (march 1961) returned Davis to the format of the quintet. Two lengthy improvisations stood out, *Teo*, again with John Coltrane, and *Pfrancing*, Davis' Quintet was so celebrated by the press that the two live albums recorded with tenor saxophonist Hank Mobley, pianist Wynton Kelly, Chambers and Cobb, **In Person** (1961) and **At Carnegie Hall** (1961), that mined his repertory and offered expanded versions of his warhorses, became best-sellers.

In a bold move, Davis ignored the lure of success and turned to a generation of very young players for his next project. Thus **Seven Steps to Heaven** (1963), whose best tracks were written by temporary pianist Victor Feldman, *Seven Steps to Heaven* and *Joshua*, debuted pianist Herbie Hancock, bassist Ron Carter and drummer Tony Williams (still a teenager). Tenor saxophonist Wayne Shorter joined in 1964 during a European tour to form the most famous of all Davis quintets. This quintet proceeded to demolish harmonic conventions of jazz music, but in a subtler way than free-jazz was doing, remaining close to the cliches of hard bop while introducing greater tonal and rhythmic freedom. Best of all, each of the five members proved to be a skilled composer, crafting themes that were ideal platforms for their sound. **E.S.P.** (january 1965), still a transitional work, contained Shorter's *E.S.P.* and *Iris*, Carter's *Mood* and *Eighty-One*, Hancock's *Little One*, Davis' *Agitation*. **Miles Smiles** (october 1966), a more spontaneous effort, highlighted Shorter both as a player and as a composer (*Orbits, Footprints, Dolores*). Edgy and neurotic, but at the same time ebullient and even childish, it turned out to be a mere detour in the progression towards the low-key transcendental ambience of **Sorcerer** (may 1967), that contained Tony Williams' *Pee Wee*, Herbie Hancock's *Sorcerer*, Shorter's *Prince of Darkness*, *Masqualero* and *Limbo*. Both the compositions and the performances were moving towards a more sophisticated style, a mannerism of emotional restraint. **Nefertiti** (june 1967) wed the neurotic feeling of **Miles Smiles** and the surreal ambience of **Sorcerer**. The result was the jangling, angular, haunting music of Hancock's *Madness*, and of Shorter's *Nefertiti* and *Fall*. The muscular sound of Williams' *Hand Jive* was the last memory of their hard-bop roots.

Davis was dispensing with the original features of jazz (syncopation, melody) and focusing on the aspect that had become more and more central to the aesthetic of post-swing jazz: textural sound (ambience, mood). At the same time he was downplaying all the elements that could break down the piece into sections, so as the achieve the smooth and seamless quality of the stream of consciousness. Davis and Shorter were altering the relative roles of instruments within jazz: instead of melodic instruments such as trumpet and saxophone accounting for the music's dynamics over a simple, stable rhythmic foundation, Davis and Shorter were simplifying their melodic layer to the limit of pure ambience or mood while shifting most of the dynamics and complexity to Williams' "drumming".

Coherently, the format was evolving towards the long monolithic jam, as displayed on the four lengthy tracks of **Miles in the Sky** (may 1968): Davis' *Stuff* (17 minutes) and *Country Son* (14 minutes), Shorter's *Paraphernalia* (12 minutes), featuring guitarist George Benson, and Williams' *Black Comedy*. More importantly, the album began to replace piano and guitar with electric piano and electric guitar. The drum themselves were played in a manner that was more "rock" than "jazz". It was not clear at all that this evolution would end up in coining a new genre, jazz-rock. But that is what it did on **Filles de Kilimanjaro** (june 1968), appropriately subtitled "directions in music" and performed by the quintet of Davis, Shorter, Williams, Chick Corea on electric piano and British bassist Dave Holland. It was in fact more than just rock and jazz, because the playing introduced doses of funk and blues as well. And this time all five tracks were signed by Davis in person: *Frelon Brun, Tout de Suite, Petits Machins, Filles de Kilimanjaro, Mademoiselle Mabry*. Jazz-rock was, in fact, a consequence of modal jazz: modal jazz had blurred the border between the two genres (and classical music itself). In an age in which rock musicians were reaching out towards jazz, jazz had inadvertently reached out towards rock. Their wedding was just a matter of time.

In a Silent Way (february 1969) marked the new beginning. The new electric octet featured Davis, Shorter, Hancock, Corea, Holland, Williams, John McLaughlin on guitar and Joe Zawinul on organ. The LP was simply divided in two continuous sides: *Shhh/Peaceful* (18 minutes) and *In a Silent Way/It's About That Time* (20 minutes).

The next album was a double LP, **Bitches Brew** (august 1969), produced by Teo Macero and released in march 1970, that included six very long jams (up to 27 minutes) performed by a revolving cast of twelve musicians (Davis, Shorter, Corea, Zawinul, McLaughlin and Holland from the "old" guard, and, among the new faces, bass clarinetist Bennie Maupin and drummer Jack DeJohnette). It became an astronomical success and it made jazz-rock a world-wide commodity. It was also one of the first albums entirely built by the producer using studio machines: Macero and Davis glued together snippets of the actual performances in order to obtain the sound they wanted. The unreleased recordings by the band were far more straightforward than what appeared on the album. Davis was again the main composer: *Bitches Brew* (27 minutes), *Spanish Key* (17 minutes), and *Miles Runs the Voodoo Down* (14 minutes), influenced by Jimi Hendrix. Other notable themes were Zawinul's *Pharaoh's Dance* (20 minutes) and Shorter's *Sanctuary* (11 minutes). But the themes were hardly visible in the finished product. Davis had created a music of impressionistic soundscapes, that relied on the beat of rock music only to anchor them down, to avoid that they disintegrate in empty space.

Teo Macero repeated the trick on **A Tribute to Jack Johnson** (1970), that was, again, divided simply into the two sides of the LP: *Right Off*, that had McLaughlin and young drummer Billy Cobham play together (and except for a stellar solo by Davis, their interplay dominates the piece), and *Yesternow*. The influence of rock (especially Jimi Hendrix) and funk music was even more overt. Again, Macero pasted together (within the same piece) material coming from different sessions by different line-ups (and even material from previous albums). Jack DeJohnette, Bennie Maupin, Dave Holland, Sonny Sharrock also featured.

Davis kept elaborating on the new sound for a few years, but was losing all of his disciples, who went on to spread the word with their own bands: Shorter and Zawinul formed Weather Report, Corea formed Return to Forever, McLaughlin formed the Mahavishnu Orchestra.

In order to capitalize on Davis' pop-star status, several subsequent releases compiled material by different line-ups and from different sessions. **Big Fun** (january 1970) delivered at least two additions to the jazz-rock canon, both almost half an hour long: Shorter's *Great Expectations* (1969), performed by a mixed Indian and jazz ensemble (sitar, tabla, trumpet, guitar, piano, clarinet, saxophone, bass, drums and even Airto Moreira on berimbau) and Davis' *Go Ahead John* (1970), performed by a quintet (Davis, McLaughlin, Holland, DeJohnette, Steve Grossman on saxophone). **Live Evil** (february 1970) was split between live and studio material, best being the live jams (of december 1970) on Davis' *Funky Tonk* (23 minutes), *What I Say* (21 minutes) and *Sivad* (15 minutes), performed by the septet of Davis, McLaughlin, DeJohnette, Moreira, Michael Henderson on bass, Gary Bartz on saxophones and Keith Jarrett on electric keyboards. **On The Corner** (1972) was a more aggressive affair, very far from the studio sophistication of **Bitches Brew**, both the four-movement *On The Corner* (again an Indian, rock, funk and jazz pastiche) and the 23-minute *Helen Butte/ Mr Freedom X*. It marked the first use of a synthesizer on a Davis album, and the assimilation of the hip-hop rhythm.

The double-LP **Get Up With It** (october 1974) compiled even more heterogeneous sessions, patched together by Macero in even more liberal ways, and extending beyond the previously sacred limit of 30 minutes: *He Loved Him Madly* (1974) and *Calypso Frelimo* (1973), both by an octet featuring flutist Dave Liebman and guitarist Pete Cosey. It also debuted *Maiysha*. The 1970s closed with two live double-LP albums that were recorded on the same day by an ensemble of trumpet, saxophone (Sonny Fortune), two guitars (Pete Cosey on the "Hendrixian" solos), bass, percussion and drums: **Agharta** (february 1975), that contained the 22-minute *Prelude* and the 27-minute *Interlude* and further increase the dose of rock and funk influences, and especially **Pangaea** (same session), simply divided in *Zimbabwe* (41 minutes) and *Gondwana* (47 minutes), two orgies of monster grooves and delirious solos.

Davis was largely missing in action during the second half of the 1970s, due to illness. He returned with two albums for sextet (or more) that featured a young Bill Evans (not the pianist) on saxophones and Marcus Miller on bass: **The Man With the Horn** (1981), with *Back Seat Betty* and *Ursula*, and **We Want Miles** (1981), with *Jean-Pierre, Fast Track, Kix* and a side-long version of Gershwin's *My Man's Gone Now*. Despite popular success, the albums that followed were the most mediocre of his career. **Star People** (january 1983), notable for the twin guitars of John Scofield and Mike Stern and for Davis' first use of the synthesizer, and **Decoy** (1983), an even more electronic work, seemed to exist only because of the title-track, as the other tracks were embarrassing. **You're Under Arrest** (january 1985) was perhaps his lowest point, playing two pop songs and Scofield's *You're Under Arrest*. **Aura** (february 1985), released in 1988, was much better, but it was a performance for big band (including McLaughlin and bassist Niels-Henning Orsted Pederson) of Danish flugelhornist Palle Mikkelbourg's ten-movement neoclassical suite *Aura*. **Tutu** (february 1986), a collection of short pieces, was a collaboration with producer Marcus Miller (who played and overdubbed several instruments himself). The format of Miller providing the soundscape for Davis' improvisations was much better realized on **Siesta** (january 1987), the soundtrack to a movie. **Amandla** (december 1989) was a more traditional group effort, but Miller still composed most of the music. His last album, **Doo-Bop** (february 1991) was a collaboration with a rapper, a saxophonist and a keyboardist. The regression back to the pop song and short pieces was surprising for a musician who used to play 30-minute jams.

The first group to consciously and unabashedly play "chamber jazz" was the Modern Jazz Quartet. The Modern Jazz Quartet was born in 1952, an offshoot of Dizzy Gillespie's rhythm section, although it stabilized in the classic line-up only in 1955: pianist John Lewis (the musical director), vibraphonist Milt Jackson, bassist Percy Heath, and Connie Kay (the last to join, replacing veteran drummer Kenny Clarke). They debuted with two 10" albums, **Modern Jazz Quartet with Milt Jackson** (june 1953) and **Modern Jazz Quartet Volume 2** (october 1953), later summarized in 1956 as the LP **Django**. It already contained some elegant Lewis compositions at the border between jazz and baroque music, such as *Vendome*, *La Ronde*, based on Dizzy Gillespie's *Two Bass Hit* and later (1955) turned into a nine-minute four-movement suite, and *Delaunay's Dilemma*, as well as Lewis' seven-minute tribute to Django Reinhardt, *Django* (1954), reminiscent of New Orleans' funeral parades, and Lewis' ballad *Milano* (1954). The plan was to architect pieces that used improvisation only to the extent that the composition required it (not for a mere display of virtuoso style), and to target the audience of the concert hall, not the night clubs.

The Kay era opened with the 12" LP **Concorde** (july 1955), containing Lewis' fugue *Concorde*, Jackson's seven-minute *Ralph's New Blues*, an eight-minute *Gershwin Medley*, and a lengthy cover of Sigmund Romberg's *Softly As in a Morning Sunrise*. For **Fontessa** (january 1956) Lewis composed another fugue, *Versailles*, and the baroque, eleven-minute suite *Fontessa*, the peak of his "neoclassical" manner. **At Music Inn** (august 1956), a collaboration with Jimmy Giuffre, contained another Lewis fugue, *A Fugue for Music Inn*, as well as the bluesy *Two Degrees East Three Degrees West*. The dynamics of these pieces was often due to the dialogue between the complementary voices of Lewis and Jackson: Lewis' piano was austere and rational, while Jackson's vibes were wild and rustic; Lewis' phrasing was rooted in blues music, while Jackson's phrasing was rooted in gospel music.

Lewis also scored movie soundtracks: **No Sun in Venice** (april 1957), that debuted the funeral music of *Cortege* and the fugue *Three Windows*; **Odds Against Tomorrow** (july 1959), with *Skatin' in Central Park* and *Odds Against Tomorrow*; *Under the Jasmine Tree*, originally composed for a documentary and inspired by Moroccan music. The Modern Jazz Quartet's **Third Stream Music** bridged the format of jazz and of chamber music via Lewis' ten-minute *Exposure* (january 1960) with a classical chamber ensemble and Schuller's eleven-minute *Conversation* (september 1959). But his interest was clearly to reach beyond jazz and towards European music: the seven-movement ballet suite **The Comedy** (january 1962), either inspired or mocking renaissance music, the ballet suite *Original Sin* (march 1961), the 14-minute three-movement suite *Three Little Feelings*, first performed in 1957 by an orchestra and recorded by the quartet on

Under the Jasmine Tree (december 1967), and the orchestral requiem *In Memoriam* (november 1973).

"Third-stream" music was mostly the invention of white composer Gunther Schuller (1925), who aimed at bridging classical and jazz music. The French horn of New York's "Metropolitan Opera Orchestra" until 1959, Schuller composed mostly classical works, but was influential on jazz music as well with this books. His **Jazz Abstractions** (december 1960) featured Ornette Coleman, Eric Dolphy, Bill Evans, Jim Hall, Scott LaFaro and many others under his conduction, and contained only two side-long pieces, *Abstraction* and *Variants On A Theme Of Thelonious Monk*.

After John Lewis, the most original of third-stream composers was perhaps another white intellectual, Bob Graettinger, whose four-movement suite *City Of Glass* (april 1948) and six-movement suite *This Modern World* (may 1953), both eventually recorded by Stan Kenton, were as subtle and imposing as anything done by the classical avantgarde, especially in the way they balanced atonality and organization, both pushed to manic extremes. Unique to Graettinger were not only the rigor but also a stylistic range that turned his pieces into labyrinthine postmodernist journeys.

White tenor saxophonist Stan Getz, a veteran of Stan Kenton (1944-45), Benny Goodman (1945-46) and Woody Herman (1947-48), was as much responsible for the evolution of bebop into cool jazz as anybody else, because his solo in *Early Autumn* (december 1948) had provided the template for the genre. He refined that idea on **Quartets** (april 1950), featuring pianist Al Haig, and containing his own ballad *Marcia*. The high point of his solo career was **Focus** (july 1961), composed and arranged by Eddie Sauter for strings. Getz was later instrumental in establishing bossanova as a worldwide phenomenon via his two hits: Antonio Jobim's *Desafinado*, off **Jazz Samba** (february 1962), a collaboration with guitarist Charlie Byrd, and Antonio Jobim's *Girl From Ipanema* off **Getz/Gilberto** (march 1963), a collaboration with Brazilian guitarist Joao Gilberto. He was rejuvenated by two collaborations with Chick Corea taken up by long improvisations: **Sweet Rain** (march 1967), including Corea's *Litha* and *Windows*, and **Captain Marvel** (march 1972), including Corea's *La Fiesta*, *Five Hundred Miles High*, *Time's Lie* and *Day Waves*. Getz was the protagonist, but the atmosphere was closer to Corea's jazz-rock fusion. Basically, Gets was an articulate guest graciously hosted in Corea's living room.

Chicago's white alto saxophonist Lee Konitz was the quintessential "cool" musician, having played with Claude Thornhill (1947), Miles Davis (1948) and Lennie Tristano (1949). His art was largely one of phrasing and timbres, not melodies and rhythms. He showed how to incorporate Charlie Parker's ideas while inventing a new kind of music. Konitz composed *Tautology* and *Subconscious-Lee* (january 1949) for the Quintet with pianist Lennie Tristano and guitarist Billy Bauer that became one of the most influential acts of post-war jazz. Konitz continued to experiment in the following years, for example in a *Duet for Saxophone and Guitar* (march 1951) with Bauer, and on **Motion** (august 1961), for a trio with drummer Elvin Jones and bassist Sonny Dallas, but mostly stuck to covers while he was playing with gurus of the cool movement such as Stan Kenton (1953), Gerry Mulligan (1953) and Jimmy Giuffre (1959). His artistic peak was probably **The Lee Konitz Duets** (september 1967), a series of duets with different instruments (tenor, piano, trombone, violin, guitar, second saxophone) that ran the gamut from traditional jazz to cool jazz to free jazz (particularly *Duplexity* with piano). Konitz's cool style permeated his (rare) compositions: *Fourth Dimension* (march 1969) for a piano-trombone quintet, *Love Choral* and *Fanfare* on **Altissimo** (july 1973), a collaboration with altoists Gary Bartz, Jackie McLean and Charlie Mariano, *Free Blues* on **Satori** (september 1974), in a quartet with pianist Martial Solal, bassist David Holland and drummer Jack DeJohnette, and several (and sometimes lengthy) improvisations on jazz and pop standards. Compared with Charlie Parker, Konitz was ethereal and aloof, preferring high tones over deep tones. His playing was less intricate and less strident. It was the epitome of "cool".

Gil Evans, the legendary Canadian-born arranger of Claude Thornhill and Miles Davis, wasted his talent with collections of jazz standards arranged for large ensemble, starting with **Gil Evans and Ten** (september 1957), that featured Steve Lacy on soprano and Lee Konitz on alto. His arranging and composing skills are better represented by **Out of the Cool** (december 1960), with his *La Nevada* and George Russell's *Stratusphunk*. **Into The Hot** (october 1961) was mainly a showcase for composer Johnny Carisi, who penned *Moon Taj* and *Angkor Wat*, two early examples of abstract soundpainting. Evans was influential in blending acoustic and electric instruments, starting with **Blues in Orbit** (may 1969), titled after George Russell's *Blues in Orbit*.

Miles Davis' white pianist Bill Evans had started in a low-key bebop vein with **New Jazz Conceptions** (september 1956), that contained his *Waltz for Debby*, and with **Everybody Digs** (december 1958), that contained his *Peace Piece*; but, after recording **Kind Of Blue** (april 1959) with Davis, he formed an all-white trio with bassist Scott LaFaro and drummer Paul Motian that introduced a new democratic relationship among the instruments and veered towards an impressionistic sound influenced by European classical music. Unfortunately, LaFaro died after their two albums, **Portrait in Jazz** (december 1959) and especially **Explorations** (february 1961). Evans overdubbed himself at the piano for **Conversations With Myself** (february 1963).

Ohio-born pianist George Russell was the apostle of modal jazz. The moment he landed in New York he showed his skills as a composer, penning *Cubano Be Cubano Bop* (september 1947) for Dizzy Gillespie and *A Bird in Igor's Yard* (april 1949) for Buddy DeFranco. In 1953 he published his influential theory of modal jazz (playing based on modes rather than harmonies) and he applied his theories of jazz composition on his first album as a leader, **Jazz Workshop** (october 1956), for a sextet with trumpeter Art Farmer, altoist Hal McKusick, guitarist Barry Galbraith and pianist Bill Evans, containing the brief *Concerto for Billy the Kid, Round Johnny Rondo, Ezz-thetic, Witch Hunt, Knights of the Steamtable* and *Ye Hypocrite Ye Beelzebub*. In these three-four minute pieces he demonstrated his focus on "vertical" form (the relationship between chords and scales), letting his cohorts do most of the playing. He contributed to third-stream music with the suite for orchestra *All About Rosie* (june 1957).

All his subsequent albums were highly innovative. The concept album **New York New York** contained two lengthy Russell compositions, *Big City Blues* (march 1959) and *Manhattan Rico* (november 1958), performed by an all-star cast of John Coltrane on tenor, Bob Brookmeyer on trombone, Art Farmer on trumpet, Bill Evans on piano, Max Roach on drums, Milt Hinton on bass, and the pioneering raps of poet Jon Hendricks.

The progression towards the big-band format was completed by **Jazz in the Space Age** (august 1960). An orchestra with two pianists (Bill Evans and Paul Bley) performed Russell's three-movement suite *Chromatic Universe*, the ten-minute *The Lydiot* (that sounds like a series of variations on the previous one's themes), the haunting *Waltz From Outer Space* and especially the ambitious 13-minute modal exploration *Dimensions*.

If **Stratusphunk** (october 1960) was perhaps too academic (despite *Stratusphunk*), **Ezz-thetics** (may 1961) topped anything he had done before, despite including only three original Russell compositions. Trumpeter Don Ellis, trombonist Dave Baker, clarinetist Eric Dolphy, bassist Steve Swallow and drummer Joe Hunt struck an eerie balance between bebop, cool jazz and free jazz (particularly in *Ezz-thetics*). A septet with Ellis, Baker and Swallow recorded the complex *Blues In Orbit* and *Stratus Seekers*, the highlights of **Stratus Seekers** (january 1962).

After the inferior **Outer View** (august 1962) that contained the title-track and a cover of Jimmie Davis' country hit *You Are My Sunshine* sung by Sheila Jordan, Russell relocated to Scandinavia and turned to extended multi-stylistic works for orchestra implementing his idea of vertical form, such as the 28-minute *Othello Ballet Suite* and the *Electronic Organ Sonata No. 1*, collected on **Othello Ballet Suite** (november 1967), and especially the **Electronic Sonata For Souls Loved By Nature** (april 1969), his masterpiece, a chaotic fusion of jazz, classical, ethnic, blues and electronic music, performed by an enthusiastic set of players (including trumpeter Manfred Schoof, tenor saxophonist Jan Garbarek, guitarist Terje Rypdal, drummer John Christensen). A new version in three movements (recorded in october 1970) appeared on **Essence** (1971), together with the *Concerto for Self-Accompanied Guitar* (january 1968).

The four-movement mass **Listen to the Silence** (june 1971) was scored for choir, organ, trumpet, tenor saxophone (Jan Garbarek), electric guitar (Terje Rypdal), electric piano (Bobo Stenson), bass and percussion. **Living Time** (may 1972) was a concept album on the stages of human life conceived together with Bill Evans (re-recorded in november 1995 for **It's About Time**), and it became the name of Russell's new orchestra, that kept expanding its stylistic range to absorb blues, rock, funk, jazz-rock (a genre that he had pioneered on **Jazz Workshop**, a decade before the term was invented), classical, electronic and ethnic elements. If possible, subsequent works were even more ambitious: the five-movement **Vertical Form 6** (march 1977), *Time Spiral*, off **So What** (june 1983), the nine-movement **The African Game** (june 1983), devoted to the evolution of the human species, etc.

White vibraphonist Teddy Charles Cohen (mainly known as "Teddy Charles") debuted as a leader in a bebop trio with a guitarist and a bassist, **The Teddy Cohen Trio** (november 1951). The EP **New Directions** (december 1952) documented a quartet that added drummer Ed Shaughnessy (*Edging Out*), while the EP **New Directions Vol 2** (january 1953) featured a trio with piano and drums (*Metalizing*). A sextet with altoist Frank Morgan and tenorist Wardell Gray was documented on the EP **West Coasters** (february 1953). Charles' music was moving out of bebop, with loose concept of tempo and harmonies that bordered on dissonance. If the material of these early recordings was mostly covers, four original Charles compositions (*Wailing Dervish, Variations On a Motive By Bud, Further Out* and *Etudiez Le Cahier*) in a much different vein, closer to cool jazz and the third stream, surfaced on the EP **New Directions Vol 3** (august 1953), for a quartet with trumpet (Shorty Rogers), bass and drums (Shelly Manne). The EP **New Directions Vol 4** (august 1953) added Jimmy Giuffre on saxophone to the quartet for *Free, Margo* and *Bobalob* that predated both modal improvisation and free jazz. After an inferior EP, **New Directions Vol 5** (january 1954) by a quintet with trombonist Bob Brookmeyer and a vocalist (*Loup-Garou*), and the EP **New Directions Quartet** (january 1955), that contained *Relaxo Abstracto* and featured a tenor saxophone and Charles Mingus on bass, Charled formed an ambitious **Tentet** (january 1956) with trumpet (Art Farmer), trombone, alto, baritone and tenor saxophones, guitar, piano (Mal Waldron), bass and drums. *Green Blues* and the eight-minute *The Emperor* gave a graver tone to Charles' fusion of classical and jazz music. Those ideas were further explored in the ten-minute *Word From Bird* for an even bigger ensemble and the ten-minute version of *Blue Greens* for the piano-quartet with Mingus, both off **Word From Bird** (october 1956), in the three extended Charles pieces (*Blues Without Woe, Hello Frisco, Dakar*) on **Touche** (february 1957), also known as **Olio**, a collaboration with trumpeter Thad Jones and tenorist Frank Wess, featuring a rhythm section with pianist Mal Waldron and drummer Elvin Jones, in the three main attractions (*Blues Become Elektra, Arlene* and *No More Nights*) of the trumpet-based **Vibe-Rant Quintet** (april 1957), again with Waldron on piano, in the eight-minute *Bunni* on **Coolin'** (april 1957) for another sextet with Waldron, and especially in the 14-minute *Take Three Parts Jazz Suite* on **The Prestige Jazz Quartet** (june 1957) in a quartet with Waldron.

The career of Boston-based white pianist Ran Blake Ran Blake (1935) was influenced by two key musicians whom he met in his twenties: vocalist Jeanne Lee (1957) and "third stream" composer Gunther Schuller (1959). Torn between abstract improvisation and structured composition, Blake quickly absorbed a broad range of musical languages, from film noir to gospel music, from Thelonious Monk to Olivier Messiaen. **The Newest Sound Around** (december 1961) was a showcase of his interaction with Lee, from the tragic (*Where Flamingos Fly*) to the comic (*Season in the Sun, Evil Blues*), as well as for his gospel-ish solo-piano style (*Church on Russell Street*). The latter was further explored on the highly original collections **Plays Solo Piano** (may 1965), with *Vanguard* and *Sister Tee*, and **Blue Potato** (april 1969), with *Blue Potato*, despite too many revisions of standards. After a long hiatus, Blake started recording solo-piano albums again, but his compositions were often hidden among tedious interpretations of standards: **Breakthru** (december 1975), with *Breakthru*, **Wende** (august 1976), the best of the decade, with *Wende, East Wind, Jim Crow* and *Airline*, **The Realization of a Dream** (june 1977), with *Racial Vertigo* and *Death of Edith Piaf*. He used a symphony orchestra on **Portfolio of Doktor Mabuse** (october 1977), with *The Frog the Fountain & Aunt Jane, Chicken Monster* and *Portfolio of Docktor Mabuse*, and recycled old compositions on **Rapport** (april 1978). The originals on **Film Noir** (january 1980), such as *Spiral Staircase, Touch Of Evil* and *Garden of Delight* scored for various chamber settings, reinvented the atmospheres of classic films. The highlight of its follow-up, **Vertigo** (november 1984), was a *Vertigo Suite*. Other notable compositions were: *Duke Dreams* on **Duke Dreams** (may 1981), *Indian Winter* on **Suffield Gothic** (september 1983) and especially the ten-minute *Sonata for Two Pianos* on **Improvisations** (june 1981) with fellow pianist Jaki Byard. The best album of the decade was **Short Life of Barbara Monk** (august 1986), both intellectual and elegant, containing *Impresario of Death, Short Life of Barbara Monk* and *Pourquoi Laurent?*.

Spectacular Detroit-born vocalist Lillie-Mae "Betty Carter" Jones, who sang with Lionel Hampton (1948-51), did more than simply use the voice as an instrument: she used the voice as "the" instrument. **The Modern Sound** (august 1960) debuted her tour de force, the seven-minute *Sounds*, that relied entirely on her creative singing. Her style became both more abstract and more personal on **Album** (1973), mostly composed by her, that was more in line with the spirit of free jazz than with the spirit of bebop. Her crowning performance was a 25-minute version of *Sounds* on the double-LP **The Audience** (december 1979).

COOL JAZZ IN LOS ANGELES

White baritone saxophonist Gerry Mulligan was the evangelist of cool jazz on the West Coast, the land of Stan Kenton and Dave Brubeck. Having spent his formative years writing arrangements for Gene Krupa (1946), such as *Disc Jockey Jump* (may 1946), Claude Thornhill (1947), such as *Elevation* (october 1948), and Miles Davis (1948), such as *Venus De Milo* (april 1949) and *Jeru* (january 1949), Mulligan scored the compositions of **Mulligan Plays Mulligan** (august 1951) for a two-baritone nonet (notably *Bweebida Bobbida*). He then moved to Los Angeles and formed a piano-less quartet with trumpeter Chet Baker and drummer Chico Hamilton. Baker's romantic phrasing was an odd counterpart to Mulligan's abstract ruminations, but the synthesis pushed the boundaries of jazz music. The 10" album **Gerry Mulligan Quartet** (Pacific Jazz, september 1952), with *Nights at the Turntable* and *Walkin' Shoes*, and **Mulligan Quartet** (Fantasy, october 1952), with *Line for Lyons* and *Bark for Barksdale*, defined once for all the antithesis between Mulligan (the brain) and Baker (the heart) that would remain the trademark of West Coast's cool jazz. His brand of cool jazz was lighter, catchier, and, ultimately, warmer. Mulligan later returned to the piano-less quartet format for *Utter Chaos* (august 1952), *Motel* (february 1953), *Turnstile* (january 1953), and the album **What Is There To Say** (january 1959), with Art Farmer on trumpet. Other notable compositions were *Westwood Walk* and *A Ballad*, off **Tentette** (january 1953) including Bud Shank, Chet Baker and Chico Hamilton, *Demanton* (september 1955), for a sextet with Bob Brookmeyer and Zoot Sims, and *Song for an Unfinished Woman* (october 1972).

Other protagonists of the Los Angeles school of cool jazz (all of them white) were: trumpeter Shorty Rogers, alto saxophonist Paul Desmond, alto saxophonist Art Pepper, clarinetist Jimmy Giuffre, drummer Shelly Manne, guitarist Jim Hall, and alto saxophonist Clifford "Bud" Shank.

Alto saxophonist Paul "Desmond" Brentenfield, a stalwart of Brubeck's groups since 1948, was the prototypical "cool" musician, almost mechanical and supernatural in the flowing, linear and prudent accompaniment and solos he provided for the group (notably for his *Take Five*).

Los Angeles-based white trumpeter Milton "Shorty Rogers" Rajonsky (1924), an alumnus of Woody Herman's orchestra (1945) and Stan Kenton's orchestra (1950), was mainly a superb arranger and subtle composer as he proved on **Modern Sounds** (october 1951), for which he recruited the likes of altoist Art Pepper, drummer Shelley Manne, tenorist Jimmy Giuffre and pianist Hampton Hawes (plus French horn, tuba and bass). After the piano quintet with Pepper of the **Popo** (december 1951), a mediocre album but that contained his signature tune *Popo*, Rogers formed his Giants, a 16-piece orchestra (featuring Pepper, Giuffre, Manne, trumpeter Maynard Ferguson, altoist Bud Shank) that recorded **Cool And Crazy** (april 1953), entirely composed by him (notably *Tales Of An African Lobster* and *Infinity Promenade*). A quintet featuring Jimmy Giuffre,

Manne and vibraphonist Theodore "Teddy Charles" Cohen (credited as the leader) predated both modal improvisation and free jazz on **New Directions Vol 4** (august 1953). A trio with Manne and Giuffre toyed with serial composition (*Three On A Row*) and free improvisation (*Abstract No 1*) on **The Three and the Two** (september 1954), credited to Manne. The collaboration with Giuffre and Manne was resumed in another quintet recording, (and quintessentially "cool"), **Swinging** (march 1955), that contained the bluesy *Martians Go Home*. Rogers was one of the most daring explorers of timbral counterpoint of cool jazz.

Los Angeles' alto saxophonist Art Pepper's favorite format was the sax-piano-bass-drums quartet, first experimented on **Discoveries**, that contained the first recording of his signature theme, *Straight Life* (august 1954). After a three-year jail stay, **Art Pepper Quartet** (august 1956), that delivered his originals *Diane, Art Opus, Pepper Pot, Blues At Twilight* and *Val's Pals*, presented him in top form. Red Garland on piano and Paul Chambers on bass helped refine the sound on the covers of **Meets the Rhythm Section** (march 1957), and on **Omega Alpha** (april 1957), that was not released for decades but contained his *Surf Ride*. His style peaked with the brief "modern jazz classics" that he recorded with the 11-piece Marty Paich Orchestra on **Plus Eleven** (march 1959). The format was augmented with Conte Candoli on trumpet for the longer tracks of **Gettin' Together** (october 1960), that featured Miles Davis' session-men (pianist Wynton Kelly, bassist Paul Chambers and drummer Jimmy Cobb), and introduced his originals *Bijou the Poodle* and *Gettin' Together*, besides reworking *Diane*. A less competent quartet recorded **Intensity** (november 1960), that contains only covers. After serving a long prison sentence and undergoing drug rehabilitation, Pepper staged an emotional comeback with **The Trip** (september 1976), featuring Elvin Jones' drumming, a sound influenced by John Coltrane, the nine-minute title-track and Michel Legrand's *The Summer Knows*. The quartet format remained his favorite also on the better **No Limit** (march 1977), that contained only four tracks, ranging from seven to 13 minutes in length, three of them original Pepper compositions: *Rita-San, My Laurie* and *Mambo de la Pinta*. **Straight Life** (september 1979), that contained an eleven-minute version of Kurt Weill's *September Song* and a ten-minute version of Eden Ahbez's *Nature Boy*, and **Winter Moon** (september 1980), with a string ensemble arranged by Bill Holman and Jimmy Bond, were slightly less imaginative, but equally touching.

Clarinetist, flutist and saxophonist Jimmy Giuffre, a former member of Shorty Rogers' group, opted for a piano-less trio, first with guitarist Jim Hall and bassist Ralph Pena, **The Jimmy Giuffre 3** (december 1956), debuting his signature tune *The Train and the River* and the *Crawdad Suite*, then with Hall and trombonist Bob Brookmeyer on **Western Suite** (december 1958), titled after its four-movement title-track.

In between he had shown his skills as a lyrical composer with the folk-ish compositions of **Tangents In Jazz** (june 1955), performed with trumpeter Jack Sheldon, bassist Ralph Pena and drummer Artie Anton, and the **Seven Pieces** (march 1959), alternating on clarinet, tenor and baritone sax, with guitarist Jim

Hall and bassist Red Mitchell (*Happy Man*, *Princess*). His skills as an architect of intimate chamber jazz were proven by the solos, duets and trios of **The Jimmy Giuffre Clarinet** (november 1956), notably the dissonant *The Side Pipers* for three flutes and drums, as well as by the pieces for four overdubbed tenor saxes (all played by Giuffre), either "solo" or accompanied by other instruments, of **The Four Brothers Sound** (september 1958), as well as by the austere **Piece for Clarinet and Strings** (july 1960) and by the large-scale *Pharoah* and *Suspensions*, that debuted on Gunther Schuller's **Music for Brass** (june 1956).

All of Giuffre's directions merged in his trio with pianist Paul Bley and bassist Steve Shallow, that developed a meditative and minimal free-jazz style with an elastic concept of time. They progressed towards a new art of sculpting sound from **Fusion** (march 1961), notably *Emphasis*, to **Thesis** (august 1961), that contained the counterpoint wizardry of Giuffre's *Sonic* and *Flight* and Carla Bley's *Ictus*, to the impressionist **Free Fall** (november 1962) that explored soundscapes for clarinet solo, for clarinet and bass and for trio (ranging from two to ten minutes), at the border between free-jazz and classical music.

It took ten years for Giuffre to resume this program of intimate zen-like atmospheres: **Night Dance** (november 1971), alternating on clarinet, flute and tenor sax with bassist Kiyoshi Tokunaga and percussionist Randy Kaye, **Music for People, Birds, Butterflies & Mosquitos** (december 1972), **Quiet Song** (november 1974) with Paul Bley on piano and Bill Connors on guitar. **Dragonfly** (january 1983), **Quasar** (may 1985) and **Liquid Dancers** (april 1989) were representative of the Jimmy Giuffre 4 (Peter Levin on electronic keyboards, plus bass and percussion), that basically adapted his cool jazz to the age of ambient music.

After leaving Gerry Mulligan, trumpeter Chet Baker recorded the septet effort of **Grey December** (december 1953), **Chet Baker & Strings** (february 1954), that wed cool jazz and a string orchestra, and especially **Chet Baker Sextet** (september 1954), with Budd Shank on saxophones and Bob Brookmeyer on trombone, but fell victim to drug addiction for most of his mature years.

Jim Hall, a East Coast guitarist who arrived in Los Angeles in 1955 and played with Chico Hamilton (1955-56) and Jimmy Giuffre (1956-59), moved back to New York in 1959 and played with Sonny Rollins (1961-62) and Art Farmer (1962-64). Hall specialized in slow and tidy solos that were the antithesis of Charlie Christian's solos. Hall's crystal-clear guitar was pure sound, predating the era of quiet, soft jazz.

A major Los Angeles-based cool musicians who was not white was drummer Chico Hamilton. After playing with Gerry Mulligan in 1952-53, Hamilton formed his (mixed-race) quintet in 1955 with guitarist Jim Hall, reed player Buddy Collette, bassist Carson Smith and cellist Fred Katz that debuted with **Spectacular** (august 1955). As in the case of the Modern Jazz Quintet, this unusual line-up often sounded like a black man's version of chamber music, except that the material was much simpler. Accordingly, Hamilton's drumming was much more than mere timekeeping, using the percussion to add color to the harmony, as shown in the solos of *Drums West* on **Quintet In Hi Fi** (february 1956) and *Mr Jo Jones* on **Quintet** (october 1956). After several changes of line-up (notably guitarist Jim Hall and flutist Paul Horn), a new quintet with Nate Gershman on cello and Eric Dolphy on reeds recorded **Gongs East** (december 1958) and **Three Faces** (february 1959), with several notable solos (*Trinkets, Happy Little Dance, No Speak No English Man*). The last of the cello albums was **Special** (november 1960), featuring Charles Lloyd on flute, after which Hamilton replaced the cello with the trombone for **Drumfusion** (february 1962), **Passin' Thru** (september 1962) and **Man from Two Worlds** (december 1963), all dominated by Lloyd's compositions and mostly devoted to hard-bop music.

Needless to say, the music of these white musicians, located thousands of kilometers away from the birthplaces of jazz, was totally removed from the heritage or reality of black life in the plantations, in the red-light districts and in the urban ghettos.

HARD BOP

Eventually, some black musicians reacted against the intellectual cliches of bebop by advocating a return to jazz music's original spontaneity and energy. A stronger rhythmic emphasis (derived from gospel and rhythm'n'blues), catchier refrains and more forceful solos revitalized the fundamental innovations of bebop (that were not refuted but simply recast in a more accessible format). Thus bebop mutated into "hard-bop" (mainly on the East Coast). Hard bop was also a reaction of sort against cool jazz: cool jazz was (mostly) white, hard bop was black; cool jazz was (mostly) West Coast, hard bop was East Coast; cool jazz was brainy, hard bop was spontaneous. Despite the aesthetic claims, both composition and arrangement were more emphasized than ever by hard bop musicians, perhaps a sign of the influence of cool jazz even on its critics.

The genealogy of hard bop begins with drummer Max Roach, who had cut his teeth with Charlie Parker (1945-49), and who in 1954 formed a quintet with trumpeter Clifford Brown (plus tenor saxophone, piano and bass). **Clifford Brown and Max Roach** (august 1954), containing Brown's *Daahoud* and *Joy Spring*, In 1956 Sonny Rollins became their tenor saxophonist but Brown died shortly afterwards. The new line-up continued to evolve Roach's vision of hard bop via **Plus Four** (september 1956), that contains a nine-minute version of George Russell's *Ezz-Thetic*, and **Jazz in 3/4 time** (march 1957), devoted to 3/4 waltz rhythms (*Blues Waltz*) and occasional forays into modal improvisation. Rollins departed before **Deeds Not Words** (september 1958), that features Booker Little on trumpet and Ray Draper on tuba.

Roach cut his masterpiece **Freedom Now Suite** (september 1960), a seven-movement suite that featured vocals (written by lyricist Oscar Brown and sang by Abbey Lincoln), with a nonet that marked a clear break with his past (trumpeter Booker Little and trombonist Julian Priester. two tenors including Coleman Hawkins, three external percussionists).

Percussion Bitter Sweet (august 1961) featured another "subversive" line-up (Little, Priester, Eric Dolphy on alto, bass clarinet, and flute, Clifford Jordan on tenor, Mal Waldron on piano, Art Davis on bass, plus a section of percussionists) and was again entirely devoted to Roach originals. He had something to say and clearly wanted to say it through his music (*Garvey's Ghost, Praise For A Martyr*).

As the politicized season faded, Roach got even more absorbed by his drumming. **Drums Unlimited** (october 1965) contained three solo-drum pieces: *The Drum Also Waltzes, Drums Unlimited* and *For Big Sid*. **Birth And Rebirth** (september 1978) was a concept album inspired to primitive beliefs and made of seven duets with Anthony Braxton framed by *Birth* and *Rebirth*, followed by **One in Two Two in One** (august 1979) that contained just one long album-size improvisation. Roach's percussion orchestra M'Boom debuted on **M'Boom** (july 1979). His main vehicle remained his quartet (Cecil Bridgewater on trumpet and

Odean Pope on tenor, flute and oboe), documented in Pope's *Mwalimu*, off **Pictures In A Frame** (september 1979), Bridgewater's 40-minute suite **Scott Free** (may 1984), and Roach's 21-minute *Survivors*, off **Survivors** (october 1984). Roach's last experiment was with the format of the double quartet on **Easy Winners** (january 1985) and **Bright Moments** (october 1986). **To the Max** was a testament to his experimental life, containing a three-movement suite *Ghost Dance* (june 1991) for M'Boom and a 21-minute *A Little Booker* (june 1991) for double quartet.

The epitome of hard bop's hard pulse was drummer Art Blakey, who already had impeccable credentials (Mary Lou Williams, Fletcher Henderson, Billy Eckstine from 1944 till 1947) when in 1954 he and pianist Horace Silver decided to form the Jazz Messengers, destined to become the premiere incubator of hard bop musicians. **Horace Silver and the Jazz Messengers** (1955) featured the quintet of Blakey on drums, Silver on piano, Kenny Dorham on trumpet, Hank Mobley on tenor and Doug Watkins on bass, and contained seven Silver compositions: due to its popularity, *The Preacher* was the piece that started the hard bop revolution. **Nica's Dream** (april 1956), with Donald Byrd replacing Dorham on trumpet, was highlighted by Silver's twelve-minute *Nica's Dream*. When Silver left, Blakey became the sole owner of the band and further increased the rhythmic intensity of his performances. By the time **Hard Bop** (1957) was recorded, all the other members had changed as well, with Jackie McLean joining on alto (and contributing the best piece, *Little Melonae*). Blakey's emphasis on rhythm increased dramatically through **Drum Suite** (1957), one of the earliest recordings that focused on drumming (two drummers and three percussionists performed on a couple of pieces), **Ritual** (1957), containing the ten-minute solo-drum piece *Ritual*, **Orgy In Rhythm** (march 1957), an African-sounding album (de facto a "world-music" album ante litteram) that featured several percussionists, Herbie Mann on African flutes, shamanic chanting and a program of captivating Blakey originals (*Buhaina Chant*, *Toffi*, *Abdullah's Delight*), and **Cu-bop** (may 1957), a Latin album featuring a congo player (as well as a new recruit, tenor saxophonist Johnny Griffin). Blakey's third quintet, with tenor saxophonist Benny Golson, pianist Bobby Timmons and trumpeter Lee Morgan, the stereotypical trumpet of hard bop, debuted on **Moanin'** (october 1958), with Timmons' nine-minute *Moanin'* (perhaps their most popular number) and Blakey's seven-minute *The Drum Thunder Suite*. **Drums Around the Corner** (november 1958) drowned trumpet and saxophone into percussions (drummers Philly Joe Jones and Roy Haynes, conga player Ray Barretto) for performances of Blakey's originals *Blakey's Blues* and *Drums in the Rain*. After scoring the film soundtrack **Les Liaisons Dangereuses** (july 1959), Blakey introduced his fourth trumpet-sax-piano-bass-drums quintet with **The Big Beat** (march 1960). The only change was in the tenor saxophone, but it was a change that dramatically altered the sound: Wayne Shorter not only introduced a different approach (slicker, less oriented towards rhythm'n'blues) but also provided compositions such as *Cheese Players* and *Lester Left Town* that better suited the dynamics of the quintet.

After **Freedom Rider** (february 1961), Blakey changed the line-up one more time keeping Shorter and introducing trumpeter Freddie Hubbard, trombonist Curtis Fuller and pianist Cedar Walton, Blakey's sextet for **Mosaic** (october 1961) and **Buhaina's Delight** (1962) now featured four formidable composers, who contributed Walton's *Mosaic*, Shorter's *Children of the Night*, Fuller's *Arabia* and Hubbard's *Crisis* to the former, and Walton's *Shaky Jake*, Fuller's *Bu's Delight* and Shorter's *Reincarnation Blues* to the latter. **Three Blind Mice** (march 1962) added Freddie Hubbard's *Up Jumped Spring* to the repertory. With Reggie Workman on bass they recorded **Caravan** (october 1962), highlighted by Shorter's *This Is For Albert* and *Sweet 'N' Sour*, **Ugetsu** (1963), containing Shorter's *One by One*, *Ping-Pong* and *On the Ginza*, as well as Walton's *Ugetsu*, and **Free For All** (1964), that included Shorter's memorable *Free For All* and Hubbard's *The Core*

Lee Morgan replaced Hubbard on **Indestructible** (1964), but real news was Fuller's promotion to main composer (*The Egyptian* and *Sortie*, both substantially more "modal" than the average of the group), although still balanced by the more traditional Walton (*When Love Is New*) and Shorter (*Mr Jin*, another gem) material. But it was the beginning of the instability that slowly marginalized the group, despite the torrential flow of recordings and the numerous talents that Blakey kept discovering, such as Wynton Marsalis on **Album of the Year** (1981) and Terence Blanchard on **Oh By The Way** (1982).

An alumnus of Bud Powell (1949), Miles Davis (1951) and Max Roach (1955-57), having contributed the compositions *Airegin*, *Doxy* and *Oleo* to Davis' **Bag's Groove** (june 1954), tenor saxophonist Theodore "Sonny" Rollins started out as a leader with the confusingly titled **Sonny Rollins with the Modern Jazz Quartet** (october 1953), that contained his *Mambo Bounce* (recorded in december 1951 by a quartet with Kenny Drew on piano, Percy Heath on bass, Art Blakey on drums). His Quintet (saxophone, trumpet, piano, Heath, Blakey) recorded **Moving Out** (august 1954), that contained four Rollins compositions (*Movin' Out*, *Swinging for Bumsy*, *Silk 'n' Satin*, *Solid*).

The quintet on **Plus Four** (march 1956) was nothing but the Clifford Brown-Max Roach Quintet (a piano-based quintet with Clifford Brown on trumpet and Max Roach on drums). Two eight-minute Rollins originals, *Valse Hot* (in 3/4 meter) and *Pent-Up House*, elevated the album above the stereotypes of hard bop.

Tenor Madness (may 1956), that borrowed Davis' quintet (Red Garland on piano, Paul Chambers on bass, Philly Joe Jones on drums), offered a twelve-minute duel between Rollins and tenor saxophonist John Coltrane in *Tenor Madness*.

A quartet with Tommy Flanagan on piano and Max Roach on drums recorded **Saxophone Colossus** (june 1956), the real launching pad for Rollins' career as a leader, containing two of his most celebrated composition: the calypso *St Thomas* and *Blue Seven*, the manifesto of his "thematic" improvisation, This was improvisation based on melody, not on chords, as bebop was, or on modes, as Davis' modal jazz was. Unlike the traditional kind of melodic improvisation (that was basically an embellishment of the original melody), Rollings'

"improvisation" was a process of recursive variation and therefore of melodic reinvention.
Tour De Force (december 1956), for a quartet with Drew and Roach, introduced Rollins' *Ee-Ah, B. Quick* and *B. Swift*.
Volume One (december 1956), for a quintet with Donald Byrd on trumpet, Wynton Kelly on piano and Max Roach on drums, delivered powerful performances of Rollins' *Decision, Bluesnote, Plain Jane*, and especially *Sonnysphere*. **Volume Two** (april 1957) was emblematic of the transition from bebop to hard bop: both Thelonious Monk and Horace Silver play piano on Monk's *Misterioso*, but elsewhere (e.g., *Why Don't I*) Rollins' quintet (Silver, trombonist James "J.J." Johnson, Chambers and Blakey) rips bebop apart.
Rollins found the ideal vehicle for his thematic improvisation in the sax-bass-drums trio of **Way Out West** (march 1957), although the material was odd at best (his own *Way Out West* excepted) to the point of sounding like a parody of the originals. Rollins was now regarded as the greatest tenor of his generation, a status confirmed by *It Could Happen to You*, his first unaccompanied solo, off **The Sound of Sonny** (june 1957), and even by mediocre albums such as **Newk's Time** (september 1957), but especially by the second album for piano-less tenor-saxophone trio, **A Night At The Village Vanguard** (november 1957), featuring drummer Elvin Jones.
Every aspect of Rollins' art culminated in the 20-minute title-track of **Freedom Suite** (march 1958), the first piece of jazz music (with Max Roach on drums and Oscar Pettiford on bass) to successfully wed politics and music.
After a mostly disappointing experiment with a large ensemble, documented on **Big Brass** (july 1958) and **Brass and Trio** (same sessions), Rollins retired from music in 1959, but promptly returned two years later in a quartet featuring Jim Hall: **The Bridge** (february 1962). Its follow-up, **What's New** (may 1962), featured two trio numbers, *Jungoso* and *Bluesongo*, that resumed his favorite format and wed it to his passion for Latin rhythms. But the real comeback was **Our Man in Jazz** (july 1962): a quartet with bass, drums and Don Cherry on cornet performing colossal versions of *Oleo* (25 minutes) and *Doxy* (15 minutes). Rollins repeated that exploit with the dissonant 20-minute *East Broadway Run Down* (may 1966), a bold thematic improvisation on the riff of Lionel Hampton's *Hey Baba Rebop* featuring Freddie Hubbard on trumpet, Jimmy Garrison on bass and Elvin Jones on drums, off **East Broadway Run Down** (1966). Then he retired again.
Few players summarized and embodied the history of jazz saxophone as well as Rollins, whose solos harked back to the classics as well as extending towards the avantgarde (and whose compositions were simply designed to maximize this ability). His art never truly progressed: he assimilated the innovations of his age only to the extent that they had become of the jazz tradition. In a sense he kept refining the shape of the "ideal solo" the same way that renaissance architects kept refining the concept of the ideal city: by continuously ad recursively reinterpreting the connection between past and future. Unlike the experiments of

many contemporaries, Rollins' style was not a tribute to himself but a tribute to jazz music.

Horace Silver was the main hard-bop pianist, influenced by both African and gospel music. On his first major recording, **Trio** (november 1953), with Art Blakey on drums and several bassists, he already displayed the essence of his exuberant style with his own compositions *Safari* (october 1952), *Quicksilver* (october 1952), *Horoscope* (october 1952) and *Opus De Funk* (november 1953). The latter also gave a name to his solid beat influenced by gospel and rhythm'n'blues. He formed the quintet with Art Blakey that started the bebop revolution by recording **Horace Silver and the Jazz Messengers** (1955), to which Silver contributed most of the tracks, particularly the hard-driving, gospel-ish *The Preacher* (february 1955), but also *Doodlin'* (november 1954) and *Room 608* (november 1954), as well as **Nica's Dream** (april 1956), containing his catchy, propulsive, Latin-tinged twelve-minute *Nica's Dream*. Then he launched his own quintet of piano, trumpet, tenor saxophone, bass and drums, to concentrate on what he liked: a bluesy piano style and a sound that borrowed as much from rhythm'n'blues as from jazz. The foundations of the line-up of **Silver's Blue** (july 1956) was the Jazz Messengers without Blakey, jamming fluently in *Shootin' Out* and *Silver's Blue*. The line-up evolved via **Six Pieces of Silver** (november 1956), containing *Senor Blues* (that became a hit) and featuring tenor saxophonist Junior Cook, **Stylings of Silver** (may 1957), featuring Art Farmer on trumpet and Hank Mobley on tenor saxophone, and containing *Home Cookin'* and *Metamorphosis*, **Further Explorations** (january 1958), featuring Clifford Jordan on tenor sax and containing the eleven-minute jam *Moon Rays*, *Safari* and *Melancholy Mood*, **Finger Poppin'** (january 1959), that established the partnership between trumpeter Blue Mitchell and tenor saxophonist Junior Cook, and contained *Swingin' the Samba*, *Juicy Lucy*, *Come on Home* and *Cookin' at the Continental*. **Blowin' the Blues Away** (september 1959) contained another exotic number, *Baghdad Blues*, and a wide stylistic excursus, from the ballad *Peace* to the driving *Break City* to the gospel-y *Sister Sadie*. The playing got even tighter on subsequent releases, that boasted the twelve-minute jam *Sayonara Blues*, off **Tokyo Blues** (july 1962), and the nine-minute jam *Silver's Serenade*, off **Silver's Serenade** (may 1963). This quintet peaked on the exotic **Song For My Father** (october 1964), that included *Calcutta Cutie*, but the most famous tracks from that album, the bossanova *Song For My Father* (his signature tune), *Que Pasa* and *The Natives Are Restless*, were already recorded by a new quintet with Joe Henderson on tenor sax. Woody Shaw on trumpet (who was much more compromised with the avantgarde than previous Silver members) and James "J.J." Johnson on trombone featured on **The Cape Verdean Blues** (october 1965), perhaps Silver's best album, that further enhanced his fusion of soul, funk and Latin music while adopting a more experimental stance, especially in *The Cape Verdean Blues*, but also in *Nutville*, *Bonita*, *The African Queen*, the waltzing *Pretty Eyes*. Unfortunately, **The Jody Grind** (november 1966), with Shaw, Tyrone Washington on tenor sax and James Spaulding on alto sax (and flute), did not continue in that experimental direction but retreated back to

Silver's trademark party-oriented funk-soul-jazz with *The Jody Grind*, *Mexican Hip Dance* and the aggressive *Grease Peace*. **Serenade to a Soul Sister** (march 1968), with new line-up fronted by trumpeter Charles Tolliver, was even more upbeat, indulging in the funk hyperdrive of *Psychedelic Sally*, the exotic grooves of *Rain Dance* and *Jungle Juice* and the *Serenade to a Soul Sister*. Trumpeter Randy Brecker and drummer Billy Cobham on drums joined for **You Gotta Take A Little Love** (january 1969), but Silver's music was now rather outdated. In 1970 he inaugurated a series of recordings under the moniker "The United States Of Mind" that included his own spiritual lyrics. The decade ended with a double LP that summarized the whole concept: **The Music of the Spheres** (december 1979), a five-movement suite for his quintet (featuring flugelhornist Tom Harrell and tenor saxophonist Larry Schneider), a string orchestra, harp and four vocalists.

The myth of Charlie Parker spawned the careers of several alto saxophonists in the hard-bop era.

Alto saxophonist Julian "Cannonball" Adderley, who had played with Miles Davis (1957), made a number of interesting recordings in 1958 (**Somethin' Else** in march with the supergroup of Miles Davis, Hank Jones, Sam Jones and Art Blakey; the nine-part four-movement suite on folk themes for jazz quartet **Alabama Concerto** in august 1958; **Things Are Getting Better** in october with Milt Jackson on vibes, Wynton Kelly on piano, Percy Heath on bass and Art Blakey on drums) and 1959 (**Cannonball and Coltrane** in february, that featured the Miles Davis Sextet minus Davis) before forming his own quintet in 1959 with his younger brother, cornetist Nat, bassist Sam Jones and pianist Bobby Timmons. After a couple of hits, Bobby Timmons' *This Here* (october 1959) and Nat Adderley's *Work Song* (march 1960), the additions of pianist Joe Zawinul and saxophonist/flutist Yusef Lateef turned it into a sextet, that debuted with **In New York** (1962) and had two more hits, Nat Adderley's *The Jive Samba* (february 1962) and Joe Zawinul's *Mercy Mercy Mercy* (july 1966), besides pioneering jazz-funk in Roebuck Staple's *Why Am I Treated So Bad* (july 1967). Influenced by Charlie Parker and faithful to the blues, Adderley was a transitional player who tried to find a sense of balance in a (stylistically) turbulent age.

Phil Woods, a white alto saxophonist, made several recordings in a shamelessly Parker-ian vein before organizing the octet (including trombonist Curtis Fuller, baritone saxophonist Sahib Shihab, French horn player Julius Watkins, pianist Tommy Flanagan) that performed his five-movement suite **Rights Of Swing** (january 1961). Another experimental project, the European Rhythm Machine, a piano quartet influenced by free jazz, debuted with **The Birth** (june 1968). But mostly Woods kept the bebop tradition alive with tracks such as *Petite Chanson* (december 1980), in a quintet with Lew Tabackin on flute, Jimmy Rowles on piano and Woods on clarinet, and *Goodbye Mr Evans* (january 1981), in a trio with pianist Tommy Flanagan and bassist Red Mitchell.

The most original of the hard-bob tenors might have been also the least prolific: Harold "Tina" Brooks, who died at 42 in 1974, recorded only one album as a leader, **True Blue** (1960), an electrifying session with trumpeter Freddie Hubbard (on one of his earliest sessions), pianist Duke Jordan, bassist Sam Jones, and drummer Art Taylor (*Good Old Soul*, *True Blue*). **Minor Move** (1958), unreleased for many years, was a straightforward hard-bop effort, counting on pianist Sonny Clark, trumpeter Lee Morgan, bassist Doug Watkins and drummer Art Blakey (*"Nutville*, *Minor Move*). He played as if he hated every single note he played. Also an excellent composer, Brooks contributed both in style and in content to countless recordings of the hard-bop era.

After stints with Max Roach (1953) and Dizzy Gillespie (1954), tenor saxophonist Hank Mobley joined Art Blakey's Jazz Messengers (1955), where he soon became one of the most recognizable "sounds" of hard bop, neither torrential like Coltrane's nor mellow like Stan Getz's. A skilled composer who focused not so much on melodic themes but on thematic development (not on sudden bursts of emotion but on quiet fire), his pieces were almost always supported by top-notch ensembles. A hard-bop supergroup of vibraphonist Milt Jackson, pianist Horace Silver, bassist Doug Watkins and drummer Art Blakey accompanied him on the five original compositions of **All Stars** (january 1957), including the ten-minute *Lower Stratosphere* and the lyrical *Mobley's Musings*. Another supergroup (Blakey, pianist Horace Silver, trumpeter Art Farmer, bassist Doug Watkins) played on the **Quintet** (march 1957) that contains *Funk in Deep Freeze*. Other formative tracks were: *Hi Groove Low Feed-Back* (april 1957) for a sextet with Donald Byrd on trumpet; *Double Exposure* (june 1957) for a sextet with Sonny Clark on piano, Bill Hardman on trumpet, Paul Chambers on bass and Art Taylor on drums; the 12-minute *Gil-Go Blues*, off **Peckin' Time** (february 1958), for a quintet with trumpeter Lee Morgan and pianist Wynton Kelly. His personal masterpiece was **Soul Station** (february 1960), recorded with Blakey, Chambers and pianist Wynton Kelly, containing the nine-minute title-track and *Dig Dis*, fluid and warm performances. Trumpeter Freddie Hubbard joined that quartet for **Roll Call** (november 1960) and introduced a discontinuity in the amalgam that somehow energized the ten-minute *Roll Call* and the nine-minute *A Baptist Beat*. A new quintet (with guitarist Grant Green, pianist Wynton Kelly, Chambers and drummer Philly Joe Jones) recorded **Workout** (march 1961), his second masterpiece, highlighted by two ten-minute "workouts", *Workout* and *Uh Huh*. The quintet remained his favorite format for a while, yielding the piece with his most famous solo, *East of the Village* (march 1963), with Donald Byrd on trumpet and Herbie Hancock on piano, *No Room for Squares* (october 1963), with Lee Morgan on trumpet and Andrew Hill on piano, the 18-bar blues *The Turnaround* (february 1965), with Hubbard, *The Vamp* (june 1965), with Morgan. These recordings marked a progression towards funk and soul music, a journey that reached its destination on the sextet release **A Caddy for Daddy** (december 1965), with trumpeter Lee Morgan, trombonist Curtis Fuller and pianist McCoy Tyner (*A Caddy for Daddy*, *The Morning After*). Mobley began experimenting with different formats, while the music was becoming more linear: *Chain Reaction* (june 1966), with Morgan and pianist McCoy Tyner, *Bossa For Baby* (may 1967), with trumpeter Donald Byrd, pianist

Cedar Walton, bassist Ron Carter and drummer Billy Higgins. *High Voltage* and *Bossa Deluxe*, off **Hi Voltage** (october 1967), by a sextet with altoist Jackie McLean, trumpeter Blue Mitchell, pianist John Hicks, were emblematic of Mobley's subtle soul-jazz fusion. As his compositions turned more austere, for example *Lookin' East* (january 1968), by a sextet with Woody Shaw on trumpet, Lamont Johnson on piano, George Benson on guitar, the touching *Feelin' Folksy* (july 1969), and the three-movement suite *Thinking Of Home* (july 1970) he seemed to reach for an inner dimension, but suffered a devastating physical collapse.

The slow rise to prominence by tenor saxophonist Joe Henderson coincided with the rise to popularity of the musicians whose style he assimilated. His first quintet featured trumpeter Kenny Dorham and pianist McCoy Tyner. The highlights of **Page One** (june 1963) were Dorham's *Blue Bossa* and *La Mesha*, besides Henderson's *Recorda Me* and *Jinrikisha*. Tyner stole the show on most tracks, but was replaced by Andrew Hill for **Our Thing** (september 1963), a rather uneven collection, partially rescued by Dorham's *Escapade*. The quality of musicianship increased dramatically on **In 'n Out** (april 1964), with the piano again in the hands of McCoy Tyner and with Elvin Jones on drums (both Coltrane sidemen): Henderson's *In 'N Out*, *Punjab* and *Serenity* were flawless hard-bop feasts enhanced with a strong Coltrane factor. That factor was even more prominent on **Inner Urge** (november 1964), containing Henderson's moody *Inner Urge* and atmospheric *Isotope*, and boasting spectacular saxophone and piano solos. Henderson's style had evolved towards a relatively free and somewhat incoherent interpretation of time and tone, that often resulted in jarring sequences of sounds and disorienting distortions of tempo. Almost as successful was **Mode For Joe** (january 1966), featuring a supergroup with trumpeter Lee Morgan, trombonist Curtis Fuller, vibraphonist Bobby Hutcherson, pianist Cedar Walton, bassist Ron Carter and drummer Joe Chambers, and containing two gems such as Henderson's *A Shade of Jade* and Walton's *Mode For Joe*. Henderson became more famous as a sideman for Horace Silver (1964-66) and Herbie Hancock (1969-70), but continued to assemble top-notch line-ups: a sextet with trumpeter Mike Lawrence, trombonist Grachan Moncur III, pianist Kenny Barron, bassist Ron Carter and drummer Louis Hayes for **The Kicker** (august 1967), but wasted on rather poor material; a trio for **Tetragon** (september 1967): a quintet with pianist Herbie Hancock, trumpeter Mike Lawrence, bassist Ron Carter and drummer Jack DeJohnette for **Power To The People** (may 1969), that contained *Black Narcissus* and the three-movement suite *Foresight and Afterthought*; a quartet with pianist Chick Corea, bassist Ron Carter and drummer Billy Higgins for **Mirror Mirror** (january 1980), that contains his *Joe's Bolero*. He finally became a star with the live trio performances of **The State of the Tenor** (november 1985), on which he sounded more like Sonny Rollins.

The trumpet counted at least five great innovators in the years between bebop and free jazz, starting with trumpeter Clifford Brown, who died very young but was a major influence on all the others with his simple, graceful phrasing that was the antithesis of bebop's jarring and convoluted phrasing.

The disjointed trumpet style of <u>Woody Shaw</u> was due to a deliberate strategy of employing between pentatonic scales/modes to mold solos and melodies. Shaw spent the best years of his life gracing the recordings of Horace Silver (1965) and Max Roach (1968). He had already composed *Moontrane* in 1965. He debuted as a leader only with the double LP **Blackstone Legacy** (december 1970), featuring two saxophonists, a pianist, two bassists and a drummer. The interplay in the 16-minute *Blackstone Legacy*, the 17-minute *New World* and the 14-minute *Boo Ann's Grand* bordered on bop, free and fusion. He changed format with every release: a sextet performed the four Shaw compositions of **Song Of Songs** (september 1972), a quintet accompanied him on **Little Red's Fantasy** (june 1976), a supergroup (Anthony Braxton on saxophones, Arthur Blythe on alto, Richard Abrams on piano, bass and drums) jammed with him in the 13-minute *Song Of Songs* off **The Iron Men** (april 1977), "concert ensembles" are featured on **Rosewood** (december 1977) and on the three-movement suite of **Woody III** (january 1979).

During a brief association with Dizzy Gillespie (1957-58) and a long association with Art Blakey (1958-65) trumpet prodigy <u>Lee Morgan</u> had a chance to develop a fiery, bluesy style that came to be seen as the quintessence of hard bop. His performance on **Candy** (november 1957), when he was still a teenager, was hailed as a major event. Already a celebrity at 21, he could afford to cut **Here's** (february 1960) accompanied by a supergroup with tenor Clifford Jordan, pianist Wynton Kelly, bassist Paul Chambers and drummer Art Blakey. That album contained his first significant compositions (*Terrible T*, *Mogie*). Suddenly, he had a hit with the lengthy title-track off **Sidewinder** (december 1963), one of the manifestos of soul-jazz. The album contained six Morgan originals, particularly *Totem Pole*. **Search for the New Land** (february 1964) was better, a sort of highbrow counterpart to the best-seller. Morgan's lighter side (the *Sidewinder* side) was overshadowed by three innovative compositions such as *Search for the New Land*, *Melancholee* and *Mr Kenyatta*, that took advantage of a stellar combo with tenor saxophonist Wayne Shorter, guitarist Grant Green, pianist Herbie Hancock, bassist Reggie Workman and drummer Billy Higgins. Morgan had matured as a composer, but his recordings focused on the lighter side, such as *Ceora*, off **Cornbread** (september 1965), and *Ca-Lee-So*, off **Delightfulee** (may 1966), rather than on the experimental side (influenced by modal improvisation and free jazz). The latter was best represented by the eleven-minute title-track of **The Gigolo** (july 1965) and the nine-minute title-track of **Cornbread** (1965), that featured Hancock, Jackie McLean on alto and Hank Mobley on tenor. Some of his best recordings weren't even released, such as *Infinity* (november 1965) with McLean, pianist Larry Willis, Workman and Higgins, or the eight-minute *The Procrastinator* (july 1967) with Hancock, Shorter, vibraphonist Bobby Hutcherson, pianist Ron Carter and Higgins. Morgan was killed in 1972 at the age of 34.

Hard Bop

The natural heir to Clifford Brown and Lee Morgan was another prodigy, Freddie Hubbard, whose pedigree included Ornette Coleman's **Free Jazz** (1960), several albums with Art Blakey (1961-66), also composing *Up Jumped Spring* (march 1962), several albums with Herbie Hancock (1962-65), Eric Dolphy's **Out to Lunch** (1964), and John Coltrane's **Ascension** (1965). His trumpet style wed crisp melodic outbursts and languid bluesy tones, making it a perfect instrument for the kind of slick fusion that became popular after Miles Davis' **Bitches Brew**. He had debuted as a leader at 22 with **Open Sesame** (june 1960), by a quintet with tenor saxophonist Tina Brooks, pianist McCoy Tyner, bassist Sam Jones and drummer Clifford Jarvis that shone on Brooks' *Open Sesame* and *Gypsy Blue* and Hubbard's *Hub's Nub* (april 1961). Similar all-star groups had helped him out on **Goin' Up** (november 1960) featuring Hank Mobley on tenor, Tyner, Paul Chambers on bass and Philly Joe Jones on drums, and contained *Blues For Brenda*, while **Hub Cap** (april 1961), a sextet session with tenor-saxophonist Jimmy Heath, trombonist Julian Priester and pianist Cedar Walton, had yielded *Hub Cap*. **Ready For Freddie** (august 1961) by a sextet with tenor saxophonist Wayne Shorter, Tyner, bassist Art Davis, drummer Elvin Jones and Bernard McKinney on euphonium, had already displayed Hubbard at his best (*Birdlike* and *Crisis*), but more experimental compositions surfaced on the following, less famous, recordings: *Bob's Place* and *Seventh Day* (july 1962), off **Artistry**, by a sextet with trombonist Curtis Fuller, tenor saxophonist John Gilmore, pianist Tommy Flanagan, bassist Art Davis and drummer Louis Hayes; *Lament for Booker* and *Hub Tones* (october 1962), off **Hub-Tones**, by a quintet with James Spaulding on alto and flute, pianist Herbie Hancock, bassist Reggie Workman and drummer Clifford Jarvis; *Aries* and *Thermo* (march 1963), off **The Body And The Soul**, by a larger ensemble featuring Wayne Shorter, Eric Dolphy and Cedar Walton; *Breaking Point* and *Far Away* (may 1964), off **Breaking Point**, by a quintet with James Spaulding on alto and flute, pianist Ronnie Matthews, bassist Eddie Khan and drummer Joe Chambers; *Blue Spirits* and *Outer Forces* (february 1965), off **Blue Spirits**, for a septet with Spaulding, tenor Hank Mobley, euphonium player Kiane Zawadi, McCoy Tyner on piano, Bob Cranshaw on bass and Pete La Roca on drums; *Little Sunflower* (october 1966), off **Backlash**; *High Blues Pressure* and *For B.P.*, off **High Blues Pressure** (november 1967), with Spaulding, tenor saxophonist Bennie Maupin, pianist Kenny Barron, Kiane Zawadi on euphonium, Howard Johnson on tuba.
The conversion to jazz-rock began with **The Black Angel** (may 1969), particularly the 17-minute *Spacetrack*, a jam highlighted by Spaulding, Workman and Barron. The new, lush style was consolidated on **Red Clay** (january 1970), by a quintet featuring tenor saxophonist Joe Henderson, pianist Herbie Hancock, bassist Ron Carter and drummer Lenny White, in lengthy, dynamic and fluid tracks such as *Red Clay* and *The Intrepid Fox*. The 17-minute *Straight Life*, off **Straight Life** (november 1970), featuring Henderson, Hancock, guitarist George Benson, bassist Ron Carter and drummer Jack DeJohnette, was the natural evolution of that chamber-jazz sound. The band (essentially the same line-up without Henderson and with Airto Moreira) for **First Light** (september 1971)

played even more electric, and the sound, arranged for chamber orchestra by Don Sebesky, was even more baroque, but the material was inferior, with only *First Light* worthy of its predecessors. The 15-minute *Povo*, on **Sky Dive** (october 1972), retained only Benson and Carter, adding Hubert Laws on flute, Keith Jarrett on piano and Billy Cobham on drums (and a horn section to provide the lush ambience). The four jams of **Keep Your Soul Together** (october 1973), instead, were performed "only" by a septet of less prestigious players (*Keep Your Soul Together*, *Spirits Of Trane*). But mostly he recorded trivial fusion jazz for lounges.

Another hard-bop musician who eventually adopted Miles Davis' electric language was trumpeter Donald Byrd, who had started out with diligent hard-bop workouts such as *The Long Two Four* off Pepper Adams' **10 to 4 at the Five-Spot** (april 1958), *Down Tempo*, on **Off to the Races** (1958), with altoist Jackie McLean, pianist Wynton Kelly, baritone saxophonist Pepper Adams, bassist Sam Jones and drummer Art Taylor, the 11-minute *Funky Mama*, off **Fuego** (1959), *Here Am I*, off **Byrd in Hand** (1959), and *Free Form*, from **Free Form** (1961), in a quintet with tenor saxophonist Wayne Shorter and pianist Herbie Hancock.

After the innovative **A New Perspective** (january 1963), for hard-bop septet (with tenor saxophonist Hank Mobley, guitarist Kenny Burrell, pianist Herbie Hancock) and gospel choir (*Elijah*, *Beast of Burden*), Byrd veered towards a funk-jazz sound that was heavily influenced by Miles Davis, and characterized by a prominent role for Duke Pearson's electric piano, longer (Byrd-composed) tracks and lush arrangements: *Fancy Free*, off **Fancy Free** (1969), *Estavianco* and *Essence*, off **Electric Byrd** (1970), *The Emperor* and *The Little Rasti*, off **Ethiopian Knights** (1971), perhaps the best of this phase.

However, **Black Byrd** (april 1972) was a commercial sell-out that opted for a more trivial format, with shorter songs (none composed by Byrd) and funky rhythms: Byrd's trumpet had become a mere ingredient in the stew concocted by producer, arranger and composer Larry Mizell. Mizell was the brain behind the concept album **Street Lady** (june 1973), that introduced a strong element of soul music, the ethnic and electronic **Stepping into Tomorrow** (december 1974), and the orchestral **Places and Spaces** (august 1975), that spawned the disco hit *Change*.

Richard "Blue" Mitchell, the trumpet of Horace Silver's quintet (1958-64), represented the "mainstream" version of hard bop with albums such as **Big Six** (july 1958), in a sextet with sextet with trombonist Curtis Fuller, tenor great Johnny Griffin, pianist Wynton Kelly, bassist Wilbur Ware and drummer Philly Joe Jones, featuring a ten-minute version of Benny Golson's *Blues March*, or **Out Of The Blue** (1958), in quintets with tenor saxophonist Benny Golson, pianists Wynton Kelly and Cedar Walton, bassists Paul Chambers and Sam Jones and drummer Art Blakey, highlighted by Golson's *Blues on My Mind*. He matured as an arranger and composer on **The Thing To Do** (july 1964), in a quintet with Chick Corea on piano.

St Louis-based trumpeter Clark Terry, who had played with Count Basie (1948-51) and Duke Ellington (1951-59), revealed his joyful personality with the hard-bop romp of **Clark Terry** (january 1955), featuring drummer Art Blakey, pianist Horace Silver and cellist Oscar Pettiford among others. He matured as a composer on **Serenade to a Bus Seat** (april 1957), in a quintet with tenor saxophonist Johnny Griffin, pianist Wynton Kelly, bassist Paul Chambers and drummer Philly Joe Jones. He then shifted to the flugelhorn and crafted **In Orbit** (1958), in a quartet with pianist Thelonious Monk, bassist Sam Jones and drummer Philly Joe Jones. Eccentric combinations such as **Top and Bottom Brass** (february 1959), in a quintet with tuba and piano, led to his most sophisticated album, **Color Changes** (november 1960), for an octet with tenor saxophone, assorted reeds (Yusef Lateef), piano (Tommy Flanagan), trombone, French horn, bass and drums.

Mal Waldron, who had played, notably, on Charles Mingus' **Pithecanthropus Erectus** (1956), was a hard-bop pianist in the philosophical tradition of Thelonious Monk. His early recordings, **Mal-1** (november 1956), **Mal-2** (may 1957), accompanied by the likes of John Coltrane and Jackie McLean, with *Potpourri*, **Mal-3 Sounds** (january 1958), with trumpeter Art Farmer and drummer Elvin Jones (besides flute, cello, bass), boasting longer and deeper compositions (*Tension*, *Ollie's Caravan* and *Portrait Of A Young Mother*, with wordless vocals), **Left Alone** (february 1959), with *Minor Pulsation* and featuring a quartet with alto saxophonist Jackie McLean, **Impressions** (march 1959), with the three-movement *Overseas Suite* for a simple piano-bass-drums trio, slowly introduced his trademark: an intimate sense of anguish. Waldron reached his artistic peak with **The Quest** (june 1961), featuring alto saxophonist Eric Dolphy, tenor-saxophonist Booker Ervin and cellist Ron Carter (plus bass and drums), a cycle of seven pensive Waldron sonatas bookended by *Status Seeking* and *Fire Waltz*. After relocating to Europe in 1965, the prolific Waldron adopted an enigmatic and minimalist style that was hardly "jazz", both in his albums of piano solos, such as **The Opening** (november 1970), containing *Sieg Haile*, and in the numerous trio and quartet sessions, such as **The Call** (february 1971), with the side-long jam *The Call* for an organ-based quartet, the trio **Number 19** (may 1971), the four solo improvisations of **Signals** (august 1971), the three improvisations for trio of **The Whirling Dervish** (may 1972), **Up Popped the Devil** (december 1973), perhaps the best of the period, thanks to bassist Reggie Workman and drummer Billy Higgins, and to the challenging material (*Up Popped the Devil*, *Snake Out*, *Changachangachang*), **What It Is** (november 1981), with tenorist Clifford Jordan, bassist Cecil McBee and a drummer (*Charlie Parker's Last Supper*, *Hymn for the Inferno*, *What It Is*), **One Entrance Many Exits** (january 1982), with tenorist Joe Henderson, bassist David Friesen and Higgins (*Golden Golson*, *One Entrance Many Exits*, *Blues in 4 by 3*), the solo **Evidence** (march 1988), with the two *Rhapsodic Interludes*, **Crowd Scene** (june 1989), two side-long improvisations for a double-sax quintet, **Where Are You** (june 1989), with the 22-minute *Waltz for Marianne* for the same quintet.

Los Angeles' trumpeter Art Farmer, a veteran of Lionel Hampton (1952-53), Oscar Pettiford (1956-57), Horace Silver (1957) and Gerry Mulligan (1958), had debuted as a leader with his **Septet** (july 1953), upon settling in New York. His favorite vehicle was the two-horn quintet, as on **Farmer's Market** (november 1956), featuring tenor saxophonist Hank Mobley and drummer Elvin Jones, on the two 10" EPs of **When Farmer Met Gryce** (may 1954 and may 1955), both with alto saxophonist Gigi Gryce (who composed all the music) and the first one featuring the rhythm section of Horace Silver (piano), Percy Heath (bass) and Kenny Clarke (drums), and on another quintet with Gryce, **Evening In Casablanca** (october 1955). **Last Night When We Were Young** (march 1957), arranged for string orchestra by Quincy Jones, and **Portrait** (may 1958), for a quartet with pianist Hank Jones, Addison Farmer and drummer Roy Haynes, led to his partnership with arranger Benny Golson, that began with **Modern Art** (september 1958) and **Brass Shout** (april 1959) for a tentet. After **Aztec Suite** (november 1959), containing Chico O'Farrill's 16-minute *Aztec Suite* for Latin big band, Farmer joined Golson's Jazztet, but continued producing music with his own quartets. **Art** (september 1960), with Tommy Flanagan on piano, was already ethereal by the standards of hard-bop, but the real breakthrough in sound came with **Perception** (october 1961) and **Listen to Art Farmer and the Orchestra** (september 1962), arranged by Oliver Nelson for big band, that emphasized his lyrical style at the flugelhorn. By switching instrument, Farmer had also changed the mood of hard bop.

Abbey Lincoln was the voice of this era. She was also one of the first explicitly political voices of jazz music. Her early collections of covers were mainly noteworthy for the cast of instrumentalists. **That's Him** (october 1957) featured tenor saxophonist Sonny Rollins, trumpeter Kenny Dorham, pianist Wynton Kelly, bassist Paul Chambers and drummer (and husband) Max Roach. **It's Magic** (august 1958) had trumpeters Kenny Dorham and Art Farmer, trombonist Curtis Fuller, tenor saxophonist Benny Golson, pianist Wynton Kelly, bassist Paul Chambers, drummer Philly Joe Jones and others. **Abbey Is Blue** (march 1959) contained her first composition. Her voice and her message blossomed in the following years on Max Roach's albums. By the time she cut **Straight Ahead** (february 1961) with tenor saxophonist Coleman Hawkins, flutist Eric Dolphy, pianist Mal Waldron, Roach and others, her voice had become one of the most sophisticated instruments or her era. After a long hiatus, she returned a more mature composer with **People In Me** (june 1973) and **Golden Lady** (february 1980), despite boasting much humbler casts.

The mellow tones and linear melodies of Indianapolis' guitarist Wes Montgomery were almost the antithesis of bebop's aesthetic. Compared with Charlie Christian and Kenny Burrell, he had neither the dynamics of the former nor the ambition of the latter. His rare compositions were short and to the point: *Jingles*, off **The Wes Montgomery Trio** (october 1959), *West Coast Blues* and *Four on Six* on **The Incredible Jazz Guitar** (january 1960), by a quartet with pianist Tommy Flanagan, *Twisted Blues*, off **So Much Guitar** (august 1961), by a quintet with pianist Hank Jones, bassist Ron Carter and the congas of Ray Barretto, *Blues Riff*, off **Portrait** (october 1963).

Hard Bop

Bud Powell-influenced pianist Duke Pearson was one of hard-bop's main composers, thanks to *Jeannine*, off **Bags Groove** (august 1961), *Cristo Redentor* for Donald Byrd's **A New Perspective** (january 1963), the memorable *Idle Moments* and *Nomad* for Grant Green's **Idle Moments** (november 1963), *Amanda* and *Bedouin* for his own best album, **Wahoo** (november 1964). Pearson was shifting towards soul-jazz, albeit in a classy and brainy way, as proven by his mature albums of original compositions for larger ensembles: **Sweet Honey Bee** (december 1966), that featured a sextet with trumpeter Freddie Hubbard, alto saxophonist James Spaulding and tenor saxophonist Joe Henderson, and **The Right Touch** (september 1967), for an octet with Hubbard, Spaulding and tenor saxophonist Stanley Turrentine.

Mingus

The art of double bass player Charlie Mingus was rooted in the same general rediscovery of blues and gospel music as hard bop, but Mingus stood out for his highbrow studies on group improvisation and jazz composition. His music was schizophrenic in that it both harked back to the New Orleans roots of jazz and looked forward to progressive chamber jazz and "third stream" jazz. His compositions ranged wildly in mood and dynamics, from pointillistic counterpoint to massive Wagner-ian explosions. He rarely employed great soloists, preferring dedicated session-men to stars with a strong personality, another way of emphasizing the compositional versus the improvisational nature of his art. Mingus was the first jazz musician since Ellington who could compete with classical composers. A proud intellectual, he publicly despised the decadent habits of many jazz stars and even the barbaric attitude of the jazz audience (compared with the audience of classical music). A precursor of "indie" music, Mingus founded his own label (1952) to avoid the commercial pressure of the major labels.

Raised in Los Angeles, he was also a rare specimen in a jazz world that was increasingly centered around New York. A child prodigy, he composed a challenging *Half-Mast Inhibition* (1941) when he was just 19 years old. He cut his teeth with Louis Armstrong (1942) and Lionel Hampton (1947-48), but had little in common with the swing era. He first displayed his true persona in a trio formed in 1950 by xylophonist Kenneth "Red Norvo" Norville with guitarist Tal Farlow. Moving to New York, he mixed with the bebop avantgarde, playing a famous date with Dizzy Gillespie, Charlie Parker, Bud Powell and Max Roach, immortalized on **Jazz at Nassey Hall** (may 1953). He also appeared on records by Bud Powell (1953), Charlie Parker (1953) and Paul Bley (1953).

He established himself as one of jazz music's main visionaries with **Pithecanthropus Erectus** (january 1956), recorded by a quintet that featured Jackie McLean on alto sax, Mal Waldron on piano, a tenor saxophonist and a drummer. The highlight of the album was the ten-minute four-movement tone poem *Pithecanthropus Erectus* (partially free-form), that influenced the birth of free jazz, but the album also contained a 15-minute *Love Chant*, a moody and cryptic suite that confirmed his narrative gift, and an eight-minute version of

Gershwin's *A Foggy Day* turned into a mini-symphony of city noises (all simulated by the instruments).

The quintet session of **The Clown** (march 1957) debuted Dannie Richmond on drums and Jimmy Knepper on trombone. The twelve-minute *Haitian Fight Song* was another tour de force of dynamics, albeit rooted in the polyphony of New Orleans' street bands (also a bassist's tour de force), matched by the closing *The Clown*, while *Reincarnation of a Lovebird* was an eight-minute tribute to bebop and to the tragedy of his greatest icon (Charlie Parker).

Tijuana Moods (june 1957), with even a vocalist and castanets, contained two ten-minute compositions that overflowed with intricate sonic events, *Ysabel's Table Dance* and *Los Mariachis*. And the list of extended experiments started growing rapidly: the ten-minute *West Coast Ghost* for a sax-trumpet-trombone-piano sextet, off **East Coasting** (august 1957), the eleven-minute *Scenes In The City* for jazz ensemble and narrating voice, off **Scenes In The City** (october 1957), the twelve-minute *Nostalgia in Times Square* for alto-tenor-piano quintet, off **Jazz Portraits** (january 1959).

Blues and Roots (february 1959) was, instead, a post-modernist tribute to the sound of New Orleans, an exercise in disassembling the cliches of a genre and rebuilding it from an analytic perspective (best the gospel-y *Wednesday Night Prayer Meeting* and the bluesy *Moanin'*). None of the exuberance was lost, but the harmonic complexity was certainly not what the old New Orleans bands had in mind. Basically, it was an entire album of pieces similar to the previous *Haitian Fight Song*.

More tributes to his idols surfaced on another accessible set, **Mingus Ah Um** (may 1959), scored for septet. *Better Get Hit in Yo' Soul* was still in the gospel vein of its predecessor, while *Goodbye Pork Pie Hat* was a moving elegy for Lester Young and other pieces were dedicated to Charlie Parker, Jelly Roll Morton and Duke Ellington. The longer *Fables of Faubus* was one of his first forays into politics.

After **Dynasty** (november 1959), that recycled the same ideas, Mingus formed a quartet with Richmond, trumpeter Ted Curson and saxophonist Eric Dolphy to record **Presents Charles Mingus** (october 1960). *Folk Forms No. 1* expanded his revisitation of New Orleans into a dreamy and sometimes nightmarish twelve-minute jam, while the 15-minute *What Love* adopted the anarchic stance of free jazz and a "conversational" approach to the double bass. After all, Mingus' quartet was modeled after Ornette Coleman's quartet that had inaugurated free jazz.

Other experiments of these years were the 20-minute *MDM* for an eleven-piece ensemble (featuring Dolphy and Paul Bley on piano), off **Mingus** (october 1960), *Peggy's Blue Skylight* (november 1961), and especially *Epitaph* (1962), his most ambitious score, first documented on the **Town Hall Concert** (october 1962) but fully reconstructed (two hours long) only posthumously in 1989.

Oh Yeah (november 1961) explored a different facet of Mingus' persona: the dadaist joker. Scored for a sextet with Knepper, Richmond, Mingus on piano, Doug Watkins on bass, Booker Ervin on tenor sax and Roland Kirk on flute and other instruments, mid-size pieces such as *Hog Callin' Blues, Devil Woman, Oh Lord Don't Let Them Drop That Atomic Bomb On Me* and *Ecclusiastics* took the postmodernist approach of **Blues and Roots** to an almost parodistic and paroxysmal extreme, while *Passions Of A Man* was again flirting with noise. It was a deviant form of traditional jazz, that kept intact the envelope while scientifically demolishing the interior.

The narrative dynamic typical of Mingus' extended works is the essence of **The Black Saint And The Sinner Lady** (january 1963), ostensibly a six-movement ballet (divided into three "tracks" and three "modes") for big band (the three modes were squeezed into a single 17-minute track on the vinyl version), and one of the masterpieces of 20th century's music. Scored for an orchestra of two trumpets, trombone, tuba, flute, baritone sax, guitar, alto (Charlie Mariano), piano (Jaki Byard), bass and drums, and painstakingly assembled by Mingus (even overdubbing several passages), it was, by definition, an exercise in colors: Mingus juxtaposed groups of instruments to maximize the contrast of tones, while using a shifting dynamic to lure ever-changing textures out of that jarring counterpoint. The resulting music was highly emotional, bordering on neurotic, merging the ancestral frustration of black slaves with the modern alienation of the urban middle class. The sense of universal tragedy was increased by the facts that instruments were clearly simulating human voices, whether the joyful singing of Mariano's sax or the sorrowful murmur of trumpet and trombone or the ghostly howls of tuba and baritone sax. The story opens with the bleak *Track A - Solo Dancer*, slides into the orchestral *Track B - Duet Solo Dancers* (reminiscent of Ellington) and delves into the melodic fantasy of *Track C - Group Dancers*, with piano and flute sculpting the leitmotiv. The "modes", *Mode D - Trio And Group Dancers, Mode E - Single Solos And Group Dance* and *Mode F - Group And Solo Dance*, wed hard bop, classical music and flamenco.

After a work of so much depth and class, Mingus paid tribute to himself on **Mingus Mingus Mingus Mingus Mingus** (september 1963), a revisitation of his popular themes, and toyed with the piano on **Mingus Plays Piano** (june 1963). The 1964 sextet with Eric Dolphy (also Clifford Jordan on tenor sax, Jaki Byard on piano, Johnny Coles on trumpet) yielded extended live jams such as *Parkeriana, Orange Was The Color Of Her Dress Then Blue Silk Meditations on Integration*, and *So Long Eric*, all of them included on **The Great Concert of Charles Mingus** (april 1964).

Teo Macero helped Mingus assemble the orchestra for **Let My Children Hear Music** (october 1971), his most daring attempt at fusing two such antithetical forms of art as classical music and free jazz. The program (*The Shoes Of The Fisherman's Wife Are Some Jive Ass Slippers*, the intricate (albeit improvised) *Adagio Ma Non Troppo, Don't Be Afraid The Clown's Afraid Too*, the breathtaking *Hobo Ho, The Chill Of Death* with narrating voice, *The I Of Hurricane Sue*) was as frantic as a Charles Ives symphony and as massive as a Wagner opera.

His last major composition were: *Opus III* (october 1973) for quintet (George Adams on tenor, Don Pullen on piano), *Sue's Changes* (december 1974) for quintet (George Adams on tenor, Don Pullen on piano, Jack Walrath on trumpet), *Todo Modo* (april 1976) for large ensemble, *Cumbia & Jazz Fusion* (march 1977) for large ensemble.

As a bassist, Mingus had developed a style that turned the instrument into something like a piano, capable of playing both the bass rhythm and the countermelody. But his achievements as a virtuoso pale compared with his achievements as a composer. A brain that was both an encyclopedia of jazz music and a laboratory of genetic synthesis had yielded the first great postmodernist artist of jazz. Mingus died in january 1979.

White Hard Bop

Jackie McLean was the only (white) alto saxophonist to create a personal style based on the spirit of Charlie Parker's accomplishments. After accompanying Sonny Rollins (1948), Miles Davis (1949), Charles Mingus (1956) and Art Blakey (1956), McLean refined his hard-bop style through a series of intriguing collaborations: his 13-minute composition *Lights Out* (january 1956), in a quintet with trumpeter Donald Byrd, pianist Elmo Hope, bassist Doug Watkins and drummer Art Taylor, an extended cover of Charlie Parker's *Confirmation* (july 1956), featuring a sextet with trumpeter Donald Byrd and tenor saxophonist Hank Mobley, his 10-minute piece *Mc Lean's Scene* (december 1956), in a quintet with trumpeter Bill Hardman, pianist Red Garland, bassist Paul Chambers and Taylor, *Beau Jack* (february 1957), with Mal Waldron on piano, Hardman, Watkins and Taylor, the 20-minute jam *A Long Drink of the Blues* (august 1957), featuring trombonist Curtis Fuller, trumpeter Webster Young, pianist Gil Coggins, bassist Paul Chambers and drummer Louis Hayes. McLean's style began to depart from standard hard bop on **New Soil** (may 1959), that displayed Ornette Coleman's influence in his *Hip Strut* and *Minor Apprehension* for a piano-trumpet quintet, on **Jackie's Bag** (september 1960), with trumpeter Blue Mitchell, tenor saxophonist Tina Brooks, pianist Kenny Drew, Chambers and Taylor, that included two exotic pieces (his *Appointment in Ghana* and Tina Brooks' *Isle of Java*, one of the few survivors of a legendary session for the Living Theater), and on **Bluesnik** (january 1961), in a quintet with trumpeter Freddie Hubbard and pianist Kenny Drew, devoted to blues pieces composed by McLean (such as the title-track). The "crying" style of his alto on **Let Freedom Ring** (march 1962), accompanied by piano, bass and drums, was the direct link between hard bop and free jazz. Its four lengthy jams (including *Melody for Melonae, Rene, Omega,*) unleashed all the emotion and creativity that had been constrained on the previous albums. The even more atmospheric **One Step Beyond** (april 1963), for a quintet with trombone (Grachan Moncur) and vibraphone (Bobby Hutcherson), merged blues, hard bop and modal improvisation into a new kind of chamber jazz, particularly in Moncour's *Frankenstein* and *Ghost Town* and in McLean's *Saturday and Sunday*. The same idea and line-up (although with a different rhythm section) were repeated on **Destination Out** (september 1963), and at least Moncour's *Esoteric* and McLean's *Kahlil the Prophet* managed to further improve the disorienting sensation of musicians playing with no proper leader. McLean fully adopted the "free" idiom on **It's Time** (august 1964), in a new quintet with trumpeter Charles Tolliver and pianist Herbie Hancock, and **Action** (september 1964), with Bobby Hutcherson's vibraphone replacing the piano. Ornette Coleman in person played trumpet for McLean on the side-long four-movement suite *Lifeline*, off **New and Old Gospel** (march 1967), his most complex composition ever. The free-jazz period ended with **Bout Soul** (september 1967), with Moncur, Woody Shaw on trumpet, piano, bass and drums (Rashied Ali), because **Demon's Dance** (december 1967), without Moncour but with Jack DeJohnette on drums, was already a more traditional work.

Detroit's white baritone saxophonist Pepper Adams represented the more aggressive side of hard-bop, especially if compared with the other famous baritonist of the era, Gerry Mulligan. His recordings include: **The Cool Sound** (november 1957), in a quintet with piano, euphonium, bass and drums (Elvin Jones); **10 to 4 at the Five-Spot** (april 1958), in a classic quintet with trumpeter Donald Byrd (the quintet's co-leader to whom all their albums were credited except this one), pianist Bobby Timmons, bassist Doug Watkins and drummer Elvin Jones; **Stardust** (1960), in a sextet with Byrd, guitarist Kenny Burrell, pianist Tommy Flanagan, bassist Paul Chambers and a drummer; **Encounter** (december 1968), in a quintet with tenor saxophonist Zoot Sims, pianist Tommy Flanagan, bassist Ron Carter and Jones.

At the turn of the decade the quintet and quartet sessions of Philadelphia's tenor saxophonist Benny Golson introduced a number of hard-bop talents, who benefited from Golson's talent in composing bluesy ballads. **New York Scene** (october 1957), with the soulful *Whisper Not*, featured trumpeter Art Farmer, pianist Wynton Kelly and bassist Paul Chambers. **The Modern Touch** (december 1957), with the eleven-minute *Blues On Down*, had Kelly, Chambers, trumpeter Kenny Dorham and drummer Max Roach. **The Other Side** (november 1958) debuted trombonist Curtis Fuller and drummer Philly Joe Jones. Fuller remained for **Gone** (june 1959), with *Blues After Dark*, **Groovin'** (august 1959), with the lengthy *My Blues House* and *Stroller* and the stellar rhythm section of pianist Ray Bryant, bassist Paul Chambers and drummer Art Blakey, **Gettin' With It** (december 1959), with the lengthy *Bub Hurd's Blues* and a new rhythm section of pianist Tommy Flanagan, bassist Doug Watkins and drummer Art Taylor, and the fascinating experiment of **Take a Number from 1 to 10** (december 1960), whose ten numbers are interpreted by progressively larger groups, starting with a sax solo and ending with *Time* for a tentet (including trumpeter Freddie Hubbard and pianist Cedar Walton).

Propelled by Golson's compositions and arrangements, Benny Golson's major project, the Jazztet, became the mainstream hard-bop experience of the early 1960s. The line-up for **Meet The Jazztet** (february 1960), containing *Blues March* (already recorded in 1958 by trumpeter Blue Mitchell) and *Killer Joe*, featured three outstanding horn players, with trombonist Curtis Fuller and trumpeter Art Farmer, and a rhythm section with pianist McCoy Tyner. **Big City Sounds** (september 1960) retained only Farmer and Golson and replaced Tyner with Cedar Walton. Walton left and trombonist Grachan Moncur joined for **Here And Now** (march 1962) and **Another Git Together** (june 1962).

Detroit's white guitarist Kenny Burrell was the premiere hard bop guitarist, although his gentle, pensive style evolved towards a more abstract form of music. The sound was carefully calibrated on the combination of guitar style, line-up and original Burrell compositions: *Fugue 'N Blues* on **Introducing Kenny Burrell** (may 1956), with pianist Tommy Flanagan, bassist Paul Chambers, drummer Kenny Clarke conga player Candido; the 17-minute *All Night Long* on **All Night Long** (december 1956), with trumpeter Donald Byrd, tenor saxophonist Hank Mobley, flutist Jerome Richardson, pianist Mal Waldron, bassist Doug Watkins and drummer Art Taylor; the 18-minute *All Day Long* on **All Day Long** (january 1957), with Byrd, tenor saxophonist Frank Foster, Flanagan, Watkins and Taylor. Perhaps his definitive testament was **Blue Lights** (may 1958), accompanied by trumpet, tenor, piano, bass (Sam Jones) and drums (Art Blakey), that contained *Yes Baby* and *Rock Salt* (with the addition of Tina Brooks on tenor) and *Phinupi* (without Brooks).

Hard Bop Big Bands

The format of the big band was kept alive in the hard-bop era mainly by black trumpeter Thad Jones, who had played in Count Basie's Orchestra from 1954 till 1963. He teamed up with white drummer Mel Lewis, who had played in Stan Kenton's orchestra from 1954 till 1957, and formed a big band in 1966. Jones provided their signature tunes and the arrangements: *Mean What You Say* (may 1966) on the first album, *A Child Is Born* on their best album, **Consummation** (may 1970), and *Central Park North* (july 1969) from the eponymous album.

The other major big band of the hard-bop era was led by Los Angeles-based white Canadian trumpeter Maynard Ferguson, a former member of Stan Kenton's orchestra. His Birdland Dream Band (formed in 1956) sounded like a simplified and less bombastic version of Kenton's orchestra, with music composed and arranged by tenor saxophonist Bill Holman.

Soul Jazz

A side-effect of hard bop was to legitimize the fusion of jazz and soul music. This sub-genre in turn opened the doors of jazz music to the most glorious of soul's instruments: the Hammond organ, with its rough, distorted sound (particularly the model introduced in 1955). The pioneer of jazz organ had been "Wild" Bill Davis, who in 1950 had organized the first of his organ-guitar-drums trios. In Philadelphia Jimmy Smith simply copied Bill Davis' style, but with one hand imitating the solos of horn players. After debuting with the spotty **A New Sound A New Star** (february 1956) and beginning to compose his material on **The Champ** (march 1956), Smith matured on **The Sermon** (february 1958), a tour de force that contained two monster jams: *J.O.S.* (august 1957), in a trio with altoist George Coleman and trumpeter Lee Morgan, and especially the 20-minute *The Sermon* (Morgan, altoist Lou Donaldson, tenor saxophonist Tina Brooks, guitarist Kenny Burrell, drummer Art Blakey). Most of his recordings were lame collections of covers, but originals such as *Open House* (1960) and *Plain Talk*, performed with altoist Jackie McLean, trumpeter Blue Mitchell, guitarist Quentin Warren and tenor saxophonist Ike Quebec, laid the groundwork for the new, improved sound of **Back at the Chicken Shack** (april 1960), featuring Burrell and tenor saxophonist Stanley Turrentine, and containing two more extended Smith gems: *Back at the Chicken Shack* and *Messy Bessy*.

Philadelphia soon became the epicenter of soul-jazz organ, Jimmy McGriffin being the most commercially successful.

After working with saxophonist Eddie "Lockjaw" Davis, notably in his hit *In the Kitchen* (1958), Shirley Scott, also based in Philadelphia, became one of the leading soul-jazz organists of the 1960s (with strong gospel and blues accents), overcoming the genre's limits at least in the eleven-minute *Chapped Chops*, off **Workin'** (may 1958) for a piano-guitar quintet, and the nine-minute *Blues For Tyrone*, off **Soul Sister** (june 1960) for a quartet with vibraphone. The quartet date of **Hip Soul** (june 1961) began the collaboration with tenor saxophonist Stanley Turrentine (her husband) that would peak on **Blue Flames** (march 1964).

Pittsburgh's tenor saxophonist Stanley Turrentine worked with Jimmy Smith (1960) and his wife Shirley Scott (1961) before starting his own career with the soul-jazz jams of *Let's Groove*, off **The Man** (january 1960), in a quartet with pianist and drummer Max Roach *Little Sheri*, off **Look Out** (june 1960), in another piano-based quartet, *Z.T.'s Blues*, off **Z.T.'s Blues** (september 1961), in a quintet with guitarist Grant Green, pianist Tommy Flanagan, bassist Paul Chambers and drummer Art Taylor. Turrentine also wrote several compositions for his wife, organist Shirley Scott: *Hip Soul* on **Hip Soul** (june 1961), *The Soul Is Willing* on **The Soul Is Willing** (january 1963), *Deep Down Soul* on **Soul Shoutin'** (october 1963), *The Hustler*, off **Hustlin'** (january 1964), in a quintet with Scott and guitarist Kenny Burrell, etc. Turrentine later veered towards to commercial fusion with groove-driven pieces such as *Get It*, off **Another Story** (march 1969), in a quintet with Thad Jones on flugelhorn and Cedar Walton on piano, the ten-minute *Sugar*, off **Sugar** (november 1970), in a sextet with guitarist George Benson, pianist Lonnie Liston Smith, and trumpeter Freddie Hubbard, and *Don't Mess With Mister T*, off **Don't Mess With Mister T** (march 1973).

St Louis' guitarist Grant Green played with the pathos and lyricism of a saxophonist. Initially, he created a unique bebop, blues and soul fusion on **Grant's First Stand** (jauary 1961) for a drum-less organ-guitar-bass trio, **Green Street** (april 1961) for a guitar-bass-drums trio and containing the ten-minute *Green With Envy*, and **Grantstand** (january 1961), in a bass-less quartet with tenor saxophonist and flutist Yusef Lateef and organist Jack McDuff, and containing the 15-minute *Blues in Maude's Flat*. He then embarked in lengthy jams of modal improvisation on **Idle Moments** (november 1963), featuring pianist Duke Pearson, tenor saxophonist Joe Henderson and vibraphonist Bobby Hutcherson and highlighted by Pearson's *Idle Moments*, **Matador** (may 1964), in a quartet with John Coltrane's pianist McCoy Tyner and drummer Elvin Jones, and **Solid** (june 1964), that added James Spaulding on alto saxophone and Joe

Henderson on tenor. He then joined organist Larry Young and Jones in a trio that debuted with **Talkin' About** (september 1964).

Larry Young had begun to play the electric organ in the soul-jazz manner pioneered by Jimmy Smith with jams such as the ten-minute *Testifying*, off **Testifying** (august 1960), and the 14-minute *Gettin' Into It*, off **Groove Street** (february 1962), but soon switched to a modal style on **Into Somethin'** (november 1964), by a quartet with tenor saxophonist Sam Rivers, guitarist Grant Green and drummer Elvin Jones, progressing via the inferior **Unity** (november 1965), with saxophonist Joe Henderson, trumpeter Woody Shaw, and drummer Elvin Jones, towards the trio with guitarist Grant Green and drummer Elvin Jones that represented the mature stage of his post-soul phase. After **Of Love and Peace** (july 1966) and **Contrasts** (september 1967), Young began another turnabout, this time towards fusion jazz on **Heaven On Earth** (february 1968) with a quintet featuring alto saxophonist Byard Lancaster and guitarist George Benson. After playing on Miles Davis's **Bitches Brew** (1969), Young was hired by Tony Williams for his Lifetime trio and turned to funk-jazz-rock fusion in earnest. **Mother Ship** (february 1969), unreleased till 1980, and **Lawrence of Newark** (1973), the first albums entirely composed by him, included elements of all his phases.

White organist Charles Earland was the heir to Philadelphia's school of soul-jazz in the era of jazz-rock due to his lightweight, poppy romps, such as *Here Comes Charlie*, off **Black Talk** (december 1969), for a sextet, *Key Club Cookout*, off **Living Black** (september 1970), featuring saxophonist Grover Washington, *Cause I Love Her*, off **Intensity** (february 1972), featuring trumpeter Lee Morgan, *Brown Eyes*, off **Leaving This Planet** (december 1973), featuring tenor saxophonist Joe Henderson and trumpeter Freddie Hubbard.

Propelled by Bob James' string arrangements, the commercial success of saxophonist Grover Washington, who had moved to Philadelphia in 1967, was emblematic of the slide of soul-jazz into utter triviality. **Soul Box** (march 1973) even featured a symphony orchestra.

The legacy of hard-bop and its myriad sub-genres was going to be felt for a long time, long after its founding fathers had retired.

Post-bop

In the early 1960s, a number of jazz musicians were caught in between the decadence of bebop and hard bop and the boom of free jazz, but still managed to coin a style that was their own and that presaged future developments.

St Louis-born alto, tenor and soprano saxophonist Oliver Nelson moved to New York in 1958. He became famous mainly as an arranger, but was also a consistent hard-bop player: **Takin' Care of Business** (march 1960), for a quintet with vibraphone, organ, bass, drums, containing *Trane Whistle*; **Afro-American Sketches** (november 1961), a concept album for big band, dedicated to the history of black people in the USA (*Emancipation Blues, Freedom Dance*); and especially **Blues and the Abstract Truth** (february 1961), with his most famous songs (*Stolen Moments, Teenie's Blues*) and a stellar cast (Nelson on tenor and alto, Eric Dolphy doubling on alto and flute, Freddie Hubbard on trumpet, Bill Evans on piano, Paul Chambers on bass, Roy Haynes on drums). Later Nelson preferred to compose for large ensemble: *Sound Piece for Jazz Orchestra*, off **Sound Pieces** (september 1966), **Black Brown And Beautiful** (october 1969), **Berlin Dialogue For Orchestra** (november 1970), containing two suites, *Berlin Dialogue for Orchestra* and *Impressions of Berlin*, and the 27-minute *Swiss Suite*, first recorded on **Swiss Suite** (june 1971).

Chicago-born pianist Andrew Hill extended hard bop way beyond its original foundations. Relocating to New York in 1962, Hill, formerly a student of classical composer Paul Hindemith, introduced a new degree of rhythmic and harmonic complexity on **Black Fire** (november 1963), with tenor saxophonist Joe Henderson, bassist Richard Davis and drummer Roy Haynes unleashed in subdued, brainy compositions (often marked by Afro-Cuban accents) such as *Land Of Nod, Pumpkin, Subterfuge* and *Black Fire*. A similar rarefied quartet session, **Smokestack** (december 1963), failed to muster the cohesiveness of the debut, but **Judgement** (january 1964), a quartet session with vibraphonist Bobby Hutcherson, bassist Richard Davis and drummer Elvin Jones, successfully merged hard bop with modal jazz and free jazz in six austere performances (including *Siete Ocho, Alfred, Yokada Yokada*). Hill's research program peaked with the more lively excursions of **Point of Departure** (march 1964), accompanied by Eric Dolphy on saxophone, clarinets and flute, Joe Henderson on saxophones, Kenny Dorham on trumpet, Richard Davis on bass and Tony Williams on drums The three longest tracks, *Refuge, Spectrum* and especially *New Monastery*, were avantgarde within the tradition, an endless reinvention of hard bop, an art of multi-horn chromatic embellishment and elusive tonality. Yet another line-up (Sun Ra's tenor saxophonist John Gilmore, drummer Joe Chambers, Hutcherson, Davis) returned to Hill's more abstract aesthetic on **Andrew** (june 1964), another set of neurotic and ever-shifting pieces that often achieve intense pathos (*The Griots* and *Le Serpent Qui Danse*). The most daring of Hill's experiments was perhaps **Compulsion** (october 1965), that contained four lengthy pieces (*Compulsion, Limbo, Legacy, Premonition*) for a septet including Gilmore, trumpeter Freddie Hubbard and three percussionists. This was as close to free jazz as Hill would ever get, as if the great hard-bopper had finally exhausted the possibilities of the genre. Alas, Hill's fortune was inversely proportional to his creativity. **Dance With Death** (october 1968), not released until 1980, contained several charming experiments (*Partitions, Dance With Death, Love Nocturne*) for trumpeter Charles Tolliver, saxophonist Joe Farrell, drummer Billy Higgins and bassist Victor Sproles, and **Passing Ships** (november 1969), rediscovered in 2001, was scored for jazz nonet and bordered on third-stream music (especially *Noon Tide*). **Lift Every Voice** (may 1969), for jazz quintet and operatic vocals, signaled that Hill was ready to try his hand at classical music, which he did by composing an opera, string quartets and orchestral works.

Hill returned to jazz with the piano-bass-drums trio of **Invitation** (october 1974), and the sax-piano-bass-drums quartet of **Blue Black** (february 1975) and especially of the 25-minute *Divine Revelation*, off **Divine Revelation** (july 1975). Hill also turned to solo piano music with the vignettes of **Hommage** (july 1975), the two side-long improvisations of **From California With Love** (october 1978), *Bayside*, off **Faces of Hope** (june 1980), and *Verona Rag*, off **Verona Rag** (july 1986). But he finally resumed his journey through chamber jazz with **Eternal Spirit** (january 1989), a quintet session with vibraphonist Bobby Hutcherson and altoist Greg Osby, **But Not Farewell** (september 1990), for a quintet with trombonist Robin Eubanks and Osby, that includes the free solo-piano improvisation *Gone*, and especially **Dusk** (october 1999), for a sextet with trumpet and two saxophones, containing some of his most elegant experiments (*Dusk, Sept, 15/8*).

White Canadian-born pianist Paul Bley, who relocated in 1950 to New York to study at a prestigious school of music and was hired by Charlie Mingus in 1952, was honored, at the young age of 21, by Mingus on double-bass and Art Blakey on drums on his debut trio sessions, **Introducing Paul Bley** (november 1953), that already featured some of his inspired originals (*Opus 1, Spontaneous Combustion*) but was still under the influence of Lennie Tristano's bebop style. Bley began to emancipate his performance from that cliche' on **Solemn Meditation** (1957), another quartet but with Dave Pike on vibraphone and Charlie Haden on double-bass (his recording debut). In 1957 Bley married composer Carla Borg, moved to Los Angeles and formed a quintet with Ornette Coleman (alto saxophone), Don Cherry (trumpet), Billy Higgins (drums) and Charlie Haden (double bass), documented on **The Fabulous Paul Bley Quintet** (october 1958), that straddled the line between bebop and free improvisation (a Coleman piece is titled *Free*). A trio with bassist Steve Swallow and drummer Pete LaRoca on **Footloose** (september 1963) evoked the contemporary experiments of Tristano and Bill Evans with a set of graceful vignettes (including Carla Bley's *Floater* and *King Korn*). Next came the quartet of **Turning Point** (march 1964), with Sun Ra's tenor saxophonist John Gilmore, double bassist Gary Peacock and drummer Paul Motian, that again flirted with free jazz but remained within the boundaries of cool jazz (notably in Paul Bley's *Turns* and Carla Bley's *Ida Lupino* and *Syndrome*). The influence of Ornette Coleman was more visible on **Barrage** (october 1964), entirely composed by Carla Bley (who also manipulated the tapes in studio to produce a thicker sound), for a quintet with Sun Ra's alto saxophonist Marshall Allen, trumpeter Dewey Johnson, bassist Eddie Gomez and drummer Milford Graves. But the composer was to be credited more than the players with the success of *Barrage* and *Ictus*.

Paul Bley came into his own with a trio formed in 1965. Abandoning all previous influences, the ten short vignettes of **Closer** (december 1965), mostly composed by Carla Bley (but Annette Peacock debuted as a composer with *Cartoon*) and accompanied by Steve Swallow on bass and Barry Altschul on drums, were in the spirit of a romantic, lyrical chamber jazz, almost "ambient music" antelitteram. Bley continued to record in the trio format (with drummer Barry Altschul and either Kent Carter or Mark Levinson on bass) for a while: **Touching** (november 1965), containing Carla Bley's *Start* and Peacock's *Touching*; **Ramblin'** (july 1966), containing Peacock's lengthy *Albert's Love Theme* and *Touching*; **Blood** (october 1966), which was mostly a Peacock album (notably *Blood* and *Mr Joy*); **Virtuosi** (june 1967), the most atmospheric and sophisticated of them all, with Gary Peacock on bass and containing even longer interpretations of two masterful Annette Peacock compositions, *Butterflies* (16 minutes) and *Gary* (17 minutes); **Ballads** (july 1967), maybe even too baroque in its delicate slow-motion mood sculpting vein (Peacock's 17-minute *Ending* and 12-minute *So Hard It Hurts*). In 1967 Paul Bley divorced Carla Bley and married another top-notch composer, Annette Peacock. The combination of Bley's smooth trio sound and Annette Peacock's elegant melodies coined a new genre, that would make the label ECM rich.

But Bley was ready to move on again. Annette Peacock became a key member of Bley's new ensemble, playing the most unusual of instruments, the synthesizer, next to Bley's electric piano. She was, in fact, one of the very first musicians to use a synthesizer (which was still a very complex machine) and probably the first one to take it on a tour. The Synthesizer Show, as their ensemble was called, recorded several pieces that eventually found their way to several milestone recordings: **Revenge** (november 1969), divided into a side played by the Bley-Peacock-Altschul trio (*Mr Joy, Daddy's Boat, Dream*) and a side played by Annette Peacock and her new ensemble (not featuring Bley) which marks the beginning of Peacock's solo career, and in which she also does her very first raps (*Loss Of Consciousness, Nothing Ever Was Anyway, I'm The One*); **Improvisie** (march 1971), with Paul Bley on synthesizer, Annette Peacock on vocals and piano, Han Bennink on percussion (which contains two lengthy improvisations, the 16-minute *Improvisie* and a 24-minute version of *Touching*); **Dual Unity** (march 1971), featuring Paul Bley on synthesizer and piano, Annette Peacock on piano and vocals, Han Bennink on drums and Mario Pavone on double bass (*Richter Scale* being the most representative and loudest of the four tracks, and the 17-minute *MJ* being the n-th version of *Mr Joy*); and the inferior **The Paul**

Bley Synthesizer Show (march 1971), that does not feature Peacock anymore, but features an all-Peacock program.
But this "synthesizer show" had been mostly Annette Peacock's personal show. Bley returned to the "ambient" sound he had pioneered during the trio years with a solo piano album, **Open To Love** (september 1972), titled yet again after a Peacock composition (and one of her best). Most of the material was made of old Carla Bley and Annette Peacock compositions, but the delivery was now emphasizing the spatial ambience and the spiritual side of things.
After divorcing Peacock, Bley formed a new trio, **Scorpio** (november 1972), playing electric and electronic keyboards next to Altschul and British double-bassist Dave Holland, and converting to the jazz-rock style in vogue at the time, but in a rather shallow manner. Bley's erratic career flirted with free jazz on **Quiet Song** (november 1974), with guitarist Bill Connors and clarinetist Jimmy Giuffre, returned to the Scorpio sound on **Pastorius Metheny Ditmas Bley** (june 1974), that marked the recording debut of both guitarist Pat Metheny and bassist Jaco Pastorius, and occasionally revived his trio with Peacock and Altschul, for example on the live 33-minute **Japan Suite** (july 1976).
He seemed more interested in innovating in other formats, particularly the visual one: in 1974 he formed a company with video artist Carol Goss to produce videos in the same improvised manner as the music was produced by free-jazz musicians.
By far his most influential output was in the format of the impressionistic piano piece: **Alone Again** (august 1974), finally relying mostly on his own material, **Axis** (july 1977), containing his lengthy *Axis*, **Tears** (may 1983), **Tango Palace** (may 1983).
Continuing to pursue his vision of baroque chamber jazz music, Bley formed a quartet with Swallow, Altschul and guitarist John Scofield for **Hot** (march 1985), one with Motian, guitarist Bill Frisell and saxophonist John Surman for **Fragments** (january 1986) and **The Paul Bley Quartet** (november 1987), the latter containing his 20-minute *Interplay*, and yet another one with Surman, Gary Peacock and drummer Tony Oxley for **In The Evenings Out There** (september 1991), and even reformed the trio with Gary Peacock and Paul Motian for **Not Two Not One** (january 1998). But mostly he continued to explore the piano on intimate recordings such as: **Blues For Red** (may 1989), **Changing Hands** (february 1991), **Synth Thesis** (september 1993), accompanying himself at the synthesizer, **Sweet Time** (1993), **Hands On** (march 1993), **Basics** (july 2000), **Nothing to Declare** (may 2003), that (abandoning his favorite "fragment" format) indulged in four lengthy improvisations, etc.
Paul Bley updated the language of Bill Evans to a new generation, even before that generation was born.

Tenor saxophonist Wayne Shorter had his breakthrough with Art Blakey's Jazz Messengers (1959-64), for which he composed *Chess Players* (march 1960) and *Lester Left Town* (november 1959) on **The Big Beat** (1960), *Children of the Night* (august 1961) on **Mosaic** (1961), *Reincarnation Blues* (november 1961) on **Buhaina's Delight** (1962) *This Is For Albert* and *Sweet 'N' Sour* on **Caravan**

(october 1962), *One by One* (june 1963), *Ping-Pong* (february 1961) and *On the Ginza* (june 1963) on **Ugetsu** (1963), *Free For All* (february 1964) on **Free For All**, *Mr Jin* (april 1964) on **Indestructible**. His tenor saxophone had a unique sound and his compositions had a unique atmosphere. Shorter's compositions for his own albums were, instead, rudimentary at best. Influenced by the hard bop played by Blakey, Shorter's first solo sessions, **Blues A la Carte** (november 1959), also known as **Introducing**, were recorded by a quintet with Lee Morgan on trumpet, Wynton Kelly on piano, Paul Chambers on bass and Jimmy Cobb on drums, while **Second Genesis** (october 1960) featured pianist Cedar Walton, bassist Bob Cranshaw and Blakey in person, and **Wayning Moments** (november 1961) a quintet with Freddie Hubbard on trumpet. He also worked for Freddie Hubbard (1962-63) and Lee Morgan (1964-67). He was hired by Miles Davis (1964-70) to work on Davis' new ideas, that eventually led to the invention of fusion jazz. Shorter was crucial for Davis' project. Not only did his saxophone sculpt much of the sound, but his compositions were among the most relevant of this phase of Davis' career: *E.S.P.* and *Iris* on **E.S.P.** (1965), *Orbits*, *Footprints* and *Dolores* on **Miles Smiles** (1966), *Prince of Darkness*, *Masqualero* and *Limbo* on **Sorcerer** (1967), *Nefertiti* and *Fall* on **Nefertiti** (1967), *Paraphernalia* on **Miles in the Sky** (1968), *Sanctuary* on **Bitches Brew** (1969), *Great Expectations* on **Big Fun** (1970). These compositions were so important, and so carefully crafted by the saxophonist, that Shorter may have been the real brain of much of Davis' music, Davis being merely the trumpet player. Shorter was a subtle and sophisticated composer who violated the rules of jazz music by indulging in ethereal melodies, slow tempos and sustained tones.
In parallel, Shorter's own albums coined an oneiric, pensive and personal sound that borrowed from John Coltrane (mainly), Art Blakey and Miles Davis while pointing towards the jazz-rock revolution. Lee Morgan on trumpet, McCoy Tyner on piano, Reggie Workman on bass and Elvin Jones on drums (Jones and Tyner being both members of the Coltrane quartet) helped him sculpt the lyrical, waltzing *Night Dreamer*, the romantic ballad *Virgo*, and the sophisticated harmonies of *Black Nile* and *Armageddon* on **Night Dreamer** (april 1964). The playing was more cohesive (especially in *JuJu*) and the compositions were more expressive (particularly *Yes or No*) on **Juju** (august 1964), recorded with the same rhythm section but without Morgan, but Shorter boldly abandoned the Coltrane paradigm on **Speak No Evil** (december 1964). Freddie Hubbard on horns, Herbie Hancock on piano, Ron Carter on bass and Jones on drums helped him find an unlikely balance of hard bop, modal jazz and free jazz while increasing the melodic intensity. The playing was not revolutionary at all, but *Witch Hunt* and *Speak No Evil* showed his compositional genius, and the album closing with two tender ballads, *Infant Eyes* (perhaps the most memorable of his career) and *Wild Flower*, that heralded a new era of emotions in jazz music.
The Soothsayer (march 1965) marked the return of Reggie Workman on bass, the replacement of Jones with Tony Williams on drums, and the addition of alto saxophonist James Spulding next to Hubbard and Shorter. Now that Jones was gone, Tyner became more than ever the anchor of Shorter's sound. The three

horns and the piano offered the composer a chance to experiment more complex structures (*The Soothsayer*, *Lost*, *The Big Push*).

After the subdued **Et Cetera** (june 1965), released only in 1980 and also known as **The Collector**, a quartet session with Hancock, Chambers and bassist Cecil McBee that featured the eleven-minute *Indian Song*, Shorter added trombonist Grachan Moncur to the horn section of himself, Hubbard and Spaulding and to the rhythm section of Hancock, Carter and Chambers for **The All Seeing Eye** (october 1965). The lush instrumental textures obscured Shorter's melodic flair and brought out the most brooding and psychological elements of his music, especially in *The All Seeing Eye*, *Genesis* and *Mephistopheles*. This album, de facto, ended Shorter's long flirtation with Coltrane's music.

After that experimental tour de force, Shorters returned to a humbler format (a quartet with Hancock, Workman and Chambers) and a simpler form of music (*Footprints*, *Adam's Apple*, *Chief Crazy Horse*) for **Adams' Apple** (february 1966). The sextet of **Schizophrenia** (march 1967), featuring Spaulding, trombonist Curtis Fuller and the rhythm section of Hancock, Carter and Chambers, continued to plow the border between bop tradition and free-jazz avantgarde in pieces such as *Tom Thumb*. The sophistication of the arrangements was rapidly becoming the main raison d'etre of Shorters' music. All in all, his compositional skills were still better served in Davis' recordings than in Shorters' own recordings. He seemed to acknowledge that much by veering sharply towards Davis' fusion sound on **Super Nova** (august 1969), employing stars of the genre such as electric guitarists John McLaughlin and Sonny Sharrock, Chick Corea, bassist Miroslav Vitous, drummer Jack DeJohnette, etc. and setting new standards of call-and-response between solo and accompaniment in the rubato *Capricorn*. **Moto Grosso Feio** (april 1970), only released in 1974, added Dave Holland to McLaughlin, Vitous, Carter and Corea and at least tried to improve on the stereotype with the lengthy *Moto Grosso Feio* and *Iska*, but **Odyssey of Iskra** (august 1970), performed by an octet with vibraphone, guitar, two basses, three percussionists, proved that Shorter was after mere living-room entertainment.

In 1970 Shorter and Joe Zawinul left Davis to form Weather Report. Shorter still recorded an album of mediocre Latin-jazz ballads, **Native Dancer** (september 1974), with Brazilian vocalist Milton Nascimento and percussionist Airto Moreira, and collaborated with singer-songwriter Joni Mitchell (1977-2002), but his creative energy was clearly reserved for the band.

Ohio-born blind saxophonist and flutist Roland Kirk, who moved to Chicago in 1960, debuted with **Triple Threat** (november 1956), a showcase for his virtuoso technique. He produced formerly unheard sounds by playing more than one instrument at once (a veritable one-man horn section), the instruments being modified saxophones. On stage he was the ultimate eccentric, but the gimmick was rapidly exhausted in the studio after a collaboration with saxophonist and trumpeter Ira Sullivan, **Introducing Roland Kirk** (june 1960), containing *The Call*, and a collaboration with organist Jack McDuff, **Kirk's Work** (july 1961), with *Funk Underneath*. Kirk focused on soul-influenced material that did not quite provide the ideal launching pad for his polyphonic saxophone technique.

Kirk began expanding in earnest the technique of the flute, particularly by incorporating circular breathing, on **I Talk With the Spirits** (september 1964), containing his signature tune *Serenade to a Cuckoo*.
The volcanic **Rip Rig & Panic** (january 1965), backed by pianist Jaki Byard, bassist Richard Davis and drummer Elvin Jones, ran the gamut from traditional jazz to avantgarde music, with dramatic peaks in *Rip Rig & Panic* and in the cacophonous, psychedelic *Slippery, Hippery, and Flippery*. The groove era opened with **Slightly Latin** (november 1965), containing *Ebrauqs*, **Now Please Don't You Cry Beautiful Edith** (may 1967), with the chaotic ballad *Now Please Don't You Cry Beautiful Edith*, the intimate **The Inflated Tear** (november 1967), and **Volunteered Slavery** (july 1969).
However, Kirk's unorthodox art was best represented by the suites *Expansions* for big band and string section, off **Left And Right** (june 1968), and *The Seeker* for chamber ensemble, off **Rahsaan Rahsaan** (may 1970). He played (almost) all the instruments on the brief sketches of **Natural Black Inventions - Root Strata** (february 1971). The best display of his self-indulgent exhibitions was perhaps the live double-LP **Bright Moments** (june 1973), with lengthy versions of *Pedal Up* and *Bright Moments*.
The soul influence returned to dominate on **Blacknuss** (september 1971), with *Blacknuss*, and especially on the three-sided LP **The Case of the 3 Sided Dream in Audio Color** (may 1975), with *Echoes of Primitive Ohio and Chili Dogs* and *Portrait of Those Beautiful Ladies*. These albums were only marred by inferior material (frequently borrowed from the soul and pop repertory).
On the other hand, Kirk transcended all styles in his most gargantuan and improbable experiments, such as the eclectic and fiery *Saxophone Concerto*, off **Prepare Thyself To Deal With A Miracle** (january 1973), and the nine-minute *Theme for the Eulipions* on **The Return of the 5000 Lb Man** (1975).

Boston's pianist Jaki Byard, who moved to New York in 1959, was relatively old when he was finally recruited by Eric Dolphy for **Outward Bound** (april 1960), **Here and There** (april 1960) and **Far Cry** (1960), the latter containing Byard's eight-minute *Mrs Parker of K.C.*, and by Charles Mingus for **The Black Saint And The Sinner Lady** (1963). The solo-piano album **Blues For Smoke** (1958) had already proven that Byard was rather unique in the way he mastered the whole spectrum of jazz piano, from stride to swing to bebop to free. The trio with bassist Ron Carter and drummer Roy Haynes of **Here's Jaki** (march 1961) allowed him even more flexibility The trio remained his favorite format, particularly for original compositions such as *Here to Hear* on **Hi-Fly** (january 1962) and the eleven-minute *Freedom Together* on **Freedom Together** (january 1966), on which he also played celeste, vibraphone, tenor sax and drums, peaking with **Sunshine Of My Soul** (october 1967), that featured Elvin Jones on drums, a set of longer pieces each of which sounds like the effortless imitation of a different style (*Sunshine, Chandra,* and especially the free-form *Trendsition Zildjian*).

Texas' pianist Cedar Walton who moved to New York in 1955 and played with Art Blakey's Jazz Messengers (1961-64), was emblematic of the musicians of the

1960s who continued to express themselves in the hard-bop vernacular ignoring most of the innovations of free jazz and fusion jazz. Walton was capable of charming compositions and playing in an unassuming melodic style, as proven on his debut album, **Cedar** (july 1967).

White guitar virtuoso Joe Pass recorded his first album, **Sound Of Synanon** (july 1962), while he was living in a drug rehabilitation center, using an electric guitar designed for rockers. Influenced by both Charlie Christian and by Django Reinhardt, he proceeded to revisit the traditions of swing and bebop music, but attained true guitar nirvana with the electric guitar solos of **Virtuoso** (august 1973), although he wasted his immense talent in covers of other people's songs. Only **Virtuoso 3** (june 1977) fully displayed his potential on a set of self-composed guitar studies.

The format of the piano-led trio experimented by Bill Evans was further explored by San Francisco-based white pianist Denny Zeitlin on albums such as **Cathexis** (february 1964), that set the theme for his research, **Carnival** (october 1964), **Zeitgeist** (march 1967), that includes *Mirage*. He was not afraid to tamper with dissonance and electronics, for example in the 14-minute *El Fuego de las Montanas*, off **Expansion** (1973), and in the four-movement suite *Syzygy*, off **Syzygy** (1977). A psychiatrist by profession, Zeitlin was pioneering a fusion of jazz, rock, classical and electronic music.

Influenced by contemporary hard-bop and soul-jazz, but already sensitive to the appeal of Miles Davis' sound, the quartet formed by tenor saxophonist Charles Lloyd with pianist Keith Jarrett, bassist Cecil McBee and drummer Jack DeJohnette penned **Dream Weaver** (march 1966), that contained the suites *Autumn Sequence* and *Dream Weaver*, and **Forest Flower** (september 1966), that contained the suite *Forest Flower*, two albums that achieved crossover success, a premonition of the jazz-rock era.

Philadelphia's white guitarist Pat Martino began his career in an uneventful while impeccable hard-bop manner on **El Hombre** (may 1967) and **Strings** (october 1967), but the four-movement Indo-Islamic suite **Baiyina** (june 1968) already displayed a passion for exotic arrangements and fusion overtones. **Desperado** (march 1970) and subsequent albums added rock, funk and soul to the mixture.

Pittsburgh's blind white alto saxophonist Eric Kloss debuted as a leader at the age of 16 in an old-fashioned hard-bop vein. He began to composed his material on albums such as **Sky Shadows** (august 1968), featuring a quintet with guitarist Pat Martino, pianist Jaki Byard, bassist Bob Cranshaw and drummer Jack DeJohnette, and **In the Land of the Giants** (january 1969), replacing the guitar with a tenor saxophone, and he attained an original pop and funk fusion when he coopted Miles Davis' rhythm section of keyboardist Chick Corea, bassist Dave Holland, and DeJohnette for **To Hear Is To See** (july 1969). More adventurous music surfaced in the 18-minute suite *One Two Free*, off **One Two Free** (august 1972), for saxophone, guitar (Pat Martino), keyboardist, bass (Dave Holland) and drums, and in the lengthy jams of **Essence** (december 1974).

Japanese pianist Toshiko Akiyoshi came to prominence with the soulful bebop fantasias of **The Toshiko Trio** (1955), but, having relocated to New York, her talent as an arranger soon led her to form an orchestra, that debuted on **Toshiko Mariano & Her Big Band** (april 1965). That idea was perfected on the albums recorded by the orchestra she formed in Los Angeles with her husband, classically trained tenor saxophonist and flutist Lew Tabackin, and that mainly relied on her compositions, for example **Kogun** (april 1974) and **Long Yellow Road** (march 1975). Her artistic zenith was represented by the 23-minute *Henpecked Old Man* on **Road Time** (february 1976) and the 21-minute *Minamata* on **Insights** (june 1976). The band continued to record alluring post-bop albums such as **March of the Tadpoles** (january 1977), **Salted Ginko Nuts** (november 1978), **Sumi-E** (february 1979). A new orchestra formed in New York premiered other ambitious Akiyoshi compositions such as: *Blues Break* on **Ten Gallon Shuffle** (may 1984), *Liberty Suite* on **Wishing Peace** (july 1986), *Desert Lady* on **Desert Lady Fantasy** (december 1993).

World-bop

The late 1950s and early 1960s were also the years when jazz culture began to embrace world-music as a natural extension of a music that was African (and therefore "world") in nature. This trend was initially limited to the dance rhythms of Latin America, but the 1960s brought an increasing awareness of the Far East and, at last, of Africa itself, the continent that jazz had largely forgotten in its quest for both commercial and artistic success.

Jewish bebop flutist Herbie "Mann" Solomon (1930) debuted with the 10" EP **Plays** (december 1954) in a straightforward bebop recordings, and became a prolific interpreter of the genre. But exotic themes popped up even on his earliest recordings, for example the lengthy *Tel Aviv* on **Flute Souffle** (march 1957) and the **African Suite** (1959). Eventually, Mann became one of the drivers of the Afro-Cuban wave via the live **Flautista** (june 1959), featuring vibraphone, bass and Latin percussion (marimba, bongos, congas), with the colorful *The Amazon River* and the catchy *Cuban Potato Chip*, via **Flute, Brass, Vibes and Percussion** (june 1960), featuring four trumpets, three percussionists and the eponymous jazz quartet, via **The Common Ground** (august 1960) for his Afro-Jazz Sextet and four trumpets (that mixed Middle-Eastern, African and Latin folk music with pop melody and bebop), and especially via **Brazil Blues** (1961) and **Do The Bossanova** (october 1962), recorded with Brazilian musicians. A serious attempt at blending Middle-Eastern and jazz music yielded **Impressions of the Middle East** (march 1966) and **The Wailing Dervishes** (september 1967).

Mann's ambitions extended to jazz-classical fusion: he composed a **Concerto Grosso in D Blues** (november 1968) for jazz quintet and symphony orchestra that was a parallel tribute to the histories of both genres, running the gamut from romantic music to dissonant music, and from dixieland to free jazz.

When the times changed, Mann easily transitioned to the funky sound of **Memphis Underground** (july 1969), featuring vibraphonist Roy Ayers, guitarists Larry Coryell and Sonny Sharrock and a soul rhythm section, to the atmospheric, strings-enhanced fusion of **Stone Flute** (1970), with *Miss Free Spirit*, and to the lively funk and rock fusion of **Push Push** (july 1971). His stylistic odyssey perhaps culminated with **Reggae** (december 1973), recorded with Jamaican musicians and containing the 19-minute romp *My Girl*. No other jazz musician had flirted so consistently with exotic music.

Latin themes had always been popular with jazz musicians. The precedents had been numerous and distinguished, beginning with Dizzy Gillespie's collaboration with Cuban conga player Chano Pozo (1947), Charlie Parker recorded Chico O'Farrel's 17-minute *Afro-Cuban Jazz Suite* (1950) with Machito's orchestra. George Shearing began his long series of Latin albums with **Latin Satin** (1953), featuring Latin musicians, vibraphonist Cal Tjader and harmonica player Toots Thielemans. Erroll Garner began his string of mambo albums with **Mambo Mores Garner** (1954). Jazz pianist Billy Taylor introduced Cuban conguero Candido Camero on **With Candido** (1954) and merged chamber jazz and Cuban music on **Four Flutes** (1959), scored for four flutes, piano, jazz rhythm section and Chino Pozo's congas. Kenny Burrell's **Introducing Kenny Burrell** (1956) featured a conga player. Art Blakey's Jazz Messengers recorded **Cu-bop** (may 1957), a Latin album featuring a conga player. Art Farmer recorded Chico O'Farrill's 16-minute *Aztec Suite* (1959). Stan Getz and Paul Winter turned bossanova into a national fad with, respectively, **Jazz Samba** (1962) and **Jazz Meets Bossanova** (1962). Cuban percussionist Ramon "Mongo" Santamaria became famous with Herbie Hancock's *Watermelon Man* (1963). But it was Herbie Mann who popularized Latin-jazz as more than just a novelty.

Los Angeles' vibraphonist <u>Roy Ayers</u> emerged from the hard-bop scene to adopt the eclectic and populist stance of his master Herbie Mann (1966-70). He had started out in the hard-bop dialect of the early 1960s on **West Coast Vibes** (july 1963), in a quintet with saxophone and piano, and **Virgo Vibes** (march 1967), featuring a stellar line-up with trumpeter Charles Tolliver, tenor saxophonist Joe Henderson, bassist Reggie Workman and pianist Herbie Hancock. He switched to soul-funk-jazz fusion on the spiritual concept **He's Coming** (1971), featuring saxophonist Sonny Fortune, bassist John Williams, keyboardist Harry Whitaker and drummer Billy Cobham. Influenced by the electric jazz-funk sound of Miles Davis and Herbie Hancock, in 1970 Ayers formed his own group, Ubiquity, that proceeded to explore that cosmic/mystic kind of fusion on **Ubiquity** (1971), although his musical vision was better represented by the haunting movie soundtrack **Coffy** (april 1973). He was clearly transitioning towards slick disco and soul music, as proven by the production tour de force of **Mystic Voyage** (1975). Ayers electrified the vibraphone, complemented it with electric keyboards and employed a laid-back syncopated rhythm. Basically, Ayers predated acid-jazz by more than a decade with pieces such as *Old One Two Move To Groove* (1975), *Everybody Loves the Sunshine* (1976), *Daylight* (1977).

San Francisco-based white vibraphonist <u>Cal Tjader</u>, the former drummer in Dave Brubeck's trio (1949-51) and vibraphonist in George Shearing's quintet (1953-54), pioneered the mambo-jazz fusion on the 10" EP **Trio** (1953). His most original album, **Latin Concert** (1958), featured Willie Bobo on timbales and Mongo Santamaria on congas. A quartet led by Tjader (with trumpet and rhythm section) also performed Lalo Schifrin's Asian suite **Several Shades of Jade** (april 1963), one of exotica's most "ambient" results.

Detroit-raised flutist, oboe player and tenor saxophonist Bill "Yusef Lateef" Huddleston (1920), who had briefly played with Dizzy Gillespie (1949-50), converted to Islam in the 1950s (as was fashionable in those days) and moved to New York in 1959 to study flute. By then he had already become a sensation in Detroit in a sextet with trombonist Curtis Fuller (plus piano, bass, drums and percussion), and a pioneer of world-music thanks to his passion for Middle-Eastern and Indian music. Lateef played tenor, flute, argol (an India double reed wind instrument) and "scraper" on **Stable Mates** (april 1957), containing his ballad *Ameena*, and established himself as a sophisticated composer on the twin release **Jazz Mood** (april 1957), playing flute in the eight-minute introduction, *Metaphor*, and penning the extended blues meditations *Yusef's Mood* and *Blues in Space* as well as the ten-minute exotic-sounding *Morning*. Lateef's lyrical post-bop melodies were beginning to migrate into a dimension beyond jazz music.
He was less creative in the quintet with Wilbur Harden on flugelhorn and Hugh Lawson on piano that recorded **Jazz and the Sounds of Nature** (october 1957), containing the six-minute *Seulb*, and its twin release **Prayer to the East** (october 1957), containing the 13-minute *Endura* (but most pieces were either covers or Harden compositions), and then (one day later) **The Sounds of Yusef** (october 1957) and its twin release **Other Sounds** (october 1957), containing the nine-minute *Minor Mood*. The instrumentation included turkish finger cymbals, rabat/rebob (a one stringed Arabic violin) and Chinese gong.
An euphonium-piano quintet recorded **The Dreamer** (june 1959), with *Moon Tree* and *Valse Bouk*, and its twin album **Fabric of Jazz** (june 1959), with *Arjuna*, *The Dreamer* and *Oboe Blues*. Lateef also played the oboe with the trumpet-piano quintet of **Cry Tender** (october 1959). But he was distracted by several conventional hard-bop albums.
After he moved to New York, Lateef drifted away from hard-bop and refined an exotic and sometimes abstract blues music that was only his own. The ensemble music of **The Centaur and the Phoenix** (june 1961) for a nonet, such as *Iqbal*, led to **Eastern Sounds** (september 1961), on which Lateef played a variety of reed instruments backed by a traditional rhythm section of piano, bass and tabla-like percussion, with pieces such as *Plum Blossom* (for a Chinese clay flute), *Snafu* (for tenor sax), *Blues For The Orient* (for oboe).
If he never quite regained the compositional power of **Jazz Mood**, and frequently stumbled into the predictable jazz of releases such as **Into Something** (december 1961) and **The Three Faces** (january 1962), Lateef had found a new mission in the contemplative world-music of **Jazz Round The World** (december 1963), a parade of ten brief ethnic pieces. The milestones of this journey were *Medula Sonata*, off **Psychicemotus** (june 1964), an album that emphasized the sound of the bamboo flute, and *1984*, off the piano-based quartet session **1984** (february 1965).

White clarinetist Tony Scott was a late comer to the scene of bebop and cool jazz, playing on **Sarah Vaughan in Hi-Fi** (may 1950) with the gotha of bebop (trumpeter Miles Davis, trombonist Benny Green, guitarist Freddie Green), and forming a Septet that recorded **Scott's Fling** (january 1955) with trombonist Kai Winding and bassist Milt Hinton. He experimented with several formats that shunned the ruling styles. An Orchestra consisting of members of Count Basie's and Duke Ellington's orchestras plus a rhythm section with pianist Bill Evans, Hinton and Green, recorded **The Touch** (july 1956), containing *Vanilla Frosting On A Beef Pie*, and **The Complete** (february 1957), containing *I'll Remember April*. Three permutations of trumpeter Clark Terry, baritonist Sahib Shihab, trombonist Jimmy Knepper, pianist Bill Evans, bassist Henry Grimes, drummer Paul Motian recorded the twin albums **My Kind of Jazz** (november 1957), **The Modern Art of Jazz** (november 1957), containing *Blues For 3 Horns*, and **Free Blown Jazz** (november 1957), with *Portrait Of Ravi*. Scott played clarinet, sax, piano, mandolin on **Sung Heroes** (october 1959), also known as **Dedications**, whose pieces were dedicated to dead musicians, the recording that, de facto, marked the debut of the Bill Evans Trio with Paul Motian and Scott LaFaro.

In 1960 Scott left the USA and went to explore the Far East. The result was **Music For Zen Meditation** (february 1964), a collaboration with koto player Shinichi Yuize and shakuhachi flute player Hozan Yamamoto (notably the trio *The Murmuring Sound of the Mountain Stream*, the koto-clarinet duets *After the Snow, the Fragrance, Prajna-Paramita-Hridaya Sutra* and *Sanzen*), that predated both new-age music, world-music and ambient music. Having contributed to create the hare krishna zeitgeist of the hippy era, Scott followed that exploit with **Homage to Lord Krishna** (november 1967) and especially **Music for Yoga Meditation and Other Joys** (february 1968), a duet with sitar player Collin Walcott. Journeys to Africa yielded the solo percussion album **Music for Voodoo Meditation** (1971), on which Scott played only African percussions, and **African Bird - Come Back Mother Africa**, with the 16-minute *African Bird Suite* (february 1981) that married Charlie Parker and African percussion.

One of the founding fathers of world-music, Pennsylvania-born white alto-saxophonist Paul Winter formed his first sextet (alto sax, baritone saxophone, trumpet, piano, bass and drums) while he was studying in Chicago to play an aggressive (and self-penned) form of bebop, as documented on **Paul Winter Sextet** (december 1961). Instead, they were dispatched to Latin America and, when they returned, they helped popularize the Brazilian sound with **Jazz Meets Bossanova** (1962) and two albums recorded in Brazil with Brazilian musicians. That Winter's interest extended beyond Brazil was proven by **Jazz Meets The Folk Song** (1964), that integrated the spirit of folksinger Pete Seeger and Woody Guthrie into the context of jazz. And that Winter's interest extended beyond popular music was proven by the Consort, the ensemble that he formed to play a hybrid of jazz, folk and classical music. **The Winter Consort** (1968) and **Something In The Wind** (1970) mixed chamber instruments such as the English horn and the cello with the saxophone's jazzy lead and African and/or Latin-American percussion, and the repertory included folk dances and classical pieces.

Last but not least, the Consort adhered to the hippies' utopian mood. **Road** (june 1970) represented the Consort at its artistic peak: cellist David Darling, classical guitarist Ralph Towner, oboe and English horn player Paul McCandless, contrabassist Glen Moore and percussionist Collin Walcott (tablas, congas). The repertory included Towner's *Icarus* and Darling's *Requiem*. Towner was the main composer of **Icarus** (1971), although the longer piece was Winter's joyful anthem *Whole Earth Chant*. The instrumentation was expanded, with McCandless also on sarrusophone, Towner also on piano and organ, Walcott on sitar and all sorts of ethnic percussion. After Towner, McCandless, Moore and Walcott left to form Oregon, Winter convened a group of friends (including Darling, McCandless, drummer Steve Gadd, guitarist Oscar Castro-Neves) at a farm and recorded **Common Ground** (1978) amalgamating the voices of the animals with the jazz improvisation. The most influential experiment were *Ocean Dream*, featuring a humpback whale on lead vocals, three human vocalists and a Latin-jazz sextet, and *Wolf Eyes* for wolf, two human vocalists and neoclassical sextet. The mesmerizing sound pattern of whales had been popularized by **Songs of the Humpback Whale** (1970), produced by the zoologist Roger Payne, but Winter turned it into an instrument of a broader ensemble. The "new age" of the 1980s recognized Winter as its spokesman, and his fusion of jazz improvisation, chamber music, world-music and natural sounds as its manifesto. The ecological and spiritual spirit of Winter's program permeated **Callings** (1980), a jam session between sea mammals (recorded all over the world) and jazz musicians playing soprano saxophone (Winter), cello (Eugene Friesen), oboe and English horn (Nancy Rumbel), pipe organ and piano and harpsichord (Paul Halley), guitar (Jim Scott) and percussion (Ted Moore), including the ten-minute *Blues Cathedral*. Resonating with the new-age spirit of the era, Winter's albums led to the **Missa Gaia** (1982), the first ever mass to feature a wolf and a whale in the choir, a work drenched in hippy, pan-ethnic and gospel spirituality (the eleven-minute *Return To Gaia*), and to the **Concert For The Earth** (june 1984).
In the meantime, the impressionist in Winter surfaced on **Sunsinger** (1983), a trio with Halley and percussionist Glen Velez, and on **Canyon** (1985), recorded in the Grand Canyon and in a cathedral. Their delicate, evanescent vignettes blended folk melody, neoclassical composure and Eastern meditation.
Whales Alive (january 1987) used the droning melodies of whales to score the chamber music for Winter and Halley. **Prayer For The Wild Things** (1994), scored for 27 animal voices, seven instruments evoking animal voices, soprano saxophone, Native American choir and three percussionists, was his most ambitious collage ever.

White reed player Paul Horn, who cut his teeth with Chico Hamilton Quintet (1956-58) in Los Angeles, went through three stages of development. At first, on **House of Horn** (1957), he was a sophisticated improviser alternating on flute, clarinet and alto saxophone in different configurations of chamber jazz. Later he formed a quintet with vibraphone and piano that mimicked Miles Davis' quintet, playing an original hybrid of cool jazz, hard bop and third stream on **Something Blue** (march 1960). His quintet recorded one of the first jazz masses, **Jazz Suite** on the **Mass Texts** (november 1964) composed by Lalo Schifrin in eight movements for orchestra, choir and jazz quintet. After accompanying Ravi Shankar (1965) and after a sojourn in India (1966), Horn changed personality and style. Instead of the cool-jazz altoist, **In India** (may 1967), a set of classical ragas performed with students of Shankar on vina, sitar, tabla and tambura, and **In Kashmir** (1967), another collaboration with Indian musicians, revealed a flute mannerist imbued with Eastern spirituality and bent on replicating Indian drones. That mood peaked with his most influential invention, the solo improvisations/meditations "inside" spectacular buildings, in which the acoustics of the place becomes part of the music. The first one was **Inside The Taj Mahal** (april 1968), and the best one was probably **Inside The Great Pyramid** (may 1977). His vocabulary of fragile mummy-like whispers that exuded millenary silence and zen ecstasy was instrumental in creating the ultimate new-age ambience. Horn also delved into the tribal, shamanic, oneiric music of **Nexus** (1975) with the Nexus percussion ensemble, collaborated with a Chinese multi-instrumentalist for **China** (1982), returned to the solo flute concept for **Inside The Cathedral** (1983), and explored both the chamber and the electronic realms on **Traveler** (1987).

After cutting the first jazz record of the African continent, **Verse I** (september 1959), with Hugh Masekela's sextet, the Jazz Epistles, in 1962 Southafrican pianist Adolph "Dollar" Brand relocated to Europe and then to New York. He debuted in the vein of Thelonious Monk, who was hardly avantgarde at that point, with **Duke Ellington Presents the Dollar Band Trio** (february 1963), containing *Ubu Suku* and *The Stride*, followed by **Round Midnight At The Montmartre** (june 1965), also in a trio, that contained *The Dream* (both also contained Monk covers). Brand's musical ambitions were better represented by the five-part orchestral suite *Anatomy of a South African Village* (first recorded for trio in january 1965), the manifesto of his fusion of African rhythms, bebop piano and European classical music, and by collections of solo piano vignettes, permeated with a solemn and spiritual sense of nostalgia and often marked by disorienting dissonance: not so much the mediocre **Reflections** (march 1965), aka **This Is Dollar Brand**, as the brilliant **African Piano** (october 1969), that still contained extended pieces such as *Bra Joe from Kilimanjaro* and *The Moon*, and **African Sketchbook** (may 1969), a sequence of brief pieces (mostly under two minutes), the longest being *African Sun* and *Tokai*. These impressionistic miniatures, organized in a stream of consciousness, struck a balance between post-bop techniques, romantic melody and Islamic ecstasy. Despite coming from a different continent, a different race and a different musical genre, Brand's piano music was not too dissimilar from Oliver Messaien's. In 1968 Brand had converted to Islam and changed name (as was fashionable at the time) to Abdullah Ibrahim.

The early 1970s were the age of Brand's majestic solo albums. **Ancient Africa** (june 1972), one long live medley of Brand compositions, was only the appetizer. One session produced material for two albums: **African Portraits** (february 1973) and **Sangoma** (february 1973). The latter, his masterpiece, contained the

three-part suite *The Alone And The Wild Rose*, the six-part suite *Fats Duke And the Monk* and the side-long three-part suite *Ancient Africa*. Besides the much inferior **Memories** (1973) and **Ode To Duke Ellington** (december 1973), the other notably solo album of the era was **African Breeze** (1974).
That magic season was sealed by Brand's masterpiece for large ensemble, **African Space Program** (november 1973), that contained two suites, the 19-minute *Tintiyana* and the 23-minute *Jabulani*, for a twelve-piece unit (piano, three trumpeters, four saxophonists including Hamiet Bluiett, flutist Sonny Fortune, trombone, bass and drums) in the vein of Charles Mingus. Also notable were the Southafrican quintet session with alto saxophonist Robbie Jansen and legendary tenor Basil Coetzee, **Mannenberg It's Where It's Happening** (1974), aka **Capetown Fringe**, that included his *Cape Town Fringe* and *The Pilgrim*: **Underground in Africa** (1974), with three wild horns undermining Brand's bluesy piano during the 23-minute *Kalahari*; **Soweto** (june 1975), aka **Africa Herbs**, that included *Soweto Is Where It's At*, *African Herbs* and *Sathima*, three extended compositions for larger combos; **Blues For A Hip King** (november 1975), for a septet of piano, two saxophones, trumpet, trombone, bass and drums; **The Children Of Africa** (january 1976), with Cecil McBee on bass and Roy Brooks on drums, that contained *Ishmael* and *Yukio-Khalifa*; the saxophone quartet **Black Lightning** (august 1976), with the side-long *Black Lightning*; and **The Journey** (september 1977), for a nonet featuring Bluiett, Dyani and Don Cherry. There was little in these romantic fantasies that could be called "avantgarde".
Each subsequent solo piano album was a tender tribute to his homeland: **Anthem For The New Nations** (1978), **Matsidiso** (1980), **South Africa Sunshine** (1980), **Autobiography** (june 1978) and especially **African Dawn** (june 1982).
A saxophone quartet penned the more pensive meditations of **Africa - Tears And Laughter** (march 1979), such as *Ishmael* and *Did You Hear That Sound*. Another simple but effective musical statement came with the eight vignettes of **African Marketplace** (december 1979) for a twelve-piece unit, and this time the nostalgic reminiscence of South Africa was almost folk music.
Opting for the septet, Brand formed Ekaya (in New York) with flutist Carlos Ward, tenor saxophonist Ricky Ford, baritone saxophonist Charles Davis, trombonist Dick Griffin, bassist David Williams and drummer Ben Riley. This line-up recorded some of the best albums of his later phase: **Ekaya** (1983), aka **The Mountain, Water From An Ancient Well** (october 1985), without Griffin, highlighted by the 12-minute *Water From An Ancient Well*, and **African River** (june 1989). A Southafrican septet (with two saxes, trumpet and guitar) recorded **Mantra Mode** (january 1991), with the nine-minute *Mantra Mode*. Solo albums of the last decades included **Desert Flowers** (december 1991) and **Knysna Blue** (october 1993), with the 16-minute *Knysna Blue*.
After the septet, Brand's favorite format was the trio: **Yarona** (january 1995), reinterpreting his classics for the 1000th time, **Cape Town Flowers** (august 1996), with the nine-minute *Joan Cape Town Flower*, **Cape Town Revisited**

(december 1997), with the suite *Cape Town to Congo Square*, and **African Magic** (july 2001).

His neoclassical Ellington-ian ambitions yielded **African Suite** (november 1997) for string orchestra and piano trio, **African Symphony** (january 1998) for an 80-piece symphony orchestra (both devoted to re-arrangements of old Brand compositions), and **Ekapa Lodumo** (june 2000) for jazz big band (mostly taken up by *Black And Brown Cherries* and *African Market*).

Another musician who explored the link between the jazz music of the USA and its ancestral black home of Africa was New York's pianist Randy Weston, who was influenced by both the swing melodies of Duke Ellington and Nat King Cole and by the challenging harmonies of bop pianists such as Thelonious Monk and Bud Powell. Weston was capable of simple but effective compositions: the nine-minute *Chessman's Delight* on **Jazz A la Bohemia** (october 1956), *Saucer Eyes* on **Piano A La Mode** (june 1957), *Little Niles, Pam's Waltz, Hi-Fly* on **Little Niles** (october 1958), a set of originals that inaugurated his collaboration with arranger Melba Liston. However, he found his mission in life with the four-movement suite **Uhuru Africa** (november 1960), particularly the three longer ones (*African Lady, Kucheza Blues, Bantu*), that were performed by an eccentric ensemble featuring jazz musicians such as tenorist Yusef Lateef, trumpeters Clark Terry and Freddie Hubbard, guitarist Kenny Burrell, bassist Ron Carter, drummer Max Roach, as well as African percussionist Babatunde Olatunji and two conga players. Weston's compositions began to reflect his experience in Africa. **African Cookbook** (october 1964), arranged by trumpeter Ray Copeland, contained the 12-minute *African Cookbook*, besides the catchy *Willie's Tune* and *Berkshire Blues*. Weston actually lived in Morocco from 1968 to 1973, when he penned the twelve-minute *Ganawa Blue Moses* and the twelve-minute *Marrakesh Blues* for **Tanjah Blue Moses** (april 1972), an album arranged by Don Sebesky and featuring trumpeter Freddie Hubbard and tenor-saxophonist Grover Washington, the eight-minute *Tanjah* for a big band on **Tanjah** (may 1973) and *Tangier Bay* on the solo-piano **Blues To Africa** (august 1974).

As his original vision was being embraced by more and more musicians of the younger generation, Weston got motivated to further expand it. The double-CD **Spirits Of Our Ancestors** (may 1991) was a satori of the Weston-Liston collaboration, notably the 16-minute *The Seventh Queen* and the 20-minute *African Sunrise*. He recorded with **The Splendid Master Gnawa Musicians of Morocco** (september 1992). And **Khepera** (february 1998) was a collaboration between his quintet (Talib Kibwe on alto sax and flute, trombone, bass, percussion) and percussionist Chief Bey, saxophonist Pharoah Sanders and pipa player Min Xiao Fen. It was one of Weston's most inspired fusions, particularly in the twelve-minute *The Shrine* and the ten-minute *Mystery Of Love*.

French-Algerian pianist Errol Parker, born Raph Schecroun, settled in New York in 1968 and turned to the drums, introducing percussive and rhythmic styles borrowed from world-music, particularly from Algerian hand drumming. The lengthy jams of **Doodles** (september 1979) and **Graffiti** (may 1980) displayed his innovative vision (polytonality, polyrhythms, overdubbing) at both the piano and the drums. After inaugurating his large horns-dominate group with **Tentet** (april 1982), Parker focused more and more on African drumming.

FREE JAZZ

    Free Jazz: the Apostles

    Free Jazz: the Disciples

    Free Jazz: Free Drumming

    Free Jazz: Free Vocals

    White Free Jazz

    Free Jazz: Borderline

FREE JAZZ: THE APOSTLES

The free-jazz revolution started at the turn of the decade with Ornette Coleman's **The Shape of Jazz to Come** (1959) and John Coltrane's **My Favorite Things** (1960). Coleman was a novice, Coltrane had played with Miles Davis. The zeitgeist had in fact been created by Davis, and the generation that debuted in that zeitgeist was eager to break with the rules of jazz harmony.

It took two giants (and probably more giants of composition than of improvisation) to kick off the revolution, but a "free" way of improvising was in the air after the experiments of cool jazz and modal jazz. George Russell and Miles Davis had shown that there were other ways for improvisers to improvise (and, although neglected at the time, for composers to compose). Several musicians were informally playing a much less organized music than the one that they were recording. Ornette Coleman was the first one who had the guts to record it and boast about it. It is not a coincidence that he grew in complete isolation from the main centers of jazz. Once the pioneers had dismantled the structure of jazz music, all the pieces came tumbling down. The most severe blow was received by the rhythm section. The traditional role of chordal instruments such as piano and guitar became useless. The bass and the drums were no longer time-keeping pulse-generating instruments but free to bedevil the harmony with melodic abstractions and polyrhythms. The idea was widely considered anathema by the generation that had been raised listening to Louis Armstrong.

It took a few years for free jazz to be accepted by the jazz establishment, that initially saw it as little more than an ephemeral novelty. In 1964 Bill Dixon organized the "October Revolution in Jazz", the first major festival for free jazz, held at the Cellar Cafe in Manhattan. That could be considered the year when free jazz became a major force in jazz.

However, it was in continental Europe that free jazz was first recognized as a peak (not a bottom) in the history of jazz music. Jazz clubs in the USA still catered to an audience that was mainly looking for entertainment. When the protagonists of free jazz landed in Europe, they found an audience that was used to the avantgarde concerts of modern classical composers and had no difficulty appreciating even the boldest forms of free jazz. John Coltrane was booed in Britain in 1961, but the tours of Cecil Taylor (1962), Archie Shepp (1963), Don Cherry (1964), Albert Ayler (1964) and finally Ornette Coleman (1965) in continental Europe did much more than inspire local scenes: they gave these USA musicians the confidence that they needed.

Free jazz erupted at about the same time that the civil-rights movement was staging its biggest demonstrations. Hard boppers such as Sonny Rollins had already introduced heavy doses of political awareness into jazz. Free jazz musicians rediscovered the West African roots of jazz, not in their sound (that was, ultimately, as European as possible) but in their identification with the sorrow and the rebellion of their ancestors.

On another level the movement for political liberation transformed into an unrelated movement for liberating music from its dogmas. It was as if the frustrated energy of the political liberation movement transferred into the unbound energy of the musical liberation movement.

In a way, free jazz was the equivalent of the Italian Renaissance for black musicians of the USA. Free jazz was about the Artist not the conventions. The Artist was entitled to ignore the conventions of tempo, tonality and consonance. The Artist was free to use multiple tempi, to have no tonal center and to use "notes" that did not belong to the classical scale. Each musician set up her or his own rules within anarchic framework, based not on the prevailing artistic dogma but on the emotions that she or he wanted to express.

Swing was a music of drums that kept the 4/4 tempo, melodies borrowed from catchy pop music, harmony that was tonal, improvisation that was restrained, meant for partying and performed by orchestras with the traditional division in three sections. Bebop was a music of percussion that contributed to the timbral sound, melodies that were convoluted, harmony that bordered on the atonal, meant for touching and performed by small combos. Free jazz was a music of polyrhythmic and improvising percussion, melodies that were warped and devastated, harmony that was frequently atonal, meant for thinking and performed by musicians pushing the limits of their instruments.

Tenor saxophonist John Coltrane honed his skills with Dizzy Gillespie (1949-51), with Miles Davis (1955-57) and briefly with Thelonious Monk (1957), refining a huge, vigorous, searing tone that competed with Sonny Rollins'. A drug addict, his career was far from linear. He debuted as a leader with **Coltrane** (1957), accompanied by trumpet, baritone saxophone, piano, bass, drums. **Blue Train** (september 1957), accompanied by trumpet (Lee Morgan), trombone (Chris Fuller), piano (Kenny Drew), bass and drums (Paul Chambers and Philly Joe Jones), was a confused collection, ranging from romantic ballads to hard bop. Four out of the five lengthy tracks were Coltrane originals: *Blue Train*, *Moment's Notice*, *Locomotion* and *Lazy Bird*. Equally uneven was **Soultrane** (february 1958), for a quartet with Chambers, Red Garland on piano and Art Taylor on drums, that had no Coltrane originals at all. That was to change soon, perhaps under the influence of the album that Coltrane was cutting with Miles Davis: **Kind of Blue**.

The original compositions of **Giant Steps** (may 1959) stemmed from the same melodic gift, but their varying intensity depicted the transition in progress: *Giant Steps* (famous for its impossible chord changes), *Syeeda's Song Flute*, *Mr P.C.*, *Spiral* and *Cousin Mary* featured a quartet with Chambers, Jones and pianist Tommy Flanagan, while the last track, *Naima* (recorded in december), featured pianist Wynton Kelly, Chambers and drummer Jimmy Cobb, i.e. the line-up of **Kind of Blue** minus Davis. And Coltrane's mission was in a sense a continuation of Davis' mission: create an art made of poignant solos; except that Coltrane's were the antithesis of Davis' solos, being a torrential, seismic, volcanic outpour of emotion ("sheets of sound"). Coltrane learned from Monk as much as from Davis, though. The subtlety of the pianist permeated his acrobatic multiphonics and his breakneck variations. **Coltrane Jazz** (october 1960) was mostly recorded by the same line-up of **Giant Steps**, but included several covers and was vastly inferior.

John Coltrane also collaborated with trumpeter Don Cherry on **The Avant-Garde** (1960), the result of a session with white bassist Charlie Haden and drummer Ed Blackwell. The title was prophetic, but the music was still acerbic, although more faithful to Davis' modal dogma.

By further increasing the role of the solo, and alternating between chord-based and mode-based improvisation, **My Favorite Things** (october 1960), recorded with a quartet that featured pianist McCoy Tyner and drummer Elvin Jones, inaugurated his brand of pseudo-free jazz (a 13-minute "modal" version of Rodgers' *My Favorite Things*, an eleven-minute version of Gershwin's *Summertime*, a nine-minute version of Gershwin's *But Not for Me*). **Africa Brass** (june 1961) was a detour of sort: three lengthy jams, arranged by Eric Dolphy, for a much larger ensemble (Coltrane's 16-minute *Africa*, a 10-minute version of the traditional *Greensleeves*, Coltrane's seven-minute *Blues Minor*).

Subsequent recordings continued the progression towards a more uncompromising rejection of structure. **Ole** (may 1961), recorded two days after **Africa Brass** by a subset of that ensemble (Freddie Hubbard on trumpet, Eric Dolphy on flute and alto, McCoy Tyner on piano, Art Davis and Reggie Workman on bass, Elvin Jones on drums), was a festival of creative solos, not just Coltrane's but everybody's. The 18-minute *Ole* and the eleven-minute *Dahomey Dance* were the tours de force, but Tyner's *Aisha* acted as the emotional center of mass.

Live at the Village Vanguard (november 1961), in quintet with Dolphy, Tyner, Workman and Jones, was the crowning achievement of this period, particularly the two colossal improvisations: the 16-minute *Chasin' the Trane* and the 15-minute *Spiritual*. That feat was repeated on the two centerpieces of **Impressions** (november 1961), *Impressions* and *India*, performed by Coltrane, Dolphy, Tyner, Workman, second bassist Jimmy Garrison and Jones.

After a terrible collection of **Ballads** (1962), and a transitional **Live At Birdland** (1963) with Tyner, Garrison and Jones (impeccable interpretations but no revolution), Coltrane's quartet (this time Tyner, Jones and Garrison) delivered the goods on the five Coltrane compositions of **Crescent** (june 1964), including *Crescent, Wise One, Lonnie's Lament* and *The Drum Thing*.

It was the prelude to Coltrane's masterpiece, and perhaps the masterpiece of the entire history of jazz music: **A Love Supreme** (december 1964). Coltrane, Tyner, Garrison and Jones concocted a multi-ethnic stew (African nationalism, Indian spirituality, western rationality) cast in the format of a four-movement mass.

Coltrane continued to push the boundaries with **Ascension** (june 1965), a free-form improvisation (although not as "free" as Ornette Coleman's **Free Jazz**) for a large ensemble that boasted three tenor saxophonists (Pharoah Sanders and Archie Shepp besides Coltrane), two alto saxophonists (Marion Brown, John

Tchicai), two trumpeters (Freddie Hubbard, Dewey Johnson), two bassists (Art Davis, Jimmy Garrison), McCoy Tyner on piano and Elvin Jones on drums. The horns improvise together in Albert Ayler's manner: an exaggerated, manic timbral orgy. This continuous 40-minute stream of consciousness was a cathartic work, a work of both freedom and subversion, affirming the artist's shamanic power while carrying out the exorcism from his sociopolitical frustration.
Sun Ship (august 1965), the last album with the classic quartet, emulated the religious ecstasy of **Ascension** with *Amen*, *Attaining* and *Ascent*.
Om (october 1965), was **Ascension**'s little brother, a 28-minute excursus featuring flute and bass clarinet plus the usual cohorts (Sanders, Tyner, Garrison, Jones).
The experiment continued, albeit with less tumult, on **Kulu Se Mama** (october 1965), particularly the side-long jam *Kulu Se Mama* with Sanders, a vocalist, a bass clarinetist and an enhanced rhythm section.
Compared with the cacophony of **Om** and **Kulu Se Mama**, the five **Meditations** (november 1965) with Sanders, Tyner, Garrison, Jones and second drummer Rashied Ali were more disciplined and somewhat rational (particularly *The Father and the Son and the Holy Ghost*, *Love* and *Consequences*).
Additional material of the time surfaced only years later: *Transition* and the 21-minute *Suite*, off **Transition** (june 1965), released in 1970, with Tyner, Garrison and Jones; *Peace On Earth* and *Leo*, off **Infinity** (february 1966), released in 1972, with Sanders, Rashied Ali on drums, Alice Coltrane on keyboards and posthumous string arrangements by Alice Coltrane; *Manifestation* and *Reverend King*, off **Cosmic Music** (february 1966), released in 1968, again with Sanders, keyboardist Alice Coltrane, Ali and Garrison; *To Be*, off **Expression** (march 1967), another mesmerizing dialogue between Coltrane and Sanders assisted by Alice Coltrane, Ali and Garrison.
Interstellar Space (february 1967), released in 1974, consists of four "cosmic" duets between John Coltrane and Rashied Ali (*Mars, Venus, Jupiter* and *Saturn*). To the last day, Coltrane's range of experiments was unbound. His career was an impressive catalog of liberating techniques. Coltrane introduced elements of Indian philosophy (if not music) into jazz, as well as a much stronger and deeper spiritual dimension.
Coltrane died in 1967, at the age of 40. Like Beethoven in classical music and Jimi Hendrix in rock music, he was so influential that very few musicians tried to imitate him.

Coltrane's intuition of a "free jazz" was further codified by a more rational brain, <u>Ornette Coleman</u>.
Texas-born alto saxophonist Ornette Coleman (1930) lived at least four lives. In the first one he was a humble rhythm'n'blues saxophonist who eventually relocated to Los Angeles. Nonetheless, he had already developed a provocative jazz aesthetic and he was able to demonstrate it on **Something Else** (march 1958), featuring a quintet with trumpeter Don Cherry, drummer Billy Higgins, bassist Don Payne and pianist Walter Norris. While drenched in the blues (the seven-minute *Jayne, The Disguise*), their music had no tonal center, sounding

literally "out of tune" (*Invisible*) or chaotic (*The Sphinx*). Coleman was grafting a free style of improvising (not based on chord sequences but on melodic fragments) onto the steady beat of bebop. Coleman toyed with melodic snippets (some of them very cliched) to the extent of approaching the psychoanalytical process of free association or the surrealist praxis of reconstructing the collective subconscious. They were further distorted by his chronic inability to follow the 12-bar or 16-bar standards of the jazz song. The sharpest observers, such as cool-jazz pioneer John Lewis, realized that Coleman was coining a new kind of music, more similar to James Joyce's "stream of consciousness" than to Louis Armstrong's entertainment via variations on a familiar melody.

After moving to the East Coast with Don Cherry, Coleman took New York's burgeoning avantgarde scene by storm with a completely revolutionary form of music, that might as well have been invented by a classical or rock musician, so little it shared with jazz (other than the general principle that improvisation matters). **Tomorrow Is The Question** (march 1959), for a quartet with Don Cherry, bassist Percy Heath and drummer Shelly Manne, contained pieces such as *Lorraine* (the archetype of his slow ballads), *Endless*, *Rejoicing*, *Giggin'* (with a celebrated Cherry solo) and the eight-minute *Turnabout* that were emblematic of Coleman's wizardry at revolutionizing the traditional roles of musical elements.

Coleman's compositions on **The Shape of Jazz to Come** (may 1959), for a quartet with white double bassist Charlie Haden, Don Cherry (on pocket trumpet) and Higgins, such as the funereal ballad *Lonely Woman*, *Congeniality* and the nine-minute *Peace* were even more notable for the way they messed with structure without losing an immediate appeal. In fact they sounded as catchy as anything done by pop singers. The idea was to make every member of the band a soloist equal to the others and to free the improvisation from musical constraints: basically, each individual was only bound to the mood of the other individuals, not to the technical aspects of the music that they were playing. Thus, for example, drums and bass hardly provided a true rhythm section. There was no piano to provide a chordal foundation. The music was more steeped in blues music than it appeared to be, but inevitably the method led to convoluted dynamics and countless detours that made it sound totally alien to the tradition of jazz (or any other form of music). By the same token, there was more tonal and chordal discipline than advertised, but Coleman's detours were so abrupt and profound that the detours (the process of instant composition) seemed to be the norm of his music. Even when they lasted only a few seconds, they could encompass dramatic explorations of microtones and pitches. Far from being mere theory, the whole irreverent apparatus of Coleman's techniques was about pathos. His own playing resembled more the contemporary style of theatrical recitation, with its sudden emotional outbursts, more than the traditional "narrative" styles of blues and jazz music. Coleman was a bold and extravagant (and prolific) composer but he actually composed for only one instrument, and in a rather instinctive way: inventing the polyphony was largely left to the other players. Coleman, Cherry, Higgins and Haden continued their mission on **Change of the**

Century (october 1960), via the relatively melodic *Ramblin'* and the chaotic *Free* and *Change of the Century*, and on **This Is Our Music** (august 1960), with Ed Blackwell replacing Higgins on drums, containing the pretty *Kaleidoscope* and *Folk Tale*, the violent *Blues Connotation* and the eerie seven-minute *Beauty Is a Rare Thing*.

Coleman's revolution climaxed with **Free Jazz** (december 1960), that contained a 37-minute collective improvisation (the longest jazz piece yet) for two reed/brass/bass/drums quartets: Coleman, Cherry, Haden and Higgins; bass clarinetist Eric Dolphy, trumpeter Freddie Hubbard, bassist Scott LaFaro and Blackwell. And the recording was no less important than the scoring: it took full advantage of stereophony, placing each quartet in one of the stereo channels. Again, his music was less revolutionary than it appeared to be: after all, Coleman's "free jazz" was largely composed, and the melodic elements (far from being inexistent) drew on bebop. It was, more appropriately, "compositional improvisation" (as Coleman himself defined it). But it was true that the roles of harmony and melody were somewhat confused by the loose organization of sound. That was going to remain a trademark of Coleman's music, one of the few constants of his career. Coleman's "free jazz" marked a return to the kind of collective improvisation of New Orleans' marching bands that marked the very beginning of jazz music, but now given a shot of dramatic tension. The improvisers were supposed to scream their angst and frustration with their instruments, the interplay simply magnifying the sense of tragedy, in a fashion similar to expressionist theater.

Ornette (january 1961), with LaFaro on bass, contained four jams, and three were colossal: *W.R.U.* (16:25), *C. & D.* (13:10), *R.P.D.D.* (9:39). **Ornette On Tenor** (march 1961) found him playing the tenor, with Jimmy Garrison on bass. However, despite two lengthy jams (*Cross Breeding* and *Mapa*), it was a bit more trivial, as if Coleman was retreating to safer terrain. So much so that **Jazz Abstractions** (december 1960) contained two structured pieces, including Gunther Schuller's *Abstraction* for alto saxophone, string quartet, two basses, guitar, percussion (a premonition of Coleman's "third stream" period), and *Variants on a Theme of Thelonious Monk* (*Criss Cross*). The second life of Coleman ended abruptly in 1962, as if he had exhausted the possibilities of jazz music.

After a three-year hiatus, Coleman, who now also played the trumpet and the violin, returned with **Chappaqua Suite** (june 1965) in four movements for large ensemble and jazz quartet (Coleman, Pharoah Sanders on tenor, David Izenzon on bass, Charles Moffett on drums), with a sax-bass-drums trio (bassist David Izenzon and drummer Charles Moffett), best documented on **Trio** (november 1965) and on the soundtrack of the film **Who's Crazy** (november 1965), and with a trio (with Haden and his own underage son Denardo Coleman) that recorded **The Empty Foxhole** (september 1966) and **Ornette at 12** (july 1968), with *Bells And Chimes*.

By now, free jazz was only a memory.

But this third life of Coleman was mainly devoted to extended compositions for large ensemble, that included: *Dedicated to Poets and Writers* (1962) for string quartet, *Forms and Sounds* for woodwind quintet (1965), and *Saints and Soldiers* (1967) and *Space Flight* (1967) for symphony orchestra, a phase that culminated in the suite **Skies of America** (may 1972), originally scored for jazz ensemble and orchestra but first recorded as a concerto for orchestra (and revised in 1983). This complex work finally found a way to link free jazz and John Cage's aleatory music. *The Artist in America* was emblematic of Coleman's "harmolodic" orchestration, "based on the four clefs bass, treble, tenor and alto... to modulate in range without changing keys" (violins in the treble, violas in the alto, cellos in the tenor, basses in the bass), but also pitting two percussionists against each other on the two stereo channels (an improvising tympanist against a time-keeping drummer) and leaving room for Coleman's soaring solo.

The transition to a new phase was signaled by recordings that did not quite fit with anything Coleman had done before. **New York Is Now** (1968) and **Love Call** (same session), with ex-Coltrane sidemen Jimmy Garrison and Elvin Jones as well as tenorist Dewey Redman, sounded like a melodic divertissment, entertaining traditionalists with the 14-minute *The Garden of Souls* (on **New York Is Now**) and the ten-minute *Airborne* (on **Love Call**).

Science Fiction (september 1971) introduced an explosive sound anchored to a volcanic rhythm section (Haden, Higgins and Blackwell) that seemed sworn to maximizing the mayhem. Coleman toyed with several different settings in *Street Woman* and *Civilization Day* (for the classic quartet of Haden, Higgins and Don Cherry), *Law Years* and *The Jungle Is a Skyscraper* (for a quintet with Haden, Blackwell, Redman and trumpeter Bobby Bradford), *Rock the Clock* (for septet, with Redman on an Arabic reed instrument and Haden on wah-wah bass, both Blackwell and Higgins on drums, and plus Indian vocalist Asha Puthli), and *Science Fiction* (with samples of crying baby and spoken-word recitation).

A brief reunion with Don Cherry yielded one of Coleman's most heartfelt compositions, *Broken Shadows* (march 1969).

During this period (1973) he also jammed with tribal musicians of Morocco on traditional instruments (plus Robert Palmer on clarinet and flute), although only four minutes of it were released three years later, titled *Midnight Sunrise*.

Coleman reinvented himself a fourth time in 1975, when he formed Prime Time, a quintet of alto saxophone (sometimes also violin and trumpet), two electric guitars, an electric bassist and a drummer (and later a second drummer, to create a "double quartet" of two guitars, two bassists, two drummers and his alto) devoted to a dense and loud stylistic jungle that ran the gamut from blues, funk, jazz and rock to dissonant music. Basically he entered the disco with the same nonchalance with which he had entered the avantgarde clubs 15 years earlier, and with the same determination to wreak havoc.

On one hand Coleman reacted to the increasing commercial turn that jazz-rock had taken, while on the other he was simply influenced by the ideas of a friend, guitarist James "Blood" Ulmer.

The highlight of **Dancing in Your Head** (december 1976) was a devastating 26-minute *Theme From a Symphony*, propelled by manic drummer Ronald Shannon Jackson and ripped apart by the twin-guitar assault of Charles Ellerbee and Bern Nix. **Body Meta** (december 1976) contained five eight/nine-minute tracks that now relied on an even funkier rhythm section (Jackson and bassist Jamaaladeen Tacuma). Coleman was reborn as a king of rocking and danceable music, although he hardly indulged in the format, repeating it only on **Of Human Feelings** (april 1979).

The great technical innovation of this period was a vaguely-defined "harmolodics", which basically stood for a hodgepodge of intricate polyrhythms, complex melodies and polytonal textures.

After a long hiatus, Coleman consolidated the "double quartet" line-up of Prime Time (two guitars, two basses, two drums plus Coleman on alto, trumpet and violin) for **Opening the Caravan of Dreams** (september 1983), for one half of the double album **In All Languages** (1987), the other half being a reunion with Coleman's original quartet (Cherry, Haden, Higgins), and for **Virgin Beauty** (1988).

However, Coleman remained more of a European composer than most jazz musicians had been, as further documented by *Time Design* (1983) for amplified string quartet and electric drum set, *The Sacred Mind of Johnny Dolphin* (1984) for chamber ensemble, *Notes Talking* (1986) for solo mandolin, *Trinity* (1986) for solo violin, *In Honor of NASA and Planetary Soloist* (1986) for oboe, English horn, mukhavina and string quartet, etc.

Coleman was also quite unique among jazz musicians of his generation because he seldom performed as a side-man on other musicians' recordings.

There had been experiments of "free jazz" before Coltrane and Coleman, notably Lennie Tristano's *Descent Into Maelstrom* and Stan Kenton's *City Of Glass*; and similar rebellions against traditional harmony were ubiquitous among contemporary classical composers. However, Coltrane and Coleman were black, not white. They injected into "free jazz" a different spirit of rebellion, one that was inevitably grounded in the racial tensions of those times. "Free" jazz happened at the same time that "freedom" was becoming the slogan for an increasing bitter confrontation with the white Establishment. Free jazz and the civil-rights movement grew in parallel. Free jazz was a new kind of music, but it was also, to some extent, a musical metaphor for the other kind of freedom, in the sociopolitical dimension.

Both white and black intellectuals got involved in the civil-rights movement, but their musical correlates were of a wildly different nature. The musical reaction of white intellectuals was the generation of folksingers such as Bob Dylan, emerging mainly from the Greenwich Village of New York. The musical reaction of black intellectuals was the generation of free-jazz musicians who reinterpreted Coltrane's and Coleman's innovations in a politicized context. They too were based in the Greenwich Village, and their lofts were favorite hang-outs for white intellectuals too. Despite the common cause and common geography, though, the two musical currents diverged in spirit and form. White folksingers were preaching, focusing on words. Black free-jazz musicians were not using words at all, just extreme instrumental music.

At the same time, free jazz represented a break with the past of black music. While previous stylistic revolutions in jazz had been carried out by musicians who had been raised in the previous style, free jazz was largely the outcome of a brand new generation of musicians, with little or no ties to bebop or cool jazz. They came out of nowhere, with a style that did not so much attack the dogmas of the previous generation (as bebop had done) as ignore them. The whole idea of the virtuoso player, of the improvisation on a pop standard, of the entertainer were thrown out of the window.

In fact, free jazz was not accepted by the jazz establishment. Most jazz musicians continued to refine their old style, ignoring and sometimes lampooning free jazz. The apostles of free jazz had to cope with a degree of negative feedback from their own community that was unprecedented in black music.

Not all of them were "free" the same way, actually. "Free" jazz was a label applied to musicians who downplayed the conventions of jazz improvisation, i.e. the elements providing for stability during an improvisation (the chord progressions or the tempo or the key). But little of their music was atonal or chaotic. Many of them played ballads and blues dirges. What they had in common was the belief that jazz music could and should explore a broader range of sounds and of combinations of sounds. Often those premises were a pretext for high-energy collective improvisations rather than for a truly self-consistent aesthetic. (Thus the decline of the piano, an instrument that was perceived to be unfit for wild improvisation). Despite its obvious contrast with the hard-bop, the bebop and the cool jazz that preceded it, free-jazz actually continued the same trend away from the melodic and rhythmic art of the progenitors and towards a more and more textural art. "Free" jazz was, ultimately, more the name of an era, a movement and a mood than the name of a specific technique.

Los Angeles-born flutist, alto saxophonist and bass clarinetist Eric Dolphy, equally influenced by bebop and by classical music, was trained at the schools of Chico Hamilton (1959), Charles Mingus (1959), Ornette Coleman (1960), John Coltrane (1961) and Gunther Schuller (1962-63). His early recordings as a leader contained relatively simple bebop workouts, often on material of his own composition, whose main purpose was to display his style at the various instruments: **Outward Bound** (april 1960), featuring trumpeter Freddie Hubbard, pianist Jaki Byard, bassist George Tucker and drummer Roy Haynes, and containing Dolphy's own *G.W.*; **Here and There** (april 1960), recorded on the same day but with only Byard, Tucker and Haynes, that contains Dolphy's *April's Fool*; and **Out There** (august 1960), featuring cellist Ron Carter, bassist George Duvivier and drummer Roy Haynes, and highlighted by his *Out There* and *Serene*.

Far Cry (december 1960) upped the ante considerably: trumpeter Booker Little, pianist Byard, Carter on bass and Haynes on drums formed a cohesive unit that did more than just support the leader. Byard's eight-minute *Mrs Parker of K.C.*

and nine-minute *Ode to Charlie Parker* provided the ideal platform, and Dolphy debuted his *Far Cry* and *Miss Ann*.

There were signs that Dolphy was not just playing around with his talent. Several recordings of the era were futuristic: *Triple Mix* (november 1960), a duet between bassist Carter and Dolphy on alto and flute, eventually released on **Naima**; the 11-minute *Improvisations and Turkas* (july 1960) for flute, tabla and tampura, the solo flute improvisations of *Inner Flight 1 and 2* (july 1960), the bass-saxophone duet of *Dolphy'n* (july 1960), all three eventually released on **Other Aspects**. Dolphy had been incorporating weird sounds, bordering on noise, into his vocabulary, and emphasized odd time signatures and wide intervals. What had been mere eccentricities were becoming a full-blown language.

Dolphy, who had been playing avantgarde music with Mingus, Coleman and Coltrane while playing more conventional music on his own albums, was ready to fully embrace the avantgarde, and did so on two albums recorded on the same day. **Conversations** (july 1963) featured a cover of Fats Waller's *Jitterbug Waltz* with trumpeter Woody Shaw and vibraphonist Bobby Hutcherson, a three-minute solo saxophone piece, and the 13-minute clarinet-bass duet on the theme of Arthur Schwartz's *Alone Together*. **Iron Man** (july 1963) was even better, highlighted by two lengthy Dolphy originals featuring Shaw and Hutcherson: *Iron Man* (nine minutes) and *Burning Spear* (twelve minutes). The latter in particular (scored for trumpet, four woodwinds, vibraphone, two basses and drums) showed the difference between the pupil and the master: Dolphy's sense of ambience and balance versus Coleman's explosions of sound). Dolphy had reached his maturity, and his satori was **Out to Lunch** (february 1964), recorded with Hutcherson, trumpeter Freddie Hubbard, bassist Richard Davis and drummer Tony Williams. This masterpiece of dissonant free-jazz sounded remarkably organic and structured, thanks in part to Dolphy's compositional skills on the five tracks: *Hat and Beard*, *Something Sweet Something Tender*, the flute piece *Gazzelloni*, the 12-minute *Out To Lunch*, *Straight Up and Down*. Those compositional skills were also on display in the 15-minute *Jim Crow* (march 1964), off **Other Aspects**. Dolphy created music by twisting every feature of sound, as if a random process were at work, while in reality a deep logic connected all the pieces. Few founding fathers of free-jazz were so blessed as composers, a fact that was a contradiction in terms, but that it might have led to a further revolution in jazz. Unfortunately, Dolphy died a few months later at 36.

In the midst of the blossoming of the free-jazz scene, pianist Cecil Taylor probably represented better than anyone else the non-jazz aspect of the movement. Many of the innovations of the 1960s were pioneered by his records. His fusion of exuberance and atonality was particularly influential. A graduate from the New England Conservatory of Music (1951-1955), where he had studied contemporary classical music, Taylor developed a radical improvising style at the piano that indulged in tone clusters, percussive attacks and irregular polyrhythmic patterns, a very "physical" style that required a manic

energy during lengthy and frenzied performances, a somewhat "cacophonous" style that relished both atonal and tonal passages. The dynamic range of his improvisations was virtually infinite.
His maturation took place via *Charge 'Em Blues*, off **Jazz Advance** (december 1955), for his first quartet, featuring white soprano saxophonist Steve Lacy, bassist Buell Neidlinger and drummer Dennis Charles, the convoluted, tonally ambiguous *Tune 2* off **At Newport** (july 1956) for the same quartet, *Toll* (the blueprint for many of his classics), *Of What* and *Excursion on a Wobbly Rail*, off **Looking Ahead** (june 1958), with Lacy replaced by vibraphonist Earl Griffith, *Little Lees* and *Matie's Trophies*, off **Love for Sale** (april 1959), with trumpeter Ted Curson, saxophonist Bill Barron and the usual rhythm section, *Air* and *E.B.*, off **The World of Cecil Taylor** (october 1960), featuring Archie Shepp on tenor saxophone and the same rhythm section, the abstract *Cell Walk For Celeste*, off **New York City R&B** (january 1961), also for the quartet of Taylor, Shepp, Charles and Neidlinger (to whom the album was credited), *Mixed*, off Gil Evans' **Into The Hot** (october 1961), featuring the brand new line-up of altoist Jimmy Lyons, tenorist Archie Shepp, bassist Henry Grimes, drummer Sunny Murray, trumpeter Ted Curson and trombonist Roswell Rudd. These albums were still anchored to the song format and wasted time on other people's material when Taylor's own compositions were so much superior; but occasionally the pianist and his cohorts launched into strident, torrential jamming that obliterated the history of jazz. Taylor's group was much bolder in their live performances, when they indulged in lengthy improvisations in front of an audience that still thought of jazz as light entertainment. Taylor's compositions at their best were wildly irregular and casually nonchalant at the same time. They were bold contradictions. Sometimes dramatic and sometimes sarcastic, they straddled the line between being and not being. At the same time, pieces such as *Tune 2*, *Toll*, *Air*, *Cell Walk For Celeste* and *Mixed* displayed the formalist concern typical of classical music.
Taylor's first major statement came with the live trio performances of **Nefertiti the Beautiful One Has Come** (november 1962), featuring Jimmy Lyons on alto and Sunny Murray on drums (the Unit), two ideal complements for Taylor's explosive style. These lengthy and complex jams, *Trance*, *Lena*, *Nefertiti The Beautiful One Has Come* and the 21-minute colossus *D Trad That's What*, were as uncompromising as Ornette Coleman's **Free Jazz** (1960) and John Coltrane's **Impressions** (1961). In fact, they were so uncompromising that very few people listened to them.
It took three years for Taylor to release another album, and it presented a larger ensemble and an even wilder sound, as violent as garage-rock, bordering on hysteria: **Unit Structures** (may 1966) featured (mostly) a septet with Lyons, Eddie Gale Stevens on trumpet, Ken McIntyre on alto sax, oboe and bass clarinet, two bassists (Henry Grimes and Alan Silva) and Andrew Cyrille on drums. These pieces (or, better, "structures") were conceived as sequences of polyphonic events rather than, say, series of variations on a theme. Nonetheless, *Unit Structure*, *Enter Evening* and *Steps* were highly structured compositions,

and therein lied Taylor's uniqueness: his "free jazz" was also "free" of the melodrama that permeated Coltrane's and Coleman's music. Despite all the furor, Taylor's music always sounded firmly under the control of a cold intelligence. Cyrille's drumming was less abstract than Murray, more integrated with the other players, but Silva now played the "decorative" role that Murray used to play.

The sextet of **Conquistador** (october 1966), featuring Bill Dixon on trumpet, Lyons, and the same three-piece rhythm section, pushed the experiment to its limits in two shockingly abrasive and expressionistic side-long jams, *Conquistador* and *With*. Their sheer size challenged the balance between disintegration and integration, looseness and cohesiveness, that constituted the soul of the previous "structures". The flow of enigmatic sounds had become a puzzle to be reconstructed. A quartet of Taylor, Lyons, Silva and Cyrille recorded **Student Studies:** (november 1966), containing the 27-minute *Student Studies*, the 20-minute *Amplitude* and the 12-minute *Niggle Feuigle*, that stepped back a bit from the edge, emphasizing the structure behind the chaos, the "jazz" soul hidden under the apparently dissolute dissonance.

However, Taylor's music was still under-appreciated and he had to spend the next seven years virtually in exile. During this period Taylor composed/improvised some of his most daring music: the four-movement *Praxis* (july 1968) for solo piano, released in 1982, the six-movement *Second Act Of A* (july 1969), for a quartet with Lyons, Cyrille and soprano saxophonist Sam Rivers, the three-movement *Indent* (march 1973) for solo piano, released on **Mysteries**, the 81-minute *Bulu Akisakila Kutala* (may 1973) for a trio with Lyons and Cyrille, released on **Akisakila** (1973).

Solo (May 1973), his first collection of solo-piano pieces, presented Taylor's "layering" technique in its most sophisticated version. The organized improvisations of *Choral of Voice*, *Lono*, *Asapk in Ame* and especially *Indent* were emblematic of the process of cooperation and competition of events operating at different levels. **Spring of Two Blue J's** (november 1973) contained two versions of the piece, one solo and one for a quartet with Lyons, Cyrille and bassist Sirone. The solo version delivered his most emotional outpour yet.

This period culminated in the five loud and noisy movements of the live solo-piano suite **Silent Tongues** (july 1974): *Abyss*, *Petals & Filaments* (combined into one 18-minute track), *Jitney* (18 minutes), *Crossing* (18 minutes divided into two tracks) and *After all* (ten minutes). This album was a compendium of Taylor's aesthetic, secreting an unlikely synthesis of the irrational and the rational that had been the contradicting pillars of his music. Its range of moods defied the laws of psychoanalysis. The sound was emblematic of his brilliant exuberance but was soon surpassed in intensity by at least two (clearly much more improvised) performances: the 62-minute *Streams and Chorus of Seed* (june 1976), released on **Dark To Themselves**, for a quintet with Lyons, trumpeter Raphe Malik, drummer Marc Edwards and tenor saxophonist David Ware, and the 76-minute solo-piano **Air Above Mountains** (august 1976). Here the music was meant to exhaust the performer, to last until it had drained every gram of psychological and physical energy out of the performer. But these live juggernauts also marked the end of the "underground" period and the beginning of a three-year artistic bonanza.

A sextet of Taylor, Lyons, trumpeter Raphe Malik, violinist Ramsey Ameen, bassist Norris "Sirone" Jones and drummer Ronald Shannon Jackson delivered the more structured and variegated jams of **Cecil Taylor Unit** (april 1978): the 14-minute *Idut*, the 14-minute *Serdab*, the 30-minute *Holiday En Masque*, and the 57-minute **3 Phasis** (april 1978). A similar sextet with Lyons, Ameen, Alan Silva on bass and cello and both Jerome Cooper and Sunny Murray on drums, recorded the 69-minute **Is it the Brewing Luminous** (february 1980). Despite the monumental proportions, this music was less magniloquent and less mysterious than the music of the 1960s.

Starting with the quartet effort **Calling it the 8th** (november 1981), featuring Lyons, bassist William Parker and drummer Rashid Bakr (all of them doubling on voice), and the solo **Garden** (november 1981), Taylor increased the production values to emphasize the nuances of his playing, adopted a jazzier style and added his poetry to the music (not a welcomed addition). A new prolific phase of his career yielded recordings for ensemble, such as **Winged Serpent** (october 1984) and the 48-minute **Legba Crossing** (july 1988); for solo piano, such as **For Olim** (april 1986), containing the 18-minute title-track, the 71-minute title-track of **Erzulie Maketh Scent** (july 1988) and the 72-minute **The Tree of Life** (march 1991), perhaps the most austere of his life; and for small groups, such as **Olu Iwa** (april 1986), containing the 48-minute *B Ee Ba Nganga Ban'a Eee* for piano, trombone, tenor sax and rhythm section, and the 27-minute *Olu Iwa* for piano and rhythm section, the precursor of his many piano and drums duets, as well as the 61-minute **The Hearth** (june 1988), for a trio with saxophonist Evan Parker and cellist Tristan Honsinger, and **Looking** (november 1989) and **Celebrated Blazons** (june 1990) for the trio with bassist William Parker and drummer Tony Oxley.

Taylor represented everything that Coleman stood against: he had studied composition (Coleman was illiterate) and he was inspired by atonal music (Coleman harked back to older black music). Coleman approached dance music from the viewpoint of the disco. Taylor's music was frequently compared (by himself) to classical ballet. Even the mood was opposite: Taylor's music was an atomic bomb compared to Coleman's passion.

Of all the protagonists of free jazz, Ohio-born tenor saxophonist Albert Ayler had the shortest career (he first recorded in 1962 and committed suicide in 1970 at 34), but he nonetheless managed to articulate one of the most radical aesthetics, second only to Cecil Taylor's. He often sounded like someone who wanted to create a virtuoso art out of anti-virtuoso playing. Ayler started out playing rhythm'n'blues. By the time he landed in New York, he had developed his idiosyncratic style (notably via an unrecorded European experience with Cecil Taylor in 1962). A quartet with trumpeter Norman Howard, drummer Sunny Murray and bassist Henry Grimes recorded **Spirits/ Witches and Devils** (february 1964), that contains four lengthy pieces: *Spirits*, the twelve-minute *Witches and Devils*, the eleven-minute *Holy Holy* and *Saints*.

Each of them sounded like it was coming from a distant past, from a remembered childhood, as it incorporated simple, naive, catchy melodies. The performance was ferocious, though, as if Ayler wanted to contrast innocence and experience, or European order and African disorder.

The live **Prophecy** (june 1964) introduced his trio with double bassist Gary Peacock and drummer Sunny Murray, and added *Ghosts* (his most famous theme), *Wizard* and *Prophecy* to his esoteric canon.

That trio was responsible for one of the most revolutionary recordings of the era, **Spiritual Unity** (july 1964), the (brief) album that made it explicit how Ayler was not interested in creating music out of notes but out of timbres, how his music was not a harmonic construction but a "soundscape". These new versions of *Ghosts*, *Spirits* and *Wizard* were delivered according to an apparently demented logic that mixed melodies inspired by folk tunes and nursery rhymes with emotional bursts of saxophone noises simulating the human voice. Murray's percussions (more cymbals than drums) had little to do with keeping the time: they produced a flow of disorienting noises that intersected and amplified Ayler's saxophone noises. By now, Ayler had refined his melodramatic vibrato. The "free" approach permeated the two side-long improvisations of **New York Eye And Ear Control** (july 1964), *AY* and *ITT*, with the trio augmented with trumpeter Don Cherry on cornet, Roswell Rudd on trombone and John Tchicai on alto, although the result was far less tight than on Ornette Coleman's **Free Jazz** (1960), proving that Ayler was a different spirit from the free-jazz crowd.

The trio and Don Cherry returned to a humbler format with **Vibrations/ Ghosts** (september 1964), that added *Children* (actually just a fast variant of *Holy Holy*), the moving ballad *Holy Spirit* (with a spectacular Cherry solo), *Vibrations* and *Mothers* to the canon, and **The Hilversum Session** (november 1964), that introduced *Angels* in a tense mid-tempo version.

Donald Ayler replaced Don Cherry for the one-sided LP **Bells** (may 1965), containing just one 20-minute track (fundamentally a madcap medley of marches and nursery rhymes) also featuring altoist Charles Tyler and bassist Lewis Worrell besides Sunny Murray.

Spirits Rejoice (september 1965), particularly its title-track (performed by Donald Ayler, Sunny Murray, altoist Charles Tyler, bassists Henry Grimes and Gary Peacock), marked a transition towards a more religious mood and a regression towards the collective improvisation of New Orleans' brass bands. *Spirits Rejoice* basically revisited the format of *Bells* in a more organic and structured way, picking up along the way an impressive amount of debris of musical stereotypes.

Holy Ghost (july 1967) documents a live performance with Don Ayler on trumpet, Michel Sampson on violin, Bill Folwell on bass and Milford Graves on drums (particularly *Truth Is Marching In/Omega* and *Our Prayer*). Ayler considerably toned down his music on **In Greenwich Village** (december 1966) and **Love Cry** (august 1967), and eventually returned to his rhythm'n'blues roots. After some kind of hippie-like spiritual crisis, Ayler turned to jazz-rock,

soul and funk music, adding lyrics by a vocal singer, notably on **Music Is The Healing Force of the Universe** (august 1969).
By employing a virtually unlimited repertory of tricks and a rich vibrato, Ayler expanded the vocabulary of the saxophone, but, most importantly, he did so while staging a multi-dimensional regression to a simpler age of music (whether the catchy folkish melodies or the military tempos or the collective improvisation of the marching bands). Ayler seemed to fuse the musical background of the pre-industrial society with an impulse towards the expressionistic cacophony of the industrial society. At the same time, his saxophone often seemed to intone shamanic invocations except to derail into frenzied explosions of vitality. Underlying all these contradictions was Ayler's exploration of sound for the sake of sound, that accounted for a completely new idea of music, away from the pillars of harmony, melody and rhythm. That was, ultimately, an exploration of the human psyche. Thus, at several levels of introspection and metaphor, Ayler's art was a mirror of society. Ayler's was the music of the collective unconscious.

One of the towering figures of 20th century's music, Alabama-born pianist and organist Herman "Sun Ra" Blount became the cosmic musician par excellence. Despite dressing in extraterrestrial costumes (but inspired by the pharaohs of ancient Egypt) and despite living inside a self-crafted sci-fi mythology (he always maintained that he was from Saturn, and no biographer conclusively proved his birth date) and despite littering his music with lyrics inspired to a self-penned spiritual philosophy (he never engaged in sexual relationships apparently because he considered himself an angel), Sun Ra created one of the most original styles of music thanks to a chronic disrespect for both established dogmas and trendy movements.

A pianist and arranger for Fletcher Henderson's band when he moved to Chicago in 1946, Sun Ra started his own big band in the old-fashioned swing style in 1952. The influence of Duke Ellington (that would remain throughout his career) and Thelonious Monk were the only discernible links to the rest of the human race. The Arkestra, as it came to be known, relied on its three colorful saxophonists: tenor saxophonist John Gilmore (from 1953), alto saxophonist Marshall Allen (1954), and baritone saxophonist Pat Patrick (1954). The rest was filled by a rotating case of musicians, whose main role was to bring as much "color" as possible to the music, particularly any number of percussionists with prominent tympani (but the other players too usually took shifts at playing one or more percussion instruments besides their own). Their albums were eccentric tonal excursions: **Supersonic Jazz/ Supersonic Sounds** (1956), with *India*, the two-part *Sunology*, *Kingdom of Not* and the first version of *Blues at Midnight*, **Sun Song/ Jazz** (july 1956), with two trumpeters and trombonist Julian Priester, and containing *Call For All Demons* and their theme song *New Horizons*, **Sound Of Joy** (november 1957), not released until 1968, with *Ankh*, *Reflections in Blue* and *Saturn*, **Jazz in Silhouette** (1958), with the first extended pieces, notably *Ancient Aethiopia* and *Blues at Midnight*, besides *Velvet*, **Lady with the Golden Stockings/ The Nubians of Plutonia** (1959), not released until 1966, with the extended percussive orgies *Lady With the Golden Stockings* and *Nubia*, **Rocket**

Number Nine/ Interstellar Low Ways (1960), not released until 1965, with the extended *Interstellar Low Ways* and *Rocket Number Nine Take off for the Planet Venus*, **Fate In a Pleasant Mood** (1960), released in 1965, with the mature percussion-driven sound of *Space Mates* and *Kingdom of Thunder*. But most of the pieces were still short bop divertissments. A chromatic fixation led Sun Ra to employ all sorts of instruments (including early electronic keyboards), a fact that made him, de facto, one of the most creative arrangers in the history of jazz music.

The Arkestra, reduced in size, relocated to New York in 1961 and Sun Ra came to be associated with the free-jazz scene, although Sun Ra had already pioneered free jazz in Chicago. The first New York albums marked a step backwards. Very few pieces continued the trend towards a percussion-dominated harmony: *Beginning* on **Futuristic Sounds/ We Are The Future** (october 1961), *Exotic Two* on **Bad and Beautiful** (december 1961), released in 1972, *Kosmos in Blue* and *Infinity of the Universe* on **Art Forms of Dimensions Tomorrow** (1962), released in 1965, *Love in Outer Space* on **Secrets of the Sun** (1962), released in 1965, that also included the proto-psychedelic *Solar Differentials* and *Solar Symbols*.

Having created his own record company, Sun Ra was now free to record anything that happened to please him. And he did not hesitate to take up Ornette Coleman's challenge with: *Calling Planet Earth* on **When Sun Comes Out** (1963), the ten-minute *Ecstasy of Being* and the 18-minute *Next Stop Mars* on **When Angels Speak of Love** (1963), released in 1966, *Adventure-Equation* and *Voice Of Space* on **Cosmic Tones For Mental Therapy** (1963), released in 1967, an album that exuded a psychedelic feeling, three years before the psychedelic explosion.

His albums became more irrational and experimental. **Other Planes of There** (1964) contained the 22-minute *Other Planes of There*, highlighted by the interplay among John Gilmore's tenor sax, Marshall Allen's oboe and Danny Davis' alto sax. **Strange Strings** (1966) contained two side-long jams, the bacchanal *Strange Strings* and the reverb-heavy *Worlds Approaching* (another parade of creative solos by the wind instruments and the electric piano). That was still accessible compared with **Featuring Pharoah Sanders and Black Harold** (june 1964), released in 1976, whose *The Voice of Pan* and *Dawn Over Israel* were childish orgies of random sounds. **Heliocentric Worlds Vol 1** (april 1965) was a minor work, that contained the hypnotic timpani-obsessed *Outer Nothingness* and *The Cosmos*. But the unrelated **Heliocentric Worlds Vol 2/ Sun Myth** (november 1965) was a colossal undertaking of space jazz, via the 17-minute abstract soundscape of *The Sun Myth*, the 14-minute satanic crescendo of *Cosmic Chaos*, and *A House of Beauty*, that belonged more to chamber music than to free jazz.

The crowning achievement of this period was **The Magic City** (september 1965), particularly the 27-minute suite *The Magic City* for a large ensemble of keyboards, trumpet, trombone, alto, tenor, baritone, flute, piccolo, clarinet, bass and percussions, but also the shorter maelstrom of *The Shadow World*.

Free Jazz: the Apostles

The end of the Sixties found Sun Ra in a more eccentric mode than ever, as documented by the live albums **Nothing Is/ Dancing Shadows** (may 1966) and **Pictures Of Infinity** (1968), by the solo-piano collection **Monorails and Satellites** (1966) and the solo-keyboard collection **The Solar Myth Approach Vol 2** (1971), by the electronic and dissonant experiments of **The Solar Myth Approach Vol 1** (1970). Years of toying with new instruments and combinations of instruments led to the new masterpieces: the epic 22-minute *Atlantis* on **Atlantis** (1967), the four tracks of **Outer Spaceways Incorporated** (1968), released in 1974, *Continuation To* on **Continuation** (1968), the electronic *The Code of Interdependence* on **My Brother the Wind** (1970) and the synthesizer solo *Space Probe* (1970).

The Arkestra moved to Philadelphia in 1970, but the lengthy, madcap jams simply became more insane: *Nidhamu* (december 1971), the 18-minute *Cosmo Fire* (may 1972), the 21-minute chant *Space Is The Place* (october 1972), the 24-minute chant *Discipline 27-II* (october 1972), *Pathways to Unknown Worlds* (1973), the free-form *Cosmo-Earth Fantasy* (september 1974), *The Soul Vibrations of Man* (november 1977), *Disco 3000* (january 1978).

Trumpeter Bill Dixon was more influential as an organizer (he conceived the first free-jazz festival, "October Revolution in Jazz", in 1964) than as a musician, but was actually one of the greatest musicians of free jazz, albeit a voluntary exile from the music industry.

His first association was with the young saxophonist Archie Shepp. They formed a quartet that recorded the Coleman-inspired **Archie Shepp-Bill Dixon Quartet** (october 1962), half of which was taken up by free improvisations titled *Trio* and *Quartet* and credited to Dixon. The album by Archie Shepp's New York Contemporary Five, known as **Consequences** (november 1963), was actually a split with Dixon's septet (march 1964) that performed two Dixon compositions, *The 12th December* and *Winter Song 1964*, of a rather different kind, mellow and restrained.

His next association was with Cecil Taylor, playing on his **Conquistador** (1966). Dixon's first album, **Intents And Purposes** (1967), released when he was already 42, included two lengthy workouts, the five-movement *Metamorphoses 1962-1966* (october 1966) for a tentet (trumpet, trombone, alto, clarinet, English horn, cello, two basses, drums and percussion) and *Voices* (january 1967) for a quintet (trumpet, clarinet, cello, bass and drums). Both works displayed Dixon's pensive, lyrical style that sounded like pure poetry among all the viscerality of free jazz. Instead of using the music as a weapon, Dixon (who was also a painter) used it to create vast canvasses of organized sounds, using space and silence in a way that predated Chicago's "creative" school, and often caressing the atmosphere with haunting bass lines.

A truly underground musician, most of his recordings of the 1970s appeared only in the 1980s. For example, **Considerations** (1980) included four extended compositions: *Orchestra Piece* (1972), *Sequences* (1972) for a quintet (trumpet, trombone, saxophone, bass and drums), *Pages* (1975) for a trumpet-saxophone-drums trio, *Places And Things* (1976) for a trio of trumpet, saxophone and bass.

Collection (1985) was a double LP of mostly solo performances dating from 1972-76. **1982** contained two sets of solo pieces (from 1970 and 1973).
Opium (august 1976) contained the side-long *For Franz* performed by a quintet with two trumpets, tenor saxophone, bass and percussion.
In Italy (june 1980) presented four of his more austere pieces performed by a sextet with three trumpets and tenor saxophone: *Summer Song, For Cecil Taylor, Dance Piece, Summer Song*.
A quartet with two trumpets recorded another set of intense jams for **November 1981** (november 1981): *November 1981, Penthesilea, Windswept Winterset, Llaattiinnoo Suite*.
Thoughts (may 1985) for septet, with *Thoughts* and the four-part suite *For Nelson and Winnie*, and **Son Of Sysiphus** (june 1988) for quartet were transitional works, but the double-CD **Vade Mecum** (august 1993) was again a mesmerizing collection, a quartet with bassists Barry Guy and William Parker and British drummer Tony Oxley crafting majestic existential moods through lengthy meditations such as *Anamorphosis, Viale Nino Bixio 20, Pellucity, Vade Mecum, Twice Upon A Time, Acanthus*. Dixon planned the narrative plot of each piece and set the constraints that the players had to obey. His own trumpet was a magical device, that attained great emotional intensity with a trickle of notes. Melodies were hinted at, rhythms disappeared in rhythmic vacuums, harmonies disintegrated as they were created. The low-key sounds made everything sound oneiric and claustrophobic. Another two-CD set, **Vade Mecum II** (august 1993), delivered the rest of those sessions, with *Tableau, Ebonite, Reflections, Incunabula, Octette #1*. Both were monumental works, worthy of Cecil Taylor's and Charles Mingus' most highbrow experiments.
The live **The Enchanted Messenger** (november 1994) featured the Tony Oxley Celebration Orchestra and Dixon in an extended improvisation of nineteen "sections".
The two volumes of **Papyrus** (june 1998) contained duets with Oxley, with many among his most poignant motifs: *Papyrus, The Statesman, Indirizzo Via Cimarose Sei, Scribbles, Palimpsest, Epigraphy, Crawlspace*. The trumpet was more subliminal than a voice, and sometimes felt like a supernatural force sending cryptic and ambiguous, but celestial, messages to the human mind. Dixon also played piano, notably in *Cinnamon*, and overdubbed a second trumpet, notably in *Four-VI-1998*.
Dixon and Oxley were joined by two double bassists on **Berlin Abbozzi** (november 1999), that contained three colossal jams: the 21-minute *Currents*, the 40-minute *Open Quiet / The Orange Bell*, and *Acrolithes*. Far from being merely an exercise in verbose improvisation, each piece was a manic, painstaking and highly emotional operation of soundsculpting. The music was dark, ghostly and ominous, like a whisper from a creature trapped in another dimension.
No other free-jazz musician managed to remain so current as Bill Dixon in his 70s.
  One of the key legacies of free jazz was to dispose of the cliches of how a jazz band should work. Previous changes had been incremental, but the free-jazz

generation introduced revolutionary changes. Ornette Coleman got rid of the piano. Cecil Taylor played with no bass. The drums were still pervasive, but they were no longer mere time-keeping devices. And the first Art Ensemble of Chicago had no drummer at all. Soon there were ensembles with more strings than horns, or with no horns at all. Free jazz was more than a Copernican revolution: it was the musical equivalent of the French revolution.

FREE JAZZ: THE DISCIPLES

The second generation of free-jazz musicians were, generally speaking, less interested in innovation and more interested in expressing meaning. Their art typically embodied a theory of the world, and tried to explain it in sounds. The emphasis kept shifting from jazz as a discipline of how to play instruments (or, worse, a device to help night clubs sell alcohol) to jazz as a lyrical discipline of how to represent the human condition in music.

Arkansas-raised tenor saxophonists Sam Rivers, who had studied at a conservatory of music, represented the highbrow alter-ego of Ornette Coleman's free jazz.
Relocating in 1964 to New York, Rivers debuted with **Fuchsia Swing Song** (december 1964), featuring a quartet with teenage drummer Tony Williams, pianist Jaki Byard and bassist Ron Carter, that was poised halfway between hard bop and free jazz. Rivers struck an unlikely balance within each piece, particularly *Luminous Monolith* and *Downstairs Blues Upstairs*, that do not seem to belong any known genre except that they evoke everything from blues to swing to free. Even in relatively straightforward tracks such as *Ellipsis* and *Fuchsia Swing Song* Rivers compensated for the simpler material with a style that was an elegant (if somewhat stiff and highbrow) synthesis of styles. The dynamic range was further broadened on **Contours** (may 1965), featuring a quintet with trumpeter Freddie Hubbard, pianist Herbie Hancock, bassist Ron Carter and drummer Joe Chambers. The five players engaged in some of the most cerebral counterpoint of the era in four lengthy tracks: the nine-minute *Point of Many Returns*, the ten-minute *Dance of the Tripedal*, the twelve-minute *Euterpe*, the nine-minute *Mellifluous Cacophony*. The sophisticated, austere, atonal Rivers persona came out vividly on the six compositions of **Dimensions And Extensions** (march 1967), for a sextet with Donald Byrd (trumpet), James Spaulding (alto saxophone, flute), Julian Priester (trombone), Cecil McBee (bass) and Steve Ellington (drums). While a lot less "humane" than John Coltrane or Ornette Coleman, Rivers was no less bold and innovative. In fact, he added the sensibility of the European avantgarde to the creative furor of free jazz. His progression towards a more abstract sound culminated in the 48-minute live improvisation of **Streams** (july 1973), that basically wed the painful exuberance of free jazz with the surgical explorations of the classical avantgarde. He employed a 64-piece orchestra for **Crystals** (march 1974), his most ambitious and complex work, that at times (*Exultation, Tranquillity, Orb*) achieved a degree of intricacy unparalleled in any musical genre, each instrument delving into labyrinthine patterns and asynchronous soliloquies. Due to budget constraints, Rivers would not be able to continue the "orchestral" experiment until **Inspiration** (september 1998) and **Culmination** (september 1998).
Another facet of Rivers' art surfaced when he formed a trio with British bassist Dave Holland and drummer Barry Altschul, documented on **The Quest** (march

1976) and **Paragon** (april 1977). He also recorded **Waves** (august 1978) and **Contrasts** (december 1979) for quartet, and at least the duets with Alexander von Schlippenbach on **Tangens** (november 1997) are noteworthy, but Rivers' talent was fundamentally crippled by a record industry that was not willing to invest in large-ensemble recordings.

Atlanta-raised alto saxophonist Marion Brown, who relocated to New York in 1965 and almost right away, still an unknown, played on John Coltrane's **Ascension**, rapidly became one of the most radical but also most romantic of the free improvisers. His **Quartet** (november 1965), featuring two basses (Ronnie Boykins and Reggie Johnson), drums (Rashied Ali) and either trumpet (Alan Shorter) or tenor-saxophone (Bennie Maupin), was one of the most forceful free session of the age, the natural successor to Coltrane's masterpiece. The 22-minute *Capricorn Moon* and the 18-minute *Exhibition* displayed two sides of his art, but both were characterized by a unique skill to mix the visceral and the lyrical. **Juba Lee** (november 1966), recorded with Boykins' bass replaced by trombonist Grachan Moncur III, Ali replaced by drummer Beaver Harris, and the notable addition of pianist Dave Burrell, was slightly less effervescent but more intimate music (*512e12*, *Juba-Lee*, *Iditus*). **Why Not** (october 1966) was also a transitional work, highlighted by Brown's skills as a composer of ballads and by the elegance of the quartet (pianist Stanley Cowell, Rashied Ali and bassist Norris "Sirone" Jones) in interpreting them (*La Sorella*, *Fortunata*, *Homecoming*). **Three for Shepp** (december 1966) was, de facto, a faithful continuation of Archie Shepp's **Four For Trane** (three of the six tracks were Shepp compositions). Acclaimed by the jazz pundits, it was actually the least original or Brown's albums. His compositional skills are much more evident on **Porto Novo** (december 1967), particularly in *Porto Novo* (a trio with bassist Maarten van Regteben Altena and percussionist Han Bennink) and the otherworldly *And Then They Danced* (a duo with trumpeter Leo Smith). The lyrical, nostalgic and melancholy aspect of Brown's art fully blossomed on **Afternoon of a Georgia Faun** (august 1970). An extended line-up, centered around Brown on alto, Anthony Braxton on all sorts of wind instruments, Bennie Maupin on three more winds, Chick Corea on piano, Andrew Cyrille on drums, Jack Gregg on bass, Jeanne Lee and Gayle Palmore on vocals, and everybody alternating at several percussion instruments, *Djinji's Corner* may have been only a pretext for virtuoso exhibition (particularly of Lee, possibly the greatest jazz vocalist of all times), but the pastoral *Afternoon of a Georgia Faun* marked a departure in Brown's art: free jazz as a music of tender feeling. This was the counterpart to Coltrane's spirituality, a return to greener pastures by the intrepid voyager. Brown pursued his newly-found soul with **Geechee Recollections** (june 1973), dedicated to his childhood and containing *Karintha* and three-part *Tokalokaloka*, and highlighted by mesmerizing alto and trumpet (Leo Smith) work, with **Sweet Earth Flying** (may 1974), that juxtaposed his sentimental alto with the keyboards of Muhal Richard Abrams and Paul Bley and was divided between the five-part *Sweet Earth Flying* and the four-part *Eleven Light City*,
Unlike most of his colleagues, who recorded too much, Brown recorded too little.

Philadelphia-raised tenor saxophonist <u>Archie Shepp</u> cut his teeth in Cecil Taylor's quartet (1960-62) and with Bill Dixon (1962), and then (1963) joined the New York Contemporary Five, a quintet with Don Cherry on cornet and John Tchicai on alto saxophone that implemented the principles of Ornette Coleman's **Free Jazz** (1960) on their **Consequences** (october 1963), particularly *Consequences* (the only track with Cherry). Shepp played on John Coltrane's **Ascension** (1965) and became one of the first saxophonists to take Coltrane's new style literally. Four tracks of **Four For Trane** (august 1964) were Coltrane compositions, performed by Shepp, trombonist Roswell Rudd, Tchicai, Coltrane's bassist Reggie Workman and Coleman's drummer Charles Moffett.
Shepp's festival of dissonance, **Fire Music** (march 1965), was no less revolutionary than Coltrane's masterpiece. In fact, it was even wilder and harsher, like a volcanic eruption of notes that superficially defied any logic, although at the end they left a sense of cathartic rebirth. Only two pieces were by Shepp, *Hambone* and *Los Olvidados*, but they both displayed innovative elements, the former relying on minimalist-like horns and the latter painting an abstract soundscape. Shepp was even more convincing on **On This Night** (august 1965), accompanied by vibraphonist Bobby Hutcherson and a rotating cast of bassists and drummers, at least in his *On This Night* and *Mac Man*. Shepp used free jazz as a pretext to build up a dramatic style of saxophone playing, that was closer in spirit to rhythm'n'blues than to bebop or swing. He never really settled on a stable group, save a quintet with Rudd documented on **Three for a Quarter One for a Dime** (february 1966).
Shepp was clearly much more influenced than Coltrane by contemporary black politics and by the African heritage. The drawback of Shepp's art is that, no matter how original, it never sounded quite as sincere and profound as Coltrane's. Where Coltrane was simply his own creation, largely independent of the times, Shepp seemed more prone to follow (whether free jazz or "Black Power" or Afrocentrism) than to lead. There were more authentic free-jazz players, there were more sincere jazz politicians, and there were more fervent Afrocentric musicians; but probably nobody else came close to fusing all three elements into one organic body of art as he did.
This socio-musical-philosophical fusion peaked with the three-part suite *A Portrait of Robert Thomson* (dedicated to revisitations of blues, gospel and jazz) and with the Middle-eastern *Basheer* on **Mama Too Tight** (august 1966), again performed by a rotating cast of avantgarde musicians. The African element became explicit with the 18-minute *The Magic of Ju-Ju* for African percussion instruments and tenor saxophone on **The Magic of Ju-Ju** (april 1967). After **The Way Ahead** (january 1968), his first recording with a pianist, that sounded like a partial retreat, Shepp penned the 20-minute *Yasmina A Black Woman* on **Yasmina** (august 1969), accompanied by three members of the Art Ensemble of Chicago and assorted percussionists. After another half-hearted effort, **Kwanza** (mostly february 1969), possibly his best ensemble ever (vocalist Jeanne Lee, trumpeter Lester Bowie, pianist Dave Burrell, bassist Malachi Favors, drummer Philly Joe Jones) helped him deliver the more meditational performances of

Blase', My Angel and *Tuareg* on **Blase'** (august 1969). Shepp played soprano on **Black Gypsy** (november 1969), basically divided into two suites (not composed by him), *Black Gipsy* and *Epitaph of a Small Winner*, but that great season was rapidly winding down. He seemed increasingly less interested in jazz (whether "free" or not) and more interested in rhythm'n'blues and funk music. This phase culminated in the more conventional and heavily-arranged "songs" of **Attica Blues** (january 1972) and **The Cry Of My People** (september 1972), quite a repudiation of free jazz.

From the very beginning, Los Angeles-raised Don Cherry displayed an anti-virtuoso attitude that contrasted with the ruling dogmas of jazz music. Cherry shunned both acrobatic exhibitions and radical experiments in favor of humility and pathos (thus appealing more to the rock crowd than to the jazz crowd). His style focused on the idiosyncratic timbres of his pocket trumpet and on languid phrases that evoked ancestral worlds via the abstraction of exotic styles, predating Jon Hassell's "fourth world" music (and the whole world-music bandwagon) by more than a decade.

His first major statement was **The Avant-Garde** (july 1960) with John Coltrane on sax, Charlie Haden on bass and Ed Blackwell on drums. When Cherry left the memorable Ornette Coleman quartet that had recorded **Something Else, The Shape of Jazz to Come** and **Free Jazz**, he joined the New York Contemporary Five, a quintet with Archie Shepp on tenor and John Tchicai on alto saxophone that implemented the principles of **Free Jazz** on their **Consequences** (november 1963).

Cherry's new musical and philosophical direction was dramatically different (especially for someone who always professed to abide by Coleman's "harmolodic" principles). He assembled a quartet with Argentinian tenor saxophonist Gato Barbieri, drummer Ed Blackwell and bassist Henry Grimes, and structured **Complete Communion** (december 1965) as two side-long improvisations, each structured as a sort of improvised suite: four melodic themes each (*Complete Communion/ And Now/ Golden Heart/ Remembrance* and *Elephantasy/ Our Feelings/ Bismallah/ Wind*), and each theme delivered to the players for "communal" improvisation (i.e., on equal terms). Cherry (at the ostensible leader) is quite subdued, his pocket trumpet unable to stand up to Barbieri's exuberant saxophone and to the creative and sometimes chaotic rhythm section: but that was precisely Cherry's point. Cherry marked the end of the "melodramatic" phase of jazz, in which the leading instrument was supposed to set the world on fire, and opened a more "existentialist" phase, in which the leading voice is one of downcast meditation.

The **Symphony For Improvisers** (september 1966) was the next logical step. With a septet that now included Karl Berger on vibraphone and piano, Pharoah Sanders on tenor saxophone and piccolo, and a second bassist, Cherry constructed two suites just like the previous ones, *Symphony for Improvisers/ Nu Creative Love/ What's Not Serious/ Infant Happiness* and *Manhattan Cry/ Lunatic/ Sparkle Plenty/ Om Nu*, except that the melodic themes were downplayed and the primal energy was emphasized. The resulting soundscape was a color version of the chiaroscuro of **Complete Communion**. **Where Is Brooklyn** (november 1966), for a quartet with Sanders, Blackwell and Grimes, closed that first creative season in a more conventional way, with five independent pieces highlighted by the 18-minute *Unite*.

Cherry moved onto his pan-ethnic phase with **Eternal Rhythm** (november 1968), featuring a looser, extended chamber orchestra with Albert Mangelsdorff and Eje Thelin on trombone, Bernt Rosengren on tenor, 0boe, clarinet and flute, Sonny Sharrock on guitar, Karl Berger on vibraphone and piano, Joachim Kuhn on piano, Arild Andersen on bass, and several of them (plus Jacques Thollot) also on percussion. Cherry managed to bestow an aura of dignified elegance and an almost religious sense of communion with far-away civilizations onto the two medleys composed/improvised by the musicians (*Baby's Breath/ Sonny Sharrock/ Turkish Prayer/ CR* and *Autumn Melody/ Lanoo/ Crystal Clear*). Cherry must have felt that a large ensemble was somewhat a contradiction in terms for his music of humility and cut the double LP **Mu** (august 1969) as a series of duets between himself (on pocket trumpet, piano, flute, percussion and vocals) and Ed Blackwell. The music was less chromatic, less cinematic, and less melodic, but it sounded a lot less abstract and a lot more personal. Cherry was pouring the artist's soul into each and every sound. The five improvisations (*Brilliant Action, Amejelo, Total Vibration, Sun of the East*, the simple apotheosis of *Terrestrial Beings*) harked back not to the tradition of Louis Armstrong or Duke Ellington but to the tradition of Saint Francis or DaoismF. *Bamboo Night* and *Teo-Teo-Can* (on the second volume) extended the symbiosis to distant musical cultures. **Mu** was instantly a hit with the rock intelligentsia (especially in Europe) but largely ignored by the jazz community (especially in the USA). On one hand there were superficial similarities with the hippy ideology, and on the other hand there was none of the narcissistic virtuoso-oriented show that the jazz world expected from a jazz musician.

Around the same time Cherry was involved in projects that shared a similar "utopian" view of music, such as Charlie Haden's **Liberation Music Orchestra** (april 1969), Carla Bley's **Escalator Over The Hill** (june 1971) and even **Human Music** (november 1969), a duet with electronic composer Jon Appleton on synclavier.

On the live European albums of that period Cherry continued to expand his ethnic horizons, from Indian karnatic chanting (he studied with Pandit Pran Nath) to Native-American percussion: *Togetherness* (his live warhorse) on **Orient** (august 1971), the 26-minute *East* on **Blue Lake** (april 1971), and *Humus* on **Actions** (november 1971), that featured an all-star cast under the moniker New Eternal Rhythm Orchestra.

Under the aegis of the Jazz Composer's Orchestra, Cherry scored for large ensemble the **Relativity Suite** (february 1973) that had debuted on the live **Organic Music Society** (august 1972). The players included saxophonists Charles Brackeen, Carlos Ward, Frank Lowe and Dewey Redman, violinist Leroy Jenkins, bassist Charlie Haden, pianist Carla Bley, two cellos, two violas, trombone, tuba, drummers Ed Blackwell and Paul Motian. A smaller (and

European) ensemble helped out on **Eternal Now** (may 1973), an album that continued his world-music travelogue. From the purest of his "folk" albums Cherry proceeded to a virtual sell-out: **Brown Rice** (1975), featuring a multitude of players (including Haden, drummers Hakim Jamil and Billy Higgins, tenorist Frank Lowe), wed his world-music to jazz-rock, although the format remained loose and extended (*Malkauns* and *Chenrezig*). Having thrown the poetry out of the window, Cherry retargeted his world-jazz for the new-age crowd of the 1980s with the atmospheric world-music of: **Hear And Now** (december 1976), the three volumes of **Old and New Dreams** (october 1976, august 1979, june 1980), quartet sessions with three other Coleman alumni (Haden, Blackwell and tenorist Dewey Redman), and the three volumes of **Codona** (september 1978, may 1980, september 1982), a graceful trio with Collin Walcott on ethnic instruments and Brazilian percussionist Nana Vasconcelos. The new duet with Blackwell, **El Corazon** (february 1982), tried in vain to recapture the charm of **Mu**. In 1985 Cherry formed Nu with altoist Carlos Ward bassist Mark Helias, drummer Ed Blackwell, and Brazilian percussionist Nana Vasconcelos, documented on the live **Nu** (july 1986). **Art Deco** (august 1988), for a quartet with tenor saxophonist James Clay, bassist Charlie Haden and drummer Billy Higgins, was free jazz played in the baroque vein of fusion jazz.

Arkansas-born tenor saxophonist Farrell "Pharoah" Sanders, who had cut his teeth in Oakland (California), moved to New York in 1962 and joined the groups of Sun Ra (where he got his nickname) and John Coltrane. His solo career, that had started with **Pharoah Sanders Quintet** (october 1964), aimed at grafting the free-jazz concept onto archetypal African rhythms and decorating the hybrid with Eastern techniques (the so called "Nubian space jazz"). The sound was perfected on **Tauhid** (november 1966), particularly by the 16-minute *Upper & Lower Egypt*, featuring Henry Grimes on bass, Dave Burrell on piano, Sonny Sharrock on guitar and two percussionists.

Distracted by recordings with Don Cherry and Alice Coltrane, Sanders did not return to his project until **Izipho Zam** (january 1969), with Howard Johnson on tuba, Sirone and Cecil McBee on bass, Lonnie Liston Smith on piano, and a whole ensemble of percussionists. The 12-minute *Balance* highlighted his sense of impressionistic counterpoint, while the 29-minute *Izipho Zam* was a colossal fresco of abstract dissonance. **Karma** (february 1969), with Smith on piano, Julius Watkins on French horn, James Spaulding on flute, Reggie Workman on bass, Ron Carter and Richard Davis on bass, and the usual army of percussionists, was mainly taken up by the 32-minute *The Creator Has A Master Plan*, a sonic excursion that ran the gamut from microscopic timbral exploration to gargantuan uncontrolled bacchanal.

The line-up was streamlined for **Jewels Of Thought** (october 1969), that is basically a piano and reed album against the backdrop of African percussion. Sanders began to play all sorts of instruments (flutes, clarinets and percussions), preferring soundpainting over virtuosity. The two suites represented the two basic forms of Sanders' art: the 15-minute *Hum-Allah-Hum-Allah-Hum Allah* was a narrative event, while the 28-minute *Sun in Aquarius* was a pure delirium of colors. **Summun Bukmun Umyun** (july 1970) repeats the same concept but the 21-minute *Summun Bukmun Umyun* extends the harmony thanks to Woody Shaw's trumpet and Gary Bartz's alto, while the 18-minute prayer *Let Us Go Into the House of the Lord* displays the spiritual side of Sanders' music. On the title-track of **Thembi** (january 1971) it was Michael White's violin that joined Sanders' saxophone and Smith's ubiquitous piano, but the album was mostly a simpler summary of previous themes.

A much better summary of Sanders' philosophy was represented by the one 37-minute improvisation of **Black Unity** (november 1971), with Marvin Peterson on trumpet, Carlos Alfredo Garnett on tenor and Joe Bonner on piano, Cecil McBee and Stanley Clarke on bass, and "only" three percussionists (notably Norman Connors). Sanders did not abandon his passion for rhythm, but this time virtuosity mattered too.

Norman Connors was responsible for the stronger funk accents of **Wisdom Through Music** (1972), and **Elevation** (september 1973) leaned towards a more rational sound, as in the lyrical 18-minute *Elevation* and the lively 14-minute *The Gathering*. **Love in Us All** (1973) was evenly split between wild experiment (*To John*) and emotional outpour (*Love Is Everywhere*). But clearly Sanders was getting softer and softer, bordering on atmospheric background music with the 20-minute *Harvest Time* on **Pharoah** (september 1976), a style that became his standard of reference for the rest of his career.

Philadelphia's pianist Alfred McCoy Tyner played on the Jazztet's **Meet The Jazztet** (february 1960) and joined John Coltrane for **My Favorite Things** (1960). While being introduced to Eastern philosophy and scales in Coltrane's group, Tyner lived a parallel life in a more conventional post-bop piano-based trios that played lightweight bebop: **Inception** (january 1962), with bassist Art Davis and drummer Elvin Jones, highlighted by the youthful ebullience of *Effendi*, or **Reaching Fourth** (november 1962), with bassist Henry Grimes and drummer Roy Haynes, containing *Blues Back*. The exceptions to the trio dogma were few, although often more creative, for example *Contemporary Focus* and *Three Flowers*, Tyner's lengthy compositions on **Today and Tomorrow** (february 1964), performed by a sextet (alto saxophone, John Gilmore on tenor-saxophone, Thad Jones on trumpet, bass and Elvin Jones on drums). After leaving Coltrane, Tyner proved to be a much more innovative musician, translating Coltrane's visceral style into his own bebop-bred language. **The Real McCoy** (april 1967), for a quartet with tenor-saxophonist Joe Henderson, bassist Ron Carter and drummer Elvin Jones, was entirely composed by him and contained intense pieces such as the ballad *Contemplation* and the modal and polyrhythmic *Passion Dance*. Having acquired confidence in his compositional skills, Tyner embarked in a personal odyssey of textural exploration. Scoring for a nonet (Lee Morgan on trumpet, Julian Priester on trombone, James Spaulding on flute, Bennie Maupin on tenor saxophone, plus French horn, tuba, bass and drums) on **Tender Moments** (december 1967), particularly *Man From Tanganika*, helped sharpen his vision. The quartet of **Time for Tyner** (may 1968) with vibraphonist Bobby Hutcherson, bassist Herbie Lewis and drummer

Freddie Waits helped the vision cohere, particularly in *African Village*. **Expansions** (august 1968) was the first mature statement of the new style, boasting four lengthy intricate pieces performed by a septet (trumpeter Woody Shaw, altoist Gary Bartz, tenorist Wayne Shorter, cellist Ron Carter, Lewis and Waits): the vibrant *Vision*, the Eastern-sounding *Song of Happiness*, the convoluted *Smitty's Place*, the melancholy *Peresina*. The miscellaneous double LP **Cosmos** (july 1970) added two innovative pieces, the eight-minute *Asian Lullaby* and the 13-minute *Forbidden Land*, for a sextet of piano, flute (Hubert Laws) oboe (Andrew White), saxophone (Gary Bartz), bass and drums. The sextet of **Extensions** (february 1970), featuring tenor/soprano saxophonist Wayne Shorter, altoist Gary Bartz, harpist Alice Coltrane, bassist Ron Carter and drummer Elvin Jones, pushed the "orchestral" quality of the sound, that had been building up since the nonet session, to an higher degree while hinting at distant echoes of Africa and Asia, particularly in the 12-minute *Message from the Nile* (half way between modal jazz and John Coltrane's style) and the blistering, 13-minute *Survival Blues*. These albums shared some of the concerns with space and time of contemporary progressive-rock.

The same format (four lengthy pieces) was repeated on **Asante** (september 1970), although the line-up of piano, alto, guitar, bass and drums, augmented with African and Latin percussion, was less colorful. The 14-minute *Malika* used vocals to increase the link with ancestral Africa, while the 14-minute *Fulfillment* was the first significant display of Tyner's uncontrollable urge.

That massive, dense, percussive, chromatic style that released clusters of chords like shrapnel, became the trademark of **Sahara** (january 1972). If previous recordings had tried to create an orchestral effect by toying with the timbres of the instruments (such as harp and cello), Tyner was now achieving the same effect simply by pushing the limits of the piano. The quartet with saxophonist/flutist Sonny Fortune, Tyner doubling on flute and percussion, bassist Calvin Hill (doubling on reeds) and drummer Alphonse Mouzon (also doubling on reeds) performed the transition from the old, abstract and impressionistic, sound to the new, visceral and explosive, sound of the 23-minute *Sahara*. The African and East Asian elements were now fully amalgamated.

Song for My Lady (1972) contained two sessions, one (november 1972) with the same quartet (that produced *Song for My Lady*) and one (september 1972) with an expanded line-up (Charles Tolliver on flugelhorn, Michael White on violin and a conga player besides the quartet) performing the longer *Native Song* and *Essence*.

Ostensibly a tribute to Coltrane, the solo piano album **Echoes of a Friend** (november 1972) actually had a centerpiece, the 17-minute *The Discovery*, that showed how different his style was from the master's. Coltrane may have been the influence to achieve such a degree of intensity, and to integrate exotic elements, but the spiritual angst of the master was replaced by a vital energy of the opposite sign.

Tyner tested the limit of his compositional skills on the music for large ensemble of **Song of the New World** (april 1973). He then applied the lesson to the more manageable format of the saxophone-based quartet for the three-movement suite *Enlightnment* and the 24-minute *Walk Spirit Talk Spirit*, off the live **Enlightnment** (july 1973). **Sama Layuca** (march 1974) again expanded the format to an octet to take advantage of a broader palette of timbres (vibraphone, oboe, flute, Latin percussion), at the same time setting his modal explorations to an insistent rhythm, the result being the ebullient texture of *Paradox*.

Detroit's classically-trained pianist and harpist Alice MacLeod married John Coltrane in 1965 and replaced McCoy Tyner when he left in 1966. After her husband's death and after converting to Hinduism (and adopting the new name Swamini Turiyasangitananda), Alice Coltrane began her career as a leader with **A Monastic Trio** (june 1968), a set that bridged Eastern spirituality and blues-jazz sensibility in humble pieces such as *Ohnedaruth* (by a quartet with Pharoah Sanders on bass clarinet) and *Gospel Trane* (by a trio with bassist Jimmy Garrison and drummer Rashied Ali). Her compositional and performing skills (both on piano and harp) blossomed on **Huntington Ashram Monastery** (may 1969), by a trio with bassist Ron Carter and Ali, especially in *IHS*, and led to the kaleidoscopic 13-minute *Ptah the El Daoud* and the simple 16-minute *Mantra* of **Ptah the El Daoud** (january 1970), her artistic peak, featuring Pharoah Sanders on tenor saxophone and alto flute, Joe Henderson on tenor saxophone and alto flute, Ron Carter on bass and Ben Riley on drums. The limits of her piano playing (that basically transposed her harp technique to the keyboard) were more than compensated by her lyrical and agile writing. The solos belonged to the jazz tradition, but the structure of the pieces inaugurated a new form of music (predating ambient, world and new-age music). **Journey in Satchidananda** (november 1970), featuring Sanders (on soprano only) and volcanic rhythm section of bassist Cecil McBee and Ali plus tampura and oud players, was another transcendent take on chamber world music, post-psychedelic droning and modal improvisation, from *Isis And Osiris* (with Charlie Haden on bass and Alice Coltrane on harp) to *Something About John Coltrane* (Alice Coltrane on piano). Alice Coltrane had reached the other end of the spectrum, compared with her husband's frenzied free-jazz, and the music was hardly jazz at all. **Universal Consciousness** (june 1971) had pieces scored for harp, string section (four violinists including Leroy Jenkins) and a dreamy rhythm section of Garrison and drummer Jack DeJohnette. The humanistic and cosmic element was now prevailing over the music itself, as in *Galaxy in Turiya* and *Galaxy in Satchidananda* on **World Galaxy** (november 1971). The strings became even more important to render that ecstatic feeling on **Lord of Lords** (july 1972), whose *Lord of Lords* and *Andromeda's Suffering* contrasted the rhythm section of Haden and Riley with a string orchestra of violins, cellos and violas. All in all, her key contribution to the history of jazz was an idea, the idea that music serves the spiritual needs of the mind. Jazz as an art of how to play instruments, or jazz as bodily entertainment was rapidly becoming obsolete.

Baritone saxophonist Charles Tyler, who had played with Albert Ayler (1965), introduced a style that was both lyrical and visceral on **First Album** (1966), in a quintet with cellist Joel Friedman, vibraphonist Charles Moffet, bassist Henry

Grimes and drummer Ronald Shannon Jackson, and on **Eastern Man Alone** (january 1967) for a drum-less quartet. After a long hiatus, he returned with an even more powerful statement, the 37-minute **Saga Out of the Outlaws** (may 1976).

Possibly the most "underground" of all free-jazz musicians, Frank Wright took the scene by storm with the three jams of his **Trio** (november 1965) and **Your Prayer** (may 1967) for a quintet with alto saxophone and trumpet, containing his zenith of pathos, the 15-minute *Your Prayer*, as well as the 12-minute *Fire Of Spirits*. While influenced by Albert Ayler, Wright was largely endowed with his own vision of earthly and supernatural sounds. His style displayed little of Ayler's populist and folkish overtones while harking back to Charlie Parker's agile delivery. A bass-less quartet with alto saxophone, piano and drums recorded **One For John** (december 1969), **Uhuru Na Umoja** (1970), on themes by Noah Howard, and especially **Church Number Nine** (1973), a massive 45-minute improvisation. Wright experimented with free-form vocals (vocalist Eddie Jefferson) on **Kevin My Dear Son** (october 1978), that featured trumpet, piano and a classic rhythm section (bassist Reggie Workman and drummer Philly Joe Jones).

Free Jazz: the West-Coast school

A mini-scene flourished in California, but it was very underground compared with the exposure that free jazz was getting in New York and even in Europe.

Los Angeles-based pianist Horace Tapscott was something of a moral leader for California's free-jazz community. In 1959 he established the multimedia Pan Afrikan Peoples Arkestra and in 1961 he helped create the Underground Musicians' Association (UGMA), but nothing surfaced on record. A quintet featuring alto saxophonist Arthur Blythe recorded the four jams of **The Giant Is Awakened** (april 1969), also known as **West Coast Hot**. The solo piano album **Songs of the Unsung** (february 1978), full of covers, was hardly representative of his compositional genius or his rhythmically eccentric style. The Arkestra (two pianos, six reeds, two trombones, tuba, cello, two basses and two percussionists) was finally documented on **Flight 17** (april 1978), that includes no Tapscott compositions, and **The Call** (april 1978), mostly composed by Tapscott. Besides a trio with bassist Art Davis and drummer Roy Haynes, **In New York** (january 1979), and the other trios of **Autumn Colors** (may 1980), and **Dissent or Descent** (1984), and the duo with a drummer of **At the Crossroads** (1980), his art was best represented on the two original pieces of **Dial B for Barbara** (1981) for a sextet (piano, trumpet, two saxophones, bass and drums). The most ambitious composition of the era was the 29-minute solo piano fantasia *Struggle X An Afro-American Dream*, documented on **Sessions 2** (november 1982). Towards the end of his life, Tapscott managed to record **Aiee The Phantom** (1996) for a trumpet-saxophone quintet with bassist Reggie Workman and drummer Andrew Cyrille, that contained the 16-minute *Mothership*, and **Thoughts of Dar es Salam** (july 1996) for another trio.

The other elderly statesman of California's free jazz was Texan-born but Los Angeles-based clarinetist John Carter, the founder and leader of the New Art Jazz Ensemble, who debuted playing saxophone on **Seeking** (january 1969). He had to wait until the 1980s before his pioneering work was widely recognized. His five-part series of concept albums devoted to the history of blacks constituted one of the boldest and most successful attempts at fusing African and USA music, focusing not so much on the stereotyped rhythms of Africa but on its melodic aspect and wedding it to the elastic application of rhythm and harmony introduced by free jazz, as well as to his own (often harrowing) sense of melodrama: **Dauwhe** (march 1982), **Castles of Ghana** (1985), **Dance of Love Ghosts** (1986), **Fields** (1988), **Shadows on a Wall** (1989).

Texas-born reed player Prince Lasha, active both on the East and West Coast, coined a more relaxed form of Ornette Coleman's free jazz on **The Cry** (november 1962), in a quartet with alto saxophonist Sonny Simmons. After playing on Elvin Jones' **Illumination** (1963) with John Coltrane's rhythm section (Jones, bassist Jimmy Garrison and pianist McCoy Tyner), he further downplayed the intensity of the free-jazz masters in the quartet (Herbie Hancock on piano, Cecil McBee on bass) of **Inside Story** (1965).

California's alto saxophonist Sonny Simmons was emblematic (although a relative rarity) of how the free-jazz improviser could wed the sophisticated composer. **Stayin' On The Watch** (august 1966) and **Music From The Spheres** (december 1966), each containing the four lengthy jams for quintets with trumpeter (and wife) Barbara Donald, were sometimes reminiscent of John Coltrane but also inherently more complex, if a bit less emotional. He remained a brilliant composer even after he started playing less confrontational music, such as on **Backwoods Suite** (january 1982), with Donald replaced by a three-piece horn section, **Global Jungle** (october 1982), in a quartet with cello, **Ancient Ritual** (december 1992), in a trio. No matter what the setting was, Simmons always managed to carve out a unique place in the history of jazz improvisation and composition.

FREE JAZZ: FREE DRUMMING

Perhaps no other instrument changed so much as the drums during the free-jazz era. The idea that percussion was merely for time keeping was turned upside down. Percussion became a component of the sound just like any melodic instrument. Basically, the free-jazz era discovered that harmony is not necessarily only built around melodies. As the gurus of free-jazz indulged more and more boldly with dissonance, percussive sounds did not sound anymore like a different dimension of music and increasingly gained peer status in the harmonic process.

One of the instruments that was more affected by the conceptual revolution of free jazz was the drums. Setting the example for others, Oklahoma-born Jimmy "Sunny" Murray, who moved to New York in 1956 and played with Cecil Taylor in 1959-62 and with Albert Ayler in 1964-67, revolutionized the role of the drums by abandoning the traditional time-keeping role in favor of a sound-making role (mostly by cymbals and snare). Basically the drums became percussion instruments whose role was to create sound (and, ultimately, contribute to the polyphony) as much as any other instrument. They differed from, say, a trumpet or a saxophone only insofar as the timbre of a wooden or metallic percussion is different from the timbre of an instrument that had been traditionally used for melodic purposes. The fact that melodic instruments were increasingly used to produce dissonance helped blurred the border. Removing the time-keeping instrument constituted, of course, a major boost to the abstraction of the music, making it even more difficult to find traces of blues or gospel or swing or anything else in the overall performance.

Murray's own recordings were more faithful to free jazz than most of the pioneers of the genre: **Sunny's Time Now** (november 1965), with the stellar cast of Albert Ayler, trumpeter Don Cherry and bassists Henry Grimes and Lewis Worrell unleashed in the jams *Virtue* and *Justice*; **Sunny Murray Quintet** (july 1966), featuring trumpet, saxophone, bass and percussion in a side-long four-movement improvisation (*Phase 1, 2, 3, 4*); **Sunny Murray** (december 1968), featuring saxophone, trumpet, clarinet, bass and piano; **Big Chief** (january 1969), with a similar line-up; **Homage to Africa** (august 1969), the manifesto of his pan-African free-jazz, with vocalist Jeanne Lee, saxophonist Archie Shepp, pianist Dave Burrell, bassist Alan Silva, Malachi Favors on balafon and two percussionists, one of his most effective ensembles ever improvising in the 17-minute *Suns Of Africa* and the ten-minute *R.I.P.*; **Sunshine** (august 1969), with the 14-minute *Flower Trane* performed by an ensemble with Burrell, Silva, trumpeter Lester Bowie, four saxophonists (including Roscoe Mitchell and Archie Shepp).

The evolution from hard-bop drumming to abstract drumming was symbolized by Michigan-born drummer Elvin Jones, the younger brother of pianist Hank and trumpeter Thad, who had moved to New York in 1955 playing on important recordings by Sonny Rollins (1957) and Miles Davis (1960). His groundbreaking work was done with John Coltrane's quartet (1960-65), particularly in their extended duet passages, although his heart always remained with hard-bop. Jones virtually liberated the hands and the feet, that seemed to play four different lines while contributing to create the unity of the piece.

New Orleans-born drummer Ed Blackwell, who relocated to Los Angeles in 1951, became a member of Ornette Coleman's legendary quartet of 1960 with trumpeter Don Cherry and bassist Charlie Haden and moved with them to New York, an association that was going to mark the rest of his life. After backing Eric Dolhy (1961) and Archie Shepp (1965-67), Blackwell was with Ornette Coleman till at least 1979 (in the group Old And New Dreams), and with Cherry from **Complete Communion** (1965) till at least 1985, when they formed the group Nu. Blackwell was the natural link between the bebop drumming of Kenny Clarke, the hard-bop drumming of Art Blakey, the proto-free drumming of Elvin Jones and folk drumming from rhythm'n'blues to African and Asian music. Blackwell was a key personality in transforming the drums into a versatile instrument, away from the purely tempo-keeping role and back to the primordial all-encompassing function. Hardly a virtuoso in the old sense of the word, Blackwell was a master of shifting tempos and timbral texturing.

Milford Graves, the percussionist who held together the improvisations of the **New York Art Quartet** (november 1964), was perhaps the boldest of the free-jazz drummers. He recorded **Percussion Ensemble** (november 1965) with another percussionist, Sunny Morgan, and then a live session with pianist Don Pullen, documented on **At Yale University** (april 1966) and **Nommo** (april 1966). These albums were about dissonance and soundscape, not about melody and rhythm. Graves became one of the most reclusive musicians of his time, rarely documented on record: a percussion duo with Andrew Cyrille, **Dialogue Of The Drums** (1974) **Babi** (march 1976), with reed players Arthur Doyle and Hugh Glover, **Meditation Among Us** (july 1977), with Mototeru Takagui on tenor, Kaoru Abe on alto, Toshinori Kondo on trumpet, and Toshiyuki Tsuchitori on percussion. He add to wait till the end of the century before he could release solo albums such as **Grand Unification** (october 1997) and **Stories** (june 2000) that fully represent his vision.

Philadelphia native Robert "Rashied Ali" Patterson, who in 1966 replaced Elvin Jones in John Coltrane's group, was one of the drummers who liberated the percussive instrument from its time-keeping cliches and made true "free jazz" possible. Faithful to Coltrane's legacy, Ali recorded bold and colossal improvisations on **New Directions in Modern Music** (1971), for a quartet with alto saxophone, violin and piano, and **Duo Exchange** (1972), a duet with tenor saxophonist Frank Lowe, before forming a **Quintet** (1973) with the young guitarist James "Blood" Ulmer that indulged in Ali's 17-minute *Address* and Ulmer's 18-minute *Theme for Captain Black*. His feverish, polytonal drumming turning each jam into a cosmic journey.

Andrew Cyrille demonstrated his blend of noisy, tribal and spacey drumming on a solo percussion album, **What About?** (1969), and on the percussion duet with Milford Graves of **Dialogue of the Drums** (january 1974). In 1975 Cyrille formed a quartet with tenor saxophonist David Ware, that delivered the 21-minute *Spiegelgasse* on **Metamusician's Stomp** (september 1978).

FREE JAZZ: FREE VOCALS

The voice was the ultimate instrument of free-jazz, although its importance was initially downplayed. It was free jazz that allowed the human voice to stand up as the powerful, expressive device that it is.

Iowa-born white vocalist Patty Waters, who relocated first to Los Angeles and then to New York, pioneered the creative vocal improvisation of free jazz and represented the connection between free jazz and the singer-songwriter of rock music. **Sings** (december 1965), containing eight brief, spare piano ballads (notably *Moon Don't Come up Tonight*) and the 14-minute interpretation of the traditional *Black is the Colour of my True Love's Hair*, a showcase of her wordless vocal acrobatics (backed by piano, bass and drums). That art of unorthodox vocal noises and atonal stream of consciousness permeated **College Tour** (april 1966), featuring pianists Ran Blake and Burton Greene and containing the seven-minute *Song Of The One* and *Hush Little Baby*.

Jeanne Lee met pianist Ran Blake at college and they began to improvise together on **The Newest Sound Around** (november 1961) Relocating to Europe in 1967, she joined Gunter Hampel's ensemble and provided vocals for his albums between 1968 and 1983. **Familie** (april 1972), for example, contained only one 55-minute improvisation for Jeanne Lee, Gunter Hampel (vibraphone, bass clarinet, flute, piano, soprano saxophone) and Anthony Braxton (alto saxophone, clarinets, flute), while **Waltz for 3 Universes in a Corridor** (june 1972) contained *Waltz for 3 Universes in a Corridor* and *Galaxie Sun Dance* for Hampel, Lee and violinist Toni Marcus. She was also featured on masterpieces of the era such as Archie Shepp's **Blase** (august 1969), Marion Brown's **Afternoon Of A Georgia Faun** (1970), Carla Bley's **Escalator Over the Hill** (1971). Her first album as a leader, **Conspiracy** (may 1974), featuring Gunter Hampel (on clarinets, vibraphone, flute and piano), Sam Rivers (on saxophones and flute), bassist Jack Gregg, drummer Steve McCall, three clarinetists and a trombonist, expanded the jazz vocabulary with elements borrowed from Tibet and India, inspired by Peruvian vocalist Yma Sumac, taking advantage not only of the voice but also of lip and throat sounds. **Freedom Of The Universe** (june 1978) was a duet with Hampel that contained another lengthy meditation. Their most ambitious collaboration was perhaps the double-LP **Oasis** (july 1978). A trio with drummer Andrew Cyrille and alto saxophonist Jimmy Lyons yielded **Nuba** (july 1979). Vocal Summit was a quintet of vocalists formed with Jay Clayton, Ursula Dudziak, Bobby McFerrin and Lauren Newton that recorded **Sorrow Is Not Forever** (november 1982). **Going Through** (1984), credited to Going Through, was one extended piece with violinist Billy Bang, tenor saxophonist Frank Lowe, bassist William Parker and two percussionists.

After **You Stepped Out Of A Cloud** (august 1989), her second collaboration with Blake, she recorded her second and last solo, **Natural Affinities** (july 1992), on which she was matched her with the likes of bassist Dave Holland, pianist Amina Claudine Myers, trumpeter Leo Smith, guitarist Jerome Harris, Hampel, etc.

She also composed the jazz opera *La Conference Des Oiseaux*, the oratorio *Prayer For Our Time* and the five-part suite *Emergence*.

Another powerful free vocalist blossomed in Poland, although relocated to New York (and married to Michal Urbaniak): Urszula Dudziak debuted as a leader with the album **Newborn Light** (november 1972), a tour de force of electronically-processed scat.

WHITE FREE JAZZ

Roswell Rudd, Steve Lacy and John Tchicai (besides Charlie Haden) were among the few white musicians to feature among the pioneers of New York's free jazz, and each of them belonged to it only in a tangential manner.

New York's white soprano saxophonist Steve "Lacy" Lackritz was the musician who restored that instrument to its original glory, and then raised it to an almost fetishist status. Coached by Cecil Taylor (1955-57) and Gil Evans (1957-64), and heavily influenced by Thelonious Monk, Lacy declared his allegiance to him while proclaiming the advent of a new soprano era on a series of quartet recordings mainly or entirely devoted to Monk compositions: **Soprano Today** (november 1957), with Wynton Kelly on piano, **Reflections** (october 1958), with Mal Waldron on piano and Elvin Jones on drums, **Evidence** (november 1959), with Don Cherry on trumpet and Billy Higgins on drums, **Straight Horn** (november 1960), with a baritone saxophonist and Roy Haynes on drums, and **School Days** (march 1963), with Roswell Rudd on trombone and Henry Grimes on bass. None of these quartets was particularly exciting or innovative, except for the fact that Lacy was interpreting the classics (Monk above the others) playing a soprano saxophone.

Perhaps inspired by the collaborations with Michael Mantler's various projects (1965-68), Lacy converted to free jazz with **Sortie** (february 1966), another quartet session (with Enrico Rava on trumpet) that this time was entirely composed by Lacy and included lengthy meditations, and with **The Forest And The Zoo** (october 1966), featuring Rava, Southafrican bassist Johnny Dyani and Southafrican drummer Louis Moholo, that contained only two side-long free-jazz pieces, *The Forest* And *The Zoo*.

Relocating to Paris in 1969, Lacy began one of the most prolific careers in the history of jazz music, re-recording countless times the same themes over and over again. His unique aesthetic was announced by the 41-minute improvisation **Roba** (june 1969) with an Italian sextet featuring trumpet (Enrico Rava), clarinet, trombone, cello (Irene Aebi) and drums, and by his first solo saxophone album, **Lapis** (september 1971). A second **Concert Solo** (august 1972), with definitive versions of *Stations*, *Weal* and *New Duck*, preceded the recording of the 30-minute four-movement anti-war suite **The Woe** (january 1973), scored for a quintet with alto, cello, bass and drums, and released only three years later. Lacy's postmodernist strategy was still embryonic but already captivating, with a passion for extra-musical noises as well as fragments of singalongs and nursery rhymes to weave intricate tapestries of harmony. The sextet of **Scraps** (february 1974), featuring saxophones (Steve Potts), piano, cello (Aebi), bass and percussion, became his favorite vehicle for the rest of his career, despite Aebi's controversial vocals. The sextet allowed him to create pieces of music that were chaotic puzzles of distorted elementary ideas, and it allowed him to run the gamut from the tonal to the cacophonous, from old-fashioned to free-jazz.

Over the years (starting at least in 1971), Lacy kept refining his "Tao suite" that was eventually finalized on **Remains** (april 1991) as a six-part *Time of Tao-Cycle*. Other themes that he performed frequently were: *I Feel A Draft*, debuted on **Journey Without End** (november 1971) by a quartet with Mal Waldron on piano; *The Crust* and *Flakes*, both debuted on **The Crust** (july 1973) by a quintet with alto (Steve Potts), guitar (Derek Bailey), bass and percussion, and both expanded on **Bura Bura** (may 1986) by a stellar quartet with drummer Masahiko Togashi, trumpeter Don Cherry and British bassist Dave Holland; *Torments*, first played by the Sextet on **Scraps** (february 1974) and revised by the sax-synth quartet of **Lumps** (september 1974); *Stalks*, debuted by the sax-bass-drums trio of **Stalks** (june 1975); *Snips*, sketched on **Solo At Mandara** (june 1975) and improved by the sax-synth quartet of **Lumps** (september 1974); *Deadline* and *Esteem*, both debuted by the Japanese sextet of **The Wire** (june 1975), and finalized (respectively) on the solo **Axieme** (september 1975) and by the two-sax quartet of **Revenue** (february 1993); *Stabs*, debuted on **Solo At Mandara** (june 1975) and finalized on the solo **Stabs** (november 1975); *The Duck* and *No Baby*, first heard on **Stabs** (november 1975), the latter refined on **Raps** (january 1977); *Blinks*, debuted by the two-sax quartet of **Raps** (1977) and revised by the Sextet on **Blinks** (february 1983); *Three Points*, first envisioned on **Points** (february 1978) but finalized only on **Blinks** (february 1983) and further expanded on **Flim-Flam** (december 1986) in duo with Potts; *Wickets* and *The Dumps*, both first heard on the Quintet's live **Stamps** (february 1978), the former expanded on **Blinks** (february 1983) and the latter on **Prospectus** (november 1983) by the Sextet plus George Lewis' trombone.

In the year of the saxophone quartet (Anthony Braxton's **New York Fall 1974** and the World Saxophone Quartet), Lacy assembled a sextet with four saxophonists (altoists Trevor Watts and Steve Potts and tenorist Evan Parker) augmented with Derek Bailey's dissonant free-form guitar and Michel Waisvisz's synthesizer. Their twisted counterpoint permeated **Saxophone Special** (december 1974), that included *Staples* and *Dreams* (with Lacy on turntable).

Bailey was added to the regular Sextet for **Dreams** (may 1975), a set that displayed an even greater degree of schizophrenia. The impressionistic chamber jazz of the quintet in pieces such as *The Oil* was devastated by Bailey's abstract doodling and both were neutralized by Lacy's irrational conversations. Several of Lacy's most radical pieces were recorded outside the Sextet. The 20-minute improvisation *Distant Voices* appeared on a trio album (Yuji Takahashi on piano, celesta and vibraphone, Takehisa Kosugi on violin, flute and vocals), **Distant Voices** (june 1975). **Clangs** (february 1976) was a duet with Italian percussionist Andrea Centazzo: Lacy played birds calls, pocket synthesizer and crackle box besides his soprano saxophone in creative pieces such as *The Owl* and *Torments*. The solo **Straws** (november 1976) included the electronic *The Rise*. **Threads** (may 1977) contained the solos *Skirts* and *Threads* as well as three brief trios with avantgarde composers Alvin Curran and Frederic Rzewski. Lacy also flirted with electronics on **Lumps** (september 1974) in a quartet with Michael Waisvisz on synthesizer, bassist Maarten Van Regteren Altena and percussionist Han Bennink. **The Owl** (april 1977) contained the three-part *The Owl Touchstones*, that augmented the Sextet with piano, kora and cornet (Butch Morris). Two trio recordings, **Capers** (december 1979) and **Flame** (january 1982), contained some of the most inspired of his extended meditations. The duo with Japanese percussionist Masahiko Togashi, **Eternal Duo** (october 1981), debuted *Twilight* and *Retreat*.

The sextet's most ambitious works were the two 40-minute **Ballets** (april 1981), *Hedges* (1980) and *The Four Edges* (1981). **Blinks** (february 1983) was perhaps the best summary of Lacy's canon, and it added *Cliches*. Sextet albums of new original material that stand out included **The Gleam** (july 1986), especially **Momentum** (may 1987), and **Live at Sweet Basil** (july 1991).

Lacy's next passion was to set poetry to jazz music: **Futurities** (january 1985), by the Sextet plus Lewis' trombone, harp and guitar; **The Condor** (june 1985) by the regular Sextet; **Anthem** (june 1989) by the Sextet plus trombone, percussion and a second vocalist; **Rushes** (november 1989) and **Packet** (march 1995) by the trio of Lacy, Frederic Rzewski on piano and Aebi on voice; the "jam opera" **The Cry** (march 1998) with Aebi, Tina Wrase on saxophones and bass clarinet, Catherine Pfeifer on accordion, Petia Kaufman on harpsichord plus bass and percussion; **The Beat Suite** (december 2001) by Lacy, Aebi, Lewis, bass and drums.

Lacy returned to the solo format for **Hocus Pocus** (december 1985), for **Solo** (december 1985), that had debuted *The Gleam* and *Morning Joy*, for **The Kiss** (may 1986), with *Blues for Aida*, and especially for **Outings** (april 1986), structured into two 20-minute improvisations, *Labyrinth* and *Island* in which he overdubbed himself.

Another intriguing project was an Indian quartet with sitar, tabla and tampura, that recorded *Saxoraga* and the 22-minute *Explorations* on **Explorations** (april 1987).

In the 1990s the ensemble kept growing. **Itinerary** (november 1990), that debuted *Sweet 16* and *Itinerary*, was performed by a 17-piece unit that was much closer to classical music than to bebop or big-band jazz. The seven jazz tributes of **Vespers** (july 1993) were performed by an octet that was basically the Sextet plus tenor saxophone and French horn. As usual with recordings centered around the sextet, these pieces were also sung by Aebi. **Sweet 16** (february 1993) was performed by a "Keptorchestra".

His last major recording was a collaboration with fellow British soprano saxophonists Evan Parker and Lol Coxhill, that resulted in the lengthy improvised saxophone duets of **Three Blokes** (september 1992).

White trombonist <u>Roswell Rudd</u> was the musician who rediscovered the trombone in the free-jazz era. After establishing his credentials with Herbie Nichols (1960-62), Cecil Taylor (1961), Steve Lacy (1963-64), Bill Dixon (1962-63) and Archie Shepp (1964-67), Rudd formed the New York Art Quartet in 1964 with John Tchicai on alto saxophone, Milford Graves on drums and Lewis Worrell on bass. **New York Art Quartet** (november 1964), one of the milestones of free jazz, displayed group improvisation at its best in four lengthy jams, particularly *Number 6* and *Rosmosis*, anchored by Graves' drumming and highlighted by the horns' fantastic counterpoint, while Leroi Jones reciting his black-revolutionary poem *Black Dada Nihilismus* offered a chance for free jazz to follow a narrative cue. Rudd greatly expanded the range of the trombone turning it into an abstract device for generating sound no less powerful than the saxophone. Rudd's stately morphing style and Tchicai's polyphonic style matured on **Mohawk** (july 1965), with Reggie Workman replacing Worrell. **Roswell Rudd** (november 1965) tested the trombone against Tchicai's alto and over a dynamic rhythm section of Dutch bassist Finn Von Eyben and Southafrican drummer Louis Moholo in three lengthy Rudd compositions: *Respects, Old Stuff* and *Sweet Smells*. **Everywhere** (february 1966) tried to repeat the same ideas but featured an inferior line-up (despite Charlie Haden on bass) and inferior material.

Rudd also composed the jazz operas *Blues for Planet Earth* and *Gold Rush*, and played in the creative orchestras of the era: Charlie Haden's **Liberation Music Orchestra** (1968) and Carla Bley's **Jazz Composers' Orchestra** (1968) and **Escalator Over The Hill** (june 1971). Rudd's own five-movement composition for the (24-piece) Jazz Composer's Orchestra, **Numatik Swing Band** (july 1973), was highlighted by *Circulation*, a multi-stylistic workout mainly for the trombone, *Lullaby For Greg* with Sheila Jordan on vocals, and the dissonant and exotic last movement, *Aerosphere*. Rudd the trombonist was transposing the New Orleans' trombone to the "creative" era while absorbing also elements of folk music.

Rudd proved to be also and mainly a significant composer on **Flexible Flyer** (march 1974), that reprised the collaboration with Sheila Jordan, backed by a quartet with piano, bass and drums (Barry Altschul), particularly in *Suh Blah Blah Buh Sibi* and the three-part 16-minute *Moselle Variations*, and on **Blown Bone** (march 1976), that delivered Rudd compositions for soprano saxophone (Steve Lacy), tenor saxophone, clarinet, electric piano, bass, drums (Paul Motian) and trombone, such as *Bethesda Fountain, Cement Blues* (also bluesman Louisiana Red on guitar and vocals) and *It's Happening* (also Louisiana Red and Enrico Rava on trumpet).

Danish-born alto saxophonist John Tchicai, son of a Danish mother and a Congolese father, was the important link between New York's original free-jazz scene and the European scene that developed in the 1970s. Tchicai followed Albert Ayler to New York in 1962 and was ubiquitous in the early pioneering experiments of free group improvisation, notably the New York Contemporary Five, a quintet with Don Cherry on cornet and Archie Shepp on tenor saxophone that implemented the principles of Ornette Coleman's **Free Jazz** (1960) on their **Consequences** (october 1963), particularly *Consequences* (the only track with Cherry); and the New York Art Quartet with Roswell Rudd on trombone, Milford Graves on drums and Lewis Worrell on bass, that experimented with expanded timbral ranges and polyphonic solos on **New York Art Quartet** (november 1964) and **Mohawk** (june 1965).

He played on several milestones of free jazz: Albert Ayler's **New York Eye And Ear Control** (1964), Archie Shepp's **Four For Trane** (1964), John Coltrane's **Ascension** (1965) and Roswell Rudd's **Roswell Rudd** (1965).

Tchicai returned to Denmark in 1966 and formed **Cadentia Nova Dancia** (october 1968), initially a nine-piece free-jazz ensemble that became a 24-piece "creative" orchestra for **Afrodisiaca** (july 1969). Tchicai, converted to Indian spirituality, was largely silent until 1977. He then formed the Strange Brothers, a quartet with a tenor saxophonist that released **Strange Brothers** (october 1977) and **Darktown Highlights** (march 1977) and split in 1981.

In the meantime, Tchicai had also released **Solo** (february 1977) for soprano, alto and flute, which also featured a duet with trombonist Albert Mangelsdorff, and especially **Real** (march 1977), twelve vignettes ranging in length from two minutes to eight minutes (*Nothing Doing in Krakow*) for a trio with guitarist Pierre Dorge and bassist Niels Henning Orsted Pedersen. These works asserted a fluid, intimate, controlled and highly rational style that sounded closer to the atmosphere of classical music than free jazz. world-music (and not only African) came natural to him and imbued many of his compositions with rhythmic and lyrical nuances that were unusual for free jazz.

FREE JAZZ: BORDERLINE

In the 1960s a number of instrumental masters remained faithful to the general framework of bebop and hard bop while incorporating the spirit (if not the letter) of free jazz.

Possibly the greatest vibraphonist of the free-jazz generation, Los Angeles-born Bobby Hutcherson, who relocated to New York in 1961, played on Jackie McLean's **One Step Beyond** (1963) and **Destination Out** (1963), as well as on Eric Dolphy's **Conversations** (1963) and **Out to Lunch** (1964), before making **Dialogue** (april 1965), the album that set the pace for the rest of his creative career. Hutcherson gathered a sextet featuring trumpeter Freddie Hubbard, saxophonist Sam Rivers, pianist Andrew Hill and drummer Joe Chambers to play music that straddled the border between hard-bop and free-jazz, particularly in Chamber's ten-minute *Dialogue*. The vibraphonist's split personality emerged clearly from **Components** (june 1965), performed by a new sextet with Hubbard, James Spaulding replacing Rivers (on alto and flute) Herbie Hancock replacing Hill (on piano and organ), Ron Carter on bass and Chambers: the album was divided between Hutcherson's lyrical compositions and Chamber's free-form pieces. Hutcherson's compositional skills matured with the quartet experience of **Happenings** (february 1966), with Hancock and Chambers, that ran the whole gamut of influences from hard-bop (*Bouquet*) to post-bop (*Aquarian Moon*) to free-jazz (*The Omen*). His zenith was perhaps *Verse*, for a quintet with tenor saxophonist Joe Henderson, pianist McCoy Tyner, bassist Herbie Lewis and drummer Billy Higgins, on **Stick-Up** (july 1966); but then **Oblique** (july 1967), another quartet with Hancock and Chambers, ventured into Latin jazz (*Subtle Neptune*) and folk melody (*My Joy*) while relinquishing the creative leadership to Chambers (*Oblique*). For a while Hutcherson was to free jazz what Lionel Hampton had been to swing or Milt Jackson to cool jazz: the vibraphone as the exotic and alien timbre of a musical revolution. Not a call to war, but the elegant dress to celebrate the triumph.

In 1967 San Francisco's tenor saxophonist Dewey Redman, who had already recorded an original **Look for the Black Star** (january 1966) for piano-based quartet, moved to New York and joined Ornette Coleman's quartet (1967-74). While his huge tenor counterpoint to Coleman's alto was mesmerizing the audience of free-jazz, Redman penned more originals for a trio session with the Art Ensemble of Chicago's bassist Malachi Favors and Don Cherry's drummer Ed Blackwell, **Tarik** (october 1969), particularly *Paris? Oui!*, *Lop-O-Lop* and *Related and Unrelated Vibrations*. Besides featuring three of the most creative minds of the free-jazz movement, it was moody and emotional music that related even to the audience of traditional jazz. He played alto on **The Ear of the Behearer** (june 1973), containing the twelve-minute bluesy *Boody* for a sextet with trumpet, cello, bass (Sirone), drums and percussion, and then also tried his hand on clarinet and zither in the trumpet-sax quartet of **Coincide** (september

1974), with the ten-minute *Qow*. Each of these albums was exploring a broad range of moods and styles, but **Musics** (october 1978), for a piano-based quartet (Mark Helias on bass), with the ten-minute *Need to Be* and the nine-minute *Unknown Tongue*, leaned towards the lighter of the spectrum. **Soundsigns** (october 1978) was its highbrow alter ego, containing a *Piece for Tenor and Two Basses* (Mark Helias and Charlie Haden on the basses) and the ten-minute *Come Earth* for harmonica, two basses and a saw. Redman formed a quartet with pianist Charles Eubanks, bassist Mark Helias, and drummer Ed Blackwell and recorded **The Struggle Continues** (january 1982), perhaps his most balanced album. Capitalizing on that sound, **Living on the Edge** (september 1989) for a similar quartet with Geri Allen on piano delivered *Boo Boodoop* and the feverish *Mirror Windows*, still straddling the line between tradition and avantgarde. Redman introduced his son Joshua on **Choices** (july 1992), whose highlights are precisely their interactions: the father on musette and the son on tenor in the 14-minute *O'Besso*, the father on alto and the son on tenor in the nine-minute *Le Clit*, both on tenor in the 13-minute *For Mo*.

Florida-born trumpeter Charles Tolliver, who had played with a number of luminaries, from Jackie Mclean (1964) to Max Roach (1967-69), gathered pianist Herbie Hancock, bassist Ron Carter, drummer Joe Chambers and alto saxophonist Gary Bartz to cut **Paper Man** (july 1968), containing the nine-minute *Peace With Myself*, a demonstration of his aesthetic at the border between hard bop and free jazz. Tolliver honed his compositional skills on **The Ringer** (june 1969), in a quartet with pianist Stanley Cowell, particularly in the twelve-minute *On The Nile*. A 17-piece orchestra centered on Tolliver and Cowell debuted on **Music Inc Big Band** (november 1971) and matured on **Impact** (january 1975), with *Plight* and *Mourning Variations*. Tolliver basically conceived of free jazz as a way to enhance the expressive power of the bebop soloist and found a way to make this sensible within the traditional structure of the big band of swing music.

Ohio-born and classically-trained pianist Stanley Cowell, who relocated to New York in 1966 and played with Marion Brown (1966-67), Max Roach (1967-70), Bobby Hutcherson (1968-71) and Charles Tolliver (1969-71), crafted cerebral and occasionally romantic compositions that straddled the border between hard bop and free jazz on **Blues for the Viet Cong** (june 1969), in a trio, such as the seven-minute *Departure*, the eight-minute *The Shuttle* and the nine-minute *Photon In A Paper World*, **Brilliant Circles** (september 1969), including the 15-minute *Brilliant Circles*, for a sextet with trumpeter Woody Shaw, Tyrone Washington on tenor, flute and clarinet, vibraphonist Bobby Hutcherson, bassist Reggie Workman and drummer Joe Chambers, and **Illusion Suite** (november 1972), in a trio, containing even more elegant and complex pieces such as *Maimoun*, *Emil Danenberg* and *Astral Spiritual*.
After forming a keyboard ensemble, the Piano Choir Inc, documented on two volumes of **Handscapes** (1973 and 1974), and wasting a quartet with alto saxophonist Marion Brown, bassist Billy Higgins and drummer Ed Blackwell playing Afro-soul-jazz-rock fusion on **Regeneration** (april 1975), Cowell

returned to the trio format for **Equipoise** (november 1978), that contained *Equipoise* and featured bassist Cecil McBee and drummer Roy Haynes, and **Sienna** (july 1989), with *Sienna, Sweet Song* and *I Think It's Time To Say Goodbye Again*. Like Tolliver, Cowell was an adventurous musician steeped in the tradition, who used the momentum of free jazz to increase the expressive potential of bebop.

An Identity Crisis

Despite the fact that jazz was mutating rapidly from decade to decade, it managed to remain "jazz", i.e. it always existed some kind of identity of jazz musicians that set them apart from, say, rock musicians, or even blues musicians.

While jazz was credited with a stronger emphasis on "improvisation", blues and rock music were also improvised, to some extent. Worse: the classical avantgarde began to experiment with improvisation (in fact, to a degree that jazz musicians had never even dreamed of). The myth that only jazz music was created as it was performed (unlike music that was written) was just that: a myth. Classical conductors also had flexibility on how to conduct a symphony, so much so that one conductor's Beethoven could sound quite different from another conductor's Beethoven. Rock musicians often improvised to much wilder extremes than jazz musicians. And almost all the greatest jazz musicians were also great composers.

Initially the white audience could distinguish blues and jazz simply based on the pace (blues music was slow, jazz music was fast) and the function (jazz music was for dancing). But bebop changed that too, while rhythm'n'blues accelerated the blues and made it "consumable" by dancehalls.

And if rock music was almost totally white, jazz became less and less black as it spread to California and to Europe.

If the color of the skin or the pace were not enough to distinguish jazz from blues, and improvisation was not enough to distinguish jazz from any other contemporary genre, it was often left to the instrumentation to label the music. A clarinet solo was "jazz" because it was a clarinet solo, whereas a guitar solo could also be (and most likely was) rock. But, again, rhythm'n'blues and rock music started using jazz instruments, while jazz started using electrical instruments. Sure, rock bands were unlikely to include a brass section, and jazz bands were unlikely to include the banjo, fiddle and mandolin section of country music, but there were too many instrumental duplications across the various genres to allow for easy categorization based on instruments.

During the early decades of jazz, it was rhythm that helped discriminate between jazz music and other kinds of music. But the evolution of jazz went precisely against that dogma, and rhythm soon became one of the many fluctuating variables rather than a stable reference point.

There was something about a jazz musician's quest for the perfect timbre that was truly a feature of jazz music. Classical musicians strove for the perfect tone, but not for a "personal" tone: in fact, they were supposed to sound as "impersonal" as possible. Blues and rock musicians were not so much interested in the timbre as on the narrative structure, of which the timbre was just an element. But jazz musicians were obsessed with the timbre of their instrument. Jazz was a music of vanity, each musician trying to play the same theme in an ever more sophisticated manner. Each musician sounded different because s/he "was" a different person. It was important in jazz to channel one's personality into an instrumental "style". Thus the "style" of the improvising soloist was something that truly set jazz apart: jazz music was the art of creating a personal, distinctive style at an instrument. While rock musicians also did that, it rarely became an obsession among rock musicians.

Jazz musicians were, fundamentally, musical peacocks, spreading their tails to an audience that was made, first and foremost, of the other peacocks: the competing soloists. From the beginning, jazz was a competitive form of music. New Orleans' bands competed in city-wide contests, and the swing bands of New York competed in clubs such as the "Savoy" that boasted the most sophisticated audience (mostly black). The best jazz soloists engaged in "battles" too. Blues music had never been so competitive, because style had never been so important.

Thus one can view the history of jazz as the history of musicians (of African, European and soon even Far Eastern descent) who continuously reinvented the art of crafting a personal sound while assimilating styles and instrumentation that they were exposed to, from ragtime to rock to ethnic folk, from the trumpet to electronic and digital equipment.

Finally there was the ultimate identity test: the music industry, which was in turn the creator and a reflection of the audience. It was the record industry that labeled music. Jimi Hendrix was a "rock" musician because it was labeled "rock" by his record label. Had he been labeled "jazz", he would have still been a revolutionary musician, but of a completely different kind: a hard-rocking jazz musician, instead of an improvising rock musician. An artist who recorded for a company specializing in jazz was a "jazz" artist. Many artists might have as well recorded for rock or blues or classical companies.

In a sense, it was not the musicians who created a symbiosis with the audience, but the labels that did it. A label created a symbiosis with a segment of the audience by providing that audience with artists that were similar enough that they could all be labeled with the same term. The audience, in turn, bought records based on similarity, and therefore demanded that the industry categorized musicians based on similarity of style. It was this loop from the industry to the audience back to the industry that was, ultimately, responsible for the consolidation of musical genres.

However, all of these elements (more or less in ascending order of importance) constituted the real definition of jazz music.

CREATIVE MUSIC

Chicago's Creative Jazz

Creative Music: the Disciples

Creative Music: the St Louis School

Jazz Post-modernism in New York

White Post-modernism in New York

Creative Music: European Creativity

Chicago's Creative Jazz

The communitarian spirit of the 1960s spawned the hippie communes, rock music's extended "families" of musicians, Detroit's radical political movement, and the militant groups of black activists such as Oakland's Black Panthers. That spirit entered free jazz in the form of organizations that grouped musicians sharing the same aesthetic intents. By the end of the 1960s there was at least one in every major city. By far the most influential came to be Chicago's Association for the Advancement of Creative Musicians (AACM), founded in may 1965. Its members shared the "creative" view (born with the most radical experiments of New York's free jazz) that music was about sound, not about musical conventions, musical tradition or musical virtuosity. Thus rhythm, melody and harmony became marginal factors: if emphasized at all, they were mere postmodern devices to reflect on the nature of jazz itself. But more often than not "creative" music was a close relative of the classical avantgarde. Basically, these Chicago musicians experimented a fusion of instrumental color, free improvisation and western-style composition, that largely transcended stylistic boundaries. They were, in fact, better appreciated in Europe than in the USA.

Ironically, the renaissance of Chicago's jazz music took place at a time when jazz was out of fashion in Chicago's clubs. The musicians of the AACM had to organize their concerts outside the network of night clubs: in theaters, in coffeehouses, in abandoned buildings, even in churches. The relative isolation of this generation of jazz musicians helped them create music that was largely indifferent to the tradition.

The style and tone of the music was fitting the environment were it was played. In contrast to the loud, passionate, intense, frantic music of New York's free-jazz elite, Chicago's creative music preferred abstract and abstruse constructs that could border on mathematics or even silence. These musicians loved dissonance and any sound or sequence of sounds that defied the laws of jazz gravity. At the same time, they emphasized discipline, not emotion. Jazz had been moving towards a deeper appreciation of timbre and logic and away from melody, but they turned the exploration of timbre and logic into a parallel science of music. Many of them relied on complex theories of music rather than on a desire for being "free". Instead of the traditional jazz instruments, Chicago's creative music liked to explore non-jazz instruments, whether classical ones or home-made ones, and eventually also electronic ones.

Free jazz had abolished the dogmas of jazz music, and therefore its stylistic borders. Chicago's creative musicians felt free to play a music that was just about anything, harking back to European chamber classical music as well as to electronic avantgarde music as well as to African shamanic folk music as well as to Far Eastern spiritual music, not to mention blues, rhythm'n'blues, street fanfares and big-band jazz. However, the underlying movement was not towards destroying music but towards "creating" it. The emphasis was consistently on creating a new form of music, as opposed to simply destroying the past. In a sense, Chicago's creative musicians simply reinterpreted the past for a society that had dramatically changed over the decades, pointing towards a future in which black music was not the music of the ghetto but the music of an epochal synthesis of civilizations.

Unlike free jazz, that still aimed for a degree of consonance with the events of the time, the "creative" school displayed a degree of detachment from the zeitgeist that was unheard of in the history of black music. With few exceptions, that sense of detachment permeated their recordings. When it was overridden, it mostly gave way to very personal, private, spiritual meditations. Whether detached or solipsistic, their stance marked a further regression of jazz towards a less social form of music.

Creative music was obviously related to experiments by John Cage, Karlheinz Stockhausen and Morton Feldman, but hardly related at all to jazz greats such as Louis Armstrong or Charlie Parker. Nonetheless it turned out to be almost exclusively "black". In fact, few schools and movements in the history of jazz music were so exclusively black. Apparently, white jazz musicians felt closer to the jazz tradition than this new generation of black musicians.

The protagonists were: pianist "Muhal" Richard Abrams, alto saxophonist Anthony Braxton, violinist Leroy Jenkins, trumpeter Leo Smith, the Art Ensemble Of Chicago (featuring saxophonist Roscoe Mitchell, saxophonist Joseph Jarman, trumpeter Lester Bowie, bassist Malachi Favors, percussionist Don Moye), Air (saxophonist Henry Threadgill, bassist Fred Hopkins, drummer Steve McCall). A 1970 performance in New York of Anthony Braxton's Creative Construction Company, introduced New York to Chicago's radical version of free jazz. Within a few years, the core of the Chicago revolution had entirely moved to New York.

"Muhal" Richard Abrams represented both a synthesis and a revolution. His piano style synthesized both ancestral traditions and avantgarde innovations in a deeply emotional and personal language. His arrangements, on the other hand, created a new kind of music, that pushed free jazz to the borders of classical music. The whole of his work laid the foundations for the "creative" music of the Association for the Advancement of Creative Musicians (AACM).

Abrams formed the Experimental Band in 1961 (featuring the young Roscoe Mitchell) that spearheaded Chicago's jazz revolution.

Levels and Degrees of Light (december 1967) was already a mature statement by a musician steeped in the blues (the ten-minute *Levels and Degrees of Light*, with Penelope Taylor's wordless vocals and Gordon Emmanuel's vibraphone) but rising towards a new level of awareness. Despite some poetry recitation, the 23-minute *The Bird Song* inaugurated a timbral counterpoint that used free jazz as the springboard but maintained a solid grip on composition, or, better, on the narrative dimension of the music (Leroy Jenkins on violin, Anthony Braxton on saxophone). **Young at Heart/ Wise in Time** (august 1969) contained two lengthy tracks: the 29-minute solo-piano excursus *Young at Heart*, highlighting his light touch and shimmering tone clusters, and the 22-minute quartet jam *Wise in Time* (Leo Smith on trumpet, Henry Threadgill on alto). After **Things to**

Come from Those Now Gone (october 1972), that contains more traditional pieces (except the austere *1 and 4 Plus 2 and 7*), Abrams returned to the intimate highbrow aesthetic that was his specialty with the seven solo-piano vignettes of **Afrisong** (september 1975), notably *Afrisong*, *Hymn to the East* and *Blues For M*. His music output then split into two. On one hand the duets, such as **Sightsong** (october 1975) with bassist Malachi Favors Maghostut, **Duets 1976** (august 1976) with Anthony Braxton (saxophones and clarinets), **Lifelong Ambitions** (march 1977) with Leroy Jenkins, and **Duet** (february 1981) with Amina Claudine Myers. On the other hand were ensemble efforts that started with two quintets, the one (led by Abrams, Braxton and Threadgill) for *Arhythm Songy* and *Charlie In The Parker* on **1-OQA+19** (december 1977), in which Abrams first experimented with the synthesizer, and the one (Joseph Jarman on bass saxophone, bassoon, clarinet, flute, soprano sax; Douglas Ewart on a plethora of reed instruments; Amina Claudine Myers on piano; Thurman Barker on percussion) for **Lifea Blinec** (february 1978), and quickly expanded to the septet of **Spihumonesty** (july 1979), in which the ominous sounds of the synthesizer prevail over the lyrical sounds of the piano, to the tentet of **Mama and Daddy** (june 1980), with the 18-minute *Malic*, and finally to the full-blown orchestra of improvisers for **Blues Forever** (july 1981), with *Chambea* and *Quartet To Quartet* (that transitions from a sax quartet to a brass quartet) and of **Rejoicing with the Light** (january 1983). While the duets were often indulgent and rarely regained the magic of his solo-piano performances, the orchestral pieces showcased timbral sensibility, dense and almost chaotic harmonies, shifting textures and, in general, continuous change.

Abrams' multiple-personality disorder continued to produce relatively uneventful duets, for example **Roots of Blue** (january 1986) with bassist Cecil McBee, **Duets and Solos** (1993) with Roscoe Mitchell and **Open Air Meeting** (august 1996) with Marty Ehrlich, impressionistic chamber recordings, such as **View from Within** (september 1984) for octet, **Colours in Thirty-Third** (december 1986) for various combos, **Familytalk** (october 1993) for sextet, **Think All Focus One** (july 1994) for septet, **Song for All** (1995) for septet, and, above all, ambitious orchestral works that were festivals of deconstructed hard bop and free jazz: **Hearinga Suite** (january 1989), **Blu Blu Blu** (november 1990) and **One Line Two Views** (june 1995). Abrams returned only occasionally to the solo-piano format, notably with the 29-minute *Piano Improvisation* on **The Visibility of Thought** (december 2000).

Abrams also composed *Variations for Solo Saxophone, Flute, and Chamber Orchestra* (1982), *Quintet for Soprano, Piano, Harp, Cello and Violin* (1982), *Improvisation Structures I - II - III - IV - V - VI* for solo piano (1983), *Odyssey of King* (1984) and *Saturation Blue* (1986) for chamber orchestra, *String Quartet #2* (1985) and *String Quartet #3* (1992), *Saxophone Quartet #1* (1994), and a symphony for orchestra and jazz quartet, *NOVI*.

One of the original members of Muhal Richard Abrams' Experimental Band, Chicago's saxophonist <u>Roscoe Mitchell</u> released the very first album of the Association for the Advancement of Creative Musicians (AACM).

Sound (august 1966), mainly taken up by the 21-minute *Sound*, truly set the standard for the rest of Chicago's creative music. The sextet (with trumpeter Lester Bowie, tenor saxophonist Kalaparusha Maurice McIntyre, trombonist/cellist Lester Lashley, bassist Malachi Favors, drummer Alvin Fiedler) challenged the dogmas of jazz improvisation and composition, venturing into dissonance and unusual timbres (even toy instruments). The instruments just did not sound like themselves: they were mere vehicles to produce abstract sounds. These sounds derived from the extended (and mostly dissonant) ranges of the instruments were made to interact and overlap. *Sound* explored the timbres of percussion instruments, and the ten-minute *Little Suite* focused on the subtleties of "little instruments". But the real breakthrough was the very notion of how to play: this was highly intellectual music, meant to be used by a brain, not by a heart, unlike New York's free jazz that was meant to be emphatic and frantic. These musicians were European scientists, not African shamans. They were scientists of the subtle. Thus the effect was that they were more interested in "silence" and in microtones than in "music". Silence was indeed the "space" in which music happened: silence was a key ingredient in the musical event.

Old/ Quartet (may 1967), mainly taken up by the 38-minute *Quartet* and released only in 1975, showed further progress/regress towards a music of minimal and primitive gestures. The live shows, that included pantomimes and clownish acts, besides the arsenal of "odd" instruments, increased the feeling that Mitchell's music was a form of theater. Free-jazz musicians, no matter how radical their experiments, had performed using bebop instrumentation and behaving like bebop performers, but the Art Ensemble showed no respect for these conventions. In 1967 the renamed Roscoe Mitchell Art Ensemble was paired down to a quartet with Bowie, Favors and a drummer. And perhaps the real manifesto of Mitchell's revolution was **Congliptious** (march 1968), an album that first redefined the jazz solo with three solos for bass (*Tutankhamen*), alto saxophone (*Tkhke*) and trumpet (*Jazz Death?*), and then resumed the project of redefining harmony with the 19-minute *Congliptious/Old*.

As the Art Ensemble of Chicago (AEOC), without a drummer and with the addition of saxophonist Joseph Jarman, took on an identity of its own, Mitchell's austere, highbrow experiment was somewhat modified to interpret a more humane, populist and even playful concept of music. Instead of a futuristic revolution, the AEOC embodied a synthesis of classical jazz, African music, American folk music and European classical music. It also embodied a strong sense of humor (unheard of in jazz since the heydays of New Orleans) and a political message. It even emphasized a circus-like theatrical element that harked back to the plantations and to Africa itself. This group was extremely prolific during its stay in Europe. Much of the music that they recorded was trivial and redundant, but some pieces do stand out: **A Jackson in Your House** (june 1969), dominated by Mitchell's 17-minute *Song For Charles*, **Tutankhamun** (june 1969), with Mitchell's 15-minute *The Ninth Room* (and a tedious version of the title-track), **The Spiritual** (june 1969), with Mitchell's 20-minute *The Spiritual*, **People in Sorrow** (july 1969), that contained just one 40-minute piece, perhaps their masterpiece, **A Message to Our Folks** (august 1969), with the 20-minute *A Brain For The Seine* and the eight-minute *Rock Out* (Jarman on guitar, Favors on bass, Mitchell and Bowie on percussion), **Reese and the Smooth Ones** (august 1969), another 40-minute piece, **Eda Wobu** (october 1969), an even longer (but far less engaging) live jam, **Certain Blacks** (february 1970), another minor album, with a 24-minute cover of Chicago Beau's *Certain Blacks*, **Go Home** (april 1970), with the 15-minute *Dance*. There were elements that acknowledged the innovations of Miles Davis and Ornette Coleman, but reinterpreted according to the quartet's unique aesthetic, that had little patience for musical dogmas. The AEOC became a quintet with the addition of drummer Famoudou "Don" Moye, whose devilish polyrhythms added a new dimension to the band's sound on **Chi Congo** (june 1970), with the 11-minute tribal maelstrom *Chi-Congo*, the 14-minute free-jazz work-out *Enlorfe* and the ten-minute orgy of *Hipparippp*, the film soundtrack **Les Stances a Sophie** (july 1970), with Fontella Bass on vocals and piano (*Theme de Yoyo*, a pioneering fusion of funk, soul and jazz), **With Fontella Bass** (august 1970), mainly divided between the 18-minute *Ole Jed* and the 19-minute *Horn Web*, and **Phase One** (february 1971), divided into two side-long jams, *Ohnedaruth* and *Lebert Aaly*.

The AEOC returned to Chicago in january 1972 and recorded **Live at Mandel Hall** (january 1972), the politicized **Bap-Tizum** (september 1972), including *Unanka* and *Ohnedaruth*, and **Fanfare for the Warriors** (september 1973), with Muhal Richard Abrams on piano, containing Mitchell's *Nonaah*, Favors' *Illistrum* and Jarman's *Fanfare For The Warriors*. Despite the publicity, the quintet had lost much of its charm. On the other hand, its music had become much more accessible.

In the meantime, Mitchell had recorded some more milestones of the creative music. The live **Solo Saxophone Concerts** (july 1974) focused on Mitchell's playing, alternating on soprano, alto, tenor and bass saxophones. **Quartet** (1975), featuring guitarist Spencer Barefield, pianist Muhal Richard Abrams and trombonist George Lewis, offered a summary of Mitchell's ideas, from the emotional *Tnoona* to the unemotional duet of *Music for Trombone and B Flat Soprano*, from the cerebral group piece *Cards* to the lyrical trombone solo of *Olobo*.

Nonaah (february 1977), featuring an all-star cast of improvisers in different combinations, delivered two expanded versions of Mitchell's most famous composition, *Nonaah* (a 22-minute solo and especially a 17-minute version for the alto saxophone quartet of Mitchell, Jarman, Threadgill and Wallace McMillan) and assorted experiments, notably *Tahquemenon* in trio with Abrams and Lewis, *A1 TAL 2LA* in duo with Favors and the 13-minute solo *Improvisation 1*.

Sketches from Bamboo (1979) tackled the large-ensemble format (which he called Creative Orchestra). Mitchell's chamber music reached a zenith with the double LP **LRG/ The Maze/ S2 Examples** (july 1978), that contained three of his most austere, complex and difficult compositions: the 17-minute soprano saxophone solo *S2 Examples*, the 36-minute *LRG* (which stands for Leo Smith,

Roscoe Mitchell and George Lewis), and the 21-minute *The Maze* for nonet, mostly on percussion (even Braxton, Threadgill, Favors and Jarman, besides Moye and Douglas Ewart) except Mitchell (saxes), Leo Smith (trumpet) and George Lewis (trombone). Not only were they fantastically disjointed, but they were more composed than they looked, being kept together by a cold logic of sound. *The Maze* ranked among the most sophisticated compositions for percussion ever.

The Art Ensemble of Chicago was still alive. They released **Nice Guys** (may 1978), with Bowie's *Ja*, Moye's *Folkus* and Jarman's *Dreaming Of The Master*, **Full Force** (1980), mainly taken up by Favors' *Magg Zelma*, the live **Urban Bushmen** (may 1980), perhaps the best of the later albums, with the 15-minute four-movement suite *Urban Magic*, Mitchell's *Uncle* and Moye's 22-minute *Sun Precondition Two*. **The Third Decade** (june 1984), and **Naked** (july 1986), the commercial sell-out.

Mitchell's career continued with his new creatures, the Sound Ensemble (trumpeter Hugh Ragin, guitarist Spencer Barefield, bassist Jaribu Shahid and percussionist Tani Tabal) and the Space Ensemble, that adopted a friendlier, more spontaneous and even "hummable" sound: **Snurdy McGurdy and Her Dancin' Shoes** (1980), **3X4 Eye** (1981), with *Cutouts for Quintet* and *3x4 Eye*, **The Sound and Space Ensembles** (1983), that added vocalist Thomas Buckner, trumpeter Michael-Philip Mossman and saxophonist Gerald Oshita,

Out of collaborations with members of these ensembles came Mitchell's most experimental recordings of the period: **More Cutouts** (february 1981), with Hugh Ragin and Tani Tabbal; **New Music for Woodwinds and Voice** (1981), with Buckner and Oshita; **An Interesting Breakfast Conversation** (1984), again with Buckner and Oshita; **First Meeting** (december 1994), with pianist Borah Bergman and Buckner; and **8 O'Clock** (2000), the third trio recording with Oshita and Buckner. Buckner's voice was a challenging factor for most of this phase.

A new quartet (Mitchell, Favors, pianist Jodie Christian, drummer Steve McCall) recorded **The Flow of Things** (september 1986). The Note Factory (Matthew Shipp on piano, Jaribu Shahid and William Parker on basses, and two percussionists) recorded **This Dance is for Steve McCall** (may 1992), that contained mostly tributes to dead friends. These ensemble works became less and less interesting, although at least the nonet of **Nine To Get Ready** (1997), with Hugh Ragin on trumpet, George Lewis on trombone, Matthew Shipp on piano, Craig Taborn on piano, Jaribu Shahid on bass, William Parker on double-bass, and two percussionists, the quartet of **In Walked Buckner** (1999), With Jodie Christian on piano, Reggie Workman on bass and Albert Heath on drums, and the nonet of **Song For My Sister** (2002) displayed sections of brilliant counterpoint.

Mitchell's career was now clearly split between jazz and classical music. Some of his classical compositions fared a lot better than his jazz combos: *Prelude* for vocals (Buckner), bass saxophone (Mitchell), contrabass sarrusophone (Gerald Oshita) and triple contrabass violin (Brian Smith) on **Four Compositions** (1988);

some of the pieces for solo woodwinds and overdubbed woodwinds and little percussion of **Sound Songs** (october 1994), entirely played by himself; *O the Sun Comes Up Up Up In The Opening* on **Pilgrimage** (1994), credited to the New Chamber Ensemble (violinist Vartan Manoogian, pianist Joseph Kubera and especially baritone Thomas Buckner); and especially **Solo 3** (2004), three discs of solo improvisations.

Mitchell also composed *Variations and Sketches From The Bamboo Terrace* for chamber orchestra (1988), *Contacts Turbulents* (1986), *Memoirs of A Dying Parachutist* for chamber orchestra (1995), *Fallen Heroes* for baritone and orchestra (1998), *The Bells of FiftyNinth Street* for alto saxophone and gamelan orchestra (2000), *59A* for solo soprano saxophone (2000), *Non-Cognitive Aspects of the City* (2002), etc.

Anthony Braxton was the "creative" musician who displayed the most obvious affinity with western classical music, scoring chamber music (both for solo instrument and for small ensembles), as well as orchestral music, that seemed aimed at extending the vocabulary of European music rather than the vocabulary of jazz music. If his was jazz music, it was the most cerebral jazz ever.

Better than any other jazz musician, Braxton represented the quantum leap forward that jazz music experienced after free jazz opened the doors of abstract composition. The music that was born as an evolution of blues and ragtime suddenly competed with the white avantgarde for radical redefinitions of the concept of harmony. Following in the footsteps of John Cage and Karlheinz Stockhausen, Braxton introduced new graphic notations to capture the subtleties of his scores, and even titled his pieces with diagrams instead of words. He invented new ways of composing and performing music. He also loved to write about his musical theory.

As a virtuoso of woodwind instruments (particularly of the alto saxophone), Braxton worked to extend the timbre and the technique. But, unlike his predecessors, Braxton was motivated by science rather than by emotion. Originally inspired by John Coltrane, he impersonated Coltrane's antithesis. In 1967 Braxton formed a trio with violinist Leroy Jenkins and trumpeter Leo Smith, the Creative Construction Company, that gladly dispensed with the rhythm section, with melody and with traditional harmony. **Three Compositions of New Jazz** (april 1968), that also featured Muhal Richard Abrams on piano, contained the 20-minute *Comp. 6E*, the manifesto of Braxton's style (at the same time abstract, visceral and geometric). The record sleeve provided the graphic scores of the music, that looked more like mathematical equations, and explained the chance-based technique that were incorporated in those scores (a` la John Cage's aleatory music). A few months later Braxton became the first musician ever to record an album of saxophone solos, **For Alto** (1969). This groundbreaking double-LP album contained eight extended pieces (each cryptically dedicated to a musician), culminating with another 20-minute juggernaut, *Comp. 8B*. His playing showed little respect for jazz traditions, but a lot of curiosity for textures and patterns. While this was mostly music of the

brain, it was performed with an almost hysterical intensity. Braxton himself seemed reluctant to continue the project.
The trio's contemporary **Silence** (july 1969), released only six years later, contained Jenkins' 17-minute *Off The Top Of My Head* and Smith's 15-minute *Silence*, two pieces that were less radical and more obviously in the free-jazz vein. The French album **Anthony Braxton** (september 1969) sounded like an appendix to the trio's music, with Smith's ten-minute *The Light On The Dalta* and Jenkins' nine-minute *Simple Like*, but also included a new Braxton vision, the 20-minute *Comp. 6G*. The line-up consisted of the trio plus drummer Steve McCall. It looked more conventional on paper, but Braxton played all sorts of woodwinds, Smith played horns and siren besides trumpet, and Jenkins toyed with viola, flute, harmonica, etc. Adding pianist Muhal Richard Abrams and drummer Steve McCall, **Creative Construction Company** (may 1970), released in 1976, was mainly taken up by a 34-minute Jenkins composition, *Muhal*. The second volume (same session) was, again, a colossal Jenkins track, *No More White Gloves*.
In the meantime, Braxton had formed Circle, a quartet with pianist Chick Corea, British double-bassist Dave Holland and drummer Barry Altschul. Their first document, **Circulus** (august 1970), credited to Corea when released as a double-LP in 1975, contained three lengthy collective improvisations titled *Quartet Piece*. **Circling In** (october 1970), again credited to Corea when released as a double-LP in 1978, was a less cryptic recording, highlighted by *Chimes* and Braxton's *Comp. 6F*. **The Complete** (february 1971) offered more of Braxton's compositions employing Holland, Altschul, Corea, plus trumpeter Kenny Wheeler and multiple tubas, in different settings. **The Gathering** (may 1971), the first studio album credited to Circle, contained only one 42-minute Corea composition, the title-track, and each of the four members played multiple instruments.
Relocating to New York in 1970, Braxton became the recognized guru of creative music. **Together Alone** (december 1971), released in 1975, inaugurated the series of Braxton duets. This one was with Joseph Jarman (both alternating at multiple instruments), highlighted by Jarman's 14-minute *Dawn Dance One* and Braxton's 15-minute *Comp. 20*.
Finally, Braxton gave **For Alto** a successor, and it almost sounded like everything he had done in between the two masterpieces was merely a long rehearsal. **Saxophone Improvisations Series F** (february 1972) was again a double-LP collection of lengthy tracks dedicated to musicians. The longest, *Comp. 26F*, was dedicated to minimalist composer Philip Glass, and for a good reason: the influence of minimalist repetition was strong, lending the album its hypnotic, otherworldly quality. Braxton's process was obscure and often not very musical, but the concentration was worthy of a physicist discovering a new substance. These pieces openly unveiled the process of distortion, variation and repetition that underlay the neurotic, claustrophobic feeling of Braxton's music.
The three-LP live album **Creative Music Orchestra** (march 1972) introduced a new side of Braxton. Four trumpets, four saxophones, tuba, piano, two bassists

and two percussionists performed twelve Braxton compositions. **Town Hall 1972** (may 1972) included the 35-minute *Comp 6P* for Braxton, Altschul, Holland, Jeanne Lee (vocals) and John Stubblefield (woodwinds). Braxton's new quartet, that basically replaced Corea's piano with Kenny Wheeler's trumpet (keeping Holland and Altschul), debuted on **Live at Moers Festival** (june 1974), a double-LP that contained six of Braxton's cryptic and overlong compositions.

But the prolific Braxton was recording non-stop, rarely replicating the powerful atmosphere of his masterpieces: **Four Compositions** (january 1973) for a trio with percussionist Masahiko Sato and bassist Keiki Midorikawa; **First Duo Concert** (june 1974) and **Royal** (july 1974) with British guitarist Derek Bailey; **Trio and Duet** (october 1974), that contained *Comp 36* for Braxton (clarinets), Smith (trumpet) and Richard Teitelbaum (synthesizer); **New York Fall 1974** (september 1974), that contained *Comp 37* for a saxophone quartet (Braxton, Julius Hemphill, Oliver Lake and Hamiet Bluiett), *Comp 38A* for saxophone and synthesizer (Richard Teitelbaum), *Comp 23A* for sax-violin-trumpet quintet (Wheeler, Jenkins, Holland, drummer Jerome Cooper); **Five Pieces** (july 1975), that contained *Comp 23E* for the quartet (Braxton, Holland, Altschul and Wheeler); etc. Most of these albums were trivial, although each contained something that opened new directions for experimental music. Braxton returned to the most ambitious idea of his career with **Creative Orchestra Music** (february 1976), six relatively short pieces for a mid-size ensemble that constituted his most eclectic output yet.

In between these seminal recordings, Braxton wasted his talent in erratic collaborations. Duets with trombonist George Lewis yielded **Elements of Surprise** (june 1976), dominated by Lewis' *Music For Trombone and Bb Soprano*, and **Donaueschingen** (october 1976), dominated by Lewis' 41-minute *Fred's Garden*. Duets with synthesist Richard Teitelbaum yielded **Time Zones** (june 1976), taken up by Teitelbaum's *Crossing* and *Behemoth Dreams*. Further collaborations accounted for **Duets** (august 1976) with pianist Muhal Richard Abrams and **Duets** (december 1976) with Roscoe Mitchell also on reeds.

Dortmund (october 1976) documented the new quartet with Lewis replacing Wheeler (especially in the long *Comp 40F*), while **Quintet** (june 1977) documented the quintet of Braxton, Lewis, Abrams, bassist Mark Helias and drummer Charles "Bobo" Shaw.

Among all these mediocre recordings one stood out: **For Trio** (september 1977), containing two versions of *Comp 76* (one with Henry Threadgill and Douglas Ewart, and one with Roscoe Mitchell and Joseph Jarman). The sheer number of instruments played by each member of the two trios was unheard of in jazz music.

He revisited two of his greatest ideas in rather inferior albums: **Solo** (may 1978) and **Creative Orchestra** (may 1978), that he only conducted (without playing). But then he outdid himself on **For Four Orchestras** (may 1978), that contained just one colossal piece, the two-hour *Comp 82* for 160 musicians and four conductors: the four orchestras surrounded the audience, that was given a chance to hear the chaotic interplay as it strove to evolve towards organic music. Braxton planned to score similar symphonies for six, eight, ten, and eventually 100 orchestras. The **Alto Saxophone Improvisations** (november 1979) were also more interesting, although a far cry from his two solo masterpieces. At last, his algorithmic music was heading for magniloquent drama.

Two of his best albums of this period were collaborations with veteran drummer Max Roach: **Birth and Rebirth** (september 1978) and **One In Two - Two In One** (august 1979).

Performance (september 1979) and **Seven Compositions** (november 1979) introduced a piano-less quartet with trombonist Ray Anderson.

In the meantime the routine of avantgarde compositions resumed. **Composition No. 94** (april 1980) contained two versions of the piece (forward and backward reading) for saxophone or clarinet, guitar and trombone. **For Two Pianos** (september 1980) contained Braxton's 50-minute *Comp. 95* performed by Frederic Rzewski and Ursula Oppens. Braxton returned to the large ensemble for **Composition N. 96** (may 1981). **Open Aspects** (march 1982) was another session with Richard Teitelbaum (now a specialist of computer interaction), but this time it was dominated by Braxton's compositions.

Composition 113 (december 1983) was a new solo album, but different from anything he had done before. First of all, Braxton played only soprano saxophone. Second, the album contained a six-movement suite that told a story. It was one of his most "humane" works.

The quartet remained Braxton's favorite format, but it began to include the piano. **Composition 98** (january 1981) documented a transitional quartet with Anderson and pianist Marilyn Crispell. The quartet consisted of pianist Anthony Davis, bassist Mark Helias and drummer Edward Blackwell on **Six Compositions - Quartet** (october 1981), and for once the players prevailed over the composer. **Four Compositions - Quartet** (march 1983) was a more composition-oriented effort by a quartet with Lewis, bassist John Lindberg and white percussionist Gerry Hemingway. **Six Compositions - Quartet** (1984) featured Crispell, Lingberg and Hemingway. **Quartet** (november 1985) had stabilized with pianist Marilyn Crispell, double-bassist Mark Dresser and drummer Gerry Hemingway, although **Five Compositions - Quartet** (july 1986) replaced Crispell with David Rosenboom.

The list of experiments was virtually infinite. **The Aggregate** (august 1986), a collaboration with the Rova Saxophone Quartet, contained *Composition 129*. **Ensemble** (october 1988) contained the 41-minute *Composition No. 141* for Braxton's saxophones, trombone (Lewis), tenor saxophone (Evan Parker), trumpet, vibraphone, bass and percussion. The **Seven Compositions** (march 1989) were scored for trio. **Eugene** (january 1989) collected eight compositions for orchestra. **Composition No. 165** (february 1992) was scored for 18 instruments. **Two Lines** (october 1992) contained duets with David Rosenboom at software-controlled piano. The twelve alto solos of **Wesleyan** (november 1992) and the **Four Ensemble Compositions** (march 1993) were, again, pale imitations of past masterpieces. **11 Compositions** (march 1995) were duets with a koto player. **Octet** (november 1995) contained *Comp. 188*, almost one-hour long. **Ensemble** (november 1995) contained *Comp. 187* for a ten-piece combo. **Tentet** (june 1996) contained the 67-minute *Comp. 193*. The most fascinating album of the period, **Composition 192** (june 1996), was a duet with vocalist Lauren Newton.

However, Braxton's focus was finally changing. **Composition 174** (february 1994) was a sort of soundtrack for a theatrical event, scored for ten percussionists and narrating voice. **Anthony Braxton with the Creative Jazz Orchestra** (may 1994) debuted his *Trillium Dialogues M*, his version of the opera. **Composition 173** (december 1994) was another piece for both actors and musicians. **Composition No. 102** (march 1996) was even music for puppet theater. **Trillium R** (october 1996) was in four acts.

Four Compositions (august 1995) for quartet and **Composition 193** (june 1996) for tentet inaugurated yet another strand of Braxton's art, "ghost trance music". And several hour-long compositions performed with the students of his classes indulged in all aspects of his musical exploration.

The "other" members of the Art Ensemble of Chicago were not as prolific as Mitchell but also produced some important recordings of the era.

Alto saxophonist Joseph Jarman headed a sextet (with tenorist Fred Anderson, piano, trumpet, bass, drums) for one of the pioneering works of the AACM, **Song For** (october 1966). Its 14-minute *Non-Cognitive Aspects of the City* and 13-minute *Song For* were typical of the soundsculpting aesthetic that was being created. Jarman, who often employed multimedia presentations (particularly poetry and dance), based the former on a poem of his, and conceived the latter as an exploration of empty space. **As If It Were the Seasons** (june 1968) contained two side-long group improvisations, *Song For Christopher* and *As If It Were the Seasons* for an even broader ensemble. Both focused on the space where music happens, the latter contrasting a naive theme with the emptiness in which it floated. Frank Lowe's **Black Beings** (march 1973) contained Jarman's *Thulani*. Jarman's albums after joining the Art Ensemble Of Chicago displayed a progression towards more and more sophisticated harmonies: the live solo **Sunbound** (december 1976), the multi-part suite **Egwu-Anwu/ Sun Song** (1977) with Don Moye, and especially **Magic Triangle** (july 1979), a trio with Moye and pianist Don Pullen. Jarman and Moye continued their partnership with more accessible works such as **Black Paladins** (december 1979), in trio with a bassist (and devoted mostly to covers), **Earth Passage** (february 1981), in quartet with a bassist and a trombonist (and containing his multi-part *Zulu Village*), **Inheritance** (december 1983), in a quartet with a bassist and pianist Geri Allen (*Inheritance* and *Love Song For A Rainy Monday*). But best was **Calypso's Smile** (march 1984), a set of duets with Moye that including *Morning Desert Song* and *Treibhaus Tribal Stomp*. After a long hiatus, Jarman returned with a duet with Marilyn Crispell, **Connecting Spirits** (january 1996), containing his *Meditation on a Vow of Compassion*, and a quartet with violinist Leroy Jenkins, pianist Myra Melford and bassist Lindsey Horner, **Out Of The Mist** (october 1997).

Unlike his cohorts in the Art Ensemble Of Chicago, trumpeter <u>Lester Bowie</u>, who relocated from St Louis to Chicago in 1965, was grounded in the jazz tradition. Unlike Roscoe Mitchell, Bowie maintained a close relationship with the idea of music as fun. In a sense, he represented Mitchell's alter-ego, complementing the partner's classical ambitions with a more populist approach. Nonetheless, Bowie was one of the most daring trumpeters of his generation, and one of the few to adopt free jazz, capable of producing a broad range of sounds. Bowie's debut album, **Numbers 1 & 2** (august 1967), contained two lengthy free-form jams that basically previewed the Art Ensemble Of Chicago (one is a trio with bassist Malachi Favors and saxophonist Roscoe Mitchell, and the other one is a quartet with Joseph Jarman). His sense of humor emerged from **Fast Last** (september 1974), an odd collection of different styles, highlighted (on the serious front) by a duet with altoist Julius Hemphill, the 13-minute *Fast Last C*, and **Rope-A-Dope** (june 1975), with Favors, Don Moye, drummer Charles Bobo Shaw and trombonist Joseph Bowie. These albums amply betrayed his tender love for blues and gospel music, a love that blossomed on **The Fifth Power** (1978), a quintet featuring altoist Arthur Blythe, pianist Amina Myers, Favors and drummer Phillip Wilson that reworked a gospel traditional into an 18-minute juggernaut; while the same quintet crafted the double LP **African Children** (1978) that synthesized all his disparate influences and moods in 20-minute pieces such as *Amina*, *Chili MacDonald* and *For Fela*. **The Great Pretender** (june 1981) marked the beginning of his conversion to a more radio-friendly form of gospel-jazz-rock fusion, that, despite the parenthesis of **All the Magic** (june 1982), whose second disc is a suite of brief satirical trumpet solos, led to Bowie's artistic demise. Whether it was a case of crossover or sell-out, the Brass Fantasy (a brass octet of four trumpets, two trombones, French horn and tuba plus a drummer) that debuted with **I Only Have Eyes for You** (february 1985) and **Avant Pop** (march 1986) ended up playing mainly pop, jazz, funk and blues covers. The best original material was provided by trombonist Steve Turre.

Famoudou <u>"Don" Moye</u> who joined the Art Ensemble Of Chicago in 1970 and moved to Chicago in 1971, employed an arsenal of percussion instruments on **Sun Percussion** (march 1975), turning it into a symphony of delicate timbres at the border between noise and trance.

Reed player "Kalaparush" <u>Maurice McIntyre</u>, another alumnus of Muhal Richard Abrams' Experimental Band, added an intense spiritual fervor to the abstract paradigms of Chicago's creative music (basically transporting the intuition of Albert Ayler and John Coltrane into a different context). He also straddled the line between rhythm'n'blues and free jazz in a spontaneous way that had few equals. **Humility in the Light of the Creator** (february 1969), featuring Leo Smith on trumpet, John Stubblefield on woodwinds, Malachi Favors on bass, Amina Claudine Meyers on piano and George Hines' wordless vocals, contained the five-movement suite *Ensemble Love* and the 19-minute *Ensemble Fate*. McIntyre formed Light (Fred Hopkins on bass, Sarnie Garrett on electric guitar, Wesley Tyus on drums, Rita Omolokun on vocals) and recorded **Forces and Feelings** (november 1970). He then relocated to New York and began teaching at the "Creative Music Studio" that vibraphonist Karl Berger had opened in Woodstock in 1972. One of the least prolific of all creative musicians, McIntyre took a decade to find the inspiration for **Peace and Blessings** (june 1979), basically a duet between Longineu Parsons (on trumpet, flugelhorn, flute, sopranino, soprano and alto) and McIntyre (on tenor, flute, clarinet, bass clarinet and percussion) plus a bassist and a drummer. The live **Ram's Run** (march 1981) featured a quartet with McIntyre on tenor, Julius Hemphill on alto, Malachi Thompson on trumpet and a drummer. After **Dream Of** (june 1998), in a trio with drummer Pheeroan Aklaff and bassist Michael Logan, McIntyre settled for a trio with a tuba player and a drummer on **South Eastern** (november 2001), the live **The Moment** (november 2001) and **Morning Song** (august 2003).

CREATIVE MUSIC: THE DISCIPLES

Once the founders of the AACM had shown how jazz musicians could lead the way in creating a new form of music for the end of the millennium, the new generation finished the program by further enhancing the status of the jazz composer.

One of the best examples of Chicago's fusion of theoretical issues and soundsculpting art during the 1970s was the career of Henry Threadgill. He is emblematic of how creative music proceeded along two parallel paths, simultaneously exploring new techniques of texture (mainly through different combinations/juxtapositions of instruments) and new techniques of composition (influenced by contemporary chamber music but also grounded in the tradition of black American music, from ragtime to free jazz).

The saxophonist cut his teeth in churches and dancehalls and military bands, playing gospel, blues and rock music. Converted to creative music while stationed with the army in St Louis, Threadgill debuted, in Chicago, both as a composer and as an alto saxophonist, on Muhal Richard Abrams's **Young at Heart Wise in Time** (august 1969). In 1972 he formed a trio, Air, with bassist Fred Hopkins and percussionist Steve McCall, that immediately revealed his strong compositional skills. Relocating to New York in 1975, Threadgill became part of a booming underworld of artists that liked to mix different kinds of art. Dance and theatre became as influential on his artistic growth as the jazz classics. **Air Song** (september 1975) contained four lengthy pieces, each for a different lead instrument: *Untitled Tango* for tenor sax, *Great Body of the Riddle* for baritone sax, *Dance of the Beast* for alto sax, and *Air Song* for flute. But the trio was truly "free" in the way they improvised around each other with no clear leader, hiding individual identity behind collective identity. **Air Raid** (july 1976) repeated the same format, with even more sophistication: the violent *Air Raid* for Chinese musette and alto sax, *Midnight Sun* for alto sax, *Release* (sixteen minutes) for flute and hubkaphone, *Through a Keyhole Darkly* for tenor sax. The research continued on **Air Time** (november 1977), that boasted even more adventurous solos, especially in three complex compositions: the obscure *No 2* for alto, the mathematical *Subtraction* and *Keep Right on Playing Thru the Mirror Over the Water*. **Open Air Suit** (february 1978) was a four-movement suite with the movements (or "cards") shuffled around. Threadgill on alto sax, tenor sax, baritone sax and flute was now dominating the proceedings. **Air Lore** (may 1979), basically a nostalgic tribute to Threadgill's musical roots, introduced a more accessible version of the band's sound, signaling the end of the experience. Nonetheless, **Air Mail** (december 1980) was still highlighted by the 18-minute *C.T., J.L.*, and **80 Degrees Below** (january 1982) was the trio's swan song, a return to the format and the magic of the early years, particularly in *The Traveller*, *80 Degrees Below '82* and *Do Tell*. As an improviser, Threadgill seemed to create a different vocabulary and a different persona for each instrument he played. All of them shared an almost scientific passion for complexity. So much so that McCall, the drummer, ended up sounding like the romantic soul of the trio (the bass was mostly running after the reed). Threadgill had already started a new project, X-75, a nonet with four reed players (Threadgill, Douglas Ewart, Joseph Jarman, Wallace McMillan), four basses and a vocalist (Amina Claudine Myers) that had debuted with **Volume 1** (january 1979), an album that replicated the four-composition format of early Air albums and showed how far his ambitions had come (notably *Celebration* and *Fe Fi Fo Fum*).

A "Sextett" (double "t") which was actually a septet (cornet player Olu Dara, trombonist Craig Harris, bassist Fred Hopkins, piccolo bassist Bryan Smith, drummers Pheeroan Aklaff and John Betsch) recorded **When Was That?** (october 1981), with *10 to 1*, *When Was That* and *Soft Suicide at the Baths*, and (replacing Smith with Diedre Murray on cello) **Just the Facts And Pass The Bucket** (march 1983), with *Gateway* and *A Man Called Trinity Deliverance*. Ancestral melodies were transformed into angelic bacchanals by a system of performance that toyed with the timbres and roles of the instruments. The Sextett was a micro-representation of the classical orchestra, divided into three sections of strings, brass and percussion. Threadgill was toying with the basic elements of the symphony without actually abandoning the jazz format. A new edition of this Sextet (Rasul Siddik on trumpet, Ray Anderson on trombone, bass, cello, two percussionists) recorded **Subject To Change** (december 1984), with *Just Trinity the Man*, *Higher Places* and *Subject to Change*, and then (with Frank Lacy on trombone) **You Know the Number** (october 1986), that offered more accessible material (such as the Caribbean *Bermuda Blues*). All these albums displayed his mesmerizing ability at deconstructing jazz music and constructing complex, twisting architectures. A new phase in Henry Threadgill's career began with **Easily Slip Into Another World** (september 1987), de jure another work by the Sextett (now featuring Hopkins, Siddick, Frank Lacy, Diedre Murray and percussionists Pheeroan Aklaff and Reggie Nicholson), but de facto a quantum leap in eclectic arrangements packed into shorter pieces, from frenzied cartoon music (*Award the Squadtett*) to nostalgic New Orleans marches (*Black Hands Bejewelled*), from moody ballads to pure chaos, to chaotic mixtures of ideas (*Spotted Dick is Pudding*, *Let Me Look Down Your Throat or Say Ah*, *My Rock*). Threadgill returned to the four-song format of Air with **Rag Bush And All** (december 1988), whose longer selections (*Off the Rag* and *Sweet Holy Rag*) displayed the growing idiosyncrasy of his compositions, ripped apart by the tension between the organized improvisation and an almost parodistic revisitation of traditional forms.

A new septet, Very Very Circus, with two brass instruments (Curtis Fowlkes on trombone and Threadgill on alto or flute), two electric guitars (Brandon Ross and Masujaa), two tubas and drums, further increased that tension between future and past. The spirited, denser and ever more eccentric standouts of **Spirit of Nuff Nuff** (november 1990), such as *Unrealistic Love*, *Drivin' You Slow and Crazy*, *Bee Dee Aff* and *First Church Of This* (Threadgill's best flute workout) coexisted with almost radio-friendly numbers (*Hope A Hope A*). Replacing the trombone with a French horn, **Too Much Sugar For a Dime** (1993) focused on sonic exploration in *Little Pocket Size Demons* and *Try Some Ammonia*; and, to increase the sense of displacement, *In Touch* and *Better Wrapped Better Unrapped* added three violins and lots of percussion (the former also vocals). With neither trombone nor French horn, **Songs Out of my Trees** (august 1993) delivered pieces without saxophone but with three guitars (*Over the River Club*, *Crea*), a piece with accordion, harpsichord and cello (*Grief*) and the gospel-y *Song Out Of My Trees* with organ. **Carry The Day** (1994) reintroduced the French horn and added Chinese stringed pipa, accordion, violin and vocals (*Come Carry the Day*, *Vivjanrondirski*, *Hyla Crucifer*), but also indulged in more linear jazz playing (*Between Orchids Lillies Blind Eyes and Crickets*). Very Very Circus' chaotic music peaked (as far as chaos goes) with **Makin' a Move** (june 1995): *Noisy Flowers* was scored for piano (Myra Melford) and guitar quartet (no sax, no French horn), *The Mockinbird Sin* for guitar quartet and cello trio, and *Refined Poverty* for alto saxophone and cello trio. The "regular" pieces (*Official Silence*, *Like It Feels*, *Dirty in the Right Places*, *Make Hot and Give*) for sax, French horn, two guitars, two tubas and drums harked back to the Sextett. Threadgill pared down the ensemble to a quintet (Ross, Tony Cedras on accordion and harmonium, Stomu Takeishi on fretless bass, drums) to form Make A Move, that debuted on **Where's Your Cup** (august 1996). Pieces such as *100 Year Old Game*, *Where's Your Cup*, *And This*, *The Flew* and *Go To Far* merely increased the sense of puzzle-like hyper-fusion musical structures. Replacing Cendras with Bryan Carrott on vibes and marimba, and introducing new Cuban drummer Dafnis Prieto, caused **Everybodys Mouth's a Book** (february 2001) to sound more constricted (albeit benefiting the austere *Platinum Inside Straight*).

A new ensemble, the acoustic, multi-ethnic and string-driven Zooid (British guitarist Liberty Ellman, Moroccan oud player Tarik Benbrahim, Puertorican tuba player Jose Davila, cellist Dana Leong, Cuban drummer Dafnis Prieto), debuted on **Up Popped the Two Lips** (april 2001), had a more exotic and neoclassical feel that better represented Threadgill's elegant eccentricity (*Around My Goose*).

The violinist Leroy Jenkins, who made his name in Anthony Braxton's Creative Construction Company (the 34-minute *Muhal* on **Creative Construction Company** of 1970), became both a virtuoso of instrument (extending the range of the instrument to become a more versatile source of abstract sound) and a composer/improviser of "creative music" (with a postmodernist take on the tradition of jazz, from spirituals to bebop).

Relocating to New York in 1970, Jenkins formed the Revolutionary Ensemble with bassist Norris "Sirone" Jones and drummer Jerome Cooper. The political nature of their music was less important than the format and the spirit. **Revolutionary Ensemble** (march 1972), also known as **Vietnam**, contained one 47-minute long jam that meant to depict the horror of the war. It was soundpainting at its most dramatic and poignant, but also at its most chromatic and dynamic. After **Manhattan Cycles** (december 1972) and **The Psyche** (1975), containing three compositions (one by each member), electronic instruments surfaced on **The People's Republic** (december 1975). Leroy Jenkins played an arsenal of instruments including synthesizer while Sirone and Jerome Cooper used all sorts of percussion instruments.

In the meantime, influenced by the Jazz Composers' Orchestra, Jenkins had assembled an all-star cast (Anthony Braxton, Kalaparusha Maurice McIntyre, Dewey Redman, Leo Smith, Joseph Bowie, David Holland, Jerome Cooper, Charles Shaw, Sirone and others) to record **For Players Only** (january 1975), two sides of avantgarde, the second being the more experimental (a sequence of solos by the various players).

Faithful to the AACM's aesthetic dogma of extended solo improvisations, Jenkins contributed to the opposite end of the spectrum **Solo Concert** (1977) and especially **Legend of Ai Glatson** (july 1978). He also cut the four duets of **Swift are the Winds of Life** (september 1975) with percussionist Rashied Ali.

His neoclassical ambitions emerged from a number of highbrow collaborations: the vignettes of **Lifelong Ambitions** (march 1977), with pianist Muhal Richard Abrams, the 21-minute electronic improvisation (with Richard Teitelbaum and George Lewis on synthesizers) of **Space Minds/ New Worlds/ Survival America** (september 1978) *Quintet No 3* for violin, French horn, clarinet, bass clarinet (Marty Ehrlich), flute (James Newton), off **Mixed Quintet** (march 1979), and *Free At Last* on **Straight Ahead/ Free at Last** (1979) with cellist Abdul Wadud. Jenkins also composed the dance opera *Mother of Three Sons* (1991), the jazz-rap opera *Fresh Faust*, the cantata *The Negro Burial Ground*, the multimedia opera *Editorio - The Three Willies* (1996). *Off-Duty Dryad*, *Themes & Improvisations on the Blues* and *Monkey on the Dragon* appeared on **Themes and Improvisations on the Blues** (1992).

Mississippi-born trumpeter Leo Smith moved to Chicago in 1967, in time to join the "creative" bandwagon and found the Creative Construction Company with saxophonist Anthony Braxton and violinist Leroy Jenkins. But his persona was fundamentally different from the "scientists" of the AACM. Like Anthony Braxton, Smith developed his own musical theory and his own notation system ("ahkreanvention" for scoring sound, rhythm and silence), but, unlike anyone else in that school, Smith viewed music as a vehicle, not as a goal; as a journey, not as a destination.

His musical vision first surfaced in the six ascetic solo "multi-improvisations" of **Creative Music 1** (december 1971). By employing other sound-producing devices besides the trumpet, he created eerie soundscapes in the seven-minute *Improvisations No 4* for found percussion and the 12-minute *Creative Music 1* for trumpet, flugelhorn and "mobile sounds". The 13-minute *aFmie-Poem DancE 3* on flugelhorn and the eight-minute *Ogotommeli - Dogon Sage* on gamelan percussion mapped vast open spaces of music philosophy. Not one note was wasted: Leo Smith was unique among creative musicians in that he aimed for the essential and the quintessential, rarely sounding rhetorical like Braxton or ornate like Abrams. He seemed to value silence more than sound itself.

That philosophy was better channeled into the two lengthy pieces of **Reflectativity** (1974) for a trio with Anthony Davis on piano and Wes Brown on bass: *Reflectativity* and *T Wmukl D*. Smith's contempt for redundance translated into loose ensemble counterpoint and a general sense of intimacy.
Smith formed New Dalta Ahkri with pianist Anthony Davis, saxophonist Oliver Lake, bassist Wes Brown and drummer Paul Maddox. The sophisticated sound of **Song of Humanity** (august 1976), permeated by Eastern spirituality, was best represented by two Davis compositions, *Lexicon* and *Of Blues and Dreams*, but also by Smith's own *Peacocks, Gazelles, Dogwood Trees & Six Silver Coins*.
A peak of Smith's lyrical imagination was the six-movement **Mass on the World** (may 1978), an extended piece blending improvisation and composition, performed by Smith (on trumpet, flugelhorn, flute), reed player Dwight Andrews and vibraphonist Bobby Naughton. The same trio penned the elegant, romantic 22-minute prayer *Divine Love* on **Divine Love** (september 1978), while Charlie Haden was added on bass for the 15-minute *Spirituals*. Smith, Andrews and Naughton were accompanied by bassist Wes Brown and drummer Pheeroan AKlaff for the 19-minute *Images* and the surreal *Spirit Catcher* on **Spirit Catcher** (may 1979), while *The Burning of Stones* (inspired by West African and Japanese music) matched Smith's trumpet with three harps for one of his most pensive chamber pieces. Smith had elaborated a theory of "rhythm units" based on Charlie Patton's blues that helped him calibrate the relationship between sound and silence, elementary sounds and compound sounds. The same trio with Wes Brown on bass was documented on the live **Go in Numbers** (january 1980), with the lengthy improvisations of *Go in Numbers* and *Illumination - The Nguzo Saba Changes*. Smith's sound was becoming precious and languid, besides pan-ethnic, almost the opposite of the standard within the Chicago school he came from. The different sound was due to a different philosophy, to a vision of jazz as a religious form of art with the power to uplift frustrated people and as a political form of art with the mission to liberate enslaved people.
On the other hand, **Ahkreanvention** (1979) was basically "Creative Music 2", as it returned to the same solo format of his debut album. Smith alternated on many instruments during the five-movement suite *Love Is a Rare Beauty* and *Life Sequence 1*. And Smith contributed the longest track, *Return To My Native Land II*, to **The Sky Cries The Blues** (january 1981) by the 17-piece Creative Musicians Improvisers Orchestra (with Oliver Lake and Marty Ehrlich on reeds). Smith's underlying concerns for humanity became more explicit in the 1980s, while the music opened up to all sorts of non-jazz influences. Smith (on trumpet, flugelhorn, flute and thumb piano) was joined by a bassist and a drummer for the live **Touch the Earth Break the Shells** (january 1981), with *Touch the Earth* and *Rastafari in the Universe*. **Human Rights** (1982) fused jazz with African, reggae and rock music, while incorporating instruments as diverse as koto, synthesizer and guitar, and maintaining the format of free jazz (the side-long improvisation *Human Rights World Music*). **Procession Of The Great Ancestry** (february 1983), featuring Naughton and Kahil El Zabar on percussion among others (electric guitar, bass, tenor sax), found him singing and pay homage to

great trumpeters of the past: *Procession of the Great Ancestry* for Miles Davis, *The Third World Grainery of Pure Earth* for Roy Eldridge, *Celestial Sparks in the Sanctuary of Redemption* for Dizzy Gillespie. Smith (now renamed "Wadada", after becoming a Rastafarian, as fashionable at the time) basically parted ways with the austere, European-inspired research of Chicago's creative musicians. The notable exception was **Rastafari** (june 1983), a free-jazz session for chamber ensemble (trumpet, soprano saxophone, violin, bass, vibraphone).

After a decade of neglect, Smith returned with **Cosmos Has Spirit** (april 1992), live duets (mainly the 32-minute title-track) between Smith (on bamboo flute, karimba and trumpet) and percussionist Yoshisaburo Toyozumi, and especially **Kulture Jazz** (october 1992), a solo album on which Smith took care of trumpet, flugelhorn, bamboo flute, koto, mbira, harmonica, percussion, and, last but not least, vocals. This album introduced a tune-oriented approach, both respectful of the jazz tradition and sentimental in revisiting his personal life.

Chamber and ethnic compositions surfaced on **Tao-Njia** (may 1996): *Another Wave More Waves*, the multi-part requiem for Don Cherry, *Double Thunderbolt*, and especially *Tao-Nija*. These classical-oriented works exuded spirituality via the careful layout of the timbres of ethnic instruments, in a way not too dissimilar from new-age music.

Smith also composed *Odwira* (1995) for twelve multi-ensemble-units, and *Heart Reflections* (1996).

The quest for a music of shadows continued with **Prataksis** (april 1997), a trio with reed player Vinny Golia and bassist Bertram Turetzky, and reached the zenith with **Golden Hearts Remembrance** (january 1997), his most intense, intimate blend of ethnic folk, blues and jazz. Performed by the sextet N'da Kulture (David Philipson on bansuri and tambura, William Roper on bass and tuba, Glenn Horiuchi on piano and shamisen, Sonship Theus on percussion, Harumi Makino on voice), the hypnotic 13-minute *Golden Hearts Remembrance A Nur Bakhshad* and the romantic 12-minute *Emmeya* the eerie soundscapes of the 12-minute *Lotus Garden*, the ten-minute *Tawhid* and the 15-minute *Condor*.

The **Golden Quartet** (2000), featuring drummer Jack DeJohnette, pianist Anthony Davis and bassist Malachi Favors, was instead one of his more conventional albums of jazz music (*Celestial Sky And All The Magic*), and the quartet's follow-up, **Year of the Elephant** (april 2002), increased the impression of a Miles Davis clone (*Al Madinah*, *Miles Star in 3 parts*).

Smith proved to be one of the most sensational soloists of his generation on **Red Sulphur Sky** (2001), that contained the lively suites (not just abstract solos) of *The Medicine Wheel* and *AFMIE - Purity and Poverty* for solo trumpet or flugelhorn.

Smith also updated his art to the digital age with **Luminous Axis** (august 2002), an ambitious set of chamber works for trumpet (or flugelhorn), live electronics (including laptop musician Ikue Mori) and percussion, notably *Caravans Of Winter And Summer* for trumpet and four laptops.

Chicago's trombonist <u>George Lewis</u>, who graduated in Philosophy from Yale University, was emblematic of the second generation of AACM musicians. He pushed the boundaries not only of jazz music but of music in general, experimenting with interactive computer music and becoming a multimedia artist. His groundbreaking **Solo Trombone Record** (november 1976) contained the 20-minute dissonant and overdubbing tour de force of *Piece For Three Trombones Simultaneously*, a journey inside the soul and the history of the instrument, and pioneered on the trombone the kind of extended techniques that had been applied mainly to the saxophone. **Shadowgraph** (1977) ventured into chamber jazz with the 13-minute *Monads* for trombone, piano (Anthony Davis), bass clarinet (Douglas Ewart), violin (Leroy Jenkins), soprano saxophone (Roscoe Mitchell) and cello (Adbul Wadud) and no bass or percussion, the nine-minute *Triple Slow Mix* for a trio of sousaphone (Lewis) and two pianos (Davis and Muhal Richard Abrams) that were recorded in separate stereo channels, and the eleven-minute *Shadowgraph 5 - Sextet* for trombone, piano (Abrams), flutes (Ewart), violin (Jenkins), saxophones (Mitchell) and cello (Wadud). The fifth was only one of the **Shadowgraph Series** (1977) for "creative orchestra". The others were only recorded in 2000. These "rhythm-less" pieces sounded oneiric and otherworldly, because Lewis sacrificed emotion and dynamics to foster textural and subliminal trance. The live in the studio 44-minute piece of **Chicago Slow Dance** (1977) for a quartet with Lewis (on electronics, trombone), Ewart (on bassoon, tenor saxophone, flute, bass clarinet), JD Parran (baritone saxophone, piccolo, Indian nagaswaram reed instrument) and Teitelbaum (synthesizer), released only four years later, presented an eerie landscape of short repetitive horn phrases, insect-like percussive noises, siren-like drones, sparse slow dirges, warped psychedelic timbres, pastoral flute melodies. The side-long *Imaginary Suite* on **George Lewis Douglas Ewart** (1978), a duo with Ewart on flutes, was Lewis' first attempt at incorporating electronic instruments and electronically-modified instruments into the grammar of jazz music. **Homage to Charles Parker** (1979) contained two side-long compositions performed by the same quartet of Lewis, Davis, Ewart and Richard Teitelbaum on synthesizers. The extremely technical structure of *Blues* contrasted with *Homage to Charles Parker*, a "tribute" to the jazz master only in spirit (highlighted by a poignant Ewart alto solo). In practice, they were both studies on how to create impressionistic soundscapes.

But Lewis was devoting more and more of his intelligence to multimedia installations such as *Voyager* (1981), his first major computer interactive composition, in which the computer manipulates the performance of the improvisers in real time.

Tenor saxophonist Chico Freeman began as a promising improviser. **Morning Prayer** (september 1976) featured a "creative" septet (Freeman on tenor, soprano, flute and pan-pipe, Henry Threadgill on alto, baritone and flute, Douglas Ewart on flute, Muhal Richard Abrams on piano, Cecil McBee on bass, Steve McCall and Ben Montgomery on percussion) stretching out on extended Freeman originals such as *Morning Prayer*, *Pepe's Samba* and *Like The Kind Of Peace It Is*. **Chico** (1977) was mostly taken up by the 24-minute three-movement suite *Moments*, a duet with bassist Cecil McBee, and the 16-minute jam *Merger*, for a piano-based quintet (McBee, pianist Muhal Richard Abrams, drummer Steve McCall, percussionist Tito Sampa). **No Time Left** (june 1977) featured a quartet with vibraphonist Jay Hoggard, bassist Rick Rozie and drummer Don Moye (and himself on tenor, soprano and bass clarinet) exploring the relationship between the traditional jazz quartet and the avantgarde jazz quartet in the 18-minute *No Time Left* and the 12-minute *Uhmla*. **Kings of Mali** (september 1977), perhaps the best of the early days, featured a stellar quintet with vibraphonist Jay Hoggard, pianist Anthony Davis, bassist Cecil McBee and drummer Don Moye performing four lengthy Freeman originals. **The Outside Within** (1978), whose centerpiece was McBee's 19-minute *Undercurrent*, but also included Freeman's *The Search*, featured a quartet with McBee, pianist John Hicks and drummer Jack DeJohnette. The interaction between color and melody was the theme of **Peaceful Heart Gentle Spirit** (march 1980) for a rich chamber octet (flutist James Newton, pianist Kenny Kirkland, vibraphonist Jay Hoggard, cello, bass, two percussionists, and Freeman on tenor sax, flute and clarinet), including some old compositions besides the new *Peaceful Heart Gentle Spirit* and *Nina's Song Dance*.

Freeman then adopted the "new traditionalist" stance in earnest and devoted the rest of his career to albums full of covers turned into muzak for yuppies. Freeman also formed the Leaders, a supergroup with trumpeter Lester Bowie, alto saxophonist Arthur Blythe, pianist Kirk Lightsey, bassist Cecil McBee and drummer Don Moye, that recorded the mediocre **Mudfoot** (june 1986) with *Freedom Swing Song* and *Midnite Train*, **Out Here Like This** (february 1987), **Heaven Dance** (may 1988), and **Unforeseen Blessings** (december 1988). The four-saxophone septet Roots (including Nathan Davis, Arthur Blythe and Sam Rivers on saxophones and Don Pullen on piano) debuted with **Salutes the Saxophone** (1991) and **Stablemates** (december 1992). Freeman pursued a fusion of pop-jazz, world-music and hip hop with Brainstorm, that released **Mystical Dreamer** (may 1989), **Sweet Explosion** (april 1990) and **Threshold** (1993).

One of the few women of Chicago's creative music, and one of the few jazz composers with a mastery of blues, gospel and soul music, Arkansas-born pianist (and, more importantly, arranger) Amina-Claudine Myers was largely missing from the great recordings of the 1960s, despite joining Muhal Richard Abrams' band in 1966. She was more interested in composing and arranging vocal music. Relocating to New York in 1976, she debuted with an album of solo piano interpretations of Marion Brown's music, **Poems For Piano** (july 1979), followed by a lyrical **Song For Mother Earth** (october 1979), a duet with percussionist Pheeroan aklaff. **Salutes Bessie Smith** (1980) in a trio with bass and drums contained her 15-minute touching *African Blues*. Another trio recording, **Circle of Time** (february 1983), contained six originals that summarized her musical roots and her spiritual persona. She converted to funk-jazz fusion with **Country Girl** (april 1986), containing three extended compositions such as *Country Girl*, *Blessings* and *Pain* performed by a sextet with Patience Higgins on flute, alto sax and soprano sax, Ricky Ford on tenor sax, Jerome Harris on bass guitar, Reggie Nicholson on drums, Bola Idowu on percussion, and Myers on piano, harmonica and vibraphone (and a few of them doubling on vocals).

There was at least one white musician who, for a while, was a match for these colossi of creative music: trombonist Ray Anderson, who moved to New York in 1972, where he worked with Anthony Braxton (1978-81) and Barry Altschul (1978-80). Anderson, a virtuoso of multiphonics and a schoolmate of trombonist George Lewis, was one of the musicians who pushed the limits of the trombone after the neglect of the bebop years. Anderson debuted on **Oahspe** (november 1978) in an all-white trio with bassist Mark Helias and drummer Gerry Hemingway that was a slicker version of Barry Altschul's free-jazz trio (in which both Anderson and Helias were playing at the time). That trio evolved via **Right Down Your Alley** (february 1984) and **You Be** (november 1985) to become BassDrumBone, the first of many Anderson projects. basically, this trio made free jazz palatable to the traditionalists with their good-humored anti-intellectual approach while surgically operating on its corpse with a postmodernist perspective in the tradition of Charles Mingus. Anderson's style at the instrument was a lot less cerebral than Lewis', and frequently downright ironic, reminiscent of New Orleans' marching bands, Chicago's rhythm'n'blues and California's funk-rock.

Anderson's schizophrenic style allowed him an equally schizophrenic career. The Slickaphonics, a quintet formed with Helias, guitarist Allan Jaffe, and saxophonist Steve Elson, played avant-funk music on **Wow Bag** (march 1982), **Modern Life** (november 1983) and **Humatomic Energy** (may 1985). His playful side emerged on **It Just So Happens** (february 1987), for a sextet (trombone, trumpet, clarinet, tuba, bass and drums) and erupted from the riotous and clownish **Blues Bred in the Bone** (march 1988), performed by a stellar quintet with pianist Anthony Davis, guitarist John Scofield, bassist Mark Dresser and drummer John Vidacovich, and **What Because** (november 1989), for a similar quintet. The *Wishbone Suite* was the centerpiece of **Wishbone** (january 1991). Anderson's comic ego found the ideal vehicle in the Alligatory Band (electric bass and guitar, drums, percussion and Lew Soloff's trumpet) that debuted with the hilarious **Don't Mow Your Lawn** (march 1994).

In the meantime, Anderson had joined George Gruntz's Concert Jazz Band for **Happening Now** (october 1987) and Charlie Haden's Liberation Music Orchestra for **Dreamkeeper** (april 1990) and played on the album by the **New York Composers Orchestra** (january 1990). He continued to be part of New York's avantgarde ventures, even if his solo and group recordings almost seemed to make fun of them.

George Gruntz's Concert Jazz Band (now featuring trumpeters Lew Soloff, Ryan Kisor, John D'Earth and Herb Robertson, saxophonists Tim Berne, Ellery Eskelin and Marty Ehrlich, violinist Mark Feldman, tuba player Howard Johnson, three trombonists, and pianist George Gruntz) performed witty Anderson music on **Big Band Record** (january 1993): *Anabel at One, Lips Apart, Seven Monsters, The Literary Lizard, Don't Mow Your Lawn.*

Louisiana-born tenor saxophonist Fred Anderson became a staple and a pillar of Chicago's creative scene despite being a bop musician at heart. He co-founded the AACM and played on Joseph Jarman's pioneering **Song For** (1966). It took him twelve years, though, to emerge as a powerful voice of the avantgarde. The fact is that he always seemed to belong to another generation. He was a player influenced by Sonny Rollins and, more importantly, a composer of the same vein as Ornette Coleman and Charles Mingus. His early recordings focused on that relatively structured aspect of his art, therefore downplaying the radical improvisation of "creative" musicians. The live **Another Place** (may 1978), by a quintet with trombonist Lewis, trumpeter Bill Brimfield and young percussionist Hank "Hamid" Drake, contained the 23-minute *Another Place*, the twelve-minute *Saxoon* and the ten-minute *The Bull*. The live **Dark Day** (may 1979), in a quartet with Drake and Brimfield and without Lewis, debuted the 18-minute *Dark Day* and the 18-minute *Three On Two*. Yet another live recording, More compositions for quartet were recorded in those years, but would be released only much later: the 16-minute *Twilight*, on **The Missing Link** (september 1979), the 17-minute *A Ballad For Rita*, on **The Milwaukee Tapes** (january 1980), etc. In 1982 Fred Anderson opened the "Velvet Lounge" that soon became the epicenter of Chicago's creative scene. For more than a decade very little was documented of his sessions. A quartet with pianist Jim Baker, bassist Harrison Bankhead and drummer Hamid Drake was finally documented on **Birdhouse** (february 1995), its highlights being, again, Anderson's compositions: the swinging 18-minute *Birdhouse* (a showcase of group interplay and solos), the bluesy 16-minute *Bernice*, the 15-minute bop excursion *Like Sonny* and the 14-minute saxophone-drums duet *Waiting for Mc*. **Chicago Chamber Music** (may 1996), for a trio with bassist Tatsu Aoki and percussionist Afifi Phillard, was more openly free jazz (the 20-minute *Grizzle* and the 14-minute *Afro Asia*).

While he did not release any record during the 1970s, white saxophonist, trumpeter, vibraphonist and drummer Harold "Hal Russell" was instrumental in keeping free jazz alive in Chicago. His NRG Ensemble, formed in 1979 and first documented on **NRG Ensemble** (may 1981), became the vehicle for his extroverted and eccentric compositions, such as the 19-minute *Cascade* on **Generation** (september 1982), featuring baritone saxophonist Charles Tyler. His sense of humor, somewhere between Albert Ayler and Frank Zappa, was influential in mitigating the grave tone of creative music.

CREATIVE MUSIC: THE ST LOUIS SCHOOL

After the AACM in Chicago, the other collective that introduced influential innovations in the history of jazz was based in St Louis, centered around the multidisciplinary arts collective Black Artists' Group (BAG), formed in 1968, and included the three great saxophonists Julius Hemphill, Oliver Lake and Hamiett Bluiett.

A reference point of the St Louis scene was the Human Arts Ensemble, founded by drummer Charles Bobo Shaw in 1971. They released **Whisper of Dharma** (1972) and **Under the Sun** (july 1973). The latter (with Smith, trumpeter Lester Bowie, alto saxophonists Marty Ehrlich and James Marshall, a reed player, a tuba player, a cellist, a bassist, a percussionist and a vocalist) contained two side-long improvisations, *A Lover's Desire* and *Hazrat the Sufi*, that contaminated free jazz with funk music.

Texas-born alto saxophonist Julius Hemphill moved to St Louis in 1968 where he became a leader of the Black Artists' Group (BAG). He staged multimedia events such as *Kawaida* (1972), *The Orientation Of Sweet Willie Rollbar* (1973) and *Obituary* (1974). His status as one of the leading composers of his time was established by pieces in which bluesy melodies became the scaffolding of complex geometric architectures. It started with the three lengthy pieces of **Dogon AD** (february 1972), featuring Baikida Carroll on trumpet, Abdul Wadud on cello and Phillip Wilson on drums: the 14-minute *Dogon A.D.*, the 15-minute flute solo *The Painter*, the eight-minute *Rites*. *The Hard Blues*, from the same session, appeared on **Coon Bid'ness** (released in 1975), that included new compositions for a sextet with baritonist Hamiet Bluiett, Wadud, altoist Arthur Blythe, drummer Barry Altschul and conga player Daniel Zebulon.

After relocating to New York in 1973 and performing in Anthony Braxton's saxophone-only ensembles, in 1976 Hemphill formed the World Saxophone Quartet with fellow saxophonists Oliver Lake (alto), David Murray (tenor) and Hamiet Bluiett (baritone). The original intention, as displayed on the freely improvised **Point Of No Return** (june 1977) and in particular with the 24-minute *Scared Sheetless*, was to pursue a bold program of dissonance. **Steppin' With** (december 1978) contained Hemphill's *Steppin'* and *R&B* as well as Murray's *P.O. in Cairo*.

The double LP **Blue Boye** (january 1977), entirely performed by Hemphill himself on alto, soprano, flute and percussion, was perhaps Hemphill's most eloquent aesthetic statement: eight elegant, intricate mid-size excursions into the secrets of sound from the perspective of an art that began with the blues. Pieces such as the 11-minute *Countryside*, the 13-minute *Hotend*, the 10-minute *OK Rubberband* and the 12-minute *C.M.E* felt much more "dense" than solos. And somehow Hemphill's jarred, fractured phrasing crafted mellow, romantic atmospheres, like a shy, nervous lover. **Roi Boye and the Gotham Minstrels** (march 1977) refined the concept in a series of performances for overdubbed instruments (alto, soprano and flute), while **Raw Materials and Residuals** (november 1977) added a lyrical element thanks to Wadud's cello and Don Moye's percussions (particularly in *Mirrors*, *Plateau* and *G Song*). The intellectual phase was closed by **Flat Out Jump Suite** (june 1980), a four-movement suite *Ear, Mind, Heart* and *Body*) for a chamber-jazz quartet with Wadud, trumpeter Olu Dara and percussionist Warren Smith.

In the meantime, Hemphill also composed the four-movement suite for seven woodwinds *Water Music* (1976) and the soundtrack to a multimedia installation, *Chile New York* (may 1980).

During the 1980s the World Saxophone Quartet absorbed most of Hemphill's energies. Hemphill continued to be the main composer of the quartet's music through **W.S.Q.** (march 1980) and **Revue** (october 1980), but the quartet soon began to play more accessible music (and often covers).

After leaving the World Saxophone Quartet in 1989, Hemphill, who had already displayed his restlessness with an album for **Big Band** (february 1988), invested more into highbrow compositions such as the multimedia opera *Long Tongues* (1989), that also debuted his saxophone sextet, the ballet *The Last Supper At Uncle Tom's Cabin/The Promised Land* (1990), *Plan B* (1993) for jazz sextet and symphony orchestra, the theatrical piece *A Bitter Glory* (1994).

His saxophone Sextet (with Marty Ehrlich, Carl Grubbs, Hames Carter, Andrew White and Sam Furnace) recorded a surprisingly fragmented album, **Fat Man and the Hard Blues** (july 1991). His health rapidly deteriorating, Hemphill organized the Sextett (altoists Tim Berne, Marty Ehrlich and Sam Furnace, tenors James Carter and Andrew White and baritonist Fred Ho) of **Five Chord Stud** (november 1993) to play his new compositions, including *Five Chord Stud*.

A ten-piece unit helped St Louis' alto saxophonist Oliver Lake on his dissonant debut, **Ntu - The Point from Which Freedom Begins**, but glory came with the various experiments of **Heavy Spirits** (february 1975), notably the 11-minute *While Pushing Down Turn* for a quintet with trumpeter Olu Dara, pianist Donald Smith, drums and bass, and the nine-minute *Rocket* for a trio with trombonist Joseph Bowie and drummer Charles "Bobo" Shaw. Relocating to New York, Lake created his own "creative" style, at the border between hard bop and free jazz, via **Holding Together** (march 1976), **Life Dance Of Is** (february 1978), the neoclassical **Shine** (october 1978), that juxtaposed electric guitar and a string quartet of three violins and cello, the live **Zaki** (august 1979), with the free improvisation of the 24-minute *Zaki* for a trio with electric guitar and drums, the Eric Dolphy tribute **Prophet** (august 1980), and **Clevont Fitzhubert** (april 1981) for a quartet with trumpeter Baikida Carroll, pianist Donald Smith and drummer Pheeroan Aklaff. Lake was one of the first improvisers to cross over into popular music. He did so with a reggae-oriented band that debuted on **Jump Up** (september 1981). **Expandable Language** (september 1984) presented Lake's quintet (guitarist Kevin Eubanks, pianist Geri Allen, bassist Fred Hopkins, drummer Pheeroan Aklaff) in a setting that shunned the most radical dissonance while remaining consistently challenging. Ditto for **Gallery** (july 1986), that featured the same musicians minus Eubanks, and **Impala** (may 1987), also for a similar piano-based quartet. **Otherside** (august 1988) applied the same principles to *Whitestone* for a piano-based quintet (Geri Allen on piano, Anthony Peterson on guitar, Fred Hopkins on bass and Andrew Cyrille on drums) and *Dedicated to Dolphy* for big band (six saxophones, four trumpets, four trombones, two French horns, piano, bass, drums). **Again And Again** (1991) returned to his specialty, the postmodernist ballad for piano-based quartet (now pianist John Hicks, bassist Reggie Workman and drummer Pheeroan Aklaff), a format that was further refined (albeit with a less cohesive line-up) by the lengthy pieces of **Edge-ing** (june 1993).

St Louis' baritone saxophonist Hamiet Bluiett moved to New York in 1969, where he refined the huge, grandiose sound of his instrument. While co-founding the World Saxophone Quartet, he recorded **Endangered Species** (june 1976) with a quintet featuring trumpeter Olu Dara, Jumma Santos on balafon, bassist Junie Booth and drummer Phillip Wilson, and the solo tour de force **Birthright** (june 1977), subtitled "a solo blues Concert", whose *Doll Baby*, *My Father's House* and *In Tribute to Harry Carney* established the threatening, deafening and challenging style of his playing. **SOS** (august 1977) contained just one 37-minute jam (*Nali Kola/ On A Cloud*) with pianist Don Pullen, bassist Fred Hopkins and percussionist Don Moye, probably his classic setting. The live **Im/Possible To Keep** (august 1977) contained a live 40-minute version of *Oasis - The Well* for a trio with Hopkins and Moye, a 37-minute version of *Nali Kola/ On A Cloud* for the quartet with Pullen and debuted *Pretty Tune* in a 35-minute version. **Resolution** (november 1977), a quintet with Don Pullen, bassist Fred Hopkins and percussionists Don Moye and Billy Hart, contained *Happy Spirit*. **Orchestra Duo And Septet** (december 1977) tried different combinations of players (cellist Abdul Wadud, trumpeter Olu Dara, pianist Don Pullen, balafon player Andy Bey, flutist Ladji Camara, bassist Reggie Workman, oud player Ahmed Abdul-Malik, drummer Thabo Michael Carvin, etc): the 14-minute orchestral *Glory - Symphony For World Peace*, the eight-minute duet *Nioka*, the 20-minute *Oasis - The Well* for septet.

Bluiett also formed an ensemble of eight clarinetists (plus bass and drums) that debuted with **The Clarinet Family** (november 1984), and a baritone saxophone quartet, the Bluiett Baritone Nation, documented by **Libation for the Baritone Saxophone Nation** (june 1997).

JAZZ POST-MODERNISM IN NEW YORK

In the 1970s in the "loft scene" of New York the border between late purveyors of free jazz and young pioneers of creative music was blurred.

Miami-born trumpeter and saxophonist Joe McPhee did not have any major experience before he started rocking the "loft scene" of New York. A quartet comprising McPhee (on tenor saxophone, trumpet, pocket cornet, alto horn), Reggie Marks (soprano and tenor saxophones, flute, organ), Tyrone Crabb (bass) and Ernist Bostic (vibraphone, drums, percussion) recorded **Underground Railroad** (april 1969), particularly the 23-minute *Underground Railroad*, a spectacular display of collective free improvisation that was frantic and spirited. John Coltrane's influence was more evident on the live **Nation Time** (december 1970), recorded with equal enthusiasm by an unusual quintet of piano, bass, two percussionists and McPhee on trumpet, soprano sax and tenor sax (the 18-minute *Nation Time*) that was expanded to an octet with propulsive alto saxophone, electric guitar and organ for the explosive, funky 13-minute *Shakey Jake*. McPhee was one step away from the funk-jazz-rock revolution. **Black Magic Man** (same concert) showed his more orthodox free-jazz side, especially in the 17-minute *Hymn of the Dragon Kings*, influenced by Cecil Taylor, as did the acrobatic 28-minute *Ionization* and the funky and bluesy *Delta* on **Trinity** (november 1971), that debuted his bass-less trio with piano and drums. **At WBAI's Free Music Store** (october 1971), credited to Survival Unit II but actually recorded by the same trio.

McPhee's intimate, lyrical, multiphonic and polychromatic language at the various instruments was crystallized on the solo album **The Willisau Concert** (october 1975), that contained *Baliamian Folksong*, *Touchstone* and *Voices*. It was followed by several more solo improvisations: **Rotation** (september 1976), **Tenor And Fallen Angels** (october 1977), the double-LP **Graphics** (june 1977), perhaps the most powerful expression of his eclectic ego (the 12-minute *Graphics 3/4*, the 15-minute *Legendary Heroes*, the 14-minute *Anamorphosis*, the eleven-minute *Trumpet*), **Variations on a Blue Line** (october 1977), **Glasses** (october 1977).

However, McPhee had been preparing to abandon the language of John Coltrane for something more futuristic. The pioneering duets between his horns and John Snyder's synthesizer (notably the 23-minute *Windows in Dreams/ Colors in Crystal*) on **Pieces Of Light** (1974) found a place for electronic music in jazz improvisation. The atonal sax-piano-guitar trio of **MFG in Minnesota** (june 1978) evoked the creative noise of Derek Bailey. **Old Eyes and Mysteries** (may 1979), including the four-movement *Women's Mysteries*, **Topology** (march 1981), including the 28-minute reed duet *Topology*, and **Oleo** (april 1982), including *Pablo* for two reeds, bass and guitar, adapted philosopher Edward DeBono's strategy of "lateral thinking" to jazz improvisation (or "po music"), which in practice meant a calmer, deeper exploration of sound. More "po music" surfaced on **A Future Retrospective** (may 1987) and **Linear B** (january 1990).

Pauline Oliveros' "deep listening" music became a major influence on **Common Threads** (october 1995), mostly taken up by the 47-minute *Spirit Traveler* (dedicated to Don Cherry) for a quintet with avantgarde composer Stuart Dempster on trombone and didjeridu, Evynd Kang on violin, bass and cello. In that vein McPhee composed **Unquenchable Fire** (premiered in august 1997).

Less interesting was his return to free improvisation, enacted via a myriad of recordings: the trio with reed player Ken Vandermark and bassist Kent Kessler of **Meeting In Chicago** (february 1996), the solo improvisations of **As Serious As Your Life** (may 1996), the duets with flutist Jerome Bourdellon of **Novio Iolu: Music for a New Place** (1997) and **Manhattan Tango** (april 2000), the duets with trombonist Jeb Bishop of **Brass City** (october 1997), the duets with bassist Dominic Duval of **The Dream Book** (august 1998) and **Rules of Engagement, Volume 2** (2004), the duets with tenor saxophonist Evan Parker of **Chicago Tenor Duets** (may 1998), the duets with bassist Michael Bisio of **Zebulon** (july 1998), the duets with drummer Johnny McLellan of **Grand Marquis** (august 1999), the duets with percussionist Hamid Drake of **Emancipation Proclamation** (june 1999), the live solos of **Everything Happens for a Reason** (november 2003), and assorted combo performances such as **Abstract** (2001), **Remembrance** (october 2001) and **Mr Peabody Goes to Baltimore** (september 2000).

McPhee mainly formed the Bluette Quartet with microtonal reed player Joe Giardullo and two bassists (Michael Bisio and Dominic Duval). After **In the Spirit** (march 1999), a tribute to spirituals, and **No Greater Love** (same session), with *Strangers In A Strange Land*, they excelled at the postmodern melodic exercise of the suite **Let Paul Robeson Sing** (september 2001), structured in four "episodes": the 21-minute *Harlem Spiritual*, the 15-minute *Peekskill 1949* in three movements, the eleven-minute *For Paul*, the ten minute *Water Boy/ Deep River/ Ol' Man River*.

The same free-melodic concept was explored by the Trio X, formed by McPhee with bassist Dominic Duval and drummer Jay Rosen, with more elegiac overtones although at times quite self-indulgent: the four-movement *Watermelon Suite* on **Watermelon Suite** (may 1998), the 47-minute *Lift Every Voice and Sing* on the live **Rapture** (december 1998), the 17-minute *Sida's Song* on the live **In Black And White** (june 2001), *Journey* and *Autograph* on **Journey** (february 2003), the 17-minute *The Sugar Hill Suite* on **The Sugar Hill Suite** (october 2004), *Burning Wood* on **Moods Playing with the Elements** (october 2004), etc.

A tenor saxophonist influenced by John Coltrane, <u>Frank Lowe</u>, a Memphis native who relocated from San Francisco to New York in 1966, participated in Alice Coltrane's **World Galaxy** ((november 1971) and Don Cherry's **Relativity Suite** (february 1973).

After a creative **Duo Exchange** (september 1972) with percussionist Rashied Ali, Lowe debuted as a leader with **Black Beings** (march 1973), leading a quintet with saxophonist Joseph Jarman, bassist William Parker, violin and drums that careened through Lowe's 25-minute *In Trane's Name* and Jarman's *Thulani*. After **Fresh** (march 1975), a skewed tribute to Thelonious Monk with trumpeter Lester

Bowie, trombonist Joseph Bowie, cellist Abdul Wadud and drummer Charles Bobo Shaw, Lowe achieved his personal form of free-jazz on **The Flam** (october 1975), unleashing his energetic playing across the 14-minute *Flam* and the ten-minute *Third St Stomp* in the company of Joseph Bowie, trumpeter Leo Smith, bassist Alex Blake and Shaw.

A quartet with Butch Morris on cornet recorded **Tricks of the Trade** (december 1976), containing *Navarro's Tomorrow*, and **The Other Side** (december 1976), while Olu Dara and Leo Smith on trumpets helped out on **Doctor Too-Much** (may 1977), containing his signature theme *Doctor Too-Much*. These recordings boasted a creative ebullience that harked back to the heydays of free jazz. Lowe began to move beyond free jazz with the eleven-piece orchestra (including Joseph Bowie, Butch Morris, Billy Bang, guitarist Eugene Chadbourne, alto saxophonist John Zorn) that he assembled for **Lowe And Behold** (october 1977). The 14-minute *Heart in Hand* and the 13-minute *Heavy Drama* presented a masterful composer and arranger disguised as a free improviser (under the influence of Morris rather than Coltrane). And Morris helped arrange again the sprightly compositions of both **Skizoke** (march 1981), for saxophone, cornet, vibraphone, guitar, bass and drums (*Originals*, *The Skizoke*, *Some Do Some Don't*, *Close to the Soul*), and **Exotic Heartbreak** (october 1981), for a quintet with Morris, pianist Amina Claudine Myers, bass and drums (the bluesy *Exotic Heartbreak*).

Lowe also played in the Jazz Doctors, a free-bop quartet with Billy Bang, that released **Intensive Care** (august 1983). Generally speaking, his music was becoming less revolutionary and more respectful of the tradition. In fact, a spectacular sextet with trumpeter Don Cherry, trombonist Grachan Moncur and pianist Geri Allen, ended up cutting his most conservative album, **Decision In Paradise** (september 1984), with *Dues and Don'ts*.

The Saxemple documented on **Inappropriate Choices** (april 1991), a four-reed ensemble featuring baritone saxophonist James Carter, bass saxophonist Michael Marcus, alto saxophonist Carlos Ward and drummer Phillip Wilson (but they played a total of eleven instruments), was basically Lowe's response to the success of the World Saxophone Quartet, displaying, yet again, a less radical side of Lowe (*Loweology* and *Fuchsia Norval*). The ensemble later expanded to six reeds but **SaxEmble** (may 1995) was largely uneventful, mixing bebop, free jazz and rhythm'n'blues.

After the conventional sax-bass-drums trios of **Bodies & Soul** (november 1995) and **Vision Blue** (february 1997), paying tribute to the giants of free jazz while toying with pop, soul and world music, the quintet with piano and trumpet of the live **Soul Folks** (february 1998) marked an attempt to refocus his program on composition (*Tubby's Night Out*, *Eddie's Dream*, *Ms Bertha's Arrival*).

The post-jazz and post-classical ambitions of Texas' trumpeter Marvin "Hannibal" Peterson, who moved to New York in 1970 and played with Gil Evans from 1971 until 1984, were revealed by the five-movement suite for orchestra **Children of the Fire** (1974), that also inaugurated his spiritual and pan-African leitmotiv. This work marked the birth of the Sunrise Orchestra, the banner under which Peterson recorded several smaller-scale works, for example the five pieces for chamber ensemble of **The Light** (may 1978). At the same time Peterson gave a personal interpretation of Don Cherry's free jazz with the trumpet-centered jams of **The Angels of Atlanta** (february 1981) with tenor saxophonist George Adams, pianist Kenny Barron, cellist Diedre Murray, bassist Cecil McBee and drummer Dannie Richmond, and with the 20-minute quintet improvisation of *Africa*, off **Poem Song** (november 1981). The crowning achievement of his career was **African Portraits** (may 1995), a large-scale oratorio for symphony orchestra, choir, African instruments and blues, gospel and operatic vocalists.

Virginia-born pianist Don Pullen, who, after playing briefly in Chicago in Muhal Richard Abrams' Experimental Band, moved to New York in 1964, was one of the musicians who bridged blues and free-jazz piano. When he backed such free-jazz gurus as saxophonist Giuseppe Logan (1964-65) and drummer Milford Graves (1966), Pullen mainly displayed a acrobatic technique (famously sounding like two pianists) that allowed him to do just about anything (as free as he wanted to be) while still playing melodies. It thus came natural to him to extend the technique at the piano to bring it in line with the experiments being carried out at the saxophone. The result sounded very similar to Cecil Taylor's style, but Pullen had reached the same point via a different path: not the brain, but, quite simply, the fingers. He composed a requiem for Malcolm X (1965), but could never perform it.

He was sidestepped for a few years until he was rediscovered by Charles Mingus (1973-74). His **Solo Piano Album** (february 1975) revealed an eclectic and mesmerizing performer, and, thanks to the 15-minute *Sweet Suite Malcolm* (the first movement of the requiem) a ten-minute *Big Alice* (destined to remain his most famous theme) and a nine-minute *Song Played Backwards*, a composer with an uncanny ear for melody and rhythm (he rarely recorded other people's compositions). Pullen then jumped from the free-jazz generation straight onto the "creative" generation, working with David Murray (1976-77), Hamiet Bluiett (1977-80) and Joseph Jarman (1979). It was the beginning of one of the most spectacular late careers in the history of jazz.

The solo concerto continued with two more imposing installments: the tour de force **Five To Go** (july 1975), that contained two side-long improvisations, *Five To Go* and *Four Move*, and **Healing Force** (october 1975), perhaps the most mature of the three although less spontaneous than the former, structured in four balanced pieces: *Pain Inside* (15:50), *Tracey's Blues* (8:30), *Healing Force* (8:25), *Keep On Steppin'* (18:40).

Another quartet with saxophonist Sam Rivers cut **Capricorn Rising** (october 1975), dominated by Rivers' compositions but also by Pullen's eleven-minute *Capricorn Rising*. And yet another quartet recorded the live **Montreux Concert** (july 1977), that included Pullen's side-long *Dialogue Between Malcolm and Betty*. Best of all these quartet sessions was **Warriors** (april 1978), with tenorist Chico Freeman, that delivered the 31-minute *Warriors* as well as the shorter (13 minutes) *Land Of The Pharoahs*. The piece de resistance, overflowing with catchy melodies and propulsive rhythms, despite the harmonic anarchy, was Pullen's definitive aesthetic statement. Somewhat influenced by Charles Mingus, the music was able to metabolize a broad spectrum of styles. Due to his versatile ambiguity, he became an unwilling evangelist of free jazz among the listeners of non-free jazz.

Milano Strut (december 1978) had four sophisticated duets with percussionist Don Moye, notably *Conversation, Communication* and *Curve Eleven* Adding Joseph Jarman on flute, piccolo, tenor, soprano and clarinet, they recorded **The Magic Triangle** (july 1979). The quartet with Adams recorded his memorable 16-minute *Double Arc Jake* on **Don't Lose Control** (november 1979).

For a while Pullen's main output was directed towards the quartet with Adams, yielding **Earth Beams** (august 1980), **Lifeline** (april 1981), with Adams' *Nature's Children* and Pullen's *Newcomer Seven Years Later*, **City Gates** (march 1983), dominated by Adams' compositions, **Live At The Village Vanguard** (august 1983), with *The Necessary Blues*, **Decisions** (february 1984), with *Trees And Grass And Thangs*, **Breakthrough** (april 1986) and **Song Everlasting** (april 1987), until Dannie Richmond died in 1988 and the quartet disbanded. This was Pullen at his more accessible. Pullen and Adams also recorded a duo album, **Melodic Excursions** (june 1982).

Until 1988 Pullen's main output was directed towards that quartet, that presented Pullen at his more accessible. However, Pullen's mature music was better represented by **Evidence Of Things Unseen** (september 1983), with *Evidence Of Things Unseen, Victory Dance* and the 18-minute *In The Beginning*. A quintet with altoist Donald Harrison and trumpeter Olu Dara penned *In the Beginning, The Sixth Sense* and *Tales From The Bright Side*, pieces that were typical of Pullen's stylistic blur, on **The Sixth Sense** (june 1985).

The sound of the quartet was further streamlined by **New Beginnings** (december 1988), a sonic gem of trio jazz with bassist Gary Peacock and drummer Tony Williams, although of little substance. Pullen's second trio album, **Random Thoughts** (march 1990), was more cerebral than the first one, thanks to longer tracks (*Random Thoughts, Indio Gitano* and *Ode To Life*) that displayed his mature technique. The quartet and trio works amounted to a commercial sell-out (short melodic pieces with an emphasis on soothing atmospheres), although they still proved Pullen's magic at the piano.

While accompanying Charles Mingus (1973-78) and Gil Evans (1974-84), tenor saxophonist George Adams, formed a quartet with pianist Don Pullen that debuted on **Jazz A Confronto** (march 1975), credited to Pullen. That quartet reached its zenith with **Suite For Swingers** (july 1976), containing Adams' 22-minute *Suite For Swingers* and the 15-minute *Melodic Rhapsody*. After indulging in the lightweight fusion jazz of *Imani's Dance* on **Sound Suggestions** (may 1979), with trumpeter Kenny Wheeler, tenorist Heinz Sauer, pianist Richie Beirach and bassist Dave Holland, and the introverted *Yamani's Passion* on the tenor-drums duet **Hand To Hand** (february 1980), Adams penned two of his best, *Mingus Metamorphosis* and *City Gates*, on the quartet's **City Gates** (march 1983), besides *Nature's Children* on **Lifeline** (april 1981).

The career of California-born tenor saxophonist David Murray went through at least three well-defined phases after he moved to New York in 1975: a confrontational free-jazz phase in which he developed a wildly dissonant style of playing, an erudite phase in which he focused on composition rather than performance, and a phase in which his performance and composition came together into an elegant (as opposed to furious) display of idiosyncratic languages at the instrument that also mirrored a rediscovery of jazz tradition.

An alumnus in Los Angeles of Horace Tapscott's Pan Afrikan Peoples Arkestra, itself an outgrowth of the Underground Musicians' Association (UGMA), formed in 1961, Murray started out as an angry young man of jazz. While he was joining the World Saxophone Quartet, Murray recorded **Flowers for Albert** (june 1976) with trumpeter Olu Dara, bassist Fred Hopkins and drummer Phillip Wilson. The album contained Murray's *Flowers For Albert* and *Ballad For A Decomposed Beauty* (virtually a long solo) as well as Butch Morris' *Joanne's Satin Green Dress*, and introduced a visceral vibrato a` la Coleman Hawkins gone awry. The trio session of **Low Class Conspiracy** (june 1976), without the trumpeter, yielded more extreme sounds in *Extriminity*, *Dewey's Circle* and *Low Class Conspiracy*, and became the name of a band, the Low Class Conspiracy, featuring cornetist Butch Morris, pianist Don Pullen, bassist Fred Hopkins and drummer Stanley Crouch. After **Solomon's Sons** (january 1977), that contained solos and duets with flutist James Newton, including Murray's *Theme For The Kidd* and *3D Family* besides Newton's *Solomon's Sons* and *Monk's Notice*, and some solo live performances, such as **Conceptual Saxophone** (february 1978), **Sur-real Saxophone** (february 1978) and **Organic Saxophone** (february 1978), and several live albums such as **3D Family** (september 1978), in a sax-drums-bass trio, containing colossal versions of his classics *Patricia* and *3D Family*, a quartet with Morris recorded **Interboogieology** (february 1978), that contained Morris' *Namthini's Shadow* and *Blues for David*, and Murray's *Interboogieology* and *Home*, and a trio (Fred Hopkins on bass and Steve McCall on drums) recorded **Sweet Lovely** (december 1979), with *The Hill* and *Hope Scope*. These recordings marked a progression towards more and more sophisticated compositions. A supergroup with altoist Henry Threadgill, trumpeter Olu Dara, cornetist Butch Morris, trombonist George Lewis, pianist Anthony Davis, bassist Wilbur Morris and drummer Steve McCall crafted *The Fast Life* and *Jasvan* on **Ming** (july 1980), much better versions of *Last Of The Hipmen* and *3-D Family*, besides the new *Santa Barbara And Crenshaw Follies* and *Choctaw Blues*, on **Home** (november 1981), and (having replaced Dara with trumpeter Bobby Bradford, and Lewis with trombonist Craig Harris, and Davis with pianist Curtis Clark) new versions of *Sweet Lovely* and *Flowers For Albert*, besides the new *Murray's Steps* and *Sing Song*, on **Murray's Steps** (july 1982). This was Murray's second period, when the radical style at the instrument was sidestepped to make room for the composer.

An outgrowth of the octet was David Murray's Big Band, documented on **At Sweet Basil** (august 1984): trumpets (Dara and Baikida Carroll), trombone (Harris), saxophones (Murray and Steve Coleman), tuba, French horn, clarinet, piano, bass, drums and Butch Morris conducting. They performed some of Murray's most exhilarating postmodernist compositions: *Bechet's Bounce*, *Duet For Big Band*, *Dewey's Circle*, *Roses*.

A new octet (with Baikida Carroll and Hugh Ragin on trumpet, John Purcell on alto) recorded **New Life** (october 1985), that contained *Train Whistle* and *Blues In The Pocket*.

In parallel Murray pursued a less ambitious (but much more prolific) career as a leader of smaller ensembles devoted to simpler material and that frequently recycled old compositions and indulged in tributes to old and new masters.

Black pianist Anthony Davis (1951), who was raised in the white intellectual milieu of Princeton University, exposed to European classical music before jazz, and educated at Yale University, formed Advent in 1973 (with Gerry Hemingway on drums, George Lewis on trombone, Wes Brown on bass and Hal Lewis on saxophone), debuted on record with Leo Smith (1974) and then relocated to New York. His solo piano album **Past Lives** (1978) was still influenced by Thelonious Monk (*Crepuscule - A suite for Monk*) but already elaborate (*Locomotif No. 1*) and poignant (*Of Blues & Dreams*). His compositional skills fully blossomed with the 29-minute three-movement *Suite for Another World*, on **Of Blues and Dream** (july 1978), featuring violinist Leroy Jenkins, cellist Abdul Wadud and drummer Pheeroan Aklaff. Another creative quartet (with vibraphonist Jay Hoggard, bassist Mark Helias and drummer Ed Blackwell) penned the 12-minute ethnic suite *Song for the Old World* and the bebop tribute *An Anthem for the Generation that Died* on **Song for the Old World** (july 1978). The series of impressive combos continued with **Hidden Voices** (march 1979), for a quintet with flutist James Newton, trombonist George Lewis, bassist Rick Rozie and drummer Pheeroan akLaff, that included Davis' *Sudden Death* and *Past Lives* as well as Newton's *Crystal Texts Set I Pre-A Reflection*.

The solo-piano masterpiece **Lady of the Mirrors** (1980) contained at least two elegant compositions that did not belong to any jazz tradition: the ten-minute *Five Moods From an English Garden* and the 12-minute *Under The Double Moon*, inspired by the Indonesian "wayang" style, besides the Duke Ellington tribute *Man on a Turquoise Cloud* and a couple of moody meditations. The same "wayang" was the centerpiece of a duo with vibraphonist Jay Hoggard, **Under The Double Moon** (september 1980), and the centerpiece again, in a version that was both more extended (29 minutes) and arranged (for octet), of **Episteme** (june 1981) The latter, performed by trombonist George Lewis, violinist Shem Guibbory, cellist Abdul Wadud, flutist/clarinetist Dwight Andrews, vibraphonist Jay Hoggard, xylophonist Warren Smith and drummer Pheeroan Aklaff, displayed a careful, calculating intelligence in the way the instruments were combined, sequenced and juxtaposed. This phase peaked with **Variations In Dream-time** (1982), scored for a sextet of piano, trombone (Lewis), cello (Wadud), clarinet/flute (JD Parran), bass and drums (Aklaff), and containing only two side-long compositions: the 24-minute *Variations in Dream-Time* and the 22-minute three-movement *Enemy of Light*. Davis, far from rejecting bebop, cool jazz or even swing music (or, for that matter, African or Indonesian music), was working outside the free-jazz paradigm, determined to restore composition to its dominating role. His non-virtuoso style at the piano was little more than a guide for the development of the composition, a practical expression of an intimidating musical plot. Despite the obvious similarities in intent, there was little in these extended suites that recalled European classical music, other than the occasional romantic melody. It was, indeed, a unique form of art.

After **I've Known Rivers** (february 1982), a trio With Newton and Wadud containing Davis' *Still Waters*, Wadud's *Tawaafa* and two Newton compositions (*Juneteenth* and *After You Said Yes*), the 39-minute five-movement ballet suite **Hemispheres** (july 1983), scored for piano, trumpet (Leo Smith), trombone (Lewis), flute/clarinet (Andrews), violin (Guibbory), cello (Eugene Friesen), vibraphone, clarinet, bass and drums (Aklaff), recycled some old themes but mainly increased the degree of structure. Davis continued to experiment with rhythmic movement and instability, pitting constant pulses against angular tempos, extracting pathos from the collision of instrumental parts in different tempos. Davis' compositions were layered, having at least a lower layer of rhythmic organization and a higher level of lyrical/melodic soundpainting, and relying on the continuous contrast between the two levels for the spontaneous emergence of meaning.

The display of sophistication continued with the 15-minute *Middle Passage*, on **Middle Passage** (1984), that also contained Earl Howard's 16-minute *Particle W* for piano and tape, Davis' first encounter with electronic music, with the four-movement *Wayang 5* (1984) for piano and symphonic orchestra, first recorded on **The Ghost Factory** (may 1988), that also contained the three-movement violin concerto *Maps* (1987), and especially with **Undine** (june 1986), that contained two 23-minute compositions, *Still Waters* and *Undine*, scored for piano, cello (Wadud), vibraphone/percussion (Gerry Hemingway), bassoon (David Miller), violin (Guibbory), flute and clarinet (Marty Ehrlich and JD Parran). Seven years after the fact, Davis returned to the format of the trio With Newton's flute and Wadud's cello **Trio2** (october 1989), with Davis' *Who's Life* (1978) and Newton's *Invisible Islands*.

Davis' most ambitions compositions were for the theater: the political opera **X - The Life and Times of Malcolm X** (premiered in 1986), the science-fiction opera **Under the Double Moon** (premiered in june 1989), the historical opera **Amistad** (premiered in november 1997), about a slave rebellion, based on the music of **Middle Passage**, the opera **Tania** (premiered in june 1992), about a famous kidnapping case, and music for two plays, Tony Kushner's **Angels in America Part I - Millennium Approaches** (premiered in april 1993) and **Angels in America Part II: Perestroika Sounds Without Nouns** (premiered in november 1994).

But Davis also composed orchestral works: *Notes from the Underground* (1988), *Violin Sonata* (1991), *Jacob's Ladder* (premiered in october 1997).

Oklahoma-born bassist Cecil McBee, who moved to New York with Paul Winter's ensemble in 1963, was an influential figure both as a bassist and as a composer. He went on to play with Andrew Hill, Sam Rivers, Jackie McLean, Wayne Shorter, Pharoah Sanders, Alice Coltrane, Dollar Brand, Chico Freeman, etc. He composed some of their material, notably the 19-minute *Undercurrent* on Freeman's **The Outside Within** (1978).

His first album, **Mutima** (may 1974), belonged to Chicago's "creative" generation rather than the free-jazz crowd he had been grown up with. With a strong spiritual emphasis, McBee intoned the eleven-minute psalm *From Within* for two overdubbed basses and their feedback, and conducted the chamber concerto of *Mutima* for small ensemble. A sextet featuring Freeman, trumpeter Joe Gardner, pianist Dennis Moorman and percussionists Don Moye and Steve McCall, was documented on two live albums: **Music From the Source** (august 1977), with the 19-minute *Agnez*, and the inferior **Compassion** (same sessions). **Alternate Spaces** (december 1977) for a sextet with Freeman, Gardner, Moye, another percussionist and pianist Don Pullen contained *Alternate Spaces*, *Consequence* and *Expression*. The zenith of his chamber jazz was perhaps the quintet of **Flying Out** (1982): violinist John Blake, cellist David Eyges, cornetist Olu Dara, drummer Billy Hart.

Los Angeles-born flutist James Newton became a full-time flutist in 1973 in a band with saxophonist David Murray, and moved to New York in 1978 where he played with pianist Anthony Davis. Classically trained, Newton absorbed Roland Kirk's and Eric Dolphy's jazz influence. He also nurtured a passion for the musical traditions of Japan, India, Africa and South America.

For his first album, **Flute Music** (september 1977), containing the first version of *Solomon's Sons*, he surrounded his flute with piano/harpsichord, guitar, bass and drums. **Paseo Del Mar** (1978), for a quartet with pianist Anthony Davis, cellist Abdul Wadud and drummer Phillip Wilson, contained two lengthy compositions, *Lake*, basically a tribute to Eric Dolphy, and *San Pedro Sketches*, a dynamic and soulful piece with some overdubbing of the flute. **From Inside** (july 1978) was his first solo effort, highlighted by his *Pinky Below*. **Binu** (august 1977) was a quartet with a koto player, bass (Mark Dresser) and drums. Newton's elegant, spiritual and eclectic form of chamber jazz blossomed with the Wind Quintet (John Carter on clarinet, John Nunez on bassoon, Charles Owens on oboe and English horn, Red Callender on tuba) that recorded **Mystery School** (march 1980), in particular the suite *The Wake*

A few Newton compositions appeared on Anthony Davis albums, notably *Crystal Texts Set I Pre-A Reflection* on **Hidden Voices** (1979) and *Juneteenth* and *After You Said Yes* on **I've Known Rivers** (1982).

James Newton (october 1982) marked another dimension of his fusion of classical music and jazz music. The septet was his first ensemble to include drums and bass, but the other instruments, flute, piano (Davis), violin, trombone and vibraphone (Jay Hoggard), engaged in highly technical counterpoint (*Ismene* was basically a tribute to Thelonious Monk). Ditto for **Portraits** (november 1979), a quintet with flute, piano (Bob Neloms), cello (Abdul Wadud), bass (Cecil McBee) and drums (Phillip Wilson). This process culminated with **Luella** (1983), scored for a three-piece string section (two violins and Wadud's cello) and a four-piece rhythm section (Hoggard's vibraphone, piano, bass and drums), particularly the mournful 17-minute *Luella*.

In between, Newton tried the solo format, the one favored by the "creative" school. However, the solo flute trance-like impressionistic improvisations of **Toil And Resolution** (1980), **Axum** (august 1981) and **Echo Canyon** (september 1984) had little of the virtuoso, scientific approach of Chicago's soloists. Newton showed little interest for timbral or textural explorations. His music was more similar to mood music. It expanded the vocabulary of the instrument only insofar as it absorbed techniques from other ethnic cultures. Thus it bordered on both world-music and new-age music.

The tentet effort **Water Mystery** (1985) for flute, clarinet, oboe, bassoon, saxophone, harp, koto, tuba, bass and drums was another zenith of Newton's chamber arrangements: *Lone Hill* juxtaposed a quintessential western instrument (the harp) and a quintessential eastern instrument (the koto) that interacted with a jazzy wind quintet, while *Water Mystery* was African folk in nature.

Newton matched that magic moment in *The Evening Leans Towards You* for an septet (Steve Turre on trombone, Geri Allen on piano, Abdul Wadud on cello, Jay Hoggard on vibraphone, bass and drums) on **Romance and Revolution** (august 1986), and in the 32-minute four-movement *Suite for Frida Kahlo* for flute, two trombones, piano, clarinet/sax, bassoon, drums and bass on **Suite for Frida Kahlo** (august 1994).

Los Angeles-based alto saxophonist <u>Arthur Blythe</u>, who played with pianist Horace Tapscott in 1960, relocated to New York in 1974, developing his baroque style at the instrument in the combos of Chico Hamilton (1975-77), Gil Evans (1976-78), Lester Bowie (1978), Jack DeJohnette (1979), McCoy Tyner (1979), etc. The live **Metamorphosis** (february 1977) and **The Grip** (same concert) by a sextet with trumpeter Ahmed Abdullah, cellist Abdul Wadud, tuba player Bob Stewart, drummer Steve Reid and percussionist Muhamad Abdullah, featured adventurous and spirited pieces such as *Metamorphosis*, *Spirits in the Field* the 18-minute *Duet for Two* (with Wadud) and (on the latter) the twelve-minute *As of Yet* that introduced a creative improviser, a proficient composer and a subtle arranger (specializing in unusual combination of instruments). The elliptic compositions of **Bush Baby** (1977) were arranged for a trio with Bob Stewart on tuba and Muhamed Abdullah on conga. **Lenox Avenue Breakdown** (1978) transposed the same idea into a more orthodox setting (electric guitarist James "Blood" Ulmer, flutist James Newton, tuba player Bob Stewart, bassist Cecil McBee and drummer Jack DeJohnette) with the 13-minute *Lenox Avenue Breakdown*, the free-form *Slidin' Through* and the haunting *Odessa*. At the same time Blythe exlored old standards with a quartet, initially comprised of pianist Stanley Cowell, bassist Fred Hopkins and drummer Steve McCall on **In The Tradition** (october 1978). The transitional **Illusions** (1980) announced the split to come. Blythe became a strange hybrid of avantgarde improviser and traditionalist, alternating between an electric funk-jazz quintet and an acoustic hard-bop piano-based quartet.

Billy "Bang" Walker (1947), a pupil of Leroy Jenkins who developed his personal style at the violin by imitating Eric Dolphy's style at the reeds (just like Stuff Smith developed his style at the violin by imitating Louis Armstrong's style at the cornet), formed the Survival Ensemble with two saxophonist (who also played all sorts of percussion), bassist William Parker and two percussionists. Their **New York Collage** (may 1978), containing lengthy jams such as *Nobody Hear the Music the Same Way* and *For Josie Part II*, was inspired by both the Art Ensemble Of Chicago and John Coltrane.

Bang's response to the success of the World Saxophone Quartet was the String Trio Of New York, formed in 1977 with white bassist John Lindberg and white guitarist James Emery. The centerpiece of their **First String** (june 1979) was Lindberg's 20-minute *East Side Suite*, that demonstrated their elegant blend of structured composition and free improvisation. Successive recordings, such as **Area Code 212** (november 1980) and **Common Goal** (november 1981), lacked the "piece de resistance" to make them worthwhile. **Rebirth of a Feeling** (november 1983) boasted Lindberg's *Utility Grey* but Bang left after **Natural Balance** (april 1986). Nonetheless the String Trio Of New York was one of the most influential free-jazz ensembles.

On the other hand, Bang's solo **Distinction Without A Difference** (august 1979) displayed both his broad range of innovative techniques and his skills at mixing free-form and melodic passages (*Theme For Masters*, *Loweski*, *Sometime Later*), while the three lengthy "improvisations", notably the 21-minute *Spiritual*, for violin and bass of **Billy Bang/ John Lindberg** (september 1979), emphasized his emotional language at the instrument.

Despite changing format with just about every record, Bang managed to establish his powerful musical vision through a series of impressive pieces. A sextet featuring tenor saxophonist Frank Lowe, alto saxophonist Luther Thomas, cornet player Butch Morris, pianist Curtis Clark bassist Wilber Morris and drummer Steve McCall, delivered the 16-minute *A Pebble Is A Small Rock* (co-arranged by Morris), on **Sweet Space** (december 1979). A trio with Parker and Japanese percussionist Toshi Tsuchitori yielded the three exuberant and cerebral pieces of **Changing Seasons** (june 1980): *Summer Night*, *Aduwa In Autumn*, *Winter Rains*. Bang employed a piano-based quintet with saxophonist Charles Tyler for the kaleidoscopic *Rainbow Gladiator*, off **Rainbow Gladiator** (june 1981), and *An Addition To Tradition*, off **Invitation** (april 1982). The quartet with trumpeter Don Cherry of **Untitled Gift** (february 1982) produced the atmospheric *Echovamp 1678* and *Maat*. A 12-piece orchestra conducted by Butch Morris (with Frank Lowe, two additional violinists, clarinetists David Murray, Charles Tyler and Henri Warner, vibraphonist Khan Jamal, percussionists Sunny Murray and John "Khuwana" Fuller) performed Bang's 19-minute volcano *Conception* and *Seeing Together* on **Outline No 12** (july 1982). *Air Traffic Control* came from a duet with drummer Dennis Charles on **Bangception** (august 1982). **Intensive Care** (august 1983), by the Jazz Doctors, a free-bop quartet with Frank Lowe, contained Bang's *Ballad with one L*.

Bang had coined his own genre, a melodic free-jazz or an abstract bebop, and proceeded to cash in on his invention with his sextet (trumpet, electric guitar, bassist William Parker and two percussionists), thanks to the Latin-tinged *The New Seers*, off **The Fire From Within** (september 1984), and *Abuella*, on **Live at Carlos 1** (november 1986).

Having left the String Trio Of New York (replaced first by Charles Burnham and then by Regina Carter), Bang was swallowed into the black hole of Sun Ra's Arkestra until 1995.

Despite *Valve No 10*, introduced by a quartet with Lowe, bassist Sirone and drummer Dennis Charles on **Valve No 10** (march 1988), and the "creative" duets with percussionist William Hooker on **Joy** (june 1994), including the 17-minute *Sweating Brain*, *Etheric Redemption* and *Joy*, Bang's output became more and more oriented towards hard-bop (or even swing). The acrobatic pieces of the period were *Spirits Gathering*, off **Spirits Gathering** (february 1996), for a guitar-based quartet, and *Spirits Entering*, off **Bang On** (april 1997), for a piano-based quartet.

The exceptions were sometimes intriguing, such as the rap-jazz fusion of **Forbidden Planet** (1997), or the solo improvisations of **Commandment** (march 1997), recorded live in a loft (notably *Daydreams*), or the trio Tri-Factor of **If You Believe** (april 2000) with percussionist Kahil El'Zabar and baritone saxophonist Hamiet Bluiett (notably *Dark Silhouette*), or the new edition of the Jazz Doctors on **One for Jazz** (june 2001), actually credited to the Billy Bang Quartet (*Echoes*), but not visionary.

Bang, who fought in Vietnam in the 1960s, invented his own form of (austere and eclectic) political art with **Vietnam - The Aftermath** (april 2001) and **Vietnam - Reflections** (may 2004). The former concept album used a piano-based quartet with pianist John Hicks as the foundation, adding other instruments as needed: a trumpet (Ted Daniel) to *Yo Ho Chi Minh is in the House* and *Tunnel Rat*, trumpet (Ted Daniel) and tenor saxophone (Frank Lowe) to *Bien Hoa Blues*, flute (Sonny Fortune) to *Fire in the Hole*, trumpet (Ted Daniel), tenor saxophone (Frank Lowe) and flute (Sonny Fortune) to *Saigon Phunk*, etc. The latter, conducted by Butch Morris, was a more homogeneous work, featuring trumpeter Ted Daniel as well as flutists James Spaulding and Henry Threadgill and structured as a series of poignant meditations (*Reflections*, *Lock & Load*, *Doi Moi*, *Reconciliation 1*, *Reconciliation 2*).

His compositions continued to straddle the line between free jazz, tradition, world music and popular music. **Transforming the Space** (february 2003), by a trio called FAB with bassist Joe Fonda and drummer Barry Altschul, contained Bang's *The Softness of Light* and *Tales from Da Bronx*. **Configuration** (november 2004), by a quartet called Sirone Bang Ensemble, contained Bang's 15-minute *Jupiter's Future*.

WHITE POST-MODERNISM IN NEW YORK

British bassist <u>Dave Holland</u> was both a melodic virtuoso of the double bass, a sound innovator who ushered in the transition of jazz music from acoustic bass to electric bass, and a composer of chamber jazz with a neoclassical sensitivity, a spiritual edge, a natural gift for naive melodies and a flair for the "conference" of timbres. After playing on the Spontaneous Music Ensemble's **Karyobin** (february 1968), Holland moved to New York and joined Miles Davis (1968-70), for whose records most of his vocabulary was originally constructed. Despite (or precisely because of) coming from a completely different background, Holland found himself in great demand in the following years, being hired by Circle (1970), a quartet with pianist Chick Corea, saxophonist Anthony Braxton and drummer Barry Altschul, Paul Bley (1972), Stan Getz (1972), Anthony Braxton (1972), and Sam Rivers (1976-81).

After **Music from Two Basses** (february 1971), mostly improvised with the other British bassist, Barre Phillips, and **Improvisations for Cello And Guitar** (january 1971) with guitarist Derek Bailey, Holland formed a quartet with two saxophonists, the ebullient Sam Rivers and the mathematical Anthony Braxton, and drummer Barry Altschul that recorded the epochal **Conference of the Birds** (november 1972). Holland found an identity between two words that were widely regarded as antithetical, "avantgarde" and "melody", not to mention "swing". Instead, Holland's compositions, propelled by one of the most swinging rhythm sections of the time, penned by a melodic talent worthy of Debussy, and never shy of venturing into dissonant, jarring and abrasive territories. Some abstract pieces (*Four Winds*) had virtually no identity, others sounded like a surreal and lyrical form of hard-bop (*Q & A*, *Interception*) and others even echoed folk music (the two shortest pieces, *Conference of the Birds* and *Now Here*, both with flute). The "sound" of this album (that became the sound of the German label ECM) was going to be more influential than anything done since Davis' conversion to electrical instruments.

In 1975 Holland, guitarist John Abercrombie and drummer Jack DeJohnette formed the all-white Gateway trio. **Gateway** (march 1975), with Holland's *May Dance* and DeJohnette's psychedelic *Sorcery I* (and the short drum-less ballad *Jamala*), and **2** (july 1977), with the 16-minute group improvisation *Opening*. This music was a close relative of progressive-rock.

Holland's aesthetic crystallized with the two solo albums **Emerald Tears** (august 1977) for solo bass and **Life Cycle** (november 1982) for solo cello, both fragmented into short pieces. The latter, perhaps his zenith as a composer, adopted the intimate, humble, restrained stance of zen Buddhism (the five-movement suite *Life Cycle*) while reminiscent of medieval folk music (*Rune, Troubadour Tale, Chanson Pour la Nuit*).

In 1982 Holland also formed his Quintet, featuring British trumpeter Kenny Wheeler, trombonist Julian Priester, altoist Steve Coleman and drummer Steve Ellington. Holland's compositions on **Jumpin' In** (october 1983) were longer and livelier (*Jumpin' In*, *New-One*, *You I Love*) but actually simpler. Holland was even less relevant on **Seeds of Time** (november 1984), that featured only three of his compositions, although he regained some of his relevance on **The Razor's Edge** (february 1987), thanks to his *Razor's Edge* and *Blues for C.M.* (contrasted with Coleman's *Vortex*).

The trio with Jack DeJohnette and Steve Coleman, **Triplicate** (march 1988), fared better, thanks to *Rivers Run* and *Triple Dance* (and to Coleman's effervescent form). On the other hand, the quartet with Steve Coleman, trombonist Kevin Eubanks and drummer Marvin Smitty Smith **Extensions** (september 1989) was even more accessible than the Quintet and penned Holland's *The Oracle*, Coleman's *Black Hole*, and Eubanks' *Nemesis* and *Color of Mind*. Holland' second solo, **Ones All** (may 1993), was also a retreat from the "avantgarde", sounding very traditional in comparison with the first one.

A new quartet with vibraphonist Steve Nelson, altoist Eric Person and drummer Gene Jackson recorded **Dream of the Elders** (march 1995) that contained several lengthy Holland originals (*The Winding Way*, *Claressence*, that would remain one of his most popular themes, *Lazy Snake*, *Ebb & Flo*, *Dream of the Elders*). This music was now elegance for the sake of elegance.

Eubanks, saxophonist Steve Wilson and drummer Billy Kilson joined Nelson and Holland for **Points of View** (september 1997), a collection that showed Holland the composer and arranger in a state of supreme confidence, eclectic and baroque, and best in the melancholy mood (*The Balance*, *Mister B.*, *Bedouin Trail*, *Ario*, *Herbaceous*, Eubanks' *Metamorphos*). **Prime Directive** (december 1998), with Chris Potter replacing Wilson, was beginning to sound like the meditation of an aging man on his own form of art, resulting in the sophisticated routine of *Wonders Never Cease*, *Looking Up*, *Jugglers Parade* (as well as Eubanks' *A Seeking Spirit*). While a bit less imaginative and spontaneous than the albums of the 1980s, these last quintet works were no less austere and profound. Having invented the new "mainstream" sound, Holland now relished in being the reactionary within his own revolution. Holland seemed to be getting tired of his own game on **Not for Nothin'** (december 2000), that featured Eubanks' *Global Citizen* but few Holland originals (mainly *Lost and Found* and *What Goes Around*).

A first big band album, **What Goes Around** (january 2001), simply revisited several of Holland's originals, but the second one, **Overtime** (2004), was highlighted by Holland's most ambitious composition, the *Monterey Suite* in four movements (*Bring It On*, *Free For All*, *A Time Remembered*, *Happy Jammy*).

White drummer Barry Altschul, one of the most intense drummers in the history of jazz music, enlivened the music of Paul Bley (1965-72), Chick Corea (1969), Anthony Braxton (1972-75), Dave Holland (1972), Sam Rivers (1976). Altschul was famous mainly for his maelstrom of percussion sounds, but could also be subtle in chamber-music settings. In fact, his first two albums, influenced by Dave Holland's **Conference Of The Birds** (1972), focused on the "conference" of the timbres, assembled the instruments in several different combinations. The centerpiece of **You Can't Name Your Own Tune** (1977) was

You Can't Name Your Own Tune that featured saxophonist Sam Rivers, pianist Muhal Richard Abrams, trombonist George Lewis, Holland and Altschul. **Another Time Another Place** (1978) presented Altschul with altoist Arthur Blythe, trombonist Ray Anderson, guitarist Bill DeArango, pianist Anthony Davis and bassist Brian Smith in *Suite for Monk*, with pianist Davis and cellist Abdul Wadud in *Chael*, with Davis, Smith and trombonist Ray Anderson in *Another Time Another Place*. Altschul, Anderson and bassist Mark Helias released two trio albums, **Somewhere Else** (1979) and **Brahma** (1980), with *Irina*.

White drummer Gerry Hemingway joined the "creative" crowd via Anthony Davis (1973-2001) and Anthony Braxton (1983-94). But his technique was also well served by the humbler all-white BassDrumBone trio with bassist Mark Helias and trombonist Ray Anderson (1978-97). Hemingway summarized his early experiments on **Kwambe** (february 1978): the four-movement suite *Kwambe*, with Anthony Davis on piano, Wes Brown on flute, Jay Hoggard on vibraphone and Mark Helias on bass (roughly Anthony Davis' group of the time), the three-movement suite *First Landscape* for a trio with George Lewis on trombone and Anthony Davis on piano, the solo-drums piece *Walking Alone the Tall Trees Sang*. They exuded a subtle intelligence, more influenced by the electroacoustic avantgarde than by Anthony Davis, with an approach that was more on the side of (richly textured) abstraction rather than narrative development. The four compositions of **Solo Works** (september 1981), ostensibly a showcase for Hemingway's extended vocabulary of the drums, was even more abstract and non-jazz, including *Black Wind* for "cymbal and drum resonances" and *The Dawntreader*, musique concrete for tape. More of his solo-percussion compositions were also collected on **Tubworks**: the 18-minute *Four Studies for Single Instruments* (1985), the polymetrical *Trance Tracks* (using rhythmic phrases of different lengths as the building blocks for the composition), *Like So Many Sails* (1985) for wood blocks and junk metal, and *Dance of the Sphygmoids* (december 1983).

Jazz music resurfaced in the quintet sessions of **Outerbridge Crossing** (september 1985), with Anderson, Helias, baritone saxophonist David Mott, Dutch cellist Ernst Reijseger. notably *Outerbridge Crossing* (that premiered his "tiered-tempo approach"), *Endorphin* and *Threnody For Charles Mingu*, and **Special Detail** (december 1990), with Don Byron on baritone sax and clarinet, bassist Ed Schuller on bass, Dutch trombonist Wolter Wierbos and Reijseger still on cello, notably the 19-minute *Special Detail* and the 14-minute *Taffia*. No matter how torrid and searing, it was still a form of jazz music that, while technically "swinging", was mostly absorbed in a manipulative analysis of form. **Down To The Wire** (december 1990), for the quartet of saxophonist and clarinetist Michael Moore, Wierbos and bassist Mark Dresser, was different in that Hemingway focused on microscopic texture (*Space 2* but also the atmospheric *If you Like*) rather than macroscopic interplay. The quintet's art was one of brains and guts, the quartet's art was one of colors and whispers. Besides BassDrumBone, Hemingway was also active with a trio that became a

quartet for **Tambastics** (march 1991): flutist Robert Dick, bassist Mark Dresser and pianist Denman Maroney. Since 1990 Hemingway was also involved in a trio with pianist Georg Graewe and cellist Ernst Reijseger that debuted on **Sonic Fiction** (march 1989).
Hemingway was also still active as an avantgarde composer, for example with his concerto for percussionist and orchestra, *Terrains* (1993). He continued to experiment with live electronic music, computer interactive music, and multimedia installations (*Waterways* for multiple slide projectors, tape and percussion). A duo with vocalist Andrea Goodman, **Divine Doorways** (april 1997), toyed with aleatory music based on tarot cards. A duo with Thomas Lehn an analogue synthesist, Tom & Gerry, yielded **Tom & Gerry** (june 1997) and **Fire Works** (march 2000). **Chamber Works** (1999) assembled: the 23-minute *Contigualis* for string quartet, *The Visiting Tank* for string quartet plus live electronics, *Aurora* for sextet, *Circus* for quintet.
Back to the jazz world, Hemingway played in several trios: the one led by clarinetist, bass clarinetist and alto saxophonist Frank Gratkowski, that debuted with **Gestalten** (september 1995); one with pianist Marilyn Crispell and bassist Barry Guy, documented by **Cascades** (june 1993); and one with Michel Wintsch and Baenz Oester, that recorded **Wintsch/ Oester/ Hemingway** (1994).
Demon Chaser (may 1993) finally presented the "transatlantic quintet" in all its glory: Hemingway, Reijseger, Dresser, Wierbos and Moore. *Slamadam* and *Demon Chaser* were the highlights. The quintet penned its masterpiece with the five-movement suite **Marmalade King** (february 1994), conceived as a fairy tale. **Perfect World** (march 1995) contained another "fairy tale" suite, *Little Suite*, the lengthy and complex narrative architecture of *Perfect World*, and *N.T.* The quintet disbanded after the live **Waltzes Two-Steps and Other Matters of the Heart** (november 1996), that contained more accessible extended pieces (*Toombow, Gospel Waltz, Gitar*).
In the meantime, Hemingway had already concocted an "American" quartet with Robin Eubanks on trombone, Ellery Eskelin on tenor saxophone and Mark Dresser on bass that debuted with the live **Johnny's Corner Song** (november 1997). This time there were echoes of blues, swing and bebop as well as African folk music although they still featured passages of elaborate abstract improvisation (the 13-minute *Johnny's Corner Song*, the eleven-minute *On It* and a 21-minute version of *Toombow*). The next release of the American quartet (and the first studio release of either quartet or quintet), **Devil's Paradise** (february 1999), featured tenorist Ellery Eskelin (who stole the show), Anderson and Dresser in a program of old Hemingway originals, while **The Whimbler** (march 2004), an all-new program (notably *The Current Underneath*, *The Whimbler*, *Curlycue*) had trumpeter Herb Robertson, Eskelin and Dresser.
The passion for the trio did not abate. Hemingway formed Thirteen Ways with pianist Fred Hersch and saxophonist Micheal Moore, that debuted with **Thirteen Ways** (july 1995), while the WHO Trio with Swiss pianist Michel Wintsch and Swiss contrabassist/cellist Baenz Oester released **Sharing the Thirst** (october 2000) and **Open Songs** (1998).

Songs (december 2001) was another groundbreaking work, although in a totally different dimension: songwriting. Performers included Lisa Sokolov on vocals, Wierbos, Hemingway, Eskelin, Lehn, Robertson, James Emery on guitars, John Butcher on tenor sax, Kermit Driscoll on bass.
Double Blues Crossing (october 2002), hardly related to the European quintet, was an ambitious suite performed by Gratkowski, Wierbos, cellist Amit Sen and bassist Kermitt Driscoll.

A long-time associate of drummer Edward Blackwell, Ray Anderson and Gerry Hemingway, white bassist Mark Helias was also a subtle composer of chamber jazz. Helias debuted as a leader with the bold, avantgarde **Split Image** (august 1984), for a quartet With tenorist Dewey Redman, altoist Tim Berne, trumpeter Herb Robertson and Hemingway, that contained Helias' extended compositions *Lands End*, *Le Tango* and *Z-5*. **The Current Set** (march 1987) was a more structured affair, delivered by a sextet with Berne, Robertson, soprano saxophonist Greg Osby, trombonist Robin Eubanks and drummer Victor Lewis, whose best pieces (*The Current Set*, *Ellipsis*, *Lism*) relished the tension between traditional form and free-form interplay. **Desert Blue** (april 1989) was even more lightweight, despite the addition of keyboardist Anthony Davis (also on synthesizer) and Marty Ehlrich on sax and clarinet to Roberson's trumpet (Jerome Harris on guitar, Pheeeman Aklaff on drums). Helias returned to form as a composer with **Attack The Future** (march 1990), that featured Robertson, Michael Moore on alto and clarinet, David Lopato on piano and Tom Rainey on drums unleashed in the 12-minute *Gnomeswalk* and the 26-minute suite *Knitting or Quitting*. Influenced by Charles Mingus as a bassist and by Dave Holland as a composer, Helias could occasionally secrete the best of the two. The composer found perhaps his best balance of avantgarde and tradition, as well as of black and ethnic music, on **Loopin' The Cool** (december 1994), highlighted by the sophisticated interplay between violinist Regina Carter and tenorist Ellery Eskelin and propelled by Rainey and Guinean percussionist Abdoulaye Epizo Bangoura (the convoluted *Seventh Sign* but also the Afro-funky *Thumbs Up*).

White soprano saxophonist Jane Ira Bloom carried out one of the most breathtaking excursions at the border between structure and improvisation. She started out in a very independent fashion with **We Are** (march 1978), a duet with bassist Kent McLagan, and **Second Wind** (june 1980), in a quintet with pianist Larry Karush and vibraphonist David Friedman, bridging Anthony Braxton and Coleman Hawkins. This attitude triumphed on **Mighty Lights** (november 1982), thanks to a quartet that featured pianist Fred Hersch and Ornette Coleman's rhythm section of two decades earlier, namely bassist Charlie Haden and drummer Ed Blackwell, and thanks to compositions such as *2-5-1* that embodied postmodernism at in its most subtle manifestation. After the transitional duets with Hersh of **As One** (september 1984), notably the nine-minute *Waiting For Daylight*, Hersh was promoted to electronic keyboards to create the brainy tapestry of **Modern Drama** (february 1987), that harked back to Paul Bley's experiments with live electronic music. The quartet with Hersh took a detour into the ballad format with **Slalom** (june 1988) before Bloom's compositional art

peaked on **Art & Aviation** (july 1992). Featuring Bloom herself on live electronics, trumpeter Kenny Wheeler, bassist Michael Formanek and electro-acoustic percussionist Jerry Granelli (again, a line-up that resembled Ornette Coleman's piano-less quartet of thirty years earlier), the album merged her passion for abstract painting and her flair for melody in sophisticated visions such as *Oshumare*, *Art & Aviation* and especially *Most Distant Galaxy*. After another light-weight divertissment, **Nearness** (july 1995), featuring Wheeler, Hersh, trombonist Julian Priester, bassist Rufus Reid and drummer Bobby Previte, the quartet session with Hersch, bassist Mark Dresser and Previte that yielded **The Red Quartets** (january 1999) were a showcase for her surgical blend of design and performance, from the torrential *Emergency* to the sparse *Tell Me Your Diamonds*.
Replacing Hersh with Vincent Bourgeyx, Bloom's quartet made another aboutface towards melody on **Sometimes the Magic** (july 2000). In a unique way of asserting her role as a transmission chain, for every step she made towards free jazz, concept art and experimental counterpoint, Bloom also made a step backwards towards the roots of jazz and pop music.
Chasing Paint (may 2002), recorded by the classic quartet with Hersch, Dresser and Previte, was her tribute to one of her influences, Jackson Pollock's abstract painting, her motion-activated synthesizer haunting the cryptic meditations of *Unexpected Light* and *Alchemy*. Replacing Hersh with Jamie Saft, **Like Silver Like Song** (july 2004) was more than the usual retreat into melody: it balanced her split personality, not only alternating catchy tunes and free-form pieces but also fusing the two into the nine-minute *Vanishing Hat*.

White pianist <u>Marilyn Crispell</u>, who was playing with Anthony Braxton (1978-86), inherited the tradition of experimental jazz pianists who were also bold composers (Thelonious Monk, Paul Bley, Cecil Taylor), and took it to a new level of sensibility and curiosity in the wild trio improvisations of **Spirit Music** (march 1981), with violinist Billy Bang and drummer John Betsch, in the passionate solo improvisations of **Rhythms Hung in Undrawn Sky** (may 1983), of **Labyrinths** (october 1987) and of **Images** (august 1991), in the cerebral duets with German pianist Irene Schweizer of **Overlapping Hands** (june 1990), in the dramatic quartet counterpoint of **Santuerio** (march 1993), with violinist Mark Feldman, cellist Hank Roberts and drummer Gerry Hemingway, in the stark duo studies with Italian saxophonist and clarinetist Stefano Maltese of **Red** (september 1999) and **Blue** (september 1999). Her focus gradually shifted from sheer extroverted expression of vital energy towards a more balanced and even introverted exploration of sound.

CREATIVE MUSIC: EUROPEAN CREATIVITY

Europe had lagged behind the USA until the 1950s. Jazz music was "black", and "blacks" were "Americans". World War II did much to export the music to Europe, but few European musicians were comparable in achievements and influence to the Americans. It was free jazz that definitely broke the barrier. European musicians enthusiastically endorsed free jazz, and soon became masters and innovators of the genre. European jazz matured at about the same time that Chicago's "creative" music was beginning to spread out of Chicago. Europe embraced their extreme form of free music. In fact, they did so much earlier than USA critics realized how important the likes of Anthony Braxton and Roscoe Mitchell were. Thus it became popular for USA musicians to sojourn in Europe for several years (Anthony Braxton in 1969, Roscoe Mitchell's Art Ensemble Of Chicago in 1969, Steve Lacy in 1969) the same way that in the past it had been the norm for Europeans to relocate to the USA.

During the 1970s the foundations were laid for important national schools to spring up in all the major western European countries, notably the northern ones.

Creative Music: Holland

In Holland the most important institution was the Instant Composers Pool, founded by Misha Mengelberg, Han Bennink and Wilhelm Breuker in 1967.

Dutch (Ukrainian-born) pianist <u>Misha Mengelberg</u> graduated from the conservatory in 1964 after participating in the John Cage-inspired artistic movement Fluxus. He debuted with **Driekusman Total Loss** (december 1964), credited to a Kwartet featuring alto saxophonist Piet Noordijk, drummer Han Bennink and bassist Gary Peacock, that contained three lengthy pieces in a free style (*Driekusman Total Loss, Nature Boy, If I Had You*) and **The Misja Mengelberg Quartet** (march 1966), containing other lengthy pieces (*Auntie Watch Your Step, Driekus Man Total Loss, Journey*). For a few years he was mainly involved in the improvised recordings of the "Instant Composers Pool" series with other improvisers, notably **Instant Composers Pool 002** (may 1968), containing *Amagabowl* for a trio with altoist John Tchicai and Bennink, **Instant Composers Pool 005** (march 1970), in a quartet with Tchicai, Bennink and guitarist Derek Bailey, **Groupcomposing** (may 1970), with trombonist Paul Rutherford, tenorist Peter Broetzmann, soprano saxophonist Evan Parker, altoist Peter Bennink, guitarist Derek Bailey and Bennink that inaugurated the ICP Orchestra (Instant Composer's Pool Orchestra), and **Instant Composers Pool 010** (march 1971) in a duo with Bennink. Other duets with Bennink (on all sorts of percussion noises) yielded **Coincidents** (june 1973), **Einepartietischtennis** (may 1974), **Midwoud 77** (march 1977), **Instant Composers Pool 023** (july 1979). The duo also recorded **Yi Yole** (september 1978) with altoist Dudu Pukuwana, and **3 Points and a Mountain** (february 1979) with Peter Broetzmann on saxophones and clarinets. These albums displayed Mengelberg's debt towards Thelonious Monk and other jazz greats, but mainly his (and

Bennink's) bizarre language of humorous noises and detours, better codified in the *Suite Banana* on his solo album **Pech Onderweg** (february 1978). A quartet with trombonist Paul Rutherford, altoist Mario Schiano and Bennink recorded the four-movement improvisation *Tristezze di Sanluigi* on **A European Proposal** (april 1978).

Mengelberg also played on and composed for the ICP Tentet's **ICP Tentet** (april 1977) and **Tetterettet** (september 1977). Mengelberg and Bennink were, above all, the pillars of the ICP Orchestra, a rotating ensemble of improvisers that recorded **Live Soncino** (september 1979), with trumpeter Enrico Rava, saxophonist Gianluigi Trovesi, tuba player Larry Fishkind and other Italian musicians, **Japan Japon** (may 1982), with trumpeter Toshinori Kondo, saxophonist Peter Broetzmann, viola player Maurice Horsthuis, Fishkind, trombonist Walter Wierbos, clarinetist Michael Moore, etc, **Caravan** (same session), **Extention Red, White & Blue** (may 1984), with soprano saxophonist Steve Lacy, cellist Ernst Reijseger, Wierbos, Fishkind, Moore, Horsthuis, etc, **Two Programs** (may 1984), with Lacy, trombonist George Lewis and others, devoted to Mengelberg's heroes, **Bospaadje Konijnehol I** (november 1986), containing Mengelberg's suite *De Purperen Sofa*, with George Lewis, Maurice Horsthuis on viola and Ernst Reijseger on cello, **Bospaadje Konijnehol II** (november 1990), containing Mengelberg's eight *K-Stukken* and Mengelberg's four-part suite *Tegenstroom*. Mengelberg's music for larger ensembles was permeated by the same absurdist circus-like atmosphere of his duets with Bennink but it augmented it with ambitions worthy of chamber music.

Mengelberg finally returned to the solo format for the 13 **Impromptus** (june 1988), another kaleidoscope of madcap proto-folk nonsense, that was followed by **Mix** (may 1994) and **Solo** (december 1999). These solo albums delivered his cacophonous vision uncensored and unedited.

The other main outlet for Mengelberg's "compositions", the ICP Orchestra, became a tighter and more focused affair on **Jubilee Varia** (november 1997), containing two more Mengelberg suites, *Jubilee Varia Suite* and *Jealousy Suite*, performed by Wierbos, Moore, Reijseger, trumpeter Thomas Heberer, clarinetist Ab Baars, cellist Tristan Honsinger, bassist Ernst Glerum and Bennink.

More than anyone else, Mengelberg found the missing link between free jazz and Dadaism and John Cage's "alea".

Dutch drummer Han Bennink, Misha Mengelberg's trusted percussionist since 1963 and a co-founder of the Instant Composer's Pool in 1967, help coin the language of European free improvisation through a number of duo and trio recordings, notably: **New Acoustic Swing Duo** (1967) with saxophonist Willem Breuker, **Instant Composers Pool 002** (may 1968) with Mengelberg and alto saxophonist John Tchicai, **Instant Composers Pool 004** (july 1969) with guitarist Derek Bailey, **The Topography of the Lungs** (july 1970) with Bailey and saxophonist Evan Parker. Bennink also anchored the trio of tenorist Peter Broetzmann and pianist Fred Van Hove on **Balls** (august 1970), **Broetzmann/ van Hove/ Bennink** (february 1973), **Einheitsfrontlied** (march 1973) and **Tschus** (september 1975); and joined the Globe Unity Orchestra in 1970 and the

Company in 1976. His gargantuan solo albums were **Solo** (1972), **Nerve Beats** (september 1973), on which he even used a rhythm machine, **Solo West/East** (october 1978), **Tempo Comodo** (september 1982).

Dutch saxophonist Willem Breuker formed a big band at the age of 22 and recorded **Contemporary Jazz for Holland** (october 1966), that contained the politically-charged *Litany for the 14th of June 1966*. However, it was a duet with Willem Breuker, **New Acoustic Swing Duo** (december 1967), that inaugurated the golden age of Dutch improvised music. He had co-founded the Instant Composers Pool with Han Bennink and Misha Mengelberg, but did not share Mengelberg's view of "instant composing" preferring a more traditional way of composing and a theatrical approach. Breuker's variant of ICP placed more emphasis on instrumentation, as proven by **Lunchconcert For Three Barrelorgans** (march 1969), and retained a passion for traditional formats, such as the opera **The Message** (january 1971), the theatrical soundtrack **De Onderste Steen** (december 1974), as well as several film soundtracks.

His masterpiece was **Instant Composers Pool 007/008** (1971), that contained two 20-minute compositions: *Song of the Lusitanian Bully* (march 1969) for trombone (Willem van Manen), gachi (Han Bennink), bagpipes (Peter Bennink) and organ (Rob du Bois), and *Lass Mich Nicht Weinen IV* (november 1969) for reeds (Breuker), piano (Rob du Bois), bass and percussion. Each was a cartoonish, collage-like, Frank Zappa-inspired accumulation of sonic events.

Breaking up with Mengelberg's concept of "instant composition", Breuker formed the Kollektief (usually a tentet) to perform his compositions, whose recordings typically bridged the swing era and the free era. Among his scores (many originally devised for the theater) performed by the Kollektief were: **De Achterlijke Klokkenmaker** (december 1974) for three saxophones, flute, piano, flugelhorn, trombone, tuba, drums (plus "voices and noises"); *La Plagiata* for three saxes, flute, trumpet, flugelhorn, two trombones, piano, bass, drums, documented on **The European Scene** (october 1975) and **Live In Berlin** (november 1975); the 16-minute *Summer Music*, off **Summer Music A Paris** (february 1978); the masterful *Kleine Amsterdam Rhapsodie* (1980) off **Muziek In Amsterdam** (march 1980); the double-LP **In Holland** (may 1981) for a tentet, with *Ouverture* and *Marche Funebre*, two of his most emotional pieces; *Spanish Wells*, off **Rhapsody in Blue** (february 1982); *Driebergen Zeist*, off **Driebergen Zeist** (september 1983); the colossal **Psalm 122** (february 1988) for jazz tentet, string ensemble, choir and barrel organ; the 11-movement suite **To Remain** (april 1989); the five-movement suite **Hunger** (august 1989); the mini-opera *Der Kritiker*, off **Heibel** (december 1990); the ballet music **Dans Plezier/ Joy Of Dance** (september 1995).

Dutch keyboardist Fred Van Hove contributed to that season with **Requiem for Che Guevara** (november 1968), that featured Willem Breuker on reeds, Han Bennink on percussion, Peter Kowald on bass, two saxophonists and a trombonist.

Dutch pianist Leo Cuypers crafted the *Johnny Rep Suite*, off **Live In Shaffy** (september 1974), and the **Zeeland Suite** (september 1977).

Dutch bassist Maarten Altena, one of Willem Breuker's trusted collaborators from 1969 till 1973 and a member of Derek Bailey's Company from 1976 till 1977, revealed his dadaist spirit with the solo albums **Handicaps** (july 1973), played with a broken wrist, and **Tuning The Bass** (may 1975). **K'ploeng** (december 1977) featured collaborations with various musicians at the border between free-noise improvisation (led by guitarist Derek Bailey), chamber music (clarinet, cello, viola, mandolin) and childish provocation (the instrumentation included cigar box, balloons, toys, crackle synthesizer). After a trio with trombonist Guenter Christmann and drummer Paul Lovens, documented on **Weavers** (june 1980), a drum-less quartet with Maurice Horsthuis on viola, Maud Sauer on oboe and Paul Termos on alto saxophone became the main vehicle for Altena's unconventional improvisations: **Op Stap** (february 1980), **Pisa** (june 1980), **Papa Oewa** (1981) and **Veranda** (1982), **Miere** (1983), **Rondedans** (1984). The rhythm-less chamber approach was further radicalized by **Tel** (october 1982), that inaugurated the octet: bassoon (Lindsay Cooper), trumpet (Kenny Wheeler), trombone (Wolter Wierbos), oboe (Sauer), alto saxophone (Termos), violin (Maartje ten Hoorn), piano (Guus Janssen) and bass (Altena). Altena progressively distanced himself from free improvisation and rediscovered composition, melody and the song format, becoming a sophisticated composer of the trans-avantgarde. **Rif** (august 1987), **Quotl** (december 1988), **Cities And Streets** (october 1989), **Code** (december 1990) refined his hyper-fusion for chamber jazz octet (typically, trumpet, trombone, clarinet, saxophone, violin, piano, bass and percussion).

Creative Music: Germany

In Germany the focal point of free jazz was the FMP collective, founded by pianist Alexander von Schlippenbach, saxophonist Peter Broetzmann and trumpeter Manfred Schoof.

German multi-instrumentalist Guenter Hampel, originally a vibraphonist, was credited with starting the free-jazz scene in continental Europe in 1964 when he formed a quintet with trumpeter Manfred Schoof and pianist Alexander von Schlippenbach that recorded **Heartplants** (january 1965). Hampel played vibraphone, flute and bass clarinet (that would remain his three main instruments), but composed only one of the five titles. The quartet of **Assemblage** (december 1966), with Willem Breuker on several saxophones and clarinets, was a far more decisive unit, and Hampel stepped up as a composer with the 22-minute *Assemblage* and the eleven-minute *Heroicredolphysiognomystery*.

Relocating to Europe in 1967, the American black vocalist Jeanne Lee joined Hampel's and Breuker's quartet on **Gunter Hampel Group + Jeanne Lee** (april 1968). Hampel's growing confidence as a leader/composer and Lee's acrobatic vocals highlighted **The 8th of July 1969** (july 1969), that also added American saxophonist Anthony Braxton to the Hampel-Breuker-Lee quintet and contained the 18-minute *Morning Song* and the 25-minute *Crepuscule*. The magic combination of Hampel's conduction and Lee's decoration permeated **Ballet-**

Symphony (january 1970) for a quintet with Hampel, Lee, cello, bass and drums; **People Symphony** (march 1970), that added Breuker on clarinet and tenor sax as well as Willem van Manen on trombone; **Out Of New York** (july 1971), for a quartet with clarinetist Perry Robison and a bassist performing Hampel's seventh and eight symphonies; **Spirits** (august 1971), a trio with Robinson; **Familie** (april 1972), a spectacular trio with Braxton, **Waltz For 11 Universes In A Corridor** (june 1972), a trio with violinist Toni Marcus containing *Waltz for 3 Universes in a Corridor* and *Galaxie Sun Dance*. Most of these albums were taken up by lengthy eponymous improvisations, that Hampel painstakingly numbered according to the conventions of classical music.

Hampel and Lee then formed the Galaxie Dream Band, still a nine-piece unit on the colossal jam **Angel** (may 1972), but, after **I Love Being With You** (july 1972), the imposing **Broadway** (july 1972), **Unity Dance** (june 1973), and **Out From Under** (january 1974), the first collection of shorter pieces, expanded to an eleven-piece ensemble for **Journey to the Song Within** (february 1974), that contained *Bolero*. The Galaxie Dream Band shrank back to an octet for the double-LP **Celebrations** (june 1974) and to a sextet for **Ruomi** (october 1974), that did not feature Lee, and then expanded again to an octet (with Lee and Braxton) for **Enfant Terrible** (september 1975). **Transformation** (september 1976), by a classic line-up featuring Lee, Robinson, Schoof and flutist Thomas Keyserling, and **All Is Real** (november 1978), by a quintet with Lee, Robinson, Keyserling and a percussionist, marked a return to the extended format. Despite being reduced to a quartet (with Robinson, Keyserling and a percussionist), the combo was still called Galaxie Dream Band on **Vogelfrei** (october 1976). The collaborations with Lee went beyond the Galaxie Dream Band: **Cosmic Dancer** (september 1975) for a quartet with Lee, Robinson and drummer Steve McCall, and especially **Freedom Of The Universe** (june 1978), that contained another lengthy meditation, and the double-LP **Oasis** (july 1978).

Hampel resurrected the Galaxie Dream Band (now a sextet with Lee) for the album-long improvisation of **All the Things You Could Be If Charles Mingus Was Your Daddy** (july 1980), and (as a quartet with Lee and Keyserling) for the shorter pieces of **A Place To Be With Us** (january 1981), and (as a quintet with Lee, Robinson and Keyserling) for **Life On This Planet** (july 1981), that contained the side-long *Infinite Transparencies*.

Hampel and Lee pursued their partnership until Lee's death in 2000, notably on **Companion** (november 1982), for a trio with Keyserling, and **Celestial Glory** (september 1991), for a quintet with Lee, Keyserling, Robinson, saxophonist Mark Whitecage, containing the 26-minute *As If It Were A Bridge*.

German trumpeter <u>Manfred Schoof</u> inaugurated the German free-jazz scene with his Quintett of 1966 (tenorist Gerd Dudek, pianist Alexander von Schlippenbach, bassist Buschi Niebergall, drummer Jacki Liebezeit) and inaugurated the FMP catalog with **European Echoes** (june 1969), credited to the Manfred Schoof Orchestra (three trumpets, Gerd Dudek and Peter Broetzmann on tenor, Evan Parker on soprano, Paul Rutherford on trombone, Derek Bailey on guitar, the three pianos of Fred Van Hove, Alex Schlippenbach and Irene

Schweizer, three basses including Peter Kowald and Buschi Niebergall, two drummers including Han Bennink).

German extremely dissonant saxophonist Peter Broetzmann, who studied visual arts and joined the Fluxus movement, accompanied Don Cherry before forming in 1965 an influential trio with bassist Peter Kowald and drummer Sven-Ake Johansson that recorded **For Adolphe Sax** (june 1967), containing the volcanic eruptions of *For Adolphe Sax* (19 minutes) and *Morning Glory* (16 minutes), and eventually merged into Alexander Schlippenbach's Globe Unity Orchestra.

His torrential, incendiary language, partially borrowed from Albert Ayler's harshest tones after removing the lyrical subtleties, set the pace for Broetzmann's 17-minute *Machine Gun*, Van Hove's ten-minute *Responsible* and Breuker's eleven-minute *Music for Han Bennink* on a seminal recording of European free-jazz, **Machine Gun** (may 1968), performed by an octet with three saxophonists (Broetzmann, Willem Breuker, Evan Parker), piano (Fred Van Hove), two basses (Kowald and Buschi Niebergall), two drummers (Han Bennink and Johansson). Sheer intensity replaced the concepts of order and structure.

Nipples (april 1969) contained the 15-minute timbral nightmare *Tell a Green Man* by a quartet with pianist Fred Van Hove, bassist Buschi Niegergall and Dutch drummer Han Bennink, and the 18-minute collective maelstrom *Nipples* by a sextet with tenor saxophonist Evan Parker, guitarist Derek Bailey, Van Hove, Niegergall and Bennink.

Another furious performance of the time, the 36-minute *Fuck de Boere* (march 1970), off **Fuck de Boere** (2001), featured Breuker, Parker, Van Hove, Bennink, guitarist Derek Bailey and four trombones (Malcolm Griffiths, Willem van Manen, Buschi Niebergall, Paul Rutherford).

Trimming down the line-up to a trio with only Van Hove and Bennink, Broetzmann recorded the exuberant **Balls** (august 1970), with the 14-minute *Balls* and the eleven-minute *De Daag Waarop Sipke Eindelijk Zijn Nagels Knipte, En Verder Alle Ander*.

Augmented with trombonist Albert Mangelsdorff, the trio indulged live in the 20-minute *Florence Nightingale*, the 15-minute *Elements*, the 21-minute *Couscouss de la Mauresque*, the 19-minute *Wenn Mein Schaetzlein auf die Pauke Haut* and the 23-minute *The End*, first documented on **Elements**, **The End** and **Couscouss de la Mauresque**, and later collected on **Live In Berlin** (august 1971).

The trio jammed with 15 children in the four-side long **Free Jazz und Kinder** (april 1972). Then, appropriately, recorded the childish **Broetzmann/ van Hove/ Bennink** (february 1973), featuring Broetzmann on alto, tenor, baritone and bass saxophones as well as on clarinet, Van Hove on piano and celesta and Bennink on all sorts of percussion including a rhythm machine. **Einheitsfrontlied** (march 1973) was issued as a single.

The two volumes of **Outspan** (april and may 1974) also featured Mangelsdorff (the 16-minute *Serieuze Serie*, the 18-minute *Outspan No 1* and the 21-minute *Ende mit Broetzophon*).

After another childish endeavour, **Tschus** (september 1975), with Van Hove also on accordion and Bennink on all sorts of noises, the celebrated trio dissolved.

A disappointing **Solo** (may 1976) was followed by duets with Han Bennink: **Ein Halber Hund Kann Nicht Pinkeln** (april 1977), on which Broetzmann played soprano, alto, tenor saxophones, a-clarinet, b-flat clarinet, bass clarinet and piano, while Bennink played piano, drums, viola, banjo and bass clarinet, and **Schwarzwaldfahrt** (may 1977), recorded in the Black Forest (Bennink plays birdcall, wood, trees, sand, land, water, air...). Broetzmann and Bennink also formed a trio with pianist Misha Mengelberg for **3 Points and a Mountain** (february 1979), containing Broetzmann's *3 Points and a Mountain*, as well as **3 Points and a Mountain Plus** (same session), containing Broetzmann's *The Bar Seems to Vanish in the Distance*.

A new trio with bassist Harry Miller and drummer Louis Moholo smoothed out the edges on **The Nearer the Bone the Sweeter the Meat** (august 1979) and the double-LP live **Opened but Hardly Touched** (november 1980), with the extended improvisations of *Special Request for Malibu*, *Opened but Hardly Touched* and *Double Meaning*. Building on the foundations of this trio, **Alarm** (november 1981), containing the 37-minute *Alarm*, featured three saxophonists (Broetzmann, Breuker, Frank Wright), Japanese trumpeter Toshinori Kondo, pianist Alex Schlippenbach, two trombones, bass (Miller) and drums (Moholo). The music had lost much of its devastating strength, as if Broetzmann had fallen under the spell of Breuker, although in 1986 Broetzmann joined Last Exit, a metal-jazz group formed in 1986 with drummer Ronald Shannon Jackson, guitarist Sonny Sharrock and rock bassist Bill Laswell.

The solo albums were always less engaging than his small-combo recordings: **14 Love Poems** (august 1984), **No Nothing** (december 1990), **Right As Rain** (august 2000).

Broetzmann's best combo of the period was the Die Like a Dog Quartet, formed with bassist Wiliam Parker, drummer Hamid Drake and trumpeter Toshinori Kondo, and documented on the live **Fragments of Music, Life and Death of Albert Ayler** (august 1993), the two volumes of **Little Birds Have Fast Hearts** (november 1997), **From Valley To Valley** (july 1998), with Roy Campbell replacing Kondo, and **Aoyama Crows** (november 1999), with Kondo back in the ranks.

In 1997 Broetzmann formed the Chicago Octet that lined up percussionists Hamid Drake and Michael Zerang, bassist Kent Kessler, cellist Fred Lomberg-Holm and trombonist Jeb Bishop around three saxophonists/clarinetists: Broetzmann, Ken Vandermark and Mars Williams. The Chicago Tentet was the octet augmented with Mats Gustafsson on baritone saxophone and fluteophone and Joe McPhee on pocket cornet, valve trombone and soprano saxophone. The trible-CD **The Chicago Octet/Tentet** (september 1997) documented the compositional versatility, ranging from Vandermark's conventional notation (*Other Brothers*) to Broetzmann's post-Cage notations (*Burning Spirit*, *Foolish Infinity*). The ensemble's tour de force was *Stonewater*, documented both on the live **Stone/Water** (1999), with Kondo's trumpet replacing Williams and William

Parker replacing Kessler, and on **Broken English** (july 2000), with Williams and Kessler (and Roy Campbell replacing Kondo).

Educated at avantgarde classical music, German pianist Alexander von Schlippenbach entered the fray of free-jazz via Gunther Hampel's and Manfred Schoof's quintets. He formed the Globe Unity Orchestra in 1966, a big band that bridged the techniques of free-jazz and the techniques of the classical avantgarde (including the twelve-tone scale).

The orchestra of **Globe Unity** (december 1966) assembled saxophonist Peter Broetzmann's trio (bassist Peter Kowald and drummer Sven-Ake Johansson), trumpeter Manfred Schoof's quintet (Schlippenbach, tenorist Gerd Dudek, bassist Buschi Niebergall and percussionist Jaki Liebezeit), plus clarinetist/flutist Gunter Hampel, saxophonist Willem Breuker, trumpeter Claude Deron, tuba player Willi Lietzmann, saxophonist Kris Wanders and drummer Mani Neumeier. The two 20-minute pieces were manifestos of two different kinds of free jazz: *Globe Unity* was a series of energetic improvised solos grafted onto the very loose structure of Von Schlippenbach's written score, while *Sun* was an even looser soundscape roamed by discrete percussion instruments, piano and vibraphone. The fundamental difference between this European kind of free-jazz and Ornette Coleman's (or John Coltrane's) free-jazz was the rhythm: the European rhythm was cold, abstract, a purely sonic element, whereas the USA rhythm was warm, bodily and, ultimately, jazz.

The 34-minute *Globe Unity 67* (october 1967), off **Globe Unity 67 & 70**, documented another loud and lively performance of continental improvisers (now also including trombonist Albert Mangelsdorff), whereas the inferior 18-minute *Globe Unity 70* (november 1970) has a cast of British improvisers (guitarist Derek Bailey, trumpeter Kenny Wheeler, drummer Paul Lovens).

Schlippenbach was also active outside the orchestra. **The Living Music** (april 1969) was recorded the same day by the same musicians who recorded Peter Broetzman's **Nipples**, but the lengthy *The Living Music* and *Tower* implemented a totally different view of group improvisation, one that was subtle instead of savage. The trio with saxophonist Evan Parker and drummer Paul Lovens of **Pakistani Pomade** (november 1972) expanded to a quartet with the addition of Kowald and for a while became the pianist's main artistic avenue; **Three Nails Left** (february 1975), with the 23-minute *Range*, the live **Hunting the Snake** (september 1975), released only in 2000, and the five-movement **Hidden Peak** (january 1977).

During the 1970s, e.g. on **Live in Wuppertal** (march 1973), the Globe Unity Orchestra briefly flirted with a more structured song-oriented format, but then returned to its free-form grandeur with a vengeance. Next to the triad of Von Schlippenbach, Broetzmann and Schoof, **Hamburg '74** (november 1974) featured Dutch drummer Han Bennink and a conspicuous British contingent (Bailey, Lovens, Wheeler, saxophonist Evan Parker, trombonist Paul Rutherford). Both *Hamburg '74* and *Contrast and Synthesis* added a choir to the collective chaos.

The Globe Unity Special of **Evidence** (march 1975) and **Into the Valley** (march 1975), later collected as **Rumbling**, was, instead, merely a nonet of four Germans (Schlippenbach, Dudek, Mangelsdorff, Kowald), four Britons (Wheeler, Parker, Lovens, Rutherford) and American soprano saxophonist Steve Lacy, dominated by Parker's compositions *Into the Valley* and *Of Dogs, Dreams, and Death*.

Pearls (november 1975), on the other hand, boasted the Globe Unity Orchestra at its international zenith: three trumpeters (Schoof, Wheeler, Enrico Rava), five saxophonists (Broetzmann, Dudek, Parker, Anthony Braxton, Ruediger Carl), three trombones (Guenter Christmann, Mangelsdorff, Rutherford), a bass clarinet (Michel Pilz), a pianist (Schlippenbach), two bassists (Kowald and Niebergall) and a drummer (Lovens). Peter Kowald engineered the two pieces of **Jahrmarkt** (june 1976): the chamber free jazz explorations of *Jahrmarkt* and the colossal fanfare of *Local Fair* for jazz ensemble, Greek bouzouki quartet, 17-piece brass band and 30-piece accordion ensemble. A slightly revised line-up with the addition of Derek Bailey and cellist Tristan Honsinger, and the notable omission of Anthony Braxton, recorded the four untitled **Improvisations** (september 1977). Steve Lacy joined for the six shorter **Compositions** (january 1979).

After the live **Detto Fra Di Noi** (june 1981) by the Schlippenbach-Parker-Lovens trio, they reformed the quartet with Alan Silva on bass and recorded the double-LP **Das Hohe Lied** (november 1981), with the 43-minute *Let This Mouth Shower Kisses On You*, and **Anticlockwise** (september 1982).

The Berlin Contemporary Jazz Orchestra (four trumpets, four trombones, six saxophones, piano, bass and drums) was built around the trio, but played more casual and organized music, at last sounding like a jazz big-band. Schlippenbach mainly conducted the music on **Berlin Contemporary Jazz Orchestra** (may 1989), that contained Kenny Wheeler's 22-minute *Ana* and Misha Mengelberg's 19-minute *Reef Und Kneebus*, and **The Morlocks** (july 1993), with the 16-minute *The Morlocks*.

German guitarist Hans Reichel recorded the solo albums **Wichlinghauser Blues** (june 1973), **Bonobo** (october 1975), **The Death of the Rare Bird Ymir** (february 1979), **Bonobo Beach** (april 1981), **The Dawn of Dachsman** (may 1987).

Sven Ake Johansson recorded one of the first solo-drums albums of creative music, **Schlingerland** (october 1972).

Swiss pianist Irene Schweizer, who had cut her teeth in a local trio with drummer Mani Neumeier. A few months after British saxophonist Joe Harriott, she pioneered Indo-jazz fusion by recording **Jazz Meets India** (october 1967), that featured a jazz quintet with trumpeter Manfred Schoof and Neumaier improvising with and a trio of Indian musicians (Diwan Motihar on sitar, Keshav Sathe on tabla, Kasan Thakur on tamboura). She achieved notoriety in a trio with bassist Peter Kowald and drummer Pierre Favre that debuted on **Santana** (october 1968), with the 14-minute *Santana*. That trio became a **Quartett** (november 1969) with the addition of British saxophonist Evan Parker (the 19-minute *Where are all the old cop sets Clancy*). **Ramifications** (september 1973) began a collaboration with tenor saxophonist Ruediger Carl (it also featured drummer Paul Lovens, trombonist Radu Malfatti, bassist Harry Miller) that continued with the quartet of **Goose Pannee** (september 1974), containing the 21-minute *Goose Pannee*. Carl and Schweizer formed a trio with drummer Louis Moholo that recorded **Messer** (may 1975) and **Tuned Boots** (november 1977), with the 20-minute *Tuned Boots*

Her first solo album, **Wilde Senoritas** (november 1976), contained two lengthy improvisations: the 15-minute *Wilde Se¤oritas* and the 18-minute *Saitengebilde*. **Hexensabbat** (october 1977) contained seven shorter pieces and the 12-minute live *Rapunzel Rapunzel*. Compared with the harsh avantgarde of the time, her style, blending classical, bebop and free-jazz elements, was folkish and oneiric.

But she was more famous for an aggressive style of playing that abused the possibilities of the keyboard and indulged in neurotic timbral detours. The duo with Carl yielded the live **The Very Centre of Middle Europe** (october 1978) and **Die V-Mann Suite** (october 1980), containing the 19-minute *Frizeit*. A trio with bassist Joelle Leandre and drummer Paul Lovens debuted in the 20-minute *Trutznachtigall*, off **Live at Taktlos** (february 1984). The collaboration with Leandre led to the 26-minute *Now And Never* for a quintet with American trombonist George Lewis, vocalist Maggie Nicols and drummer Guenter Sommer, off the live **The Storming of The Winter Palace** (march 1988).

She relished a series of piano-drum duos (Andrew Cyrille, Pierre Favre, Han Bennink, Louis Moholo, Mani Neumeier), best probably being the one with Sommer that yielded the ebullient 19-minute *Schweizersommer* (february 1987). The trio of Schwiezer, vocalist Maggie Nichols, and bassist Joelle Leandre, all members of EWIG (the European Women's Improvising Group), recorded **Les Diaboliques** (april 1993), a series of brief absurdist skits.

German trombonist Albert Mangelsdorff, a veteran who joined Alex von Schlippenbach's Globe Unity Orchestra in 1967, displayed his allegiances on **And His Friends**, a series of collaborations (recorded between 1967 and 1969) with trumpeter Don Cherry, altoist Lee Konitz, pianist Wolfgang Dauner, vibraphonist Karl Berger and drummer Elvin Jones. He first proved his compositional and improvisational skills with the 22-minute *Room 1220*, off **Room 1220** (august 1970), a collaboration with John Surman on baritone saxophone. His technique of multiphonics (playing multiple notes simultaneously) was centerstage on the solo-trombone album **Trombirds** (december 1972). Thanks to his "invention", Mangelsdorff was able to explore a vast territory of subtleties on **Tromboneliness** (march 1976) and **Solo** (february 1982).

His versatility allowed him to play in different configurations, from the trio of **The Wide Point** (may 1975), featuring Palle Daniellson on bass and Elvin Jones on drums, to the trio of the live **Trilogue** (november 1976), with Weather Report's bassist Jaco Pastorius and drummer Alphonse Mouzon; from the quartet of **Solo Now** (june 1976), with Gunter Hampel on vibraphone, Joachim Kuehn on piano and Pierre Favre on drums, to the Mumps quartet of **A Matter Of Taste** (march 1977), with John Surman (saxophones, piano, synthesizer), Barre Phillips (bass), Stu Martin (percussion and synthesizer); from the quartet of **A Jazz Tune I Hope** (august 1978), with pianist Wolfgang Dauner, bassist Eddie Gomez and Elvin Jones, to the **Trombone Summit** (may 1980) for four trombones and rhythm section; from the collaboration with Dauner, **Two Is A Company** (1982), to the collaboration with altoist Lee Konitz, **Art Of The Duo** (june 1983); from the quartet of **Hot Hut** (1985) with Dauner and Jones, to the percussion ensemble (plus Dauner's piano) of **Moon At Noon** (april 1987). Mangelsdorff more than simply dialogued with his partners: he could simulate an entire band.

After the solo albums **Purity** (1990) and **Lanaya** (november 1993), Mangelsdorff entered the digital age with **Movin' On** (1990), for a quartet that featured Bruno Spoerri on saxophones and electronics, as well as Ernst Reijseger on cello.

German (Polish-born) trombonist Guenter Christmann invented a new, almost clownish but at times expressionist, language at the instrument by finding the common elements between the grotesque excesses of the old Dixieland style and the furious excesses of the new free-jazz style. His technique blossomed in the duets of **We Play** (february 1973) and **Topic** (november 1975) with percussionist Detlef Schonenberg, in the albums with the Globe Unity Orchestra, that he joined in 1973. on the solo album **Solomusiken Fuer Posaune und Kontrabasse** (september 1976), in the duets of **Earmeals** (may 1978) with cellist Tristan Honsinger, on **Weavers** (december 1979), by a trio with bassist Maarten Altena and drummer Paul Lovens.

The surreal and Cage-inspired element of his music surfaced on **Off** (1979), that contained sound collages, compositions for breath, *Mandolympia* for mandolin and typewriter, etc. This interest for event/chance art led Christmann to organize multimedia events titled "Vario", that included acrobats and dancers as well as musicians, an idea that eventually evolved into the "Deja-vu" events that also incorporated theater and cinema. The former were documented on **Vario II** (june 1980), with music performed by the trio (Altena and Loves) plus vocalist Maggie Nicols and guitarist John Russell,

These radical experiments translated into music that was abstract and apparently absurd in the dadaistic tradition, notably **White Earth Streak** (february 1981), basically trombone jams with three stringed instruments (viola and violin player LaDonna Smith, guitarist Davey Williams and Torsten Mueller).

Italian percussionist Andrea Centazzo organized the spectacular sextet of **Environment for Sextet** (november 1978) with John Zorn on reeds, Toshinori Kondo on trumpet, Tom Cora on cello, Eugene Chadbourne on guitars and Polly Bradfield on violin. His solo-percussion triple-LP **Indian Tapes** (1980) was inspired by Native-American percussion and birdsongs of the American Southwest. He formed the Mitteleuropa Orchestra to perform larger-scale works. First documented on the live **Mitteleuropa** (december 1980), the orchestra specialized in concertos for small orchestra such as *Doctor Faustus* (1983), **Cjant** (1983) and **Omaggio a Pier Paolo Pasolini** (1985).

The Ganelin Trio was the greatest ensemble of free-jazz in continental Europe, namely in Russia. Like other European improvisers, pianist Vyacheslav Ganelin,

Creative Music: European Creativity

woodwind player Vladimir Chekasin and percussionist Vladimir Tarasov too found a common ground between free-jazz and Dadaism. Their shows were as much music as they were provocative antics. The music of albums such as **Con Anima** (1976), **Concerto Grosso** (1978), the double-LP **Ancora Da Capo** (november 1980), **Poi Segue** (1981), **Non Troppo** (1983) and especially **Semplice/ Con Affetto** (1983) was a gross exercise in mis-interpreting Cecil Taylor, as if played by a circus ensemble affected by deep neurosis but with the skills of classical musicians. After emigrating to Israel in 1987, they recorded the frantically moving **Jerusalem February Cantible** (1989).

Austrian trumpeter Franz Koglmann founded the Chamber Jazz Emsembles Pipetet that debuted with **Schlaf Schlemmer Schlaf Magritte** (december 1984), a vehicle for his brainy scores that embedded everything from Arnold Schoenberg's dodecaphony to swing to free jazz, all done with a Dadaist attitude worthy of Pere Ubu (notably in the four-movement *Tanzmusick Fuer Paszstueckem*). Evolving through fragmented albums such as **Ich** (october 1986), his manyfold art of composition and deconstruction bloomed on the nine-movement suite **The Use of Memory** (october 1990), almost a colossal compendium of 20th century music. A theorist not so much of post-modern but of post-classical music, Koglmann continued to rehearse a cryptic vision of music on albums such as **L'Heure Bleue** (april 1991) only to unleash another massive, powerful reconceptualization of the century's music with **Cantos I-IV** (october 1992) for orchestrated improvisers. Koglmann had coined a moving music of contradictions, misunderstandings and, ultimately, of mistakes. His monumental and demented synthesis of improvised and composed music continued on **O Moon My Pin Up** (march 1997), explicitly dedicated to poet Ezra Pound. After **Make Believe** (november 1998) for a quintet, he also ventured outside chamber music with the electroacoustic opera **Fear Death By Water** (march 2003) and the "imaginary play" **Let's Make Love** (september 2004). One of the greatest composers of his generation, Koglmann metabolized the past in order to create the future.

Creative Music: Britain

British free music found two early reference points in John Stevens' Spontaneous Music Ensemble and Chris McGregor's Brotherhood of Breath. From 1963 to 1966 drummer Tony Oxley, guitarist Derek Bailey and bassist Gavin Bryars formed the trio Joseph Holbrooke that pioneered free jazz in Sheffield. Later, the London Jazz Composers' Orchestra (formed in 1972 by bassist Barry Guy) and the Company (started by guitarist Derek Bailey in 1976) united many of the British improvisers.

However, one man had preached free jazz even before the USA musicians brought it to Europe. Jamaican-born alto saxophonist Joe Harriott relocated to Britain in 1951, initially playing the bebop music that was popular at the time. While recovering from tuberculosis in 1958, Harriott invented free jazz independently from Ornette Coleman, although he used a piano-based quintet (sax, trumpet, piano, drums, bass). They recorded **Free Form** (1960) and

Abstract (1962), the manifestos of British free-jazz, and an even more radical experiment, **Movement** (1963).

In 1965 Harriott met Indian violinist John Mayer, who had relocated to Britain in 1952 and was experimenting a fusion of Indian and European classical music. The two musicians formed the mixed-race ensemble Indo-Jazz Fusions. Harriott thus pioneered the fusion with Indian music culminating with **Indo-Jazz Fusions** (september 1966) and the **Indo-Jazz Suite** (october 1966), two albums (mostly composed by Mayer) recorded by a double quintet: Harriott's jazz quintet and an Indian quintet led by Mayer plus Diwan Motihar on sitar, flute, tambura and tabla. He pursued this idea on **Hum-Dono** (1969), featuring Indian guitarist Amancio D'Silva, trumpeter Ian Carr and vocalist Norma Winstone.

The Spontaneous Music Ensemble was formed in 1965 by British drummer John Stevens and saxophonist Trevor Watts with the intent of creating a jazz version of Cornelius Cardew's AMM avantgarde collective. In reality, after **Challenge** (march 1966), that featured Kenny Wheeler on flugelhorn, Paul Rutherford on trombone, Trevor Watts on alto and soprano saxophone, bass and drums, the ensemble started playing music that was as free, chaotic and atonal as the music of AMM, but focused on the interplay instead of the contrasts.

The line-up of the Spontaneous Music Ensemble changed with every concert and every recording. The ensemble was a sextet with Evan Parker on saxophones, Wheeler on trumpet and flugelhorn, Rutherford on trombone, Watts on oboe and alto, Barry Guy on bass and Stevens on percussion for the four-movement film soundtrack *Withdrawal* (october 1966). **Withdrawal** (march 1967), released only in 1997, added Derek Bailey on dissonant guitar for the three *Withdrawal Sequences* and the four-movement chamber suite *Seeing Sounds And Hearing Colors*. **Summer '67** (august 1967), released in 1996, contained the 15-minute *First Cousins*, a duet between bassist Peter Kowald and Stevens, and the eleven-minute *Second Cousins*, a trio with Parker. The unreleased *Willow Trio* (october 1967) was a lengthy improvisation by Parker (on soprano), Stevens and bassist Barre Phillips, and the unreleased *Familie* (january 1968) was recorded by Stevens, Watts, Parker, Bailey, bassist Dave Holland and several others.

The jazz component had all but disappeared by the time that Stevens, Wheeler, Parker, Bailey and bassist Dave Holland recorded the six-movement **Karyobin** (february 1968), perhaps the ensemble's artistic peak. **Oliv** (1969) contained the 19-minute *Oliv I* for a larger cast (Stevens, Wheeler, Bailey, Watts, bassist John Dyani, vocalist Maggie Nichols and more) and the 16-minute *Oliv II* for just Stevens, Watts, Dyani and Nicols. **For You To Share** (may 1970) contained two lengthy duets by Stevens and Watts, *Peace Music* and *For You To Share*. Another milestone, **The Source - From And Towards** (november 1970), was a five-movement suite for three saxophones (including Watts), trumpet (Wheeler), two trombones, piano, two basses and drums (Stevens).

So What Do You Think (january 1971) boasted the classic quintet of Stevens, Watts, Wheeler, Bailey and Holland in one lengthy improvisation. British vocalist Julie Tippetts fronted a quartet with Stevens and Watts on **Birds of a Feather** (july 1971).

Creative Music: European Creativity

A quintet with Parker, Bailey, Stevens and Watts was documented on **Quintessence 1** (october 1973) and **Quintessence 2** (february 1974), released in 1987. **Face To Face** (november 1973) was another Stevens-Watts duet. The 20-minute *In Relationship to Silence* and the 24-minute *Mouthpiece* on **Mouthpiece** (november 1973) documented Stevens' "compositions" for large ensemble, Stevens "devised" these pieces that the improvisers were free to bend at will. Stevens only imposed constraints on the improvisers' moves to make sure that they would participate and not alienate each other. In a sense, Stevens was working on a more humane natural of "harmony".

The South African influence on British jazz started with Chris McGregor, a white pianist who in 1964 had organized in South Africa a mixed-race group, the Blue Notes: Mongezi Feza on trumpet, Dudu Pukwana on alto saxophone, Nikele Moyake on tenor saxophone, Johnny Dyani on bass and Louis Moholo on drums. After emigrating to Britain, the group expanded to include young British improvisers such as saxophonists John Surman, Mike Osborne and Alan Skidmore, trombonists Malcolm Griffiths and Nick Evans, and trumpeter Marc Charig, and became the Brotherhood Of Breath. The sound of this big band blended Duke Ellington's paradigmatic swing style with ethnic township rhythms, jazz-rock and free jazz, with McGregor's arrangements enabling challenging scores such as the 21-minute *Night Poem* on **Chris McGregor's Brotherhood of Breath** (october 1970). **Brotherhood** (1971), also featuring Gary Windo, was less cohesive but contained *Joyful Noises Of The Lord*. Evan Parker, Paul Rutherford and Kenny Wheeler also played in the band at different points in time.

Another visionary precursor of the British jazz avantgarde was bassist Graham Collier. The ensemble that he debuted on **Deep Dark Blue Centre** (january 1967) was a septet with trumpeter Kenny Wheeler, trombonist Mike Gibbs, Karl Jenkins on saxophones, oboe and piano, and drummer John Marshall. It already displayed the leader's skills at composing and organizing soloists that blossomed with the four-movement **Symphony Of Scorpions** (1977), and then with the four-part suite **Workpoints** (composed in 1968 but released only in 2005), inspired by Charlie Mingus and first performed (in march 1968) by a large ensemble featuring saxophonist John Surman besides the previous talents.

The three British improvisers who lent the British scene its unique (and quite radical) character were Evan Parker, Derek Bailey and Tony Oxley, the founders of Incus (1970).

An alumnus of the Spontaneous Music Ensemble of 1967, immensely prolific British saxophonist Evan Parker coined a wildly dissonant, incoherent and violent language at the instrument via the Music Improvisation Company (formed in 1968 with guitarist Derek Bailey), via Peter Broetzmann's **Machine Gun** (1968), via Derek Bailey's Music Improvisation Company (that he co-founded in 1968), via Tony Oxley's groups (from 1969), via Barry Guy's London Jazz Composers' Orchestra (that he joined in 1972), and via Alexander von Schlippenbach's Trio and Globe Unity Orchestra (that he joined in 1972).

The manifesto of Parker's art was **The Topography of the Lungs** (july 1970), notably the 20-minute *Titan Moon* and the twelve-minute *Dogmeat*, for a trio with guitarist Derek Bailey and percussionist Han Bennink.

For the next few years a duo with drummer Paul Lytton became Parker's main vehicle for experimenting with noise and home-made instruments. That duo was best documented in the 13-minute each *Shaker* and *Lytton Perdu*, off **Collective Calls** (april 1972), in the 28-minute *The Theatre of the World and Photic Diversions* (june 1973) and the 29-minute *The Night the Ariel Left Harwich and Other Synchronicities* (july 1974), off **Three Other Stories** (Parker on soprano and tenor saxophones, lyttonophone, dopplerphone, khene, ocarina and voice, Lytton on percussion and live electronics), then in the 42-minute *Two Horn'd Reasoning Cloven Fiction* (november 1975), off **Two Octobers** (Parker on soprano and tenor saxophones, Lytton on percussion and live electronics), and finally in the 38-minute live **Ra 1+2** (june 1976).

But Parker soon became, first and foremost, the British master of the soprano saxophone solo: the barbaric **Saxophone Solos** (september 1975), the virtuoso **Monoceros** (april 1978), the live **At the Finger Palace** (november 1978) and the almost supernatural **Six of One** (june 1980) implemented the view of the improviser as a unity of body and mind. He himself described it as a circus-like art of juggling and acrobatics in order to fill the acoustic space. He achieved that goal by employing both circular breathing (a` la Roland Kirk) in order to extend duration and tongue techniques that enabled rapid successions of notes of very short durations. He could thus mix sustained overtones and the saxophone equivalent of polyrhythms, and create an extremely versatile language that mirrored the way people speak more than the way musicians usually play music. The Parker-Lytton duo became a trio with the addition of bassist Barry Guy and, while losing some of its irreverent, dadaistic, provocative overtones, heralded an austere form of trio improvisation as both Guy and Lytton kept expanding the range of their instruments by using amplification and live electronics. **Tracks** (january 1983), with the 19-minute *Sidetrack*, and **Hook Drift and Shuffle** (february 1983), a collaboration with American trombonist George Lewis that included the 34-minute *Drift*, led to **Atlanta** (december 1986), containing four lengthy improvisations *Atlanta* (25 minutes), *The Snake as Road Sign* (17 minutes) and *Geometry* (20 minutes). The trio became a staple of the improvising community thanks to yearly recordings: **Imaginary Values** (march 1993), the twelve **Breaths and Heartbeats** (december 1994), the live **The Redwood Session** (june 1995), **Natives and Aliens** (may 1996), a collaboration with pianist Marilyn Crispell, the live **At The Vortex** (june 1996), the live **At Les Instants Chavires** (december 1997), with the 38-minute *Three-legged Chicken*, the double-CD **After Appleby** (june 1999), a second collaboration With pianist Marilyn Crispell, highlighted by the 20-minute *Blue Star Kachina*, the 25-minute *Where Heart Revive* and the 51-minute live jam *Capnomantic Vortex*.

Parker's solo work continued to pursue a more intense form of music (although a bit more introverted) via **The Snake Decides** (january 1986), the monumental **Conic Sections** (june 1989), the sixteen short pieces of **Process and Reality** (may 1991), that first used overdubs, **Chicago Solo** (november 1995), his first solo tenor album, and **Lines Burnt in Light** (october 2001). His duos included **Obliquities** (december 1994) with Barry Guy, **Tempranillo** (november 1995) with Spanish pianist Agusti Fernandez, **Most Materiall** (february 1997) with American percussionist Eddie Prevost, **Here Now** (january 1998) with cellist and trombonist Guenter Christmann.

In the 1990s Parker got intrigued by the electronic sounds that he experimented on **Hall of Mirrors** (february 1990), a collaboration with Walter Prati, and **Dividuality** (february 1997) and **Solar Wind** (january 1997), two collaborations With Lawrence Casserley. The Parker-Lytton-Guy trio became an Electro-acoustic Ensemble with the addition of Philipp Wachsmann (violin, viola, live electronics, and sound processing of Guy's and his own playing), Walter Prati (live electronics, and sound processing of Parker's playing) and Marco Vecchi (live electronics and sound processing of Lytton's playing) on the groundbreaking **Toward the Margins** (may 1996), the elegantly alien **Drawn Inward** (december 1998), that also featured Lawrence Casserley (also on live electronics and sound processing), the live **Memory/Vision** (october 2002), with Agusti Fernandez on prepared piano and Joel Ryan on computer besides Wachsmann, Prati, Vecchi and Casserley, and **The Eleventh Hour** (november 2004), that added sampling keyboards (operated by Richard Barrett and Paul Obermayer) to the acoustic, electronic and digital arsenal of **Memory/Vision**. Parker was moving towards a music for soundsculptors, not just post-jazz improvisers, but, after all, he had always been a soundsculptor himself.

Parker added the ethnic element to his electro-acoustic experiments on the live **Synergetics: Phonomanie III** (september 1993), that mixed Vecchi and Prati with George Lewis, Korean vocalist Sainkho Namchylak, bassist Motoharu Yoshizawa, African percussionist Thebe Lipere, Vietnamese komungo harpist Jin Hi Kim and Carlos Mariani on "luaaneddas" (sort of electronic bagpipes).

Foxes Fox (july 1999) debuted a quartet with Steve Beresford on piano, John Edwards on bass and Louis Moholo on drums, that returned after a five-year hiatus with **Naan Tso** (october 2004).

At the turn of the century Parker also collaborated with the drum'n'bass duo Spring Heel Jack, and recorded the two **Dark Rags** (january 2000) with Keith Rowe.

The double-CD **Needles** (april 2001) debuted a trio with violinist Philipp Wachsmann and bassist Teppo Hauta-aho.

The double-CD **America 2003** (may 2003) was a collaboration with Alex Schlippenbach and Paul Lytton. The idea was expanded on **Bishop's Move** (march 2003) to include Peter Broetzmann, bassist William Parker and drummer Hamid Drake.

In the 1970s British guitarist Derek Bailey became synonymous with wildly dissonant music. His unconventional methods evoked John Cage's dadaistic provocations, but Bailey was less interested than Cage in the process and more interested in sound for the sake of sound. In his hands the guitar mutated from a melodic and rhythmic instrument into a non-rhythmic percussion instrument. Of all the British musicians who turned soundsculptors, Bailey was the most obviously removed from the traditional approach to musical instruments. His guitar was merely a medium to produce sounds that were "not" musical. He was not interested in romancing the human race, but in cataloging what sounds the human race can produce and what happens when they are combined. He played in four of the pioneering free-jazz acts of Britain (Joseph Holbrooke in Sheffield in 1963, the Spontaneous Music Ensemble in London in 1966, Tony Oxley's sextet in 1968, Peter Broetzmann's group in 1969, Paul Rutherford's Iskra 1903 in 1970, Barry Guy's London Jazz Composers' Orchestra in 1972). In 1968 he founded the Music Improvisation Company with Evan Parker on soprano saxophone, Hugh Davies on live electronics and Jamie Muir on percussion, as documented on **The Music Improvisation Company 1968-1971** (june 1970).

The Topography of the Lungs (july 1970) with saxophonist Evan Parker and percussionist Han Bennink, the **Improvisations for Cello And Guitar** (january 1971) with David Holland on cello, and **Solo Guitar** (february 1971) were the albums that provided a shock therapy for the world of improvised music: nobody had ever abused the guitar like that. By comparison, Jimi Hendrix was a classical musician.

More solos followed: **Lot 74** (may 1974), **Improvisations** (september 1975), **Domestic & Public Pieces** (january 1976), the live double-LP **New Sights Old Sounds** (may 1978). Bailey called for "non-idiomatic improvisation," or improvisation that did not hark back to any pre-existing musical genre. Thus he was aiming for improvisation that would be as personal and subjective as possible, completely removed from the cultural conditioning of history.

Extending the idea of the Music Improvisation Company, in 1976 Bailey founded the Company, an "orchestra" of free improvisers like him, with a fluctuating line-up. **Company 1** (may 1976) featured four trio pieces by four different combinations of Dutch bassist Maarten van Regteren Altena, Honsinger, Parker and Bailey taken from their first concert. That concert also consisted of a quartet piece and of all possible duo combinations. **Company 2** (august 1976) was instead a trio with Parker and Braxton. **Company 3** (september 1976) was a duo with Bennink. **Company 4** (november 1976) was a duo with American soprano saxophonist Steve Lacy, another master of noise. **Company 5** (may 1977), perhaps the best of the series, contained the 25-minute *LS/MR/DB/TH/AB/SL/EP* for trumpeter Leo Smith, Braxton, Parker, Lacy, Bailey, Honsinger and Altena. **Company 6** (may 1977) also featured soprano saxophonist Lol Coxhill, pianist Steve Beresford and Bennink. **Fictions** (august 1977) was for Bailey, Coxhill, Beresford and pianist Misha Mengelberg, but was ruined by spoken-word sections. **Fables** (may 1980) employed Bailey, Parker, Holland and American trombonist George Lewis. **Epiphany** (july 1982) was a 47-minute improvisation by Bailey, Lewis, classical pianist Ursula Oppens, rock guitarist Fred Frith, glass-harmonica virtuoso Akio Suzuki, harpist Anne LeBaron, pianist Keith Tippett, violinist Phil Wachsmann, bassist Moto Yoshizawa and vocalist Julie Tippetts. **Epiphanies** (same session) was a set of brief sketches by the same

Creative Music: European Creativity

musicians organized in smaller groups. **Trios** (may 1983) contained trios, a duo and a collective improvisation by musicians such as Bailey, Muir, Reijseger, Parker, saxophonist Peter Broetzmann, trombonist Vinko Globokar, bassist Joelle Leandre, electronic musician Hugh Davies, etc. **Once** (may 1987) collected a 22-minute guitar-less *Quartet* (for keyboardist Richard Teitelbaum, saxophonist Lee Konitz, bassist Barre Phillips and percussionist Steve Noble), a twelve-minute *Sextet* (for Bailey, Teitelbaum, Konitz, Phillips, violinist Carlos Zingaro and cellist Tristan Honsinger), and a *Trio 1* with Konitz and Honsinger. The solo albums (never his favorite format) of the period were: **Music and Dance** (july 1980), **Aida** (august 1980), perhaps the best of the decade, with the 19-minute *Paris*, the inferior **Notes** (july 1985), **Lace** (december 1989), with the 30-minute *Let's Hope We're All in the Right Place*, and **Solo Guitar Volume 2** (june 1991).

During the 1990s the Company moved further away from the stalwarts of British improvised music that had created its reputation. The triple-LP **Company 91** (1991) featured Bailey, John Zorn, electronic musician Pat Thomas, trombonist Yves Robert, violinist Alexander Balanescu, bassist Paul Rogers, percussionist Paul Lovens and vocalist Vanessa Mackness, The double-CD **Company in Marseille** (january 1999) merely documented a quartet with harp, bass and cello. The last Company festival was held in 1994.

Bailey finally returned to the solo format for **Takes Fakes & Dead She Dances** (september 1997), but his last decade was mostly devoted to a deluge of mediocre collaborations.

British drummer Tony Oxley, who had pioneered British free-jazz in the trio Joseph Holbrooke, was one of the most influential figures of the 1970s. His first album as a leader, **The Baptised Traveller** (january 1969), featured a quintet with guitarist Derek Bailey, saxophonist Evan Parker, trumpeter Kenny Wheeler and bassist Jeff Clyne, and contained four lengthy improvisations (notably The **Four Compositions for Sextet** (february 1970), notably *Amass*, added trombonist Paul Rutherford. **Ichnos** (1971) featured Oxley playing solo (the twelve-minute *Oryane*) as well as with a quartet (the 12-minute *Cadilla*) and a sextet (the eight-minute *Crossing*) with the same personnel except for Clyne being replaced by Barry Guy. The evolution of his style (both in terms of its role in improvisation and in terms of expressive range) was documented by pieces such as *Never Before or Again* (1972), off **Tony Oxley**, for a sextet (with Guy, Parker, Riley, Rutherford, trumpeter Dave Holdsworth), and *Quartet 1*, off **February Papers** (february 1977), with Guy on bass and two violins. A trio with pianist Howard Riley and bassist Barry Guy produced increasingly adventurous albums: **Flight** (march 1971), with the 21-minute *Motion*, **Synopsis** (october 1973), with the 14-minute *Quantum* and Oxley toying with amplified percussion, **Overground** (november 1975), with the 20-minute *Overground* and Oxley doubling on live electronics.

The Celebration Orchestra debuted on **Tomorrow is Here** (october 1985), split between two lengthy improvisations: *Invitation to Karlovyvary* and *Third Triad*. The orchestra consisted of three saxophones (including Gerd Dudek and Larry

Stabbins), two violins (including Phil Wachsmann), trombone, piano, cello, three basses (including Guy) and five percussionists (including Oxley).

Oxley's experiments with electronics ranged from **The Glider and the Grinder** (april 1987), that featured Wolfgang Fuchs on reeds, Phil Wachsmann on violin and electronics and Hugh Metcalfe on guitar and electronics, to the 16-minute *Quartet 1*, off **The Tony Oxley Quartet** (april 1992), with Bailey, Matt Wand on drum machine and Pat Thomas on electronic keyboards, to **Floating Phantoms** (february 2002) for the B.I.M.P. Quartet (with Wachsmann, Thomas on electronics and Wand on sampling).

Oxley's collaboration with American pianist Cecil Taylor began with the live duets of **Leaf Palm Hand** (july 1988) and blossomed with the Feel Trio (himself, Cecil Taylor and American bassist William Parker) that recorded the live **Looking** (november 1989) and **Celebrated Blazons** (june 1990).

A new improved Celebration Orchestra (Wachsmann, Thomas, Wand, plus trumpeter Bill Dixon, vocalist Phil Minton, violin, cellos, two saxophones, trombone and three percussionists) recorded the more electronic **The Enchanted Messenger** (november 1994).

An alumnus of John Stevens' Spontaneous Music Ensemble and a member of Iskra 1903 with guitarist Derek Bailey and trombonist Paul Rutherford, British composer and bassist <u>Barry Guy</u> organized the London Jazz Composers' Orchestra to transfer the epos of improvised music into the orchestral format of classical music. The seven-movement suite of **Ode** (april 1972) featured three trumpeters (Harry Beckett, Dave Holdsworth, and Marc Charig), three trombonists (Paul Rutherford, Mike Gibbs and Paul Nieman), six saxophonists (including Trevor Watts, Mike Osborne, Evan Parker and Karl Jenkins), guitarist Derek Bailey, a tuba player, a pianist, a flutist, two bassists and two percussionists Tony Oxley and Paul Lytton). The four-movement *Stringer* (march 1980), off **Study II**, was scored for five saxophonists (Trevor Watts, Evan Parker, Peter Broetzmann, Larry Stabbins, Tony Coe), two trombones (Paul Rutherford and Paul Nieman), piano, violin, tuba, bass (Peter Kowald), percussion (Tony Oxley and John Stevens). Other significant Guy "compositions" for the orchestra included: *Polyhymnia* (november 1987), off **Zurich Concerts**; **Harmos** (april 1989); **Double Trouble** (april 1989); **Theoria** (february 1991), a collaboration with pianist Irene Schweizer; **Three Pieces for Orchestra** (december 1995); **Double Trouble II** (december 1995), a collaboration with pianists Marilyn Crispell and Irene Schweizer. In the new century, Guy renamed it New Orchestra and recorded the seven-movement suite **Inscape** (may 2000) and the three-movement suite **Entropy** (july 2004), works that were even more ambitious and sophisticated than the earlier ones.

British trombonist <u>Paul Rutherford</u> an alumnus of the Spontaneous Music Ensemble (1966), of Mike Westbrook's orchestra (1967), of the Globe Unity Orchestra (1970), and of pretty much every major ensemble of British improvised music, kept refining and expanding the language of his instrument until the solo **The Gentle Harm of the Bourgeoisie** (december 1974) demonstrated what it could do by itself. Rutherford's trombone record used the simplest of means to produce complex, extroverted and humorous music. Given his charisma, Rutherford recorded very little as a leader. The live **Old Moers Almanac** (june 1976) and **Neuph** (january 1978), that alternates trombone and euphonium and adds overdubs, closed his solo discography of the heydays of improvised music.

Derek Bailey (guitar), Barry Guy (double bass) and Paul Rutherford (trombone) formed Iskra 1903 in 1970. The double-LP **Iskra 1903** (may 1972) collected improvisations of the first two years.

Rutherford, saxophonist Harrison Smith, cellist Tony Moore and drummer Eddie Prevost formed the Free Jazz Quartet and recorded **Premonitions** (july 1989).

British percussionist Paul Lytton, a member of Evan Parker's groups (1969) and of the London Jazz Composers' Orchestra (1972), used self-made percussion and live electronics to animate the soundscapes of **The Inclined Stick** (july 1979).

The duets with drummer Paul Lovens of **Was It Me?** (january 1977), the 23-minute *Moinho da Asneira* (december 1978) and the 25-minute *A Cerca da Bela Vista a Graca* (november 1979), off **Moinho da Asneira**, the 30-minute *Catching* (june 1980), off **Fetch**, as well as their trio with Japanese trumpeter Toshinori Kondo **Death is our Eternal Friend** (september 1982), reintroduced a jazz element, although in a waste land of discrete noises.

Lytton was one of the original and stable members of the King Ubu Orchestru with reed player Wolfgang Fuchs, trombonist Radu Malfatti and violinist Phil Wachsmann. The line-up for **Music Is Music Is** (december 1984) included guitar, cello, bass, trumpet and a second reed player. **Binaurality** (june 1992) instead augmented the core quartet with trombonist Guenter Christmann, Georg Katzer on computer and electronics, reed players Luc Houtkamp and Peter van Bergen, tuba player Melvyn Poore and bassist Torsten Muller. The notable addition on **Trigger Zone** (november 1998) was trumpeter Axel Doerner.

British guitarist Keith Rowe, a member since 1965 of the avantgarde collective AMM, was one of the improvisers who most contributed to the definition of a new vocabulary for the guitar; or, better, for the "tabletop" guitar, a guitar plugged into the cacophony of the "perfectly ordinary reality" (usually, a barrage of radios and electronic devices). Starting with the chaotic, cryptic and apparently meaningless "guitar solos" of **A Dimension of Perfectly Ordinary Reality** (july 1989), notably the 24-minute *Untitled* and the 17-minute *'73*, Rowe played the guitar virtually in every possible manner and with every possible tool, to the point that the guitar became a mere object that could be used to produce unusual sounds. His body of work that referenced Paul Klee's abstract painting, Dada, Edgar Varese and John Cage, was the quintessence of "noise" guitar music, culminating in the three improvisations recorded in a garage for tabletop-guitar and electronics of **Harsh** (november 1999).

He updated his concepts to the digital age via the ensemble of electronic and digital improvisers Music In Movement Electronic Orchestra (including violinist Phil Durrant, pianist Cor Fuhler, guitarist Rafael Toral, electronic keyboardist Thomas Lehn, electronic soundsculptor Gert-Jan Prins as well as computer musicians Marcus Schmickler, Kaffe Matthews, Christian Fennesz and Peter "Pita" Rehberg), documented on the albums **MIMEO** (november 1997) and **Electric Chair + Table** (december 1999). Rowe also engineered **Rabbit Run** (june 2002), a colossal jam with Lehn's synthesizers and Schmickler's computers, and the two massive CDs of **Duos for Doris** (january 2003) with AMM's pianist John Tilbury.

British jazz saxophonist John Butcher was already in his thirties when he abandoned Physics to join the ranks of creative musicians inspired by Evan Parker (as well as by the new realm of electronic music). After cutting his teeth in Chris Burn's Jazz Ensemble and Jon Corbett's Freelance, Butcher recorded duets with Burn on piano (composed by Burn), **Fonetiks** (december 1984), and formed a trio with guitarist John Russell and violinist Phil Durrant documented on the eleven short pieces of **Conceits** (april 1987). The trio expanded to a quintet with the addition of drummer Paul Lovens and trombonist Radu Malfatti, and assumed the name News from the Shed. The ten brief pieces on **News from the Shed** (february 1989) were studies in contrast, texture and silence. Butcher leaned towards cerebral, not aggressive, improvisation, relying on all sorts of effects at his instrument. In the meantime, Butcher had also joined Embers, formed in 1986 by Australian classically-trained reed player Jim Denley (a member of Burn's ensemble) with Burn himself and cellist Marcio Mattos. The four lengthy improvisations of their **Live** (november 1988) also employed a sampler. Butcher was also active in Georg Graewe's quartet Frisque Concordance (1991), in John Stevens' Spontaneous Music Ensemble (1993) and in Barry Guy's London Jazz Composers Orchestra.

His art of methodical and surgical exploration, of painstaking coloring, of abstract dissonant soundpainting peaked with his solo-saxophone albums, veritable concertos for microtones and overtones: **Thirteen Friendly Numbers** (december 1991), that first experimented with multi-tracking (notably in *Bells and Clappers*, *Mackle Music*), the live **London & Cologne** (august 1998), that finally included longer pieces such as the nine-minute *Some Kind Of Memory* and the 13-minute *A Thing or Two*, besides *Shrinkdown* for four overdubbed sopranos, and the live **Fixations 14** (collecting pieces from 1997 to september 2000). These three works marked a progress from a purely scientific approach to a more emotional stance.

In the meantime, Butcher also engaged in countless duets with countless improvisers, notably the electroacoustic duets with Phil Durrant (playing only electronics) on **Secret Measures** (november 1997), besides joining the Austrian quartet Polwechsel in 1997 (replacing Malfatti) and resurrecting his acoustic trio with Durran and Russell for the live juggernauts of **The Scenic Route** (may 1998).

The Contest of Pleasures (august 2000), in a trio with French clarinetist Xavier Charles and German trumpeter Axel Doerner, **Tincture** (march 2001), with cellist Fred Lonberg-Holm and percussionist Michael Zerang, and **Equation** (may 2002), with turntablist Mike Hansen and percussionist Tomasz Krakowiak, were emblematic of Butcher's pioneering role in subdued, spare, subliminal, free-form soundpainting.

Creative Music: The other side of British creative music

London in the 1970s was a strange place for jazz music. The influence of Derek Bailey (Britain's premier improviser) was gigantic, but somehow London developed a surreal and almost self-parodistic take on the whole "creative" scene. The British improvisers of this generation often flirted with folk, pop and rock music, emphasizing irony at the same time that they were embracing the most hostile techniques. The works of some of the most austere improvisers was actually British humor at its best.

Lol Coxhill, a soprano saxophonist of the Canterbury school of progressive-rock (a former member of Kevin Ayers's group) penned **Ear Of The Beholder** (january 1971), a chaotic mosaic of fragments in the British tradition of the nonsense, inspired by the musichall, nursery rhymes, dancehalls, marching bands as well as free-jazz. An even more explicit tribute to street musicians, **Welfare State** (1975), was his political and aesthetic manifesto: avantgarde music for ordinary folks. Coxhill's humane and poetic approach surfaced even in his most reckless improvisations: the *Duet For Soprano Saxophone And Guitar* off **Fleas In Custard** (1975), *Wakefield Capers* off **Joy Of Paranoia** (1978), *11/5/78* off **Digswell Duets** (may 1978), the *Floz Variations* off the **Johnny Rondo Duo** (may 1980) with Dave Holland (on piano) and guitarist Mike Cooper, *Distorted Reminiscences* off **Dunois Solos** (november 1981), the *Variations pour Violoncelle, Contrabasse, Sopranino et Piano* (Coxhill, bassist Joelle Leandre, pianist Steve Beresford, cellist Georgie Born) off **Couscous** (september 1983), *Music for Feathery Fronds* off **Out To Launch** (april 2002), in a bewildering, disorienting, superhuman variety of styles, ranging from nostalgic/subversive echoes of antiquated genres to cacophonous and chaotic streams of consciousness.

The South African musicians who had flown to Britain following Chris McGregor's Brotherhood created an influential fusion of township music and free jazz (and a bit of jazz-rock). Alto saxophonist Dudu Pukwana, who had written the Brotherhood's signature tune, *Mra*, recorded **In The Townships** (november 1973) in a quartet with trumpeter Mongezi Feza and drummer Louis Moholo, and **Diamond Express** (november 1973), with Feza, Moholo, saxophonist Elton Dean, pianist Keith Tippett and trombonist Nick Evans, albums of jams that relied on the infectious African melodies and rhythms while adopting open-ended structures.

Ditto for drummer Louis Moholo's **Spirits Rejoice** (january 1978), featuring tenor saxophonist Evan Parker, trumpeter Kenny Wheeler, trombonists Nick Evans and Radu Malfatti, pianist Keith Tippett and bassist Johnny Dyani.

British pianist Steve Beresford debuted with **The Bath Of Surprise** (1977), which included pieces scored for toy instruments, bath water, whistles, tubes, euphonium and ukelele (besides piano, guitar and trumpet), and then delivered the atonal duets of **Double Indemnity** (august 1980) with cellist Triston Honsinger.

British clarinet and saxophone player Tony Coe was no less casual, Spanning a diverse spectrum of jazz styles. **Tournee du Chat** (april 1982), featuring the 17-minute *The Jolly Corner*, **Le Chat Se Retourne** (1984) and the soundtrack for **Mer de Chine** (1987) revealed a surreal storyteller and a painter of florid vignettes.

British progressive-rock hero and Keith Rowe's disciple Fred Frith developed a technique of brief vignettes that straddled the border between dissonant and folk music on **Gravity** (january 1980) and **Speechless** (august 1980). In the meantime, starting with **Guitar Solos** (july 1974), he had joined the ranks of the improvisers. Through collaborations with guitarist Henry Kaiser, cellist Tom Cora, harpist Zeena Parkins, saxophonist Lol Coxhill, keyboardist Bob Ostertag and percussionist Charles Noyes as well as with fellow Henry Cow member Chris Cutler, Frith perfected a collage-style art that juxtaposed improvised jams and cells of composed music. Notable were the colossal jams with Ostertag of **Getting A Head** (june 1980) and **Voice Of America** (august 1981), and the folk-neoclassical-atonal fusion of Skeleton Crew's **Learn To Talk** (january 1984) with Cora. The compositional aspect also led him to compose chamber music such as **Quartets** (december 1992) and **The Previous Evening** (june 1996) that paid tribute to the USA avantgarde of the previous decades (such as John Cage and Morton Feldman). He also founded the trio Maybe Monday with Miya Masaoka on koto and electronics and with saxophonist Larry Ochs of the Rova Saxophone Quartet. Their **Saturn's Finger** (july 1998) was perhaps his most mature venture into creative jazz, containing three lengthy improvisations that sample ambient, industrial and exotic overtones.

British violinist Jon Rose, after debuting his "relative violin" theory with two volumes of **Solo Violin Improvisations** (1978), experimented with numerous home-made instruments, mostly solo, on **Towards a Relative Music** (may 1978), for electronics, vibes, gongs and even furniture, **Relative String Music** (april 1980) for solo violin or sarangi, **Devils and Angels** (november 1984) for amplified violin or cello. Then **Paganini's Last Testimony** (1988) for voice and violin marked the beginning of his mock neoclassical phase, continued with **Die Beethoven Konversationen** (june 1989) and **2 Real Violin Stories** (1991). His surrealistic phase was highlighted by **The Virtual Violin** (1990), a comic "opera" relying on a rapid fire of samples triggered by more or less random sounds of the violin, and a series of radio works (that often sounded like Dada making fun of Dada making fun of humankind). **The Fence** (august 1996) was the first installment of the "Fence" series, two suites for giant string installations: the speech opera *Bagni Di Dolabella* (september 1993) and the sociopolitical radiodrama *The Fence* (august 1996). It was followed by **Great Fences of Australia** (2002), on which Rose literally played very long wooden, metal, barbed and electrified fences spread all over Australia like they were musical instruments. It all seemed to come together (John Cage-derived aleatory music, sense of humor, and free improvisation) on **The Hyperstring Project** (august 1999), a study on counterpoint for violin and interactive software.

Creative Music: Japan

The Japanese scene for free improvisers boomed in the 1970s thanks to a group of visionary musicians.

Japanese pianist Yosuke Yamashita formed a bass-less trio in 1969 that over the years featured alto saxophonist Akira Sakata and several drummers. The jams of the trio (and the pianist's stormy style) were captured on **Live 1973** (july 1973), that contained a 19-minute version of Yamashita's *Ballad for Takeo* (19:01) and a 22-minute version of Akira Sakata's *Zubo* (22:22), **Clay** (june 1974), with his signature theme *Clay*, **Chiasma** (june 1975), **Banslikana** (1976), **Arashi** (1976), while **Breath Take** (1975) and **Inner Space** (june 1977) were solo-piano collections. In 1988 Yamashita formed a New York Trio with bassist Cecil McBee and drummer Pheeroan AkLaff, documented on **Kurdish Dance** (may 1992) and **Dazzling Days** (may 1993).

Motoharu Yoshizawa recorded solo acoustic bass improvisations on **Cracked Mirrors** (1975) and then developed a cacophonous five-string bass for more disjointed works such as **Empty Hats** (1994). The elegant style of percussionist Masahiko Togashi was documented on **Rings** (1975), on which he also played vibraphone and celesta.

The most influential musician of this generation was probably guitarist Masayuki Takayanagi, who became one of the earliest noise guitar improvisers, recording extremely cacophonous works such as **Free Form Suite** (1972), with his New Directions combo, and the brutal solo improvisations of **Action Direct** (1985), **Inanimate Nature** (1991) and **Three Improvised Variations on a Theme of Quadhafi** (1991), recorded just before his death. Saxophonist Kaoru Abe (who died at 29) emerged through three galactic duets with Takayanagi: **Kaitaiteki Koukan/ Deconstructive Communication** (1970), **Gradually Projection** (1970) and **Mass Projection** (1970).

NOISE JAZZ

The white San Francisco-based Rova Saxophone Quartet was the alternative and experimental alter-ego of the more famous World Saxophone Quartet. Formed in 1977 by Jon Raskin, Larry Ochs, Andrew Voigt and Bruce Ackley, on respectively baritone, tenor, alto and soprano saxophone it straddled the border between free jazz and classical music of the 20th century. Raskin had already founded several multimedia projects and worked with composer John Adams. Their first concert became also their first album, **Cinema Rovate'** (august 1978), highlighted by Raskin's chaotic and cacophonous 21-minute *Ride Upon the Belly of the Waters* After **The Bay** (december 1978) with Italian percussionist Andrea Centazzo, the noise strategy of the group was perfected on **The Removal of Secrecy** (february 1979), particularly Ochs' 19-minute *That's How Strong*. There was method in their madness, but it was not easily detected within the dense structures of their scores. After **Daredevils** (february 1979) with guitarist Henry Kaiser, and the transitional **This This This This** (august 1979), with Raskin's eleven-minute *Flamingo Horizons*, **Invisible Frames** (october 1981) boasted another peak of their expressionist art, Voigt's 22-minute *Narrow Are the Vessels*. Ochs' 19-minute *Paint Another Take of the Shootpop*, off **As Was** (april 1981), was dedicated to both classical composer Olivier Messiaen and soul vocalist Otis Redding. Rova's style was becoming more accessible while still being abstract, absurd and atonal. After the live double-LP **Saxophone Diplomacy** (june 1983), with a 24-minute *Detente or Detroit*, and the Steve Lacy tribute of **Favorite Street** (november 1983), the Rova Saxophone Quartet sculpted the titanic jams of **Crowd** (june 1985), such as the 19-minute *The Crowd*, Ochs' 29-minute *Knife In the Times* and Raskin's 16-minute *Terrains*.

Black drummer William Hooker, who moved to New York in 1974, remained fundamentally faithful to the aesthetic of free-jazz (despite a passion for esoteric/spiritual themes), starting with the double-LP **Is Eternal Life** (may 1976 - Reality Unit Concepts, 1978), a set of collaborations with other improvisers (including tenor saxophonists David Murray and David Ware, notably the lengthy trio *Soy* with Murray and a bassist) and with **Brighter Lights** (Reality Unit Concepts, 1982) in a trio with flutist Alan Braufman and pianist Mark Hennen.

Drumming and poetry coexisted on the albums of his relatively traditional period: **Great Sunset** (1988) with Mark Hennen (piano), Lewis Barnes(trumpet), Charles Compo (tenor and baritone sax, flute); **Lifeline** (1989) for a quartet with piano and alto plus tenor saxophonist Charles Compo and trombonist Masahiko Kono; **Colour Circle** (1989) for a trio with saxophonist Booker Williams and trumpeter Roy Campbell; **Firmament Fury** (1992), in a quintet with alto saxophonist Claude Lawrence, tenor saxophonist Charles Compo, trombonist Masahiko Kono and Borbetomagus' guitarist Donald Miller; and **Subconscious** (1992), that documented a live performance by a sextet.

Rediscovered by Sonic Youth's guitarist Thruston Moore for the rock audience, Hooker returned to a more abstract and free-form kind of creative improvisation in the main works of his prolific middle age: *Darkness* (november 1992) and *The Spirits Return* (april 1994) on **Radiation**, by Hooker's band featuring Miller, electronic musician Brian Doherty, Compo, Kono; a duet with Moore (*Sirius*) and an electroacoustic duet with guitarist Elliott Sharp (*The Hat*) on **Shamballa** (1993); the 40-minute *The Coming One* and the 24-minute *Big Mountain* off **Tibet** (march 1994), with piano (Mark Hennen), saxophone (Compo) and guitar (Donald Miller); the 31-minute duet with Sonic Youth's wildly dissonant guitarist Lee Ranaldo *Matches* on **Envisioning** (april 1994). the 17-minute live duet with violinist Billy Bang *Sweating Brain* (june 1994) on **Joy**; the 51-minute *Stamina* that added Zeena Parkins' harp to the Ranaldo-Hooker duo on the live **Gift of Tongues** (1995); the eight-movement solo-percussion sonata **Heat Of Light** (august 1995). The albums with Ranaldo were heavily influenced by his screeching sounds, just like the albums with Donald Miller were heavily influenced by his turbulent wall of noise.

Armageddon (february 1995) marked a change in direction, both because the improvisations turned towards a more sophisticated kind of soundpainting and because the stylistic palette expanded dramatically, ranging from a dadaistic duet with turntablist Gregor "DJ Olive" Asch to the 16-minute free jam *State Secrets* for drums and two guitars. However, **Hard Time** (december 1995) was one of his most violent albums ever, featuring an electro-acoustic quintet with Donald Miller, electronic keyboardist Doug Walker, guitarist Jesse Henry and saxophonist Richard Keene. Nonetheless, the experiment with the turntable was continued on **Mindfulness** (august 1996), that featured DJ Olive as well as reed player Glenn Spearman, on **Bouquet** (april 1999), a cacophonous live jam with turntablist Christian Marclay and Sonic Youth's wildly atonal guitarist Lee Ranaldo, and on the live **Complexity #2** (september 2000), containing the 41-minute *Twelve Windows* for ocean waves, drumming, electronic keyboards (Doug Walker) and turntable (DJ Olive).

Percussionist Charles Noyes conceived some of the most cerebral improvised music on **Free Mammals** (1980), for guitar and percussion, and **The World And The Raw People** (1983), featuring John Zorn and Henry Kaiser.

New York's white trio Borbetomagus produced hurricanes of free-jazz music for two saxophones (Jim Sauter and Don Dietrich), guitar (Donald Miller) and electronic distortion. Their delirious improvised bacchanals constituted a sort of "baroque" style of the ugly and the noisy. The devastating early "concordats" of **Borbetomagus** (april 1980) and **Work On What Has Been Spoiled** (april 1981), the cacophonous symphony **Barbet Wire Maggot** (may 1982), perhaps their most extreme statement, the abstract and grotesque soundpainting of **Borbeto Jam** (october 1981), that seemed to exhaust the expressive power of the "concordats", and **Fish That Sparkling Bubble** (march 1988), a ferocious collaboration with noise-meisters Voice Crack (Norbert Moeslang and Andy Guhl), had little in common with the traditional quest for "sound" in jazz, a quest for an atmospheric, romantic and, ultimately, pleasant sound.

Voice Crack, the duo of Swiss musicians Andy Guhl (percussion and bass) and Norbert Moeslang (reeds), made music with broken objects found in garbage cans and adopted the extreme improvisation of free-jazz. Albums such as **Knack On** (october 1982) and the live **Concerto for Cracked Everyday-Electronics and Chamber Orchestra** (may 1994) were Dadaist acts of musical rebellion.

Latvian collective ZGA specialized in playing found, self-made and traditional instruments in a percussive way, starting with **ZGA** (recorded between 1984 and 1988).

The 1980s also witnessed a new generation of creative vocalists.

White wordless vocalist Jay Clayton created one of the most cerebral languages of free-jazz singing. She came into her own only much later than her counterpart Jeanne Lee, debuting with b>All Out (october 1980).

San Francisco-based vocalist Bobby McFerrin cut **The Voice** (1984), the first solo vocal album in the history of jazz music. His vocal style was among the most versatile since the days of Jeanne Lee and Jay Clayton, although the material had often the effect of turning his improvisations into novelties rather than avantgarde. In fact, he later crossed over into pop and even classical music, returning to creative improvisation only with **Circlesongs** (1997).

FUSION

Fusion Jazz: the Pioneers

Pre-fusion Pianists

White Jazz Between Free Jazz and Fusion

Latin Jazz

Fusion Groups

Fusion Stylists

Guitar Heroes

Pop-fusion

Euro-fusion

Fusion Jazz: the Pioneers

Miles Davis's quintet featuring drummer Tony Williams, bassist Ron Carter, pianist Herbie Hancock and tenor saxophonist Wayne Shorter had pioneered a sound that was just that: "sound". When Davis fused jazz with rock rhythm and soul melody (and even dissonance) on **Bitches Brew** (1969), Davis legitimized a new genre, "fusion jazz". All in all, this revolution paralleled the revolution that was finally picking up steam in free (or pseudo-free) jazz. The revolution had to do with rhythm. Since the earliest experiments with replacing the tuba with the double bass and with removing the piano from the rhythm section, the changes in the rhythm section had reverberated so wildly to create entire new genres. In the 1960s, basically, jazz musicians took two opposite views of where to go next: free musicians decided to turn the rhythm section into a decorative element (percussion is a coloring device, not a time-keeping device), which almost inevitably led to the demise of melody, whereas Miles Davis and the other jazz-rock pioneers decided to anchor bebop/cool jazz to the most solid of all rhythms, the loud and steady rhythm of rock music (nothing more than an evolution of rhythm'n'blues), a decision that almost inevitably led to the rise of melody.

Several rock groups (Soft Machine, Colosseum, Caravan, Nucleus, Chicago, and, above all, Frank Zappa) had the same idea at the same time, except that they turned it upside down: instead of focusing on sound, rockers focused on dynamics. Davis' fusion jazz was slick, smooth and elegant, while "progressive-rock" was typically convoluted and abrasive.

Once jazz music had been contaminated by rock music, it was merely natural that jazz musicians also adopted the instruments of rock music. This juncture marked the first major revolution in instrumentation since the early days of New Orleans jazz. In a few years jazz adopted the electric guitar, the bass guitar (replacing the double bass), the Hammond organ and all its successors (electric piano and electronic keyboards). Jazz-rock also adopted the rock way of using them. For example, the guitar and the keyboards as leading instruments, not part of the rhythm section. the rhythm section was pared down to bass and drums. organ,

Credit for "inventing" jazz-rock goes to Indiana-born white vibraphonist <u>Gary Burton</u>, originally an enfant prodige of country music in Nashville. After a stint in Stan Getz's quartet (1964-66), Burton began to experiment with rock rhythms on **The Time Machine** (1966), that featured bassist Steve Swallow, and attempted a fusion of jazz and country music on **Tennessee Firebird** (september 1966). The quartet with guitarist Larry Coryell, Swallow and drummer Roy Haynes, recorded the first jazz-rock album, **Duster** (april 1967), highlighted by mesmerizing Coryell playing, followed by **Lofty Fake Anagram** (august 1967). After performing Carla Bley's composition **A Genuine Tong Funeral** (1967), Burton came full circle by adding country music to the mix on **Country Roads and Other Places** (september 1968), recorded by a new quartet that simply replaced Coryell with guitarist Jerry Hahn, and on **Throb** (june 1969), added country violinist Richard Greene to that quartet. And then Burton embraced electronic keyboards for **Good Vibes** (september 1969), which was basically a rhythm'n'blues album. Pioneering a four-mallet technique, Burton owed little to the jazz pioneers of the instrument (Lionel Hampton, Red Norvo, Milt Jackson) and seemed unaware of the innovations introduced by the most influential vibraphonist of the era, Bobby Hutcherson.

Then Burton decisively joined the jazz-rock bandwagon. After **Gary Burton & Keith Jarrett** (july 1970), that had a quintet almost entirely devoted to Jarrett compositions, and **Crystal Silence** (november 1972), a collaboration with Corea that, again, mainly belonged to the pianist, Burton formed a **New Quartet** (march 1973) but continued to play other people's music with little or no personality. Burton inaugurated a quintet with guitarists Mick Goodrick and Pat Metheney, bassists Steve Swallow and drummer Bob Moses on **Ring** (july 1974), also featuring bassist and jazz-rock star Eberhard Weber, and **Dreams So Real** (december 1975), devoted to Carla Bley material (without Weber). Even better was **Passengers** (november 1976), with the same duo of bassists but only one guitarist (Metheny) and Dan Gottlieb on drums. Permutations of the quartet continued stoically. The problem with all of Burton's visionary experiments was that the material was of extremely poor quality (mostly covers).

Foremost among the propounders of fusion jazz were, instead, the Miles Davis alumni, starting with Tony Williams.

Boston-raised drummer Tony Williams moved to New York in 1962 (when he was barely 17) and was almost immediately hired by Miles Davis for **Seven Steps to Heaven** (1963). After playing on Eric Dolphy's **Out to Lunch** (1964), Williams became Davis' trusted drummer, popularizing a subtle convergence of traditional time-keeping and avantgarde free drumming that smoothly blended polyrhythms and variable time-signatures.

At the same time he recorded a milestone of drums-driven jazz music, **Life Time** (august 1964), that also revealed his skills as a composer. *Memory*, an eight-minute free-form jam with vibraphonist Bobby Hutcherson and pianist Herbie Hancock, and especially the 19-minute two-part suite *Two Pieces of One* for a quartet with tenor saxophonist Sam Rivers and two bassists, displayed his skills at merging different moods and styles. The same territory at the border between Miles Davis' music and free jazz was explored on **Spring** (august 1965) by a supergroup with Herbie Hancock, saxophonists Wayne Shorter and Sam Rivers, and bassist Gary Peacock, via more convoluted compositions (*Extras, Love Song, Tee*). In the meantime his drumming style had evolved to incorporate a repertory of tricks that used every part of the instrument for the purpose of crafting the textural qualities of the piece (Davis' ideology, after all).

After he left Davis in 1969, Williams formed the jazz-rock group Lifetime, a trio with organist Larry Young and guitarist John McLaughlin. Their debut album, the double-LP **Emergency** (may 1969), pretty much defined the genre via Williams' *Emergency, Beyond Games* and *Sangria for Three*, and McLaughlin's *Where* and *Spectrum*, pieces that were both intense, colorful and romantic. The addition of rock bassist and vocalist Jack Bruce of Cream tilted the balance towards the pop-song format on **Turn It Over** (july 1970), de facto a recreation of Cream with Williams instead of Ginger Baker and McLaughlin instead of Eric Clapton. Williams regained control of the compositions on **Ego** (march 1971), a completely different album that showcased an intriguing fusion of psychedelic-rock and free-jazz elements (*Lonesome Wells*, again sung by Bruce, and *The Urchins of Shermese*). After McLaughlin's departure, and a lame **The Old Bum's Rush** (1972) that emphasized electronic keyboards and vocals, Williams reorganized Lifetime as a quartet with bass, guitar and keyboards. The highlight of **Believe It** (july 1975) and **Million Dollar Legs** (june 1976) was the incendiary guitar work of British rock guitarist Allan Holdsworth (basically a John Coltrane of the guitar). The former was an energetic instrumental album (particularly *Fred*, also known as *Kinder*), while the latter destroyed the magic with vocals and a much more relaxed mood.

PRE-FUSION PIANISTS

Arguably, the foundations for the success and the evolution of fusion jazz came from the pianists raised in Davis' ensembles: Herbie Hancock, Chick Corea, Keith Jarrett and Joe Zawinul.

Chicago's pianist Herbie Hancock was perhaps the ultimate synthesis of the fusion movement, cross-breeding jazz with everything from rock to hip hop. After **Takin' Off** (may 1962), a hard-bop effort that featured Dexter Gordon on sax and Freddie Hubbard on trumpet and included his *Watermelon Man* and *Empty Pockets*, and **My Point of View** (march 1963), a more original take on hard-bop (*Blind Man Blind Man*) for a septet with trumpeter Donald Byrd, tenor saxophonist Hank Mobley, trombonist Grachan Moncur, guitarist Grant Green, bassist Chuck Israels and drummer Tony Williams, Hancock was hired by Miles Davis. In the trumpeter's quintet, Hancock developed an "orchestral" style of accompaniment and a passion for labyrinthine variations on a melodic theme. Hancock's more experimental side and his passion for Latin jazz came out on **Inventions and Dimensions** (august 1963), an improvised jam with bassist Paul Chambers and two Latin percussionists (*Succotash*, *Mimosa*). A more traditional trumpet-based quartet (Hubbard, Williams, Ron Carter on bass) sculpted the four lengthy tracks of **Empyrean Isles** (june 1964), including his signature funky theme *Cantaloupe Island* and the 14-minute bustling jam *The Egg*. By magnifying the point where hard-bop meets modal jazz and free jazz, Hancock had coined his own language: impressionistic, cerebral, sophisticated and sometimes even danceable.

Adding saxophonist George Coleman to the quartet, the elaborate pieces of **Maiden Voyage** (may 1965), namely *Eye of the Hurricane*, the eight-minute *Maiden Voyage*, the nine-minute *Little One* and the nine-minute *Dolphin Dance*, turned that language into an archetype, one that somehow resonated with the zeitgeist, expressing a sort of fantastic and graceful neurosis, almost an antidote to psychedelic ecstasy. While the atmosphere was mostly mellow and soothing, the ten-minute *Survival Of The Fittest* added a sense of poignancy. Hancock also composed the score for Michelangelo Antonioni's film **Blow Up**(1966), another figment of the zeitgeist, employing a large band and playing organ. But in those years he was mostly busy with Miles Davis.

Despite boasting three horns (flugelhorn, bass trombone and alto flute), **Speak Like A Child** (march 1968) focused on the "uneventful" (mellow) component of Hancock's new style and on his piano playing (the other instruments acting like mere wallpaper).

After ending his five-year tenure with Davis in 1968, Hancock penned a mournful tribute to Martin Luther King, **The Prisoner** (april 1969), through five lengthy pieces scored for a nonet (basically, the previous sextet plus three more winds, tenor sax, bass clarinet and trombone), as well as a soundtrack for the cartoon show **Fat Albert Rotunda** (december 1969), notable as his first venture into lively rhythm'n'blues and funk music.

Now based in California and converted to Buddhism, Hancock formed a sextet with trumpeter Eddie Henderson, trombonist Julian Priester, reed player Bennie Maupin, drummer Billy Hart and bassist Buster Williams, that allowed him to vent his secret passions: flirting with rhythm'n'blues and rock music, toying with electronic keyboards. **Mwandishi** (december 1970) the funky 13-minute *Ostinato* and the laid-back ten-minute *You'll Know When You Get There* By comparison, Julian Priester's 21-minute *Wandering Spirit Song* was a wild beast, spanning both free jazz and fusion jazz. Hancock's attention to tone and texture resulted in his musicians alternating between different instruments.

Crossings (november 1972) featured a full-time synthesizer player, Patrick Gleeson (in addition to some electronic keyboards played by Hancock himself), an experiment already tried by Paul Bley. Hancock's haunting 25-minute five-movement suite *Sleeping Giant* was influenced by progressive and psychedelic rock, but added danceable, funky overtones. Bennie Maupin contributed two abstract, ethereal pieces, *Quasar* and *Water Torture*, that exploited the textural qualities of the keyboards and of the trumpet in the opposite direction, not narrative but atmospheric. Hancock's blend of modal jazz, free jazz and fusion jazz was far more versatile than any of the three styles by itself, as each the three styles of the three tracks of **Sextant** (february 1973) proved: the twenty-minute *Hornets* was another dense, dynamic narrative juggernaut, while *Hidden Shadows* showcased the funk element (in a 19/4 meter) and *Rain Dance* indulged in pure ambience. Roughly the same sextet recorded two albums credited to (and mostly composed by) Henderson, **Realization** (february 1973) and **Inside Out** (october 1973).

Hancock's funk alter-ego eventually won: **Headhunters** (october 1973), inspired by Sly Stone's psychedelic funk music but heavily electronic in nature, and performed by a new quintet with Maupin (playing several woodwinds), a bassist and two percussionists, created a sensation with its unabashed dance rhythm and front-stage synthesizers. It became the biggest selling jazz record yet, thanks mainly to the 16-minute *Chameleon*. On **Thrust** (august 1974) Hancock seemed more interested in exploring the latest technological innovations than in playing music, but, besides three stereotyped electronic funk tracks, he also penned the eleven-minute *Butterfly*, one of his most romantic themes.

Despite his commercial sell-out, Hancock was eager to participate in nostalgic operations such as V.S.O.P. (1977), the Miles Davis Quintet (Herbie Hancock, Wayne Shorter, Ron Carter, Tony Williams) minus Davis himself, replaced by Freddie Hubbard, and **Quartet** (july 1981), i.e. the Miles Davis rhythm section (Hancock, Carter, Williams) plus Wynton Marsalis on trumpet. Their retro albums of acoustic jazz set the trend for the 1990s. Ironically, Hancock, who had pioneered electronic fusion (and was still cashing in on his invention), ended up also pioneering the neo-traditionalist movement.

Bill Laswell employed Hancock on three electronic albums the industrial-tinged **Future Shock** (august 1983), the African-tinged **Sound-System** (1984) and the digital funky **Perfect Machine** (1988). The first one was notable for the single

Rockit, that featured scratching and de facto introduced hip hop to jazz and viceversa.

The best project of the decade was probably the least publicized, **Village Life** (august 1984), a duet between Hancock on electronic machines and Gambian kora player Foday Musa Suso, particularly the twenty-minute *Kanatente*. Other jazz musicians had mixed jazz and West-African music, but Hancock added his electronic and funk background, i.e. the temporal contrast of ancient and modern.

Boston's white pianist Armando "Chick" Corea moved to New York in 1961 and cut his teeth in Latin-jazz combos. He rapidly transitioned from the hard bop of **Tones For Joan's Bones** (december 1966), also released as **Inner Space**, with the lengthy *Litha* and *Straight up and Down* (Woody Shaw on trumpet, Joe Farrell on flute and tenor saxophone, Steve Swallow on bass, Joe Chambers on drums), to the free jazz of **Now He Sings Now He Sobs** (march 1968), with *Steps Now He Sings Now He Sobs*, in a trio with bassist Miroslav Vitous and drummer Roy Haynes. Corea used Bud Powell's style as a launching pad but expanded it with a lyrical, chromatic, percussive and fibrillating technique. After collaborating with Stan Getz on **Sweet Rain** (1967), Corea was hired by Miles Davis to replace Herbie Hancock on electric piano.

After leaving Davis, Corea formed Circle, a quartet with avantgarde saxophonist Anthony Braxton, double-bassist Dave Holland and drummer Barry Altschul. **The Gathering** (may 1971) contained only one 42-minute Corea composition, the title-track, and each of the four members played multiple instruments. Circle was exploring the boundaries of free jazz and classical avantgarde, and Braxton would make an entire career out of that idea.

At first Corea continued that exploration of extremely free forms with **Is** (june 1969), mainly taken up by the 29-minute *Is*, and **Sundance** (may 1969), both in the company of trumpeter Woody Shaw, flutist Hubert Laws, tenor saxophonist Bennie Maupin, bassist Dave Holland and drummer Jack DeJohnette and a second drummer, and with **The Song of Singing** (april 1970) and **A.R.C.** (january 1971), both in a trio with Holland and Altschul, although the material was often uneven and inconclusive.

But then he pulled back from the brink of the abyss of the avantgarde. He penned two volumes of **Piano Improvisations** (april 1971), including *Sometime Ago*, the eight-movement suite *Where Are You Now* and (on the second volume) the five-movement *A New Place*, that were romantic and impressionistic. He devoted a collaboration with vibraphonist Gary Burton, **Crystal Silence** (november 1972), to melodic chamber jazz. And he formed one of the pioneering fusion bands, Return to Forever, with Brazilian vocalist Flora Purim, reed player Joe Farrell, bassist Stanley Clarke and Brazilian percussionist Airto Moreira, and rediscovered his Latin roots. **Return To Forever** (february 1972) introduced a new standard of light jazz via the melodic *Return To Forever*, the oneiric *Crystal Silence*, and the 23-minute medley of *Sometime Ago* and the effervescent *La Fiesta*. **Light as a Feather** (october 1972) was even more relaxed (bordering on balladry) and included *Light as a Feather*, *500 Miles High* and one of Corea's most famous compositions, *Spain* (basically a rewrite of *Steps*). Compared with the other fusion bands of the time, this first version of Return To Forever displayed more of a spiritual than an earthly tone. The rock element was kept in the background, overwhelmed by a neoclassical sensibility. But the sound changed dramatically on **Hymn of the Seventh Galaxy** (august 1973), recorded by a Return To Forever that was a rocking (and not so much Latin) quartet with Corea on electric keyboards, Clarke, electric guitarist Bill Connors (specialized in the distorted sound of psychedelic rock) and drummer Lenny White. The influence of Herbie Hancock and the Mahavishnu Orchestra was felt in *Captain Senor Mouse* and *Space Circus*. With the virtuoso guitarist Al DiMeola replacing Connors, Clarke coining a funky style at the electric bass and Corea embracing the synthesizer, Return To Forever cut the very popular trilogy of **Where Have I Known You Before** (july 1974), with the 14-minute *Song to the Pharoah Kings*, **No Mystery** (january 1975), with the *Celebration Suite* and *No Mystery*, and the medieval concept **Romantic Warrior** (february 1976), with *Romantic Warrior* and *Duel of the Jester and the Tyrant*, that mimicked British progressive-rock of the early 1970s both in sound and in theme. **MusicMagic** (february 1977) was a Return To Forever album only in name because it featured a 13-piece orchestra and vocals (and no electric guitar)

In the meantime Corea was flooding the market with erratic recordings, ranging from the gargantuan **The Leprechaun** (1975), that included *The Leprechaun*, to **My Spanish Heart** (october 1976), featuring vocals, synthesizer, string quartet and brass section, that included the multi-movement suites *El Bozo* and *Spanish Fantasy*.

Corea's classical ambitions surfaced unabashedly on *Quintet No 2*, performed on **Live in Montreaux** (july 1981) by a quartet with Joe Henderson on tenor sax, Gary Peacock on bass and Roy Haynes on drums; the acoustic **Three Quartets** (february 1981) with tenor saxophonist Michael Brecker, bassist Eddie Gomez and drummer Steve Gadd; *Quintet No 3*, that appeared on **Again & Again** (march 1982); *Duet Suite*, off **Duet** (1979), his second collaboration with Gary Burton; the seven-movement **Lyric Suite for Sextet** (september 1982), for piano, bass (Burton) and a string quartet; the five-movement **Septet** (october 1984); and *Piano Concerto*, performed on **Corea Concerto** (april 1999) by a symphony orchestra and jazz trio (Origin).

In 1985 Corea formed the Elektrik band with virtuoso electric bassist John Patitucci, drummer Dave Weckl and a guitarist, indulging himself in the synthesizer. The band peaked with **Inside Out** (january 1990), that contained the 20-minute four-movement suite *Tale Of Daring*. This project was followed by its antithesis, the Akoustic Band, a traditional jazz trio with Weckl and Patitucci. Lacking memorable compositions, their albums mainly highlighted the virtuoso playing of the bassist and the drummer.

Pennsylvania-born pianist <u>Keith Jarrett</u> moved to New York in 1965. After stints with Art Blakey and Charles Lloyd, Jarrett formed his own trio with bassist Charlie Haden and drummer Paul Motian (Ornette Coleman's rhythm section), that recorded **Life Between The Exit Signs** (may 1967) and **Somewhere Before** (october 1968). Having proven his passion for the styles of Bill Evans and Paul

Bley, besides a familiarity with Ornette Coleman's free-jazz idiom, Jarrett was briefly hired by Miles Davis in 1970 to play electric keyboards. After leaving Davis' group and after the piano-vibraphone collaboration **Gary Burton & Keith Jarrett** (july 1970), composed almost entirely by Jarrett (*Fortune Smiles*, *The Raven Speaks*), he returned to acoustic keyboards. In 1971 he made three sessions that set the standard for the rest of his career. The first session of his quartet with Haden, Motian and tenor saxophonist Dewey Redman (the "American Quartet") was documented on three albums: **The Mourning of a Star** (july 1971), containing the nine-minute *The Mourning of a Star* (without Redman), **Birth** (july 1971), with *Spirit*, and **El Juicio** (july 1971), with *Gypsy Moth* and the free-form jam *El Juicio*. The second session, **Expectations** (october 1971), collapsed their talents into lyrical reinventions of Latin jazz (*Common Mama*), jazz-rock (*Take Me Back*) and free jazz (the 17-minute *Nomads*).

His first solo acoustic piano album, **Facing You** (november 1971), was more articulate in defining his eclectic and visionary personality, that already absorbed influences ranging from gospel to classical music via cool jazz and free jazz, and metabolized them thanks to a melodic and visceral talent for filling the musical space like a living orchestra (*In Front*, *My Lady My Child*, *Lalene*).

The double-LP **In The Light album** (february 1973), collecting various chamber pieces, including a 21-minute *Brass Quintet*, a 16-minute *String Quartet* and the 19-minute *Metamorphosis* for flute and string orchestra, offered the first clue to Jarrett's neoclassical ambitions. **Luminessence** (april 1974) contained Jarrett compositions for saxophone (Garbarek) and string orchestra, notably *Luminessence* and *Numinor*, that hardly belonged to the jazz (or classical) tradition.

The American quartet delivered the live **Fort Yawuh** (february 1973), with the 13-minute *Misfits*, the 18-minute *Fort Yawuh* and the dramatic 12-minute *De Drums*, while the triple-LP **Solo Concerts** (july 1973) documented two completely improvised solo concerts, each more than one hour long. His ensemble work may have been intriguing, but these colossal improvisations were unique. They created a warm, soothing ambience and organic structures out of the mutation and replication of minimal gestures, a musical example of self-organization and emergent properties.

The American quartet recorded **Treasure Island** (february 1974), with *The Rich And The Poor*, while **Belonging** (april 1974) inaugurated the "European Quartet", formed with saxophonist Jan Garbarek, bassist Palle Danielsson and drummer Jon Christensen, and devoted to less intense and less cerebral music (*Blossom*, *Solstice*).

The American quartet, now augmented with Brazilian percussionist Guilherme Franco, cut **Death and the Flower** (october 1974), mainly devoted to the 23-minute suite *Death and the Flower*, **Backhand** (leftovers from the same session), **Mysteries** (december 1975), that contained the 15-minute free-form jam *Mysteries* and **Shades** (december 1975), with *Shades Of Jazz*.

The double-LP of **The Koeln Concert** (january 1975) perfected his style of solo improvisation, transforming the stream of his tense, introverted, semi-philosophical ruminations into static zen-like spiritual meditations, and became one of the best-selling jazz albums of all times, besides foreshadowing the boom of new-age music.

On the neoclassical front, **Arbour Zena** (october 1975) contained abstract music for strings and jazz improvisers (Jarrett, Garbarek and Haden), notably the 27-minute *Mirrors*. The 32-minute piano sonata *Ritual* (june 1976) tried to decouple Jarrett the composer from Jarrett the performer (he doesn't play it), emphasizing the pensive and sentimental elements of his art.

Back to the quartet, Jarrett played piano, soprano sax, bass flute, celesta and percussion on the 48-minute **The Survivor's Suite** (april 1976) that seemed to bring together his three personas: the jazz ensemble player, the avantgarde classical composer and the solo piano improviser. The composer crafted the stately architecture, the ensemble breathed life into it and the improviser injected a soul into it. The live 33-minute *Eyes of the Heart*, off the three-sided LP **Eyes of the Heart** (may 1976), was a loose corollary to the **Survivor's Suite**.

However, Jarrett's interest in the American quartet (without Franco) was fading, as proven by the lack of Jarrett compositions on **Bop-Be** (october 1976) and **Byablue** (same session).

His solo albums also became too self-indulgent. The suites of **Staircase** (may 1976), namely the three-movement *Staircase*, two-movement *Hourglass*, three-movement *Sundial* and three-movement *Sand*, were languid and uneventful. The nine-movement *Spheres* for pipe organ, off **Hymns & Spheres** (september 1976), was baroque and redundant. The ten-LP **Sun Bear Concerts** (november 1976), containing five improvisations (each a double-LP), was more megalomania than music.

The European quartet, with its folkish overtones, became the best vehicle for Jarrett's intimate lyricism starting with **My Song** (november 1977), that included the romantic theme of *My Song* but also the supernatural atmospheres of *Questar*, *Tabarka*, *Mandala* and *The Journey Home*. Their live **Nude Ants** (may 1979) further stretched the temporal dimension with the 17-minute *Chant of the Soul*, the 20-minute *Processional*, the 30-minute juggernaut *Oasis*, *New Dance* and *Sunshine Song*, pieces that seem to float rather than flow.

The new solo effort, **Invocations/ The Moth and the Flame** (november 1979), contained *Invocations*, a seven-movement suite for pipe organ and saxophone (both played by him) recorded in an abbey to take advantage of the acoustics (an idea popularized by Paul Horn), and *The Moth and the Flame*, a five-movement suite for grand piano. The triple-LP **Concerts** (may 1981) returned to his favorite live improvised format.

His interest in classical music increased over the years, leading to **The Celestial Hawk** (march 1980), a three-movement concerto for piano, percussion and orchestra, **Book of Ways** (july 1986) was a studio album of clavichord studies. **Bridge of Light** (1994) collected *Elegy for Violin and String Orchestra* (1984),

Adagio for Oboe and String Orchestra (1984), *Sonata for Violin and Piano* (1984) and *Bridge of Light for Viola and Orchestra* (1990).
He wasted a trio (the "Standards Trio") with bassist Gary Peacock and drummer Jack DeJohnette on collections of jazz standards (the first one in 1983). The trio rarely performed Jarrett originals, but, when it did, they ranked among his most challenging works, such as the 30-minute *Flying*, off **Changes** (january 1983), and the 15-minute *Endless*, off **Changeless** (october 1987).
Solo improvised concerts of the latter days included **Dark Intervals** (april 1987), **Paris Concert** (october 1988), **Vienna Concert** (july 1991), **La Scala** (february 1995), and, after a long hiatus due to illness, **Radiance** (october 2002).
The Standards trio finally delivered some innovative music with the live recordings **Inside Out** and **Always Let Me Go** (2001) that contained lengthy free-form jams such as *From the Body*, *Inside Out* and *341 Free Fade* (on the former) and the 40-minute *Hearts In Space* on the latter. Jarrett's "fusion jazz" rarely fused jazz with rock or funk, but it was still a fusion of jazz with other genres, namely folk and classical music.

Philadelphia's pianist Alfred McCoy Tyner played on the Jazztet's **Meet The Jazztet** (1960) and joined John Coltrane for **My Favorite Things** (1960). While being introduced to Eastern philosophy and scales in Coltrane's group, Tyner lived a parallel life in a more conventional post-bop piano-based trios that played lightweight bebop: b>Inception (1962), with bassist Art Davis and drummer Elvin Jones, highlighted by the youthful ebullience of *Effendi*, or **Reaching Fourth** (1963), with bassist Henry Grimes and drummer Roy Haynes, containing *Blues Back*. The exceptions to the trio dogma were few, although often more creative, for example *Contemporary Focus* and *Three Flowers*, Tyner's lengthy compositions on **Today and Tomorrow** (1963), performed by a sextet (alto saxophone, John Gilmore on tenor-saxophone, Thad Jones on trumpet, bass and Elvin Jones on drums).
After leaving Coltrane, Tyner proved to be a much more innovative musician, translating Coltrane's visceral style into his own bebop-bred language. **The Real McCoy** (april 1967), for a quartet with tenor-saxophonist Joe Henderson, bassist Ron Carter and drummer Elvin Jones, was entirely composed by him and contained intense pieces such as the ballad *Contemplation* and the modal and polyrhythmic *Passion Dance*. Having acquired confidence in his compositional skills, Tyner embarked in a personal odyssey of textural exploration. Scoring for a nonet (Lee Morgan on trumpet, Julian Priester on trombone, James Spaulding on flute, Bennie Maupin on tenor saxophone, plus French horn, tuba, bass and drums) on **Tender Moments** (december 1967), particularly *Man From Tanganika*, helped sharpen his vision. The quartet of **Time for Tyner** (1968) with vibraphonist Bobby Hutcherson, bassist Herbie Lewis and drummer Freddie Waits helped the vision cohere, particularly in *African Village*. **Expansions** (august 1968) was the first mature statement of the new style, boasting four lengthy intricate pieces performed by a septet (trumpeter Woody Shaw, altoist Gary Bartz, tenorist Wayne Shorter, cellist Ron Carter, Lewis and Waits): the vibrant *Vision*, the Eastern-sounding *Song of Happiness*, the convoluted *Smitty's*

Place, the melancholy *Peresina*. The miscellaneous double LP **Cosmos** (july 1970) added two innovative pieces, the eight-minute *Asian Lullaby* and the 13-minute *Forbidden Land*, for a sextet of piano, flute (Hubert Laws) oboe (Andrew White), saxophone (Gary Bartz), bass and drums.

The sextet of **Extensions** (february 1970), featuring tenor/soprano saxophonist Wayne Shorter, altoist Gary Bartz, harpist Alice Coltrane, bassist Ron Carter and drummer Elvin Jones, pushed the "orchestral" quality of the sound, that had been building up since the nonet session, to an higher degree while hinting at distant echoes of Africa and Asia, particularly in the 12-minute *Message from the Nile* (half way between modal jazz and John Coltrane's style) and the blistering, 13-minute *Survival Blues*. These albums shared some of the concerns with space and time of contemporary progressive-rock.

The same format (four lengthy pieces) was repeated on **Asante** (september 1970), although the line-up of piano, alto, guitar, bass and drums, augmented with African and Latin percussion, was less colorful. The 14-minute *Malika* used vocals to increase the link with ancestral Africa, while the 14-minute *Fulfillment* was the first significant display of Tyner's uncontrollable urge.

That massive, dense, percussive, chromatic style that released clusters of chords like shrapnel, became the trademark of **Sahara** (january 1972). If previous recordings had tried to create an orchestral effect by toying with the timbres of the instruments (such as harp and cello), Tyner was now achieving the same effect simply by pushing the limits of the piano. The quartet with saxophonist/flutist Sonny Fortune, Tyner doubling on flute and percussion, bassist Calvin Hill (doubling on reeds) and drummer Alphonse Mouzon (also doubling on reeds) performed the transition from the old, abstract and impressionistic, sound to the new, visceral and explosive, sound of the 23-minute *Sahara*. The African and East Asian elements were now fully amalgamated.

Song for My Lady (1972) contained two sessions, one (november 1972) with the same quartet (that produced *Song for My Lady*) and one (september 1972) with an expanded line-up (Charles Tolliver on flugelhorn, Michael White on violin and a conga player besides the quartet) performing the longer *Native Song* and *Essence*.

Ostensibly a tribute to Coltrane, the solo piano album **Echoes of a Friend** (november 1972) actually had a centerpiece, the 17-minute *The Discovery*, that showed how different his style was from the master's. Coltrane may have been the influence to achieve such a degree of intensity, and to integrate exotic elements, but the spiritual angst of the master was replaced by a vital energy of the opposite sign.

Tyner tested the limit of his compositional skills on the music for large ensemble of **Song of the New World** (april 1973). He then applied the lesson to the more manageable format of the saxophone-based quartet for the three-movement suite *Enlightnment* and the 24-minute *Walk Spirit Talk Spirit*, off the live **Enlightnment** (july 1973). **Sama Layuca** (march 1974) again expanded the format to an octet to take advantage of a broader palette of timbres (vibraphone, oboe, flute, Latin percussion), at the same time setting his modal explorations to an insistent rhythm, the result being the ebullient texture of *Paradox*.

WHITE JAZZ BETWEEN FREE JAZZ AND FUSION

Despite having contributed to the decline of bebop on Paul Bley's **Solemn Meditation** (1957) and to the birth of free jazz with his performances on Ornette Coleman's **The Shape of Jazz to Come** (1959) and John Coltrane's **The Avant-Garde** (1960), Los Angeles-based white bassist Charlie Haden was rarely faithful to his roots in the rest of his career. Raised in the Midwest to country music, Haden brought to jazz the typical sensitivity of provincial America, of simple things for simple people, a populist viewpoint that his political beliefs turned into a Woody Guthrie-like weapon. The Noam Chomsky of jazz music, he always seemed more interested in the message than in the music Surprisingly for such an outspoken critic of mainstream USA culture, Haden's music has tended to gravitate around relatively conservative musical paradigms, emphasizing melody, graceful counterpoint and mellow atmospheres. Thus Haden has actually been one of the jazz musicians who crossed over into pop and folk music in the most deliberate manner.

In 1967 Haden joined Keith Jarrett's trio with Paul Motian, one of the most distinctive acts of fusion jazz. While he worked with Jarrett (and Ornette Coleman, whom he never abandoned), Haden made only one recording as a leader, but it was a sensational one. He formed the Liberation Music Orchestra with a huge cast of improvisers: Don Cherry on cornet and flutes, Dewey Redman on alto and tenor saxophones, Gato Barbieri on tenor saxophone and clarinet, Michael Mantler on trumpet, Roswell Rudd on trombone, Perry Robinson on clarinet, Bob Northern on French horn, Howard Johnson on tuba, Sam Brown on guitar, Carla Bley on piano, Charlie Haden on bass. Paul Motian on percussion. Their **Song for Che** (april 1969), that sold well to the rock audience, focused on protest songs arranged by Carla Bley, but the real standout was Haden's *Song For Che*.

The second Liberation Music Orchestra album, **The Ballad Of The Fallen** (november 1982), a collaboration with arranger Carla Bley, was devoted to communist-inspired folk tunes from all over the world. The terrific players (Don Cherry on trumpet, Michael Mantler on trumpet, Gary Valente on trombone, Sharon Freeman on French horn, Jack Jeffers on tuba, Steve Slagle on saxophones, clarinet and flute, Jim Pepper on saxophones and flute, Dewey Redman on tenor saxophone, Mick Goodrick on guitar, Charlie Haden on bass, Carla Bley on piano, Paul Motian on drums) were wasted on poor material (*La Pasionaria* was the only major contribution by Haden).

Haden was mostly active as a sessionman for other leaders (Ornette Coleman till 1987, Alice Coltrane in 1971-75, Art Pepper 1975-82, Pat Metheny 1980-85, Geri Allen 1987-90, Paul Motian 1988-91, John Scofield 1988-91, Gonzalo Rubalcaba 1989-92, Abbey Lincoln 1990-94), but in 1987 he formed his own quartet (with tenor saxophonist Ernie Watts, pianist Alan Broadbent and drummer Larance Marble), that recorded old-fashioned bebop album, mostly devoted to covers, starting with **Quartet West** (december 1986) and **In Angel**

City (june 1988), with his celebrated *First Song*. In the 1990s the Quartet West became a postmodernist project of deconstruction of Hollywood soundtracks of the black and white era ("noir jazz"). **Haunted Heart** (october 1991), **Always Say Goodbye** (august 1993), **Now Is The Hour** (july 1995) and **The Art Of The Song** (february 1999) were stylish, translucent, largely devoid of substance and added samples of old recordings to the mix. This commercially successful venture was emblematic of the ideological and aesthetic surrender of the avantgarde.

The third Liberation Music Orchestra album, **Dream Keeper** (april 1990), was highlighted by Carla Bley's 17-minute *Dreamkeeper Suite*. The fourth political sermon by the Liberation Music Orchestra, **Not In Our Name** (august 2004), was highlighted by a 17-minute thematic collage, *America the Beautiful*, again arranged by Carla Bley.

White Oakland-born pianist Carla Bley married Paul Bley in 1957 and moved with him to Los Angeles. After composing *Bent Eagle* for George Russell's **Stratusphunk** (1960) and *Ictus* for Jimmy Giuffre's **Thesis** (1961), she became her husband's main composer, penning: *Floater* and *King Korn* on **Footloose** (1963), *Ida Lupino* and *Syndrome* on **Turning Point** (1964), the entire **Barrage** (1964), most of **Closer** (1965), *Start* on **Touching** (1965). She left Paul Bley for trumpeter Michael Mantler in 1965.

Mantler and Bley formed a large star-studded jazz orchestra, the Jazz Composers' Orchestra, that debuted with **Communication** (april 1965) and **Jazz Composers' Orchestra** (june 1968), obtaining immense critical success. In between those albums, Mike Mantler on trumpet, Steve Lacy on soprano saxophone, Carla Bley on piano and two bassists recorded **Jazz Realities** (january 1966), including Bley's *Oni Puladi* (the habanera *Ida Lupino* played in reverse).

Those collaborations would have been enough to establish her as a major figure of the decade, but she also composed the whole of Gary Burton's **A Genuine Tong Funeral** (1967) and most of Charlie Haden's **Liberation Music Orchestra** (1969), two milestones of jazz. By the end of the decade, she could vie for the title of greatest living jazz composer with Mingus and Ellington.

Her public image was quite schizophrenic, on one hand a living advertisement for the bohemian lifestyle of the hippie generation, on the other hand an austere and uncompromising modernist. Her compositional ambitions clearly collided with the aesthetic of free-jazz, although she displayed an ideological affinity with free jazz. Perhaps these contradictions were precisely what made her music so unique and powerful.

Bley topped everything she had done so far with the colossal three-LP jazz opera **Escalator Over The Hill** (1971), the result of three years of recordings, one of the greatest albums in the history of jazz music. The large orchestra was actually structured in four orchestras. The Orchestra proper (and Hotel Lobby Band) was a 19-piece unit with Carla Bley (piano), Jimmy Lyons (alto saxophone), Gato Barbieri (tenor saxophone), Chris Woods (baritone saxophone), Michael Mantler and Enrico Rava (trumpets), Roswell Rudd, Sam Burtis and Jimmy Knepper (trombones), Jack Jeffers (bass trombone), Bob Carlisle and Sharon Freeman

(French horns), John Buckingham (tuba), Nancy Newton (viola), Karl Berger (vibraphone), Charlie Haden (bass), Paul Motian (drums), Roger Dawson (congas), Bill Morimando (bells, celeste). The Desert Band featured Bley (organ), Don Cherry (trumpet), Souren Baronia (clarinet), Leroy Jenkins (violin), Calo Scott (cello), Sam Brown (guitar), Ron McClure (bass) and Motian (percussion). The Original Hotel Amateur Band comprised Bley (piano), Mantler (valve trombone), Motian (drums), Michael Snow (trumpet), Howard Johnson (tuba), Perry Robinson and Peggy Imig (clarinets), Nancy Newton (viola), Richard Youngstein (bass). Jack's Traveling Band consisted of Carla Bley on organ and the power-trio of John McLaughlin (guitar), Jack Bruce (bass) and Paul Motian (drums). Finally, the "silent music" was performed by Michael Mantler on prepared piano, Don Preston on synthesizer and Carla Bley on organ, celeste and calliope. The singers ranged from country star Linda Ronstadt to avantgarde vocalist Jeanne Lee. Bley's score, spanning jazz, electronic, rock and Indian music, was of Wagner-ian proportions and ambitions, combining pathos and epos in a way that had not been tried before in jazz music. Most of the pieces were brief, like a lattice of morphing ideas, except for *Hotel Overture*, *Rawalpindi Blues* and the closing *And It's Again*. Her intricate dissonant unstable multi-stylistic structures amounted to a refounding of jazz music.

By comparison, **Tropic Appetites** (february 1974) was a mini-opera for vocalists (Julie Driscoll, Karen Mantler) and jazz septet (Gato Barbieri on tenor, Michael Mantler on trumpet and trombone, Howard Johnson on clarinets, saxophones and tuba, Toni Marcus on violin and viola, Dave Holland on bass and cello, Carla Bley on piano and organ, Paul Motian on percussion), but the stylistic excursion was no less breathtaking, from the *What Will Be Left Between Us and the Moon Tonight?* to *Indonesian Dock Sucking Supreme* to *Song of the Jungle Stream*. The humbler setting shifted the emphasis from creative chaos and abandon to impressionistic timbral and textural exploration.

Bley proved that she could also excel in neoclassical music with the lyrical *3/4* for piano and orchestra, on **Michael Mantler - Carla Bley** (august 1975). **Dinner Music** (september 1976) was Bley's version of slick muzak (*Sing Me Softly of the Blues*, *A New Hymn* and *Song Sung Long*), featuring herself, Mantler, Richard Tee (piano), Carlos Ward (alto and tenor saxophones and flute), Roswell Rudd (trombone), Bob Stewart (tuba), and a funky rhythm section of two guitars, bass and drums.

Her mood seemed to have relaxed considerably, and **Musique Mecanique** (november 1978) was the ultimate proof, almost a divertissment for tentet. The 23-minute three-movement *Musique Mecanique* and *Jesus Maria and Other Spanish Strains* were bizarre but not too cerebral (and frequently humorous) compositions, highlighted by the solos of tenor saxophonist Gary Windo and trombonist Roswell Rudd. The other players (besides Bley and Mantler) included Alan Braufman on reeds, John Clark on French horn, Bob Stewart on tuba, Terry Adams on piano, Steve Swallow and Charlie Haden on basses, and Eugene Chadbourne on guitar. Like all of her best works, this was both jazz, rock and classical music, while being blasphemous to them all.

Social Studies (december 1980) was highlighted by a postmodernist *Reactionary Tango* scored for a surreal nonet (Bley, Mantler, Ward, Valente, Swallow, tenor saxophone, euphonium, tuba, drums).

The ambient/melodic side of her art returned to the fore with the adventurous tentet music of **Heavy Heart** (october 1983), that relied on Bley's synthesizer and Valente's trombone, more than on the other horns (Mantler's trumpet, tuba, flute, saxophones), and on the delicate rhythm section (Kenny Kirkland's piano, Hiram Bullock's guitar, Steve Swallow's bass and two percussionists), to sculpt the relaxed atmospheres of *Heavy Heart* and *Light or Dark*. The Bley-Swallow mellow-fusion sound was formalized by the **Sextet** (december 1986) with guitarist Hiram Bullock, pianist Larry Willis and two percussionists, in particular by *The Girl Who Cried Champagne* and *Healing Power*.

The 18-piece **Very Big Carla Bley Band** (october 1990), featuring four soloists (Valente, trumpeter Lew Soloff, saxophonists Wolfgang Puschnig and Andy Sheppard), failed to resurrect the original Carla Bley spirit, despite the 15-minute *United States* and especially *All Fall Down*. But the 17-minute *Dreamkeeper Suite* for Charlie Haden's third Liberation Music album, **Dreamkeeper** (april 1990), fared a bit better. Bley's 18-piece orchestra (same four soloists, main addition the violinist Alex Balanescu) fared even better in the 20-minute suite *Birds of Paradise* on **Big Band Theory** (july 1993). Also notable for big band was the 24-minute *Setting Calvin's Waltz* on the live **Goes To Church** (july 1996).

Her truly serious compositions (the 19-minute *Tigers in Training*, the nine-minute *End of Vienna*, the 14-minute *Wolfgang Tango*) finally appeared on **Fancy Chamber Music** (december 1997), featuring Bley on piano, a string section (violin, viola, cello, bass), flute, clarinet and percussion. The return to form continued with **4x4** (july 1999), for a double quartet of sort (Bley on piano, Larry Goldings on organ, Steve Swallow on bass, Victor Lewis on drums, Lew Soloff on trumpet, Wolfgang Puschnig on alto, Andy Sheppard on tenor, Gary Valente on trombone), that contained *Blues in Twelve Bars* and the three-movement *Les Trois Lagons*.

Looking For America (october 2002), a work for big band with the same four horn soloists, was political satire with a high degree of musical sophistication, as demonstrated by the 22-minute postmodernist audio-collage *National Anthem*.

Bley debuted a quartet with Sheppard, Swallow and drummer Billy Drummond on **The Lost Chords** (october 2003). It was mostly taken up by two suites: *3 Blind Mice*, that displayed her knowledge of blues and jazz tradition, and *Lost Chords*, that showed Bley the melodic poet in her most romantic mood.

White Austrian-born trumpeter Michael Mantler relocated to New York in 1964 and formed the Jazz Composer's Orchestra Association (JCOA) to promote compositions for jazz orchestra. Mantler and pianist Carla Bley formed a large star-studded jazz orchestra, the Jazz Composer's Orchestra, that debuted with **Communication** (april 1965) and **Jazz Composer's Orchestra** (june 1968), obtaining immense critical success. The former featured Steve Lacy on soprano saxophone, Jimmy Lyons on alto saxophone, Robin Kenyatta on alto saxophone,

Ken McIntyre on alto saxophone, Bob Carducci on tenor saxophone, Fred Pirtle on baritone saxophone, Mike Mantler on trumpet, Ray Codrington on trumpet, Roswell Rudd on trombone, Paul Bley on piano, Steve Swallow on bass, Kent Carter on bass and Barry Altschul on drums, and included Mantler's *Day - Communications No 4* and *Communications No 5*. The latter featured six soloists (Don Cherry on cornet, Gato Barbieri on tenor saxophone, Larry Coryell on guitar, Roswell Rudd on trombone, Pharoah Sanders on tenor saxophone, Cecil Taylor on piano), piano (Carla Bley), seven saxophones (including Steve Lacy, Jimmy Lyons, Lew Tabackin), seven brass instruments, five basses (Steve Swallow, Charlie Haden, Reggie Workman, Eddie Gomez, Ron Carter), and two drummers (Andrew Cyrille and Beaver Harris), and included Mantler's *Communications No.8*, *Communications No.9*, *Communications No.10*, *Preview - Communications No.11*.

In between those albums, Mike Mantler on trumpet, Steve Lacy on soprano saxophone, Carla Bley on piano and two bassists recorded **Jazz Realities** (january 1966), including Mantler's *Communication No 7*. Mantler featured on all subsequent Carla Bley recordings until 1983.

But Mantler's soul was European to the core. **Michael Mantler - Carla Bley** (august 1975) contained his *13 for Piano and Two Orchestras*, a terrifying expressionist work. He fully realized his ambitions in the sphere of highbrow progressive chamber jazz with **No Answer** (february 1973), a cycle of lieder on Samuel Beckett texts sung by rock vocalist Jack Bruce, accompanied by an organ-trumpet-bass trio (Carla Bley, Don Cherry, Jack Bruce), although the cerebral, disjointed music sounded closer in spirit to the Canterbury school of progressive rock. The proximity to that school increased on **The Hapless Child** (july 1975), with words by Edward Gorey, featuring rock vocalist Robert Wyatt, Carla Bley on piano and synthesizer, Norwegian guitarist Terje Rypdal, bassist Steve Swallow and drummer Jack DeJohnette. This time the brooding lieder were even more in the hands of the vocalist, one of the greatest of all times, with the musicians following his cues and filling the gaps. The rock element further increased on the next cycle, **Silence** (june 1976), based on the Harold Pinter play and scored for a trio of piano/organ (Bley), guitar (Chris Spedding) and bass (Ron McClure) fronted by Kevin Coyne and Wyatt (and Bley herself). These albums of erudite, ponderous chamber jazz songs set the standard for the rest of his career.

Mantler abandoned the human voice and finally played in person on the eight-movement suite **Movies** (march 1977) in a quintet with Bley (on both acoustic and electronic keyboards), guitarist Larry Coryell, bassist Steve Swallow and drummer Tony Williams. The line-up shifted the emphasis of the sound towards orthodox fusion jazz. **More Movies** (march 1980) replaced Coryell with Belgian guitarist Philip Catherine and added tenor saxophonist Gary Windo.

Something There (june 1982) returned to his classical obsession, scoring another suite for jazz-rock quintet (guitarist Mike Stern, Bley on piano, Swallow and Pink Floyd's drummer Nick Mason) and a string orchestra. The duets with Don Preston on synthesizer, **Alien** (july 1985), were de facto another orchestral album, a sort of concerto for trumpet and (electronic) orchestra, because Mantler used the synthesizer to add color to the solo instrument's meditations.

Mantler returned to the song cycle with **Many Have No Speech** (december 1987), for rock vocalists such as Jack Bruce, Robert Wyatt and Marianne Faithfull backed by a symphony orchestra, but he fragmented too much the material. Having relocated to Denmark, Mantler greatly reduced his frequency of recordings, preferring to focus on the format of classical music. Even more ambitious was the 29-minute suite *Folly Seeing All This* on **Folly Seeing All This** (july 1992), scored for the Balanescu String Quartet and a jazz quintet (trumpet, guitar, alto flute, piano, vibraphone). Another cycle of lieder, **Cerco Un Paese Innocente** (january 1994), featured vocalist Mona Larsen backed by a chamber ensemble (trumpet, guitar, piano and a string quartet) and a big band with synthesizer. The opera **The School of Languages** (august 1996) featured eight vocalists (including rock vocalists Robert Wyatt, Jack Bruce, John Greaves and Mantler's daughter Karen) backed by a ten-piece ensemble and a string orchestra. *One Symphony* on **Songs And One Symphony** (november 1998) was his largest orchestral composition yet. Wyatt dominated again the song cycle **Hide And Seek** (september 2000) for an eleven-piece ensemble.

The format of the piano-led trio experimented by Bill Evans was further explored by Chicago's white pianist Denny Zeitlin (who had relocated to San Francisco in 1964) on albums such as **Cathexis** (march 1964) for a trio, that set the theme for his research, **Carnival** (october 1964), for another trio (Charlie Haden on bass), and **Zeitgeist** (march 1967), for the same trio, that included the free-form *Mirage*. He was not afraid to tamper with dissonance and electronics, for example in the 14-minute *El Fuego de las Montanas*, off **Expansion** (1973), in the four-movement suite *Syzygy*, off **Syzygy** (1977) and in the melodramatic film soundtrack **Invasion of the Body Snatchers** (1978). A psychiatrist by profession, Zeitlin was pioneering a fusion of jazz, rock, classical and electronic music.

White drummer Paul Motian, who had cut his teeth with the likes of Thelonious Monk and Lennie Tristano, had an intense career, first pioneering a more proactive role for the drums with Bill Evans (1959-61), and then abstracting the drums to match the soundscape with Paul Bley (1963-64) and drumming in an almost "melodic" way with Keith Jarrett (1967-76). All his "bosses" were pianists, a fact that had an impact on his musical mindset.

The revelation of his debut album, **Conception Vessel** (november 1972), was, in fact, Motian as a composer: *Georgian Bay* and *Rebica* for a trio of Motian, bassist Charlie Haden and guitarist Sam Brown, *Conception Vessel*, a duet with Keith Jarrett, and *Inspiration from a Vietnamese Lullaby* for a quartet with Haden, violinist Leroy Jenkins and flutist Becky Friend, were exceptional open post-bop structures that radiated ideas in all directions. *Sod House*, on **Tribute** (may 1974), added another format: a quintet with two guitars, bass (Haden) and alto sax (Charles Ward).

After he finished his tenure with Jarrett, Motian unleashed his compositional skills in the realm of sophisticated chamber jazz. This phase was begun by two trio albums with saxophonist Charles Brackeen and a bassist: **Dance** (september 1977), that contained the relatively short and lively *Waltz Song, Asia* and *Lullaby*, and **Le Voyage** (march 1979), that contained the longer and more pensive *Folk Song For Rosie* and *Le Voyage*.

A breakthrough for Motian's research on sound was represented by **Psalm** (december 1981), performed by a piano-less quintet featuring saxophonists Joe Lovano and Billy Drewes, bassist Ed Schuller and guitarist Bill Frisell that Motian conducted through graceful and soulful excursions such as *Second Hand*, *Fantasm* and *Yahllah*. Part of the success was due to the exuberant talents of Frisell and Lovano. The two youngsters were, again, the main feature of **The Story Of Maryam** (july 1983), with Jim Pepper replacing Drewes, an album with even more baroque pieces such as *9 X 9* and *The Owl of Cranston*, and of **Jack Of Clubs** (march 1984), with *Cathedral Song*. This piano-less quintet broke up after **Misterioso** (july 1986), ostensibly a Monk tribute but also including Motian's lyrical *Dance*.

Motian's melodic flair was now irrepressible, and it erupted with the trio albums that followed, both because Motian was more fully in control of his music and because limiting the group to the interplay between Frisell's guitar (the ebullient persona) and Lovano's saxophone (the subtle persona) actually optimized the pathos of his glossy chamber jazz. *Fiasco* and *India*, on the trio's debut album, **It Should've Happened A Long Time Ago** (july 1984), were emblematic of the style that exerted a huge influence on fusion jazz of the era.

LATIN JAZZ

Argentinian tenor saxophonist Gato Barbieri relocated to Italy in 1962 and collaborated with Don Cherry on **Complete Communion** (1965) and The **Symphony For Improvisers** (1966). Barbieri expanded that experiment on **In Search Of Mystery** (march 1967), a wild free-jazz session in a quartet with cello, bass and drums, centered around the theme of *Michelle* and the two movements of *Cinematheque*, and on the lengthy **Obsession** (june 1967), recorded by a trio of sax, bass and drums. After a collaboration with Dollar Brand, **Confluence** (march 1968), and a participation to both Mike Mantler's **Jazz Composer's Orchestra** (1968) and Charlie Haden's **Liberation Music Orchestra** (1969) Barbieri found his mission in life with **The Third World** (november 1969), that mixed free jazz and Latin music in a visceral, exuberant manner. Three of the four compositions paid tribute to great Argentinian composers, and the fourth was his *Antonio Das Mortes*. Barbieri became more interested in offering the USA public jazzy versions of Latin classics, a less spontaneous but more elegant version of the concept of **Third World**, but each album contained at least one Barbieri composition that also represented his artistic ambitions: *Carnavalito* on **Fenix** (april 1971), featuring Pharoah Sanders' pianist Lonnie Liston Smith guitarist Joe Beck, bassist Ron Carter, drummer Lenny White and Brazilian percussionist Nana Vasconcelos, *El Pampero* on the live **El Pampero** (june 1971), *El Parana* on **Under Fire** (recorded in 1971), featuring Smith, guitarist John Abercrombie bassist Stanley Clarke and percussionist Airto Moreira.

The worldwide success of Barbieri's sensual, melancholy soundtrack for Bertolucci's **Last Tango In Paris** (november 1972), released in its entirety only in 1998, stood as a much more personal statement.

Even more emotional was **Bolivia** (recorded in 1973), by the same players of **Under Fire**, with *Merceditas* and *Bolivia*.

Barbieri's vision of Latin-tinged melodic and rhythmic soundscapes was fully realized with a tetralogy that employed larger units and Latin-American musicians: **Latin America** (april 1973), his artistic zenith, with *Encuentros* and the four-part suite *La China Leoncia*, **Hasta Siempre** (april 1973), with *Encontros*, **Viva Emiliano Zapata** (june 1974), accompanied by a big band in four of his short pieces (notably *Lluvia Azul*), and the live **Alive In New York** (1975).

After leaving Miles Davis (1970) and Chick Corea (1972), Brazilian percussionist Airto Moreira enjoyed a brief moment of notoriety during which he concocted a trivial world-funk-jazz-soul-rock fusion on albums, frequently featuring his wife, vocalist Flora Purim, such as **Free** (april 1972), that contained his first original composition, the twelve-minute *Free*, and **Fingers** (april 1973), with *Tombo in 7/4*, **Virgin Land** (june 1974).

Brazilian vocalist Flora Purim, who had joined Chick Corea's Return to Forever in 1972, was the exotic vocalist par excellence of the decade, although her own albums, such as **Butterfly Dreams** (1973), featuring saxophonist Joe Henderson, keyboardist George Duke, guitarist David Amaro, bassist Stanley Clarke and percussionist (and husband), were vastly inferior to her work with Corea.

Classically trained, Brazilian multi-instrumentalist Egberto Gismonti (guitar, flute, piano), who had already composed the song *O Sonho* (1968) for a 100-piece orchestra, fused European classical music, jazz-rock, bossanova and Brazilian choro folk music on albums such as **Sonho 70** (1970), inspired by the movie soundtracks of the 1960s, **Academia De Dancas** (1974), with orchestral and electronic arrangements, and especially the suite **Dance Das Cabecas** (november 1976) for guitar, piano, flute (all played by Gismonti) and percussion (Nana Vasconcelos). basically bossanova's version of free-jazz improvisation, **Sol Do Meio Dia** (november 1977), another venture with Vasconcelos and others (saxophonist Jan Garbarek, percussionist Collin Walcott, guitarist Ralph Towner) into the Brazilian jungle, and **Solo** (november 1978), a set of melancholy solos on different instruments, notably the 21-minute *Selva Amazonica* for guitar. Despite turning towards new-age music in the 1980s, Gismonti continued to produce profound pieces of music, increasingly classical sounding, such as **Danca Dos Escravos** (november 1988), another concept album, this time for guitar only, *Natura Festa Do Interior*, off **Musica de Sobrevivencia** (april 1993), *Mestiso and Caboclo* for a Brazilian trio, off **Zig Zag** (april 1995). Classical compositions included: *Musica de Sobrevivencia* (composed in 1990) for orchestra, the five-movement cantica *Cabinda* (composed in 1992) for orchestra, *Strawa no sertao* (composed in 1991) for chamber orchestra.

Despite being inspired by McCoy Tyner and enlightened by Roland Kirk, pianist Hilton Ruiz opted for an infectious party-oriented fusion of Cuban music and free jazz. After debuting in a trio with the sophisticated meditations of **Piano Man** (july 1975), Ruiz merged Cuban rhythms and funk music on **Rhythm in the House** (1976). His danceable zenith was reached with the salsa-infected albums **Something Grand** (october 1986) and **El Camino** (october 1987), the latter including the 15-minute *Eastern Vibration* and featuring Sam Rivers on saxophones.

After playing with Gato Barbieri in 1971, Brazilian-born percussionist Nana Vasconcelos established his credentials as a virtuoso of the berimbau with **Africadeus** (1972). While contributing to Jon Hassell's masterpieces, Vasconcelos conceived a fusion of berimbau and symphony orchestra on **Saudades** (1979). His percussions adorned Don Cherry and Pat Metheny records of the 1980s. He used voices and the percussive sounds of the human body on **Zumbi** (1983) and meticulously-tuned drum-machines on **Nanatronics** (1985), that was never released. The soundscape of **Bush Dance** (1986) was crafted by electronic keyboards and Arto Lindsay's atonal guitar. A more spontaneous, almost childish, form of music surfaced on **Asian Journal** (1988), recorded by a world quartet of bansuri flute, bass and tablas.

Brazilian band Azymuth, formed in 1973 by keyboardist Jose Roberto Bertrami, mixed samba, funk and jazz in dance hits such as *Linha do Horizonte* (1975) and *Jazz Carnival* (1978).

Fusion Groups

Rock music was largely a genre oriented towards the group, that downplayed the individual musician. Fusion jazz ended up imitating the praxis of rock music. The "stars" of fusion jazz were, first and foremost, the leaders of jazz-rock groups that, for all purposes, might have been simply rock groups.

Another candidate to inventor of jazz-rock was Texas-born white guitarist Larry Coryell. Relocating to New York in 1965, he formed an early jazz-rock group, the Free Spirits, that released **Out of Sight And Sound** (1966). After working in Gary Burton's quartet (1967-68), Coryell emerged as one of the most innovative electric and noisy guitarists of all time, competing with his more famous contemporary Jimi Hendrix. His early classics, frequently recorded in guitar-bass-drums trios, included: *Stiff Neck* on **Lady Coryell** (1968), featuring Elvin Jones on drums, that focused on Coryell's youthful speed and metal overtones (and, alas, his monotonous singing), *The Jam With Albert* on **Coryell** (april 1969), *Wrong Is Right* on **Spaces** (july 1970), featuring the stellar cast of John McLaughlin on guitar, Miroslav Vitous on bass and Billy Cobham on drums, *Souls Dirge* on **Fairyland** (june 1971). Coryell approached the intensity of progressive-rock with the 20-minute jam *Call to the Higher Consciousness* on **Barefoot Boy** (1971), featuring Steve Marcus on saxophones, Micheal Mandel on piano, Roy Haynes on drums, bass and percussion, and by now he was less interested in acrobatic solos than in group improvisation. After **Offering** (january 1972), a more straightforward quintet with Mandel and Marcus (*Foreplay*), and **The Real Great Escape** (1973), a pop album heavy on the vocals and the synthesizers, Coryell settled down with the quintet Eleventh House, soon destined to become one of the most famous jazz-rock groups of the 1970s (trumpet, bass, Alphonse Mouzon on percussion, Mike Mandel on piano and synthesizer), that released **Introducing The Eleventh House** (july 1974) and **Level One** (1975).

Austrian-born conservatory-trained pianist Josef Zawinul emigrated to the United States in 1958 and joined Cannonball Adderley's quintet in 1962, rapidly becoming one of the most respected hard-bop pianists. After the prophetic **The Rise And Fall Of The Third Stream** (october 1967), mostly composed by tenor saxophonist William Fischer, Zawinul contributed to the electronic period of Miles Davis, and penned some of his best compositions, such as *Pharaoh's Dance* on **Bitches Brew** (1969). Zawinul de facto coined the atmospheric sound of Weather Report with **Zawinul** (august 1970), featuring trumpeter Woody Shaw, soprano saxophonist Earl Turbinton, pianist Herbie Hancock and bassist Miroslav Vitous. The ten-minute *Double Image* and the 14-minute *Doctor Honoris Causa* bridged hard-bop and jazz-rock, bypassing cool jazz and free jazz. Zawinul perfected his vision of the keyboards in the electronic age on the Weather Report albums. He and Annette Peacock can be credited with introducing electric and electronic keyboards into the jazz mainstream.

Fusion Groups

Zawinul's intuition led to the birth of the second major group of jazz music (after the Modern Jazz Quartet). In 1970 tenor and soprano saxophonist Wayne Shorter and Austrian keyboardist Joe Zawinul (both veterans of Miles Davis' groups) joined forces with Czech bassist Miroslav Vitous, Brazilian percussionist Airto Moreira and drummer Alphonse Mouzon to form Weather Report. **Weather Report** (february 1971) introduced a sophisticated blend of jazz improvisation, rock and funk rhythms, folk melodies and ethnic accents. Every member contributed with its own style of improvisation to the ethereal and delicate textures, but Zawinul towered over the others, defining the thick and slick arrangements with his electric and electronic effects, and penning the most ambitious compositions (*Waterfall* and especially *Orange Lady*). The personality of **I Sing the Body Electric** (january 1972), featuring two new percussionists and partly recorded live, was better distributed, with Zawinul's *Unknown Soldier* (an ambitious excursus from haunting to elegiac), Vitous' *Crystal* and Shorter's *Surucucu* (Roger Powell played synthesizer, one of the first on a jazz album). Weather Report popularized a kind of ensemble playing that was not quite group improvisation but was born out of the same principle of equality. All instruments contributed to the overall economy of the sound, each bringing both melodic and rhythmic elements. Emotional peaks were achieved when there was no soloist. The emancipation of the rhythm section from timekeeping roles liberated bass and percussion. The general attention to textural playing (instead of the traditional roles) contrived a homogeneous distribution of sound. Zawinul cast a huge shadow again on **Sweetnighter** (february 1973), an album that veered towards funky and Latin rhythms, indulged in the sound of the synthesizer, and relied almost entirely on two lengthy Zawinul compositions, *Boogie Woogie Waltz* and *125th Street Congress*, that relied less on improvisation than on structure.

Alphonso Johnson replaced Vitous for **Mysterious Traveller** (may 1974), that included Zawinul's *Nubian Sundance* (with vocals) and Shorter's *Mysterious Traveller*. **Tale Spinnin'** (february 1975) was less subtle than its predecessors, showing how limited the possibilities were. But Jaco Pastorius replaced Alphonso Johnson on **Black Market** (january 1976), and his flamboyant style (guitar-like solos and electronic enhancements of the instrument) became the band's new attraction on **Heavy Weather** (october 1976), an album propelled in the charts by Zawinul's *Birdland*. **Mr Gone** (may 1978) sealed the marriage of Zawinul's presentation and Pastorius' verve with overdoses of electronics, dance rhythms and ethnic arrangements.

The group's albums were now highly predictable, a careful balance of danceable grooves and instrumental virtuosity, addressing a lucrative market with the surgical precision of a marketing analyst. Their last albums were mainly notable for Zawinul's reinvention of the synthesizer as a swinging and melodic instrument.

British guitarist John McLaughlin was a product of the same British blues revival that spawned rock groups such as the Rolling Stones and Cream. When he formed his first quartet, with soprano and baritone saxophonist John Surman, a bassist and drummer Tony Oxley, McLaughlin was already 26. His debut album, **Extrapolation** (january 1969), entirely composed by him but mostly driven by Surman's improvisations, was a brilliant transposition of new trends (whether free jazz or progressive-rock or post-bop melody) into the open-minded milieu of the British intelligentsia. McLaughlin both jazz and rock listeners with the crisp sound of his guitar (fitted with an electric pickup and heavy gauge strings).

The following month McLaughlin relocated to New York and joined both Miles Davis' group and Tony Williams' Lifetime.

His second album, **My Goal's Beyond** (march 1971), declared his passion for Indian music (*Peace One* and *Peace Two*) and experimented with the acoustic guitar on simple melodic themes (*Follow Your Heart*). **Devotion** (february 1970) was, for all practical purposes, an album of instrumental psychedelic-rock (guitar, organ, drum and bass), with the electric guitar unleashed to produce all sorts of ferocious sound effects. Nonetheless the eleven-minute *Devotion* still maintained the Indian attitude.

In july 1971 McLaughlin formed the Mahavishnu Orchestra, one of the premier electric fusion groups, with violinist Jerry Goodman, keyboardist Jan Hammer, electric bassist Rick Laird and drummer Billy Cobham. Despite the strong influence of Jimi Hendrix on their visceral solos and swirling rhythms, their virtuoso playing and delirious interplay created a new stereotype of fusion jazz. *The Dance Of Maya* and *Meeting Of The Spirits*, off **The Inner Mounting Flame** (august 1971), the ten-minute *One Word*, off **Birds Of Fire** (october 1972), the colossal *The Dream*, off the live **Between Nothingness And Eternity** (september 1973), were the most mind-bending work-outs, but many of their pieces had more to do with show business than with music. McLaughlin also vented his late-hippy spiritual enlightenment in duo with rock guitarist Carlos Santana, the cycle of devotional songs **Love Devotion Surrender** (march 1973). The original Mahavishnu Orchestra disbanded in 1973, but McLaughlin organized a new edition, featuring violinist Jean-Luc Ponty, that embarked in an ambitious collaboration with a symphony orchestra, **Apocalypse** (march 1974), arranged by Michael Gibbs. While less hyped than the early albums, this work, particularly the 20-minute *Hymn To Him*, was a truly innovative fusion of jazz, rock, Indian and classical elements. This edition of Mahavishnu Orchestra was terminated after the mediocre **Visions Of The Emerald Beyond** (december 1974) and the slightly more energetic and electronic **Inner Worlds** (august 1975).

McLaughlin formed the quintet Shakti with four Indian musicians (virtuoso violinist Lakshminarayana Shankar, tabla player Zakir Hussain and a mridangam player) to play acoustic music inspired to Indian music and Hindu religion, but preserving the high-octane, rocking approach of the Mahavishnu Orchestra. The music decayed rapidly from the avantgarde **Shakti** (july 1975), with the 29-minute pseudo-raga *What Need Have I For This*, to the delicately melodic **A Handful Of Beauty** (august 1976), to the almost poppy **Natural Elements** (july 1977).

McLaughlin also composed a *Concerto for Guitar and Symphony Orchestra* (1985), documented on **Mediterranean Concerto** (september 1988), and the three-movement suite *Thieves And Poets* for acoustic guitar and chamber orchestra, on **Thieves And Poets** (july 2002).

Chicago-born drummer Jack DeJohnette briefly flirted with the AACM avantgarde but moved to New York and cut his teeth in Charles Lloyd's quartet (1966-67). After replacing Tony Williams in Miles Davis' group (1968-70), and after a few conventional records, his more experimental side came out with the two lengthy trio improvisations (Bennie Maupin on tenor saxophone and Gary Peacock on bass) of **Have You Heard** (april 1970), a 20-minute version of *Papa-Daddy and Me* and the 21-minute *Have You Heard*. His first group was a trio with a bassist and a drummer, documented on **Compost** (1971), on which he also played electric clavinet, organ and vibraphone. **Sorcery** (may 1974) collected two sessions, one (march) with Bennie Maupin on bass clarinet and John Abercrombie and Mick Goodrick on guitars (the 14-minute *Sorcery #1*) and one (may) with Dave Holland on bass (the seven-movement *The Reverend King Suite*). DeJohnette also played in Abercrombie's Gateway, a trio with bassist Dave Holland that released **Gateway** (1975) and **Gateway 2** (1977). **Pictures** (february 1976), a duo album with Abercrombie, contained his extended percussion solo *Picture 2* and his extended piano solo *Picture 6*.

His experiments deconstructing the cliches of jazz-rock continued with the quartet Directions (saxophones, Abercrombie's guitar, bass and drums) and its cerebral extended pieces: the 14-minute *Flying Spirits*, on **Untitled** (february 1976), also featuring a pianist, *Minya's the Moon* and *New Rags* on **New Rags** (may 1977), with DeJohnette doubling on piano, *Bayou Fever* and *Where or Wayne* on **New Directions** (june 1978), that introduced a new line-up (Abercrombie, Chicago trumpeter Lester Bowie and bassist Eddie Gomez).

A new quartet with David Murray on tenor and bass clarinet, Arthur Blythe on alto, Peter Warren on bass and cello, that ranked as one of the most innovative fusion groups of the era, debuted on **Special Edition** (march 1979), containing some of DeJohnette's most challenging music: the ten-minute *One For Eric*, the eleven-minute *Zoot Suite* and the eight-minute *Journey To The Red Planet*. Replacing the saxophonists with tenorist Chico Freeman and altoist John Purcell, **Tin Can Alley** (september 1980) and **Inflation Blues** (september 1982) further broadened the stylistic palette via adventurous pieces such as *Tin Can Alley* and the 13-minute *Pastel Rhapsody* on the former, *Ebony*, *Islands* and *Starbust* on the latter. While technically not particularly revolutionary, DeJohnette was proving to be one of the most accomplished composers among the drummers of all times. Special Edition became a quintet for **Album Album** (june 1984), with David Murray returning on tenor and the addition of Howard Johnson's tuba, and the music (with the exception of *Third World Anthem*) was becoming not only more eclectic but also much more accessible.

After a futuristic soundtrack for a videogame, **Zebra** (may 1985), scored only for synthesizer (DeJohnette himself) and trumpet (Lester Bowie), DeJohnette resurrected the moniker Special Edition for **Irresistible Force** (january 1987)

and **Audio-Visualscapes** (february 1988), but the players were all new (reed player Gary Thomas, saxophonist Greg Osby, electric bass and electric guitar) and the sound was updated to the new fashions of funk-jazz fusion. **Earthwalk** (june 1991) added Michael Cain's electronic keyboards and further stretched the compositions (*On Golden Beams*, *Earth Walk*, *Monk's Plumb*).
Another intriguing project was the shamanic **Music For The Fifth World** (february 1992), for a rock-ish quintet featuring guitarists Vernon Reid and John Scofield and a choir, drummer Will Calhoun and bassist Lonnie Plaxico (and with DeJohnette doubling on vocals and synthesizer). The pagan and spiritual phase led to the 20-minute *Dancing With Nature Spirits* and the 22-minute *Healing Song For Mother Earth* for a trio of keyboards, reeds and percussion, off **Dancing with Nature Spirits** (may 1995). It then transitioned to the spiritual and intimate **Oneness** (january 1997) and imploded into the 61-minute keyboard meditation **Music In the Key of Om** (august 2003).

While still playing with Art Blakey and Max Roach, alto saxophonist Gary Bartz debuted as a leader with **Libra** (june 1967). His style was still derivative of bebop but his compositions were already first-rate, and the 24-minute suite *Another Earth* for a sextet featuring trumpeter Charles Tolliver, tenor saxophonist Pharoah Sanders, pianist Stanley Cowell and bassist Reggie Workman, off **Another Earth** (june 1968), proved it. After **Home** (march 1969), Bartz replaced Wayne Shorter in Miles Davis' group. Influenced by Davis as well as by John Coltrane and by rock guitarist Jimi Hendrix, Bartz formed NTU Troop in 1970 to play a high-energy fusion of soul, funk, jazz and rock on **Harlem Bush Music - Taifa** (november 1970), ruined by Andy Bey's vocals (and lyrics), **Juju Street Songs** (october 1972), that flirted with soul music between the mildly exotic *Teheran* and the Coltrane-ian *Sifa Zote*, **Follow The Medicine Man** (october 1972), with the funk workout *Dr Follow's Dance*, the live **I've Known Rivers And Other Bodies** (july 1973), with pianist Hubert Eaves replacing Bey and the Afro-spiritual hymns *Ju Ju Man* and *I've Known Rivers* ruined by Bartz's own vocals, and **Singerella - A Ghetto Fairy Tale** (february 1974), with Bartz also playing synthesizer. That marked the beginning of Bartz's career as a guru of electronic funk, starting with **The Shadow Do** (1975) and **Music Is My Sanctuary** (1977).

After drumming in the jazz-rock group Dreams, that included trumpeter Randy Brecker, saxophonist Michael Brecker and guitarist John Abercrombie, and a brief stint with Miles Davis, Billy Cobham joined John McLaughlin's Mahavishnu Orchestra (1971-73) and his drumming maelstroms soon became one of the most characteristic elements of their sound. After parting with McLaughlin, Cobham formed Spectrum, one of the premier groups of jazz, funk and rock fusion. **Spectrum** (may 1973), featuring a quartet with keyboardist Jan Hammer, heavy-metal guitarist Tommy Bolin and electric bassist Lee Sklar, upped the ante of fusion jazz with incendiary jams such as *Stratus*. **Crosswinds** (august 1973) featured his old fellow Dreams members Abercrombie, Randy Brecker and Michael Brecker, plus keyboardist George Duke, trombone and bass and Latin percussion. It contained the 17-minute four-movement suite *Spanish*

Moss, that proved Cobham was also a sophisticated composer. **Total Eclipse** (1974) featured a similar line-up in extended (the suite *Solarization*, the ten-minute *Sea Of Tranquillity*) as well as concise (the catchy *Moon Germs*) pieces that relied more on group interplay than on individual bombastic playing. The live **Shabazz** (july 1974) added two lengthy jams, *Shabazz* and *Tenth Pin*. While not even remotely subtle, the sound was becoming more cerebral and introspective. Later, with John Scofield replacing Abercrombie, the sound veered towards danceable funk music.

White guitarist John Abercrombie made a sensation in 1970 when he joined Dreams, a jazz-rock group led by Michael and Randy Brecker. His debut album **Timeless** (1974), in a trio with keyboardist Jan Hammer and drummer Jack DeJohnette, wed a lyrical while rocking approach to the guitar (more prominent in the eleven-minute *Timeless*) with visceral keyboards-driven fusion jazz (Hammer's 12-minute *Lungs*). At the same time, in 1974 Abercrombie joined Billy Cobham's Spectrum, a group that basically reunited him with the Breckers. His command of tone became legendary. Abercrombie, DeJohnette and bassist Dave Holland formed the trio Gateway, that released **Gateway** (march 1975) and **Gateway 2** (july 1977), mostly composed by Holland. Abercrombie also played in DeJohnette's Directions (1976) and New Directions (1978). However, Abercrombie's musical persona was better represented by the most humble records of that period. **Sargasso Sea** (may 1976), a duo album with fellow guitarist Ralph Towner, contrasted Abercrombie's lively and intricate style with Towner's impressionistic and transcendent style in some of Abercrombie's most atmospheric compositions (*Fable*). The solo album **Characters** (november 1977) was a showcase of his vibrant technique and of his unnerving compositions (*Parable*, *Ghost Dance*, *Evensong*).

Abercrombie recycled his elegant fusion style in the company of different line-ups: the quartet with pianist Richard Beirach that debuted on **Arcade** (december 1978), with *Arcade*, the trio with bassist Marc Johnson and drummer Peter Erskine that debuted on **Current Events** (1985), with the dreamy *Still*, the new guitar-organ-drums trio, best heard on **Open Land** (september 1998), that also featured violinist Mark Feldman, trumpeter Kenny Wheeler and tenorist Joe Lovano.

Best was the quartet that he formed with violinist Mark Feldman, drummer Joey Baron and bassist Marc Johnson. The guitarist's compositions, such as the waltzing *A Nice Idea* and *Soundtrack* on **Cat'n'Mouse** (december 2000), or *Dansir* and *Descending Grace* on **Class Trip** (february 2003), were majestic and haunting, while the performances were often mesmerizing (Feldman's work in *Third Stream Samba* on the former and in *Excuse My Shoes* on the latter).

Philadelphia-born white tenor saxophonist Michael Brecker and his brother, trumpeter Randy Brecker, an original founder of the rock group Blood, Sweat and Tears, formed the jazz-rock outfit, Dreams, that included John Abercrombie on guitar and Billy Cobham on drums, and released **Dreams** (december 1970) and **Imagine My Surprise** (1971). Michael Brecker also joined Billy Cobham's group (1974), where they basically reunited with the members of Dreams.

However, Michael and Randy Brecker also created a fusion band out of a group of veteran session-men such as alto saxophonist David Sanborn and keyboardist Don Grolnick. Most of their sophisticated and intricate material was composed by Randy Brecker. The compositions and the improvisation on **Brecker Brothers** (1975), with their signature tune *Some Skunk Funk* and the lengthy *A Creature Of Many Faces*, made for some of the most adventurous and innovative fusion sound of the era, bridging the world of bebop and hard bop with the world of funk-jazz, although subsequent albums rapidly descended into trivial dance music: **Back to Back** (1975), that also added guitarist Steve Kahn, **Don't Stop the Music** (1977), with *Funky Sea Funky Dew* and *Squids*, **Heavy Metal Bebop** (1978), that added *Inside Out* to their repertory and was perhaps the best display of their electronically-modified horns, **Detente** (1980), dominated by keyboardist George Duke, and **Straphangin'** (1980).

In the meantime, Michael Brecker played on many albums by other artists, including Joni Mitchell and Paul Simon. In particular, he participated in the recording of veteran pop-jazz arranger Claus Ogerman's ballet *Some Times* (originally composed in 1972) for **Gate of Dreams** (october 1976). They collaborated again on **Cityscape** (january 1982), that contained Ogerman's three-movement suite *In The Presence And Absence Of Each Other* arranged for jazz band and strings.

Michael Brecker then joined Mike Mainieri's Steps Ahead (1981-86), with whom he refined his electronic sound.

He finally debuted as a leader with **Michael Brecker** (1986), that featured guitarist Pat Metheny, keyboardist Kenny Kirkland, bassist Charlie Haden, and drummer Jack DeJohnette, emphasized Brecker's unique style at the "electronic wind instrument" and introduced Becker's compositional skills, very much in the bebop vein (*Syzygy*). The music rapidly progressed towards a facile mainstream sound engineered by the producer, and group interplay more and more reminiscent of John Coltrane, on **Don't Try This at Home** (1988), with *Don't Try This at Home* and *Itsbynne Reel* (both co-written by pianists Don Grolnick), **Now You See It Now You Don't** (1990), that added a synthesizer, **Tales from the Hudson** (january 1996), with *African Skies*, **Two Blocks from the Edge** (december 1997), with *Two Blocks from the Edge* and with pianist Joey Calderazzo frequently stealing the show, **Time Is of the Essence** (1999), virtually a Coltrane tribute thanks to Brecker's extended compositions *Arc of the Pendulum* and *Outrance*.

Wide Angles (january 2003), credited to the Quindectet, a 15-piece ensemble with trumpet, trombone (Robin Eubanks), oboe, French horn, violin (Mark Feldman), cello (Eric Friedlander), bass (John Patitucci), guitar and accordion, but no keyboards, was the first significant change in his career. Showing that he matured immensely as a composer, Brecker crafted the luxuriant *Scylla* and *Timbuktu*, while displaying his introspective bebop side.

The all-white group <u>Oregon</u> was an offshoot of Paul Winter's Consort, featuring four of Winter's best discoveries: acoustic guitarist Ralph Towner (also on piano), bassist Glen Moore (also on flute), percussionist Collin Walcott (tabla, sitar) and oboe player Paul McCandless (also on English horn). Oregon (named after Towner's and Moore's home state) basically continued Winter's mystical exploration of ethnic styles but shifting the emphasis on textures and timbres, and, ultimately, on chamber music. Their sophisticated interplay of improvisation and composition, jazz and classical music, world and folk music secreted the metaphysical miniatures of **Music Of Another Present Era** (1972) and the complex spiritual journeys of **Distant Hills** (1973). The latter showed the members maturing also as composers, not only soundsculptors, notably with *Mi Chinita Suite* and Towner's *Aurora* and *Distant Hills*. Towner rapidly became the main composer of the group, specializing in chromatic kaleidoscopes that incorporated elements of jazz, raga, flamenco, classical music and medieval dance: *Tide Pool* and *Ghost Beads* on **Winter Light** (1974), *Le Vin* and *Brujo* on **Together** (january 1976), a collaboration with veteran drummer Elvin Jones, *Interstate* on **Friends** (1977), *Raven's Wood* on **Violin** (1978), that also contained the (unusual for them) group improvisation *Violin* with Polish violinist Zbigniew Seifert, *Yellow Bell* and *Waterwheel* on **Out Of The Woods** (1978), *Vessel* on **Roots In The Sky** (1979). The basic medium remained the same: baroque calligraphy, lyrical longing and austere composure. A touch of electronics and jazzier overtones accounted for the more introspective and hermetic sound of **Oregon** (1983) and **Crossing** (1985).

In 1973 Miles Davis' pianist Lonnie-Liston Smith formed the Cosmic Echoes (sax, guitar, piano, bass, drums and exotic percussions). **Astral Traveling** (1973) offered a mellow and mostly melodic sound imbued with Eastern spirituality. But Smith soon turned towards even smoother elements of funk and soul music on albums such as **Expansions** (november 1974).

Steps Ahead was formed by vibraphonist Mike Mainieri as a vehicle to bring together some white New York virtuosi in a fusion group. The line-up on **Step By Step** (december 1980) included tenor saxophonist Michael Brecker, pianist Don Grolnick, bassist Eddie Gomez and drummer Steve Gadd. The supergroup continued to supply technical mastery but little emotion on **Paradox** (1982), with Peter Erskine replacing Gadd, and **Steps Ahead** (1983), with Eliane Elias replacing Grolnick (who nonetheless contributed the best track, *Pools*), before going electronic with **Modern Times** (Elektra, 1984), thanks to new keyboardist Warren Bernhardt.

Texan drummer Ronald Shannon Jackson, who relocated to New York in 1966, was influenced by his three main sessions of his career, Ornette Coleman's **Dancing in Your Head** (1976), Cecil Taylor's **Unit** (1978) and James "Blood" Ulmer's **Are You Glad To Be In America** (1980), to start his own group, the Decoding Society. Their debut album, **Eye On You** (1980), for an octet with violinist Billy Bang, saxophonists Byard Lancaster and Charles Brackeen, guitarist Vernon Reid, two bassists (including Melvin Gibbs), was still a transitional work fragmented into short unpretentious pieces (notably the catchy *Apache Cry Love*), but **Nasty** (march 1981), featuring a tighter nonet with Reid, Gibbs, three saxophonists and vibraphonist Khan Jamal, boasted the ten-minute *Black Widow* and the eleven-minute *When We Return* that clearly stated

Jackson's purpose: revise Ornette Coleman's harmolodic principle, as embodied by his Prime Time, while adding disproportionate doses of funk and rock. Jackson pursued a turbulent and intricate synthesis of composition and improvisation not in the sense that they coexist and complement each other but in the sense that they contrast and antagonize each other. This hybrid of free and fusion jazz was perfected on **Street Priest** (june 1981), with two new saxophonists and **Mandance** (june 1982), with a trumpet and only one saxophone, with the drumming hanging halfway between Tony Williams and Sunny Murray, but leaning towards the former, and further stimulated by the dual bass attack and by Reid's explosive (and sometimes electronic) guitar riffs. A complacent routine led from **Barbeque Dog** (march 1983) to less and less consistent albums.

Out of St Louis' avantgarde community came trombonist Joseph Bowie, Lester's younger brother, but he had a completely different agenda. After moving in 1973 to New York with Bobo Shaw's Human Arts Ensemble, Joseph Bowie got involved with various rhythm'n'blues projects and with "no wave" saxophonist James Chance.
Despite playing with the likes of Cecil Taylor, Frank Lowe, Anthony Braxton, Henry Threadgill, Charlie Haden and David Murray, Bowie continued to mine the danceable side of the equation and in 1978 formed his own funk-jazz-rock band, Defunkt, whose dancefloor hits were *Make Them Dance*, off **Defunkt** (1980), the single *Razor's Edge* (1981), and *Avoid the Funk*, off **Thermonuclear Sweat** (1982).

Former Pat Metheny's bassist Mark Egan and drummer Danny Gottlieb formed Elements in 1982 with saxophonist Bill Evans and keyboardist Clifford Carter. Albums such as **Elements** (january 1982), **Illumination** (august 1987) and **Spirit River** (february 1990) were quintessential examples of relaxing pop-jazz ambience.

Fusion Stylists

Fusion jazz changed the instrumental focus of the music. Just like rock music was centered on the guitar and the keyboards, and used the horns only as decoration, fusion jazz downplayed the traditional solo instruments of jazz music (trumpet, saxophone) and emphasized "unusual" instruments such as the guitar and the violin. Thus a side effect of fusion jazz was to raise a generation of virtuosi on instruments that previously had been largely neglected by jazz musicians.

At the same time, another side effect was to greatly expand the geography of jazz music. Many of the protagonists of fusion jazz came from the Midwest, an area that traditional had few jazz musicians (and, for that matter, few black people at all) and from Europe.

French violinist Jean-Luc Ponty was the musician who took the violin into the electric/electronic age and made it a pivotal force of the jazz-rock movement. Originally employed in a symphony orchestra, Ponty debuted at the age of 22 with **Jazz Long Playing** (july 1964). His first important composition was *Suite For Claudia* on **Sunday Walk** (june 1967) for a quartet with pianist Wolfgang Dauner, bassist Niels Pedersen and drummer Daniel Humair. Ponty had already developed a style at the instrument that basically imitated the phrasing of the bebop soloist and occasionally flirted with free jazz.

He more than flirted with jazz-rock when, relocated to Los Angeles, he started working with rock composer Frank Zappa (1968). Ponty joined forces with pianist George Duke to form the ensemble of **Electric Connection** (1968), that contained his *Hypomode Del Sol*, and the ensemble of **King Kong** (october 1969), that performed music by Zappa (notably *Music for Electric Violin and Low Budget Orchestra*, a masterpiece of jazz, rock and classical fusion).

Ponty's main compositions of the time reflected the Zappa influence: *Contact* on **Experience** (september 1969) for a quartet with Duke on piano, the 20-minute three-movement suite *Flipping* and the 15-minute *Open Strings* on the sublime **Open Strings** (december 1971) for a quintet with keyboardist Joachim Kuhn and Belgian guitarist Philip Catherine, *Astrorama* on **Astrorama** (august 1970), *Concerto for Jazz Violin and Orchestra* on **With Kurt Edelhagen & His Orchestra** (july 1969), and especially the five-movement **Sonata Erotica** (june 1972), recorded live with Ponty on acoustic violin and echo box, Joachim Kuhn on electric piano, Nana Vasconcelos on percussion, plus a bassist and a drummer, basically a reworking of the concerto for jazz violin and orchestra. After playing with John McLaughlin's Mahavishnu Orchestra, a more electronic and energetic sound surfaced on **Upon the Wings of Music** (january 1975), with en electronic keyboardist and with Ponty playing electronically-modified violins (the overdubbed solo violin workout *Echoes Of The Future*). It also displayed the first symptoms of Ponty's African passion (percussionist Ndugu Leon Chancellor). That album's energetic and futuristic fusion set the pace for the subsequent albums, that mostly replicated the line-up of the Mahavishnu

Orchestra (electric violin, guitar, keyboards, bass, drums): **Aurora** (december 1975), **Imaginary Voyage** (august 1976), highlighted by the 20-minute four-movement suite *Imaginary Voyage*, **Enigmatic Ocean** (july 1977), with Allan Holdsworth added a second guitar and two multi-part suites, *Enigmatic Ocean* (twelve minutes) and *The Struggle Of The Turtle* (13 minutes), **Cosmic Messenger** (1978), with Ponty doubling on synthesizer and with Peter Maunu and Joaquin Lievano splitting guitar chores (*Egocentric Molecules*). The 24-minute five-movement suite *Mystical Adventures* on **Mystical Adventures** (september 1981) de facto closed an era.

Detroit's classically-trained cellist and bassist Ron Carter, who relocated to New York in 1959 and played with Eric Dolphy (1960), Randy Weston (1960), Jaki Byard (1961) and especially Miles Davis (1963-68), becoming one of the most prolific musicians ever, dedicated his recordings as a leader to demonstrating the virtues of the double bass. For that purpose he used and reused a few original compositions. **Uptown Conversation** (october 1969), that contains *Little Waltz*, toyed with various instrumental configurations including several extended bass solos to show how the bass can lead and inspire. On the other hand, albums such as **Blues Farm** (january 1973), that contained his *Blues Farm* and *Hymn for Him*, and **All Blues** (october 1973), with a nine-minute *All Blues* and a seven-minute *117 Special*, focused on the ability of the instrument to contract and dilate time within a regular combo. The double-LP **Piccolo** (march 1977), with the 18-minute *Saguaro*, featured a quartet with pianist Kenny Barron and Carter on the piccolo bass, a new instrument pitched between the bass and cello range. Other noteworthy showcases were: ten-minute *Arkansas* on **Spanish Blue** (november 1974), *Blues for D.P.* on **A Song For You** (june 1978), *Parade* on **Parade** (march 1979), *Alternate Route* on **New York Stick** (december 1979), *Nearly* on the Brazilian **Patrao** (may 1980). His last major recording was **Etudes** (september 1982) in a quartet with trumpeter Art Farmer, saxophonist Bill Evans and drummer Tony Williams.

Czech bassist Miroslav Vitous, a child prodigy who moved to the USA in 1966 and immediately generated a sensation, being adopted by the likes of Chick Corea and Jack DeJohnette, debuted as a leader at 22 with **Infinite Search** (october 1969), that featured guitarist John McLaughlin, keyboardist Herbie Hancock, tenor saxophonist Joe Henderson and drummer Jack DeJohnette, almost an offshoot of the sessions for Wayne Shorter's **Super Nova** (august 1969). It was a pioneering work of jazz-rock jamming and also a showcase for the leader's multifaceted technique that granted a melodic and textural role to the bass (the eleven-minute *I Will Tell Him On You*). **Purple** (august 1970), featuring McLaughlin, keyboardist Joe Zawinul and drummer Billy Cobham, contained even more elegant compositions, such as *Purple* and *Water Lilie*. The following year he joined Weather Report.

Stanley Clarke was one of the bassists who created a language for the electric bass in the context of fusion music. Starting out with Pharoah Sanders (1971) and especially Chick Corea (1972), Clarke turned the electric bass into a force of nature, both in terms of percussive power and in terms of chromatic spectrum.

Fusion Stylists

His compositions were ambitious the 16-minute *Sea Journey* on **Children of Forever** (december 1972), that still featured Chick Corea on keyboards; the 14-minute *Life Suite* on the heavily arranged **Stanley Clarke** (1974); the 14-minute *Concerto for Jazz-rock Orchestra* on **Journey to Love** (1975). **School Days** (june 1976) was a hit, thanks to the nine-minute *Life Is Just A Game* and the catchy *School Days*. The double-LP **I Wanna Play For You** (september 1979) marked the transition from the old progressive fusion (still represented by the nine-minute *Quiet Afternoon*) to the electronic pop-soul-funk music concocted by keyboardist George Duke. The latter became his main preoccupation during the 1980s, notably in the funk group **The Clarke/Duke Project** (1981).

Florida-raised flamboyant white electric bassist Jaco Pastorius, who had debuted on **Pastorius Metheny Ditmas Bley** (june 1974) with Paul Bley and Pat Metheny, became a sensation with **Jaco Pastorius** (october 1975), one of the most innovative albums ever led by a bass player, also featuring keyboardist Herbie Hancock, saxophonists David Sanborn, Wayne Shorter and Michael Brecker, flutist Hubert Laws, Peter Gordon on French horn, drummer Lenny White, percussionist Don Alias. Pieces such as *Opus Pocus* and *Cha Cha* matched bold arrangements and an eclectic array of musical styles (from soul to neoclassical) with an insanely obsessive instrumental technique. His solos in the higher registers and the fat, colored tones that frequently turned into his distinctive "growl", the dense, eerie chords and harmonics, wed rhythmic and textural playing in one instrument. The album not only popularized the fretless electric bass, but turned the bass into one of the most expressive instruments of the fusion era.
Pastorius became a star during his tenure with Weather Report (1976-81). During that time, Pastorius also played for Joni Mitchell (1976-80). After Weather Report split in 1981, Pastorius formed his big band, Word of Mouth, featuring dozens of musicians (including Hancock, Shorter, Laws, Shorter, Brecker, Alias, reed player Tom Scott, harmonica player Toots Thielemans trumpeter Chuck Findley, tuba player Howard Johnson, drummers Jack DeJohnette and Peter Erskine). **Word of Mouth** (1981) focused more on his skills as a composer than on his virtuoso playing, particularly in the lengthy *Liberty City* and *John and Mary*. Another orchestra (five trumpets, five reeds, four trombones, two French horns, harmonica, drums, percussion and steel drum) performed the wildly inferior **Invitation** (december 1983), mostly devoted to covers. Word of Mouth disbanded in 1984.

White contrabassist David Friesen cycled from the mostly solo-contrabass experiments of **Color Pool** (october 1975) to the mellow ethnic-tinged chamber jazz-rock of **Star Dance** (november 1976), in a quartet with horn and oboe player Paul McCandless, guitarist John Stowell and percussionist Steve Gadd, and of **Waterfall Rainbow** (august 1977), featuring McCandless, Stowell, guitarist Ralph Towner, flutist Nick Brignola and two percussionists, back to the solo album **Paths Beyond Tracing** (february 1980), but in a spiritual new-age vein. Longer compositions and a more intimate mood characterized **Storyteller** (april 1981), in a quartet with McCandless and Stowell, and especially **Amber Skies** (january 1983), with tenor saxophonist Joe Henderson, flutist Paul Horn, pianist Chick Corea, drummer Paul Motian and percussionist Airto Moreira.

The members of Oregon were all brilliant solo artists. Oregon's percussionist Collin Walcott was in fact one of the most innovative percussionists of the era, exploring his personal brand of Indian jazz-rock on **Cloud Dance** (march 1975), featuring guitarist John Abercrombie, bassist Dave Holland and drummer Jack DeJohnette, and on **Grazing Dreams** (february 1977), featuring Don Cherry and Abercrombie besides bass and percussion.

White pianist Art Lande, who moved to San Francisco in 1969, specialized in calm, bucolic atmospheres both in the duets with saxophonist Jan Garbarek of **Red Lanta** (november 1973) and on his solo piano album **The Eccentricities Of Earl Dant** (february 1977). He also formed a quartet with Mark Isham on trumpet that recorded **Rubisa Patrol** (may 1976), with *Corinthian Melodies*, and **Desert Marauders** (june 1977), with the 16-minute *Desert Marauders*, both dominated by languid tones. Quasi-classical ambitions surfaced in the 23-minute solo-piano sonata *The Story Of Ned Tra-La* (august 1977), off **The Story Of Ba-Ku** and the 19-minute *The Story Of Ba-Ku* (august 1978) for piano, three reed players, bass and drums off **The Story Of Ba-Ku**.

White saxophonist John Klemmer, based in Los Angeles since 1968, electrified the saxophone in order to obtain the evocative sound more appropriate for his smooth fusion-tinged excursions. He had one of the big hits of that season, *Touch* (1975).

White pianist Steve Kuhn established his fusion style that flirted with free jazz and classical music (and therefore exhibited a lot more dynamics and instability than the average smooth fusion-jazz of the era) with the brilliant solo **Ecstasy** (november 1974) and **Trance** (november 1974), accompanied by bassist Steve Swallow and drummer Jack DeJohnette. **Playground** (july 1979) inaugurated Kuhn's collaboration with avantgarde vocalist Sheila Jordan.

White bassist Steve Swallow's credentials were already colossal thanks to high-caliber tenures with Paul Bley (1960-65), Jimmy Giuffre (1960-62), George Russell (1961-62), Art Farmer (1962-65), Stan Getz (1965-67), Gary Burton (1967-70), before he switched to the electric bass, playing it like a high-toned guitar, almost a contradiction in terms. His best work was probably done with Carla Bley, starting in 1978. **Swallow** (november 1991), with *Soca Symphony*, was perhaps his best display of technique, but his solo work was mostly hampered by inferior material.

Later in the decade, Prime Time's bassist Jamaaladeen Tacuma crafted two of the most virulent albums of funk-jazz, **Show Stopper** (1983) and **Renaissance Man** (1984), both translating Ornette Coleman's invention into a diverse range of scenarios.

GUITAR HEROES

By the mid 1970s, the fusion of jazz with rock had had the effect of greatly increasing the status of the guitar in jazz music. In fact, after decades of neglect, the guitar came to dominate jazz music in the last quarter of the century the way the saxophone had dominated until the 1960s.

After playing free jazz with Pharoah Sanders (1966-68) while he was playing funk-jazz with Herbie Mann (1969-72), guitarist Warren "Sonny" Sharrock recorded three albums with his wife Linda Sharrock's wordless vocals: **Black Woman** (may 1969), featuring trumpeter Teddy Daniel, pianist Dave Burrell, bassist Norris "Sirone" Jones and drummer Milford Graves, that displayed the influence of free jazz (*Peanut*, *Portrait of Linda* and the first version of his signature tune *Blind Willy*); **Monkey-Pockie-Boo** (june 1970), possibly his most personal album, crowned by the 17-minute stream of consciousness of *27th Day* (mostly on slide whistle instead of guitar) and the nine-minute *Monkey-Pockie-Boo*; and **Paradise** (july 1975), introducing electronic keyboards in the sound of the couple and emphasizing Linda's Jeanne Lee-like vocal workouts (*Miss Doris*, *Gary's Step*), an avant-funk experiment that predated the new wave of rock music. The background of his guitar playing was fundamentally the blues, but at the same time he erupted a loud, aggressive, feedback-laden, quasi heavy-metal technique. Sharrock was trying to emulate both the visceral style of John Coltrane on the saxophone and the dissonant, decadent style of Jimi Hendrix.

For six years Sharrock did not make a single record. It was white bassist Bill Laswell, a protagonist of the new wave, who rediscovered him for Material's **Memory Serves** (1981). **Dance with Me Montana** (march 1982), not released until 1986, contained embryonic versions of his classics *She's Only Fourteen*, *Dance With Me Montana* and *Dick Dogs*.

Laswell also organized Last Exit, an avant-funk mixed-race quartet with Sharrock, German saxophonist Peter Brotzmann and drummer Ronald Shannon Jackson that played virulent jazz-rock, influenced by both the brutal edge of punk-rock and the cerebral stance of the new wave. Laswell was the brain, but Sharrock was the epitome: Last Exit played the kind of loud, savage jazz-rock and free jazz that Sharrock had pioneered. The catch, of course, was that Laswell had put together four mad improvisers, ranging from the cacophonic Brotzmann to the hysterical Sharrock to Laswell's dub bass. **Last Exit** (february 1986) was a set of totally improvised jams, with frantic peaks in *Redlight* and *Crackin'*, but pale in comparison with the massive 18-minute *Hard School* on the live **Koln** (february 1986). The other Last Exit live recording, **The Noise of Trouble** (october 1986), was a humbler study in contrasts, despite *Panzer Bebop*. Sharrock overdubbed himself for the solo **Guitar** (february 1986), achieving both his most challenging technique and emotional pathos in the four-movement suite *Princess Sonata*. He then partnered with rock bassist Melvin Gibbs and avantgarde drummer Pheeroan Aklaff for **Seize the Rainbow** (may 1987), that attempted a fusion of heavy metal and fusion jazz (a ten-minute version of *Fourteen*).

In the meantime, Last Exit's punk-jazz achieved a different kind of intensity on **The Iron Path** (1988), a set of ten short pieces, and the live **Headfirst Into The Flames** (1989).

Sharrock also played on two albums by Machine Gun, a free-form improvising group, **Machine Gun** (1988) and **Open Fire** (1989).

A quartet with two free-jazz veterans, Pharoah Sanders and Elvin Jones, on **Ask the Ages** (1991) restored Sharrock's status as a unique guitarist and composer (*Promises Kept, Many Mansions*) and pushed it to new insane heights, but he died in 1994.

South Carolina-born electric guitarist James "Blood" Ulmer relocated to New York in 1971. After playing with Ornette Coleman (1972-74), he developed an aggressive, edgy, jangled, dissonant style at the instrument that transposed Coleman's "harmolodic" free jazz coupled with Jimi Hendrix's psychedelic funk-blues-rock fusion (and loud amplification).

Revealing (1977), in a quartet with tenor saxophonist George Adams, bassist Cecil McBee and drummer Doug Hammond, contained four lengthy jams (particularly *Revealing* and *Overtime*). Ulmer used the same kind of quartet, but with Ornette Coleman on alto saxophone and Jamaladeen Tacuma on bass, on the more famous but less adventurous **Tales From Captain Black** (december 1978), containing eight short pieces. The difference was not so much Coleman, but Tacuma, thanks to whom the sound became visceral and funky. **Are You Glad To Be In America** (january 1980), with the formidable rhythm section of drummer Ronald Shannon Jackson and bassist Amin Ali, was structured again as a series of (ten) demonstrations (notably *Lay Out* and *Time Out*) of Ulmer's potential, somewhere between the Pop Group and Bill Laswell's Material. Ulmer returned to the extended free-jam format of **Revealing** with the Music Revelation Ensemble, a quartet with tenor saxophonist David Murray, bassist Amin Ali and drummer Ronald Shannon Jackson. **No Wave** (june 1980) contained four energetic pieces, particularly *Time Table*, *Big Tree* and *Baby Talk*. But the albums under his own name valued instead structure and brevity. Increasing the ferocity of his attack via **Free Lancing** (1981), whose *Timeless* was almost punk-rock, Ulmer achieved the brutal peak of **Black Rock** (1982), debuting flutist Sam Sanders and coupling Ali's bass with drummer Grant Calvin Weston, a collection that ran the gamut from hardcore (*Open House*) to free-jazz (*We Bop*) and focused on the middleground, a radio-friendly fusion of hard-rock and funk music (*Black Rock*). The idea was ready for mass consumption, and Ulmer, accompanied only by violin and drums, and relying ever more on his vocals, found a huge audience with **Odyssey** (1983),

Ulmer teamed up with tenor saxophonist George Adams and created the quartet Phalanx. Their **Got Something Good For You** (september 1985) featured Ali and Weston, whereas **Original** (february 1987) and **In Touch** (1988) boasted bassist Norris "Sirone" Jones and drummer Rashied Ali.

America Do You Remember the Love? (september 1986) was a jazz-rock quartet session with guitarist Nicky Skopelitis, bassist Bill Laswell and Ronald Shannon Jackson, heavily influenced by Laswell's ambient/world philosophy.
Ulmer finally resurrected the Music Revelation Ensemble (with Jamaaladeen Tacuma replacing Ali) for **Music Revelation Ensemble** (february 1988), indulging in six free-form jams (notably *Body Talk*, *Playtime*, *Nisa*). The rhythm section changed (Amin Ali and drummer Cornell Rochester) for **Elec Jazz** (march 1990), that had the free-jazz workout *Big Top* (in two parts), *Exit* (also in two parts), the eight-minute ballad *No More* and the ten-minute *Taps Dance*.
After Dark (october 1991) contained *Maya*, the 12-minute avant-ballad *Never Mind*, and *After Dark*, his first experiment with a string quartet. Basically, as Ulmer moved away from free jazz in his albums, he moved back into free jazz with the Ensemble.
Ulmer's most ambitious album, **Harmolodic Guitar with Strings** (july 1993) contained three multi-movement suites for guitar and string quartet (*Arena*, *Page One*, *Black Sheep*), each movement being very short.
With Murray replaced by guest saxophonists (Arthur Blythe on alto in *Non-Believer*, Hamiet Bluiett on baritone in *The Dawn*, or Sam Rivers on soprano in *In Time*, on tenor in *Help* and on flute in *Mankind*), the Music Revelation Ensemble rode the cacophonic maelstrom of **In The Name Of** (december 1993). The funkier **Knights of Power** (april 1995) was less terrifying, but still contained powerful pieces such as *Convulsion* (with Bluiett) and *The Elephant* (with Blythe). **Cross Fire** (december 1996), with bassist Calvin Jones replacing Ali, used Pharoah Sanders' tenor saxophone (notably in *My Prayer*) and John Zorn's alto saxophone. These Ensemble albums were also vehicles for Ulmer to showcase his supernatural technique at the guitar, freed from the song-oriented constraints of his solo albums.

Oregon's guitarist <u>Ralph Towner</u>, who had been Oregon's main composer, was not much of a virtuoso, but had few rivals in crafting seductive atmospheres. Towner introduced the acoustic twelve-string guitar to jazz. **Diary** (april 1973), a milestone of introspective and meditational jazz, ran the gamut from *Dark Spirit*, a neoclassical sonata for guitar and piano (both played by Towner), to the jazzy saraband of *Ogden Road*. After the mediocre **Matchbook** (july 1974) with vibraphonist Gary Burton, Towner reach a zenith of magic and bliss on **Solstice** (december 1974), in a quartet with saxophonist Jan Garbarek, bassist Eberhard Weber and drummer Jon Christensen, weaving the oneiric filigrees of *Drifting Petals*, intoning the exuberant *Oceanus* and riding the sax-flute dances of *Nimbus*. After the evanescent **Sargasso Sea** (may 1976) with guitarist John Abercrombie, Towner refined his format on the second Solstice album, **Sound And Shadows** (february 1977), a set of five lengthy pieces, each one shimmering melancholy from the haunting *Balance Beam* to the feathery *Arion* to the quasi-psychedelic *Songs of the Shadows* and to Oregon's *Distant Hills*. Towner's compositional skills peaked with **Batik** (january 1978), in a trio with bassist Eddie Gomez and drummer Jack DeJohnette, boasting the 16-minute jazz-rock juggernaut *Batik*, as well as the fragile *Trellis* and the lively *Waterwheel*. After another jazzy effort, **Old Friends New Friends** (july 1979), featuring trumpeter Kenny Wheeler, cellist David Darling, bassist Eddie Gomez and drummer Michael DiPasqua, and containing the catchy *Beneath An Evening Sky*, Towner adopted a simpler language for **Solo Concert** (october 1979), spinning colloquial, folkish proto-ballads (*Chelsea Courtyard*) and wordless fairy tales (*Spirit Lake*).

Missouri-born white guitarist Pat Metheny debuted on **Pastorius Metheny Ditmas Bley** (1974) with Paul Bley and Jaco Pastorius, and played on Gary Burton's **Dreams So Real** (1975) and **Passengers** (1976), albums that popularized the twelve-string electric guitar.

His debut as a leader, **Bright Size Life** (december 1975), a trio session featuring Pastorius and drummer Bob Moses (also fresh from Burton's group), introduced more than just an electric instrument (two with Pastorius' bass) to jazz music: the key factor was the domestic and naturalistic mood of the Midwest's white farming culture that permeated every piece (especially *Midwestern Nights Dream*). The experimental (*Sirabhorn*) and melodic (*Unity Village*, an overdubbed duet between two electric guitars) were mere variations on the same theme. The album also relied on the spontaneous equilibrium between Metheny, who was shaping the sound of the electric guitar, and Pastorius, who was revolutionizing the electric bass.

Watercolors (february 1977) debuted a quartet with pianist Lyle Mays, bassist Eberhard Weber and drummer Danny Gottlieb. As the title implied, Metheny's compositions were shifting towards an impressionistic, chromatic aesthetic. The idyllic *Watercolors*, the turbulent *Icefire*, and the ten-minute odyssey *Sea Song* relied on elegant counterpoint, crystalline tones and youthful exuberance.

Adopting those elements as dogmas, the following year Metheny formed his fusion Group with Mays, Gottlieb and bassist Mark Egan. Mays was co-responsible for most of the material (notably the edgy ten-minute *San Lorenzo*, as well as a couple of eight-minute rhapsodies, *Phase Dance* and *April Joy*) and the overall atmosphere of **Group** (january 1978), a symbiosis that was to become the essence of the Group's music.

If, before Metheny, fusion jazz had to pretend to be "black" in order to qualify for a slot in jazz magazines and record stores, with Metheny any pretense was set aside. Metheny's jazz was as white as country or folk music. The closest relative to his guitar picking was Jerry Garcia of the Grateful Dead. That he did not acknowledge much of the history of jazz was also implied by the fact that his material was mostly self-penned and hardly referenced any of the masters. The jazz heritage was a mere technicality, just like the guitar was originally invented in Spain but that didn't imply that every guitar piece had to pay tribute to Spanish music.

His solo work paled in comparison: **New Chautauqua** (august 1978) contained pieces for overdubbed electric guitars (acoustic, six-string electric, twelve-string electric, electric bass and even fifteen-string harp guitar) that rarely achieved the same intensity and mostly indulged in a bucolic feeling (*Daybreak*).

The Group's **American Garage** (june 1979), instead, skyrocketed to the top of the charts, thanks to the catchy *Heartland* and streamlined arrangements, although the 13-minute *Epic* displayed the quartet's experimental side. The Group moved towards progressive-rock with the convoluted 21-minute suite *As Falls Wichita So Falls Wichita* on **As Falls Wichita So Falls Wichita** (september 1980), that debuted Brazilian percussionist Nana Vasconcelos.
Metheny showed his jazz credentials on the double-LP **80/81** (may 1980), a collaboration with tenor saxophonists Dewey Redman and Michael Brecker, bassist Charlie Haden and drummer Jack DeJohnette, highlighted by the folk-bop fusion of the 21-minute *Two Folk Songs*, the 14-minute Coleman-ian group improvisation of *Open*, the cerebral *Pretty Scattered* and the 13-minute ballad *Everyday I Thank You*. The "jazz" trilogy was completed by **Rejoicing** (november 1983), a trio session with Haden and Billy Higgins, more important for Metheny's *The Calling* (that popularized the guitar synthesizer) than for the Coleman covers, and **Song X** (december 1985), a collaboration with Ornette Coleman that was mostly Coleman's.
The Group, on the other hand, was progressively moving towards Brazilian pop-jazz muzak via **Offramp** (october 1981), with bassist Steve Rodby replacing Egan (*Are You Going with Me*, *Au Lait*), **First Circle** (february 1984), featuring Argentinian multi-instrumentalist Pedro Aznar and with drummer Paul Wertico replacing Gottlieb (*End of the Game*, *The First Circle*), **Still Life** (april 1987), featuring Brazilian percussionist Armando Marcal (*Third Wind*, *Minuano*), and **Letter from Home** (1989), with *Every Summer Night*.
Metheny's releases became more and more erratic and the Group wandered aimlessly through pop muzak, on **We Live Here** (1994), acoustic folk, on **Quartet** (may 1996), and world-music, on **Imaginary Day** (1997), which was the best recording of the decade.
An artistic rebirth of sorts took place in the new millennium. The Group's live double-CD **Speaking of Now** (2001) featured Mays, Rodby, Mexican drummer Antonio Sanchez, trumpeter Cuong Vu and Cameroonian bassist Richard Bona (*Gathering Sky*, *Proof*). Adding Swiss harmonica player Gregoire Maret to the line-up, the Group's 68-minute four-movement suite **The Way Up** (2004) was Metheny's and Mays' most ambitious and eclectic composition ever, running the gamut from minimalist repetition to romantic melody.

Japanese guitarist Kazumi Watanabe, who had debuted with the four lengthy suites of **Endless Way** (july 1975), accompanied by saxophone (Hidefumi Toki), trombone, bass and drums, attained celebrity with the smooth fusion music of ensemble recordings such as **Kylyn** (may 1979) and **Mobo I** (september 1983), but his more original take on the genre was perhaps **To Chi Ka** (march 1980), featuring keyboardist Kenny Kirkland and vibraphonist Mike Manieri. **Spice Of Life** (november 1986) debuted a trio with rock drummer Bill Bruford and bassist Jeff Berlin.

After playing on albums by Billy Cobham (1974-76) and Charles Mingus (1977), Ohio-born white guitarist John Scofield embarked on a solo career as a purveyors of funk-jazz fusion with **East Meets West** (august 1977), a trio session highlighted by the lengthy *Public Domain* and *V.*, **Live** (november 1977), for a piano-based quartet that indulged in the 15-minute *Gray and Visceral*, **Rough House** (november 1978), with *Rough House* for another piano-based quartet, and **Who's Who** (1979), with *How The West Was Won*. While he was playing in Dave Liebman's group (1978-80), Scofield formed a trio with bassist Steve Swallow and drummer Adam Nussbaum that helped refine both his playing and his composing via **Bar Talk** (august 1980), with *Fat Dancer*, **Shinola** (december 1981), with *Yawn*, and the live **Out Like a Light** (december 1981), with the spectacular *Holidays*.

While he was playing with Miles Davis (1983-87), Scofield toyed with different formats: a quintet with altoist David Sanborn, trombonist Ray Anderson, synthesizer and drums for **Electric Outlet** (may 1984), containing his signature tune *Pick Hits*; a quartet with electronic keyboardist Don Grolnick, electric bassist Darryl Jones and drummer Omar Hakim for **Still Warm** (june 1985), containing the lyrical *Still Warm* and the quirky *Techno* and *Rule Of Thumb*; a quintet with keyboards, bass, drums and percussion for **Blue Matter** (september 1986), containing the funky *Blue Matter* and *Time Marches On*; the same quintet plus keyboardist George Duke for **Loud Jazz** (december 1987), that further reduced the length of the pieces (*Dirty Rice*, *Spy Vs Spy*); an organ-based quartet (Don Grolnick on organ) inspired by New Orleans' rhythm'n'blues for **Flat Out** (december 1988). Best was the piano-less quartet a` la Ornette Coleman with tenor saxophonist Joe Lovano, bassist Charlie Haden and drummer Jack DeJohnette that recorded **Time on my Hands** (november 1989), and inspired Scofield to compose *Wabash III*, *Stranger To The Light* and *Farmacology*. And Lovano stole the show on **Meant To Be** (december 1990), with a new rhythm section (bassist Marc Johnson and drummer Bill Stewart) and inventive solos in *Big Fun* and *Go Blow*. This was high-caliber funk-jazz, despite the fact that Scofield refrained from venturing into group improvisation or the kind of suites favored by progressive-rock.

If James "Blood" Ulmer came from the free-jazz tradition, Scofield stood solidly in the bebop tradition, but filtered through his roots in white rhythm'n'blues, his upbringing in fusion jazz and a pervasive rock influence on his guitar technique. At the same time, Scofield quickly matured as a composer in a Mingus-ian vein.

Thus **Grace Under Pressure** (december 1991), featuring fellow guitarist Bill Frisell, Haden and drummer Joey Baron, excelled at both straight-ahead jazz (*Grace Under Pressure*) and at jazz-rock on the brink of insanity (*Scenes From a Marriage*). Scofield was beginning to feel more comfortable with longer and more eccentric tracks also with the Lovano-led quartet on **What We Do** (may 1992), with *Camp Out*, *Call 911* and *Why Nogales*.

Scofield moved towards an old-fashioned sound with the funk-soul-jazz fusion of **Hand Jive** (october 1993), featuring veteran soul-jazz saxophonist Eddie Harris as well as organist Larry Goldings (*Do Like Eddie*, *Golden Gaze*, *Dark Blue*), and **Groove Elation** (1995), on which Goldings became Scofield's alter-ego (*Carlos*).

Guitar Heroes

Italian-American electric guitarist Al DiMeola, who made his name in Chick Corea's Return To Forever (1974-76) when he was still a teenager, was emblematic of the mix of technical mastery and relaxing material (but devoid of innovation or challenge) that came to be expected from fusion guitarists. His first album, **Land of the Midnight Sun** (july 1976), coined a delicate blend of baroque fusion-jazz and melodic progressive-rock in two nine-minute pieces, *Land of the Midnight Sun* and the three-movement suite *Golden Dawn*. DiMeola's style rapidly converged towards a stereotyped kind of Latin-tinged fusion via **Elegant Gypsy** (january 1977), that included an acoustic duet with fellow guitarist Paco de Lucia (*Mediterranean Sundance*), an electric-guitar tour de force (*Race With Devil on Spanish Highway*) and another nine-minute suite (*Elegant Gypsy*), **Casino** (september 1977), with another tour de force (the multi-tracked *Fantasia Suite for Two Guitars*), catchy numbers (*Senor Mouse, Egyptian Danza*) and the customary nine-minute suite, *Casino*, and the double-LP **Splendido Hotel** (1979), a sort of self-celebration in various configurations (*Alien Chase On Arabian Desert, Dinner Music Of The Gods*). In the 1980s DiMeola reemerged as an acoustic Pat Metheny-inspired guitarist of sentimental moods at the intersection of new-age and world-music. The new classics were: the eleven-minute *Cielo E Terra* on **Cielo E Terra** (1985), *Beijing Demons* and *Rhapsody of Fire* on **Tirami Su** (1987), *Morocco* and *Phantom* on **Kiss My Axe** (may 1991), and, after declaring his love for Argentinian tango composer Astor Piazzolla on the all-acoustic **World Sinfonia** (october 1990), *Grande Passion* on **Grande Passion** (april 2000) and *Zona Desperata* on **Flesh on Flesh** (april 2002).

Minnesota's white guitarist Steve Tibbetts coined a dreamy, intimate version of jazz-rock, occasionally bordering on spiritual new-age music, on the solo **Steve Tibbetts** (1976), rich in studio effects, on **Yr** (1980) for overdubbed guitars, bass, exotic percussion and recording techniques (that become an instrument in themselves) and on **Northern Song** (october 1981), an evocation of supernatural landscapes by guitar and percussion, notably the lengthy *Nine Doors*. On the other hand, **Safe Journey** (november 1983), that returned to the guitar-bass-percussion configuration, and **Exploded View** (1986), that added wordless vocals to the exotic jazz-rock stew, bordered on psychedelic rock and heavy metal. The broad palette of Tibbetts' music was further expanded on **Big Map Idea** (1988) by *Three Letters*, a study in chamber world-music with ethnic samples, and on **The Fall Of Us All** (1994), a visceral set of intrepid solos over complex polyrhythmic patterns with an ever stronger ethnic accent. The tone of Tibbetts' neurotic sacred music became more hypnotic on **Cho** (january 1996), a collaboration with Tibetan nun Choying Drolma, and **A Man About A Horse** (2002), that returned to his preferred configuration of guitar, bass, exotic percussion and field recordings. Tibbetts' career was one unlikely symbiosis between urban emotional imbalance and pastoral spiritual equilibrium.

White guitarist Steve Khan refined his smooth, tuneful and delicate fusion music over two albums, **Tightrope** (april 1977) and **The Blue Man** (february 1978), that featured trumpeter Randy Brecker, tenor saxophonist Michael

Brecker, alto saxophonist David Sanborn, pianist Don Grolnick, bassist Bob James and drummer Steve Gadd. A looser, more improvised style emerged with **Eyewitness** (november 1981).

White guitarist Mike Stern, who had made his name with Billy Cobham (1979) and Miles Davis (1981), crafted a string of albums overflowing with energetic jazz-rock interplay and longer and longer solos: **Neesh** (september 1983), featuring alto saxophonist David Sanborn, **Upside Downside** (april 1986), **Time In Place** (december 1987), **Jigsaw** (february 1989), **Odds or Evens** (1991), **Is What It Is** (1994), **Between The Lines** (february 1996). He reached a zenith of virtuoso sophistication with **Play** (september 1999), after which he was able to harmoniously import pop melody, world music and wordless singing into **Voices** (september 2001).

His wife, German guitarist Leni Stern, had a keen sense of how to arrange pieces straddling the border between pop, jazz and rock, demonstrated since **Clairvoyant** (december 1985).

POP-FUSION

The mellow, bland, romantic music that came to be called "fusion jazz" in the following decade was largely the product (a very commercial product) of mediocre musicians such as Chuck Mangione and Al Jarreau, and of derivative bands such as Spyro Gyra and Yellowjackets.

Pittsburgh-born guitarist and vocalist George Benson, who cut his teeth in Jack McDuff's group (1962) with a style reminiscent of Wes Montgomery and Charlie Christian, became the epitome of commercial fusion jazz of the 1970s. **The New Boss Guitar** (may 1964), with McDuff on organ, presented Benson as a composer and performer of hard-bop at the border with soul (*Shadow Dancers*) and blues (*I Don't Know*). His lightning-speed technique matured via **It's Uptown** (1964) and **Cookbook** (october 1966), both enhanced with Lonnie Smith's organ, **Giblet Gravy** (february 1968) and **Shape of Things to Come** (october 1968), both enhanced with organ, Herbie Hancock's piano and pop arrangements. On his way to stardom, Benson was forced to use more covers and less originals, and to accent the groove of his soul-jazz for the dancehalls, but he still managed to deliver some noteworthy originals: *Somewhere In The East* on **Beyond the Blue Horizon** (february 1971), with drummer Jack DeJohnette and bassist Ron Carter, the eleven-minute *El Mar* on **White Rabbit** (november 1971), with Hancock, percussionist Airto Moreira, bassist and Ron Carter and drummer Billy Cobham, the funky workouts *Body Talk* and *Dance* on **Body Talk** (july 1973), with the rhythm section of Carter and DeJohnette. The musical surgery of arranger Don Sebesky **Bad Benson** (may 1974), with the samba *My Latin Brother* and Sebelsky's funky 12-minute *Serbian Blue*, and of Claus Ogerman on **Breezin'** (january 1976), whose only song (an eight-minute cover of Leon Russell's *This Masquerade*) climbed the charts, succeeded in depressing Benson's guitar craft and turning him into a smooth crooner specializing in covers of slick, formulaic pop-soul ballads, peaking with the Quincy Jones-produced **Give Me The Night** (1980)

White flugelhorn player Chuck Mangione specialized in orchestral ballads that mixed the most atmospheric aspects of bebop music and the most melodic aspects of pop music. The double-LP **Friends And Love** (may 1970), with the anthemic *Hill Where the Lord Hides* and the 26-minute pop-folk-jazz-classical fantasia *Friends And Love*, and **Land Of Make Believe** (1973) for jazz quartet and orchestra, with the twelve-minute *Land Of Make Believe* and *Legend of the One-Eyed Sailor*, were live concerts that spanned a vast stylistic territory. **Chase the Clouds Away** (1975) and **Bellavia** (1975), instead, pioneered the "smooth" sound of fusion of the 1980s. Mangione achieved mass-market success when he, basically, replicated the lightweight orchestral sound with a jazz quintet of flugelhorn, reeds, guitar, bass and drums on **Feels So Good** (1977). The catchy *Maui Waui* and *Theme From Side Street*, the gentle *Hide And Seek* and *Last Dance*, the epic *The Eleventh Commandment* were summarized in the *Feels So Good*, one of the biggest hits of the era.

Pop-fusion

Widely considered one of the most uninspired jazz bands of all times, Spyro Gyra was also one of the most commercially successful, particularly among the non-jazz audience. They were therefore influential in evangelizing the white pop audience. Formed in 1974 by alto saxophonist Jay Beckenstein and electric pianist Jeremy Wall, the band's two main composers, and centering around the setting of a small chamber ensemble (notably keyboardist Tom Schuman), Spyro Gyra succeeded where others had failed because they shamelessly focused on the lightweight pop, soul and jazz fusion that the jazz establishment considered debasing. Instead, their hits, such as *Shaker Song*, from **Spyro Gyra** (1976), *Morning Dance* and *Heliopolis*, from **Morning Dance** (1979), *Carnaval*, from **Carnaval** (1980), *Autumn Of Our Love* and *Catching The Sun*, from **Catching The Sun** (1980), *Freetime* and Schuman's *Pacific Sunrise*, from **Freetime** (1981), *Incognito*, *Harbor Nights* and *Old San Juan*, from **Incognito** (1982) *Shakedown* from **Alternating Currents** (1985), Schuman's *Conversations*, *Serpent In Paradise* and *Islands In The Sky*, from **City Kids** (1983), that introduced vibraphonist/marimba player Dave Samuels, emphasized dance rhythms, catchy melodies, relaxed counterpoint and slick arrangements, a format that was the epitome of yuppie intellectual torpor. By the time of the electronic **Breakout** (1986), Spyro Gyra's sound had become pure routine, that any member of the band (not only Beckenstein and Wall) could compose.

Los Angeles-based vocalist Al Jarreau started out as a promising purveyor of improvised vocals on **We Got By** (1975), around themes entirely composed by him. That art mutated into elegant pop-jazz ballads such as *Alonzo* on **This Time** (may 1980), *Roof Garden* on **Breakin' Away** (1981), but his fame came as an interpreter of faceless soul ballads, such as *Mornin'* and *Boogie Down* on **Jarreau** (1983), later penned by his producers or professional songwriters.

Yellowjackets, fronted by alto saxophonist Marc Russo and keyboardist Russell Ferrante (the band's main composer), coined a sound halfway between Weather Report's melodic atmospheres (Ferrante's Zawinul-inspired synthesizer) and the instrumental equivalent of the pop-soul ballad. Pieces such as *Daddy's Gonna Miss You*, *Homecoming* and *Samurai Samba*, from **Samurai Samba** (1984), *Claire's Song* and *Top Secret*, from **Mirage a Trois** (1983), *Sightseeing*, from **Four Corners** (1987), *Local Hero* and *Evening Dance*, from **Politics** (1988), *Geraldine* and *Storytellers* from **Spin** (1989), represented the "jazzy" version of Spyro Gyra's fusion pop.

When saxophonist Bob Mintzer replaced Russo, the band rediscovered its funk-jazz roots, stretching out in the nine-minute *Green House*, on **Green House** (1990), *My Old School*, on **Like A River** (1992), and *Wisdom*, on **Run For Your Life** (1993).

Dreamland (1995), instead, marked a return to the melodic focus (*Summer Song*, with Bobby McFerrin on vocals, and *The Chosen*). But the group had grown, both in terms of musicianship and composition, and **Blue Hats** (1997) turned ballads such as *Savanna* and *Angelina* into intricate mini-sonatas. The double-CD **Mint Jam** (2001) was the crowning achievement of this craft thanks to longer elaborations such as *Statue of Liberty* and *Motet*.

While not exactly fusion, a couple of innovative vocalists belonged to this generation and brought a lot more to the "fusion" concept, besides quite simply expanding the role of the human voice in an instrumental context.

Leon Thomas, who moved to New York in 1958, became a legend thanks to his vocal performances on Pharoah Sanders' **Karma** (1969) and **Jewels Of Thought** (1970). His intense and acrobatic vocabulary included scats, melismas, yodels, shrieks, growls, shouts. His own albums, particularly **Spirits Known and Unknown** (october 1969), featuring saxophonist Pharoah Sanders, flutist James Spaulding, pianist Lonnie Liston Smith, bassist Cecil McBee and drummer Roy Haynes, and containing his signature theme *The Creator Has A Masterplan* and the poignant hymn *Malcom's Gone* and **Album** (1970), with a revolving cast of instruments, mostly devoted to the side-long *The Journey*, artfully mixed jamming that borrowed from blues, soul-jazz and free-jazz with overtones derived from Eastern spirituality and agit-prop politics.

Gil Scott-Heron, a Chicago poet and novelist turned musician, predated rap music with his spoken-word pieces. Accompanied by keyboardist and flutist Brian Jackson, Scott-Heron made an album of his poems, **Small Talk At 125th & Lenox Ave** (1970), which included *The Revolution Will Not Be Televised* and *Whitey On The Moon*. The duo's Miles Davis-inspired fusion of jazz, funk and rock, and Scott-Heron's agit-prop lyrics reached maturity on **Pieces Of A Man** (april 1971), that included *Lady Day And John Coltrane* and *Home Is Where The Hatred Is*. **Winter In America** (october 1973) was his most "musical" statement.

EURO-FUSION

Britain was the first country to adopt the new language of fusion jazz and, in fact, to merge it with the contemporary languages of progressive-rock and of the classical avantgarde. In fact, this was the first time in history that British jazz did not trail USA jazz but almost predated it. The fact was not surprising because British jazz musicians shared the same stages (and therefore the same groups) with blues musicians. During the boom era of the "swinging London" this movement found an audience that was eager for something more exciting than pop singers. Alexis Korner organized his Blues Incorporated in 1962, hiring musicians that played more than just rhythm'n'blues: he combined a solid rhythm section (Jack Bruce, Charlie Watts, Ginger Baker) with a jazzy horn section (Graham Bond, Dick Heckstall-Smith) and fronted them with blues singers (mainly Cyril Davies but also Mick Jagger). Graham Bond did something similar with his Organization, that came to include John McLaughlin, Bruce and Baker. Jagger and Watts went on to form the Rolling Stones, Bruce and Baker formed Cream (fall of 1966). Cream introduced jazz improvisation into blues-rock music, simply fulfilling Korner's vision. Heckstall-Smith formed Colosseum (summer of 1968), that, since it featured a horn, became one of the earliest jazz-rock outfits. Soft Machine (formed in 1966) were even more important because their starting point was psychedelia, the vogue of 1966 in rock music. Soft Machine moved towards jazz improvisation because it made sense for a psychedelic group that aimed at crafting extended pieces that relied more on the instrumental backing than on the catchy melody.

Neil Ardley was probably the British composer/arranger who was closer to the tradition of Duke Ellington and Gil Evans. His New Jazz Orchestra, that had debuted in 1965, recorded his first compositions on **Le Dejeuner Sur L'Herbe** (september 1968), boasting four trumpets (including Ian Carr), four trombones (including Zimbabwe expatriate Michael Gibbs), four reeds (including Dick Heckstall-Smith), tuba, vibraphone, bass (Jack Bruce) and drums (Jon Hiseman). Ardley's main legacy was the great "chromatic" trilogy of **The Greek Variations** (october 1969) for a nine-piece jazz ensemble plus string quintet (including Carr, Gibbs, Bruce, drummer John Marshall, oboe and English horn player Karl Jenkins), the four movement *A Symphony of Amaranths* for a large orchestra and jazz quartet (Dick Heckstall-Smith on woodwinds, Karl Jenkins on electric piano, Ardley himself on prepared piano, plus piano, harp, celeste, viola, cellos, violins, vibraphone, harpsichord, oboe, bassoon, glockenspiel, trumpets, trombones, saxes, tuba, bass, drums), his most spectacular experiment with mixing composition and improvisation, contained in **A Symphony of Amaranths** (june 1971), and **Kaleidoscope of Rainbows** (march 1976), based on Balinese scales and scored for a smaller ensemble (including Ian Carr on trumpet, Tony Coe on sax, Paul Buckmaster on cello, Dave McRae on electric piano). Ardley mixed acoustic and electronic instruments (besides voices) on **Harmony of the Spheres** (september 1978), featuring John Martyn on guitar, Ardley on synthesizer and a jazz septet (including Tony Coe and Ian Carr). This experiment led to the "live electronic jazz orchestra" of **Virtual Realities** (july 1991), actually a quartet with Ardley and John Walters on electronic keyboards, Carr on trumpet and a guitarist.

Mike Westbrook was perhaps the most influential of the band leaders of British jazz fusion. His Concert Band originally featured Westbrook on piano, John Surman on baritone saxophone, soprano saxophone and bass clarinet two altoists, one tenorist, French Horn, trombone, valve trombone, trumpet, tuba, bass, drums, and debuted with **Celebration** (august 1967), co-composed by Mike Westbrook and John Surman. After the inferior **Release** (august 1968), a larger band (still featuring Surman) performed the pacifist concept of the double-LP **Marching Song** (april 1969), entirely composed by Westbrook and inspired by Charlie Haden's Liberation Music Orchestra. A smaller band with Chris Spedding on guitar and Paul Rutherford on trombone, besides Surman, recorded **Love Songs** (april 1970). The zenith of Westbrook's dense and smooth arrangements was the nine-movement symphony **Metropolis** (august 1971), recorded by a 24-piece band (without Surman but with trumpeter Kenny Wheeler), followed by the eleven-part suite **Citadel/ Room 315** (march 1975), with Surman back in the ranks. An 18-piece orchestra (including Rutherford, pianist Dave McRae, guitarist Brian Godding) was employed for **Love/Dream and Variations** (february 1976). Later, Westbrook seemed to abandon his ambitious fusion-jazz aesthetic and turned to the more popular formats heralded by **Mama Chicago** (june 1979), a "jazz cabaret" originally scored in 1976 for a musical about mafia boss Al Capone, and **The Cortege** (composed in 1979) for voices and 16-piece jazz orchestra.

Zimbabwe-born Mike Gibbs scored his albums for orchestras that helped several British talents mature: **Michael Gibbs** (december 1969) for seven reeds (including John Surman and Alan Skidmore), six trumpets (including Kenny Wheeler), four French horns, seven trombones, tuba, cello, piano, celeste, guitar (Chris Spedding), bass (Jack Bruce), drums (John Marshall and Tony Oxley), with *Family Joy Oh Boy*; **Tanglewood '63** (december 1970), for a very similar line-up (the notable addition being Roy Babbington on bass) with the 13-minute *Canticle*, **Just Ahead** (may 1972), for a smaller ensemble (that still included Wheeler, Skidmore, Marshall, Babbington and Spedding); **In The Public Interest** (june 1973) for another large band that included several USA musicians (vibraphonist Gary Burton, trumpeter Randy Brecker, saxophonist Michael Brecker, bassist Steve Swallow); **Seven Songs For Quartet and Chamber Orchestra** (december 1973), credited to Gary Burton; and his masterpiece, **Only Chrome Waterfall** (1974), for another large orchestra that included saxophonist Charlie Mariano, Belgian guitarist Philip Catherine, Mike Gibbs on keyboards, Tony Coe on reeds, besides Skidmore, Wheeler, Swallow, and many others.

Canada-born trumpeter Kenny Wheeler moved to London in 1952 and joined John Dankworth's Boporchestra in 1959. His first major composition was **Windmill Tilter** (march 1968), a concept album on Cervantes' "Don Quixote" performed by Dankworth's big band. Wheeler simultaneously played jazz-rock in

Mike Gibbs' orchestra (1969-75) as well as free jazz in John Stevens' Spontaneous Music Ensemble (1966-70), Tony Oxley's group (1969-72), Alexander von Schlippenback's Globe Unity Orchestra (1970) and Anthony Braxton's group (1971-76). Wheeler's own **Song For Someone** (january 1973) was an odd combination of Wheeler's split personas: a set of jazz songs featuring vocalist Norma Winstone and two lengthy free-jazz jams with saxophonist Evan Parker, *Causes Are Events* and *The Good Doctor*. The imbalance was healed on **Gnu High** (june 1975), particularly the 21-minute suite *Heyoke*, one of his artistic peaks, angelically performed by a quartet with Keith Jarrett on piano, Dave Holland on bass and Jack DeJohnette on drums. Wheeler had coined his own personal version of elegant fusion jazz that acquired an almost mystical quality on **Deer Wan** (july 1977), featuring saxophonist Jan Garbarek, guitarists John Abercrombie and guitarist Ralph Towner, Holland and DeJohnette (*Peace for Five, Sumother Song, Deer Wan*). The sextet of **Around 6** (august 1979), featuring Parker, trombonist Eje Thelin and vibraphonist Tom VanDerGeld, was more experimental (*Mai We Go Around, Follow Down*), but **Double Double You** (may 1983), featuring saxophonist Michael Brecker, pianist John Taylor, Holland and DeJohnette, returned to his lyrical suite format (the 23-minute *Three for d'Reen/ Blue for Lou/ Mark Time*, the 14-minute *Foxy Trot*). In 1982 Wheeler joined Holland's quintet and neglected his own compositions and arrangements. At last, the quintet session of **Flutter By Butterfly** (may 1987) resurrected his lyrical extended ballads (*Everybody's Song But My Own, Flutter By Butterfly*). A quintet with Abercrombie, Taylor, Holland and drummer Peter Erskine crafted the six melodic abstractions of **Widow in the Window** (february 1990), particularly *Ana*. But the real highlights of this season were the seven-movement *Sweet Time Suite*, off **Music for Large and Small Ensemble** (february 1990), **Kayak** (may 1992), featuring a ten-piece orchestra, and the 20-minute *Little Suite*, off **Siren's Song** (october 1996), two larger works that displayed Wheeler's skills at the border between neoclassical and free-jazz music.

British saxophonist John Surman, the baritonist of Mike Westbrook's orchestra, coined an elegant form of chamber fusion on **John Surman** (august 1968), particularly in the 21-minute suite *Incantation/ Episode/ Dance* for an eleven-piece ensemble (including trumpeter Kenny Wheeler, trombonist Paul Rutherford, bassist Dave Holland), **How Many Clouds Can You See** (march 1969), with the 15-minute *Galata Bridge* for an octet (Surman on baritone saxophone, plus alto, Alan Skidmore's tenor, trumpet, trombone, piano, bass, drums) and the 18-minute *Event* for a quartet with pianist John Taylor, bassist Barre Phillips and drummer Tony Oxley (and Surman on baritone sax, soprano sax and bass clarinet), and **Way Back When** (october 1969), released only 26 years later, containing the 21-minute four-movement suite *Way Back When* for a piano-based quartet. Surman then lost a bit of his inspiration. He formed **The Trio** (march 1970) with bassist Barre Phillips and drummer Stu Martin, a format repeated on **Conflagration** (1970), collaborated with guitarist John McLaughlin on **Where Fortune Smiles** (may 1970), that contains his *Glancing Backwards*, and with Canadian reeds player John Warren (who composed the music) on the

horns-heavy **Tales of the Algonquin** (april 1971), that mimicked the band-oriented albums of Neil Ardley, Mike Westbrook and Mike Gibbs.
Finally he reinvented himself as an electronic musician on **Westering Home** (september 1972), entirely composed, played and overdubbed by himself on baritone and soprano saxophones, bass clarinet, recorder, piano, synthesizer, percussion.
Surman played soprano saxophone and bass clarinet on **Morning Glory** (march 1973) with guitarist Terje Rypdal, pianist John Taylor, drummer John Marshall, bassist Chris Laurence and trombone. *Cloudless Sky/ Iron Man* was the first piece in years to match the graceful intensity of his early albums. Electronics was also employed for the all-saxophone project **S.O.S.** (february 1975) with altoist Mike Osborne and tenorist Alan Skidmore, as well as for the duets with keyboardist Stan Tracey, **Sonatinas** (april 1978) and for Surman's second solo album, **Upon Reflection** (march 1979), that embraced the ruling aesthetic of ambient jazz, and the first collaboration with Jack DeJohnette, **The Amazing Adventures Of Simon Simon** (january 1981).
After repeating the same idea on **Such Winters Of Memory** (december 1982), with Norwegian vocalist Karin Krog and drummer Pierre Favre, and especially on the new solos **Withholding Pattern** (december 1984), **Private City** (december 1987), originally a ballet score and his best-selling album, and **The Road to St Ives** (april 1990), with an increasingly impressionistic approach, Surman finally began to experiment new avenues on **Adventure Playground** (september 1991) and **In The Evenings Out There** (september 1991), two albums derived from a quartet session with pianist Paul Bley, bassist Gary Peacock and drummer Tony Oxley, and on **The Brass Project** (april 1992), another collaboration with John Warren.
Surman fundamentally continued to sculpt ethereal, atmospheric jazz muzak based on a superficial blend of folk, jazz and classical elements. **Stranger Than Fiction** (december 1993) inaugurated the quartet with pianist John Taylor, bassist Chris Laurence and drummer John Marshall, paralleled by the drum-less **Nordic Quartet** (august 1994) with vocalist Karin Krog, guitarist Terje Rypdal, and pianist Vigleik Storaas. The new solo, **A Biography of the Reverend Absalom Dawe** (october 1994), showed Surman at his most conservative, but he was also venturing into choral music, on **Proverbs and Songs** (june 1996) for saxophone, pipe organ and an 80-voice chorus, world music, on **Thimar** (march 1997) for a trio with Tunisian oud-player Anouar Brahem and bassist Dave Holland, and chamber music, on **Coruscating** (january 1999) for saxophone/clarinet and string quintet.

A former member of Chris MacGregor's Blue Notes (where he met drummer Louis Moholo, cornetist Mongezi Feza and saxophonist Dudu Pukwana), British pianist Keith Tippett formed his first combo in 1967. By the time Miles Davis revolutionized jazz-rock, Tippett had assembled an impressive group of talents, including Elton Dean (alto sax), Mark Charig (trumpet), Nick Evans (trombone), Roy Babbington (bass), John Marshall (drums). Their albums **You Are Here I Am There** (september 1969), containing the 14-minute *I Wish There Was A*

Nowhere, and **Dedicated To You But You Weren't Listening** (september 1970) came out at the same time that Nucleus and Soft Machine were moving towards jazz-rock. The three families of musicians began an incestuous relationship that would last many years. Tippett's Centipede, a 50-piece orchestra with players drawn from the jazz, rock, folk and classical worlds (drummer Robert Wyatt, guitarist Brian Godding, trombonist Paul Rutherford, oboe player Karl Jenkins, tenorist Brian Smith, tenorist Gary Windo, tenorist Alan Skidmore, trumpeter Ian Carr, vocalists Julie Driscoll, Zoot Money and Maggie Nicols and a string section, in addition to his cohorts Dean, Marshall, Charig, Evans and Babbington and to old friends Pukwana and Feza) recorded the monolithic four-movement suite **Septober Energy** (june 1971), the ultimate testament of British jazz-rock (over 80-minute long). After **Ovary Lodge** (december 1972), a trio with Babbington and percussionist Frank Perry, Tippett tried to repeat the exploit of Centipede with Ark, a 22-piece orchestra that recorded the four-movement suite **Frames** (may 1978), and with the septet (Dean, Charig, Nick Evans, saxophonist Larry Stabbins, bassist Paul Rogers, drummer Tony Levin) of the four-movement suite **A Loose Kite In A Gentle Wind Floating With Only My Will For An Anchor** (october 1984). Tippett's technique of "spontaneous composition" was tested with Mujician, a quartet featuring Paul Dunmall (reeds), Rogers and Levin, in the hour-long meditation of **The Journey** (june 1990), reminiscent of Arnold Schoenberg and George Gershwin as well as of cool jazz and free jazz, and in the much more disjointed and dissonant 71-minute "five-verse" **Poem About The Hero** (february 1994). Mujician's most uncompromising statement, the four-movement **Colours Fulfilled** (may 1997), was a massive, hysterical free-jazz mayhem. By the time of the 45-minute **There's No Going Back Now** (june 2005), Mujician had refined an art of merging hyper-free music of discrete, dissonant, glitchy soundsculpting and festive albeit chaotic group fanfares.

 Nucleus, featuring Ian Carr on trumpet and flugelhorn (a veteran of the British bebop scene), Brian Smith on saxophone and flute, Chris Spedding on guitar and bouzouki, Jeff Clyne on bass and two members of Graham Collier's ensemble, namely Karl Jenkins on oboe and piano and John Marshall on drums, proved on **Elastic Rock** (january 1970) that Britain had state-of-the-art jazz-rock players. **We'll Talk About It Later** (september 1970) refined Carr's aesthetics to an almost baroque degree and at an almost rocking pace. Nucleus' evolutionary process led to the "orchestral" sound of **Solar Plexus** (december 1970), augmented with a three-piece horn section led by trumpeter Kenny Wheeler and the synthesizer, the 21-minute suite *Torso / Snakehips' Dream* representing a new peak for their fluid style of improvisation. A new line-up with virtuoso rock guitarist Allan Holdsworth, keyboardist Dave MacRae, pianist Gordon Beck, bassist Roy Babbington, continued Ian Carr's elegant, orchestral, baroque trip, while furthering his exploration of timbres and tempos, on **Belladonna** (july 1972). Carr's status as a conductor, composer and arranger of large ensembles kept increasing via albums such as **Labyrinth** (march 1973).

 British alto saxophonist Elton Dean, hired by pianist Keith Tippett in 1968 and by Soft Machine the following year, revealed a warm soul that could be both poetic and scientific on **Elton Dean** (may 1971), in a quartet with Mark Charig on cornet, containing *Banking On Bishopsgate* (a 20-minute fit of post-cool neurosis). His Ninesense with Alan Skidmore (saxophone), Tippett, two trumpets and two trombones offered a modern interpretation of the "big band" concept in the four jams of **Happy Daze** (july 1977). The quintet with Charig and Tippett of **Boundaries** (february 1980) and the quintet with pianist Sophia Domancich and three members of Tippett's Mujician (trumpeter Paul Dunmall, bassist Paul Rogers and drummer Tony Levin) of **Silent Knowledge** (june 1995), containing the 28-minute *Gualchos* (perhaps his artistic peak), sounded like a smaller-scale version of Ninesense, and led to Ninesense's successor band, **Newsense** (november 1997), featuring three trombones (Paul Rutherford, Roswell Rudd, Annie Whitehead), trumpet, piano and a cello-driven rhythm section.

If Britain was looking for a national language, Germany was the country that found one and that turned it into a universal language. In 1969 Manfred Eicher founded the ECM label in Germany that eventually coined a smooth, elegant, slick jazz sound, usually in chamber-like settings (solo or small ensemble). That sound was largely "invented" by Jan Garbarek, with **Dansere** (1975), and found a fertile milieu in Scandinavia.

Norwegian saxophonist Jan Garbarek established his credentials by playing on George Russell's **Electronic Sonata For Souls Loved By Nature** (1969) and **Listen to the Silence** (1971), as well as in Keith Jarrett's "European Quartet" (1974-79).
He was a member of Esoteric Circle, a quartet with guitarist Terje Rypdal, bassist Arild Anderson and drummer Jon Christensen that played a unique hybrid of jazz-rock, free jazz and progressive-rock on **Esoteric Circle** (october 1969), particularly the longer *Rabalder*, *SAS 644* and *Karin's Mode*, on **Afric Pepperbird** (september 1970), with the twelve-minute *Beast of Kommodo*, *Blow Away Zone* and the catchy *Afric Pepperbird*, and on **Sart** (april 1971), that added pianist Bobo Stenson to the quartet and contained the 14-minute *Sart*, *Song of Space* and *Irr*. The ambience of these recordings was permeated by the zen-like quality of his long tones and pauses and by the folk-like quality of his melodies. A trio with Anderson and Finnish percussionist Martii-Juhani "Edward" Vesala yielded the darker and more strident **Triptykon** (november 1972). After a collection of covers, **Witchi-Tai-To** (november 1973), notable only for a 20-minute version of Don Cherry's *Desireless* (Cherry's original was only one-minute long), and collaborations with Art Lande and Keith Jarrett, Garbarek entered a new phase of his career. Leaving behind both the rock and the free excesses of his classics, Garbarek employed a new quartet with Stenson, Christensen and bassist Palle Danielsson for **Dansere** (november 1975), a far less experimental and much more baroque work that defined the soothing "ECM sound" (particularly the 16-minute *Dansere*). The new format led to the drumless **Dis** (december 1976), ostensibly a sax-guitar duo (Garbarek on tenor, soprano and wood flute, Ralph Towner on 12-string and classical guitars), whose *Vandrere* (with windharp), *Skygger* (with brass) and *Dis* (with windharp) basically transposed Brian Eno's ambient music into jazz music, one of the most

influential ideas in the history of post-bop jazz. That idea got a bit out of control on the four lengthy tracks of **Places** (december 1977), including *Reflections, Going Places* and *Passing*, performed by a quartet with Garbarek on tenor, soprano and alto, guitarist Bill Connors, John Taylor on organ and piano, and drummer Jack DeJohnette, and on **Photo With Blue Sky, White Cloud, Wires, Windows and a Red Roof** (december 1978), featuring a quintet with Connors, Taylor, bassist Eberhard Weber and Christensen and containing *White Cloud, The Picture, Red Roof*.

Garbarek then embarked in an idiosyncratic exploration of world-music via **Folk Songs** (november 1979) and **Magico** (june 1979), two collaborations with bassist Charlie Haden and Brazilian guitarist Egberto Gismonti, **Aftenland** (december 1979), a (more adventurous) collaboration with Pipe organist Kjell Johnsen, **Eventyr** (december 1980), a collaboration with guitarist John Abercrombie and Brazilian percussionist Nana Vasconcelos devoted to Scandinavian melodies, Afro-Latin rhythms and Far-Eastern atmospheres (*Soria Maria, Eventyr, Once Upon a Time, East of the Sun*).

Garbarek returned to his ethereal brand of "ambient jazz" with **Paths Prints** (december 1981), featuring Garbarek on tenor and soprano, Bill Frisell on guitar, Weber and Christensen. *Footprints* represented the state of the art in coloring and breathing life into fragile melodies. The collaboration with Frisell and Weber continued on **Wayfarer** (march 1983), that contains *Pendulum*, whereas **It's OK To Listen To The Gray Voice** (december 1984), containing *White Noise of Forgetfulness*, replaced Frisell with the more robust guitar of David Torn and closed the guitar trilogy.

Norwegian guitarist <u>Terje Rypdal</u>, raised at the intersection of classical and rock music, converted to jazz as a member of Jan Garbarek's Esoteric Circle (1969). His first album as a leader, **Terje Rypdal** (august 1971), was orchestrated for oboe, English horn, flute, clarinet, tenor saxophone (Jan Garbarek), electric piano (Bobo Stenson or Tom Halversen), bass (Arild Andersen) and percussion (Jon Christensen), and sounded like a cross of Weather Report's jazz-rock, Soft Machine's progressive-rock and Pink Floyd's psychedelic-rock (*Keep It Like That Tight* and especially *Electric Fantasy*), and it already signaled a significant departure from the prevailing (much more aggressive) style of guitar-based fusion jazz. The same gentle tone permeated *Bend It* and especially *What Comes After* on **What Comes After** (august 1973), recorded by a smaller ensemble (that retained oboe and English horn, but neither the horns nor the piano). Instead **Whenever I Seem To Be Far Away** (1974) explored the other end of the spectrum: the 14-minute *Silver Bird Is Heading For The Sun* was a majestic piece of progressive-rock with mellotron and French horn, while the 18-minute *Whenever I Seem To Be Far Away* for electric guitar, strings, oboe and clarinet was an ambitious neoclassical suite. The double-LP **Odyssey** (august 1975), recorded by an ensemble with soprano saxophone, trombone, organ, strings, bass and drums, was the crowning achievement of the early phase of his career, representing all the poles of his art, from vibrant jazz-rock (the 26-minute *Rolling Stone*) to neoclassical ambience (*Adagio*), from progressive-rock (*Midnite*) to atmospheric jazz (*Farewell*). Rypdal played all the instruments (electric and acoustic guitars, string ensemble, piano, electric piano, soprano saxophone, flute, tubular bells, bells) on **After the Rain** (august 1976) and downgraded his ambitions to the humbler format of impressionistic vignettes such as *Autumn Breeze* and *After The Rain*. Continuining in his stylistic zigzag, Rypdal turned to a more traditional format for **Waves** (september 1977), recorded by a quartet with trumpeter Palle Mikkelborg and containing the effervescent, polyrhythmic *Per Ulv*. Yet another departure came with **Descendre** (march 1979) that featured a trio of guitar, trumpet and drums crafting emotional multi-faceted atmospheres that represented Rypdal's sonic peak (*Circles, Innseiling, Men of Mystery*).

Two collaborations with bassist Miroslav Vitous and drummer DeJohnette, namely **Rypdal/ Vitous/ DeJohnette** (june 1978) and **To Be Continued** (january 1981), failed to sustain the interest, but one with cellist David Darling, the electronic **Eos** (may 1983), boasted pieces such as *Eos* and *Mirage* that ranked among his most futuristic endeavors.

After indulging in conventional jazz-rock and fronting a guitar-bass-drums power-trio on **The Chasers** (may 1985), with *Ambiguity*, **Blue** (november 1986) and **The Singles Collection** (august 1988), Rypdal rediscovered his classical soul and focused on larger-scale compositions: *Undisonus* (1990) for violin and orchestra, *Ineo* (1990) for choir and chamber orchestra, the five-movement **Q.E.D.** (december 1991) for electric guitar, string ensemble, and woodwinds, the sinfonietta *Out Of This World*, off **Skywards** (february 1996), *Double Concerto* (1998) for two electric guitars and orchestra, *5th Symphony* (1998), the five-movement **Lux Aeterna** (july 2000) for chamber ensemble.

Danish bassist <u>Niels-Henning Orsted-Pedersen</u> was not only a virtuoso but proved at least once that he could also be an accomplished composer: on **Dancing On The Tables** (august 1979), in a quartet with saxophonist Dave Liebman, guitarist John Scofield and drummer Billy Hart, and containing the 15-minute *Dancing On The Tables*.

German pianist <u>Wolfgang Dauner</u> was a reluctant pioneer of free improvisation on **Dream Talk** (september 1964) by a trio with Eberhard Weber on bass and **Free Action** (1967) by a quintet with French violinist JeanLuc Ponty, percussionist Mani Neumeier, Weber and tenorist Gerd Dudek. **Fuer** (april 1969), by a quartet featuring Eberhard Weber mainly on cello, and **The Oimels** (july 1969) instead embraced the hippy age with an acid-soul-jazz sound replete with fuzz guitars and sitar. So inconsistent as creative, Dauner flirted with choral music in *Psalmus Spei*, off Fred van Hove's **Requiem For Che Guevara** (november 1968), fusion on **Rischka's Soul** (november 1969), with swing on **Music Zounds** (february 1970) and with electronics on **Output** (october 1970), mostly for trios with Weber. **Dauner-eschingen** (october 1970) repeated the experiment with the choir. Dauner even formed the jazz-rock group Et Cetera, that released **Et Cetera** (1971), **Knirsch** (march 1972), featuring guitarist Larry Coryell and Colosseum's drummer Jon Hiseman, and **Live** (1973). And even more ambitious was the United Jazz and Rock Ensemble, that Dauner formed in

1975 by gathering progressive jazz and rock musicians such as guitarist Volker Kriegel, trumpeter Ack Van Rooyen, trombonist Albert Mangelsdorff, saxophonist Charlie Mariano, flutist Barbara Thompson, Nucleus' trumpeter Ian Carr, bassist Eberhard Weber, and Colosseum's drummer Jon Hiseman. Their albums, starting with **Live im Schutzenhaus** (1977) and peaking with **The Break Even Point** (1979), that featured trumpeter Kenny Wheeler, ranked among the bestsellers of German jazz.

He also co-founded the ensemble **Free Sound And Super Brass** (october 1975). In the meantime, Dauner had released his first solo album, **Changes** (september 1978), followed by **Piano Solo** (1983) and **Zeitlaufe/ Kalender Suite** (1988).

German bassist Eberhard Weber, Wolfgang Dauner's trusted partner for many years, never quite sounded like a jazz musician, his lyrical and oneiric tones being more reminiscent of classical chamber music and minimalist avantgarde music than of the jazz tradition. The 19-minute *No Motion Picture* was the centerpiece of **The Colours of Chloe** (december 1973), virtually a trio with a keyboardist (Rainer Brueninghaus) and a drummer (Weber played bass, cello and ocarina), the album that coined his "orchestral" style, simultaneously abstract and sentimental.

Yellow Fields (september 1975), featuring soprano saxophonist Charlie Mariano, Brueninghaus and drummer Jon Christensen, was a uniform sea of languid tones, with three main pieces (the 15-minute *Sand-Glass*, the ten-minute *Yellow Fields*, the 13-minute *Left Lane*) straddling the line between melody and hypnosis.

Continuing this trend towards ethereal atmospheres, **The Following Morning** (august 1976) gave up the drums and retained only Brueninghaus' keyboards while adding western classical instruments (*T. On A White Horse*, *Moana I*, *The Following Morning*).

Colours, the quartet formed with Mariano, Brueninghaus and drummer John Marshall, recorded **Silent Feet** (november 1977), whose 17-minute *Seriously Deep*, had a jazzier feeling, and **Little Movements** (july 1980), with *A Dark Spell*.

Other highlights of Weber's career were: the graceful 17-minute *Quiet Departures*, off **Fluid Rustle** (january 1979), that featured guitarist Bill Frisell and vibraphonist Gary Burton and two vocalists; the lively 16-minute *Death In The Carwash*, off **Later That Evening** (march 1982), with Frisell, pianist Lyle Mays, drummer Michael DiPasqua and Paul McCandless on soprano saxophone, oboe, English horn and bass clarinet; the seven-movement **Chorus** (september 1984), with saxophonist Jan Garbarek, classical instruments and Weber on synthesizer; the almost baroque *Seven Movements* for chamber ensemble (two flugelhorns, three trombones, two French horns, tuba, bass), off **Orchestra** (august 1988); the solo-bass *Pendulum*, off **Pendulum** (1993). Weber's focus was "sound" per se, with little or no interest for musical genres and traditions.

East German pianist Joachim Kuehn, a classical musician by training, shifted to hard-bop in 1961, possibly under the influence of his brother, clarinetist Rolf Kuehn. After defecting to West Germany in 1966, the brothers formed a free-jazz quartet. Relocating to France in 1968, Joachim Kuehn joined JeanLuc Ponty for his album **Experience** (1969) and stayed with him till 1972. His musical emancipation began with the seven **Solos** (march 1971) and the jazz-rock quartet of **Cinemascope** (1973). After moving to California, Kuehn adopted a more atmospheric fusion style that led to **Hip Elegy** (november 1975), featuring Japanese trumpeter Terumasa Hino, American drummer Alphonse Mouzon, bassist John Lee, Brazilian percussionist Nana Vasconcelos and Belgian guitarist Philip Catherine, and containing his *Hip Elegy In Kingsize*, and to **Springfever** (april 1976), that pared down the group to a quartet with Catherine and contained the ten-minute *Lady Amber*. **Night Time In New York** (april 1981), featuring tenor saxophonists Michael Brecker and Bob Mintzer, bassist Eddie Gomez and drummer Billy Hart, achieved perhaps the most sophisticated sound (*Yvonne Takes A Bath*, *April In New York*, *Nightline*). These were pieces that straddled the border between progressive-rock and jazz-rock. Other highlights of this period were the nine-minute *Horror Dream*, off **Don't Split** (june 1982), a collaboration with Rolf Kuehn, and the ten-minute *Heavy Birthday*, off **I'm Not Dreaming** (march 1983), a chamber experiment with cellist Ottomar Borwitzky, trombonist George Lewis, percussionist Mark Nauseef and marimba player Herbert Foersch. Back in Germany, Kuehn rediscovered his classical upbringing and turned to the grand piano and composed some austere pieces for solo piano such as the eleven-minute *Norddeutschland* on **Distance** (may 1984), the 18-minute *Italienische Sonate* and the ten-minute *Wandlungen* on **Wandlungen/ Transformations** (may 1986), and the 15-minute *Bank Of Memory* on **Dynamics** (june 1990), besides the ballet music of **Quintus - Dark** (1988) in collaboration with Walter Quintus. At the same time he also led a conventional be-bop trio that also flirted with free-jazz on **Easy To Read** (june 1985), with *Details*, **From Time To Time Free** (april 1988), with *Trio Music*, and especially **Carambolage** (september 1991), containing the 20-minute *Carambolage*. But Kuehm never quite seemed to fall in love with jazz, and eventually returned to classical music again.

Italian trumpeter Enrico Rava, who moved to New York in 1967, was influenced by Miles Davis' haunting ambience which he augmented with soulful interplay and smooth dynamics on the albums for quartets with guitar, bass and drums: **Il Giro Del Giorno in 80 Mondi** (february 1972), **The Pilgrim and the Stars** (june 1975) and **The Plot** (august 1976), the last two with John Abercrombie on guitar. **Quartet** (march 1978), featuring trombonist Roswell Rudd and containing Rava's 15-minute suite *Tramps*, was perhaps his most conceptual work.

Polish violinist Michael Urbaniak moved to the USA in 1973 and formed Fusion in concert with his wife, vocalist Urszula Dudziak, two keyboardist and a drummer, a group largely inspired by JeanLuc Ponty and progressive-rock (notably Frank Zappa) when they debuted on **Fusion** (june 1973). By **Fusion III** (february 1975) the sound had become even more electronic and included guitars. However, the highlight remained Dudziak's mesmerizing vocals.

Russian pianist Sergey Kuryokhin offered a dadaistic, hysterical and acrobatic fusion of avantgarde classical, jazz and rock music with his satirical multimedia events of "pop mechanics" and on solo-piano albums such as **The Ways of**

Freedom (april 1981) **Some Combinations Of Fingers And Passion** (june 1991). His Pop Mekhanika Orchestra pioneered a cultural fusion of the arts ("total performance").

JAZZ TRADITIONALISM

The sudden boom of "neo-traditionalists" (jazz musicians who basically staged a revival of traditional jazz) marked the peak of a crisis that had started when rock music was invented. Jazz had made sense not so much as the music of black USA citizens but as the popular alternative to classical music. Rock displaced its ideological position in the firmament of the arts. Then jazz began a convoluted journey towards (free jazz) and against (fusion jazz) the classical avantgarde. What free jazz and fusion jazz had in common was that they were both movements away from... jazz music. That crisis was never resolved and continued to weaken the case for jazz music during the 1980s, particularly at a time when so many white musicians were entering the fray of jazz music (often selling more records than black musicians). At the end of the 1970s it almost felt like "jazz" was merely a word for "instrumental music" as opposed to rock music that was mostly vocal. The music itself was not all that different from progressive-rock, and, in general, less adventurous. The jazz world was living in denial. The neo-traditionalists called the bluff. Instead of trying to move away from the jazz tradition, they staged a massive and shameless revival of it.

The neo-traditionalists changed the debate. Instead of a debate between avantgarde (free jazz) and commercial music (fusion), it became a debate between the revival of jazz values (neo-traditionalists) and the continuing progress towards non-jazz values (both free jazz and fusion and later acid-jazz, jazztronica, etc). While rock music was undergoing a stylistic meltdown and fragmentation that virtually created a waterfall of new musical genres, from heavy metal to punk-rock to drone-rock (plus all the variations on dance-music), jazz music seemed to converge towards just two opposite camps, a yin and yang of sorts.

The revival of traditional jazz started in earnest when white tenor saxophonist Scott Hamilton burst onto the scene with **A Is a Good Wind Who Is Blowing Us No Ill** (march 1977), a mediocre collection of covers. But that was the beginning of the avalanche.

Philadelphia-born pianist Kenny Barron featured prominently in the groups of Dizzy Gillespie (1962-66), Freddie Hubbard (1966-70), Yusef Lateef (1970-75), Ron Carter (1976-80) and Stan Gets (1984-91) before launching a career as an elegant evangelist of hard-bop music for the Wynton Marsalis generation. His style was a sprightly cocktail of Art Tatum, Thelonious Monk, McCoy Tyner and Herbie Hancock, using piano, electric piano, clavinet and synthesizer. However, his real strength came from his compositional skills, as proven by: the nine-minute *Sunset* on **Sunset to Dawn** (april 1973), the ten-minute *Peruvian Blue* and the ten-minute *Two Areas* on **Peruvian Blue** (march 1974), the nine-minute *Spirits* and the 13-minute *Hellbound* on **Lucifer** (april 1975), the 12-minute *Sunshower* (already debuted in 1975) and the ten-minute *Innocence* on **Innocence** (1978), *Row House* and *Dew Drop* on **Golden Lotus** (april 1980). In the 1980s Barron began to play more and more standards and notable originals became rarer: the solo-piano *Enchanted Flower* on **At the Piano** (february 1981), the twelve-minute *And Then Again* on **Imo Live** (june 1982), that debuted the trio with bassist Buster Williams and drummer Ben Riley, the eleven-minute *Spiral* on **Spiral** (june 1982), *Lemuria* on **Autumn in New York** (december 1984), the ten-minute *Water Lily* on **Scratch** (march 1985), in a trio with Dave Holland on bass, *Phantoms* on **What If** (february 1986), in a quintet with trumpet and tenor saxophone. The music was not revolutionary but the repertory was impressive. At the same time, Barron formed Sphere, i.e. Barron's trio plus tenor saxophonist Charlie Rouse, that, after a Thelonious Monk tribute album, and a mediocre **Flight Path** (january 1983), gave him the opportunity to write *Baiana* and *Lunacy* for **Four For All** (march 1987). Barron, now a star, was devoting himself to terrifyingly tedious collections of standards and old originals, notably wasting a trio with bassist Charlie Haden and drummer Roy Haynes for the awkward selections of **Wanton Spirit** (february 1994). Only a few compositions displayed the old touch: the bossanova *The Moment* and the romantic *Tear Drop* on **The Moment** (august 1991), *Gardenia* on **Sambao** (may 1992), *Mythology* and *Nikara's Song* on **Other Places** (february 1993). Then Barron staged the spectacular rebirth of **Things Unseen** (march 1995), featuring an unusually large ensemble (for someone who always preferred the trio format) of tenorist John Stubblefield, trumpeter Eddie Henderson, guitarist John Scofield, violin, bass, drums and percussion. It contained several lengthy originals that displayed his old magic: the 13-minute *Marie Laveau*, the nine-minute *The Sequel, Rose Noire, Things Unseen, Joy Island*. Then the consummate pianist started delivering again his melodic, swinging and occasionally adventurous compositions: *Twilight Song* on **Night And The City** (september 1996), a duet with Charlie Haden, *The Wizard* on **Spirit Song** (may 1999), *Zumbi* and *Clouds* on **Canta Brasil** (february 2002), with a Brazilian rhythm section, and (possibly his swan song) the 18-minute *Images* on **Images** (october 2003), in a quintet with saxophonist/flutist Anne Drummond, vibraphonist Stefon Harris, bassist Kiyoshi Kitagawa and drummer Kim Thompson.

Los Angeles' white pianist <u>Joanne Brackeen</u> who moved to New York in 1965 and played in Art Blakey's Jazz Messengers (1969-72). She debuted as a leader at 36 with **Snooze** (march 1975), reissued as **Six Ate**, in a trio with bassist Cecil McBee and drummer Billy Hart. A similar trio cut **Invitation** (july 1976), a better display of her lengthy, erudite and intricate post-bop compositions (*Six Ate, Echoes, C-Sri*). Tenor saxophonist Michael Brecker joined Brackeen, Hart and McBee on **Tring-A-Ling** (march 1977), the first album entirely devoted to original compositions (the twelve-minute *Shadowbrook-Aire*, the nine-minute *Echoes*, the twelve-minute *Haiti-B*). **Aft** (december 1977), in a trio with guitarist Ryo Kawasaki and bassist Clint Houston, emphasized textural and timbral nuances of her playing (*Haiti B, Aft, Winter Is Here*, the nine-minute *Green Voices of Play Air*). The closest reference point for her piano playing would be McCoy Tyner.

In the meantime she had been playing with Joe Henderson (1972-1975) and Stan Getz (1975-1977), but now she began to focus on her solo career. Her first solo-piano album, **Mythical Magic** (september 1978), sounded a bit shy (except *Mythical Magic*), as did **Keyed In** (may 1979), in a trio with bassist Eddie Gomez and drummer Jack DeJohnette, devoted to relatively simpler pieces. On the contrary, the four lengthy originals of **Ancient Dynasty** (may 1980), that added tenor saxophonist Joe Henderson to the rhythm section of Gomez and DeJohnette, boasted both the intensity and the brains of her most inspired moments. **Special Identity** (december 1981), again in a trio with Gomez and DeJohnette, was even more adventurous in terms of group interplay and solos (*Special Identity*).

She never quite recaptured the magic of the 1970s, despite featuring trumpeters Terence Blanchard and Branford Marsalis on **Fi-Fi Goes To Heaven** (august 1986). **Live At Maybeck Recital Hall** (june 1989) debuted several new originals for solo piano (*Dr Chu Chow, Curved Space, African Aztec*) among a plethora of predictable standards. She returned to her favorite format of the trio on **Is It Really True** (july 1991), that delivered more evidence of her compositional mastery (the eleven-minute *Haiti-B*, the nine-minute *Dr Chu Chow*, the nine-minute *Estilo Magnifico*), and reunited with Gomez and DeJohnette on **Where Legends Dwell** (september 1991) for a set of impeccable post-bop and pre-fusion demonstrations (notably *Picasso* and *Asian Spell*).

White San Francisco-based pianist Jessica Williams began to improvise in the vein of Thelonious Monk but in a rather shy manner, both as a solo performer, for example in the psychological vignettes of **Portal of Antrim** (1976), and as a member of a small ensemble, notably on **Orgonomic Music** (1979). During the 1980s she recorded very little but her technique achieved supernatural status, a worthy disciple of Art Tatum although in an altogether different voice. By the time she resurfaced with **And Then There's This** (february 1990) in a trio, she had become one of the greatest living virtuosi of the piano. Unfortunately the consequence was that she devoted most of her recordings to interpretations of jazz standards, returning to creative terrain only with **Inventions** (january 1995) and **Joy** (january 1996).

Cleveland's white tenor saxophonist Ernie Krivda coined an incendiary style on **Satanic** (1977), **The Alchemist** (january 1978) and **Glory Strut** (1979).

White trumpeter Jack Walrath (Charlie Mingus' last trumpeter) was emblematic of the slightly more experimental contingent of traditionalists during his golden decade, from **Demons In Pursuit** (august 1979) till **Neohippus** (august 1988).

Ohio-born white tenor saxophonist Joe Lovano studied music in Boston and moved to New York in 1980. He refined his style while playing with Paul Motian (from 1981) and John Scofield (from 1989). His relationship to free jazz was ambivalent. Lovano basically bridged bebop, hard-bop, fusion jazz and free jazz as if he wanted to transform John Coltrane into a mainstream jazz musician.

The short pieces of **Village Rhythms** (june 1988), by a quintet with Werner, trumpeter Tom Harrell, bassist Marc Johnson and drummer Paul Motian, struck a balance between impressionism and abstraction while exuding humility. Lovano assembled a "wind ensemble" (Lovano on tenor sax, soprano sax and alto clarinet, trumpeter Tim Hagans, trombonist Gary Valente, two guitarists, bass and drums) that included Motian and Bill Frisell, to accompany improvising vocalist Judi Silvano (Lovano's wife) on the live **Worlds** (march 1989), featuring extended pieces (*Tafabalewa Square*, *Worlds*, *Round Dance*) that were in the tradition while introducing a personal jazz language. **From the Soul** (december 1991) was the best of the early albums, thanks to soulful accompaniment by pianist Michel Petrucciani, bassist Dave Holland and drummer Ed Blackwell, and to at least one Lovano gem, *Evolution*. **Universal Language** (june 1992) marked the return of Judi Silvano's wordless soprano singing, "backed" by a piano-sax-trumpet sextet with Hagans, Werner, Charlie Haden or Steve Swallow on bass and Jack DeJohnette on drums. Lovano played soprano and alto saxophones, flute, alto clarinet and even some percussion. The vocals were just one of the instruments, and each piece sounded like a tribute to a different jazz style, with some (*Sculpture*, *The Dawn of Time*, *Chelsea Rendez-Vous*) being more adventurous than others, but none being avantgarde by any stretch of the imagination. Except for **Trio Fascination** (september 1997), a trio with drummer Elvin Jones and bassist Dave Holland (and Lovano, as usual, on both tenor and alto sax, plus alto clarinet), Lovano later turned to mainstream pop-jazz muzak.

On his own, Pat Metheny's white keyboardist Lyle Mays, an instrumentalist equally brilliant at the acoustic piano as at the synthesizer, and a prolific composer who penned many of Metheny's classics, showcased his articulate, elegant contrapuntal craft in the 14-minute *Alaskan Suite*, off **Lyle Mays** (april 1985), and in the 20-minute suite *Street Dreams*, a kaleidoscopic blend of progressive-rock, electronic music, new-age music and world-music, off **Street Dreams** (1988).

New Orleans-born trumpeter Wynton Marsalis, one of the most popular jazz musicians of all times, was educated to classical music but, after joining Art Blakey's Jazz Messengers (1980), adopted the hard-bop trumpet styles of Clifford Brown, Lee Morgan and Freddie Hubbard, as mediated by the sound of Miles Davis' acoustic quintet of the 1960s, and flirted with the spirit of the swing era. He became the ultimate neo-traditionalist with **Wynton Marsalis** (august 1981), whose best compositions (*Father Time* and *Twilight*) were performed by a quintet with pianist Kenny Kirkland and his saxophonist brother Branford Marsalis (although the others featured Miles Davis's rhythm section of pianist Herbie Hancock, bassist Ron Carter and drummer Tony Williams). The mediocre **Think Of One** (february 1983), with *Knozz-Moe-King* featuring the quintet with Branford Marsalis, Kirkland and drummer Jeff "Tain" Watts, and the terrible **Hot House Flowers** (may 1984) introduced a cynical entertainer, more interested in melodic standards for atmospheric background than in original compositions.

On the other hand, Marsalis impersonated a superb Miles Davis imitator on **Black Codes** (january 1985), a collection of seven originals (including *Black Codes* and *For Wee Folks*) for the quintet with his brother and Kirkland. Scaled down to a quartet with pianist Marcus Roberts, **J Mood** (december 1985) was less charming if still effective (*J Mood*).

His mission was to restore the "moral values" of jazz music that had been lost in the intellectual turmoil of cool jazz and free jazz. Faced with the schism of the 1960s, that opposed free jazz and fusion jazz, Marsalis chose to disavow both and retreat to the previous era. His music therefore tended to be rather predictable and dejavu, no matter how elegant and passionate.

His ambitions as a composer (as well as his nostalgic view of his birth town) surfaced on **The Majesty Of The Blues** (october 1988), that contained the 15-minute *The Majesty Of The Blues* for sextet (Roberts, Todd Williams on tenor and Wes Anderson on alto) and the 36-minute three-movement suite *The New Orleans Function* (ruined by a lengthy spoken-word performance).

Marsalis better fine-tuned his arrangements for the septet (Roberts, Williams, Anderson, trombonist Wycliffe Gordon, bassist Reginald Veal and drummer Herlin Riley) on **Blue Interlude** (1991), whose centerpiece, the 37-minute *Blue Interlude*, achieved the grace and romance of Duke Ellington's classic years. Eric Reed replaced Roberts on piano for the large-scale suite **In This House On This Morning** (march 1993), premiered in may 1992, basically a neoclassical mass inspired by black church music, and including a suite within a suite, the 28-minute *In the Sweet Embrace of Life*.

Marsalis was now a master of the extended composition, and proceeded to score the three-movement ballet **Citi Movement** (july 1992), leaving behind the Ellington model for a post-modernist cacophony. However, the dance scores *Jump Start* (january 1993) and *Jazz - Six Syncopated Movements* (august 1995), documented on **Jump Start and Jazz**, *Sweet Release* for jazz orchestra and *Ghost Story* for a quartet without Marsalis, documented on **Sweet Release and Ghost Story** (august 1999), and *Them Two's* (june 1999), were more traditional in their quotation of the jazz tradition. So was **Big Train** (december 1998), a suite for big band that was shamelessly in the tradition of Duke Ellington. The film soundtrack **Reeltime** (october 1999) was utterly trivial in the way it quoted folk, blues and jazz music. This prolific period culminated with the 13-movement childishly impressionistic **Marciac Suite** (february 1999) for jazz septet. Notable among his classical compositions (straddling the border between Charles Ives, Duke Ellington and Igor Stravinsky) were: the seven-movement first string quartet, *At the Octoroon Balls* (premiered in may 1995), dedicated to New Orleans; the colossal oratorio *Blood on the Fields* (premiered in april 1994), that draws from the entire history of black music; the twelve-movement suite *All Rise* (premiered in december 1999) for jazz big band, symphony orchestra and 100-unit gospel choir.

There was no question, though, that Wynton Marsalis' commercial and critical success (both in jazz and classical quarters) helped revitalize mainstream jazz at a time when it seemed incapable to connecting with the audience, and doomed to an inferior status than avantgarde jazz.

New Orleans-born saxophonist <u>Branford Marsalis</u> cut his teeth with Art Blakey (1980-81) and younger brother Wynton Marsalis (1982-1985), developing a style reminiscent of John Coltrane while retaining the romantic flavor of the mainstream jazz whose demise Coltrane had caused. After a stint with pop singer

Gordon "Sting" Sumner, Branford Marsalis debuted as a leader on **Scenes In The City** (november 1983), with *Solstice*, **Royal Garden Blues** (july 1986), the mediocre **Renaissance** (january 1987), **Random Abstract** (august 1987), with *Crescent City* and *Broadway Fools* (on soprano saxophone), **Trio Jeepy** (january 1988), with *Housed From Edward* and *Random Abstract* (on soprano saxophone). Specializing at the tenor saxophone but doubling on soprano, and employing variable ensembles, Marsalis failed to exhibit an original persona or a musical program.

His group finally stabilized as a quartet with pianist Kenny Kirkland, bassist Bob Hurst and drummer Jeff "Tain" Watts on **Crazy People Music** (march 1990), containing *Spartacus* and *Wolverine* (on soprano saxophone). Marsalis did even better in a trio without the pianist on **The Beautiful Ones Are Not Yet Born** (june 1991), possibly his compositional peak, from *The Beautiful Ones Are Not Yet Born* (on soprano saxophone) to *Gilligan's Isle*, from *Dewey Baby* to *Xavier's Lair*, turning the apparent contradiction of his Coltrane-ish traditionalism into a personal language.

After collaborating with blues greats on **I Heard You Twice The First Time** (october 1991), Branford Marsalis formed Buckshot LeFonque with disc-jockeys, rappers and an army of jazz musicians to concoct an exuberant fusion of hip-hop, jazz and rhythm'n'blues on **Buckshot LeFonque** (july 1993) and **Music Evolution** (1996). That experiments helped Marsalis craft the stylistic Babel (hard-bop, rock, funk) of the trio's **The Dark Keys** (august 1996), notably *The Dark Keys*, *Sentinel* and *Lykief* on soprano.

The piano-based quartet of **Requiem** (december 1998) wed this acquired eclecticism with the original Coltrane-ish stance (*A Thousand Autumns*, *16th St Baptist Church*) although the recording was left unfinished after the death of Kirkland (a trio-only version of *Elysium*). He was replaced by Joey Calderazzo on **Contemporary Jazz** (december 1999), that featured the full-blown 16-minute version of *Elysium* for piano-based quartet. The 18-minute *Eternal* was a comparable tour de force for the same quartet on **Eternal** (october 2003), a postmodernist take on the form of the ballad that managed to bridge the lyrical Duke Ellington and the metaphysical John Coltrane. The smooth, eloquent and austere tone of these lengthy compositions finally granted Branford Marsalis a major ranking among the neo-traditionalists after a much tortuous journey.

Kansas-born alto saxophonist Bobby Watson, yet another alumnus of Art Blakey's Jazz Messengers in the 1970s, led the hard-bop revival of the 1980s (both through his own recordings and the recordings with the 29th Street Saxophone Quartet, which was de facto the hard-bop equivalent of the World Saxophone Quartet) and gave it some of its most popular compositions: *The Punjab of Java Po* from **Post-Motown Bop** (september 1980), *Beatitudes* from **Beatitudes** (april 1983), *Appointment in Milano* from **Appointment in Milano** (february 1985), *The Misery of Ebop* from **Love Remains** (november 1986), etc. His group, named Horizon, also relied on the compositions of bassist Curtis Lundy, such as *Orange Blossom* on **Jewel** (april 1983) and *Present Tense* on

Present Tense (december 1991). With **Tailor Made** (december 1992) Watson began to venture into big-band jazz.

Memphis-born pianist James Williams, a former gospel organist and yet another alumnus of Art Blakey's Jazz Messengers, merged soul music and hard bop on his most personal albums, such as **Alter Ego** (july 1984).

White trumpeter Tom Harrell, a member of Phil Woods' quintet in the 1980s, penned atmospheric cool-toned hard-bop in two-horn settings with expanded rhythm sections. **Play Of Light** (february 1982) and **Moon Alley** (december 1985) set the standard of his carefully sculpted and orchestrated compositions. The free-jazz detour of **Form** (april 1990), with Joe Lovano on saxophones and the rhythm section of bassist Charlie Haden and drummer Paul Motian, heralded the introspective mood of the more mainstream collections of **Stories** (january 1988), with Harrell on flugelhorn, and **Passages** (october 1991), another collaboration with Lovano. Harrell switched to three horns for **Upswing** (june 1993), with Harrell on flugelhorn, Joe Lovano on tenor and Phil Woods on alto, **Labyrinth** (january 1996) and the Latin-tinged **Art Of Rhythm** (july 1997). Continuing that progression towards more and more complex harmonies, Harrell ventured into big-band jazz with **Time's Mirror** (march 1999).

New Orleans-born trumpeter Terence Blanchard, another alumnus of Art Blakey's Jazz Messengers (1982-86) like Wynton Marsalis (whom he replaced), was, like Marsalis, heavily influenced by Freddie Hubbard's sound, shot to the forefront of the hard-bop revival when he formed the quintet with altoist Donald Harrison and pianist Mulgrew Miller that debuted on **New York Second Line** (october 1983). The more original **Crystal Stair** (april 1987) and **Black Pearl** (january 1988) featured pianist Cyrus Chestnut. His "solo" career (still leading a sax-piano-trumpet quintet) began with **Terence Blanchard** (december 1990), with the 13-minute Afro-Cuban shuffle *Azania*, and **Simply Stated** (october 1991). The soundtrack for a Spike Lee film was turned into **The Malcolm X Jazz Suite** (december 1992), again scored for his quintet. That was his first major accomplishment as a composer (*Blues For Malcolm*, *Malcolm At Peace*) and as an original (not derivative) arranger. **Romantic Defiance** (december 1994) and especially **Wandering Moon** (june 1999), with *Joe & O*, perfected his baroque mastery of the hard-bop quintet. Blanchard's romantic ambience had become a cliche' within the cliche'. **Bounce** (february 2003) expanded the quintet to a sextet by adding electronic keyboardist Robert Glasper and guitarist Lionel Loueke, but marked a retreat by the composer.

While still a member of Art Blakey's Jazz Messengers (1983-86), pianist Mulgrew Miller refined a modal style of playing that evoked McCoy Tyner's more mainstream work. It took a while for Miller to also emerge as a composer and an arranger. **Wingspan** (may 1987) featured him in a small-ensemble context (a quintet), playing relatively harmless originals. The idea was applied to **Countdown** (august 1988), in a quartet with tenor saxophonist Joe Henderson, bassist Ron Carter and drummer Tony Williams, and especially to the septet of **Hand In Hand** (december 1992), that contained his most sophisticated art yet.

White pianist <u>Fred Hersch</u> coined a lyrical and sentimental style through the trio recordings that peaked with **Horizons** (1984), the first album of mainly original material, definitely maturing with the lullabies and elegies of **Heartsongs** (december 1989) and **Forward Motion** (july 1991).

White soprano saxophonist <u>Dave Liebman</u>, who played with Miles Davis (1973-74), had demonstrated his austere compositional ambitions and his multi-reed skills (soprano sax, tenor sax, flute and clarinet) on the live **Open Sky** (june 1972), in a trio with bassist Frank Tusa and drummer Bob Moses. Liebman mixed ideas from classical music, progressive-rock, Ornette Coleman, Charles Mingus and Lennie Tristano in the 13-minute *Places*, the ten-minute *Questions* and the eight-minute *Constellation*. **Lookout Farm** (october 1973), the project with pianist Richie Beirach, offered an original blend of cool jazz and free jazz in the 14-minute *Pablo's Story* and the 24-minute *M.D. /Lookout Farm*. **Drum Ode** (may 1974) veered towards a baroque and exotic fusion (*The Iguana's Ritual* and *Loft Dance*), thanks to a line-up that featured Liebman on soprano sax, tenor sax and alto flute Beirach, Moses, guitarist John Abercrombie, percussionists Barry Altschul and Collin Walcott, vocalist Elene Sternberg, as well as bongo, conga and tabla players. The group (including Beirach, Abercrombie, bassists Charlie Haden and Frank Tusa, percussionist Don Alias, sitarist Arooj Lazewal, tabla player Badal Roy, tampura player Gita Roy) toyed with Indian-jazz fusion on **Sweet Hands** (july 1975), but the highlight was the funk-jazz-rock workout *Dr Faustus*. **Forgotten Fantasies** (november 1975) was, instead, just a duo of Liebman and Beirach, straddling the border of fusion jazz, cool jazz and free jazz in Beirach's 13-minute *Obsidian Mirrors*.

After briefly flirting with Herbie Hancock's funk-jazz, and recording a straightforward hard-bop album such as **Pendulum** (february 1978) with a quintet featuring Beirach, Tusa, trumpeter Randy Brecker and drummer Al Foster, mostly devoted to Beirach's 18-minute *Pendulum*, in 1978 Liebman formed his Quintet with veteran Japanese trumpeter Terumasa Hino and guitarist John Scofield. Their **Opal Heart** (february 1979), **Doin' It Again** (august 1979) and especially **If They Only Knew** (july 1980), with their most mature post-bop compositions (*If They Only Knew*, *Capistrano* and *Move On Some*), were much more structured and linear than the music of Lookout Farm.

Liebman's chamber music surfaced on the drum-less **Dedications** (september 1979), containing pieces for soprano saxophone, piano (Beirach), bass (Eddie Gomez) and a string section (*The Delicacy of Youth* and *The Code's Select Code*) as well as a duo of soprano sax and cello (*Ode for Leo*) and a duo of soprano and violin (*Mr K*).

Its ludic alter-ego was **What It Is** (december 1979), featuring Scofield, pianist Kenny Kirkland, vibraphonist Mike Mainieri, bassist Marcus Miller, drummer Steve Gadd, percussionist Don Alias.

The project of Lookout Farm was de facto reprised with Quest, another collaboration with Beirach but this time in a quartet with Liebman on soprano only and in a lighter context: **Quest** (december 1981), with *Napanoch*, **Quest II**

(april 1986), the live **NY Nites** (march 1988), **Natural Selection** (june 1988), bordering on new-age music, **Of One Mind** (july 1990), devoted to free jazz, etc. More important were Liebman's solo-saxophone (with overdubs) concept album **The Loneliness Of A Long-distance Runner** (december 1985), **Trio + One** (may 1988), a set of creative improvisations with bassist Dave Holland and drummer Jack DeJohnette, the neoclassical **Chant** (july 1989), a new duo project with Beirach including three Beirach *Incantations* and three Liebman *Invocations*, and a second solo concept **The Tree** (april 1990), all of them focusing on the soprano saxophone.
While the David Liebman Group featuring keyboardist Phil Markowitz and guitarist Vic Juris largely disappointed in the linear, structured pieces of **Songs for My Daughter** (may 1994), Liebman's most intense work was for the chamber setting, whether the impressionistic vignettes of **The Seasons** (january 1993), for a chamber trio with bassist Cecil McBee and drummer Billy Hart, and of **The Elements - Water** (january 1997), for the same trio augmented with guitarist Pat Metheny, or the solo meditations of **Time Immemorial** (november 1997), four lengthy suites for soprano, tenor, alto and baritone, as well as bamboo flute and dudek, further processed by producer Walter Quintus, and of **Colors** (1998) for tenor saxophone.

California-born tenor saxophonist Joshua Redman, the son of tenor saxophonist Dewey Redman, who moved to New York in 1991, was hyped as the next Sonny Rollins or John Coltrane when he debuted at 22 with **Joshua Redman** (september 1992), although his technique was a humble blend of soul and hard-bop cliches, and, other than the Coltrane-ian *Sublimation* and *Wish*, he was still a rudimentary composer and arranger. **Wish** (1993), by a piano-less quartet featuring guitarist Pat Metheny, bassist Charlie Haden and drummer Billy Higgins, was, globally, an amazing waste of talents, as it persevered in that conservative approach to hard bop and soul music. The enfant prodige finally matured on **Moodswing** (march 1994), a set of originals for a quartet with pianist Brad Mehldau, bassist Christian McBride and drummer Brian Blade, that, while derivative to the point of sounding like standards, nonetheless displayed his true voice (*Rejoice, Sweet Sorrow*). A similar quartet was documented on the live double-CD **Spirit of the Moment** (march 1995) containing quite a few extended originals (the waltzing soprano-led *Second Snow*, the ebullient and funky *Herbs and Roots*, the Coltrane-ian ballad *Neverend*, the teetering *Lyric*). Adding a guitar to his favorite quartet, Redman ventured into funk and hip-hop rhythms on **Freedom in the Groove** (april 1996), his sax solos imitating gospel and soul vocals (*Invocation, Stream of Consciousness*). His most ambitious and introspective album yet, **Beyond** (may 1999), experimented with different time signatures, looser improvisation and Eastern modes (*Leap of Faith, Last Rites of Rock'n'Roll, Twilight and Beyond*). The seven-movement suite **Passage of Time** (june 2000) was the natural evolution of that experiment, finally delving into the psyche of the musician rather than into the tradition of jazz (*Our Minuet, Bronze, Enemies Within*). As his music became more profound, his melodic gift actually became more striking. On the other hand the trio formed with organist Sam

Yahel and drummer Brian Blade, first named **Yaya3** (january 2002) and then **Elastic** (march 2002), indulged in eclectic groove-oriented funk-soul-jazz feasts.

St Louis-raised white alto saxophonist David Sanborn, who had played with Paul Butterfield (1967) and Stevie Wonder (1972), specialized in catchy and danceable pseudo-jazz drenched in rhythm'n'blues, funk and pop music. Trivial collections such as **Hideaway** (1979) and **Voyeur** (1980), mostly inspired by bassist Marcus Miller, became best-selling albums.

Texan trumpeter Roy Hargrove debuted at 20 with **Diamond In The Rough** (december 1989) as one of the "young lions" of the hard-bop and bebop revival. His solos were praised by the establishment but added very little to the history of jazz.

Detroit-born tenor saxophonist James Carter, who relocated to New York in 1988 and already a teenage sensation, established himself as one of the faceless stylists of his generations with **J.C. on the Set** (april 1993), playing tenor, alto and baritone in a quartet with piano, bass and drums (notably on the 14-minute *Blues For A Nomadic Princess*). Carter flirted with funk and rock on **Layin' in the Cut** (june 2000), accompanied by rock guitarist Marc Ribot, bassist Jamaaladeen Tacuma and drummer Calvin Weston.

Cuban-born trumpeter Arturo Sandoval, a founding member of the Orquesta Cubana de Musica Moderna, exploited the Latin element on **Tumbaito** (1985) and **Danzon** (november 1993), but more appropriately displayed his unusual range, fire and speed on the hard-bop originals of **Swingin'** (january 1996).

Stanley Jordan was perhaps the first real innovator of the guitar since Jimi Hendrix. He invented a way to play the guitar as if it were a piano, with two independent hands. In fact, he occasionally played two guitars at the same time. Albums such as **Touch Sensitive** (1982) and **Magic Touch** (september 1984) created a sensation but, like many in the neo-trad generation, Jordan wasted his talent playing rather tedious material.

Blind pianist Marcus Roberts, Wynton Marsalis' pianist since 1985, coined an original neo-traditionalist style based on the lessons of Duke Ellington and Thelonious Monk on **The Truth is Spoken Here** (july 1988). He went even as far as to rediscover archaic jazz techniques such as stride piano on **As Serenity Approaches** (november 1991). However, he best expressed his tormented persona on the Ellingtonian suites of **Blues for the New Millennium** (may 1997).

White pianist Brad Mehldau specialized in Bill Evans-style trios propelled by his lyrical but rather lightweight playing. After establishing his voice on **Introducing** (april 1995) and **Art of the Trio - 1** (september 1996), Mehldau began to adopt the austere approach to the piano of a Keith Jarrett with the solo piano meditations of the **Elegiac Cycle** (february 1999) and the trio concept of **Places** (march 2000). Further expanding his horizons, the chamber pieces of **Largo** (april 2002) ran the gamut from droning to dissonance to electronics.

White trombonist Steve Turre, who also became a virtuoso of the conch shell while accompanying Roland Kirk, reinvented chamber jazz through ever more complex and longer compositions and diverse settings that ranged from ensembles of conch shells to traditional jazz combos. The depth of his music kept increasing via **Fire and Ice** (february 1988), **Right There** (april 1991) and **Rhythm Within** (1995) until the delicately baroque take on Latin music of **Turre** (1996).

British black tenor saxophonist Courtney Pine (1964) grew up with funk, soul and reggae music, influences that were still discernable on **Journey to the Urge Within** (july 1986), containing the hit song *Children of the Ghetto*. The influence of John Coltrane and of the neo-traditionalists merged instead on the acoustic **Destiny's Song + the Image of Pursuance** (august 1987), but that turned out to be only the beginning of a tortuous stylistic itinerary that took him from Jamaica to Africa to India and that peaked with **To The Eyes Of Creation** (1992). Even the strictly jazzy **Modern Day Jazz Stories** (1996), featuring keyboardist Geri Allen, trumpeter Eddie Henderson and vocalist Cassandra Wilson, turned out to be a detour rather than a maturation because **Underground** (1997) employed turntables, drum-machines and digital programming.

Canadian-born pianist and vocalist Diana Krall, who relocated to New York in 1989, was the most successful pop-jazz crossover artist of the 1990s, selling millions of copies of her album **The Look of Love** (january 2001), but her ballads were the quintessence of mediocrity.

The Death of Jazz

Many of the musicians of the older generations thought that jazz music was rapidly dying. What was dying was the traditional concept of jazz as a history of how to play instruments. Older musicians and critics had always analyzed and appreciated jazz first and foremost as a set of instrumental techniques. A jazz musician was deemed to be a classic if his/her style was immediately recognizable, unique, profoundly personal. In the 1990s, instead, jazz was entering an era in which few jazz musicians could boast such a personal style.

Bebop, cool jazz and free jazz had changed a lot of features of jazz, but not its fundamental attribute: of being the art of how to play instruments. While both merely a development of previous styles (hard bop and free jazz), jazz-rock and creative music shifted the emphasis from the instrument towards the atmosphere, the overall "sound", the soundscape. The effect was to downplay the importance of the instrumental technique. Thus the death of jazz for those who thought that the history of jazz was the history of how Louis Armstrong played the cornet and how Charlie Parker played the saxophone and how Miles Davis played the trumpet. The new jazz was a descendant of Duke Ellington not of Louis Armstrong.

NON-JAZZ OF THE 1980S

M-Base

In 1984 a group of young New York musicians started the "M-Base Collective" ("macro-basic array of structured extemporization"). Inspired by Ornette Coleman's "harmolodic" blend of free jazz and funk music, they defined a program of spontaneous composition that generally mixed free-jazz improvisation and elements of West African music. (It was also adorned with spiritual and philosophical theories that rarely amounted to much else than a naive excitement for primitive societies). The resulting style was intellectual music that had a ludic appeal, basically turning funk music into avantgarde music. Despite the fact that they denied the existence of an M-Base style, the M-Base style that they (willingly or unwillingly) coined was one of the most influential of the decade. The collective included: saxophonists Steve Coleman and Greg Osby, trumpeter Graham Haynes, trombonist Robin Eubanks, guitarist Jean-Paul Bourelly, pianist Geri Allen, bassist MeShell N'degecello, vocalist Cassandra Wilson. An influence on the saxophonists was the eccentric and emotional style of veteran saxophonist Bunky Green, notably on **Places We've Never Been** (february 1979).

Chicago's alto saxophonist Steve Coleman relocated to New York in 1978 and in 1984 was instrumental in starting the M-Base Collective. His solo debut, **Motherland Pulse** (march 1985), was the first manifestation of the concept (it also featured pianist Geri Allen, vocalist Cassandra Wilson and trumpeter Graham Haynes). The M-Base Collective truly came into its own when Coleman formed the Five Elements (with vocalist Cassandra Wilson, trumpeter Graham Haynes, electronic keyboardist Geri Allen, guitarist Kelvyn Bell, a bassist and two percussionists) and released **On the Edge of Tomorrow** (january 1986), the manifesto of Coleman's non-Western forms of musical expression, in particular his indifference towards the time signature. The idea was repeated with less imagination on **World Expansion** (november 1986) and **Sine Die** (january 1988), despite the fact that they featured pretty much the same crowd (Wilson, Allen, Bell, Haynes, trombonist Robin Eubanks, bass, drums on the former, plus saxophonists Branford Marsalis, Greg Osby and Gary Thomas on the latter). Steve Coleman's music sounded simply like an update to the 1990s of Ornette Coleman's harmolodic jazz of the 1980s. Different combinations of instruments (some including Dave Holland on bass) did not fare any better on **Rhythm People** (february 1990).

The "official" M-Base Collective debut albums, both credited to the Strata Institute (basically a loose group led by Coleman and Osby), **Cypher Sintax** (april 1988) and **Transmigration** (january 1991), were actually less representative of the movement. Coleman's involvement was marginal on their

third album, this time credited directly to the M-Base Collective, **Anatomy of a Groove** (january 1992).
Though still lacking memorable numbers, **Black Science** (december 1990) was a mature formalization of Coleman's aesthetic. The first M-Base album featuring all-acoustic piano (James Weidman), besides bass (Dave Holland), guitar and drums, it supported the funky improvisation of the leader with multi-layered rhythmic cycles (more or less inspired by West African music), and it revolutionized the concept of tempo, each instrumentalist playing in a different meter. The result was a neurotic form of funk music, but less jarring than in the past. After the inferior **Drop Kick** (january 1992), Coleman reached another M-Base zenith on **Tao of Mad Phat** (may 1993), a set of lengthy live improvisations in the studio with more regular meters (*Tao of Mad Phat, Collective Meditations, Polymaid Nomads* for tentet, *Little Girl on Fire*).
Influenced by a trip to West Africa and ever more spiritual in nature, Coleman refined his anti-Western jazz on **Def Trance Beat** (june 1994) the EP **A Tale of 3 Cities** (1994), credited to the Metrics (alto, tenor, piano, trumpet, bass, drums and samples) but merely a rap-jazz experiment, and on the (uneven) trilogy derived from one live event: **Myths Modes and Means** (march 1995), credited to the Mystic Rhythm Society (sax, trumpet, koto, bass, percussion, keyboards) and containing three colossal improvisations (*Finger Of God, Song of the Beginnings, Transits*), **The Way of The Cipher** (march 1995), credited to the Metrics (mostly rap tunes), and **Curves of Life** (march 1995), credited to the Five Elements but performed by a keyboards-based quartet and containing two more lengthy improvisations (*Muliplicity of Approaches* and *Country Bama*). Despite the pretentious titles, the music was mostly light-weight funk-jazz. The Afro-Cuban album **The Sign and The Seal** (february 1996), a collaboration with a Cuban band, added the Latin ingredient to the stew, again under the pretense of a new theory of music.
The metaphysical element was better expressed on the eight-movement suite **Genesis** (june 1997), a concept on the seven Biblical days of the Creation for an orchestra (the Council of Balance) featuring a massive horn section (six saxophones, three trumpets, five trombones), a string section (viola, cello, violin), guitar, piano, bass, drums, ethnic percussions. Likewise the seven lengthy movements of **The Sonic Language of Myth - Believing Learning Knowing** (may 1999), thanks to the tension between the shamanic vocals and the timbral counterpoint of horns, vibraphone, piano and strings.
After a long period of travel, Coleman resumed his Five Elements project with the austere **The Ascension To Light** (june 1999), the live double-CD **Resistance is Futile** (august 2001), featuring a mid-size band and extended funk-jazz jams (*Resistance is Futile, Wheel Of Nature, 9 to 5*), the demonstrative **Alternate Dimension Series I** (march 2002), the lightweight **On the Rising of the 64 Paths** (april 2002), **Lucidarium** (may 2003), that toyed with different combinations of instruments and voices, the ambitious double-CD **Weaving Symbolics** (may 2005), alternating retreats to fusion music and great leaps

forward into uncharted post-jazz territory, all of them dedicated to pompous pseudo-pantheistic philosophical theories.

St Louis-born alto saxophonist Greg Osby relocated to New York in 1984 where he joined Jack DeJohnette's group and became a member of the M-Base Collective. The funk-jazz style of the latter permeated the albums of his guitar and keyboards quintets: **Sound Theatre** (june 1987) and **Mind Games** (may 1988). **Season of Renewal** (july 1989) added wordless vocals by Amina Claudine Myers and Cassandra Wilson to the leader's dissonant solos over funky rhythm. Osby pioneered the fusion of jazz and hip-hop music on **3D Lifestyles** (october 1992).

Mississippi-born vocalist Cassandra Wilson relocated to New York in 1982 where she became the most famous member of the M-Base Collective. She blossomed with **New Moon Daughter** (1995), when she started borrowing from the whole canon of popular music (folk, blues, country, soul, rock) to mold her own voice, a project continued on **Belly of the Sun** (2002) and **Glamoured** (march 2003), that feature more of her own compositions.

Detroit-born pianist Geri Allen, a graduate in ethnomusicology, moved to New York in 1982. She collaborated with Oliver Lake (1984-87) and with Steve Coleman (1986-88), and joined the M-Base collective. Allen's debut album, **The Printmakers** (february 1984), in a trio with bassist Anthony Cox and percussionist Andrew Cyrille, was an original offering of dissonant and free jazz, but subsequent recordings moved rapidly towards the lightweight and superficial end of the spectrum. She preferred to fragment her albums into short pieces rather than attempt the epic-length suite or jam. Collections of original compositions were **The Nurturer** (january 1990), featuring Marcus Belgrave on trumpet and flugelhorn, Kenny Garrett on alto saxophone, bass and two percussionists, and especially **Maroons** (february 1992) with one or more trumpet, bass and drums (*Feed The Fire, Laila's House, Mad Money*). **Some Aspects of Water** (march 1996) contained two of her longest compositions ever: the ten-minute *Skin* for a piano-bass-drums trio, and the 19-minute *Some Aspects of Water* for nonet. **Gathering** (february 1998) was another collection of (Allen-composed) atmospheric chamber-jazz pieces for various combinations of instruments, but faithful to a radio-friendly ideology that ran the gamut from new-age music to jazz-rock. After a six-year hiatus, Allen led a more serious trio with bassist Dave Holland and drummer Jack DeJohnette on **The Life Of A Song** (january 2004), although the material was still rather lightweight, with few notable exceptions (*Mounts And Mountains, The Experimental Movement*).

Tenor saxophonist and flutist Gary Thomas established himself as one of the most jarring soloists of his generation, especially against somewhat chaotic backdrops such as the electronic-tinged accompaniment of guitar, keyboards, bass and drums on **Seventh Quadrant** (april 1987) and **Code Violations** (july 1988). He kept antagonizing the tradition of jazz with **By Any Means Necessary** (may 1989), featuring (among others) alto saxophonist Greg Osby, keyboardist Geri Allen, guitarist John Scofield, bassist Anthony Cox and percussionist Nana Vasconcelos, and **The Kold Kage** (june 1991), that experimented with synthesizer, turntable and rapping, always displaying a passion for uncharted territories..

Texan pianist Jason Moran found a compromise between impressionist classical music, energetic bebop and moody new-age music on **Soundtrack to Human Motion** (september 1998), arranged for a small ensemble, and **Black Stars** (march 2001), for a quartet with Sam Rivers. The solo piano program of **Modernistic** (2002) used studio effects to bridge ancient jazz piano and contemporary sound.

Acid Jazz

In 1988 the British disc-jockey Gilles Peterson coined the term "acid jazz" for his mixes of jazz records (mostly funk-jazz) and hip-hop. This style became a sensation in London and eventually migrated to the USA. The term "acid-jazz" came to denote the successor of fusion jazz, a hybrid style that borrowed from funk, soul, rock, jazz and, last but not least, the post-disco dance styles (such as "acid house", that was peaking at about the time that acid-jazz was starting out).

The "acid-jazz" scene of San Francisco was pioneered by the Broun Fellinis, formed in 1991 by saxophonist David Boyce, bassist Ayman Mobarak and drummer Kevin Carnes, (a former member or the rock group Beatnigs), and the Alphabet Soup, formed in 1991 by saxophonist Kenny Brooks, pianist Dred Scott, rapper Chris Burger, and drummer Jay Lane. San Francisco, an ideal meeting point of the most open-minded traditions of rock, jazz and hip-hop music, soon became the headquarter of the movement.

In 1993 San Francisco's white guitarist Charlie Hunter, a former musical partner of white rapper Michael Franti and member of his rap-rock group Disposable Heroes of Hiphoprisy (1992), formed a bass-less trio with tenor saxophonist Dave Ellis and drummer Jay Lane (a former member of the rock group Primus) that heralded the golden age of acid-jazz. After the funky mini-orgies of **Charlie Hunter Trio** (may 1993), Hunter embraced a custom-made eight-string guitar (that allowed him to play rhythm and melody simultaneously) and added a more sophisticated jazz touch to **Bing Bing Bing** (1995). Scott Amendola replaced Lane before **Ready Set Shango** (1996), that also added saxophonist Calder Spanier to the line-up, thus turning the trio into a quartet. Ellis was replaced by Kenny Brooks of Alphabet Soup while trumpeter Chuck MacKinnon, vibraphonist Stefon Harris and percussionist John Santos were added to form a septet, renamed Pound For Pound. However, Hunter disposed of the horns and pared down the band to a quartet of guitar, drums, percussion and vibraphone for **Return of the Candyman** (september 1997). These were all fun albums that were popular with the intellectual disco crowd because they focused on the groove.

In the 1990s the New York scene of groove-based jazz was dominated by Medeski Martin & Wood: keyboardist John Medeski, bassist Chris Wood and drummer Billy Martin, all of them white. The acoustic **Notes From the Underground** (january 1992), on which Medeski played a grand piano and penned the lengthy *Querencia*, achieved an inspired fusion of jazz tradition with funky and hip-hoppish rhythms. But the highlights of the electric and commercial **It's a Jungle in Here** (august 1993) were Afro-funk and reggae covers. They settled on a compromise on **Friday Afternoon In The Universe** (july 1994), that was basically an album of old-fashioned soul-jazz with the neurotic accent of the 1990s (*The Lover, We're So Happy*). They plunged into late-night lounge-music with the languid **Shack Man** (june 1996), but resurrected with **Farmer's Reserve** (february 1997), a set of free improvisations, with **Combustication** (1998), featuring collaborations with turntablist Jason "DJ Logic" Kibler as well as acoustic pieces (*Latin Shuffle*), with the dense soundscape of **The Dropper** (2000), featuring cellist Jane Scarpantoni and guitarist Marc Ribot, and with the even more abstract **Uninvisible** (2001), enhanced with horns and turntables.

New-age Jazz

In 1975 Palo Alto-based guitarist William Ackerman coined the term "new-age music" and founded a record label, Windham Hill, to promote atmospheric instrumental acoustic music. New-age music was, first and foremost, a synthesis, straddling the border between jazz, classical and folk music (and eventually also psychedelic and electronic music). The term "new age" was a reference to the spiritual mood that had taken hold of the hippy generation. The former hippies now constituted an appealing market segment (many of them having become yuppies). Thus new-age music was peaceful music meant to reflect the harmony of nature, music permeated by a spiritual, pantheistic and pan-ethnic mood, and therefore music heavily influenced by Eastern religion/philosophy. Since it targeted the middle-aged urban professionals, new-age music was music made by white folks for white folks, and therefore related to the ECM generation of white jazz musicians. It was also mostly based on the West Coast. Tony Scott's **Music For Zen Meditation** (1964) and Paul Horn's **In India** (1967) were largely responsible for the marriage of jazz and Eastern music that laid the foundations for new-age music of the 1980s.

San Francisco-based white trumpeter Mark Isham, a former member of Art Lande's Rubisa Patrol in Scandinavia (1976) and of the prog-rock quartet Group 87 (1978) with guitarist Peter Maunu, bassist Patrick O'Hearn and drummer Terry Bozzio, wed his oneiric Miles Davis-influenced technique with chromatically haunting synthesizers on **Vapor Drawings** (may 1983), a cycle of meticulously-arranged impressionistic vignettes (with all instruments played by him except drums). Less electronics and a real group (guitarist David Torn, Oregon's reed-player Paul McCandless, Japan's bassist Mick Karn plus former Group 87 buddies Maunu, O'Hearn and Bozzio) gave **Castalia** (1988) a sound closer to Weather Report-style jazz-rock. It all came together on the five-movement symphony **Tibet** (1989) for a chamber ensemble (including flutist Bill Douglas, guitarists Maunu and Torn), a majestic fusion of jazz, electronics, ambient music and world-music.

White cellist David Darling, a member of Paul Winter's Consort, specialized in solemn, highly chromatic and almost baroque meditations straddling classical, jazz and Eastern music. **Journal October** (october 1979), his first solo, and

Cycles (november 1981), that featured saxophonist Jan Garbarek, pianist Steve Kuhn, sitarist Collin Walcott, guitarist Oscar Castro-Neves and bassist Arild Andersen in various configurations, were mainly demonstrations of his glacial technique. After a long hiatus, Darling penned a trilogy of performances in solo settings, often overdubbing his acoustic and electric cellos: **The Tao Of Cello** (1989), a set of 22 brief improvised interludes reminiscent of Chinese philosophy; **Cello** (january 1992), that debuted the medieval-inspired "Darkwood" series of adagios; **Darkwood** (july 1993), containing four more multi-part suites of the "Darkwood" series (4 to 7), his most austere effort in the realm of neoclassical music; and finally **Eight String Religion** (1993), recorded over eleven years, that added his own piano playing and natural sounds.

The emphasis of new-age music on solo acoustic instruments yielded pensive and impressionistic albums that were basically structured as free-form melodic fantasias: George Winston's **Autumn** (june 1980) for the piano, Georgia Kelly's **The Sound Of Spirit** (october 1981) for the harp, Daniel Kobialka's **Echoes Of Secret Silence** (1982) for the violin, Frank Perry's **Deep Peace** (october 1980) for percussion instruments, etc. Pianists outnumbered any other instrumentalists.

Canadian pianist Michael Jones, the new-age master of the lyrical stream of consciousness, penned the psychological double-CD concept **Pianoscapes** (january 1981), the impressionistic trilogy of **Windsong** (may 1982), **Seascapes** (january 1984) and **Sunscapes** (december 1985), the sophisticated cello-piano duets of **Amber** (march 1987) with David Darling, the majestic chamber music of **After The Rain** (december 1987) with Darling and oboe player Nancy Rumbel, one of new-age's melodic zeniths, and the four ambitious suites of **Air Born** (february 1994).

Seattle-born white pianist David Lanz specialized in domestic vignettes based on folkish melodies and tempos, such as **Heartsounds** (june 1983) and especially the longer ones of **Nightfall** (september 1984) and **Cristofori's Dream** (april 1988). While baroque pomp permeated the **Skyline Firedance** (may 1990), conceived as micro-symphonic poems. Lanz was emblematic of new-age music's strategy of ransacking the vocabulary of classical music, from the madrigal to the adagio.

The introspective art of California pianist Liz Story on **Solid Colors** (1983), **Speechless** (1988) and **Escape Of The Circus Ponies** (1991) evoked the brilliancy of Keith Jarrett's style but remained anchored to the folk and classical tradition.

Another category of soloists that found a broader audience thanks to new-age music was that of percussionists.

New York's percussionist Mark Nauseef combined Indonesian, Indian, African, rock, jazz and minimalist techniques on the esoteric **Sura** (1983), featuring the jazz supergroup with Steve Kuhn on keyboards, Markus Stockhausen on horns, Trilok Gurtu on percussion, David Torn on guitar and a cornucopia of exotic instruments, and on the solo tour de force of **Wun Wun** (may 1984), with rock vocalist Jack Bruce, a timbral feast at times reminiscent of avantgarde electronic music. Nauseef partnered with Serbian guitarist Miroslav Tadic for a series of notably **The Snake Music** (june 1993), that featured Bruce, Markus Stockhausen, guitarist David Torn, German saxophonist Wolfgang Puschnig and Walter Quintus on computers, and **Still Light** (march 1993), a trio with German reed player Markus Stockhausen. Nauseef also tried to coin "sufi-jazz" on two collaborations with Turkish ney virtuoso Kudsi Erguner: **Ottomania** (may 1998) and **Islam Blues** (may 2000), which also featured Vietnamese guitarist Nguyen Le, French contrabassist Renaud Garcia-Fons and Turkish singers and musicians.

Texan percussionist Glen Velez, who had worked with Steve Reich (1972) and Paul Winter (1983), devoted himself to the frame drum on **Handance** (1983) and **Internal Combustion** (may 1985), accompanied only by fellow percussionist Layne Redmond. **Seven Heaven** (may 1987) added flutist Steve Gorn, and **Assyrian Rose** (june 1989), his first "melodic" work, added French horn, harmonica and piano to the frame drums and the flute. The 45-minute *Doctrine Of Signatures* for five frame drums, off **Doctrine Of Signatures** (1991), was his aesthetic peak.

Indian percussionist Trilok Gurtu, the son of vocalist Shobha Gurtu, who had played with Don Cherry (1976), with Oregon (1984) and with John McLaughlin (1989), perfected a technique that draws equally from Indian tabla and dhol drums, from jazz music (cymbals, hi-hats) and from other ethnic cultures (gongs, congas, cowbells, snares). He even dipped resonating instruments in buckets of water to produce sounds that he could not produce with traditional instruments. He began his mission with the intense mixture of Indian music, jazz-rock and world-music of the double-CD **Usfret** (1988), featuring the likes of trumpeter Don Cherry, guitarist Ralph Towner, Indian violinist Lakshminarayana Shankar, Swedish bassist Jonas Hellborg, French keyboardist Daniel Goyone and his own mother, vocalist Shobha, although the album still downplayed the exotic overtones and emphasized instead supernatural spirituality. His world horizons further expanded on **Living Magic** (march 1991), performed by a multinational septet with Goyone, Norwegian saxophonist Jan Garbarek, Brazilian percussionist Nana Vasconcelos, Belgian bassist Nicolas Fiszman, British kora player Tunde Jegede and Indian veena player Shanthi Rao.

Electronic keyboards and a lot more jazz reduced the world-music element on the trilogy that followed: **Crazy Saints** (june 1993), featuring Goyone, keyboardist Joe Zawinul, guitarist Pat Metheny, Dutch cellist Ernst Reijseger, French bassist Marc Bertaux; **Believe** (july 1994), for a more regular quartet (Goyone, Vietnamese bassist Chris Minh Doky and guitarist David Gilmore); and the live **Bad Habits Die Hard** (october 1996) by the same quartet but with Andy Emler replacing Goyone on keyboards (and saxophonist Bill Evans and violinist Mark Feldman guesting).

However, Gurtu later embarked on a project to fuse African and Indian music while retaining the western song-oriented format on the following trilogy: **The Glimpse** (september 1996), whose core was an Oregon-like ensemble with Emler, Bulgarian flutist Teodosii Spassov and Indian-American guitarist Jaya Deva; **Kathak** (december 1997), an Afro-Indian-jazz jam with Swedish bassist Kai Eckhardt de Camargo, Moroccan guitarist Jaya Deva, Indian sitar player

Ravi Chary and vocalist Neneh Cherry; and **African Fantasy** (2000), performed by a mixed African-Indian ensemble (Chary, Fiszman, Deva and several African vocalists).

New York-based steel-pans virtuoso Andy Narell introduced Trinidad's national instrument to jazz music with the exuberant, melodic pan-ethnic sonatas of **The Hammer** (1987) and **Little Secrets** (1989).

California's contrabassist Bob Wasserman borrowed from David Grisman's progressive bluegrass, acid-rock and free jazz to pen his first album **Solo** (1983) and the **Trios** (1994) that featured rock, jazz, folk and blues musicians.

New-age instrumentalists also merged in configurations of simple counterpoint that evoked both chamber jazz and chamber classical music. San Francisco-based guitarist Teja Bell presided over three of the best examples of chamber new-age music. Pianist Marcus Allen assembled a quartet with Bell, lyricon player Dallas Smith and vibraphonist John Bernoff for his **Petals** (1981). Then the three without Allen recorded **Summer Suite** (1983). And Mahavishnu Orchestra's violinist Steve Kindler's **Dolphin Smiles** (1987) featured Bell and a percussionist.

Shadowfax created the standard for the new-age acoustic ensemble with chromatically-rich and melodically-relaxing albums such as **Shadowdance** (1983). Significant contributions to the "chamber" wing of new-age music came from former members of David Grisman's quintet, whose "jazzgrass" lent itself to a neo-classical interpretation. Violinist Darol Anger, pianist Barbara Higbie, mandolinist Mike Marshall, and bassist Michael Manring formed Montreux, that released borderline albums such as **Sign Language** (february 1987) and **Let Them Say** (january 1989), and Anger led their spin-off, the Turtle Island String Quartet (Anger, violinist David Balakrishnan, cellist Mark Summer, viola player Irene Sazer), whose **Turtle Island String Quartet** (july 1987), mostly composed by Balakrishnan, perfected those ideas.

The subtle fusion of different musical universes (jazz, rock, minimalism, ambient) was not lost on the next generation of jazz groups.

Post-fusion

Los Angeles-based guitarist Nels Cline opened a new front of jazz-rock cross-fertilization, being both a fusion guitarist who played post-rock and a post-rock guitarist who played jazz. As a composer, he matured on **Angelica** (august 1987), featuring saxophonist Tim Berne, Von Essen, drummer Alex Cline and trumpeter Stacey Rowles. Cline formed a power trio in a fashion similar to what Bill Frisell had done, and recorded equally eclectic tours de force, such as **Silencer** (december 1990) and **Chest** (july 1995). However, it was **The Inkling** (may 1999), recorded by a quartet (with Zena Parkins on harp), and the **Instrumentals** (august 2001), with the free-form jam *Blood Drawing*, that succeeded in redefining fusion jazz in the age of post-rock.

The Necks, an Australian combo formed by three veteran session-men (pianist Chris Abrahams, drummer Tony Buck, bassist Lloyd Swanton), specialized in lengthy (usually album-length), trancey jams anchored to simple melodic lines and sometimes propelled by swinging, funky grooves. These "jams" were actually studio constructions, i.e. the result of a painstaking mixing and editing process. The insistent repetition of harmonic elements harked back to minimalism while the fluid and atmospheric interplay evoked jazz-rock. **Sex** (1989) was the archetype of how to make cascading piano notes coalesce in hypnotic streams of casual tones. The subdued rhythm and slightly syncopated tempo created a delicate texture for the intermittent patterns of neoclassical piano and sensual trumpet wails. The way Abrahams caressed the piano was both abstract, exotic and romantic. The style of their meditations, based on slow, fragile, colloquial interplay, reached maturity with *White*, off the double-CD **Silent Night** (september 1995). The formula was repeated on **Hanging Gardens** (january 1999), a cryptic if not gothic piece that underwent several mutations, and especially **Aether** (2000), perhaps the most "ambient" of their hour-long pieces, in which a simple chord was repeated like a mantra to elicit a cosmic drone that led the music into an ecstatic crescendo of counterpoint. The latter was, in turn, the blueprint for the dreamy ambience and fluent dynamics of **Drive By** (2003), the ultimate secretion of Miles Davis, Terry Riley and Brian Eno, while *See Through*, off **Mosquito/ See Through** (2005), was both a miracle of contained chaos and suspense and a showcase of piano jazz soliloquy.

Yeah No (clarinetist and saxophonist Chris Speed, Vietnamese-born trumpeter Cuong Vu, Icelandic-born bassist Skuli Sverrisson, drummer Jim Black) were jazz musicians playing Eastern European folk melodies and dance rhythms, starting with Yeah No (1997), a concept similar to Lol Coxhill's Welfare State.

The Claudia Quintet, formed in 1997 by drummer John Hollenbeck and featuring Yeah No's clarinetist and saxophonist Chris Speed, merged chamber music, jazz improvisation and minimalist

POST-JAZZ MUSIC

Post-jazz Creativity in New York

Post-jazz Soloists and Hyper-fusion

Post-jazz Big Bands

The Great Chicago Jazz Rebirth

The Return of the Jazz Improviser

20th Century Post-creativity

Freer jazz

The Digital Improviser

Turntables

Post-jazz Creativity in New York

New York experienced a "new wave" of musical creativity around the mid 1970s. Rock music was reborn thanks to a multitude of independent musicians who avoided the mainstream cliches. Jazz and avantgarde music felt the effects of that revolution. It was a revolution that blurred the borders between the genres. One reason was racial: it was mainly a white revolution (unlike the previous stylistic revolutions of free jazz or creative improvisation, that were led by black musicians). Black musicians were de facto segregated from rock music and classical music, but white musicians were not. White musicians of all different genres enjoyed a far greater degree of synergy than the superficial one of the past between black jazz musicians and white rock or classical musicians. The traditional "cross-over" for jazz musicians had been with blues, funk and soul music, i.e. with the other "black" genres, not with the rock and classical avantgarde, i.e. not with the "white" genres. This generation of mainly white musicians who played jazz instruments (hardly "jazz musicians" in the traditional sense of the expression) "cross over" into precisely those genres. The music itself (that had been honed through cool jazz, third stream, free jazz and creative improvisation) lend itself to cross-fertilization with rock and classical avantgarde music.

Jewish saxophonist John Zorn emerged from the milieu of the solo creative improvisers, but his concept of "improvisation" was more closely related to John Cage's aleatory music than to Ornette Coleman's free jazz. Game-pieces such as **Lacrosse** (first recorded in june 1977 with soprano saxophonist Bruce Ackley and guitarists Eugene Chadbourne and Henry Kaiser), *Hockey* (composed in 1978 but first recorded in march 1980 by Chadbourne, keyboardist Wayne Horvitz and electronic musician Bob Ostertag), **Archery** (composed in 1979 but first recorded in september 1981 with flutist Robert Dick, trombonist George Lewis, keyboardists Mark Kramer, Anthony Coleman and Wayne Horvitz, guitarists Chadbourne and Bill Horvitz, bassist Bill Laswell, violinist Polly Bradfield, cellist Tom Cora, drummer David Moss) and **Pool** (also composed in 1979, recorded in march 1980 with violinist Polly Bradfield, vibraphonist Mark Miller, percussionist Charles Noyes, Ostertag and trumpeter Lesli Dalaba) were partially structured improvisations that defined rules within which a cast of improvisers could improvise (improvisation being bound more by mathematical than emotional constraints, a` la Anthony Braxton). True to Cage's indeterminate aesthetics, Zorn composed uncomposed music and conducted unrepeatable performances. Zorn played indifferently alto or soprano saxophones and clarinets. But instrumental style was definitely not what his musical "games" were about.

Zorn embraced the aesthetic of the new wave and of punk-rock with the hysterical and laconic fragments of **Locus Solus** (september 1983), that employed both jazz musicians (keyboardist Wayne Horvitz) and rock musicians (including DNA's guitarist Arto Lindsay, Golden Palominos' drummer Anton Fier, DNA's drummer Ikue Mori) plus turntablists (notably Christian Marclay). This time his own demented saxophone playing stood out as a major and shocking stylistic innovation. Hot on the heels of the large-scale game piece *Track And Field* (1982), **Cobra** (may 1986), a game piece originally conceived in 1984, marked another zenith of Zorn's chaotic and abrasive vision, a dadaistic symphony structured in twenty classical movements that, despite the pretentious premises, was the musical equivalent of a Marx Brothers' slapstick. The studio version featured Jim Staley on trombone, Carol Emanuel and Zeena Parkins on harps, Bill Frisell, Elliott Sharp and Arto Lindsay on guitars, Anthony Coleman and Wayne Horvitz on organ, piano, harpsichord and celeste, David Weinstein on sampling keyboards, Guy Klucevsek on accordion, Bob James on tapes, Christian Marclay on turntables, Bobby Previte on percussion. Vestiges of popular music, from Jimi Hendrix's glissandos to cajun accordion, kept surfacing with frantic exuberance from the shroud of random dissonance, perhaps a metaphor for the post-modernist conflict between nostalgia and futurism, amid a concrete collage of power-drills and electronic oscillations, jackhammer rhythms and expressionist overtones.

Xu Feng (composed in 1985, recorded by guitarists Fred Frith and John Schott, electronic musicians Chris Brown and David Slusser, percussionist William Winant and Slayer's drummer Dave Lombardo) closed the "infinite series" of game pieces (games in which the participants contribute to keep the game alive) and opened a new series, in which Zorn tried to recreate an environment via sound (in this case, kung-fu martial arts).

A number of hyper-kinetic collages of subcultural genres such as **The Bribe** (1986) for small orchestra (with Marty Ehrlich on saxophones and bass clarinet, Jim Staley on trombone, Zeena Parkins and Carol Emanuel on harps, Robert Quine on guitar, Anthony Coleman and Wayne Horvitz on keyboards, Christian Marclay on turntables, David Hofstra on bass, Bobby Previte on percussion, Ikue Mori on drum machines) and *Spillane* (june 1986), off **Godard Spillane**, a melodic fantasia for almost the same ensemble (minus Ehrlich, Parkins, Horvitz, Marclay, Mori but with Frisell, Bob James on tapes and David Weinstein on sampling keyboards) that paid homage to the atmospheres of film noir, announced the new Zorn: the post-modernist (or, better, cubist) artist who "quoted", deconstructed and reconstructed musical stereotypes while injecting the cacophony, frenzy and violence of the 20th century; capable of revising established canons in ways that bordered on blasphemy.

That artist moved closer to the world of rock music with **Naked City** (1989), a venture with rock guitarists Bill Frisell and Fred Frith, Boredoms's psychotic vocalist Yamatsuka Eye, keyboardist Wayne Horvitz and drummer Joey Baron offering brief bursts of irreverent jazz-surf-punk fusion music that referenced a broad spectrum of musical stereotypes, albeit drenched in urban neurosis. Zorn's works now fully revealed the influence of the epileptic discontinuity of Carl Stalling's cartoon soundtracks, literally applied on **Cynical Hysterie Hour** (october 1988), one of his most ambitious attempts at deconstructing the western musical civilization. Even more uncompromising, Naked City's **Torture Garden** (1990) and **Heretic** (1991), without Laswell and with Frith on bass, were whirlwinds of recombinant pieces that applied John Cage to atonal improvisation. The two Painkiller albums (for a "jazzcore" trio with bassist Bill Laswell and Napalm Death's drummer Mick Harris), **The Guts Of A Virgin** (april 1991) and especially **Buried Secrets** (october 1991), were kaleidoscopic frescoes of unfulfilled semiotic events. Zorn's music of abrupt shifts of style (whether within the same song or from one song to the next) was the equivalent of turning the tuning dial of a radio.

Zorn was also active as a composer of chamber music, as proven by *For Your Eyes Only* (1989), another Carl Stalling-style score, and **Elegy** (november 1991), a four-movement tribute to French writer Jean Genet scored for flute, viola, guitar, turntables, percussion and voice. Zorn's combinatorial exercises and cut-up techniques were in fact better pursued in his chamber music, which yielded large-scale works such as **Kristallnacht** (november 1992), for a Jewish ensemble (Mark Feldman on violin, Marc Ribot on guitar, Anthony Coleman on keyboards, Mark Dresser on bass, William Winant on percussion, David Krakauer on clarinet), **Redbird** (1995) for string trio (Carol Emanuel on harp, Jill Jaffe on viola, Erik Friedlander on cello), **Aporias** (1998) for piano and orchestra, and **Chimeras** (january 2003) for the same ensemble (voice and twelve instruments) as Schoenberg's *Pierrot Lunaire*, as well as the wind octet *Angelus Novus* (1993) and several string quartets: *Cat o' Nine Tails* (1988), *The Dead Man* (1990), *Memento Mori* (1992), *Kol Nidre* (1996), *Necronomicon* (2003). Some of them betrayed the influence of Morton Feldman's latter-day chamber music.

After Naked City's **Radio** (april 1993), another (and perhaps the ultimate) exercise in quotation and collage at manic speed, Painkiller's double-disc **Execution Ground** (june 1994) dominated by the ambient-dub aesthetic of Laswell and Harris, Zorn (disguised under silly monikers) concocted two noise-fests with Yamatsuka Eye: **Nani Nani** (march 1995) and Mystic Fugu Orchestra's **Zohar** (Tzadik, 1995).

In one of his typical turnarounds, Zorn also formed Masada, a more traditional jazz quartet (trumpeter Dave Douglas, bassist Greg Cohen and drummer Joey Baron) with an emphasis on klezmer melody, to explore the same vision of **Kristallnacht**, i.e. Jewish history, over the course of ten albums, from **Alef** (february 1994) to **Yod** (september 1997), with an artistic peak in **Hei** (july 1995). Masada's music was also re-arranged first for chamber ensemble on **Bar Kokhba** (march 1996) and **The Circle Maker** (december 1997), and then for guitar only (Bill Frisell, Tim Sparks, Marc Ribot) on **Masada Guitars** (2003). Masada-style klezmer jazz also surfaced on some of his movie soundtracks, notably *The Port of Last Resort* (november 1997), scored for jazz sextet (Feldman, Friedlander, bassist Greg Cohen, guitarist Marc Ribot, pianist Anthony Coleman and pipa virtuoso Min Xiao Fen).

An endless series of albums titled **Filmworks** collected Zorn's monumental (quantity-wise) output for the cinema. Mostly mediocre, his soundtracks recycled all sorts of disparate ideas from jazz, rock, avantgarde music and cartoon music.

Post-jazz Creativity in New York

For example: *She Must Be Seeing Things* (1986), with Staley, Frisell, Emanuel, Coleman, Horvitz, Weinstein, Previte, Hofstra, Nana Vasconcelos on percussion, Shelley Hirsch on vocals, Marty Ehrlich on tenor saxophone and clarinet, Tom Varner on French horn; *The Golden Boat* (1990), with Coleman, Quine, Emanuel, Dresser, Previte, Vicki Bodner on oboe, David Shea on turntable, Cyro Baptista on percussion; *The Thieves Quartet* (1993), that debuted the Masada line-up of Zorn, Douglas, Cohen and Baron; *A Lot of Fun for the Evil One* (released in 1997), a computer collage of musical samples; *Tears Of Ecstasy* (october 1995), 48 one-minute fetishes of popular music performed by guitarists Robert Quine and Marc Ribot and percussionist Cyro Baptista; *Trembling Before G-d* (released in 2000), his first feature-length soundtrack, scored only for clarinet (Chris Speed), organ (James Saft) and percussion (Baptista); *In the Mirror of Maya Deren* (2001), one of the most romantic, with tender cello (Friedlander) and piano (Zorn and Saft) counterpoint and exotic overtones (Baptista); *Secret Lives* (2002) for string trio (Cohen, Feldman, Friedlander), one of his simplest compositions; *Invitation to a Suicide* (june 2002), perhaps the best one, performed by Ribot, Freidlander, Tin Hat Trio's accordionist Rob Burger, rock bassist Trevor Dunn and percussionist Kenny Wollesen; *Hiding and Seeking* (april 2003), a virtually Jewish fantasia for classical guitar (Ribot), vibraphone (Wollesen), Brazilian percussion (Baptista), acoustic bass (Dunn) and voice (Ganda Suthivarakom); *Protocols of Zion* (october 2004) for an ethnic trio (Zorn himself on piano, Baptista and bassist Shanir Ezra Blumenkranz); the electronic *Workingman's Death* (2005) for Saft, Zorn, Ikue Mori (all on keyboards), Blumenkranz and Baptista; *Notes on Marie Menken* (2005) for a free-jazz trio (Zorn on alto, Blumenkranz and Wollesen) plus guitarist Jon Madof; the exotic *The Treatment* (2005) for Latin-jazz quartet (Feldman, Burger, Blumenkranz and Wollesen).

Zorn's main contribution to the history of music was the invention of an anti-jazz style, a frantic and chaotic hodgepodge of cartoon music, chamber music, punk-rock and sheer dissonance grafted onto the body of improvised music. The sense of an agonizing civilization radiated from his multi-faceted musical neurosis.

Hyper-active guitarist <u>Elliott Sharp</u> was perhaps the most incoherent experimentalist of his age, almost adopting a different technique for each recording, but his wildly multiform activity came to symbolize the ultimate synthesis of dissonance, repetition and improvisation, the three cardinal points of the classical, rock and jazz avantgarde. Sharp emerged from the sociomusical revolution of the new wave of rock music and entered a jazz world that was still recovering from the destructive process of the creative improvisers. His early groups, such as the ones documented on **ISM** (october 1981), with cornetist Olu Dara, trombonist Art Baron, bassist Bill Laswell and drummer Charles Noyes, **Carbon** (1984), with Lesli Dalaba on trumpet and Charles Noyes on percussion, and **Semantics** (july 1985), with Sam Bennett on drums and Ned Rothenberg on saxophone, applied cacophony and deconstruction to funk, blues and rock. His atonal guitar style was looking for patterns, not melody.

Soon he was transcending free jazz in the savage sonic assault of *Sili/Contemp/Tation* (april 1985) for quintet (Sharp on reeds and guitars, two trombones, bassist David Hofstra, Previte), and pioneering the computer and the sampler in *Virtual Stance*, off **Virtual Stance** (1986), a collaboration with drummer Bobby Previte, later re-recorded on **Looppool** (1988) in a purely digital version for computer, sampler and drum machine (all operated by Sharp himself). Last but not least, Sharp was abusing Mathematics, notably in two pieces for guitar, trombones and percussions, the tribal *Marco Polo's Argali*, off **Six Songs** (february 1985), and the dissonant ballet suite *Not Yet Time* off **Fractal** (1986), but also in the string quartet *Tessalation Row* (1986), all chamber works with tunings, counterpoint and dynamics based on the Fibonacci series, fractal geometry and chaos theory. His musico-mathematical studies culminated in the 40-minute pseudo-ethnic six-movement suite **Larynx** (october 1987) for a geometrically-organized 13-piece ensemble (Sharp on sax, clarinet, guitar and sampler, four brass players such as trumpeter Lesli Dalaba and three trombones, the four stringed instruments of the classical string quartet and four drummers including Previte, Bennett and Noyes), inspired by the overtones of Tibetan chanting. His "digital" adventures, instead, peaked with the structured improvisation *Twenty Below* for keyboard sextet (Anthony Coleman on toy piano and organ, Wayne Horvitz and Zeena Parkins on electronic keyboards, a reed organ and two musicians on samplers) off **K!L!A!V!** (august 1989).

Carbon remained his "rock'n'roll" alter-ego, that indulged in brief, frantic bursts of sound running the gamut from punk-jazz to funk-blues, as documented on vibrant, eclectic, acrobatic and reckless albums such as **Datacide** (1989), featuring Zeena Parkins on harp and two drummers, and **Tocsin** (1991), with Parkins and Sharp complemented by bass, percussion and sampler.

At the same time, he continued to score wildly dissonant works for chamber ensembles such as: *Ferrous* for "pantars" and "violinoid" (both homemade instruments), off **Twistmap** (june 1991); the atonal and very rhythmic chamber "orchestral" suite **Abstract Repressionism - 1990-99** (april 1992) for guitar, string quartet and percussion, something halfway between Anthony Braxton, Iannis Xenakis and Glenn Branca; the electroacoustic piece *Intifada* (composed in 1992) with Sharp processing (via real-time MIDI control) the sound of his own guitar and clarinet and of a string quartet, off **Xenocodex** (1996); *Cryptid Fragments* (march 1992) for cello, violin and computer (Sharp himself), off **Cryptid Fragments**; *Zappin' the Pram* for Sharp's guitar improvisations over the music he composed for a guitar trio, off **Dyners Club** (december 1993); the guitar-harp duet *Peregrine*, off the Parkins-Sharp collaboration **Blackburst** (1996); **Spring & Neap** (october 1996) for Zeena Parkins on harp, Makoto Nomura on piano, Michiyo Yagi on koto, Yumiko Tanaka on shamisen, Yoshiko Fujio on shamisen, Tamiki Sawa and Mio Abe on violins, Hiromichi Sakamoto and Kota Miki on cellos, Hiroaki Mizutani and Masaaki Kikuchi on contrabasses, Guam Kumada and Kenji Ito on percussions.

Tectonics was yet another project, this time in the realm of dance music: **Tectonics** (1995), **Field And Stream** (1997) and **Errata** (1999) were solo albums for guitar, sax and massive electronic/digital processing that crafted a futuristic, groove-based fusion of jazz, drum'n'bass and glitch music.

As a guitar improviser, Sharp penned the guitar solos of **Sferics** (1996), **The Velocity of Hue** (june 2003) and **Quadrature** (june 2005), that are dictionaries of incorrect guitar techniques. **Suspension Of Disbelief** (2001) was a solo album on which Sharp played guitar, clarinet, saxophone, zither, bass, synthesizer and computers.

While drawing from a kaleidoscope of rock and jazz guitar techniques as well as from the chaotic structures of Charles Ives' symphonies and Frank Zappa's dadaistic pieces, Eugene Chadbourne was a free improviser whose roots were in rural white music. However, exposure to Derek Bailey's and Anthony Braxton's creative improvisation and a demented sense of humor bestowed a tone of punk irreverence on **Solo Acoustic Guitar Volume One** (1975), including the cacophonous *Music for Mr Anthony Braxton*, **Solo Acoustic Guitar Volume Two** (june 1976), mostly for prepared stringed instruments and including *Making It Go Away*, and especially the **Collected Symphonies** (1985) for guitar.

A childish dadaism permeated a formidable orchestral piece created in june 1979 under the aegis of John Cage's aleatory music, **The English Channel**, credited to the 2000 Statues (featuring Lesli Dalaba and Toshinori Kondo on trumpets, Mark Kramer on organ, John Zorn on saxophone, Bob Ostertag on synthesizer, Steve Beresford on toy instruments, Fred Frith on guitar, Polly Bradfield on violin, LaDonna Smith on viola, Tom Cora on cello, Wayne Horvitz on piano, Andrea Centazzo on drums, Mark Miller on percussion, etc) that was reassembled in 1981 and mixed with all sorts of samples and sonic debris to obtain an abominable organism similar to Frank Zappa's satirical post-modernist collages. Chadbourne, also a proficient banjoist, promoted an unlikely marriage of country music and creative improvisation on **Country Music from Southeastern Australia** (1983), featuring David Moss on percussion and drum-machine, Jon Rose on violin and piano, and Rik Rue on field recordings and noises.

Chadbourne's erratic career continued to alternate between home-made lo-fi audio collages such as **Dinosaur On The way** (1979), featuring Tom Cora, Toshinori Kondo and John Zorn, or **Wombat on the Way** (1985), and mocking protest songs in the vein of Nashville's country music such as **Chad-Born Again** (1991). The latter form peaked with the satirical country & western opera **Jesse Helms Busted for Pornography** (1996), while his audio collage reached a new dimension with *House by the Cemetery* (premiered in 1998), off **Horror Part One**.

The aesthetic culmination of Chadbourne's insanity was probably the monumental project of *Insect And Western* (1996) for "symphony orchestra, gamelan and high-school jazz stage band", partially documented on **Insect Attracter**, **Insect and Western Party** and **The Intellectual and Emotional World of the Cockroach**. Parts of it were reorganized as **Termite Damage** (1998) and the series was later extended with **Bed Bugs** (2000). His madcap chamber music included *I Talked to Death in Stereo* (premiered in

1998) for electric guitar, strings, reeds, theremin and percussion, off **I Talked to Death in Stereo**.
His rare ventures into structure improvisation were best represented by *The Post Day of the Dead Ritual* (premiered in 1994) for ensemble.
Chadbourne was quite unique in the history of music for being at the same time an avantgarde composer in the classical tradition, a jazz improviser, a folk musician and a member of a rock band. Only Frank Zappa could compete with such eclecticism.

San Francisco-based guitarist Henry Kaiser adopted Derek Bailey's approach to creative atonal improvisation and Captain Beefheart's approach to post-psychedelic timbral and rhythmic mayhem on **Ice Death** (1977), featuring both solos and collaborations with improvisers such as guitarist Eugene Chadbourne and alto saxophonist John Oswald, the duets of **Protocol** (december 1978), with the Japanese trumpeter Toshinori Kondo and the Italian percussionist Andrea Centazzo, the chaotic guitar duets with Fred Frith of **With Friends Like These** (july 1979), that was also his first experiment in using the studio as an instrument, and finally the solo album **Outside Pleasure** (august 1979). The double-LP album **Aloha** (september 1981) contained two lengthy solo showcases for his extended technique *The Shadow Line*, a vast catalog of abominable blues, jazz, rock and Indian mistakes, and the studio-processed *Aloha Gamera* (a remix ante-litteram). Kaiser successfully wed creative improvisation and ethnic music on **Invite The Spirit** (august 1983), for a trio with Korean zither and percussion (Charles Noyes).
Instead the 27-minute *It's A Wonderful Life*, off **It's A Wonderful Life** (september 1984), began to display his twisted genius for composition, freely adapting elements of bluegrass, blues, rock, Indian and Japanese stringed instruments. The hypnotic scales, the fractured melodies and the intricate tonal zigzagging framed by neurotic tempos were closer in spirit to an acid-rock jam or to a melodic fantasia than to Derek Bailey's blasts of noise.
Other notable pieces of bizarre improvisation were the live duet with Bill Frisell, *Last Of The Few* (november 1985), off **Marrying For Money** (1982); the live duet with guitarist Jim O'Rourke, *A Long Life Is A Slow Death*, off **Tomorrow Knows Where You Live** (march 1991); the 25-minute solo *The Five Heavenly Truths*, off **The Five Heavenly Truths** (june 1992).

Cellist Tom Cora, who moved to New York in 1979, formed the original Curlew line-up with bassist Bill Laswell, guitarist Nicky Skopelitis, drummer Bill Bacon and reed player George Cartwright, that recorded **Curlew** (march 1980), but he also joined **Nimal** (1987), a combo formed by Swiss multi-instrumentalist Jean "Momo" Rossel that straddled the line between jazz, folk and progressive-rock. He remained a pillar of Cartwright's Curlew on **North America** (august 1984), **Live In Berlin** (march 1987), **Bee** (november 1990) and **A Beautiful Western Saddle** (1993), and a pillar of Nimal on **Voix De Surface** (1989), but he also played with Dutch anarcho-punk rockers Ex (1991-93). Cora's technique, that balanced the brutal and the lyrical, was the subject of the solo-cello albums **Live at The Western Front** (may 1986) and especially **Gumption** in **Limbo** (september 1990). In his hands the cello became both a guitar and a percussion, Cora continued to roam a broad horizon, from Third Person, the trio of Cora, percussionist Samm Bennett and rotating members that recorded **The Bends** (december 1990), **Trick Moon** (june 1990) and especially **Lucky Water** (june 1994) with Japanese saxophonist Umezu Kazutoki, to the abstract punk-noise experiment Roof, that recorded **The Untraceable Cigar** (february 1996).

Switzerland-based Irish guitarist Christy Doran established his credentials as a creative musicians through the solo albums **Harsh Romantics** (1984), **Phoenix** (april 1990) and **What a Band** (june 1991). Among his projects were **Corporate Art** (june 1991), a tight quartet with saxophonist Gary Thomas, bassist Mark Helias and drummer Bobby Previte, and the abstract jazz-rock quartet with vocals New Bag, that debuted with **Confusing the Spirit** (1999).

Alto saxophonist Tim Berne coined a neurotic language that mixed composition and improvisation. His wittily iconoclastic style, that toyed with counterpoint like in a marriage of cool jazz's rationality and free jazz's effervescence, matured via **Five Year Plan** (april 1979), containing *NYC Rites* for a sax-bass-drums trio augmented with clarinetist John Carter, baritone saxophonist Vinny Golia and a trombonist, **7X** (january 1980), containing *Showtime* for alto, baritone (Golia), guitar (Nels Cline), bass, trombone and percussion, and **Spectres** (february 1981), containing *For Charles Mingus* with cornetist Olu Dara, trombone, bass and percussion.
The live double-LP **Songs And Rituals In Real Time** (july 1981), in a quartet with tenor saxophonist Mack Goldsbury, bassist Ed Schuller and drummer Paul Motian, sounded like a compromise between melodic tunesmith and ceremonial music. The linguistic nonsense of *The Unknown Factor*, the cubistic game of decomposition and recomposition of *The Mutant of Alberan* and especially the 25-minute *The Ancient Ones*, that achieved a delicate balance of the lyrical and the expressionistic in music, relying on showers and rainbows of chromatic interplay, revealed Berne's unique compositional genius.
The sextet with trumpet (Herb Robertson), trombone (Ray Anderson), tenor saxophone (Goldsbury), bass (Schuller) and drums (Motian) documented on **The Ancestors** (february 1983), with the uncontrollable variations of the 34-minute two-part *Shirley's Song*, and pared down to a quartet without trombone or tenor on **Mutant Variations** (march 1983), brought Berne closer to the jazz tradition while continuing to invest on his compositional ideas. The atonal duets with guitarist Bill Frisell of **Theoretically** (september 1983), notably the horror cosmic music of *2001*, abandoned any pretense of jazz form.
Acrobatic pieces such as *The Ancient Ones*, *Shirley's Song* and *2011* were the preludes to the captivating balance of complex structure and anarchic solos achieved on **Fulton Street Maul** (august 1986), featuring Hank Roberts on cello, Bill Frisell on electric guitar and Alex Cline on percussion, a pastiche of pieces that could be both wildly dissonant (*Icicles Revisited*), melancholy romantic (*Betsy*) and frantically tribal (*Federico*).
Berne's musical chaos increased on **Sanctified Dreams** (october 1987), for a sax-trumpet-cello quintet (cellist Hank Roberts, trumpeter Herb Robertson, bassist

Mark Dresser, drummer Joey Baron), with almost clownish (but always intricate) revisitations of the jazz tradition (*Mag's Groove*); and reached a zenith on **Fractured Fairy Tales** (june 1989), that added violin (Mark Feldmann) and electronics (played by Baron) to the quintet. The dissonant chamber jazz of *Evolution Of A Pearl* bridged Frank Zappa's madcap stylistic soups and the classical avantgarde's studies on timbre and texture.
Berne then proceeded to apply the same twisted and schizophrenic logic to different combinations of musicians and styles.
Miniature, i.e. the trio of Berne, Baron and Roberts, used "electronic processing" and veered towards futuristic ethno-jazz-funk music on **Miniature** (march 1988) and **I Can't Put My Finger On It** (january 1991);
Caos Totale, a sextet including Robertson, Dresser, trombonist Steve Swell, drummer Bobby Previte and guitarist Marc Ducret, continued the progression towards lengthy and convoluted compositions such as *Legend of P1* on **Pace Yourself** (november 1990) and the imposing triad of **Nice View** (august 1993), that added keyboardist Django Bates: *It Could Have Been A Lot Worse* (21:15), *The Third Rail* (17:32), *Impacted Wisdom* (38:03).
Berne switched to baritone sax for **Loose Cannon** (october 1992), a trio with bassist Michael Formanek and drummer Jeff Hirshfield that penned the 16-minute *Fibrigade*.
The live **Lowlife** (september 1994), with the monoliths *Bloodcount* and *The Brown Dog Meets The Spaceman*, was, de facto, the first document of Bloodcount, a band featuring Ducret, Formanek, reed player Chris Speed, drummer Jim Black, and devoted to colossal live jams such as the 51-minute *Eye Contact*, off **Memory Select** (september 1994).

The live **Visitation Rites** (1996), whose highlight is the 30-minute *Piano Justice*, debuted Paraphrase, a more conventional sax-bass-drums trio also devoted to endless live jams.
After many mediocre live albums, Berne returned to studio recording with the ambitious **Open Coma** (july 2000) for big band, that revisited three of his masterpieces, with **The Shell Game** (2001), in a trio with percussionist Tom Rainey and electronic keyboardist Craig Taborn, containing the 30-minute *Thin Ice*. That trio added Ducret and became the Science Friction Band (a sax-guitar-keyboards-drums quartet), a project that harked back to Berne's cartoonish phase, thus closing the loop.

Elusive trumpeter Lesli Dalaba, a New York resident since 1978 (and a member of Wayne Horvitz's, Elliott Sharp's and La Monte Young's ensembles) contributed to renovate the vocabulary of the instrument with a style that turned even the most cerebral sounds into lyrical poems. Except for the solos and duets of **Trumpet Songs and Dances** (march 1979), her own compositions surfaced much later. **Core Samples** was mainly devoted to two multi-movement suites: *Core Sample* (1989), with two movements performed by the 10-piece Zlatne Ustne brass band (two alto saxophones, three baritone saxophones, a tuba, three Eastern European "truba" wooden trumpets and percussion), two duets with trumpeter Herb Robertson, two duets with guitarist Elliott Sharp and vocalist

Sussan Deihim; and *Violin Sentiment* (1989), with Sharp, violinist Jim Katzin and a drummer. **Dalaba Frith Glick-Rieman Kihlstedt** (Accretions, 2003), a collaboration with guitarist Fred Frith, pianist Eric Glick Rieman and violinist Carla Kihlstedt, relished Dalaba's sustained tones colliding against Frith's dadaistic noises in pieces such as *Ant Farm Morning* and *Worm Anvils*. **Timelines** (2004), featuring a quintet of veteran female musicians (Zeena Parkins on harp, Amy Denio on vocals, Ikue Mori on keyboards, Carla Kihlstedt on violin), was a concept album dedicated to the history of the world. **Lung Tree** (january 2004) was a set of slow-motion, pointillistic, desolate elegies with Eric-Glick Rieman on prepared piano and Stuart Dempster on trombone.

Jewish drummer Joey Baron, who had played with Bill Frisell (1988), Tim Berne (1989) and John Zorn (1989), debuted as a leader with **Tongue in Groove** (may 1991) and **Raised Pleasure Dot** (february 1993), both in a bizarre trio (Barondown) featuring trombonist Steve Swell and tenor saxophonist Ellery Eskelin performing sets of brief unpredictable sketches. Having proven how little he cared for the conventions of rhythm, Baron proceeded to form Down Home, a much more orthodox quartet with alto saxophonist Arthur Blythe, guitarist Bill Frisell and bassist Ron Carter whose **Down Home** (april 1997) featured longer pieces such as *Little Boy*, *Wide Load* and *What* that straddled the border between free jazz and rhythm'n'blues. In the meantime, Barondown changed format, delivering two lengthy and convoluted skits, *Games On A Train* and *Sittin' On A Cornflake*, on **Crackshot** (august 1995). Down Home, instead, crafted **We'll Soon Find Out** (april 2000), in an even more conventional vein, almost a postmodernist take on bebop.

The Microscopic Septet was a creative ensemble (soprano saxophonist Philip Johnston, alto saxophonist Don Davis, tenor saxophonist Paul Shapiro, baritone saxophonist Dave Sewelson, pianist Joel Forrester, bassist Dave Hofstra and drummer Richard Dworkin) that concocted an eccentric and sometimes clownish stew of free jazz, progressive-rock and rhythm'n'blues. The effervescent **Take the Z Train** (january 1983), **Let's Flip** (november 1984), **Off Beat Glory** (april 1986), and **Beauty Based on Science** (1988) were full of twists and turns but remained true to a homogeneous consistent ideology of passionate irreverence and unbound imagination. Forrester and Johnston were the main composers. Their mutant scores were collages of stylistic quotations that evoked Frank Zappa's madcap romantic orchestral themes.

POST-JAZZ SOLOISTS AND HYPER-FUSION

The influence of rock, world and avantgarde music on the white jazz community of New York was felt in both the kind of material that they embraced and in the kind of techniques that they employed for their improvisation.

Reed player Ned Rothenberg cut his teeth in Fall Mountain, an experimental trio with Bob Ostertag (electronics) and Jim Katzin (violin), that recorded the extended cacophonous pieces of **Early Fall** (december 1978). But Rothenberg established himself among creative improvisers with *Trials Of The Argo* (september 1980), a lengthy experiment of overdubbing saxophones, flutes, clarinets, shakuhachi flute and ocarina, *Continuo After The Inuit* (march 1981), that only used circular breathing and multiphonics (but no overdubbing) to imitate the vocal music of the Inuits on alto saxophone, both off **Trials Of The Argo**, with the three solos (november 1982) for alto saxophone, bass clarinet, soprano saxophone and ocarina as well as the duet with drummer Gerry Hemmingway, *Polysemy* (april 1983), off **Portal**, with the alto saxophone solo *Caeneus* and the clarinet-sax duet *Kakeai* with John Zorn off **Trespass** (august 1985).

He largely abandoned creative improvisation when he formed the New Winds, a trio of "multi-reedists" (Robert Dick on flute and piccolo, J.D. Parran mainly on clarinets, Rothenberg mainly on alto), that indulged in the complex and ambitious textures of **The Cliff** (september 1986), **Traction** (1991) and **Digging it Harder From Afar** (june 1994). He then formed the Double Band (with reed player Thomas Chapin, two bassists and two drummers) that debuted on **Overlays** (may 1991), playing high-energy funk-jazz inspired by Ormette Coleman's Prime Time.

Continuing that progression towards larger and more intricate constructions, the crowning achievement of his career was a big-band effort, **Power Lines** (august 1995), that explored dense, unpredictable structures replete with his favorite rhythmic experiments (Hanrahan on reeds, Mark Feldman on violin, Ruth Siegler on viola, Erik Friedlander on cello, Mark Dresser on bass, Dave Douglas on trumpet, Josh Roseman on trombone, Kenny Berger on reeds, Mike Sarin on drums, Glen Velez on percussion).

The chamber jazz compositions of **Ghost Stories** (april 2000), namely the *Duet for Alto Saxophone and Percussion* with Japanese percussionist Satoshi Takeishi, *Arbor Vitae* with shakuhachi player Riley Lee, and *Ghost Stories*, a quartet with Chinese pipa player Min Xiao-Fen, cellist Erik Friedlander and Takeishi, and the solos of the double-CD **Intervals** (Animul, 2002), one disc for alto sax and one disc for clarinet or shakuhachi, displayed his extended techniques at the reeds in the new context of his sophisticated sense of timbral counterpoint.

Jewish percussionist Kip Hanrahan came to prominence with a project of "neighborhood music" which looked like the urban, American equivalent of Lol Coxhill's "welfare state" project. **Coup De Tete** (1980), featuring several Latin percussionists, rock percussionist Anton Fier, atonal guitarist Arto Lindsay,

Post-jazz Soloists and Hyper-fusion

flutist Byard Lancaster and an army of guests, **Desire Develops An Edge** (june 1983), for vocalist Jack Bruce and an orchestra of rotating musicians, influenced by Carla Bley's Jazz Composers Orchestra, **Conjure** (october 1983), with blues vocalist Taj Mahal fronting Murray, Scherer, Lindsay and the usual arsenal of Latin percussions, and **Vertical Currency** (february 1984), for a smaller orchestra with rock vocalist Jack Bruce, Lindsay, tenor saxophonist David Murray, electronic keyboardist Peter Scherer, bassist Steve Swallow, four percussionists (including himself) and assorted guests, offered exotic progressive jazz-rock performed by all-star casts and drenched in a jungle of congas, bongos and the likes.

Hanrahan's exquisitely Latin-tinged "weltanschauung" permeated the percussion-heavy funk-jazz world-music of **Days And Nights Of Blue Lucy Inverted** (march 1987), with Allen Toussaint arranging the horns, of the colossal and eclectic **Tenderness** (march 1990), with a huge cast of musicians (including rock vocalist Gordon "Sting" Sumner, pianist Don Pullen, tenor saxophonist Chico Freeman and drummer Andrew Cyrille) of **Exotica** (may 1992), with Jack Bruce again fronting the big band, and **A Thousand Nights and a Night - Shadow Night** (march 1996), the first installment in a nine-part composition.

The career of drummer Sam Bennett bridged the solo percussion album **Metafunctional** (1983) and the abstract soundpainting of Skist, a duo with Haruna Ito that wed percussions with sampling and electronics, via the new-wave groups he co-founded with guitarist Elliott Sharp and saxophonist Ned Rothenberg, such as Semantics.

Trombonist Jim Staley tested different trios of musicians on **Mumbo Jumbo** (june 1986), with keyboardist Wayne Horvitz, guitarist Elliott Sharp, vocalist Shelley Hirsch, drummer Samm Bennett, guitarist Bill Frisell, percussionist Ikue Mori, guitarist Fred Frith and saxophonist John Zorn.

Saxophonist and clarinetist Marty Fogel penned **Many Bobbing Heads At Once** (march 1989), featuring David Torn on guitar, Michael Shrieve on drums and Dean Johnson on bass, a lyrical work incorporating and mixing elements of funk, pop, samba, Africa, reggae and bebop music.

Among the most original composers of his generation was a virtuoso of the French horn, Tom Varner, who coined a sophisticated idea of post-jazz from the five lengthy pieces of **Quartet** (august 1980), accompanied by an alto saxophonist, to the varied repertory of **Swimming** (june 1999).

New York-born accordionist Guy Klucevsek delighted the avantgarde world with a combination of austere compositions, such as *The Flying Pipe Organ* for multiple accordions, off **Scenes From a Mirage** (july 1987), or the eight-movement *Citrus My Love* for accordion, violin, cello and double bass, off **Citrus My Love** (1995), or *Tesknota* for accordion, violin, cello and bass, off **Stolen Memories** (1996); and surreal folk dance scores such as *Union Hall* (composed in 1989) for accordion, tenor saxophone and double bass, off **Flying Vegetables of the Apocalypse**, or *The Heart Of the Andes* for solo accordion, off **The Heart of the Andes** (september 2001).

As removed as possible from the austere tone of the solo creative improvisation, guitarist <u>Bill Frisell</u>, who moved to New York in 1980, a staple of Paul Motian's ensemble (1981-84), assimilated rock and jazz innovations while harking back to old-time church and folk music, and sometimes to marching bands and cafe orchestras, on **In Line** (august 1982), a collection of guitar solos and duets with bassist Arild Andersen, and on **Rambler** (august 1984), that featured trumpeter Kenny Wheeler, tuba player Bob Stewart, bassist Jerome Harris and drummer Paul Motian. The heavy-metal jazz trio Power Tools, with Ronald Shannon Jackson on drums and Melvin Gibbs on bass, that debuted on **Strange Meeting** (january 1987), highlighted Frisell's vast vocabulary of guitar techniques and ambient cacophony. In the meantime, Frisell's eclectic and eccentric postmodernist art peaked with the unstable chamber music of **Lookout For Hope** (march 1987), by a quartet with Hank Roberts on cello and Joey Baron on drums, and especially **Before We Were Born** (august 1988), featuring several distinguished guests (Baron, Roberts, guitarist Arto Lindsay, keyboardist Peter Scherer, saxophonists Julius Hemphill, Doug Wieselman and Billy Drewes) and offering a broad range of stylistic experiments, from bluegrass to noise (all condensed in *Hard Plains Drifter*).

Is That You (august 1989), in a bass-less trio with Wayne Horvitz on keyboards and Baron, and especially **Where in the World** (february 1991), virtually a continuation of **Lookout For Hope**, were calmer works that sounded like nostalgic tributes to his civilization, albeit distorted by evergreen strains of neurosis.

This Land (october 1992), by a sextet juxtaposing a horn section (clarinetist Don Byron, trombonist Curtis Fowlkes, alto saxophonist Billy Drewes) to his moody guitar technique, scoured the American musical subconscious. Continuing to drift away from jazz music and into a pastoral mood, Frisell reinvented his musical roots in a series of quiet stylistic tours de force: the country-music detour (with mandolin, banjo, dobro, bass, harmonica and Robin Holcomb's vocals) of **Nashville** (november 1996); **Ghost Town** (2000), on which he played all of the instruments by himself; the deceptively ambitious **Blues Dream** (2001), played by a septet (with Drewes, Fowlkes, trumpeter Ron Miles, steel guitarist Greg Leisz, bass and drums). All stood as a mad incursion into the American psyche. And **The Intercontinentals** (2003), featuring a multi-national ensemble, pushed Frisell's musical explorations even beyond the USA.

White bassist Marc Johnson formed a quartet with drummer Peter Erskine and guitarists Bill Frisell and John Scofield that recorded **Bass Desires** (may 1985) and **Second Sight** (march 1987), emphasizing the post-modernist dialogue between the guitars.

Guitarist <u>David Torn</u>, a former member of the Everyman Band (with Martin Fogel on saxophones), bridged Jimi Hendrix and Sonny Sharrock when he coined the space and psychedelic jazz-rock style of the solo **Best Laid Plans** (july 1984) and the baroque, oneiric and cerebral style of **Cloud About Mercury** (march 1986), featuring Bill Bruford on drums, Tony Levin on bass and Mark Isham on trumpet (*Networks Of Sparks*). He left behind the last vestiges of progressive-

Post-jazz Soloists and Hyper-fusion

rock and jazz-rock on **Tripping Over God** (november 1994), an electroacoustic post-rock industrial ambient blues raga crafted by augmenting his guitar with all sorts of sound effects and overdubs, and **What Means Solid Traveller?** (november 1995), with stronger elements of electronics, world-music, heavy-metal and noise, and almost all digital, electric and ethnic instruments played by himself.

The music of cellist Hank Roberts was mainly influenced by free jazz but also incorporated elements of soul, blues and classical music. His technique at the cello often mimicked other instruments, both western (harp), rock (guitar) and eastern (sarod, kora), while his falsetto indulged in metaphysical croons a` la Robert Wyatt. Roberts' output ranged from the experimental **Black Pastels** (december 1987), featuring guitarist Bill Frisell, saxophonist Tim Berne, drummer Joey Baron and three trombonists, to **Arcado** (1989), a string trio with Mark Dresser and Mark Feldman, to the compositions for large ensemble of **The Truth and Reconciliation Show** (2002), to the solo cello and vocals meditations of **22 Years From Now** (january 1996); but perhaps his zenith was *Saturday Sunday*, off **Little Motor People** (december 1992), a veritable collage of musical styles of the American heartland in the tradition of Aaron Copland and Charles Ives.

Former Santana's drummer Michael Shrieve built a unique repertory that focused on percussion. Energetic and creative albums such as the solo-percussion tour de force **In Suspect Terrain** (1984), **Stiletto** (july 1988), that featured Mark Isham on trumpet and Andy Sumners and David Torn on guitars, and **The Big Picture** (1989), which was virtually a concerto for an orchestra of percussion instruments, relied on a visionary and frequently oneiric concept of percussive sounds. **Fascination** (november 1993), with Bill Frisell and Wayne Horvitz, lent him a new life in post-jazz soundsculpting.

POST-JAZZ BIG BANDS

The second half of the 1990s saw a resurgence of music for largest ensembles, away from the solo creative music of the 1970s/1980s.

The trend had been pioneered by one the most original composers and arrangers of the 1980s, bassist Saheb Sarbib, whose music for big band included the 34-minute *Concerto for Rahsaan*, premiered on **Live at the Public Theater** (october 1980), and the four-movement suite *Aisha*, off **Aisha** (august 1981),

Black cornet player Butch (Lawrence Douglas) Morris was perhaps the most revolutionary conductor of big bands of the post-swing era. An alumnus in Los Angeles of Horace Tapscott's Pan Afrikan Peoples Arkestra, itself an outgrowth of the Underground Musicians' Association (UGMA), formed in 1961, Morris relocated to New York in 1976 and became a member of David Murray's band (1982-97). The aim of multimedia events such as the 47-minute **Current Trends In Racism** (february 1985) was to transform the performance of an orchestral work into an improvised duet between the conductor (Morris) and the orchestra (Frank Lowe on tenor sax, John Zorn on alto sax, Zeena Parkins on harp, Tom Cora on cello, Christian Marclay on turntables, and others on vibraphone, piano, guitar, percussion, voice). The conductor expressed himself through gestures and the orchestra expressed itself through sounds. Both contributed creatively to defining the result. Thus the concepts of improvisation, composition and performance get blurred to the point that the composer is an improviser, the improvisers are as much in charge as the conductor, etc. This album contained *Conduction 1*, where "conduction" means "conducted improvisation" (the conductor uses both signs and gestures to direct the development of the composition). The music was as "un-orchestral" as it could be. The instruments were basically playing against each other rather than together. There was little or no sense of synchronicity, harmony or coherence. The sheer amount of instruments made it virtually impossible to achieve any degree of organic improvisation. Morris' orchestra redefined counterpoint as a chaotic eruption of timbres, and Morris' counterpoint redefined the orchestra as a loose assembly of individual urges. The focus was in finding a balance between the conductor's stream of consciousness and the collective stream of consciousness of the players. That goal entailed developing a common vocabulary of musical blocks, and most of the piece was just that: the slow, painful development of a new language of piano clusters, guttural moans, sax squeals, etc.

The idea of conducting a big band of improvisers was further developed on the eight-movement suite **Homeing** (june 1987), for cornet, French horn, oboe, trombone, vibraphone, piano, violinist Jason Hwang, guitarist Pierre Dorge, electronic musician David Weinstein, vocalist Shelley Hirsch, bass and drums, in the two colossal live jams with Hirsch, Hwang, trombone, reeds, cello, guitarist Hans Reichel and drummer Paul Lovens of **Mass-X-Communication** (december 1990), and on **Dust To Dust** (november 1990), that toyed with multiple aspects of musical presentation, scored for English horn, trombone, vibraphone, bassoon, oboe, clarinetist Marty Ehrlich, keyboardist Wayne Horvitz, violinist Jason Hwang, pianist Myra Melford, harpist Zeena Parkins, guitarist Jean-Paul Bourelly and drummer Andrew Cyrille (no Morris and no bass).

The ten-disc **Testament** collects "conductions" experimented with different combinations of instruments: *Conduction #11/ Where Music Goes* (december 1988) for the Rova Saxophone Quartet, electronics, piano, trombone, guitar, cello, violin, bass and percussion; *Conduction #15/ Where Music Goes II* (november 1989) for alto saxophone (Arthur Blythe), violin (Hwang), harp (Zeena Parkins), flute, vibraphone, French horn, piano, trombone, bassoon, guitars and percussion; *Conduction #22* (june 1992) for turntablist Christian Marclay, percussionist Le Quan Ninh, electronic musician Gunter Muller, trombone and cello; *Conduction #23/ Quinzaine de Montreal* (april 1992) for violin, five cellos, trombone, piano, vibraphone and bass (and no percussion); *Conduction #25/ The Akbank Conduction* (october 1992) and *Conduction #26/ Akbank II* (october 1992), both for a Turkish ensemble (kemence, oud, kanun, ney) plus percussionist Le Quean Ninh, vibraphone, trombone, harp, guitar, piano and trumpet; *Conduction #28/ Cherry Blossom* (march 1993) for a Japanese ensemble of traditional instruments (nokan, ohtsuzumi, shomyo, tugaru syamisen, shakuhachi) plus violin, piano, clarinet, computer, vocals, turntablist Yoshihide Otomo, bass and percussion, with Butoh dancers; *Conduction #31* (may 1993) for soprano saxophone, trombone, piano (Steve Beresford), guitar (Hans Reichel), cello (Tom Cora), vocals (Catherine Jauniaux), bass (Peter Kowald), percussion (Han Bennink) and drum machines (Ikue Mori); *Conduction #35/ American Connection 4* (may 1993) and *Conduction #36/ American Connection 4* (may 1993) for flute, clarinet, guitar, violin, piano, trombone, vocals, bass (Maarten Altena) and drums; *Conduction #38/ In Freud's Garden* (december 1993) for three cellos, viola, clarinets, saxophones, pianist Myra Melford, harpist Zeena Parkins, vibraphone, guitar, trombone, bass and percussionist Le Quan Ninh: percussion; *Conduction #39* (november 1993) and *Conduction #40* (november 1993) for turntablist Christian Marclay, guitarist Elliott Sharp, three violins, two cellos, harp, vibraphone, piano (Melford), three bassists (William Parker, Mark Helias and Fred Hopkins); *Conduction #41/ New World* (february 1994) for two clarinets, two saxophones, two trombones, shakuhachi, guitar and vocals; *Conduction #50* (march 1995) for Japanese instruments (otuzumi, koto, gidayu, zheng, tugaru syamisen), piano, violin, percussion, turntablist Yoshihide Otomo, vocals and two basses. The music of these "conductions" borrowed freely from the classical avantgarde, free jazz, ethnic music, Brian Eno's ambient music, but the development was eccentric to say the least.

More works for large ensemble followed: the double-CD **Berlin Skyscraper**, containing *Conduction #51, #52, #55, #56* for a 17-piece ensemble (piano, bassoon, oboe, cello, trumpet, clarinet, saxophone, flute, vibraphone, guitar, three violins, harp, trombone, bass and two percussionists); **Conduction #70/ Tit For Tat** (september 1996) for turntable, electronics, noise sculptors Voice Crack (Norbert Moeslang and Andy Guhl), electronic musician Gunter Muller, clarinet, violin, cello, violin, guitar, vocals and drums; **Holy Sea**, containing *Conduction #57, #58, #59* (february 1996) for turntablist Otomo Yoshihide, sampling, drum-machine, electronics, piano and an Italian orchestra (four violins, three violas, two cellos, contrabass, flute bassoon, horn, trumpet, trombone, tuba, harp, timpani, percussion); the four-section **Conduction 117** (2001), credited to the Jump Arts Orchestra, an orchestra of 24 improvisers drawn from rock, classical, jazz and ethnic music (two trumpets, two trombones, French horn, tuba, flute, four clarinets, bassoon, three saxophones, piano, two violas, two cellos, two basses, two percussionists); etc.

White keyboardist <u>Wayne Horvitz</u> was "the" composer of his generation. While he was playing with John Zorn, Horvitz rehearsed his ideas about progressive chamber jazz with the four swinging suites of **No Place Fast** (june 1979), featuring both Horvitz and his wife Robin Holcomb on keyboards, plus percussion, saxophone and flute, the two radio pieces of **Cascando** (may 1979), namely *Cascando* for trumpet (Lesli Dalaba) and vocalists and *Words And Music* for trumpet, vocalists, contrabass and percussion, **Simple Facts** (may 1980), that featured Holcomb's first compositions, and the two lengthy suites for piano (Horvitz), cornet (Butch Morris) and bass (William Parker) of **Some Order Long Understood** (february 1982), *Some Order Long Understood* and especially *Psalm*.

After **Dinner At Eight** (september 1985), a post-fusion hodgepodge of funk, jazz, rock and ethnic music (with Horvitz on electronic keyboards and drum-machine, Elliott Sharp on guitars, Doug Wieselman on clarinet and tenor saxophone, Chris Brown on percussion), and a jazzier trio with cornet player Butch Morris and drummer Bobby Previte, **Nine Below Zero** (january 1986), in 1986 Horvitz and Holcomb the New York Composers' Orchestra to perform compositions for jazz orchestra, at a time when everybody else seemed more and more fascinated by freer and freer improvisation.

At the same time, Horvitz entertained an electric fusion band, the President, formed in 1985 with himself on electronic keyboards, Doug Wieselman on tenor saxophone, Elliot Sharp and Bill Frisell on guitars, David Hofstra on bass and Bobby Previte on drums, and basically a continuation of the trans-stylistic song-oriented program of **Dinner At Eight**. **The President** (1987), **Bring Yr Camera** (february 1988), with Dave Tronzo replacing Frisell, and **Miracle Mile** (1991), with Frisell and several new additions, took frequent detours into progressive rock, rhythm'n'blues and ethnic music.

The acoustic jazz career with the New York Composers Orchestra continued on a parallel track via **New York Composers Orchestra** (january 1990), featuring alto saxophone, flute, reeds (Wieselman, Marty Ehrlich), two trombones (including Ray Anderson's), two French horns, three trumpets (including Herb Robertson and Lesli Dalaba), two pianos (Holcomb and Horvitz), bass and drums (Previte), and via **First Program in Standard Time** (january 1992), by a less star-studded version of the orchestra (without Robertson, Dalaba, Previte).

A full-time member of John Zorn's Naked City, Horvitz continued to explore other kinds of music with his own groups: sampled-laden progressive-rock with

Pigpen, a quartet of alto saxophone, keyboards, bass (Fred Chalenor) and drums, as on **V As In Victim** (may 1993) and **Miss Ann** (december 1993); electronic dance music (funk, trip-hop, acid-jazz) with Zony Mash (keyboards, guitar, bass, drums) on **Cold Spell** (1997) and **Brand Spankin' New** (1998); eerie soundscapes for piano, violin (Eyvind Kang), trombone (Julian Priester) and electronic keyboards (Reggie Watts) with the 4+1 Ensemble on **4+1 Ensemble** (1996) and its follow-up **From a Window** (august 2000); straight-forward funk-jazz jams with Ponga (a quartet with keyboardist Dave Palmer, drummer Bobby Previte and saxophonist "Skerik") on the live **Ponga** (1997); elegant chamber jazz with the Gravitas Quartet (trumpeter Ron Miles, cellist Peggy Lee, bassoonist Sara Schoenbeck) on **Way Out East** (august 2005).

A member of Elliott Sharp's and Wayne Horvitz's ensembles, white drummer Bobby Previte found a bizarre compromise between ECM's baroque jazz and Frank Zappa's nonsensical rock on **Bump The Renaissance** (june 1985), for a jazz quintet (Lenny Pickett on saxophone and clarinet, David Hofstra on bass, Richard Schulman on piano, Tom Varner on French horn) and running the gamut from avantgarde to jazz to rock to blues to ragtime music, and on **Pushing The Envelope** (april 1987), featuring Hofstra, Varner, Wayne Horvitz on keyboards and Marty Ehrlich on tenor sax. The more electronic and "industrial" **Dull Bang, Gushing Sound, Human Shriek** (november 1986), entirely played by Previte on keyboards and percussion, displayed his skills as an oneiric and apocalyptic arranger. His eclectic and iconoclastic imagination was in full bloom on **Claude's Late Morning** (1988), featuring Horvitz, Bill Frisell on guitar, Joey Baron on drums, Ray Anderson on trombone, Carol Emanuel on harp, Guy Klucevsek on accordion (plus steel guitar and sampler), and especially **Empty Suits** (may 1990), a stylistic cauldron that reached back to his chaotic beginnings with an expanded orchestration (Robin Eubanks on trombone, Marty Ehrlich on alto sax, Elliott Sharp on guitar, Carol Emanuel on harp, David Shea on turntables, plus electronic keyboards, guitar, vocals, steel guitar). His knack for assembling creative ensembles was also responsible for the calmer, more complex and more melodic **Weather Clear Track Fast** (january 1991), featuring Don Byron and Marty Ehrlich on clarinets and saxophones, Graham Haynes on cornet, Anthony Davis on piano, Robin Eubanks on trombone, Anthony Cox on bass. His skills as a composer, on the other hand, emerged from the humorous suite of **Music of the Moscow Circus** (august 1991), featuring a typical electroacoustic chamber ensemble (violinist Mark Feldman, trumpeter Herb Robertson harpist Carol Emanuel, bassist Mark Helias, opera singers electronic keyboards and percussion), from the four lengthy, intricate and anti-classical compositions (notably *Fantasy And Nocturne*, *Walz* and *Prelude And Elegy*) of **Slay The Suitors** (june 1993), credited to the Empty Suits (Eubanks, Horvitz, electronic keyboards, bass and percussion), from the keyboards-heavy incursions into melodic jazz of **Hue And Cry** (december 1993), credited to Weather Clear Track Fast (Byron, Cox, Davis, Ehrlich, Eubanks, Haynes, and Larry Goldings on organ), from the hysterical suites (*Three Minute Heels*, *The Eleventh Hour*, *Box End Open End*) of **Too Close To The Pole** (april 1996), that engaged a completely new ensemble (saxophone, trumpeter Cuong Vu, clarinet, keyboardist Jamie Saft, trombone, bass, percussion) and from many other projects under different names, each devoted to a different style. Latin For Travelers' **My Man In Sydney** (january 1997) was progressive rock for an electric quartet with guitarist Marc Ducret, organist Jamie Saft and bassist Jerome Harris. Bump's **Just Add Water** (june 2001) mimicked the playful, funky, bluesy sound of New Orleans' street bands (Ray Anderson on trombone, Joseph Bowie on trombone, Marty Ehrlich on tenor saxophone, Wayne Horvitz on piano, Steve Swallow on bass and Previte on drums). Bump's **Counterclockwise** (october 2002) (Ehrlich, trombonist Curtis Fowlkes, Horvitz, Swallow, Previte), retained the pulsation but deconstructed Previte's funk-blues-jazz fusion. Groundtruther's **Latitude** (2004), a collaboration with guitarist Charlie Hunter and alto saxophonist Greg Obsy, was heavily electronic and percussive.

Previte's progressive embracing of neoclassical structures peaked with **The 23 Constellations of Joan Miro** (july 2001), a suite of 23 lyrical chamber vignettes performed by an all-star cast.

St Louis-raised white multi-instrumentalist Marty Ehrlich (mainly clarinet, saxophone, and flute), a veteran improviser who had played in the Human Arts Ensemble (1973), Anthony Braxton's Creative Orchestra (1978), George Russell's Big Band (1978), Roscoe Mitchell's Creative Orchestra (1979), Leo Smith's Creative Improvisers Orchestra (1979), Leroy Jenkins' Mixed Quintet (1979) and Muhal Richard Abrams' Orchestra (1981), was initially influenced by Anthony Braxton and Henry Threadgill on **The Welcome** (march 1984) for a trio with bassist Anthony Cox and drummer Pheeroan AkLaff. However, he bridged the worlds of traditional jazz, creative improvisation, melodic music and avantgarde classical music on **Pliant Plaint** (april 1987), with Bobby Previte on drums, Anthony Cox on bass and Stan Strickland on sax, and especially **Traveller's Tale** (june 1989), with a similar quartet (Lindsey Horner replacing Cox on bass), elegant and eccentric, linear and imaginative, and **Side by Side** (january 1991), in a quintet with Wayne Horvitz on piano, Frank Lacy on trombone, Cox on bass and Andrew Cyrille on drums. At the same time Ehrlich was among the most ubiquitous members of the big bands of the 1990s (Bobby Previte, Wayne Horvitz, Butch Morris, John Zorn).

His proximity to chamber music was emphasized by the trio with cellist Abdul Wadud and Horner on **Emergency Peace** (december 1990), and by **Just Before the Dawn** (april 1995), in a quintet with Vincent Chancey on French horn, Erik Friedlander on cello, Mark Helias on bass and Don Alias on drums. His specialty was probably the lyrical cello-tinged "song".

The jazzier side of Ehrlich, in which improvisation prevailed over composition, basically constituted a parallel life: the quartet with Strickland, Previte and bassist Michael Formaniek of **Can You Hear a Motion** (september 1993); the quintet with Strickland, Formanek, Michael Cain on piano and Bill Stewart on drums of **New York Child** (february 1995); the duo with pianist Muhal Richard Abrams of **Open Air Meeting** (august 1996); the trio with bassist Mark Dresser

and drummer Andrew Cyrille of **C/D/E** (october 1998); the trio with Formanek and drummer Peter Erskine of **Relativity** (may 1999).
The piano-based quartets with bassist Formanek and drummer Billy Drummond of **Song** (october 1999), featuring pianist Uri Caine, and **Line On Love** (december 2002), featuring pianist Craig Taborn, made up yet another artistic avenue, confessing his passion for melody.
The chamber-jazz program was continued on **Sojourn** (february 1999), which added guitarist Marc Ribot to the trio of cello (Friedlander), bass (Helias) and reeds, and by the Traveler's Tales, a quartet of two horns (Ehrlich and saxophonist Tony Malaby) and rhythm section (bassist Jerome Harris and Previte), on **Malinke's Dance** (december 1999). The project was given an almost baroque format on **The Long View** (april 2002), a seven-movement suite that managed to display both neoclassical and jazz overtones, with orchestrations ranging from the ten-piece unit of the first movement to the chamber ensemble with reeds, strings (Helias, violinist Mark Feldman, Friedlander), piano (Horvitz), trombone (Ray Anderson) and drums (Pheeroan AkLaff) of the fifth to the quartet with Horvitz, Dresser and Previte of the fourth to the duet with Horvitz of the seventh. It got stretched to the limit on **News On The Rail** (november 2004), one of his most erudite studies on timbral counterpoint (for a sextet with three horns, piano, bass and drums).
Marty Ehrlich was both the natural heir of Eric Dolphy as a multi-instrumental stylist, and a composer in the vein of Charles Mingus.

Yugoslavian-born pianist <u>Stevan Tickmayer</u>, a composer of chamber music in various settings, co-founded the Science Group with percussionist Chris Cutler, bassist Bob Drake and assorted guests. Their **A Mere Coincidence** (january 1999) and **Spoors** (2003) are yet another take on the fusion of chamber and improvised music.

Minnesota-born composer <u>Maria Schneider</u>, who moved to New York in 1985, resurrected the style of Gil Evans for the generation of the 1990s on albums for orchestra such as **Evanescence** (1992) and **Coming About** (november 1995), all the way to the big-band effort of **Concert In The Garden** (2004).

British reed player <u>Paul Dunmall</u>, a member of Keith Tippett's Mujician, also led his own octet, that recorded the five-part suites **Bebop Starburst** (june 1997) and **The Great Divide** (march 2000), and toyed with the big-band format on **I Wish You Peace** (march 2003), all three milestones of revisionist avant-garde jazz that run the gamut from soulful melodies to abrasive solos, from dissonant counterpoint to noir ambience, from fanfares to litanies.

THE GREAT CHICAGO JAZZ REBIRTH

Chicago's pianist <u>Myra Melford</u>, who moved to New York in 1984, debuted with the solo-piano meditations **One For Now** (august 1986) but established herself as a poignant composer in the vein of Henry Threadgill with a trio that recorded **Jump** (june 1990), **Now and Now** (august 1991) and the live **Alive In The House of Saints** (february 1993). Their playing revisited all the elements of jazz improvisation within a structured context. In order to pursue these erudite studies, she formed The Same River Twice with saxophonist Chris Speed, trumpeter Dave Douglas, cellist Erik Friedlander and drummer Michael Sarin, that recorded **The Same River Twice** (january 1996) and **Above Blue** (april 1998), albums whose music was frequently cryptic and disorienting. However, they all paled in comparison with the 25-minute combinatorial game of *La Mezquita Suite*, off **Even the Sounds Shine** (march 1994), for a quintet with trumpeter Dave Douglas and saxophonist Marty Ehrlich. A blend of lyrical inspiration and musical mastery fueled the ever more sophisticated architectures of **Dance Beyond the Color** (may 1999) and **The Tent** (april 2003).

White saxophonist and clarinetist <u>Ken Vandermark</u>, who relocated to Chicago in 1989, started his career in rock groups such as the Flying Luttenbachers (1992-95). In 1993 his quartet (guitarist Todd Colburn, bassist Kent Kessler, drummer Michael Zerang) debuted with a pyrotechnic display of rhythms, melodies and musical mistakes on **Big Head Eddie** (february 1993), equally dedicated to Thelonious Monk, funk guru George Clinton and (most appropriately) rock eccentric Captain Beefheart, the elusive musician who in the late 1960s had pioneered the fusion of psychedelic rock, free jazz, classical avantgarde and pop music that Vandermark took as a starting point. His other influence was Hal Russell's anarchic project, the NRG Ensemble, in which Vandermark played (1993-95). **Solid Action** (may 1994), with Daniel Scanlan replacing Colburn, and containing his first major compositions (*Catch 22* and *Bucket*), indulged in the postmodernist ambiguity of playing music that deconstructed all sorts of musical cliches (blues, dub, funk, jazz, rock) and it did so with a vengeance.

Vandermark was also exploring the format of the trio, first with the Steelwood Trio (Vandermark, Kessler, drummer Curt Newton) on **International Front** (september 1994) and then with the DKV Trio (basically, the Steelwood Trio with percussionist Hamid Drake replacing Newton) on the wild **Baraka** (february 1997), that contained the 35-minute free-form amoeba *Baraka*.

Vandermark 5, instead, the quintet with reed player Mars Williams, guitarist/trombonist Jeb Bishop, bassist Kent Kessler and drummer Tim Mulvenna, played visceral free jazz at neurotic speed that was cohesive enough to sound closer in spirit to progressive-rock than to creative improvisation. **Single Piece Flow** (august 1996) and especially **Target Dr Flag** (october 1997), collapsed Charles Mingus, John Coltrane, Eric Dolphy, Albert Ayler and Ornette Coleman into one disorienting vortex. Dave Rempis replaced Williams on **Simpatico** (december 1998), and **Burn The Incline** (december 1999), with

Distance, that were basically post-modernist tributes to his favorite jazz players, passionate distillations from the history of post-bop jazz. Vandermark's wild sax style became a classic despite sounding like a clown aping the greats of the past. Now rooted in the jazz tradition, the compositions of **Acoustic Machine** (january 2001) were lengthy tests of Vandermark's mastery of jazz counterpoint (*Stranger Blues, Auto Topography, Fall to Grace, Close Enough, Wind Out*). After **Airports for Light** (august 2002), the ambitions of the composer of his quintet further expanded with the 20-minute suite *Six of One*, off **Elements of Style** (july 2003), with the 19-minute *Camera*, off the double-CD **The Color Of Memory** (july 2004), with the 14-minute *Some Not All*, off **A Discontinuous Line** (december 2005), on which cellist Fred Lonberg-Holm replaced Bishop; pieces that felt like distorted mirror images of the history of jazz music. Vandermark then embraced the trend towards chamber jazz and big-band jazz with the Territory Band, whose spectacular line-ups created music that was both accessible and unpredictable. Vandermark took advantage of the larger ensembles to create larger-scale constructions and trigger larger-scale improvisation. **Transatlantic Bridge** (february 2000) featured the quintet (Bishop, Kessler, Rempis, Mulvenna) plus trumpeter Axel Doerner, pianist Jim Baker, cellist Fred Lonberg-Holm and drummer Paul Lytton in what was basically a concept about abstract painting in four lengthy movements (*Collage, RM, Mobile, Stabile*). **Atlas** (february 2001) and the double-CD **Map Theory** (september 2002) added Kevin Drumm on electronics to concoct the glitchy electroacoustic improvisations for chamber orchestra of *Neiger* and *Now* (on the former) and *A Certain Light for Peter Kowald, Framework for Rob Vandermark, Image As Text for Richard Hull* (on the latter). Another double-CD album, **Company Switch** (september 2004), replaced Drumm with electronic musician Lasse Marhaug towards a more introspective form of electroacoustic improvisation (*Killing Floor, Local Works, Franja*). The triple-disc **A New Horse for the White House** (october 2005) for a 12-piece unit explored an even deeper soundscape across four complex atonal fantasias (*Fall With A Vengeance, Untitled Fiction, Corrosion, Cards*), largely dominated by Doerner's trumpet, Lonberg-Holm's cello, Lytton's percussion and Lasse Marhaug's electronics. Despite the epic proportions of the music, the Territory Band sounded like Vandermark's most private and anguished statement yet.

After playing in klezmer and rock groups in New York, cellist Fred Lonberg-Holm moved to Chicago and founded the Light Box Orchestra, a rotating orchestra of jazz musicians (so named because the improvisers were switched on and off by a box of lights). While also a member of several Chicago post-rock bands, he joined the ranks of the creative improvisers with the solo performances of **Personal Scratch** (february 1996), and the duets of **Site-Specific** (september 1998) with rock and jazz musicians on guitar (Jim O'Rourke, Kevin Drumm, Michael Zerang, Ben Vida, Michael Krassner, Jeb Bishop, etc).

Possibly inspired by the Modern Jazz Quartet, Terminal 4 was his attempt at composing rock music for a pseudo-jazz quartet of cello, guitar (Ben Vida), bass (Josh Abrams) and trombone (Jeb Bishop). **Terminal 4** (2001), featuring vocalist

Terria Gartelos, and **When I'm Falling** (2003), with bassist Jason Roebke replacing Abrams, contained delicate chamber arias, noisy ballads and surrealist fanfares.

Pillow was a quartet with Fred Lonberg-Holm on cello, Michael Colligan on reeds, and two members of Town And Country, Liz Payne on bass and Ben Vida on guitar. Their **Pillow** (1998), **Field On Water** (2000) and **Three Henries** (2001) were sets of free improvised jams.

The cello solos of **Dialogs** (january 2002), that sounded like a repertory of ways to "destroy" the sound of the cello, the duets of **Object 1** (2003) with German trumpeter Alex Dorner, and **Eruption** (2003), a trio with electronic musician Kevin Drumm and the Flying Luttenbachers' drummer Weasel Walter, moved the cellist further into the dissonant realm.

Chicago-based saxophonist, flutist and clarinetist Scott Rosenberg, a pupil of Anthony Braxton, expanded the vocabulary of jazz music with an anarchic polyphony of extended techniques and illicit sounds, best documented on **V - Solo Improvisations** (may 2000) and on the Skronktet West's dadaistic albums **Toad In The Hole** (december 1999) and **El** (april 2001), for a quintet with clarinet (Matt Ingals), guitar (John Shiurba), contrabass (Morgan Guberman) and percussion (Gino Robair). Rosenberg's "noise-jazz" was an art straddling the border between tradition and insanity, rationality and randomness, semiotics and psychoanalysis, sense and nonsense. His works for large ensembles, such as the four-part symphony **IE** (august 1997) for 27-piece orchestra (five violins, viola, cello, two guitars, five clarinets, two saxophones, tuba, trumpet, accordion, three basses, three percussions plus two vocalists), whose movements range from apocalyptic to clownish, and **Creative Orchestra Music** (march 2001) for 26-piece orchestra (vocals, flute, oboe, six reeds, two trumpets, two trombones, tuba, two guitars, viola, two cellos, piano, three basses and three percussions), a music of complex scores and grand gestures that ran the gamut from dramatic dissonance to trancey fanfares.

His passion for dense and convoluted scores and for reckless improvisation, also permeated his music for quartet: **Owe** (march 2001) and **Blood** (may 2004) for Red, a quartet of tenor sax, bass, drums and cornet (Todd Margasak) that replicated the configuration of Ornette Coleman's quartet with Don Cherry, and **New Folk New Blues** (august 2003) for a quartet of improvisers (Rosenberg on sax, keyboardist Jim Baker, bassist Anton Hatwich and percussionist Tim Daisy).

The Return of the Jazz Improviser

Zeena Parkins, a veteran of Lindsay Cooper's progressive outfit News From Babel (1983-85), was the harpist who introduced the instrument in the context of creative improvisation. She was also the closest thing to a composer of chamber music within New York's "creative" milieu. **Something Out There** (january 1987) collected solos, duets and trios with the likes of drummer Ikue Mori, cellist Tom Cora, turntablist Christian Marclay, percussionist Samm Bennett, etc. She continued to straddle the line between rock and jazz, playing in Chris Cochrane's No Safety (1989-92) while partnering with the likes of Butch Morris and Elliott Sharp. The prototype for her lengthy compositions was *Ursa's Door* (june 1991), off **Ursa's Door**, scored for chamber trio (harp, violin, cello), guitar and electronics, with Ikue Mori's computer-generated "concrete" sounds haunting Parkins' alien harp-based soundscapes.
After the brief harp solos of **Nightmare Alley** (1992), she began to stretch out. The ten-movement suite **Isabelle** (september 1993) for harp, piano, cello, violin and sampler; the nine-movement suite *Maul* (december 1995) and the six-movement suite *Blue Mirror* (february 1996), both off **Mouth=Maul=Betrayer** and also scored for small chamber ensembles (electric harp, sampler, piano, cello, violin, percussion, vibraphone, guitar, didjeridu) displayed her skills at composing counterpoint and at conducting improvisers; while the 24-minute *Peregrine*, a collaboration with Elliott Sharp off Psycho-Acoustic's **Blackburst** (1996) that employed electronics and digital manipulation, the sample-driven dissonant solo **No Way Back** (december 1997), and especially the three suites of **Pan-Acousticon** (december 1998) for found sounds, strings and percussion, as well as the impressionistic/futuristic vignettes of **Phantom Orchard** (2004), a collaboration with Ikue Mori, moved her art towards more and more abstract and looser structures.
Persuasion for string quartet and electronic processing and the three-movement *Visible/Invisible* for string quartet, off **Necklace** (2006), were stoic exploration of the sonic space, from sharp drones to percussive dissonance. In her most inspired moments Parkins carried out dense and complex experiments on texture and dynamics that rivaled the contemporary classical avantgarde.

The style of Japanese trumpet player Toshinori Kondo, who moved to New York in 1978, evolved from creative improvisation, best represented by the neurotic solo **Fuigo From a Different Dimension** (may 1979), towards solo electronic trumpet meditations such as the six-movement suite **Panta Rhei** (november 1993).

The second life of Love Child's, Blue Humans' and Run On's prog-rock guitarist Alan Licht concentrated on anarchic and dadaistic noise with the lengthy improvisations of *Betty Page*, off **Sink The Aging Process** (1994), *Rabbi Sky*, off **Rabbi Sky** (1998), and *Remington Khan*, off **Plays Well** (july 2000).

White flutist Robert Dick explored extended techniques at the instrument on **Venturi Shadows** (january 1991) and applied them to a surreal kind of chamber music in the duets with violinist Mari Kimura of **Irrefragable Dreams** (1994).

Trombonist Peter Zummo coined a deviant fusion of chamber music and free jazz on **Experimenting with Household Chemicals** (august 1991).

Jewish, Philadelphia-born, classically-trained pianist Uri Caine debuted with **Sphere Music** (may 1992), ostensibly dedicated to Thelonious Monk but in reality running the gamut from melodic classical music to dissonant free jazz (the eight-minute *Mr B.C.* for a quartet with clarinetist Don Byron, bassist Anthony Cox and drummer Ralph Peterson, *This Is a Thing Called Love* for a trio, the free-form *Jelly* and the ten-minute *Jan Fan* also featuring tenor saxophonist Gary Thomas and trumpeter Graham Haynes). That eclectic range was at least matched, if not surpassed, by **Toys** (march 1995), thanks to an improved pool of collaborators (Byron, Thomas, Peterson, trumpeter Dave Douglas, trombonist Joshua Roseman, bassist Dave Holland, and percussionist Don Alias) and engaging stylistic hybrids (the Latin-tinged and Wagner-quoting *Time Will Tell*, the sprightly *Or Truth*, the abstract *Yellow Stars in Heaven*).

White trumpeter Dave Douglas was emblematic of the neo-traditionalist who, far from being merely a nostalgic revivalist, actually enacts a synthesis of an entire civilization. Backed by a string trio (violin, cello and bass), Douglas opened his career with **Parallel Worlds** (march 1993), an eclectic excursion into hard bop, free jazz and classical music via kaleidoscopes such as *Parallel Worlds* and *For Every Action*.
In Our Lifetime (december 1994), dedicated to Booker Little, particularly the stuttering 17-minute *Bridges*, the post-modernist *Four Miniatures After Booker Little* and *In Our Lifetime* (the latter with bass clarinetist Marty Ehrlich). The Sextet's second chapter, **Stargazer** (december 1996), was dedicated to Wayne Shorter, recreating his haunting atmospheres in *Goldfish* and *Intuitive Science* while indulging in sinister cacophony in *Four Sleepers*.
Tiny Bell Trio (december 1993) inaugurated a collaboration with guitarist Brad "Shepik" Schoeppach and drummer Jim Black devoted to the integration of Balkan folk music and jazz improvisation. Their world-jazz fusion matured on **Constellations** (february 1995), a more overtly political work in the vein of Charlie Haden (*Maquiladora*, *Hope Ring True*). *Zeno* was the centerpiece of **Live In Europe** (april 1997). By the Trio's third chapter, **Songs for Wandering Souls** (december 1996), the fusion was becoming formulaic (*Songs for Wandering Souls*).
Five (august 1995) marked the debut of yet another project, the String Group, featuring violinist Mark Feldman, cellist Erik Friedlander, bassist Mark Dresser and drummer Michael Sarin. Its programmatic nature was embedded in the dedications: the 13-minute *Actualities* for Woody Shaw, *Over Farrell's* for John Cage, *Mogador* for John Zorn, etc.
In 1994 Douglas started contributing to John Zorn's various projects. The effect could be heard on the double-CD live **Sanctuary** (august 1996), a chaotic (not merely eclectic) creative set with tenorist Chris Speed, trumpeter Cuong Vu,

bassists Mark Dresser and Hilliard Greene, and drummer Dougie Bowne providing the pseudo-jazz fuel while Anthony Coleman and Cibo Matto's Yuka Honda derailed the sound on samplers (*Apparition*, *Heavenly Messenger*, *The Lantern*).
The versatile Douglas used different quartets for different (albeit humbler) purposes. **Music Triangle** (may 1997), with tenor saxophonist Chris Potter, bassist James Genus and drummer Ben Perowsky, was truly a jazz album, exploring the continuum from hard bop to free jazz. The same line-up cooked up *Continental Divide* on the more daring **Leap Of Faith** (september 1998). **Charms of the Night Sky** (september 1997) and **A Thousand Evenings** (october 2000), both recorded by a drum-less quartet with Guy Klucevsek on accordion, Feldman on violin and Greg Cohen on bass, marked one of his eccentric detours, blending Eastern European folk music, chamber music and post-modernist jazz. **Moving Portrait** (december 1997), by another harmless quartet (with pianist Bill Carrothers, Genus and drummer Billy Hart) and dedicated to singer-songwriter Joni Mitchell, was rather impressionistic by his wild standards (*Moving Portrait* and *Romero*).
The String Group's **Convergence** (january 1998), replacing Dresser with Drew Gress, summarized all of Douglas' experiments via morphing pieces such as the 13-minute *Goodbye Tony* and the 16-minute *Meeting at Infinity*. The Sextet returned with **Soul on Soul** (september 1999), dedicated to Mary Lou Williams and including the refined *Multiples*.
Sanctuary's futuristic program was continued on the ambitious political concept **Witness** (december 2000), scored for an electro-acoustic chamber ensemble (Douglas, Speed, Roseman, Feldman, Friedlander, Gress, Sarin, vibraphonist Bryan Carrott, tuba player Joe Daley, electronic percussionist Ikue Mori and Yuka Honda on sampling). The 24-minute *Mahfouz* included a spoken-word piece by singer-songwriter Tom Waits. It basically combined the String Group, the Charms of the Night Sky, half of the Sextet and a bit of Sanctuary.
The Charms of the Night Sky was also the core of the ensemble for the dance score **El Trilogy** (premiered in june 2000), structured in three multi-part suites (*Groove and Countermove*, *Weather Invention*, *Rapture to Leon James*) and closer in spirit to the classical avantgarde than to the jazz avantgarde.
A New Quintet (Potter, Caine, Genus, drummer Clarence Penn) debuted on **The Infinite** (december 2001), that contained covers of pop musicians as well as extended originals in a jazz-rock vein such as *Penelope*. **Strange Liberation** (january 2004) added guitarist Bill Frisell to the quintet. The Miles Davis influence was even stronger on the New Quintet's third album, **Meaning and Mystery** (february 2006), notably in *Culture Wars*.
The fusion element wed to Sanctuary's electronic sound permeated **Freak In** (september 2002), with *Traveler There Is No Road*, featuring Speed, Sarin, Baron, Ikue Mori, saxophonist Seamus Blake, guitarist Marc Ribot, electronic keyboardist Jamie Saft and electric pianist Craig Taborn. A smaller electronic combo (saxophonist Marcus Strickland, Saft, turntablist Gregor "DJ Olive" Asch,

bass and drums) crafted **Keystone** (may 2005), dedicated to silent-cinema star Roscoe 'Fatty' Arbuckle.

In 2003 a new acoustic quintet called Nomad (saxophonist/clarinetist Michael Moore, cellist Peggy Lee, tuba player Marcus Rojas and drummer Dylan van der Schyff) premiered the suite **Mountain Passages** (june 2004), to be performed at high altitude only, a work that focused on textural and melodic interplay.

Brazilian tenor saxophonist Ivo Perelman, who relocated to New York in 1989, initially paid tribute to his roots (folk songs, composer Heitor Villa-Lobos) employing the free-jazz devices first experimented by Albert Ayler. His maturation as a (emotional and almost mystic) composer started with the drum-less trio of **Cama de Terra** (july 1996), featuring bassist William Parker and pianist Matthew Shipp, and the trio of **Sad Life** (june 1996), featuring Parker and Rashid Ali on drums. **Seeds, Visions and Counterpoint** (september 1996), in another trio, achieved a synthesis of Perelman the improviser and Perelman the composer through the 20-minute *Seeds, Visions and Counterpoint* and the 26-minute *Cantilena*, his wildest musical excursions yet (but also the first fully-realized expression of his spirituality). Equally dissonant and intense was **Sound Hiearchy** (october 1996), for a quartet with pianist Marilyn Crispell, bassist William Parker and drummer Gerry Hemingway. Perelman's horizons further expanded via a collaboration with a string quartet, the eight-movement **The Alexander Suite** (may 1998), that was, if possible, even more jarring and chaotic than his trios and quartets, to the point that "free" sounded like an understatement, and via the seven-movement suite **The Seven Energies of the Universe** (april 1998) for a bass-less trio. Density rather than dissonance stood out on the colossal expressionist **Suite for Helen F** (2003) for a double trio, basically a 107-minute total immersion in the inner nightmare of a devastated psyche.

White pianist Denman Maroney introduced a new kind of prepared piano with the three solo piano sonatas of **Hyperpiano** (1998) and then employed it for the six-part chamber concerto *Fluxations* (april 2001), mixing improvisation and "pulse field", a polyrhythmic sequence denoted as a rhythmic relationship between instruments.

20TH CENTURY POST-CREATIVITY

At the end of the 20th century the wake of new creative music extended well beyond New York.

San Francisco's bassist Michael Formanek debuted with the creative watercolors of **Wide Open Spaces** (january 1990), featuring saxophonist Greg Osby, violinist Mark Feldman, guitarist Wayne Krantz and drummer Jeff Hirshfield. Longer compositions such as *Dominoes* gave **Extended Animation** (november 1991), with Tim Berne replacing Osby, a completely different feeling, almost like a philosophical version of the previous album's impressionism. The progression towards a more pensive and plaintive style continued on **Low Profile** (october 1993), for a septet including Berne, trumpeter Dave Douglas, saxophonist and clarinetist Marty Ehrlich, trombone, piano and drums, that included the 12-minute *Great Plains*, and reached a peak with the 12-minute *Thick Skin/ Dangerous Crustaceans* on **Nature of the Beast** (april 1996), in a quartet with trumpeter Douglas, trombonist Steve Swell and drummer Jim Black, recorded while Formanek was a member of Tim Berne's Bloodcount. These albums had rarely been showcases for his technique, but the solo-bass tour de force of **Am I Bothering You** made amend, offering a dazzling catalogue of bass inventions.

Boston-based white composer Joe Maneri, a member of the classical avantgarde who had composed microtonal music in his youth, released his first jazz album at the age of 68. **Kavalinka** (january 1989), for tenor and clarinet (Maneri himself), violin (his son Mat) and percussion introduced the notion of "free" improvisation that was relaxed (instead of incendiary or overly intellectual) and tonal (instead of wildly dissonant). Adding bassist Cecil McBee to form a quartet, Maneri indulged in the three lengthy improvisations of **Dahabenzapple** (may 1993). Similar quartets recorded **Coming Down the Mountain** (october 1993), **Tenderly** (1993), **Get Ready To Receive Yourself** (1995), **Let The Horse Go** (june 1995) and **In Full Cry** (june 1996), always in the same subdued and introverted microtonal style, while **Three Men Walking** (november 1995) was by a trio of reeds, violin and guitarist Joe Morris, and **Blessed** (october 1997) was a duet with violinist Mat Maneri. **Tales of Rohnlief** (1998) and **Angels Of Repose** (may 2002) were trios with the Maneris and bassist Barre Phillips. The Maneris' experiments with free jazz and microtonal music culminated with **Going To Church** (june 2000), featuring trumpeter Roy Campbell, pianist Matthew Shipp, bassist Barre Phillips and drummer Randy Peterson (notably the 31-minute *Blood And Body*).

Argentinean clarinetist and alto saxophonist Guillermo Gregorio basically played classical avantgarde in a jazz context. He began with the brief lyrical pieces for small ensemble of **Approximately** (june 1995), featuring Eric Pakula on saxophones, Mat Maneri on violin, Pendelis Karayorgis on piano and John Lockwood on bass, and **Ellipsis** (february 1997), featuring Gene Coleman on bass clarinet, Jim O'Rourke on acoustic guitar and accordion, Carrie Biolo on vibraphone and Michael Cameron on bass. Then he turned to a music influenced by cool jazz and third-stream jazz with the longer *A Tiny Bit More* and the three-movement *Just About Five*, off **Background Music** (january 1998), featuring Mats Gustafsson on saxophones and Kjell Nordeson on percussion, and the disorienting whirlwinds of **Red Cubed** (march 1998), featuring Pandelis Karayorgis on piano and Mat Maneri on electric violin. **Degrees of Iconicity** (february 1999), featuring Carrie Biolo on vibes, Fred Lonberg-Holm on cello and cornet, Michael Cameron and Kent Kessler on acoustic basses, was an even more chaotic experience, evoking the aesthetics of the Italian futurists. The highlights of **Faktura** (december 2000), namely the five-movement *Rodchenko Suite* and the *Systems and Variations for Piano*, roam an even vaster and more unstable territory (Francois Houle on clarinet, Robbie Lynn Hunsinger on English horn, Jeb Bishop on trombone, Kyle Bruckmann on oboe, Fred Lonberg-Holm on cello, Jen Paulson on viola, Jim Baker on piano, Jeff Parker on guitar, Michael Cameron on bass, Carrie Biolo on percussion).

Canadian pianist Paul Plimley took Cecil Taylor's exuberant style into the 1990s, while wedding the acrobatic and intense aspects of it with atmospheric and pensive threads. The similarities with the master declined rapidly from **When Silence Pulls** (november 1990), a trio session with bassist Lisle Ellis and drummer Andrew Cyrille, to the impressionistic piano vignettes of **Everything in Stages** (april 1995) to the duets with bassist Barry Guy of **Sensology** (november 1995) to the wildly eclectic and virtuoso parade of **Safe-Crackers** (january 1999), another trio session.

Boston-based trumpet player Greg Kelley unleashed the improvised noise of **Trumpet** (2000) and **If I Never Meet You In This Life** (october 2001), besides attempting a fusion of concrete music and free jazz on **Field Recordings** (2000). Nmperign, the duo of Greg Kelley on trumpet and Bhob Rainey on saxophone, developed a program of absurd, cacophonous, irrational duets from **Nmperign** (1998) to **We Devote Every Effort To Offer You The Best That You Deserve To Have For Your Enjoyment** (2003), Nmperign's ultimate statement: two lengthy tracks that cover a gigantic spectrum of possibilities.

Canada-raised violinist Eyvind Kang was one of the most eclectic musicians of his generation, playing in both rock, jazz and classical contexts. The more intimate and spiritual (and ethnic) aspect of his art was documented on the five-movement suite **The Story Of Iceland** (2000), on the 19-minute gamelan-inspired *Doorway to the Sun* for chamber orchestra, off **Virginal Co-ordinates** (may 2000), and on the 27-minute mostly-droning *Binah* for guitar, violin and bass, off **Live Low to the Earth in the Iron Age** (2002).

San Francisco-based multi-instrumentalist improviser and electronic composer Eric Glick-Rieman was a virtuoso of the prepared electric piano, as documented on the solo improvisations of **Ten To The Googolplex** (may 2000).

Freer Jazz

Towards the end of the 20th century the legacy of free jazz was more visible than ever among the black jazz community, notably in New York.

John Coltrane-influenced tenor saxophonist David Ware became the leading proponent of free jazz after graduating from the groups of Cecil Taylor (1976) and Andrew Cyrille (1978). His huge, agile and, at times, frantic sound, first experimented on **Birth of a Being** (april 1977) and **From Silence to Music** (september 1978), became the pillar of his groups with bassist William Parker and drummer Marc Edwards, first the trio of **Passage To Music** (april 1988), with *The Elders Path*, and then the quartet formed with pianist Matthew Shipp that debuted on the double-CD **Great Bliss** (january 1990), with *Forward Motion*, *One Two Three* and *Stritchland*. Ware played tenor sax, flute, saxello and stritch, showcasing not only his manyfold virtuosity but also his keen instinct for timbral exploration. Despite the cryptic *Infi-Rhythms #1*, **Flight Of I** (december 1991) smoothed the edges of Ware's free-jazz approach. Edwards was replaced by Whit Dickey on **Third Ear Recitation** (october 1992), that contained stronger avant-retro contrasts as well as flights of the imagination such as *The Chase*. A more radical approach, and phenomenal playing by Shipp and Parker, turned **Earthquation** (may 1994), with *Cococana*, and especially **Cryptology** (december 1994), with *Cryptology*, into incendiary shows. The quartet's form peaked on **Oblations and Blessings** (september 1995), with *Oblations and Blessings*, and the apparently chaotic **Dao** (september 1995), with *Dao Forms* and *Dao*. Ware's sonic attack was matched by the creative turbulence of Parker, Shipp and Dickey. If Ware was reenacting John Coltrane's spiritual fervor, Shipp was charting a territory beyong McCoy Tyner's psychotic exuberance. The dynamics was breathtaking, with moments of trance-like transcendence followed by moments of absolute delirium and by ecstatic pauses. Susie Ibarra replaced Dickey on **Godspelized** (may 1996), an album more influenced by Albert Ayler and Sun Ra than by Coltrane's legendary group (*Godspelized*). Ware's understated compositional style was beginning to emerge more clearly (as in "there is method in his madness"), and **Wisdom of Uncertainty** (december 1996) boasted pieces such as *Utopic*, *Continuum* and *Acclimation* that relied on a powerful logic besides pure energy. Ware began to concentrate more on composition than improvisation.

Craig Harris emerged as an irreverent trombonist, capable of indulging in catchy folk melodies as well as harsh dissonance on **Black Bone** (january 1983), **Aboriginal Affairs** (1983), on which he debuted his didjeridu playing, and **Tributes** (1984). A living summary of the history of jazz trombone playing, his madcap art probably peaked with the 17-minute *Shelter Suite*, off **Shelter** (december 1986). **Blackout in the Square Root of Soul** (november 1987) added the synthesizer to his odd palette of sounds.

Washington's pianist Matthew Shipp, who relocated to New York in 1984, established his reputation in 1990 as a follower of Cecil Taylor's percussive style in saxophonist David Ware's quartet along with bassist William Parker. After ten **Sonic Explorations** (february 1988) with alto saxophonist Rob Brown, Shipp formed his own quartet, featuring Brown, Parker and drummer Whit Dickey, and turned to free jazz of the 1960s with the lengthy vehement improvisations of **Points** (january 1990). A trio with Parker and Dickey yielded the four-movement suite **Circular Temple** (october 1990) and the live **Prism** (march 1993), two creative sessions worthy of Cecil Taylor. Between a stark duo with Parker **Zo** (may 1993), the live solo performances of **Before the World** (june 1995), the duets of **2-Z** (august 1995) with saxophonist Roscoe Mitchell and the brief solo post-bop vignettes of **Symbol Systems** (november 1995), all of them more indebted towards Chicago's and London's "creative" scenes, Shipp emancipated himself from the cliches of free jazz via a quartet featuring violinist Mat Maneri, Parker and Dickey (who in the meantime had also joined Ware with Shipp and Parker). Their **Critical Mass** (september 1994) and **The Flow of X** (may 1995) moved towards abstract soundpainting of the kind practiced by electronic musicians, albeit rooted in the tradition of jazz instruments.

A String Trio with Maneri and Parker crafted the brief watercolors of **By the Law of Music** (august 1996). This marked the end of the verbose, youthful, dense, free-jazz period. Shipp adopted a more concise style and rediscovered the "song" format. His irrational and chaotic free-jazz style metamorphosed into a close relative that was actually both rational and romantic.

After **Thesis** (january 1997) with guitarist Joe Morris, **The Multiplication Table** (july 1997), recorded by a trio with Parker and drummer Susie Ibarra, even included jazz standards. Another drum-less ensemble, the Horn Quartet, featuring Parker, trumpeter Roy Campbell and alto saxophonist Daniel Carter, penned the 14 solos, duets, trios and quartets of **Strata** (december 1997), one of his most cerebral works and the one that revealed Shipp's debt to classical music.

Shipp's numerous collaborations, that included **Gravitational Systems** (may 1998) with Mat Maneri, **DNA** (january 1999) with Parker, and the solos, duets and trios with Parker and Brown of **Magnetism** (january 1999), were mere teasers and/or detours. The real "meat" was to be found in his trios and quartets: the trio with Maneri (on electric violin) and drummer Randy Peterson of **So What** (august 1998), the String Trio of **Expansion Power Release** (november 1999), the quartet with Campbell, Parker and drummer Gerald Cleaver of **Pastoral Composure** (january 2000), one of his most romantic works, the quartet with Leo Smith replacing Campbell of **New Orbit** (september 2000), and the trio with reed player Charles Waters and drummer Andrew Barker of **Apostolic Polyphony** (april 2001).

At the turn of the century, Shipp was ready to shift gear once more. He began a collaboration with the electronic dance project Spring Heel Jack (2001-02), then he experimented with hip-hop music on **Nu Bop** (august 2001) in the company of saxophonist/flutist Daniel Carter, Parker, drummer Guillermo Brown, and Chris Flam on synthesizer, drum machine and sampler. That was only the appetizer, because soon Shipp was playing with the hip-hop group Antipop Consortium (2002), with DJ Spooky (2002) and with rapper El-P (2003). The problem is that

Shipp never fully integrated his style with the dance style of his partners. The "nu bop" idea was continued on **Equilibrium** (june 2002) with Parker, Flam, Cleaver and vibraphonist Khan Jamal, perhaps the most "sentimental" of the series, on **The Sorcerer Sessions** (january 2003) with Parker, Flam, Cleaver, clarinetist Evan Ziporyn and violinist Daniel Bernard Roumain, and on **Harmony and Abyss** (february 2004), with just Parker, Flam and Cleaver.
The solo-piano album **One** (april 2005) was also consistent with the "nu bop" program, as its short pieces echoed Thelonious Monk more clearly than it did Cecil Taylor.

Classically-trained clarinetist Don Byron erupted on the scene of New York's avantgarde in 1991 thanks to a series of collaborations with the established protagonists (such as Bobby Previte) and to his own **Tuskegee Experiments** (july 1991), a set of colorful and passionate pieces for various configurations that featured guitarist Bill Frisell and even poet Sadiq (*Tuskegee Strutter's Ball, Next Love, Diego Rivera*). However, anchored to a relatively traditional sextet (cornetist Graham Haynes, pianist Edsel Gomez, bass, drums and congas plus Frisell and Sadiq), **Music for Six Musicians** (1995) delved into Byron's obsession with Latin music, adding strong political overtones (*Ross Perot, Rodney King, Al Sharpton*). Even more conventional was the live **No-Vibe Zone** (january 1996) for a quintet with guitarist David Gilmore and pianist Uri Caine (*Sex/Work*). Byron lampooned funk music on **Nu Blaxploitation** (january 1998), again diluted by spoken-word segments but boasting a live *Schizo Jam* with rapper Marcell "Biz Markie" Hall. The more serious **Romance With The Unseen** (march 1999), by a quartet with Frisell and drummer Jack DeJohnette, aimed for a romantic mood (*Homegoing*). After toying with swing, classical and soul music, and reenacting the Latin-tinged "Music for Six Musicians" on **You Are #6** (october 2001), with *Dark Room*, Byron switched to tenor saxophone on **Ivey-Divey** (september 2004) in order to deconstruct several more eras of music. The Bang On A Can All-Stars performed his nine-movement *Red Tailed Angels* on **A Ballad for Many** (june 2006).

Formed in 1987 by saxophonist Roy Nathanson and trombonist Curtis Fowlkes (both former members of no-wave combo the Lounge Lizards), the Jazz Passengers debuted with **Broken Night/ Red Light** (1987), that showed their evolution from a duo to a full-fledged band with vibraphonist Bill Ware, bassist Brad Jones, etc. Their Dadaesque wit, hyper-fusion of ethnic, rock and funk music, free improvisation and elegant post-modernist quotations blossomed on **Deranged & Decomposed** (1989) and especially **Implement Yourself** (1990), containing *Indian Club Bombardment*, and featuring guitarist Marc Ribot and violinist Jim Nolet. **Live at the Knitting Factory** (january 1991), adding Yuka Honda on sampler and Marcus Rojas on tuba, contained *Tikkun*. A bit too anarchic even by Frank Zappa's standards, **Plain Old Joe** (1993) signaled the end of the epic era.

The Los Angeles-based BSharp Jazz Quartet (saxophonist Randall Willis, pianist Eliot Douglass, bassist Reggie Carson and drummer Herb Graham) debuted on **B Sharp Jazz Quartet** (1994), mostly composed and arranged by

Graham, in a vein that bridged hard-bop and free-jazz styles, culminating with the lengthy *Hoopty*.

The Digital Improviser

The revolution of computer-driven instrumentation began to make a difference in creative improvisation at the turn of the century. The new generation of "digital improvisers" coming from the free-jazz background basically merged with the generation of "sound sculptors" coming from the classical avantgarde.

Ben Neill played the "mutantrumpet" (an electro-acoustic instrument producing a Jon Hassell-ian tone) both in LaMonte Young's ensemble and on his own **Green Machine** (1995).

Chicago-based tabletop guitarist and synthesizer player Kevin Drumm developed a style that stood as the guitar equivalent of digital/glitch electronica: an art of static soundscapes roamed by sporadic, arctic, minimal events. The result often appeared to be a psychoacoustic study on the flow of time. Sonic odysseys such as the seven untitled tracks of **Kevin Drumm** (october 1996), *Cynicism*, off **Second** (october 1998), and *Organ*, off **Comedy** (1999), took the ideas of Keith Rowe and Fred Frith and relocated them to another era and another planet. On the other hand, the brutal orgies of **Sheer Hellish Miasma** (2002) and **Land of Lurches** (2003) seemed to renege on Drumm's aesthetic of silence.

Swiss percussionist Guenter Mueller (Günter Müller) established his credentials as an electro-acoustic improviser via a series of duets, trios and quartets beyond the conventions of (classical, jazz, rock) traditions, blending naturally into the soundscapes created by his collaborators (Christian Marclay, Jim O'Rourke, Taku Sugimoto, Otomo Yoshihide, Voice Crack, Keith Rowe, Taku Sugimoto, Oren Ambarchi). Different kinds of "noise" fueled his **Eight Landscapes** (june 2002).

The eclectic San Francisco-based composer Miya Masaoka expanded the techniques of the improvisers with **Compositions/Improvisations** (1993) for solo koto and **While I Was Walking I Heard A Sound** (2003) for mixed choir of 100-150 voices, while straddling the border between jazz, classical, electronic and Japanese music on **What is the Difference Between Stripping and Playing the Violin?** (march 1997), and mixing solo improvisation and field recordings on **For Birds, Planes & Cello** (2005).

Japanese guitarist and cellist Taku Sugimoto learned the importance of silence on his **Unaccompanied Violoncello Solo** (may 1994) and **Fragments of Paradise** (june 1997) and **Opposite** (june 1997) for solo guitar. He then applied those lessons to post-rock and digital-noise settings. By the same token, his austere **Chamber Music** (may 2003), namely the *Sonata for Violin and Piano Music for Violin, Cello and Piano* (each half an hour long), mixed western timbral exploration and eastern rarefied meditation. Both his solo, group and chamber music were based on silence, not sound, and thus each piece tended to be an incredibly slow and sparse flow of tones. Silence prevailed over sound. In a sense, his works were pauses interrupted by sounds, rather than sounds with long pauses. He often let background noise take center stage, his guitar occasionally interrupting the coughing, the footsteps and the raindrops with a distant strum.

The improvising guitarist seemed to meditate on the sounds that he heard, and only every now and then was he willing to emit a sign of life.

Tyondai Braxton improvised the digital/electronic tours de force of **The Grow Gauge** (1999) and especially **History That Has No Effect** (2002), that displayed his art of "orchestrated loops" manipulating voice and guitar.

French sound sculptor and jazz saxophonist Jean-Luc Guionnet, a member of the musique concrete ensemble Afflux with Eric LaCasa and Eric Cordier, conceived **Synapses I & IV** (1999), a collaboration with Cordier, in which plucking the strings of a stringed instrument caused a chain reaction of sounds from another set of instruments.

Los Angeles-based guitarist Greg Headley proceeded from the solo tabletop guitar meditations of **Adhesives** (march 1999) to the abstract manipulation of guitar sounds of **A Table of Opposites** (june 2000) to the noisy, frantic electronic soundscapes of **Similis** (september 2001).

Los Angeles-based virtuoso saxophonist Earl Howard (1951) concentrated on superimposing electronic/manipulated sounds to live improvised performances, such as in the five-movement *Strong Force* (november 1999) for synthesizer, piano, percussion, harp and cello, or *ILEX* (2004) for vocals, electronics, percussion and pipa. These cold, disjointed, loose, open-ended streams end up sounding like summaries of 20th-century chamber music. His **Five Saxophone Solos** (2004) are complex sequences built out of simple units, cascades of primal speech units not meant to create abstract sound patterns but to deliver primal emotions (like a child who is just beginning to utter the rudiments of language).

Japanese guitarist Kazuhisa Uchihashi, a former member of the experimental ensembles First Edition, Altered States and Ground Zero, recorded several albums of solo guitar improvisations and formed **Phantasmagoria** (april 1999), a six-piece unit of guitar, sampler, sax, trumpet and rhythm section.

Australian improvising trio Triosk (Adrian Klumpes on keyboards, Laurence Pike on drums, Ben Waples on double bass) diluted jazz music into a maze of post-processing techniques on **Moment Returns** (2004).

Zanana, i.e. the New York-based duo of vocalist Kristin Norderval and trombonist Monique Buzzarte, blended improvisation, acoustic instruments, electronics, samples, field recordings and live processing to create the spectral landscapes of **Holding Patterns** (2005).

TURNTABLES

Next to electronic and digital instruments, another instrument debuted in the world of improvised music and it was an old-fashioned analogic instrument: the turntable.

The turntablist as an instrumentalist was an artistic figure that migrated from hip-hop music into avantgarde, rock and jazz music during the 1990s. The turntable allowed musicians to achieve two goals (that were frequently overlapped): 1. "quote" from a musical source by another musician (and therefore create collages of quotations), and 2. produce sequences of extreme noise. Since the turntable is inherently an instrument that plays recorded music, whatever turntablists played was, in theory, an audio montage of found sounds, but, in practice, the sources were rarely intelligible.

Christian Marclay spearheaded the trend towards "composing", performing and improvising using phonographic records. De facto, he applied John Cage's indeterminism and, in general, Dadaism's provocative principles of aesthetic demystification, to the civilization of recorded music. His specialty was to devise mechanisms for letting a record evolve a sound over time, typically by having people somehow degrade its sound (as in *Record Without a Cover* of 1985, a record sold with no cover and no jacket so that it keeps deteriorating after every playing, or *Footsteps* of 1990, a totally random composition resulting from hundreds of people walking on a record).

British turntablist, sampling engineer and sound sculptor Philip Jeck fused the turntable creativity of Christian Marclay and David Shea with the sampling terrorism of John Oswald and Negativland. Obsessed with vintage vinyl, with the noises that the "performer" can extract from the process and with the "sounds" that the records contain, Jeck created the chaotic cacophony of *Vinyl Requiem* (1993) for 180 turntables and the solo improvisations titled *Vinyl Coda* (2000) in which snippets of old records are mixed with a jungle of turntable noises.

Japanese composer Otomo Yoshihide, Ground Zero's guitarist, reinvented himself as a turntablist and engaged in duets between the turntable and the laptop, such as Nobukazu Takemura's laptop on **Turntables and Computers** (2003), the turntable and the sampler, such as Sachiko M's sampler on **Filament 1** (1998), or the turntable and another turntable, such as Martin Tetreault's turntable on **Grrr** (2004).

It was fitting that the century of jazz ended with the introduction of a new instrument, an instrument that was the very device that had made jazz the soundtrack of the first half of the century.

APPENDIX: RECOMMENDED DISCOGRAPHY BY DECADE

This discography only includes original albums (not compilations or reissues) and starts from the age of the LP. A much more complete list can be found on my website www.scaruffi.com

1950s
1. Charles Mingus Pithecanthropus Erectus (1956)
2. Ornette Coleman: The Shape of Jazz To Come (1959)
3. Thelonious Monk: Brilliant Corners (1956)
4. Miles Davis: Kind Of Blue (1959)
5. Stan Kenton: City of Glass (1951)
6. Sonny Rollins: Freedom Suite (1958)
7. John Coltrane: Giant Steps (1959)
8. Lennie Tristano: Manhattan Studio/ New York Improvisations (1956)
9. Modern Jazz Quartet: Fontessa (1956)
10. Miles Davis: Birth of the Cool (1950)
11. George Russell: New York New York (1959)
12. Charles Mingus: Tijuana Moods (1957)
13. Lennie Tristano: Lennie Tristano (1955)
14. Sonny Rollins: Saxophone Colossus (1956)
15. Horace Silver: Horace Silver and the Jazz Messengers (1955)
16. George Russell: Jazz Workshop (1956)
17. Sun Ra: Jazz in Silhouette (1958)
18. Art Blakey: Orgy In Rhythm (1957)
19. Jimmy Giuffre: Western Suite (1958)
20. Yusef Lateef: Jazz Mood (1957)
21. Gerry Mulligan: Mulligan Quartet (1952)

1960s
1. Charles Mingus: The Black Saint And The Sinner Lady (1963)
2. John Coltrane: A Love Supreme (1964)
3. Cecil Taylor: Unit Structures (1966)
4. John Coltrane: Ascension (1965)
5. Anthony Braxton: For Alto (1969)
6. Albert Ayler: Spiritual Unity (1964)
7. Michael Mantler: Jazz Composers' Orchestra (1968)
8. Sun Ra: Atlantis (1967)
9. Don Cherry: Mu (1969)
10. Miles Davis: Bitches Brew (1969)
11. Ornette Coleman: Free Jazz (1960)
12. Gary Burton: A Genuine Tong Funeral (1967)
13. Eric Dolphy: Out to Lunch (1964)
14. Roscoe Mitchell: Sound (1966)
15. Sam Rivers: Dimensions And Extensions (1967)
16. Pharoah Sanders: Karma (1969)
17. Albert Ayler: New York Eye And Ear Control (1964)
18. Miles Davis: In a Silent Way (1969)

Recommended Discography

19. Roscoe Mitchell: Old Quartet (1967)
20. Don Cherry: Symphony For Improvisers (1966)
21. Max Roach: Freedom Now Suite (1960)
22. Art Ensemble of Chicago: People in Sorrow (1969)
23. Roscoe Mitchell: Congliptious (1968)
24. Bill Dixon: Intents And Purposes (1967)
25. Charles Mingus: Presents (1960)
26. Cecil Taylor: Nefertiti (1962)
27. Sun Ra: Cosmic Tones For Mental Therapy (1963)
28. Jimmy Giuffre: Free Fall (1962)
29. Albert Ayler: Witches and Devils (1964)
30. Marion Brown: Quartet (1965)
31. Gunther Schuller [John Lewis]: Jazz Abstractions (1960)
32. Cecil Taylor: Conquistador (1966)
33. Joe Harriott: Movement (1963)
34. Art Ensemble of Chicago: Reese and the Smooth Ones (1969)
35. George Russell: Electronic Sonata For Souls Loved By Nature (1969)
36. George Russell: Jazz in the Space Age (1960)
37. Eric Dolphy: Far Cry (1960)
38. Tina Brooks: True Blue (1960)
39. Charles Mingus: Mingus (1960)
40. Joe Harriott: Free Form (1960)
41. Alex Schlippenbach: Globe Unity (1966)
42. Ornette Coleman: Ornette (1961)
43. John Coltrane: Impressions (1961)
44. Andrew Hill: Point of Departure (1964)
45. Sam Rivers: Fuchsia Swing Song (1964)
46. Archie Shepp: Mama Too Tight (1966)
47. Steve Lacy: The Forest And The Zoo (1966)
48. Don Cherry: Complete Communion (1965)
49. Sam Rivers: Contours (1965)
50. George Russell: Othello Ballet Suite (1967)
51. MUhal Richard Abrams: Levels and Degrees of Light (1967)
52. Charles Mingus: Oh Yeah (1961)
53. Yusef Lateef: Eastern Sounds (1961)
54. Don Cherry: Eternal Rhythm (1968)
55. Miles Davis: Filles de Kilimanjaro (1968)
56. Kalaparusha Maurice McIntyre: Humility In The Light Of Creator (1969)
57. Andrew Hill: Black Fire (1963)
58. Joe Harriott: Abstract (1962)
59. Archie Shepp: The Magic of Ju-Ju (1967)
60. Bill Evans: Explorations (1961)
61. Peter Broetzmann: Machine Gun (1968)
62. George Russell: Ezz-thetic (1961)
63. John Surman: John Surman (1968)
64. Randy Weston: Uhuru Africa (1960)
65. Wayne Shorter: Speak No Evil (1964)
66. Herbie Hancock: Empyrean Isles (1964)
67. Jackie McLean: New and Old Gospel (1967)

Recommended Discography

1970s:
1. Anthony Braxton: Saxophone Improvisations (1972)
2. Carla Bley: Escalator Over The Hill (1971)
3. Keith Jarrett: Survivors Suite (1976)
4. Sam Rivers: Streams (1973)
5. Paul Bley: Improvisie (1970)
6. Marion Brown: Afternoon of a Georgia Faun (1970)
7. Leo Smith: Mass on the World (1978)
8. Sam Rivers: Crystals (1974)
9. Cecil Taylor: Silent Tongues (1974)
10. Steve Lacy: Saxophone Special (1974)
11. Rova Saxophone Quartet: Removal of Secrecy (1979)
12. Charlie Haden: Liberation Music Orchestra (1970)
13. George Lewis: Solo Trombone Record (1976)
14. Roland Kirk: Prepare Thyself To Deal With A Miracle (1973)
15. Dave Holland: Conference of the Birds (1972)
16. Alice Coltrane: Ptah The El Daoud (1970)
17. McCoy Tyner: Extensions (1970)
18. Roscoe Mitchell: LRG-Maze-S II Examples (1978)
19. Leroy Jenkins: Legend of Ai Glatson (1978)
20. Charles Mingus: Let My Children Hear Music (1971)
21. McCoy Tyner: Sahara (1972)
22. Art Ensemble of Chicago: Les Stances A Sophie (1970)
23. Jeanne Lee: Conspiracy (1974)
24. Keith Jarrett: The Koeln Concert (1975)
25. Revolutionary Ensemble: The People's Republic (1975)
26. Miles Davis: Pangaea (1975)
27. Evan Parker: Saxophone Solos (1975)
28. Leroy Jenkins: For Players Only (1975)
29. George Lewis: Shadowgraph (1977)
30. Air: Air Time (1977)
31. Paul Bley: Dual Unity (1971)
32. Air: Air Raid (1976)
33. Leo Smith: Reflectativity (1974)
34. Art Ensemble of Chicago: Phase One (1971)
35. Joe McPhee: Graphics (1977)
36. Gerry Hemingway: Kwambe (1978)
37. Rova Saxophone Quartet: Cinema Rovate (1978)
38. David Murray: Flowers for Albert (1976)
39. Air: Air Song (1975)
40. Weather Report: I Sing the Body Electric (1972)
41. Kenny Wheeler: Gnu High (1975)
42. Derek Bailey: Company 1 (1976)
43. Jan Garbarek: Dis (1976)
44. Jean-Luc Ponty: Sonata Erotica (1972)
45. James Ulmer: Revealing (1977)
46. Pat Metheny: Watercolors (1977)
47. Sonny Sharrock: Monkey-Pockie-Boo (1970)
48. London Jazz Composers Orchestra: Ode (1972)
49. Toshiko Akiyoshi: Road Time (1976)

Recommended Discography

50. Irene Schweizer: Wilde Senoritas (1976)

1980s:
1. Anthony Davis: Variations In Dream-time (1982)
2. Borbetomagus: Barbed Wire Maggot (1983)
3. George Lewis: Chicago Slow Dance (1981)
4. Anthony Davis: Lady of the Mirrors (1980)
5. John Zorn: Cobra (1986)
6. Butch Morris: Current Trends In Racism (1985)
7. Anthony Davis: Episteme (1981)
8. Henry Threadgill: Easily Slip Into Another World (1987)
9. Anthony Davis: Hemispheres (1983)
10. Anthony Davis: Undine (1987)
11. Rova Saxophone Quartet: Invisible Frames (1980)
12. Henry Threadgill: When Was That (1982)
13. John Zorn: Locus Solus (1984)
14. Marty Ehrlich: Traveller's Tale (1989)
15. Tim Berne: Fractured Fairy Tales (1989)
16. Bill Frisell: Before We Were Born (1988)
17. Joe McPhee: Topology (1981)
18. Paul Motian: Psalm (1981)
19. Rova Saxophone Quartet: As Was (1981)
20. Air: 80 Degrees Below (1982)
21. Evan Parker: Atlanta (1986)
22. Anthony Davis: Undine (1987)
23. Henry Threadgill: Rag Bush And All (1988)
24. Turtle Island String Quartet: Turtle Island Quartet (1988)
25. ICP Orchestra: Bospaadje Konijnehol I (1986)
26. Marilyn Crispell: Spirit Music (1981)
27. Pat Metheny: As Falls Wichita So Falls Wichita (1980)
28. Billy Bang: Changing Seasons (1980)
29. Julius Hemphill: Flat Out Jump Suite (1980)
30. MUhal Richard Abrams: Blues Forever (1981)
31. Billy Bang: Outline No 12 (1982)
32. Dave Holland: Life Cycle (1982)
33. Terje Rypdal: Eos (1983)
34. Don Pullen: Evidence of Things Unseen (1983)
35. David Murray: Murray's Steps (1982)
36. Bobby Previte: Bump The Renaissance (1985)
37. Henry Kaiser: Aloha (1981)
38. James Newton: Luella (1983)
39. George Russell: The African Game (1985)
40. Rova Saxophone Quartet: Crowd (1985)
41. Joe Maneri: Kavalinka (1989)

1990s:
1. Guillermo Gregorio: Approximately (1996)
2. Franz Koglmann: Cantos I-IV (1993)
3. Ivo Perelman: Seeds, Visions and Counterpoint (1996)
4. Jane Ira Bloom: Art & Aviation (1992)

Recommended Discography

5. Myra Melford: Even the Sounds Shine (1994)
6. Butch Morris: Testament (1995)
7. Guillermo Gregorio: Ellipsis (1997)
8. Franz Koglmann: The Use of Memory (1990)
9. Matthew Shipp: Circular Temple (1990)
10. Maria Schneider: Evanescence (1992)
11. Bill Dixon: Vade Mecum (1993)
12. Michael Formanek: Extended Animation (1991)
13. Jane Ira Bloom: The Red Quartets (1999)
14. Steve Coleman: The Sonic Language of Myth - Believing Learning Knowing (1999)
15. Matthew Shipp: Strata (1997)
16. Steve Coleman: Genesis (1997)
17. Marcus Roberts: Blues for the New Millennium (1997)
18. Toshiko Akiyoshi: Desert Lady (1994)
19. Matthew Shipp: Critical Mass (1994)
20. Dave Douglas: In Our Lifetime (1995)
21. Geri Allen: Maroons (1992)
22. Wynton Marsalis: Citi Movement (1992)
23. Joe Lovano: Universal Language (1992)
24. Terence Blanchard: The Malcolm X Jazz Suite (1992)
25. Matthew Shipp: The Flow of X (1995)
26. Sergey Kuryokhin: Some Combination of Fingers and Passion (1992)
27. Medeski Martin and Wood: Notes From the Underground (1992)
28. Marilyn Crispell: **Santuerio** (1993)
29. Michael Formanek: Nature of the Beast (1996)
30. Marty Ehrlich: Malinke's Dance (1999)
31. Dave Douglas: Convergence (1998)

2000s:
1. Spring Heel Jack: Disappeared (2000)
2. Franz Koglmann: Fear Death By Water (2003)
3. Ivo Perelman: Suite for Helen F (2003)
4. Denman Maroney: Fluxations (2001)
5. Jane Ira Bloom: Chasing Paint (2002)
6. Guillermo Gregorio: Faktura (2000)
7. Spring Heel Jack: Amassed (2002)
8. Marty Ehrlich: The Long View (2002)
9. Joe Maneri: Going To Church (2000)
10. Brad Mehidau: Largo (2002)
11. Myra Melford: Dance Beyond the Color (2000)
12. Andrew Hill: Dusk (2000)
13. Dave Douglas: El Trilogy (2000)
14. Dave Douglas: Mountain Passages (2005)

ALPHABETICAL INDEX

- A complete alphabetical index would have been too long and costly to produce. This index is a compromise between providing help to locate a musician and saving space/money.
- Each musician is located via the number of the chapter. See the numbered list of chapters below.
- For each musician only one entry is given: the chapter in which her/his/their main recordings are discussed (that is the place where the name appears underlined).
- Therefore the names listed in this index are the names that are underlined in the text. Musicians that are only mentioned in passing (no matter how many times) are not listed in this index.
- If you want to find out all the places where a certain musician is mentioned, you can go to www.scaruffi.com and use the search engine.

1	The Beginnings: New Orleans
2	Chicago: White Jazz
3	New York: Stride Piano
4	New York: Big Bands
5	New York: The Swing Era
6	New York: The Swing Soloists
7	Kansas City: Big Bands
8	Bebop
9	Bebop Pianist
10	Bebop Big Bands
11	Cool Jazz
12	Cool Jazz In Los Angeles
13	Hard Bop
14	Post-Bop
15	Free Jazz
15.1	Free Jazz: The Apostles
15.2	Free Jazz: The Disciples
15.3	Free Jazz: Free Drumming
15.4	Free Jazz: Free Vocals
15.5	White Free Jazz
15.6	Free Jazz: Borderline
16	Creative Music
16.1	Chicago's Creative Jazz
16.2	Creative Music: The Disciples
16.3	The St Louis School
16.4	Jazz Post-Modernism In New York
16.5	White Post-Modernism
16.6	European Creativity
16.7	Noise-Jazz
17	Fusion
17.1	Fusion Jazz: The Pioneers
17.2	Pre-Fusion Pianists
17.3	White Jazz Between Free Jazz And Fusion
17.4	Latin Jazz
17.5	Fusion Groups
17.6	Fusion Stylists
17.7	Guitar Heroes
17.8	Pop-Fusion
17.9	Euro-Fusion
18	Jazz Traditionalism
19	Non-Jazz Of The 1980s
20	Post-Jazz Music

Abercrombie John 17.5
Abrams Richard 16.1
Adams George 16.4
Adams Pepper 13
Adderley Cannonball 13
Akiyoshi Toshiko 14
Ali Rashied 15.3
Allen Geri 19
Allen Marcus 19
Allen Red 1
Altena Maarten 16.6
Altschul Barry 16.5
Anderson Fred 16.2
Anderson Ray 16.2
Ardley Neil 17.9
Armstrong Louis 1
Ayers Roy 14
Ayler Albert 15.1
Azymuth 17.4
Bailey Derek 16.6
Baker Chet 12
Bang Billy 16.4
Barbieri Gato 17.4
Baron Joey 20
Barron Kenny 18
Bartz Gary 17.5
Basie Count 7
Bechet Sidney 1
Bell Teja 19
Bennett Sam 20
Bennink Han 16.6
Benson George 17.8
Beresford Steve 16.6
Berne Tim 20
Blackwell Ed 15.3
Blake Ran 11
Blakey Art 13
Blanchard Terence 18
Bley Carla 17.3
Bley Paul 14
Bloom Jane-Ira 16.5
Bluiett Hamiet 16.3
Blythe Arthur 16.4
Bolden Buddy 1
Borbetomagus 16.7
Bowie Joseph 17.5
Bowie Lester 16.1
Brackeen Joanne 18

Brand Dollar 14
Braxton Anthony 16.1
Braxton Tyondai 20
Brecker Michael 17.5
Breuker Willem 16.6
Broetzmann Peter 16.6
Brooks Tina 13
Brown Clifford 13
Brown Marion 15.2
Brubeck Dave 9
BSharp Jazz Quartet 20
Burrell Kenny 13
Burton Gary 17.1
Butcher John 16.6
Byard Jaki 14
Byrd Donald 13
Byron Don 20
Caine Uri 20
Calloway Cab 4
Carter Benny 6
Carter Betty 11
Carter James 18
Carter John 15.2
Carter Ron 17.6
Centazzo Andrea 16.6
Chadbourne Eugene 20
Charles Teddy 11
Cherry Don 15.2
Christian Charlie 6
Christmann Guenter 16.6
Clarke Stanley 17.6
Claudia Quintet 19
Cline Nels 19
Cobham Billy 17.5
Coleman Ornette 15.1
Coleman Steve 19
Collier Graham 16.6
Coltrane John 15.1
Cora Tom 20
Corea Chick 17.2
Coryell Larry 17.5
Cowell Stanley 15.6
Coxhill Lol 16.6
Crispell Marilyn 16.5
Cyrille Andrew 15.3
Dalaba Lesli 20
Darling David 19
Dauner Wolfgang 17.9

Davis Anthony 16.4
Davis Miles 11
Dean Elton 17.9
DeJohnette Jack 17.5
Desmond Paul 12
Dick Robert 20
DiMeola Al 17.7
Dixon Bill 15.1
Dolphy Eric 15.1
Doran Christy 20
Dorsey Tommy 5
Douglas Dave 20
Drumm Kevin 20
Dudziak Urszula 15.4
Dunmall Paul 20
Durham Eddie 7
Earland Charles 13
Ehrlich Marty 20
Eldridge Roy 6
Elements 17.5
Ellington Duke 4
Evans Bill 11
Evans Gil 11
Farmer Art 13
Ferguson Maynard 13
Fitzgerald Ella 6
Fogel Marty 20
Formanek Michael 20
Freeman Chico 16.2
Friesen David 17.6
Frisell Bill 20
Frith Fred 16.6
Garbarek Jan 17.9
Garner Erroll 9
Getz Stan 11
Gibbs Mike 17.9
Gillespie Dizzy 8
Gismonti Egberto 17.4
Giuffre Jimmy 12
Glick-Rieman Eric 20
Globe Unity Orchestra 16.6
Golson Benny 13
Goodman Benny 5
Gordon Dexter 8
Graettinger Bob 11
Grappelli Stephane 6
Graves Milford 15.3
Green Grant 13

357

Gregorio Guillermo 20
Guionnet Jean-Luc 20
Gurtu Trilok 19
Guy Barry 16.6
Haden Charlie 17.3
Hall Jim 12
Hamilton Chico 12
Hampel Guenter 16.6
Hampton Lionel 10
Hancock Herbie 17.2
Handy William 1
Hanrahan Kip 20
Hargrove Roy 18
Harrell Tom 18
Harriott Joe 16.6
Harris Craig 20
Hawkins Coleman 6
Headley Greg 20
Helias Mark 16.5
Hemingway Gerry 16.5
Hemphill Julius 16.3
Henderson Fletcher 4
Henderson Joe 13
Herman Woody 10
Hersch Fred 18
Hill Andrew 14
Hines Earl 1
Holiday Billie 6
Holland Dave 16.5
Hooker William 16.7
Horn Paul 14
Horvitz Wayne 20
Howard Earl 20
Hubbard Freddie 13
Human Arts Ensemble 16.3
Hunter Charlie 19
Hutcherson Bobby 15.6
Isham Mark 19
Jackson Ronald-Shannon 17.5
Jamal Ahmad 9
Jarman Joseph 16.1
Jarreau Al 17.8
Jarrett Keith 17.2
Jazz Passengers 20
Jazztet 13
Jeck Philip 20
Jenkins Leroy 16.2
Johnson J.J. 8
Johnson James 3
Jones Elvin 15.3
Jones Michael 19
Jones Thad 13
Jordan Stanley 18
Kaiser Henry 20
Kang Eyvind 20
Kelley Greg 20
Kenton Stan 10
Keppard Freddie 1
Khan Steve 17.7
Kindler Steve 19
Kirby John 6
Kirk Roland 14
Kloss Eric 14
Klucevsek Guy 20
Koglmann Franz 16.6
Kondo Toshinori 20
Konitz Lee 11
Krupa Gene 5
Kuehn Joachim 17.9
Kuhn Steve 17.6
Kuryokhin Sergey 17.9
Lacy Steve 15.5
Lake Oliver 16.3
Lande Art 17.6
Lang Eddie 6
Lanz David 19
Lateef Yusef 14
Lee Jeanne 15.4
Lewis George 16.2
Licht Alan 20
Liebman Dave 18
Lincoln Abbey 13
Lloyd Charles 14
Lonberg-Holm Fred 20
Lovano Joe 18
Lowe Frank 16.4
Lunceford Jimmie 4
Lytton Paul 16.6
MacLeod Alice 15.2
Maneri Joe 20
Mangelsdorff Albert 16.6
Mangione Chuck 17.8
Mann Herbie 14
Mantler Michael 17.3
Marclay Christian 20
Maroney Denman 20
Marsalis Branford 18
Marsalis Wynton 18
Martino Pat 14
Masaoka Miya 20
Mays Lyle 18
McBee Cecil 16.4
McFerrin Bobby 16.7
McGregor Chris 16.6
McIntyre Maurice 16.1
McLaughlin John 17.5
McLean Jackie 13
McPhee Joe 16.4
Medeski Martin & Wood 19
Mehldau Brad 18
Melford Myra 20
Mengelberg Misha 16.6
Metheny Pat Pat 17.7
Microscopic Septet 20
Miller Glenn 5
Miller Mulgrew 18
Mingus Charlie 13
Mitchell Blue 13
Mitchell Roscoe 16.1
Mobley Hank 13
Modern Jazz Quartet 11
Monk Thelonious 9
Montgomery Wes 13
Montreux 19
Moran Jason 19
Moreira Airto 17.4
Morgan Lee 13
Morris Butch 20
Morton Jelly-Roll 1
Moten Bennie 7
Motian Paul 17.3
Moye Don 16.1
Mueller Guenter 20
Mulligan Gerry 12
Murray David 16.4
Murray Sunny 15.3
Myers Amina-Claudine 16.2
Narell Andy 19
Nauseef Mark 19
Necks 19
Neill Ben 20
Nelson Oliver 14
New Orleans Rhythm Kings 1
Newton James 16.4
Nichols Herbie 9
Nichols Red 5
Noyes Charles 16.7
Nucleus 17.9

Oliver King 1
Oregon 17.5
Original Dixieland Jass Band 1
Orsted-Pedersen Niels-Henning 17.9
Ory Kid 1
Osby Greg 19
Oxley Tony 16.6
Page Walter 7
Parker Charlie 8
Parker Errol 14
Parker Evan 16.6
Parkins Zeena 20
Pass Joe 14
Pastorius Jaco 17.6
Pearson Duke 13
Pepper Art 12
Perelman Ivo 20
Peterson Hannibal 16.4
Peterson Oscar 9
Pine Courtney 18
Plimley Paul 20
Ponty Jean-Luc 17.6
Powell Bud 9
Previte Bobby 20
Prince Lasha 15.2
Pukwana Dudu 16.6
Pullen Don 16.4
Purim Flora 17.4
Raeburn Boyd 10
Rava Enrico 17.9
Redman Dewey 15.6
Redman Joshua 18
Reinhardt Django 6
Rivers Sam 15.2
Roach Max 13
Roberts Hank 20
Roberts Luckey 3
Roberts Marcus 18
Rogers Shorty 12
Rollins Sonny 13
Rose Jon 16.6
Rosenberg Scott 20
Rothenberg Ned 20
Rova Saxophone Quartet 16.7
Rudd Roswell 15.5
Ruiz Hilton 17.4
Russell George 11
Russell Hal 16.2
Rutherford Paul 16.6
Rypdal Terje 17.9
Sanborn David 18
Sanders Pharoah 15.2
Sandoval Arturo 18
Sarbib Saheb 20
Schlippenbach Alexander 16.6
Schneider Maria 20
Schoof Manfred 16.6
Schuller Gunther 11
Schweizer Irene 16.6
Scofield John 17.7
Scott Shirley 13
Scott Tony 14
Scott-Heron Gil 17.8
Shadowfax 19
Sharp Elliott 20
Sharrock Sonny 17.7
Shaw Artie 5
Shaw Woody 13
Shearing George 9
Shepp Archie 15.2
Shipp Matthew 20
Shorter Wayne 14
Shrieve Michael 20
Silver Horace 13
Simmons Sonny 15.2
Smith Jabbo 6
Smith Jimmy 13
Smith Leo 16.2
Smith Lonnie-Liston 17.5
Smith Willie-The-Lion 3
Solal Martial 9
Spontaneous Music Ensemble 16.6
Spyro Gyra 17.8
Staley Jim 20
Steps Ahead 17.5
Stern Mike 17.7
Story Liz 19
Sugimoto Taku 20
Sun Ra 15.1
Surman John 17.9
Swallow Steve 17.6
Takayanagi Masayuki 16.6
Tapscott Horace 15.2
Tatum Art 3
Taylor Cecil 15.1
Tchicai John 15.5
Terry Clark 13
Thomas Gary 19
Thomas Leon 17.8
Thornhill Claude 11
Threadgill Henry 16.2
Tibbetts Steve 17.7
Tickmayer Stevan 20
Tippett Keith 17.9
Tjader Cal 14
Tolliver Charles 15.6
Torn David 20
Towner Ralph 17.7
Trio Ganelin 16.6
Triosk 20
Tristano Lennie 9
Turre Steve 18
Turrentine Stanley 13
Turtle Island String Quartet 19
Tyler Charles 15.2
Tyner McCoy 15.2
Tyner McCoy 17.2
Uchihashi Kazuhisa 20
Ulmer James-Blood 17.7
Urbaniak Michael 17.9
Vandermark Ken 20
Varner Tom 20
Vasconcelos Nana 17.4
Velez Glen 19
Vitous Miroslav 17.6
Voice Crack 16.7
Walcott Collin 17.6
Waldron Mal 13
Waller Fats 3
Walton Cedar 14
Ware David 20
Wasserman Bob 19
Watanabe Kazumi 17.7
Waters Patty 15.4
Watson Bobby 18
Weather Report 17.5
Webb Chick 4
Weber Eberhard 17.9
Webster Ben 7
Westbrook Mike 17.9
Weston Randy 14
Wheeler Kenny 17.9
Whiteman Paul 5
Williams Clarence 1

Williams James 18
Williams Jessica 18
Williams Mary-Lou 7
Williams Tony 17.1
Wilson Cassandra 19
Winter Paul 14
Woods Phil 13

Wright Frank 15.2
Yamashita Yosuke 16.6
Yeah No 19
Yellowjackets 17.8
Yoshihide Otomo 20
Young Larry 13
Young Lester 7

Zanana 20
Zawinul Josef 17.5
Zeitlin Denny 14
Zeitlin Denny 17.3
ZGA 16.7
Zorn John 20
Zummo Peter 20